Random Data

WILEY SERIES IN PROBABILITY AND STATISTICS

Established by WALTER A. SHEWHART and SAMUEL S. WILKS

Editors: *David J. Balding, Noel A. C. Cressie, Garrett M. Fitzmaurice, Iain M. Johnstone, Geert Molenberghs, David W. Scott, Adrian F. M. Smith, Ruey S. Tsay, Sanford Weisberg*
Editors Emeriti: *Vic Barnett, J. Stuart Hunter, Jozef L. Teugels*

A complete list of the titles in this series appears at the end of this volume.

Random Data

Analysis and Measurement Procedures

Fourth Edition

JULIUS S. BENDAT
ALLAN G. PIERSOL

WILEY

Random Data
Analysis and Measurement Procedures
Second Edition

Authorized reprint by Wiley India Pvt. Ltd., 4435-36/7, Ansari Road, Daryaganj, New Delhi – 110002.

Copyright © 2010 by John Wiley & Sons, Inc.
Published by John Wiley & Sons, Inc., Hoboken, New Jersey. All rights reserved.

No part of this book, including interior design, cover design, and icons, may be reproduced or transmitted in any form except with the permission of John Wiley & Sons Inc., 111 River Street, Hoboken, NJ 07030, (201) 748-6011.

Limit of Liability/ Disclaimer of Warranty: The publisher and the author make no representations or warranties with respect to the accuracy or completeness of the contents of this work and specifically disclaim all warranties, including without limitation warranties of fitness for a particular purpose. No warranty may be created or extended by sales or promotional materials. The advice and strategies contained herein may not be suitable for every situation. This work is sold with the understanding that the publisher is not engaged in rendering legal, accounting, or other professional services. If professional assistance is required, the services of a competent professional person should be sought. Neither the publisher nor the author shall be liable for damages arising here from. The fact that an organization or Website is referred to in this work as a citation and/or a potential source of further information does not mean that the author or the publisher endorses the information the organization or Website may provide or recommendations it may make. Further, readers should be aware that Internet Websites listed in this work may have changed or disappeared between when this work was written and when it is read.

Trademarks: Wiley and the Wiley logo are trademarks or registered trademarks of John Wiley & Sons, Inc. and/or its affiliates, in the United States and other countries, and may not be used without written permission. SQL Server is a registered trademark of Microsoft Corporation. All other trademarks are the property of their respective owners. John Wiley & Sons, Inc. is not associated with any product or vendor mentioned in this book.

This edition is authorized for sale in the Indian Sub-continent only.

Reprint: 2014

Printed at: *Radha Offset Press, Delhi*

ISBN: 978-81-265-4604-6

To Allan G. Piersol
1930-2009

To Allan G. Piersol
1930-2009

Contents

Preface	xv
Preface to the Third Edition	xvii
Glossary of Symbols	xix

1. Basic Descriptions and Properties ... 1

    1.1. Deterministic Versus Random Data, 1
    1.2. Classifications of Deterministic Data, 3
        1.2.1. Sinusoidal Periodic Data, 3
        1.2.2. Complex Periodic Data, 4
        1.2.3. Almost-Periodic Data, 6
        1.2.4. Transient Nonperiodic Data, 7
    1.3. Classifications of Random Data, 8
        1.3.1. Stationary Random Data, 9
        1.3.2. Ergodic Random Data, 11
        1.3.3. Nonstationary Random Data, 12
        1.3.4. Stationary Sample Records, 12
    1.4. Analysis of Random Data, 13
        1.4.1. Basic Descriptive Properties, 13
        1.4.2. Input/Output Relations, 19
        1.4.3. Error Analysis Criteria, 21
        1.4.4. Data Analysis Procedures, 23

2. Linear Physical Systems ... 25

    2.1. Constant-Parameter Linear Systems, 25
    2.2. Basic Dynamic Characteristics, 26
    2.3. Frequency Response Functions, 28
    2.4. Illustrations of Frequency Response Functions, 30
        2.4.1. Mechanical Systems, 30

2.4.2. Electrical Systems, 39
2.4.3. Other Systems, 41
2.5. Practical Considerations, 41

3. Probability Fundamentals   45

3.1. One Random Variable, 45
   3.1.1. Probability Density and Distribution Functions, 46
   3.1.2. Expected Values, 49
   3.1.3. Change of Variables, 50
   3.1.4. Moment-Generating and Characteristic Functions, 52
   3.1.5. Chebyshev's Inequality, 53
3.2. Two Random Variables, 54
   3.2.1. Expected Values and Correlation Coefficient, 55
   3.2.2. Distribution for Sum of Two Random Variables, 56
   3.2.3. Joint Moment-Generating and Characteristic Functions, 57
3.3. Gaussian (Normal) Distribution, 59
   3.3.1. Central Limit Theorem, 60
   3.3.2. Joint Gaussian (Normal) Distribution, 62
   3.3.3. Moment-Generating and Characteristic Functions, 63
   3.3.4. N-Dimensional Gaussian (Normal) Distribution, 64
3.4. Rayleigh Distribution, 67
   3.4.1. Distribution of Envelope and Phase for Narrow Bandwidth Data, 67
   3.4.2. Distribution of Output Record for Narrow Bandwidth Data, 71
3.5. Higher Order Changes of Variables, 72

4. Statistical Principles   79

4.1. Sample Values and Parameter Estimation, 79
4.2. Important Probability Distribution Functions, 82
   4.2.1. Gaussian (Normal) Distribution, 82
   4.2.2. Chi-Square Distribution, 83
   4.2.3. The t Distribution, 84
   4.2.4. The F Distribution, 84
4.3. Sampling Distributions and Illustrations, 85
   4.3.1. Distribution of Sample Mean with Known Variance, 85
   4.3.2. Distribution of Sample Variance, 86
   4.3.3. Distribution of Sample Mean with Unknown Variance, 87
   4.3.4. Distribution of Ratio of Two Sample Variances, 87

CONTENTS

- 4.4. Confidence Intervals, 88
- 4.5. Hypothesis Tests, 91
    - 4.5.1. Chi-Square Goodness-of-Fit Test, 94
    - 4.5.2. Nonparametric Trend Test, 96
- 4.6. Correlation and Regression Procedures, 99
    - 4.6.1. Linear Correlation Analysis, 99
    - 4.6.2. Linear Regression Analysis, 102

5. Stationary Random Processes — 109

- 5.1. Basic Concepts, 109
    - 5.1.1. Correlation (Covariance) Functions, 111
    - 5.1.2. Examples of Autocorrelation Functions, 113
    - 5.1.3. Correlation Coefficient Functions, 115
    - 5.1.4. Cross-Correlation Function for Time Delay, 116
- 5.2. Spectral Density Functions, 118
    - 5.2.1. Spectra via Correlation Functions, 118
    - 5.2.2. Spectra via Finite Fourier Transforms, 126
    - 5.2.3. Spectra via Filtering–Squaring–Averaging, 129
    - 5.2.4. Wavenumber Spectra, 132
    - 5.2.5. Coherence Functions, 134
    - 5.2.6. Cross-Spectrum for Time Delay, 135
    - 5.2.7. Location of Peak Value, 137
    - 5.2.8. Uncertainty Relation, 138
    - 5.2.9. Uncertainty Principle and Schwartz Inequality, 140
- 5.3. Ergodic and Gaussian Random Processes, 142
    - 5.3.1. Ergodic Random Processes, 142
    - 5.3.2. Sufficient Condition for Ergodicity, 145
    - 5.3.3. Gaussian Random Processes, 147
    - 5.3.4. Linear Transformations of Random Processes, 149
- 5.4. Derivative Random Processes, 151
    - 5.4.1. Correlation Functions, 151
    - 5.4.2. Spectral Density Functions, 154
- 5.5. Level Crossings and Peak Values, 155
    - 5.5.1. Expected Number of Level Crossings per Unit Time, 155
    - 5.5.2. Peak Probability Functions for Narrow Bandwidth Data, 159
    - 5.5.3. Expected Number and Spacing of Positive Peaks, 161
    - 5.5.4. Peak Probability Functions for Wide Bandwidth Data, 162
    - 5.5.5. Derivations, 164

6. Single-Input/Output Relationships — 173

- 6.1. Single-Input/Single-Output Models, 173

6.1.1. Correlation and Spectral Relations, 173
6.1.2. Ordinary Coherence Functions, 180
6.1.3. Models with Extraneous Noise, 183
6.1.4. Optimum Frequency Response Functions, 187
6.2. Single-Input/Multiple-Output Models, 190
6.2.1. Single-Input/Two-Output Model, 191
6.2.2. Single-Input/Multiple-Output Model, 192
6.2.3. Removal of Extraneous Noise, 194

7. Multiple-Input/Output Relationships 201

7.1. Multiple-Input/Single-Output Models, 201
7.1.1. General Relationships, 202
7.1.2. General Case of Arbitrary Inputs, 205
7.1.3. Special Case of Mutually Uncorrelated Inputs, 206
7.2. Two-Input/One-Output Models, 207
7.2.1. Basic Relationships, 207
7.2.2. Optimum Frequency Response Functions, 210
7.2.3. Ordinary and Multiple Coherence Functions, 212
7.2.4. Conditioned Spectral Density Functions, 213
7.2.5. Partial Coherence Functions, 219
7.3. General and Conditioned Multiple-Input Models, 221
7.3.1. Conditioned Fourier Transforms, 223
7.3.2. Conditioned Spectral Density Functions, 224
7.3.3. Optimum Systems for Conditioned Inputs, 225
7.3.4. Algorithm for Conditioned Spectra, 226
7.3.5. Optimum Systems for Original Inputs, 229
7.3.6. Partial and Multiple Coherence Functions, 231
7.4. Modified Procedure to Solve Multiple-Input/Single-Output Models, 232
7.4.1. Three-Input/Single-Output Models, 234
7.4.2. Formulas for Three-Input/Single-Output Models, 235
7.5. Matrix Formulas for Multiple-Input/Multiple-Output Models, 237
7.5.1. Multiple-Input/Multiple-Output Model, 238
7.5.2. Multiple-Input/Single-Output Model, 241
7.5.3. Model with Output Noise, 243
7.5.4. Single-Input/Single-Output Model, 245

8. Statistical Errors in Basic Estimates 249

8.1. Definition of Errors, 249
8.2. Mean and Mean Square Value Estimates, 252
8.2.1. Mean Value Estimates, 252

- 8.2.2. Mean Square Value Estimates, 256
- 8.2.3. Variance Estimates, 260
- 8.3. Probability Density Function Estimates, 261
  - 8.3.1. Bias of the Estimate, 263
  - 8.3.2. Variance of the Estimate, 264
  - 8.3.3. Normalized rms Error, 265
  - 8.3.4. Joint Probability Density Function Estimates, 265
- 8.4. Correlation Function Estimates, 266
  - 8.4.1. Bandwidth-Limited Gaussian White Noise, 269
  - 8.4.2. Noise-to-Signal Considerations, 270
  - 8.4.3. Location Estimates of Peak Correlation Values, 271
- 8.5. Autospectral Density Function Estimates, 273
  - 8.5.1. Bias of the Estimate, 274
  - 8.5.2. Variance of the Estimate, 278
  - 8.5.3. Normalized rms Error, 278
  - 8.5.4. Estimates from Finite Fourier Transforms, 280
  - 8.5.5. Test for Equivalence of Autospectra, 282
- 8.6. Record Length Requirements, 284

9. Statistical Errors in Advanced Estimates — 289

- 9.1. Cross-Spectral Density Function Estimates, 289
  - 9.1.1. Variance Formulas, 292
  - 9.1.2. Covariance Formulas, 293
  - 9.1.3. Phase Angle Estimates, 297
- 9.2. Single-Input/Output Model Estimates, 298
  - 9.2.1. Bias in Frequency Response Function Estimates, 300
  - 9.2.2. Coherent Output Spectrum Estimates, 303
  - 9.2.3. Coherence Function Estimates, 305
  - 9.2.4. Gain Factor Estimates, 308
  - 9.2.5. Phase Factor Estimates, 310
- 9.3. Multiple-Input/Output Model Estimates, 312

10. Data Acquisition and Processing — 317

- 10.1. Data Acquisition, 318
  - 10.1.1. Transducer and Signal Conditioning, 318
  - 10.1.2. Data Transmission, 321
  - 10.1.3. Calibration, 322
  - 10.1.4. Dynamic Range, 324
- 10.2. Data Conversion, 326
  - 10.2.1. Analog-to-Digital Converters, 326
  - 10.2.2. Sampling Theorems for Random Records, 328

- 10.2.3. Sampling Rates and Aliasing Errors, 330
- 10.2.4. Quantization and Other Errors, 333
- 10.2.5. Data Storage, 335
- 10.3. Data Qualification, 335
  - 10.3.1. Data Classification, 336
  - 10.3.2. Data Validation, 340
  - 10.3.3. Data Editing, 345
- 10.4. Data Analysis Procedures, 349
  - 10.4.1. Procedure for Analyzing Individual Records, 349
  - 10.4.2. Procedure for Analyzing Multiple Records, 351

11. Data Analysis 359

- 11.1. Data Preparation, 359
  - 11.1.1. Data Standardization, 360
  - 11.1.2. Trend Removal, 361
  - 11.1.3. Digital Filtering, 363
- 11.2. Fourier Series and Fast Fourier Transforms, 366
  - 11.2.1. Standard Fourier Series Procedure, 366
  - 11.2.2. Fast Fourier Transforms, 368
  - 11.2.3. Cooley–Tukey Procedure, 374
  - 11.2.4. Procedures for Real-Valued Records, 376
  - 11.2.5. Further Related Formulas, 377
  - 11.2.6. Other Algorithms, 378
- 11.3. Probability Density Functions, 379
- 11.4. Autocorrelation Functions, 381
  - 11.4.1. Autocorrelation Estimates via Direct Computations, 381
  - 11.4.2. Autocorrelation Estimates via FFT Computations, 381
- 11.5. Autospectral Density Functions, 386
  - 11.5.1. Autospectra Estimates by Ensemble Averaging, 386
  - 11.5.2. Side-Lobe Leakage Suppression Procedures, 388
  - 11.5.3. Recommended Computational Steps for Ensemble-Averaged Estimates, 395
  - 11.5.4. Zoom Transform Procedures, 396
  - 11.5.5. Autospectra Estimates by Frequency Averaging, 399
  - 11.5.6. Other Spectral Analysis Procedures, 403
- 11.6. Joint Record Functions, 404
  - 11.6.1. Joint Probability Density Functions, 404
  - 11.6.2. Cross-Correlation Functions, 405
  - 11.6.3. Cross-Spectral Density Functions, 406
  - 11.6.4. Frequency Response Functions, 407
  - 11.6.5. Unit Impulse Response (Weighting) Functions, 408
  - 11.6.6. Ordinary Coherence Functions, 408

11.7. Multiple-Input/Output Functions, 408
- 11.7.1. Fourier Transforms and Spectral Functions, 409
- 11.7.2. Conditioned Spectral Density Functions, 409
- 11.7.3. Three-Input/Single-Output Models, 411
- 11.7.4. Functions in Modified Procedure, 414

12. Nonstationary Data Analysis — 417

12.1. Classes of Nonstationary Data, 417
12.2. Probability Structure of Nonstationary Data, 419
- 12.2.1. Higher Order Probability Functions, 420
- 12.2.2. Time-Averaged Probability Functions, 421

12.3. Nonstationary Mean Values, 422
- 12.3.1. Independent Samples, 424
- 12.3.2. Correlated Samples, 425
- 12.3.3. Analysis Procedures for Single Records, 427

12.4. Nonstationary Mean Square Values, 429
- 12.4.1. Independent Samples, 429
- 12.4.2. Correlated Samples, 431
- 12.4.3. Analysis Procedures for Single Records, 432

12.5. Correlation Structure of Nonstationary Data, 436
- 12.5.1. Double-Time Correlation Functions, 436
- 12.5.2. Alternative Double-Time Correlation Functions, 437
- 12.5.3. Analysis Procedures for Single Records, 439

12.6. Spectral Structure of Nonstationary Data, 442
- 12.6.1. Double-Frequency Spectral Functions, 443
- 12.6.2. Alternative Double-Frequency Spectral Functions, 445
- 12.6.3. Frequency Time Spectral Functions, 449
- 12.6.4. Analysis Procedures for Single Records, 456

12.7. Input/Output Relations for Nonstationary Data, 462
- 12.7.1. Nonstationary Input and Time-Varying Linear System, 463
- 12.7.2. Results for Special Cases, 464
- 12.7.3. Frequency–Time Spectral Input/Output Relations, 465
- 12.7.4. Energy Spectral Input/Output Relations, 467

13. The Hilbert Transform — 473

13.1. Hilbert Transforms for General Records, 473
- 13.1.1. Computation of Hilbert Transforms, 476
- 13.1.2. Examples of Hilbert Transforms, 477
- 13.1.3. Properties of Hilbert Transforms, 478
- 13.1.4. Relation to Physically Realizable Systems, 480

13.2. Hilbert Transforms for Correlation Functions, 484
  13.2.1. Correlation and Envelope Definitions, 484
  13.2.2. Hilbert Transform Relations, 486
  13.2.3. Analytic Signals for Correlation Functions, 486
  13.2.4. Nondispersive Propagation Problems, 489
  13.2.5. Dispersive Propagation Problems, 495
13.3. Envelope Detection Followed by Correlation, 498

14. Nonlinear System Analysis 505

14.1. Zero-Memory and Finite-Memory Nonlinear Systems, 505
14.2. Square-Law and Cubic Nonlinear Models, 507
14.3. Volterra Nonlinear Models, 509
14.4. SI/SO Models with Parallel Linear and Nonlinear Systems, 510
14.5. SI/SO Models with Nonlinear Feedback, 512
14.6. Recommended Nonlinear Models and Techniques, 514
14.7. Duffing SDOF Nonlinear System, 515
  14.7.1. Analysis for SDOF Linear System, 516
  14.7.2. Analysis for Duffing SDOF Nonlinear System, 518
14.8. Nonlinear Drift Force Model, 520
  14.8.1. Basic Formulas for Proposed Model, 521
  14.8.2. Spectral Decomposition Problem, 523
  14.8.3. System Identification Problem, 524

Bibliography 527

Appendix A: Statistical Tables 533

Appendix B: Definitions for Random Data Analysis 545

List of Figures 557

List of Tables 565

List of Examples 567

Answers to Problems in Random Data 571

Index 599

Preface

This book is dedicated to my coauthor, Allan G. Piersol, who died on March 1, 2009. I met Allan in 1959 when we were both working at Ramo-Wooldridge Corporation in Los Angeles. I had just won a contract from Wright-Patterson Air force Base in Dayton, Ohio, to study the application of statistics to flight vehicle vibration problems. I was familiar with statistical techniques but knew little about aircraft vibration matters. I looked around the company and found Allan who had previous experience from Douglas Aircraft Company in Santa Monica on testing and vibration problems. This started our close association together that continued for 50 years.

In 1963, I left Ramo-Wooldridge to become an independent mathematical consultant and to form a California company called Measurement Analysis Corporation. I asked Allan to join me where I was the President and he was the Vice President. Over the next 5 years until we sold our company, we grew to 25 people and worked for various private companies and government agencies on aerospace, automotive, oceanographic, and biomedical projects. One of our NASA projects was to establish requirements for vibration testing of the Saturn launch vehicle for the Apollo spacecraft to send men to the moon and return them safely to earth. Allan was a member of the final certification team to tell Werner Von Braun it was safe to launch when the Apollo mission took place in 1969.

In 1965, Allan and I were invited by the Advanced Group on Aeronautical Research and Development of NATO to deliver a one-week series of lectures at Southampton University in England. Some 250 engineers from all over Europe attended this event. Preparation for these lectures led to our first book *Measurement and Analysis of Random Data* that was published by John Wiley and Sons in 1966. This first book filled a strong need in the field that was not available from any other source to help people concerned with the acquisition and analysis of experimental physical data for engineering and scientific applications. From further technical advances and experience by others and us, we wrote three updated editions of this *Random Data* book published by Wiley in 1971, 1986, and 2000. We were also able to write two companion books *Engineering Applications of Correlation and Spectral Analysis* published by Wiley in 1980 and 1993.

In all of our books, Allan and I carefully reviewed each other's work to make the material appear to come from one person and to be clear and useful for readers. Our books have been translated into Russian, Chinese, Japanese, and Polish and have had world sales to date of more than 100,000 copies. We traveled extensively to do consulting work on different types of engineering research projects, and we gave many educational short courses to engineering companies, scientific meetings, universities, and government agencies in the United States as well as in 25 other countries.

The preface to the third edition and the contents should be read to help understand and apply the comprehensive material that appears in this book. Chapters 1–6 and Chapter 12 in this fourth edition are the same as in the third edition except for small corrections and additions. Chapters 7–11 contain new important technical results on mathematical formulas and practical procedures for random data analysis and measurement that replace some previous formulas and procedures in the third edition. Chapter 13 now includes a computer-generated Hilbert transform example of engineering interest. Chapter 14, Nonlinear System Analysis, is a new chapter that discusses recommended techniques to model and identify the frequency-domain properties of large classes of nonlinear systems from measured input/output random data. Previous editions deal only with the identification of linear systems from measured data.

This fourth edition of *Random Data* from 50 years of work is our final contribution to the field that I believe will benefit students, engineers, and scientists for many years.

JULIUS S. BENDAT

Los Angeles, California
January 2010

Preface to the Third Edition

This new third edition of *Random Data: Analysis and Measurement Procedures* is the third major revision of a book originally published by Wiley in 1966 under the title *Measurement and Analysis of Random Data*. That 1966 book was based upon the results of comprehensive research studies that we performed for various agencies of the United States government, and it was written to provide a reference for working engineers and scientists concerned with random data acquisition and analysis problems. Shortly after its publication, computer programs for the computation of complex Fourier series, commonly referred to as fast Fourier transform (FFT) algorithms, were introduced that dramatically improved random data analysis procedures. In particular, when coupled with the increases in speed and decreases in cost of digital computers, these algorithms led to traditional analog data analysis instruments being replaced by digital computers with appropriate software. Hence, in 1971, our original book was extensively revised to reflect these advances and was published as a first edition under the present title.

In the mid-1970s, new iterative algorithms were formulated for the analysis of multiple-input/output problems that substantially enhanced the ability to interpret the results of such analyses in a physically meaningful way. This fact, along with further advances in the use of digital computers plus new techniques resulting from various projects, led to another expansion of our book that was published in 1986 as the second edition. Since 1986, many additional developments in random data measurement and analysis procedures have occurred, including (a) improvements in data acquisition instruments, (b) modified iterative procedures for the analysis of multiple-input/output problems that reduce computations, and (c) practical methods for analyzing nonstationary random data properties from single sample records. For these and other reasons, this book has again been extensively revised to produce this third edition of *Random Data*.

The primary purpose of this book remains the same, namely, to provide a practical reference for working engineers and scientists in many fields. However, since the first publication in 1966, this book has found its way into a number of university classrooms as a teaching text for advanced courses on the analysis of random processes. Also, a different companion book written by us entitled *Engineering*

Applications of Correlation and Spectral Analysis, published by Wiley–Interscience in 1980 and revised in a second edition in 1993, includes numerous illustrations of practical applications of the material in our 1971 and 1986 books. This has allowed us in the third edition of *Random Data* to give greater attention to matters that enhance its use as a teaching text by including rigorous proofs and derivations of more of the basic relationships in random process theory that are difficult to find elsewhere.

As in the second edition, Chapters 1, 2, and 4 present background material on descriptions of data, properties of linear systems, and statistical principles. Chapter 3 on probability fundamentals has been revised and expanded to include formulas for the Rayleigh distribution and for higher order changes of variables. Chapter 5 presents a comprehensive discussion of stationary random process theory, including new material on wavenumber spectra and on level crossings and peak values of normally distributed random data. Chapters 6 and 7 develop mathematical relationships for the detailed analysis of single-input/output and multiple-input/output linear systems that include modified algorithms. Chapters 8 and 9 derive important practical formulas to determine statistical errors in estimates of random data parameters and linear system properties from measured data. Chapter 10 on data acquisition and processing has been completely rewritten to cover major changes since the publication of the second edition. Chapter 11 on data analysis has been updated to include new approaches to spectral analysis that have been made practical by the increased capacity and speed of digital computations. Chapter 12 on nonstationary data analysis procedures has been expanded to cover recent advances that are applicable to single sample records. Chapter 13 on the Hilbert transform remains essentially the same.

We wish to acknowledge the contributions to this book by many colleagues and associates, in particular, Paul M. Agbabian, Robert N. Coppolino, and Robert K. Otnes, for their reviews of portions of the manuscript and helpful comments. We also are grateful to the many government agencies and industrial companies that have supported our work and sponsored our presentation of short courses on these matters.

JULIUS S. BENDAT
ALLAN G. PIERSOL

Los Angeles, California
January 2000

Glossary of Symbols

a, b	Sample regression coefficients, arbitrary constants
A	Amplitude, reverse arrangements, regression coefficient
$A(f)$	Frequency response function after linear or nonlinear operation
$b[\;]$	Bias error of $[\;]$
B	Cyclical frequency bandwidth, regression coefficient
B_e	Frequency resolution bandwidth
B_n	Noise spectral bandwidth
B_s	Statistical bandwidth
c	Mechanical damping coefficient, arbitrary constant
C	Electrical capacitance
C_{xy}	Covariance
$C_{xx}(\tau)$	Autocovariance function
$C_{xy}(\tau)$	Cross-covariance function
$C_{xy}(f)$	Coincident spectral density function (one-sided)
$e(t)$	Potential difference
$E[\;]$	Expected value of $[\;]$
f	Cyclical frequency
Δf	Bandwidth resolution (Hz)
$\mathscr{F}[\;]$	Fourier transform of $[\;]$
$G_{xx}(f)$	Autospectral density function (one-sided)
$G_{xy}(f)$	Cross-spectral density function (one-sided)
$G_{yy \cdot x}(f)$	Conditioned autospectral density function (one-sided)
$G_{x_i y \cdot x_j}(f)$	Conditioned cross-spectral density function (one-sided)
$G(\kappa)$	Wavenumber spectral density function (one-sided)
$\mathscr{G}(f)$	"Energy" spectral density function
$h(\tau)$	Unit impulse response function
$H(f)$	Frequency response function
$|H(f)|$	System gain factor
$\mathscr{H}[\;]$	Hilbert transform of $[\;]$
i	Index
$i(t)$	Current
$\text{Im}[\;]$	Imaginary part of $[\;]$
j	$\sqrt{-1}$, index

k	Mechanical spring constant, index
K	Number of class intervals
L	Electrical inductance, length
$L(f)$	Frequency response function for conditioned inputs
m	Mechanical mass, maximum number of lag values
n	Degrees of freedom, index
N	Sample size, number of sample records
$p(x)$	Probability density function
$p(x, y)$	Joint probability density function
$P(x)$	Probability distribution function
$P(x, y)$	Joint probability distribution function
Prob[ ]	Probability that [ ]
PSNR	Peak signal-to-noise ratio
PS/N	Peak signal-to-noise ratio in dB
q	Number of inputs
$q(t)$	Electrical charge
$q(R)$	Rayleigh probability density function
$Q(R)$	Rayleigh probability distribution function
$Q_{xy}(f)$	Quadrature spectral density function (one-sided)
r	Number of outputs, number of lag values
r_{xy}	Sample correlation coefficient
R	Electrical resistance
$R(t)$	Envelope function
$R_{xx}(\tau)$	Autocorrelation function
$R_{xy}(\tau)$	Cross-correlation function
$R(t_1, t_2)$	Double-time correlation function
$\mathscr{R}(\tau, t)$	Alternate double-time correlation function
Re[ ]	Real part of [ ]
s	Sample standard deviation
s^2	Sample variance
s_{xy}	Sample covariance
s.d.[ ]	Standard deviation of [ ]
$S_{xx}(f)$	Autospectral density function (two-sided)
$S_{xy}(f)$	Cross-spectral density function (two-sided)
$S_{yy \cdot x}(f)$	Conditioned autospectral density function (two-sided)
$S_{x_i y \cdot x_j}(f)$	Conditioned cross-spectral density function (two-sided)
$\mathscr{S}(f)$	"Energy" spectral density function (two-sided)
$S(f_1, f_2)$	Double-frequency spectral density function (two-sided)
$\mathscr{S}(f, g)$	Alternate double-frequency spectral density function (two-sided)
SNR	Signal-to-noise ratio
S/N	Signal-to-noise ratio in dB
$SG(f, t)$	Spectrogram
t	Time variable, Student t variable
Δt	Sampling interval
T	Record length

GLOSSARY OF SYMBOLS

T_n	Noise correlation duration
T_r	Total record length
u_n	Raw data values
$u(t), v(t)$	Time-dependent variables
Var []	Variance of []
W	Amplitude window width
$W(f, t)$	Frequency-time spectral density function (one-sided)
$\mathscr{W}(f, t)$	Frequency-time spectral density function (two-sided)
$WD(f, t)$	Wigner distribution
$x(t), y(t)$	Time-dependent variables
$\bar{x}$	Sample mean value of x
$\overline{x^2}$	Sample mean square value of x
$\tilde{x}(t)$	Hilbert transform of $x(t)$
X	Amplitude of sinusoidal $x(t)$
$X(f)$	Fourier transform of $x(t)$
$X(f,T)$	Fourier transform of $x(t)$ over record length T
z	Standardized normal variable
$|[]|$	Absolute value of []
$[\hat{\ }]$	Estimate of []
α	A small probability, level of significance, dummy variable
β	Probability of a type II error, dummy variable
$\gamma^2_{xy}(f)$	Ordinary coherence function
$\gamma^2_{y:x}(f)$	Multiple coherence function
$\gamma^2_{x_iy \cdot x_j}(f)$	Partial coherence function
δ	Spatial variable
$\delta()$	Delta function
Δ	Small increment
ε	Normalized error
κ	Wavenumber
λ	Wavelength
θ	Phase angle
$\theta_{xy}(f)$	Argument of $G_{xy}(f)$
μ	Mean value
ρ	Correlation coefficient
$\rho(\tau)$	Correlation coefficient function
σ	Standard deviation
σ^2	Variance
τ	Time displacement
$\phi(f)$	Phase factor
ϕ	Arbitrary statistical parameter
χ^2	Statistical chi-square variable
ψ	Root mean square value
ψ^2	Mean square value
ζ	Mechanical damping ratio

CHAPTER 1

Basic Descriptions and Properties

This first chapter gives basic descriptions and properties of deterministic data and random data to provide a physical understanding for later material in this book. Simple classification ideas are used to explain differences between stationary random data, ergodic random data, and nonstationary random data. Fundamental statistical functions are defined by words alone for analyzing the amplitude, time, and frequency domain properties of single stationary random records and pairs of stationary random records. An introduction is presented on various types of input/output linear system problems solved in this book, as well as necessary error analysis criteria to design experiments and evaluate measurements.

1.1 DETERMINISTIC VERSUS RANDOM DATA

Any observed data representing a physical phenomenon can be broadly classified as being either deterministic or nondeterministic. Deterministic data are those that can be described by an explicit mathematical relationship. For example, consider a rigid body that is suspended from a fixed foundation by a linear spring, as shown in Figure 1.1. Let m be the mass of the body (assumed to be inelastic) and k be the spring constant of the spring (assumed to be massless). Suppose the body is displaced from its position of equilibrium by a distance X and released at time $t=0$. From either basic laws of mechanics or repeated observations, it can be established that the following relationship will apply:

$$x(t) = X\cos\sqrt{\frac{k}{m}}t \quad t \geq 0 \tag{1.1}$$

Equation (1.1) defines the exact location of the body at any instant of time in the future. Hence, the physical data representing the motion of the mass are deterministic.

Random Data: Analysis and Measurement Procedures, Fourth Edition. By Julius S. Bendat and Allan G. Piersol
Copyright © 2010 John Wiley & Sons, Inc.

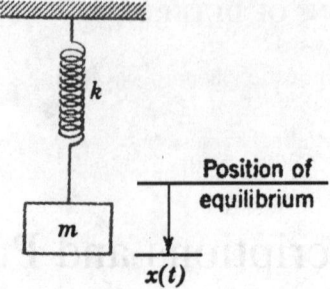

Figure 1.1 Simple spring mass system.

There are many physical phenomena in practice that produce data that can be represented with reasonable accuracy by explicit mathematical relationships. For example, the motion of a satellite in orbit about the earth, the potential across a condenser as it discharges through a resistor, the vibration response of an unbalanced rotating machine, and the temperature of water as heat is applied are all basically deterministic. However, there are many other physical phenomena that produce data that are not deterministic. For example, the height of waves in a confused sea, the acoustic pressures generated by air rushing through a pipe, and the electrical output of a noise generator represent data that cannot be described by explicit mathematical relationships. There is no way to predict an exact value at a future instant of time. These data are random in character and must be described in terms of probability statements and statistical averages rather than by explicit equations.

The classification of various physical data as being either deterministic or random might be debated in many cases. For example, it might be argued that no physical data in practice can be truly deterministic because there is always a possibility that some unforeseen event in the future might influence the phenomenon producing the data in a manner that was not originally considered. On the other hand, it might be argued that no physical data are truly random, because an exact mathematical description might be possible if a sufficient knowledge of the basic mechanisms of the phenomenon producing the data were available. In practical terms, the decision of whether physical data are deterministic or random is usually based on the ability to reproduce the data by controlled experiments. If an experiment producing specific data of interest can be repeated many times with identical results (within the limits of experimental error), then the data can generally be considered deterministic. If an experiment cannot be designed that will produce identical results when the experiment is repeated, then the data must usually be considered random in nature.

Various special classifications of deterministic and random data will now be discussed. Note that the classifications are selected from an analysis viewpoint and do not necessarily represent the most suitable classifications from other possible viewpoints. Further note that physical data are usually thought of as being functions of time and will be discussed in such terms for convenience. Any other variable, however, can replace time, as required.

1.2 CLASSIFICATIONS OF DETERMINISTIC DATA

Data representing deterministic phenomena can be categorized as being either periodic or nonperiodic. Periodic data can be further categorized as being either sinusoidal or complex periodic. Nonperiodic data can be further categorized as being either "almost-periodic" or transient. These various classifications of deterministic data are schematically illustrated in Figure 1.2. Of course, any combination of these forms may also occur. For purposes of review, each of these types of deterministic data, along with physical examples, will be briefly discussed.

1.2.1 Sinusoidal Periodic Data

Sinusoidal data are those types of periodic data that can be defined mathematically by a time-varying function of the form

$$x(t) = X \sin(2\pi f_0 t + \theta) \tag{1.2}$$

where

$X =$ amplitude
$f_0 =$ cyclic frequency in cycles per unit time
$\theta =$ initial phase angle with respect to the time origin in radians
$x(t) =$ instantaneous value at time t

The sinusoidal time history described by Equation (1.2) is usually referred to as a sine wave. When analyzing sinusoidal data in practice, the phase angle θ is often ignored. For this case,

$$x(t) = X \sin 2\pi f_0 t \tag{1.3}$$

Equation (1.3) can be pictured by a time history plot or by an amplitude–frequency plot (frequency spectrum), as illustrated in Figure 1.3.

The time interval required for one full fluctuation or cycle of sinusoidal data is called the period T_p. The number of cycles per unit time is called the frequency f_0.

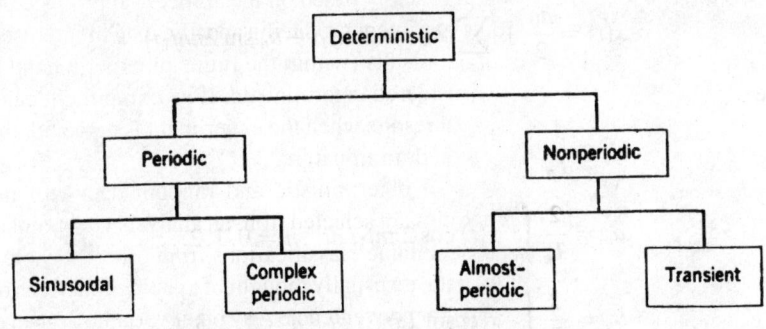

Figure 1.2 Classification of deterministic data.

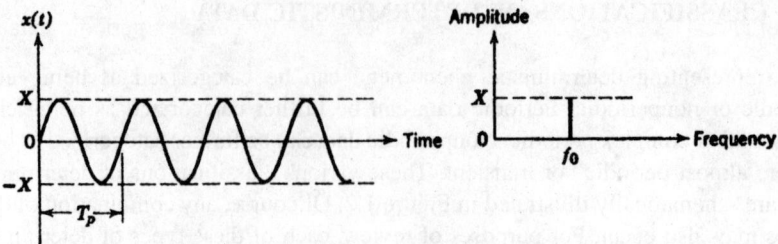

Figure 1.3 Time history and spectrum of sinusoidal data.

The frequency and period are related by

$$T_p = \frac{1}{f_0} \tag{1.4}$$

Note that the frequency spectrum in Figure 1.3 is composed of an amplitude component at a specific frequency, as opposed to a continuous plot of amplitude versus frequency. Such spectra are called *discrete spectra* or *line spectra*.

There are many examples of physical phenomena that produce approximately sinusoidal data in practice. The voltage output of an electrical alternator is one example; the vibratory motion of an unbalanced rotating weight is another. Sinusoidal data represent one of the simplest forms of time-varying data from the analysis viewpoint.

1.2.2 Complex Periodic Data

Complex periodic data are those types of periodic data that can be defined mathematically by a time-varying function whose waveform exactly repeats itself at regular intervals such that

$$x(t) = x(t \pm nT_p) \quad n = 1, 2, 3, \ldots \tag{1.5}$$

As for sinusoidal data, the time interval required for one full fluctuation is called the *period* T_p. The number of cycles per unit time is called the *fundamental frequency* f_1. A special case for complex periodic data is clearly sinusoidal data, where $f_1 = f_0$.

With few exceptions in practice, complex periodic data may be expanded into a Fourier series according to the following formula:

$$x(t) = \frac{a_0}{2} + \sum_{n=1}^{\infty} (a_n \cos 2\pi n f_1 t + b_n \sin 2\pi n f_1 t) \tag{1.6}$$

where

$$f_1 = \frac{1}{T_p}$$

$$a_n = \frac{2}{T_p} \int_0^{T_p} x(t) \cos 2\pi n f_1 t \, dt \quad n = 0, 1, 2, \ldots$$

$$b_n = \frac{2}{T_p} \int_0^{T_p} x(t) \sin 2\pi n f_1 t \, dt \quad n = 1, 2, 3, \ldots$$

An alternative way to express the Fourier series for complex periodic data is

$$x(t) = X_0 + \sum_{n=1}^{\infty} X_n \cos(2\pi n f_1 t - \theta_n) \tag{1.7}$$

where

$$X_0 = a_0/2$$
$$X_n = \sqrt{a_n^2 + b_n^2} \quad n = 1, 2, 3, \ldots$$
$$\theta_n = \tan^{-1}(b_n/a_n) \quad n = 1, 2, 3, \ldots$$

In words, Equation (1.7) says that complex periodic data consist of a static component X_0 and an infinite number of sinusoidal components called harmonics, which have amplitudes X_n and phases θ_n. The frequencies of the harmonic components are all integral multiples of f_1.

When analyzing periodic data in practice, the phase angles θ_n are often ignored. For this case, Equation (1.7) can be characterized by a discrete spectrum, as illustrated in Figure 1.4. Sometimes, complex periodic data will include only a few components. In other cases, the fundamental component may be absent. For example, suppose a periodic time history is formed by mixing three sine waves that have frequencies of 60, 75, and 100 Hz. The highest common divisor is 5 Hz, so the period of the resulting periodic data is $T_p = 0.2$ s. Hence, when expanded into a Fourier series, all values of X_n are zero except for $n = 12$, $n = 15$, and $n = 20$.

Physical phenomena that produce complex periodic data are far more common than those that produce simple sinusoidal data. In fact, the classification of data as being sinusoidal is often only an approximation for data that are actually complex. For example, the voltage output from an electrical alternator may actually display, under careful inspection, some small contributions at higher harmonic frequencies. In other cases, intense harmonic components may be present in periodic physical data. For example, the vibration response of a multicylinder reciprocating engine will usually display considerable harmonic content.

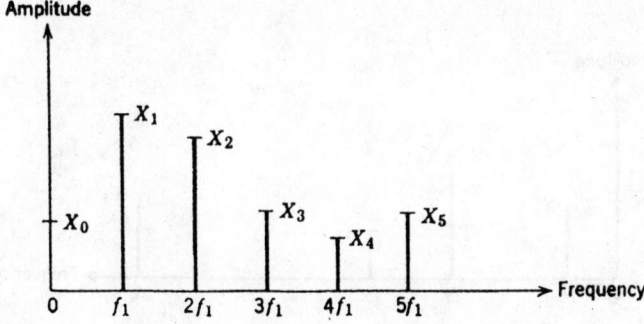

Figure 1.4 Spectrum of complex periodic data.

1.2.3 Almost-Periodic Data

In Section 1.2.2, it is noted that periodic data can generally be reduced to a series of sine waves with commensurately related frequencies. Conversely, the data formed by summing two or more commensurately related sine waves will be periodic. However, the data formed by summing two or more sine waves with arbitrary frequencies generally will not be periodic. Specifically, the sum of two or more sine waves will be periodic only when the ratios of all possible pairs of frequencies form rational numbers. This indicates that a fundamental period exists that will satisfy the requirements of Equation (1.5). Hence,

$$x(t) = X_1 \sin(2t + \theta_1) + X_2 \sin(3t + \theta_2) + X_3 \sin(7t + \theta_3)$$

is periodic because $\frac{2}{3}$, $\frac{2}{7}$, and $\frac{3}{7}$ are rational numbers (the fundamental period is $T_p = 1$). On the other hand,

$$x(t) = X_1 \sin(2t + \theta_1) - X_2 \sin(3t + \theta_2) + X_3 \sin(\sqrt{50}\, t + \theta_3)$$

is not periodic because $2/\sqrt{50}$ and $3/\sqrt{50}$ are not rational numbers (the fundamental period is infinitely long). The resulting time history in this case will have an almost-periodic character, but the requirements of Equation (1.5) will not be satisfied for any finite value of T_p.

Based on these discussions, almost-periodic data are those types of nonperiodic data that can be defined mathematically by a time-varying function of the form

$$x(t) = \sum_{n=1}^{\infty} X_n \sin(2\pi f_n t + \theta_n) \qquad (1.8)$$

where $f_n/f_m \neq$ rational number in all cases. Physical phenomena producing almost-periodic data frequently occur in practice when the effects of two or more unrelated periodic phenomena are mixed. A good example is the vibration response in a multiple-engine propeller airplane when the engines are out of synchronization.

An important property of almost-periodic data is as follows. If the phase angles θ_n are ignored, Equation (1.8) can be characterized by a discrete frequency spectrum similar to that for complex periodic data. The only difference is that the frequencies of the components are not related by rational numbers, as illustrated in Figure 1.5.

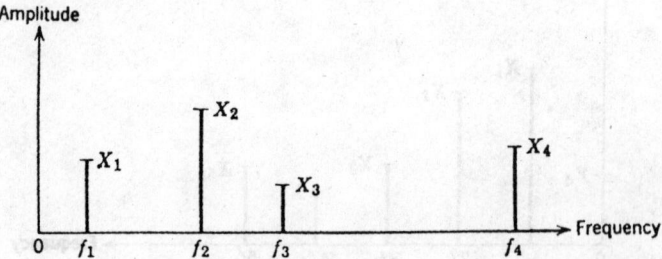

Figure 1.5 Spectrum of almost-periodic data.

CLASSIFICATIONS OF DETERMINISTIC DATA

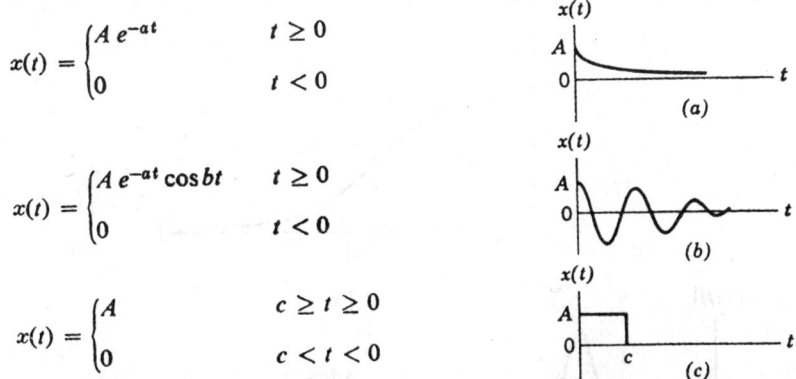

Figure 1.6 Illustrations of transient data.

1.2.4 Transient Nonperiodic Data

Transient data are defined as all nonperiodic data other than the almost-periodic data discussed in Section 1.2.3. In other words, transient data include all data not previously discussed that can be described by some suitable time-varying function. Three simple examples of transient data are given in Figure 1.6.

Physical phenomena that produce transient data are numerous and diverse. For example, the data in Figure 1.6(a) could represent the temperature of water in a kettle (relative to room temperature) after the flame is turned off. The data in Figure 1.6(b) might represent the free vibration of a damped mechanical system after an excitation force is removed. The data in Figure 1.6(c) could represent the stress in an end-loaded cable that breaks at time c.

An important characteristic of transient data, as opposed to periodic and almost-periodic data, is that a discrete spectral representation is not possible A *continuous* spectral representation for transient data can be obtained in most cases, however, from a Fourier transform given by

$$X(f) = \int_{-\infty}^{\infty} x(t)e^{-j2\pi ft}dt \qquad (1.9)$$

The Fourier transform $X(f)$ is generally a complex number that can be expressed in complex polar notation as

$$X(f) = |X(f)|e^{-j\theta(f)}$$

Here, $|X(f)|$ is the magnitude of $X(f)$ and $\theta(f)$ is the argument. In terms of the magnitude $|X(f)|$, continuous spectra of the three transient time histories in Figure 1.6 are as presented in Figure 1.7. Modern procedures for the digital computation of Fourier series and finite Fourier transforms are detailed in Chapter 11.

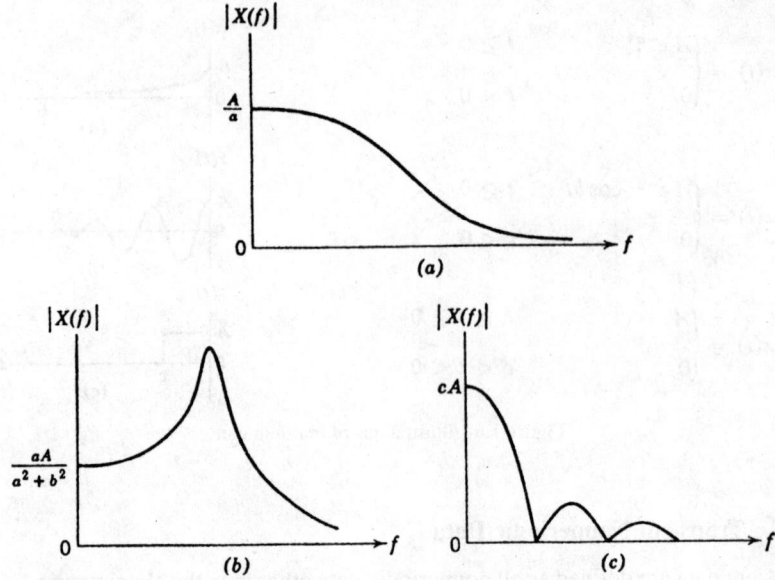

Figure 1.7 Spectra of transient data.

1.3 CLASSIFICATIONS OF RANDOM DATA

As discussed earlier, data representing a random physical phenomenon cannot be described by an explicit mathematical relationship because each observation of the phenomenon will be unique. In other words, any given observation will represent only one of many possible results that might have occurred. For example, assume the output voltage from a thermal noise generator is recorded as a function of time. A specific voltage time history record will be obtained, as shown in Figure 1.8. If a second thermal noise generator of identical construction and assembly is operated simultaneously, however, a different voltage time history record would result. In fact, every thermal noise generator that might be constructed would produce a different voltage time history record, as illustrated in Figure 1.8. Hence, the voltage time history for any one generator is merely one example of an infinitely large number of time histories that might have occurred.

A single time history representing a random phenomenon is called a *sample function* (or a *sample record* when observed over a finite time interval). The collection of all possible sample functions that the random phenomenon might have produced is called a *random process* or a *stochastic process*. Hence, a sample record of data for a random physical phenomenon may be thought of as one physical realization of a random process.

Random processes may be categorized as being either stationary or nonstationary. Stationary random processes may be further categorized as being either ergodic or nonergodic. Nonstationary random processes may be further categorized in terms of

CLASSIFICATIONS OF RANDOM DATA

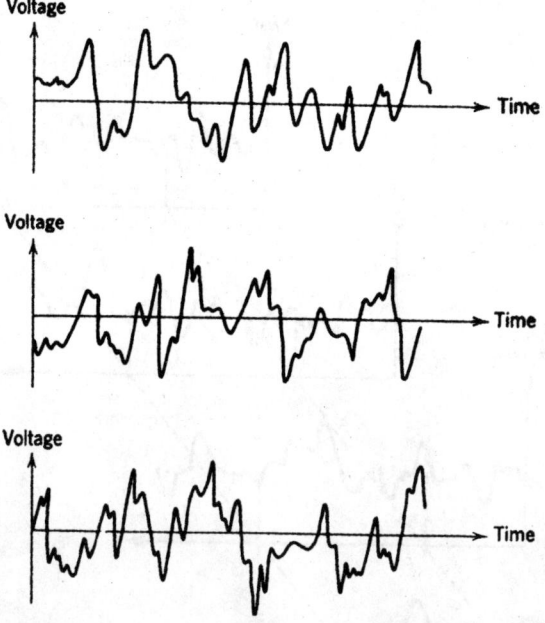

Figure 1.8 Sample records of thermal noise generator outputs.

specific types of nonstationary properties. These various classifications of random processes are schematically illustrated in Figure 1.9. The meaning and physical significance of these various types of random processes will now be discussed in broad terms. More analytical definitions and developments are presented in Chapters 5 and 12.

1.3.1 Stationary Random Data

When a physical phenomenon is considered in terms of a random process, the properties of the phenomenon can hypothetically be described at any instant of time by computing

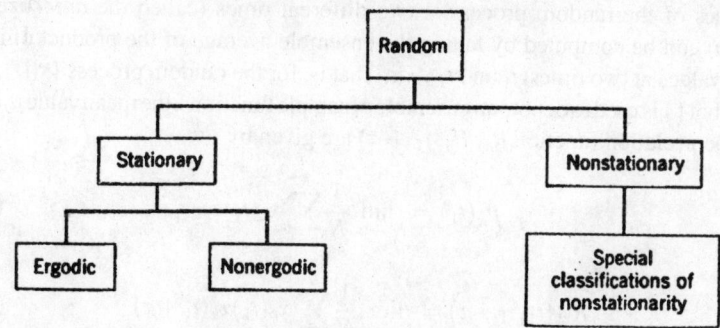

Figure 1.9 Classifications of random data.

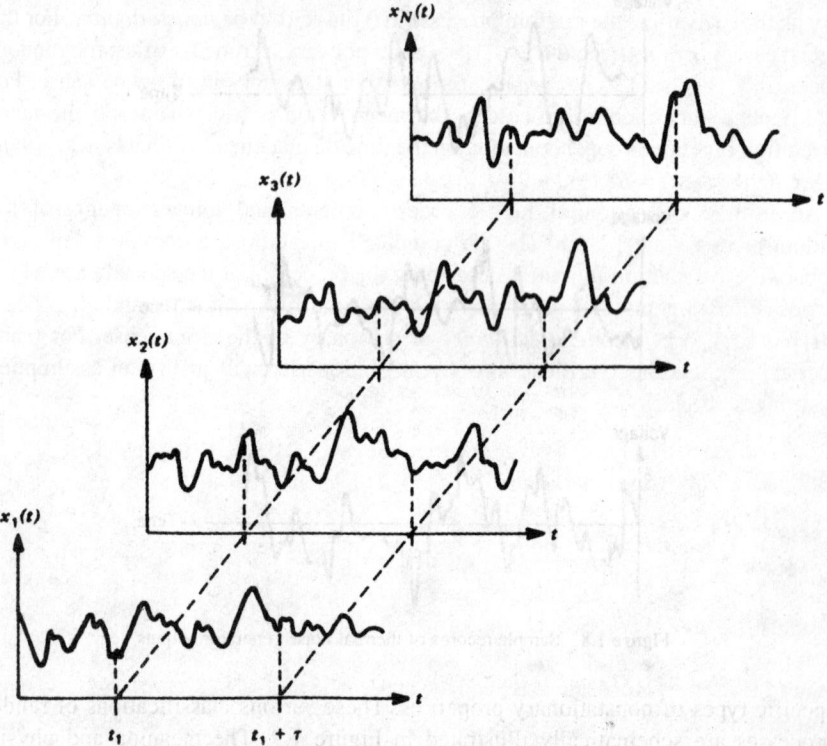

Figure 1.10 Ensemble of time history records defining a random process.

average values over the collection of sample functions that describe the random process. For example, consider the collection of sample functions (also called the *ensemble*) that forms the random process illustrated in Figure 1.10. The *mean value* (first moment) of the random process at some t_1 can be computed by taking the instantaneous value of each sample function of the ensemble at time t_1, summing the values, and dividing by the number of sample functions. In a similar manner, a correlation (joint moment) between the values of the random process at two different times (called the *autocorrelation function*) can be computed by taking the ensemble average of the product of instantaneous values at two times, t_1 and $t_1 + \tau$. That is, for the random process $\{x(t)\}$, where the symbol $\{\ \}$ is used to denote an ensemble of sample functions, the mean value $\mu_x(t_1)$ and the autocorrelation function $R_{xx}(t_1, t_1 + \tau)$ are given by

$$\mu_x(t_1) = \lim_{N \to \infty} \frac{1}{N} \sum_{k=1}^{N} x_k(t_1) \qquad (1.10a)$$

$$R_{xx}(t_1, t_1 + \tau) = \lim_{N \to \infty} \frac{1}{N} \sum_{k=1}^{N} x_k(t_1) x_k(t_1 + \tau) \qquad (1.10b)$$

where the final summation assumes that each sample function is equally likely.

CLASSIFICATIONS OF RANDOM DATA

For the general case where $\mu_x(t_1)$ and $R_{xx}(t_1, t_1 + \tau)$ defined in Equation (1.10) vary as time t_1 varies, the random process $\{x(t)\}$ is said to be *nonstationary*. For the special case where $\mu_x(t_1)$ and $R_{xx}(t_1, t_1 + \tau)$ do not vary as time t_1 varies, the random process $\{x(t)\}$ is said to be *weakly stationary* or stationary in the wide sense. For weakly stationary random processes, the mean value is a constant and the autocorrelation function is dependent only on the time displacement τ. That is, $\mu_x(t_1) = \mu_x$ and $R_{xx}(t_1, t_1 + \tau) = R_{xx}(\tau)$.

An infinite collection of higher order moments and joint moments of the random process $\{x(t)\}$ could also be computed to establish a complete family of probability distribution functions describing the process. For the special case where all possible moments and joint moments are time invariant, the random process $\{x(t)\}$ is said to be *strongly stationary* or stationary in the strict sense. For many practical applications, verification of weak stationarity will justify an assumption of strong stationarity.

1.3.2 Ergodic Random Data

In Section 1.3.1, it is noted how the properties of a random process can be determined by computing ensemble averages at specific instants of time. In most cases, however, it is also possible to describe the properties of a stationary random process by computing time averages over specific sample functions in the ensemble. For example, consider the kth sample function of the random process illustrated in Figure 1.10. The mean value $\mu_x(k)$ and the autocorrelation function $R_{xx}(\tau, k)$ of the kth sample function are given by

$$\mu_x(k) = \lim_{T \to \infty} \frac{1}{T} \int_0^T x_k(t)\, dt \qquad (1.11a)$$

$$R_{xx}(\tau, k) = \lim_{T \to \infty} \frac{1}{T} \int_0^T x_k(t) x_k(t + \tau)\, dt \qquad (1.11b)$$

If the random process $\{x(t)\}$ is stationary, and $\mu_x(k)$ and $R_{xx}(\tau, k)$ defined in Equation (1.11) do not differ when computed over different sample functions, the random process is said to be *ergodic*. For ergodic random processes, the time-averaged mean value and autocorrelation function (as well as all other time-averaged properties) are equal to the corresponding ensemble-averaged values. That is, $\mu_x(k) = \mu_x$ and $R_{xx}(\tau, k) = R_{xx}(\tau)$. Note that only stationary random processes can be ergodic.

Ergodic random processes are clearly an important class of random processes since all properties of ergodic random processes can be determined by performing time averages over a single sample function. Fortunately, in practice, random data representing stationary physical phenomena are generally ergodic. It is for this reason that the properties of stationary random phenomena can be measured properly, in most cases, from a single observed time history record. A full development of the properties of ergodic random processes is presented in Chapter 5.

1.3.3 Nonstationary Random Data

Nonstationary random processes include all random processes that do not meet the requirements for stationary defined in Section 1.3.1. Unless further restrictions are imposed, the properties of a nonstationary random process are generally time-varying functions that can be determined only by performing instantaneous averages over the ensemble of sample functions forming the process. In practice, it is often not feasible to obtain a sufficient number of sample records to permit the accurate measurement of properties by ensemble averaging. This fact has tended to impede the development of practical techniques for measuring and analyzing nonstationary random data.

In many cases, the nonstationary random data produced by actual physical phenomena can be classified into special categories of nonstationarity that simplify the measurement and analysis problem. For example, some types of random data might be described by a nonstationary random process $\{x(t)\}$, where each sample function is given by $x(t) = a(t)u(t)$. Here, $u(t)$ is a sample function from a stationary random process $\{u(t)\}$ and $a(t)$ is a deterministic multiplication factor. In other words, the data might be represented by a nonstationary random process consisting of sample functions with a common deterministic time trend. If nonstationary random data fit a specific model of this type, ensemble averaging is not always needed to describe the data. The various desired properties can sometimes be estimated from a single sample record, as is true for ergodic stationary data. These matters are discussed in detail in Chapter 12.

1.3.4 Stationary Sample Records

The concept of stationarity, as defined and discussed in Section 1.3.1, relates to the ensemble-averaged properties of a random process. In practice, however, data in the form of individual time history records of a random phenomenon are frequently referred to as being stationary or nonstationary. A slightly different interpretation of stationarity is involved here. When a single time history record is referred to as being stationary, it is generally meant that the properties computed over short time intervals do not vary significantly from one interval to the next. The word *significantly* is used here to mean that observed variations are greater than would be expected due to normal statistical sampling variations.

To help clarify this point, consider a single sample record $x_k(t)$ obtained from the kth sample function of a random process $\{x(t)\}$. Assume a mean value and an autocorrelation function are obtained by time averaging over a short interval T with a starting time of t_1 as follows:

$$\mu_x(t_1, k) = \frac{1}{T} \int_{t_1}^{t_1+T} x_k(t)\, dt \qquad (1.12a)$$

$$R_{xx}(t_1, t_1 + \tau, k) = \frac{1}{T} \int_{t_1}^{t_1+T} x_k(t) x_k(t+\tau)\, dr \qquad (1.12b)$$

For the general case where the sample properties defined in Equation (1.12) vary significantly as the starting time t_1 varies, the individual sample record is said to be nonstationary. For the special case where the sample properties defined in Equation (1.12) do not vary significantly as the starting time t_1 varies, the sample record is said to be stationary. Note that a sample record obtained from an ergodic random process will be stationary. Furthermore, sample records from most physically interesting nonstationary random processes will be nonstationary. Hence, if an ergodic assumption is justified (as it is for most actual stationary physical phenomena), verification of stationarity for a single sample record will effectively justify an assumption of stationarity and ergodicity for the random process from which the sample record is obtained. Tests for stationarity of individual sample records are discussed in Chapters 4 and 10.

1.4 ANALYSIS OF RANDOM DATA

The analysis of random data involves different considerations from the deterministic data discussed in Section 1.2. In particular, because no explicit mathematical equation can be written for the time histories produced by a random phenomenon, statistical procedure must be used to define the descriptive properties of the data. Nevertheless, well-defined input/output relations exist for random data, which are fundamental to a wide range of applications. In such applications, however, an understanding and control of the statistical errors associated with the computed data properties and input/output relationships is essential.

1.4.1 Basic Descriptive Properties

Basic statistical properties of importance for describing single stationary random records are

1. Mean and mean square values
2. Probability density functions
3. Autocorrelation functions
4. Autospectral density functions

For the present discussion, it is instructive to define these quantities by words alone, without the use of mathematical equations. After this has been done, they will be illustrated for special cases of interest.

The mean value μ_x and the variance σ_x^2 for a stationary record represent the central tendency and dispersion, respectively, of the data. The mean square value ψ_x^2, which equals the variance plus the square of the mean, constitutes a measure of the combined central tendency and dispersion. The mean value is estimated by simply computing the average of all data values in the record. The mean square value is similarly estimated by computing the average of the squared data values. By first subtracting the mean value estimate from all the data values, the mean square value computation yields a variance estimate.

The probability density function $p(x)$ for a stationary record represents the rate of change of probability with data value. The function $p(x)$ is generally estimated by computing the probability that the instantaneous value of the single record will be in a particular narrow amplitude range centered at various data values, and then dividing by the amplitude range. The total area under the probability density function over all data values will be unity because this merely indicates the certainty of the fact that the data values must fall between $-\infty$ and $+\infty$. The partial area under the probability density function from $-\infty$ to some given value x represents the probability distribution function, denoted by $P(x)$. The area under the probability density function between any two values x_1 and x_2, given by $P(x_2) - P(x_1)$, defines the probability that any future data values at a randomly selected time will fall within this amplitude interval. Probability density and distribution functions are fully discussed in Chapters 3 and 4.

The autocorrelation function $R_{xx}(\tau)$ for a stationary record is a measure of time-related properties in the data that are separated by fixed time delays. It can be estimated by delaying the record relative to itself by some fixed time delay τ, then multiplying the original record with the delayed record, and finally averaging the resulting product values over the available record length or over some desired portion of this record length. The procedure is repeated for all time delays of interest.

The autospectral (also called *power* spectral) density function $G_{xx}(f)$ for a stationary record represents the rate of change of mean square value with frequency. It is estimated by computing the mean square value in a narrow frequency band at various center frequencies, and then dividing by the frequency band. The total area under the autospectral density function over all frequencies will be the total mean square value of the record. The partial area under the autospectral density function from f_1 to f_2 represents the mean square value of the record associated with that frequency range. Autocorrelation and autospectral density functions are developed in Chapter 5.

Four typical time histories of a sine wave, sine wave plus random noise, narrow bandwidth random noise, and wide bandwidth random noise are shown in Figure 1.11. Theoretical plots of their probability density functions, autocorrelation functions, and autospectral density functions are shown in Figures 1.12, 1.13, and 1.14, respectively. Equations for all of these plots are given in Chapter 5, together with other theoretical formulas.

For pairs of random records from two different stationary random processes, joint statistical properties of importance are

1. Joint probability density functions
2. Cross-correlation functions
3. Cross-spectral density functions
4. Frequency response functions
5. Coherence functions

ANALYSIS OF RANDOM DATA

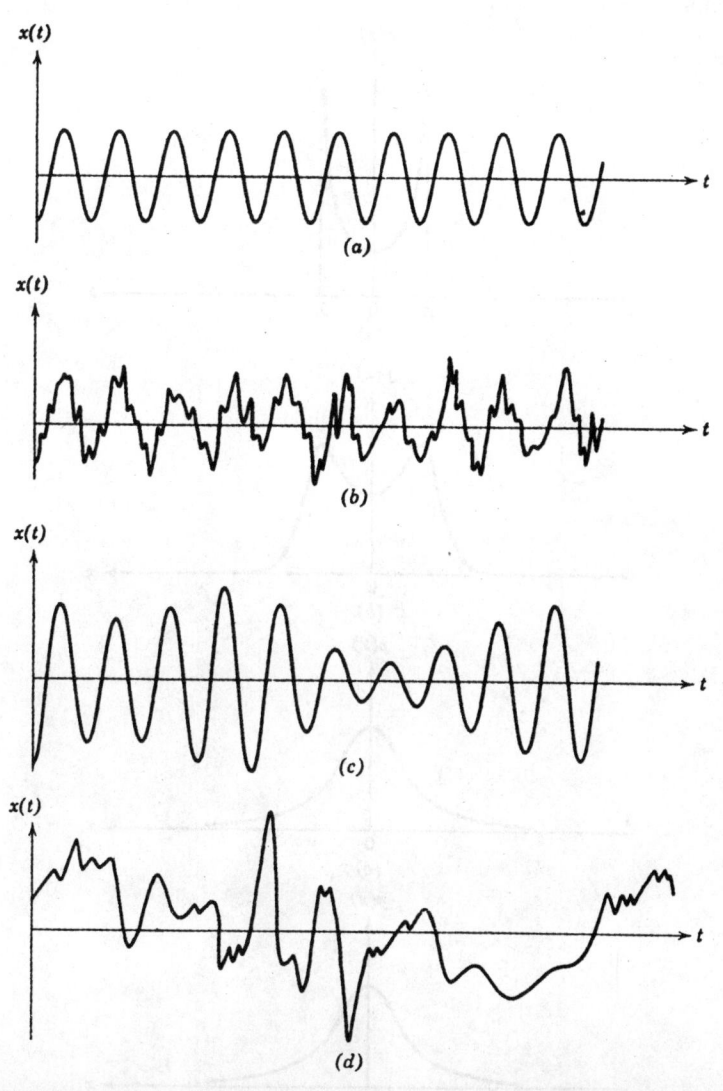

Figure 1.11 Four special time histories. (*a*) Sine wave. (*b*) Sine wave plus random noise. (*c*) Narrow bandwidth random noise. (*d*) Wide bandwidth random noise.

The first three functions measure fundamental properties shared by the pair of records in the amplitude, time, or frequency domains. From knowledge of the cross-spectral density function between the pair of records, as well as their individual autospectral density functions, one can compute theoretical linear frequency response functions (gain factors and phase factors) between the two records. Here, the two records are treated as a single-input/single-output problem. The coherence function is a measure of the accuracy of the assumed linear input/output model and can also be computed from the measured autospectral and cross-spectral density functions. Detailed discussions of these topics appear in Chapters 5, 6, and 7.

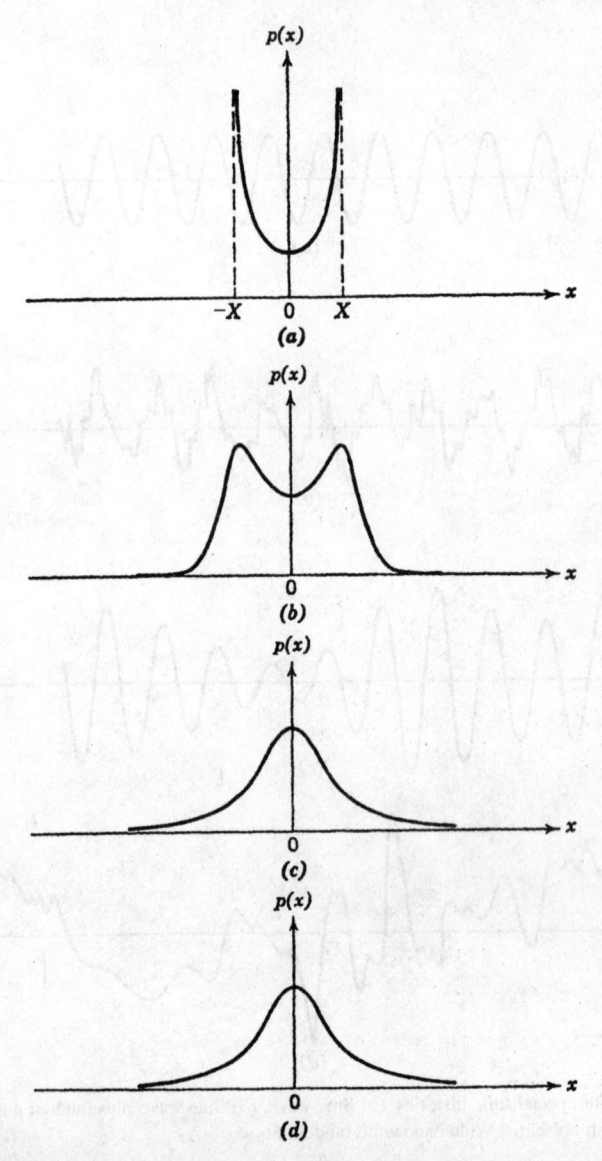

Figure 1.12 Probability density function plots. (*a*) Sine wave. (*b*) Sine wave plus random noise. (*c*) Narrow bandwidth random noise. (*d*) Wide bandwidth random noise.

Common applications of probability density and distribution functions, beyond a basic probabilistic description of data values, include

1. Evaluation of normality
2. Detection of data acquisition errors
3. Indication of nonlinear effects
4. Analysis of extreme values

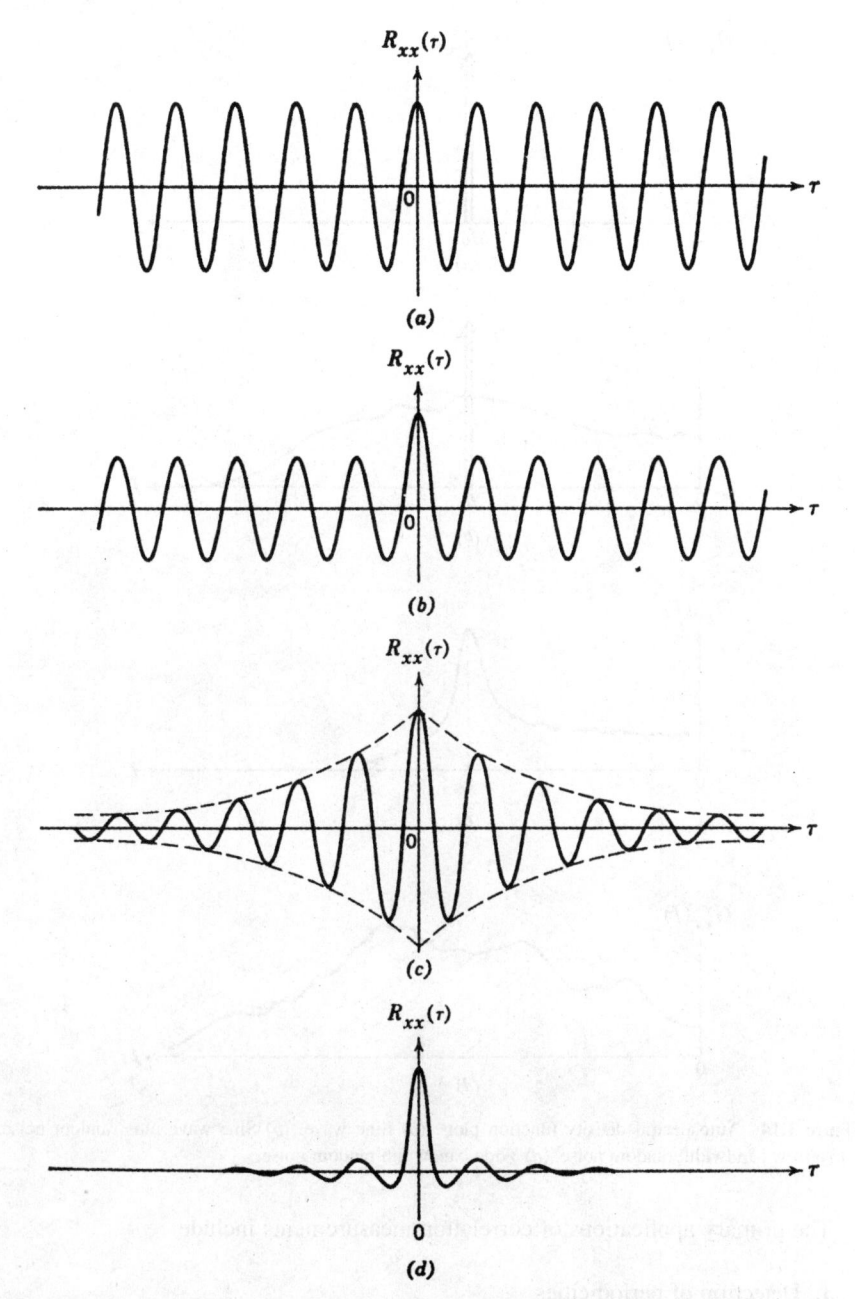

Figure 1.13 Autocorrelation function plots. (*a*) Sine wave. (*b*) Sine wave plus random noise. (*c*) Narrow bandwidth random noise. (*d*) Wide bandwidth random noise.

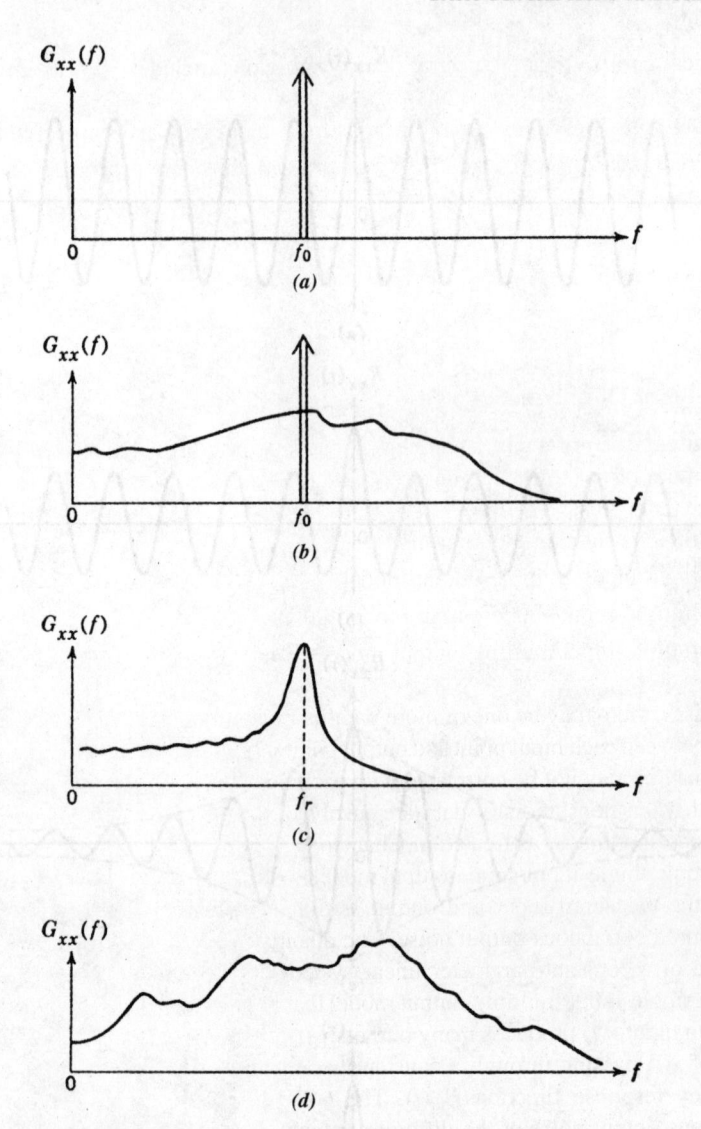

Figure 1.14 Autospectral density function plots. (*a*) Sine wave. (*b*) Sine wave plus random noise. (*c*) Narrow bandwidth random noise. (*d*) Wide bandwidth random noise.

The primary applications of correlation measurements include

1. Detection of periodicities
2. Prediction of signals in noise
3. Measurement of time delays
4. Location of disturbing sources
5. Identification of propagation paths and velocities

ANALYSIS OF RANDOM DATA

Typical applications of spectral density functions include

1. Determination of system properties from input data and output data
2. Prediction of output data from input data and system properties
3. Identification of input data from output data and system properties
4. Specifications of dynamic data for test programs
5. Identification of energy and noise sources
6. Optimum linear prediction and filtering

1.4.2 Input/Output Relations

Input/output cases of common interest can usually be considered as combinations of one or more of the following linear system models:

1. Single-input/single-output model
2. Single-input/multiple-output model
3. Multiple-input/single-output model
4. Multiple-input/multiple-output model

In all cases, there may be one or more parallel transmission paths with different time delays between each input point and output point. For multiple-input cases, the various inputs may or may not be correlated with each other. Special analysis techniques are required when nonstationary data are involved, as treated in Chapter 12, or when systems are nonlinear, as treated in Chapter 14.

A simple single-input/single-output model is shown in Figure 1.15. Here, $x(t)$ and $y(t)$ are the measured input and output stationary random records, and $n(t)$ is the unmeasured extraneous output noise. The quantity $H_{xy}(f)$ is the frequency response function of a constant-parameter linear system between $x(t)$ and $y(t)$. Figure 1.16 shows a single-input/multiple-output model that is a simple extension of Figure 1.15, where an input $x(t)$ produces many outputs $y_i(t)$, $i = 1, 2, 3,\ldots$ Any output $y_i(t)$ is the result of $x(t)$ passing through a constant-parameter linear system described by the frequency response function $H_{xi}(f)$. The noise terms $n_i(t)$ represent unmeasured extraneous output noise at the different outputs. It is clear that Figure 1.16 can be considered as a combination of separate single-input/single-output models.

Appropriate procedures for solving single-input models are developed in Chapter 6 using measured autospectral and cross-spectral density functions. Ordinary coher-

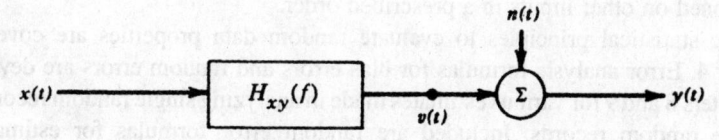

Figure 1.15 Single-input/single-output system with output noise.

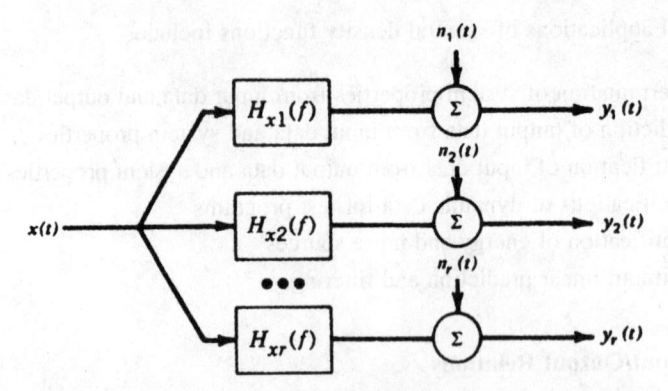

Figure 1.16 Single-input/multiple-output system with output noise.

ence functions are defined, which play a key role in both system-identification and source-identification problems. To determine both the gain factor and the phase factor of a desired frequency response function, it is always necessary to measure the cross-spectral density function between the input and output points. A good estimate of the gain factor alone can be obtained from measurements of the input and output autospectral density functions only if there is negligible input and output extraneous noise.

For a well-defined single-input/single-output model where the data are stationary, the system is linear and has constant parameters, and there is no extraneous noise at either the input or output point, the ordinary coherence function will be identically unity for all frequencies. Any deviation from these ideal conditions will cause the coherence function to be less than unity. In practice, measured coherence functions will often be less than unity and are important in determining the statistical confidence in frequency response function measurements.

Extensions of these ideas can be carried out for general multiple-input/multiple-output problems, which require the definition and proper interpretation of multiple coherence functions and partial coherence functions. These general situations can be considered as combinations of a set of multiple-input/single-output models for a given set of stationary inputs and for different constant-parameter linear systems, as shown in Figure 1.17. Modern procedures for solving multiple-input/output problems are developed in Chapter 7 using conditioned (residual) spectral density functions. These procedures are extensions of classical regression techniques discussed in Chapter 4. In particular, the output autospectral density function in Figure 1.17 is decomposed to show how much of this output spectrum at any frequency is due to any input conditioned on other inputs in a prescribed order.

Basic statistical principles to evaluate random data properties are covered in Chapter 4. Error analysis formulas for bias errors and random errors are developed in Chapters 8 and 9 for various estimates made in analyzing single random records and multiple random records. Included are random error formulas for estimates of frequency response functions (both gain factors and phase factors) and estimates of

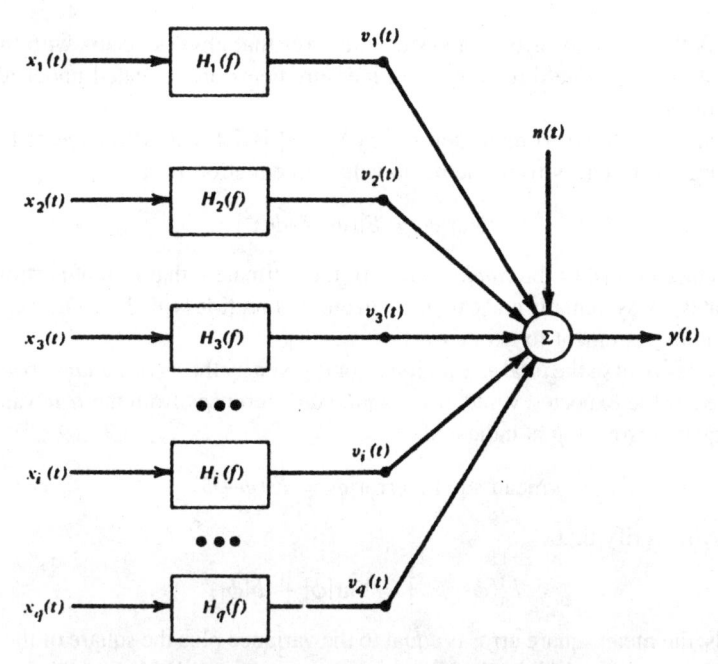

Figure 1.17 Multiple-input/single-output system with output noise.

coherence functions (ordinary, multiple, or partial). These computations are easy to apply and should be performed to obtain proper interpretations of measured results.

1.4.3 Error Analysis Criteria

Some error analysis criteria for measured quantities will now be defined as background for the material in Chapters 8 and 9. Let a hat (^) symbol over a quantity ϕ, namely, $\hat{\phi}$, denote an estimate of this quantity. The quantity $\hat{\phi}$ will be an estimate of ϕ based on a finite time interval or a finite number of sample points.

Conceptually, suppose $\hat{\phi}$ can be estimated many times by repeating an experiment or some measurement program. Then, the expected value of $\hat{\phi}$, denoted by $E[\hat{\phi}]$, is something one can estimate. For example, if an experiment is repeated many times to yield results $\hat{\phi}_i$, $i = 1, 2, \ldots, N$, then

$$E[\hat{\phi}] = \lim_{N \to \infty} \frac{1}{N} \sum_{i=1}^{N} \hat{\phi}_i \qquad (1.13)$$

This expected value may or may not equal the true value ϕ. If it does, the estimate $\hat{\phi}$ is said to be unbiased. Otherwise, it is said to be biased. The *bias* of the estimate, denoted $b[\hat{\phi}]$, is equal to the expected value of the estimate minus the true value—that is,

$$b[\hat{\phi}] = E[\hat{\phi}] - \phi \qquad (1.14)$$

It follows that the bias error is a systematic error that always occurs with the same magnitude in the same direction when measurements are repeated under identical circumstances.

The *variance* of the estimate, denoted by $\mathrm{Var}[\hat{\phi}]$, is defined as the expected value of the squared differences from the mean value. In equation form,

$$\mathrm{Var}[\hat{\phi}] = E[(\hat{\phi}-E[\hat{\phi}])^2] \qquad (1.15)$$

The variance describes the *random error* of the estimate—that is, that portion of the error that is not systematic and can occur in either direction with different magnitudes from one measurement to another.

An assessment of the total estimation error is given by the *mean square error*, which is defined as the expected value of the squared differences from the *true* value. The mean square error of $\hat{\phi}$ is indicated by

$$\text{mean square error}[\hat{\phi}] = E[(\hat{\phi}-\phi)^2] \qquad (1.16)$$

It is easy to verify that

$$E[(\hat{\phi}-\phi)^2] = \mathrm{Var}[\hat{\phi}] + (b[\hat{\phi}])^2 \qquad (1.17)$$

In words, the mean square error is equal to the variance plus the square of the bias. If the bias is zero or negligible, then the mean square error and variance are equivalent.

Figure 1.18 illustrates the meaning of the bias (systematic) error and the variance (random) error for the case of testing two guns for possible purchase by shooting each gun at a target. In Figure 1.18(*a*), gun A has a large bias error and small variance error. In Figure 1.18(*b*), gun B has a small bias error but large variance error. As shown, gun A will never hit the target, whereas gun B will occasionally hit the target. Nevertheless, most people would prefer to buy gun A because the bias error can be removed (assuming one knows it is present) by adjusting the sights of the gun, but the random

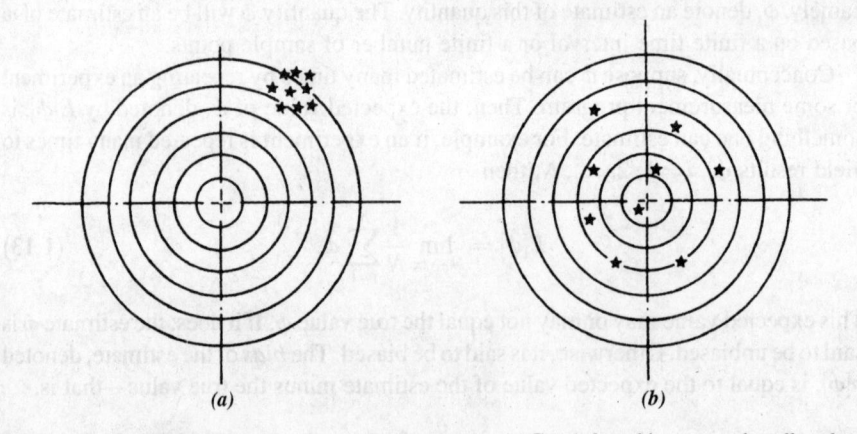

Figure 1.18 Random and bias errors in gun shoots at a target. (*a*) Gun A: large bias error and small random error. (*b*) Gun B: small bias error and large random error.

error cannot be removed. Hence, gun A provides the potential for a smaller mean square error.

A final important quantity is the *normalized rms error* of the estimate, denoted by $\varepsilon[\hat{\phi}]$. This error is a dimensionless quantity that is equal to the square root of the mean square error divided by the true value (assumed, of course, to be different from zero). Symbolically,

$$\varepsilon[\hat{\phi}] = \frac{\sqrt{E[(\hat{\phi}-\phi)^2]}}{\phi} \qquad (1.18)$$

In practice, one should try to make the normalized rms error as small as possible. This will help to guarantee that an arbitrary estimate $\hat{\phi}$ will lie close to the true value ϕ.

1.4.4 Data Analysis Procedures

Recommended data analysis procedures are discussed in more detail in Chapters 10–14. Chapter 10 deals with data acquisition problems, including data collection, storage, conversion, and qualification. General steps are outlined for proper data analysis of individual records and multiple records, as would be needed for different applications. Digital data analysis techniques discussed in Chapter 11 involve computational procedures to perform trend removal, digital filtering, Fourier series, and fast Fourier transforms on discrete time series data representing sample records from stationary (ergodic) random data. Digital formulas are developed to compute estimates of probability density functions, correlation functions, and spectral density functions for individual records and for associated joint records. Further detailed digital procedures are stated to obtain estimates of all of the quantities described in Chapters 6 and 7 to solve various types of single-input/output problems and multiple-input/output problems. Chapter 12 is devoted to separate methods for nonstationary data analysis, and Chapter 13 develops Hilbert transform techniques. Chapter 14 discusses models for nonlinear system analysis.

PROBLEMS

1.1 Determine the period of the function defined by

$$x(t) = \sin 11t + \sin 12t$$

1.2 For the following functions, which are periodic and which are nonperiodic?
- (a) $x(t) = 3 \sin t + 2 \sin 2t + \sin 3t$.
- (b) $x(t) = 3 \sin t + 2 \sin 2t + \sin \pi t$.
- (c) $x(t) = 3 \sin 4t + 2 \sin 5t + \sin 6t$.
- (d) $x(t) = e^{-t} \sin t$.

1.3 If a stationary random process $\{x(t)\}$ has a mean value of μ_x, what is the limiting value of the autocorrelation function $R_{xx}(\tau)$ as the time delay τ becomes long?

1.4 An estimate is known to have a mean square error of 0.25 and a bias error of 0.40. Determine the variance of the estimate.

1.5 In Problem 1.4, if the quantity being estimated has a true value of $\phi = 5$, what is the normalized rms error of the estimate?

In Problems 1.6–1.9 state which properties are always true.

1.6 A stationary random process must
 (a) be discrete.
 (b) be continuous.
 (c) be ergodic.
 (d) have ensemble-averaged properties that are independent of time.
 (e) have time-averaged properties that are equal to the ensemble-averaged properties.

1.7 An ergodic random process must
 (a) be discrete.
 (b) be continuous.
 (c) be stationary.
 (d) have ensemble-averaged properties that are independent of time.
 (e) have time-averaged properties that are equal to the ensemble-averaged properties.

1.8 A single sample function can be used to find all statistical properties of a random process if the process is
 (a) deterministic.
 (b) ergodic.
 (c) stationary.
 (d) all of the above.

1.9 The autocorrelation function of a stationary random process
 (a) must decrease as $|\tau|$ increases.
 (b) is a function of the time difference only.
 (c) must approach a constant as $|\tau|$ increases.
 (d) must always be nonnegative.

1.10 How do the answers to Problem 1.9 change if the stationary random process is mixed with a periodic process?

CHAPTER 2

Linear Physical Systems

Before the measurement and analysis of random physical data is discussed in more detail, it is desirable to clarify some pertinent concepts and fundamental definitions related to the dynamic behavior of physical systems. This chapter reviews the theoretical formulas for describing the response characteristics of ideal linear systems and illustrates the basic ideas for simple physical examples.

2.1 CONSTANT-PARAMETER LINEAR SYSTEMS

An ideal system is one that has *constant parameters* and is *linear* between two clearly defined points of interest called the input or excitation point and the output or response point. A system has constant parameters if all fundamental properties of the system are invariant with respect to time. For example, a simple passive electrical circuit would be a constant-parameter system if the values for the resistance, capacitance, and inductance of all elements did not change from one time to another. A system is linear if the response characteristics are additive and homogeneous. The term *additive* means that the output to a sum of inputs is equal to the sum of the outputs produced by each input individually. The term *homogeneous* means that the output produced by a constant times the input is equal to the constant times the output produced by the input alone. In equation form, if $f(x)$ represents the output to an input x, then the system is linear if for any two inputs x_1, x_2, and constant c,

$$f(x_1 + x_2) = f(x_1) + f(x_2) \quad \text{additive property} \qquad (2.1a)$$

$$f(cx) = cf(x) \quad \text{homogeneous property} \qquad (2.1b)$$

The constant-parameter assumption is reasonably valid for many physical systems in practice. For example, the fundamental properties of an electrical circuit or a mechanical structure will usually not display significant changes over any time interval of practical interest. There are, of course, exceptions. The value of an

---

Random Data: Analysis and Measurement Procedures, Fourth Edition. By Julius S. Bendat and Allan G. Piersol
Copyright © 2010 John Wiley & Sons, Inc.

electrical resistor may change owing to a high-temperature exposure, or the stiffness of a structure may change because of fatigue damage caused by continual vibration. Furthermore, some physical systems are designed to have time-varying parameters that are fundamental to the desired purpose of the system. Electronic communication systems are an obvious example. However, such conditions are generally special cases that can be clearly identified in practice.

A linearity assumption for real systems is somewhat more critical. All physical systems will display nonlinear response characteristics under sufficiently extreme input conditions. For example, an electrical capacitor will ultimately arc as the applied voltage is increased and, hence, will no longer pass a current that is directly proportional to the applied voltage, or a metal cable will ultimately break as the applied load is increased and, hence, will no longer display a strain that is proportional to the applied load. To make the problem more difficult, common nonlinearities usually occur gradually rather than abruptly at one point. For example, the load-strain relationship for the metal cable would actually start deviating from a linear relationship long before the final abrupt break occurs. Nevertheless, the response characteristics for many physical systems may be assumed to be linear, at least over some limited range of inputs, without involving unreasonable errors. See Chapter 14 and Ref. 1 for detailed discussions of analysis procedures for nonlinear systems.

Example 2.1. **Illustration of Nonlinear System.** Consider a simple square law system where the output is given by

$$y = f(x) = ax^2$$

For any two inputs x_1 and x_2,

$$f(x_1 + x_2) = a(x_1 + x_2)^2 = ax_1^2 + 2ax_1x_2 + ax_2^2$$

but the additive property in Equation (2.1a) requires that

$$f(x_1 + x_2) = ax_1^2 + ax_2^2$$

Furthermore, for an arbitrary constant c,

$$f(cx) = a(cx)^2 = c^2 ax^2$$

but the homogeneous property in Equation (2.1b) demands that

$$f(cx) = cax^2$$

Hence, the system is not linear, in that it fails to comply with both the additive and homogeneous properties of a linear system.

2.2 BASIC DYNAMIC CHARACTERISTICS

The dynamic characteristics of a constant-parameter linear system can be described by an *impulse response function* $h(\tau)$, sometimes called the *weighting function*, which

BASIC DYNAMIC CHARACTERISTICS

is defined as the output of the system at any time to a unit impulse input applied a time τ before. The usefulness of the impulse response function as a description of the system is due to the following fact. For any arbitrary input $x(t)$, the system output $y(t)$ is given by the *convolution integral*

$$y(t) = \int_{-\infty}^{\infty} h(\tau)x(t-\tau)\,d\tau \qquad (2.2)$$

That is, the value of the output $y(t)$ is given as a weighted linear (infinite) sum over the entire history of the input $x(t)$.

In order for a constant-parameter linear system to be *physically realizable (causal)*, it is necessary that the system respond only to past inputs. This implies that

$$h(\tau) = 0 \quad \text{for } \tau < 0 \qquad (2.3)$$

Hence, for physical systems, the effective lower limit of integration in Equation (2.2) is zero rather than $-\infty$.

A constant-parameter linear system is said to be *stable* if every possible bounded input function produces a bounded output function. From Equation (2.2),

$$|y(t)| = \left| \int_{-\infty}^{\infty} h(\tau)x(t-\tau),d\tau \right| \leq \int_{-\infty}^{\infty} |h(\tau)||x(t-\tau)|\,d\tau \qquad (2.4)$$

When the input $x(t)$ is bounded, there exists some finite constant A such that

$$|x(t)| \leq A \quad \text{for all } t \qquad (2.5)$$

It follows from Equation (2.4) that

$$|y(t)| \leq A \int_{-\infty}^{\infty} |h(\tau)|\,d\tau \qquad (2.6)$$

Hence, if the constant-parameter linear weighting function $h(\tau)$ is absolutely integrable, that is,

$$\int_{-\infty}^{\infty} |h(\tau)|\,d\tau < \infty \qquad (2.7)$$

then the output will be bounded and the system is stable.

Example 2.2. Illustration of Unstable System. Consider a simple system with a unit impulse response function of the form

$$h(\tau) = \begin{cases} Ae^{a\tau} & \tau \geq 0 \\ 0 & \tau < 0 \end{cases}$$

Because $h(\tau) = 0$ for $\tau < 0$, the system is physically realizable by definition. However,

$$\int_{-\infty}^{\infty} |h(\tau)|\,d\tau = \int_{0}^{\infty} |Ae^{a\tau}|\,d\tau = \frac{A}{a}(e^{a\infty} - 1)$$

It follows that the system is unstable if $a \geq 0$, but stable if $a < 0$. Specifically for $a = -b < 0$,

$$\int_0^\infty |Ae^{-b\tau}| d\tau = \frac{A}{-b}(e^{-\infty} - 1) = \frac{A}{b}$$

This completes Example 2.2.

A constant-parameter linear system can also be characterized by a *transfer function* $H(p)$, which is defined as the Laplace transform of $h(\tau)$. That is,

$$H(p) = \int_0^\infty h(\tau) e^{-p\tau} d\tau \quad p = a + jb \tag{2.8}$$

The criterion for stability of a constant-parameter linear system (assumed to be physically realizable) takes on an interesting form when considered in terms of the transfer function $H(p)$. Specifically, if $H(p)$ has no poles in the right half of the complex p plane or on the imaginary axis (no poles where $a \geq 0$), then the system is stable. Conversely, if $H(p)$ has at least one pole in the right half of the complex p plane, then the system is unstable.

An important property of constant-parameter linear systems is frequency preservation. Specifically, consider a constant-parameter linear system with an impulse response function $h(\tau)$. From Equation (2.2), for any arbitrary input $x(t)$, the nth derivative of the output $y(t)$ with respect to time is given by

$$\frac{d^n y(t)}{dt^n} = \int_{-\infty}^\infty h(\tau) \frac{d^n x(t-\tau)}{dt^n} d\tau \tag{2.9}$$

Now, assume the input $x(t)$ is sinusoidal, that is,

$$x(t) = X \sin(2\pi f t + \theta) \tag{2.10}$$

The second derivative of $x(t)$ is

$$\frac{d^2 x(t)}{dt^2} = -4\pi^2 f^2 x(t) \tag{2.11}$$

It follows from Equation (2.9) that the second derivative for the output $y(t)$ must be

$$\frac{d^2 y(t)}{dt^2} = -4\pi^2 f^2 y(t) \tag{2.12}$$

Thus, $y(t)$ must also be sinusoidal with the same frequency as $x(t)$. This result shows that a constant-parameter linear system cannot cause any frequency translation but can only modify the amplitude and phase of an applied input.

2.3 FREQUENCY RESPONSE FUNCTIONS

If a constant-parameter linear system is physically realizable and stable, then the dynamic characteristics of the system can be described by a *frequency response function* $H(f)$, which is defined as the Fourier transform of $h(\tau)$. That is,

$$H(f) = \int_0^\infty h(\tau)e^{-j2\pi f\tau}d\tau \tag{2.13}$$

Note that the lower limit of integration is zero rather than $-\infty$ since $h(\tau)=0$ for $\tau<0$. The frequency response function is simply a special case of the transfer function defined in Equation (2.8) where, in the exponent $p=a+jb$, $a=0$ and $b=2\pi f$. For physically realizable and stable systems, the frequency response function may replace the transfer function with no loss of useful information.

An important relationship for the frequency response function of constant-parameter linear systems is obtained by taking the Fourier transform of both sides of Equation (2.2). Letting $X(f)$ be the Fourier transform of an input $x(t)$ and letting $Y(f)$ be the Fourier transform of the resulting output $y(t)$, assuming these transforms exist, it follows from Equation (2.2) that

$$Y(f) = H(f)X(f) \tag{2.14}$$

Hence, in terms of the frequency response function of a system and the Fourier transforms of the input and the output, the convolution integral in Equation (2.2) reduces to the simple algebraic expression in Equation (2.14).

The frequency response function is generally a complex-valued quantity that may be conveniently thought of in terms of a magnitude and an associated phase angle. This can be done by writing $H(f)$ in complex polar notation as

$$H(f) = |H(f)|e^{-j\phi(f)} \tag{2.15}$$

The absolute value $|H(f)|$ is called the system *gain factor*, and the associated phase angle $\phi(f)$ is called the system *phase factor*. In these terms, the frequency response function takes on a direct physical interpretation as follows. Assume a system is subjected to a sinusoidal input (hypothetically existing over all time) with a frequency f producing an output that, as illustrated in Section 2.2, will also be sinusoidal with the same frequency. The ratio of the output amplitude to the input amplitude is equal to the gain factor $|H(f)|$ of the system, and the phase shift between the output and the input is equal to the phase factor $\phi(f)$ of the system.

From physical realizability requirements, the frequency response function, the gain factor, and the phase factor of a constant-parameter linear system satisfy the following symmetry properties:

$$\begin{aligned} H(-f) &= H^*(f) \\ |H(-f)| &= |H(f)| \\ \phi(-f) &= -\phi(f) \end{aligned} \tag{2.16}$$

Furthermore, if one system described by $H_1(f)$ is followed by a second system described by $H_2(f)$, and there is no loading or feedback between the two systems, then the overall system may be described by $H(f)$, where

$$\begin{aligned} H(f) &= H_1(f)H_2(f) \\ |H(f)| &= |H_1(f)||H_2(f)| \\ \phi(f) &= \phi_1(f)+\phi_2(f) \end{aligned} \tag{2.17}$$

Thus, on cascading two systems where there is no loading or feedback, the gain factors multiply and the phase factors add.

It is important to note that the frequency response function $H(f)$ of constant-parameter linear system is a function of only frequency and is not function of either time or the system excitation. If the system were nonlinear, $H(f)$ would also be a function of the applied input. If the parameters of the system were not constant, $H(f)$ would also be a function of time.

2.4 ILLUSTRATIONS OF FREQUENCY RESPONSE FUNCTIONS

A clearer understanding of the frequency response function of common physical systems will be afforded by considering some examples. The examples chosen involve simple mechanical and electrical systems because these particular physical systems are generally easier to visualize. The analogous characteristics relating mechanical and electrical systems to other physical systems are noted.

2.4.1 Mechanical Systems

Assume a simple mechanical structure can be represented by a lumped parameter system consisting of a mass, a spring, and a viscous damper (also called a *dashpot*), where the motion of the mass is restricted to translation in only one direction, as shown in Figure 2.1. In this figure, m is the mass in kilograms (kg), k is the spring constant in newtons/meter (N/m), and c is the damping coefficient in newton-seconds/meter (Ns/m). The system in Figure 2.1 is commonly referred to as a *single degree-of-freedom (dof) system* because its response can be described by a single coordinate.

Before a frequency response function can be determined, it is necessary to define the input and output parameters of interest. There are a number of possibilities for the system in Figure 2.1, as will be illustrated now.

2.4.1.1 Force Input and Displacement Output

Assume the input of interest is a force applied to the mass, and the output of interest is the resulting displacement of the mass, as illustrated in Figure 2.2. Here, $F(t)$ is an applied force in newtons and $y(t)$ is the resulting output displacement of the mass in meters.

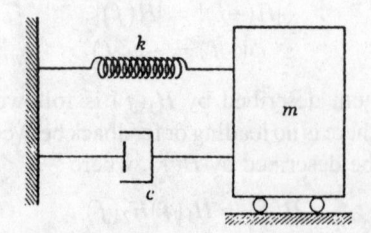

Figure 2.1 Simple mechanical system.

ILLUSTRATIONS OF FREQUENCY RESPONSE FUNCTIONS

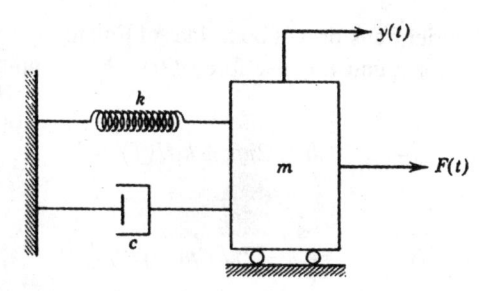

Figure 2.2 Mechanical system with force input.

The first step toward establishing an appropriate frequency response function for this system is to determine the equation of motion. This is accomplished by using the relationship from basic mechanics that the sum of all forces acting on the mass must equal zero, as follows:

$$F(t) + F_k(t) + F_c(t) + F_m(t) = 0 \qquad (2.18)$$

where

$$F_k(t) = -ky(t) = \text{spring force} \qquad (2.18a)$$

$$F_c(t) = -c\dot{y}(t) = \text{damping force} \qquad (2.18b)$$

$$F_m(t) = -m\ddot{y}(t) = \text{inertial force} \qquad (2.18c)$$

$$\dot{y}(t) = \frac{dy(t)}{dt} = \text{velocity}$$

$$\ddot{y}(t) = \frac{d^2y(t)}{dt^2} = \text{acceleration}$$

Hence, the equation of motion for this system is

$$m\ddot{y}(t) + c\dot{y}(t) + ky(t) = F(t) \qquad (2.19)$$

In Section 2.3, the frequency response function is defined as the Fourier transform of the output of the system to a unit impulse. For this case, the output of the system is the displacement $y(t)$ whose Fourier transform is given by

$$Y(f) = \int_0^\infty y(t)e^{-j2\pi ft}\,dt = H(f) \qquad (2.20)$$

It follows that

$$\text{Fourier transform}[\dot{y}(t)] = j2\pi f\, H(f) \qquad (2.20a)$$

$$\text{Fourier transform}[\ddot{y}(t)] = -(2\pi f)^2 H(f) \qquad (2.20b)$$

Now, by taking the Fourier transform of both sides of Equation (2.19) and noting that the Fourier transform for a unit impulse force $F(t) = \delta(t)$ is unity, one obtains the following result:

$$[-(2\pi f)^2 m + j2\pi fc + k]H(f) = 1 \qquad (2.21a)$$

Thus

$$H(f)_{f-d} = [k - (2\pi f)^2 m + j2\pi fc]^{-1} \qquad (2.21b)$$

where the subscript f–d is added to indicate that this particular $H(f)$ relates a force input to a displacement output.

It is desirable to write Equation (2.21) in a different form by introducing two definitions:

$$\zeta = \frac{c}{2\sqrt{km}} \qquad (2.22a)$$

$$f_n = \frac{1}{2\pi}\sqrt{\frac{k}{m}} \qquad (2.22b)$$

The term ζ in Equation (2.22a) is a dimensionless quantity called the *damping ratio*. The term f_n in Equation (2.22b) is called the *undamped natural frequency* and has units of cycles per second (Hz). When these definitions are substituted into Equation (2.21), the following result is obtained:

$$H(f)_{f-d} = \frac{1/k}{1-(f/f_n)^2 + j2\zeta f/f_n} \qquad (2.23)$$

Writing Equation (2.23) in complex polar notation gives the frequency response function in terms of a gain factor $|H(f)|$ and a phase factor $\phi(f)$ as follows:

$$H(f) = |H(f)|e^{-j\phi(f)} \qquad (2.24)$$

where

$$|H(f)|_{f-d} = \frac{1/k}{\sqrt{[1-(f/f_n)^2]^2 + [2\zeta f/f_n]^2}} \qquad (2.24a)$$

$$\phi(f)_{f-d} = \tan^{-1}\left[\frac{2\zeta f/f_n}{1-(f/f_n)^2}\right] \qquad (2.24b)$$

Note that $|H(f)|_{f-d}$ has units of $1/k$ or meters/newton. This particular function is sometimes called a *magnification function*.

Plots of $|H(f)|_{f-d}$ and $\phi(f)_{f-d}$ as defined in Equation (2.24) are presented in Figure 2.3. Three characteristics of these plots are of particular interest. First, the gain factor has a peak at some frequency less than f_n for all cases where $\zeta \leq 1/\sqrt{2}$. The frequency at which this peak gain factor occurs is called the *resonance frequency* of

ILLUSTRATIONS OF FREQUENCY RESPONSE FUNCTIONS

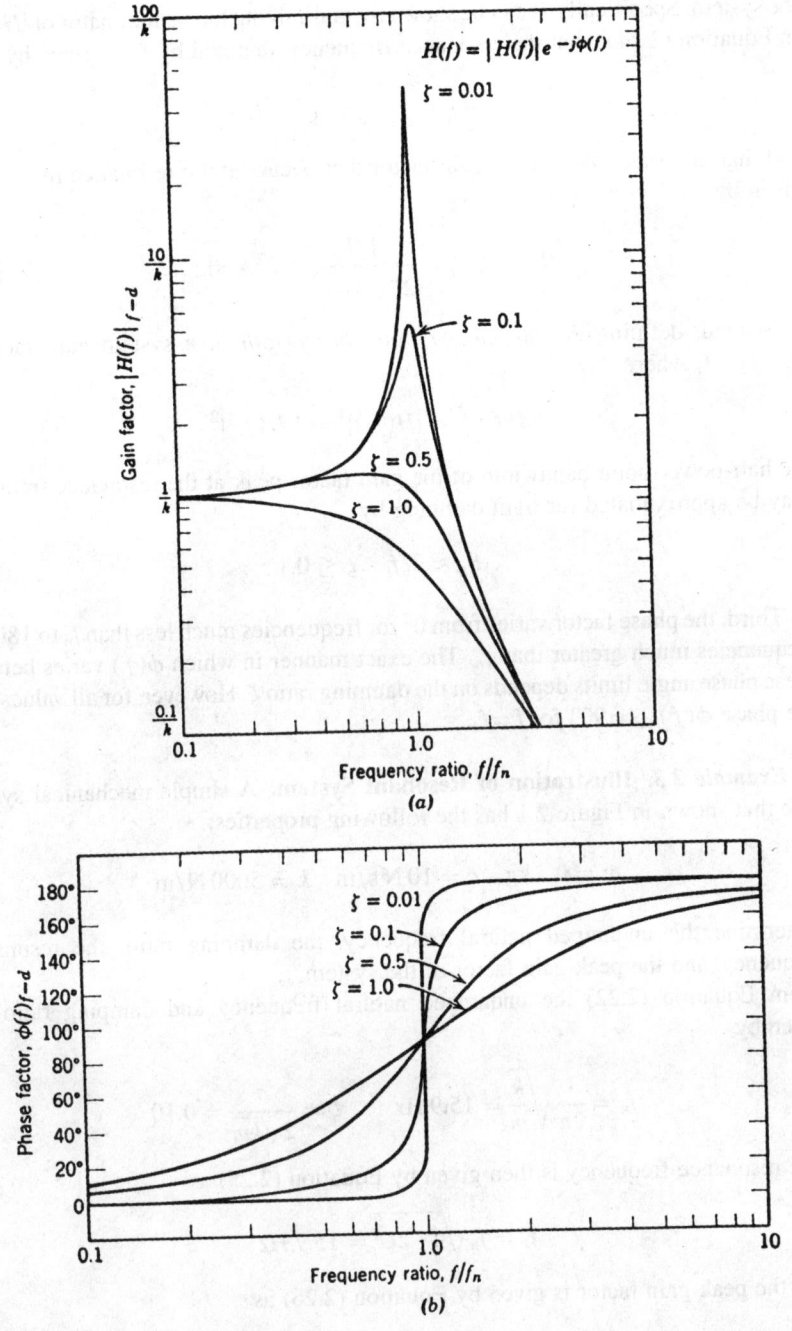

Figure 2.3 Frequency response function of mechanical system with force input. (*a*) Gain factor. (*b*) Phase factor.

the system. Specifically, it can be shown by minimizing the denominator of $|H(f)|_{f-d}$ in Equation (2.24a) that the resonance frequency, denoted by f_r, is given by

$$f_r = f_n\sqrt{1-2\zeta^2} \qquad \zeta^2 < 0.5 \qquad (2.25)$$

and that the peak value of the gain factor that occurs at the resonance frequency is given by

$$|H(f_r)|_{f-d} = \frac{1/k}{2\zeta\sqrt{1-\zeta^2}} \qquad \zeta^2 < 0.5 \qquad (2.26)$$

Second, defining the *half-power point bandwidth* of a system gain factor as $B_r = f_2 - f_1$ where

$$|H(f_1)|^2 = |H(f_2)|^2 = \tfrac{1}{2}|H(f_r)|^2$$

the half-power point bandwidth of the gain factor peak at the resonance frequency may be approximated for light damping by

$$B_r \approx 2\zeta f_r \qquad \zeta \leq 0.1 \qquad (2.27)$$

Third, the phase factor varies from 0° for frequencies much less than f_n to 180° for frequencies much greater than f_n. The exact manner in which $\phi(f)$ varies between these phase angle limits depends on the damping ratio ζ. However, for all values of ζ, the phase $\phi(f)_{f-d} = 90°$ for $f = f_n$.

Example 2.3. Illustration of Resonant System. A simple mechanical system like that shown in Figure 2.1 has the following properties:

$$m = 0.5 \text{ kg} \quad c = 10 \text{ N s/m} \quad k = 5000 \text{ N/m}$$

Determine the undamped natural frequency, the damping ratio, the resonance frequency, and the peak gain factor of the system.
From Equation (2.22) the undamped natural frequency and damping ratio are given by

$$f_n = \frac{1}{2\pi}\sqrt{\frac{k}{m}} = 15.9 \text{ Hz} \qquad \zeta = \frac{c}{2\sqrt{km}} = 0.10$$

The resonance frequency is then given by Equation (2.25) as

$$f_r = f_n\sqrt{1-2\zeta^2} = 15.7 \text{ Hz}$$

and the peak gain factor is given by Equation (2.26) as

$$|H(f_r)| = \frac{1/k}{2\zeta\sqrt{1-\zeta^2}} = 0.001 \text{ m/N}$$

It is common in practice to present gain factors for physical systems in dimensionless terms by multiplying out the stiffness term, that is,

$$k|H(f_r)| = \frac{1}{2\zeta\sqrt{1-\zeta^2}} = 5.0$$

This is often called the *quality factor* of the system, denoted by Q. The reciprocal of Q is usually referred to as the *loss factor* of the system denoted by η. For the system in question, $Q = 5.0$ and $\eta = 0.2$ ($\eta = 2\zeta$).

2.4.1.2 Foundation Displacement Input and Displacement Output

Now consider a different case, where the input of interest is a motion of the foundation and the output of interest is the displacement of the mass, as illustrated in Figure 2.4. Here, $x(t)$ is an applied foundation displacement in meters measured from a mean foundation position, and $y(t)$ is the resulting output displacement of the mass in meters measured from the position of equilibrium.

As before, the equation of motion for the system can be determined from basic principles as follows:

$$F_k(t) + F_c(t) + F_m(t) = 0 \tag{2.28}$$

where

$$F_k(t) = -k[y(t)-x(t)] = \text{spring force} \tag{2.28a}$$

$$F_c(t) = -c[\dot{y}(t)-\dot{x}(t)] = \text{damping force} \tag{2.28b}$$

$$F_m(t) = -m\ddot{y}(t) = \text{inertial force} \tag{2.28c}$$

Hence, the equation of motion for this system is

$$m\ddot{y}(t) + c\dot{y}(t) + ky(t) = kx(t) + c\dot{x}(t) \tag{2.29}$$

Once again the frequency response function of the system will be given by the Fourier transform of the response displacement $y(t)$ for a unit impulse foundation displacement $x(t) = \delta(t)$. By taking the Fourier transform of both sides of Equation (2.29), and noting that Fourier transform $[\dot{\delta}(t)] = j2\pi f$, one obtains the following result:

$$[-(2\pi f)^2 m + j2\pi fc + k]Y(f) = [k + j2\pi fc]$$

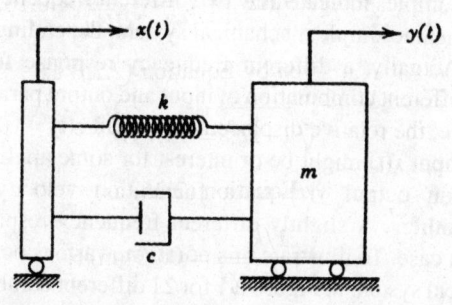

Figure 2.4 Mechanical system with foundation motion input.

Thus,

$$Y(f) = H(f)_{d-d} = \frac{k + j2\pi fc}{k - (2\pi f)^2 m + j2\pi fc} \qquad (2.30)$$

where the subscript d–d means that this particular $H(f)$ relates a displacement input to a displacement output.

Using the definitions from Equation (2.22), the result in Equation (2.30) may be written as

$$H(f)_{d-d} = \frac{1 + j2\zeta f/f_n}{1 - (f/f_n)^2 + j2\zeta f/f_n} \qquad (2.31)$$

In complex polar notation, Equation (2.31) reduces to the following gain factor and phase factor:

$$H(f) = |H(f)|e^{-j\phi(f)} \qquad (2.32)$$

where

$$|H(f)|_{d-d} = \left(\frac{1 + [2\zeta f/f_n]^2}{[1 - (f/f_n)^2]^2 + [2\zeta f/f_n]^2} \right)^{1/2} \qquad (2.32a)$$

$$\phi(f)_{d-d} = \tan^{-1} \left[\frac{2\zeta (f/f_n)^3}{1 - (f/f_n)^2 + 4\zeta^2 (f/f_n)^2} \right] \qquad (2.32b)$$

Note that $|H(f)|_{d-d}$ is dimensionless. This particular function is often called a *transmissibility function*. Plots of $|H(f)|_{d-d}$ and $\phi(f)_{d-d}$ are presented in Figure 2.5. Note that the gain factor displays a single peak similar to the example for a force input illustrated in Figure 2.3. However, the details of the gain factor as well as the phase factor in Figure 2.5 are quite different from the factors in Figure 2.3. In particular, $|H(f)|_{d-d} = 1$ at $f = \sqrt{2}f_n$, independent of ζ, and $\phi(f)_{d-d} \neq 90°$ at $f = f_n$ except for $\zeta = 0$.

2.4.1.3 Other Input and Output Combinations

The previous two examples indicate how two different frequency response functions are applicable to the same simple mechanical system, depending on the type of input to be considered. Actually, a different frequency response function is generally required for every different combination of input and output parameters that might be desired. For example, the relative displacement output $z(t) = y(t) - x(t)$ to a foundation displacement input $x(t)$ might be of interest for some applications, whereas the absolute acceleration output $\ddot{y}(t)$ to a foundation velocity input $\dot{x}(t)$ would be appropriate for others. A slightly different frequency response function would be required for each case. To illustrate this point, the various possible gain factors of the simple mechanical system in Figure 2.1 for 21 different combinations of input and output parameters are presented in Table 2.1.

ILLUSTRATIONS OF FREQUENCY RESPONSE FUNCTIONS

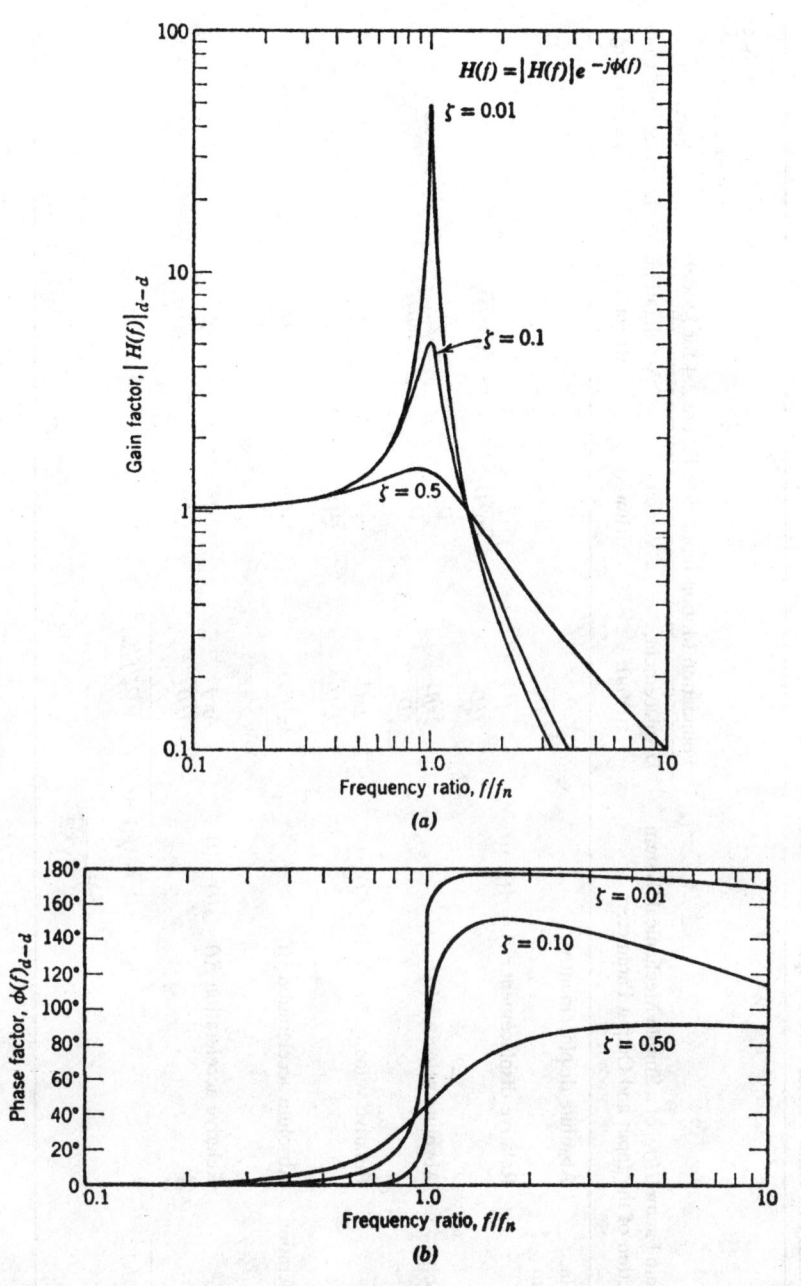

Figure 2.5 Frequency response function of mechanical system with foundation motion input. (a) Gain factor. (b) Phase factor.

Table 2.1 Summary of Gain Factors for Simple Mechanical System

Values for the Gain Factor $|H(f)|$ of a Simple Mechanical System as a Function of the Input and Output Parameters	Foundation Motion Input (See Figure 2.4 for Model)			Force Input (See Figure 2.2 for model)
	Displacement, $x(t)$ (m)	Velocity, $\dot{x}(t)$ (m/s)	Acceleration, $\ddot{x}(t)$ (m/s²)	Force (in Displacement Units), $x(t) = F(t)/k$ (m)
In terms of displacement output, m				
Absolute displacement $y(t)$	$\dfrac{D_1}{D_2}$	$\dfrac{D_1}{2\pi f D_2}$	$\dfrac{D_1}{4\pi^2 f^2 D_2}$	$\dfrac{1}{D_2}$
Relative displacement $z(t) = y(t) - x(t)$	$\dfrac{f^2}{f_n^2 D_2}$	$\dfrac{f}{2\pi f_n^2 D_2}$	$\dfrac{1}{4\pi^2 f_n^2 D_2}$	
In terms of velocity output, m/s				
Absolute velocity $\dot{y}(t)$	$\dfrac{2\pi f D_1}{D_2}$	$\dfrac{D_1}{D_2}$	$\dfrac{D_1}{2\pi f D_2}$	$\dfrac{2\pi f}{D_2}$
Relative velocity $\dot{z}(t) = \dot{y}(t) - \dot{x}(t)$	$\dfrac{2\pi f^3}{f_n^2 D_2}$	$\dfrac{f^2}{f_n^2 D_2}$	$\dfrac{f}{2\pi f_n^2 D_2}$	
In terms of acceleration output, m/s²				
Absolute acceleration $\ddot{y}(t)$	$\dfrac{4\pi^2 f^2 D_1}{D_2}$	$\dfrac{2\pi f D_1}{D_2}$	$\dfrac{D_1}{D_2}$	$\dfrac{4\pi^2 f^2}{D_2}$
Relative acceleration $\ddot{z}(t) = \ddot{y}(t) - \ddot{x}(t)$	$\dfrac{4\pi^2 f^4}{f_n^2 D_2}$	$\dfrac{2\pi f^3}{f_n^2 D_2}$	$\dfrac{f^2}{f_n^2 D_2}$	

$$D_1 = \sqrt{1 + [2\zeta(f/f_n)]^2}$$

$$D_2 = \sqrt{[1-(f/f_n)^2]^2 + [2\zeta(f/f_n)]^2}$$

$$f_n = \frac{1}{2\pi}\sqrt{\frac{k}{m}} \qquad \zeta = \frac{c}{2\sqrt{km}}$$

ILLUSTRATIONS OF FREQUENCY RESPONSE FUNCTIONS

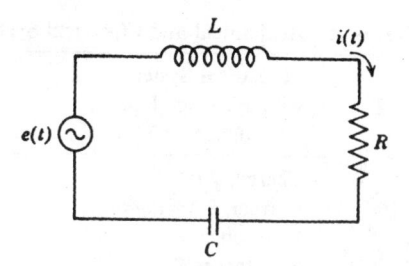

Figure 2.6 Electrical system with voltage input.

2.4.2 Electrical Systems

Assume that a simple electrical circuit can be represented by a lumped parameter system consisting of an inductor, a resistor, and a capacitor. Further assume that the input to the system is a potential difference as shown in Figure 2.6. In this figure, C is a capacitance in farads, R is a resistance in ohms, L is an inductance in henries, $e(t)$ is an applied potential in volts, and $i(t)$ is the resulting current in amperes. Note that $i(t) = dq(t)/dt$, where $q(t)$ is charge in coulombs.

Assume the input of interest is an applied voltage and the output of interest is the resulting charge. As for the case of mechanical systems in Section 2.4.1, the first step toward establishing a proper frequency response function is to determine the differential equation describing the system. From basic circuit theory, the sum of all potential differences across the circuit elements must equal zero. That is,

$$e(t) + e_C(t) + e_R + e_L(t) = 0 \quad (2.33)$$

where

$$e_C(t) = -\frac{1}{C}q(t) = \text{potential difference across capacitor} \quad (2.33a)$$

$$e_R(t) = -R\dot{q}(t) = \text{potential difference across resistor} \quad (2.33b)$$

$$e_L(t) = -L\ddot{q}(t) = \text{potential difference across inductor} \quad (2.33c)$$

Hence, the differential equation for this system is

$$L\ddot{q}(t) + R\dot{q}(t) + \frac{1}{C}q(t) = e(t) \quad (2.34)$$

Note the similarity between Equation (2.34) and the equation of motion for a force excited mechanical system given by Equation (2.19). Using the same analysis procedures outlined in Section 2.4.1, it follows directly that the frequency response function of this simple electrical system is

$$H(f)_{e-q} = \left[\frac{1}{C} - (2\pi f)^2 L + j2\pi fR\right]^{-1} \quad (2.35)$$

Table 2.2 Analogous Terms for Mechanical and Electrical Systems

	Electrical System with a Voltage Input	Mechanical System with a Force Input
Input	Voltage, $e(t)$	Force, $F(t)$
Output	Charge, $q(t)$	Displacement, $y(t)$
	Current, $i(t) = dq/dt$	Velocity, $v(t) = dy/dt$
Constant parameters	Inductance, L	Mass, m
	Resistance, R	Damping, c
	Capacitance, C	Compliance, $1/k$

where the subscript e–q means that this particular $H(f)$ relates a voltage input to a charge output. Note that $H(f)_{e-q}$ has the units of coulombs/volt.

The plot for $H(f)_{e-q}$ would be identical to the plot for the mechanical frequency response function $H(f)_{f-d}$ presented in Figure 2.3, where the damping ratio ζ and the undamped natural frequency f_n of the electrical circuit are given as follows:

$$\zeta = \frac{R}{2}\sqrt{\frac{C}{L}} \qquad (2.36a)$$

$$f_n = \frac{1}{2\pi}\sqrt{\frac{1}{LC}} \qquad (2.36b)$$

It should now be clear that a direct analogy may be made between mechanical and electrical systems as presented in Table 2.2.

A more common frequency response function for electrical systems is one that relates a voltage input to a current output. This particular frequency response function is given by

$$H(f)_{e-i} = \left[R + j\left(2\pi f L - \frac{1}{2\pi fC}\right)\right]^{-1} \qquad (2.37)$$

where $H(f)_{e-i}$ has the units of amperes/volt. The reciprocal of Equation (2.37), which may be denoted by $H(f)_{i-e}$, is called an *impedance function*:

$$H(f)_{i-e} = R + j\left(2\pi f L - \frac{1}{2\pi fC}\right) \qquad (2.38)$$

Note that the mechanical analogy to Equation (2.38) is given from Table 2.2 by $H(f)_{v-f}$ as follows:

$$H(f)_{v-f} = c + j\left(2\pi fm - \frac{k}{2\pi f}\right) \qquad (2.39)$$

The function in Equation (2.39) is often called a *mechanical impedance function* because of its analogy to the common electrical impedance function.

Table 2.3 Analogous Characteristics for Several Physical Systems

System	Input	Output	Constant Parameters		
Electrical	Voltage	Current	Inductance	Resistance	Capacitance
Mechanical (translational)	Force	Velocity	Mass	Damping	Compliance
Mechanical (rotational)	Torque	Angular velocity	Moment of inertia	Angular damping	Angular compliance
Acoustical	Pressure	Particle velocity	Inertance (acoustical mass)	Acoustical damping	Acoustical capacitance
Thermal	Temperature	Heat flow	—	Thermal resistance	Thermal capacitance
Magnetic	Magneto-motive force	Flux	—	Reluctance	—

2.4.3 Other Systems

By the same analytical procedures outlined in Section 2.4.1, an appropriate frequency response function can be developed, at least in theory, for any clearly defined constant-parameter linear system that is physically realizable and stable. Moreover, the frequency response functions of different physical systems will often display analogous parameters, just as illustrated for mechanical and electrical systems in Section 2.4.2 and Table 2.2. A summary of analogous characteristics for several common physical systems is presented in Table 2.3.

2.5 PRACTICAL CONSIDERATIONS

The analytical determination of frequency response functions of physical systems has been illustrated in Section 2.4. To facilitate the development and clarification of basic ideas, examples were limited to simple mechanical and electrical systems. It should not be implied from these examples that the analytical determination of frequency response functions of physical systems is always so easy.

Consider, for example, a mechanical system in the form of a continuous elastic structure where the various parameters (mass, damping, and stiffness) are distributed rather than lumped as hypothetically assumed for the examples in Section 2.4.1. Such a mechanical system would have many different possible input and output points that might be of interest. Furthermore, the frequency response function of each input/output combination would generally display many peaks representing many resonant frequencies, as opposed to a single resonance as illustrated for the examples in Section 2.4.1. For relatively uncomplicated continuous structures such as beams, plates, and shells, appropriate frequency response functions may still be established with reasonable accuracy by direct analytical procedures [2]. For more complicated structures, as well as fluids and other physical systems, computer modeling procedures such as finite element methods [3] might be used to estimate frequency response functions and other response properties. If the physical system of interest has been constructed and is available for experimental studies, frequency response functions can be estimated by empirical procedures. The most straightforward empirical approach is to subject the system to a sinusoidal input and measure the output amplitude and phase as the input frequency is varied. From Section 2.3, the ratio of the output to input amplitudes at any given frequency equals the gain factor, and the phase of the output relative to the input at any given frequency equals the phase factor. However, the same results can be obtained with substantially less experimental time by applying either random or transient inputs to the system, either natural or artificial, and measuring the system response. The estimation of frequency response functions from random and transient input/output data will be dealt in detail in Chapters 6 and 7.

PROBLEMS

2.1 If an input $x(t)$ produces an output $y(t) = x(t)|x(t)|$, prove that the input/output relationship is nonlinear.

2.2 Write a single equation that defines the required conditions for linearity of physical systems.

2.3 To define the dynamic properties of a system by a single-valued weighting function $h(\tau)$, which of the following requirements apply? The system must

(a) have constant parameters.

(b) be linear.

(c) be physically realizable.

(d) be stable.

2.4 Determine the frequency response function of a physical system with a weighting function $h(\tau) = Ae^{-a\tau}$, where $a > 0$.

2.5 Assume the mechanical system shown in Figure 2.2 has a spring constant of $k = 2000$ N/m, a viscous damping coefficient of $c = 10$ N s/m, and a mass of $m = 5$ kg. Determine the

(a) undamped natural frequency f_n.

(b) damping ratio ζ.

(c) force excited resonance frequency f_r.

(d) peak value of the gain factor $|H(f)|$.

2.6 Determine the weighting function of the force excited mechanical system shown in Figure 2.2.

2.7 Prove that the resonance frequency of the force excited mechanical system shown in Figure 2.2 is $f_r = f_n\sqrt{1-2\zeta^2}$, $\zeta^2 < 0.5$, as stated in Equation (2.25).

2.8 The half-power point bandwidth of a resonant physical system is defined as $B_r = f_2 - f_1$, where $|H(f_1)|^2 = |H(f_2)|^2 = \frac{1}{2}|H(f_r)|^2$. Given the force excited mechanical system shown in Figure 2.2, prove that $B_r \approx 2\zeta f_r$ for small ζ, as stated in Equation (2.27).

2.9 Assume the mass of the mechanical system shown in Figure 2.1 is displaced from its position of equilibrium and then released. Prove that the time between crossings of the position of equilibrium in the resulting oscillation is $T = \frac{1}{2}[f_n\sqrt{1-\zeta^2}]^{-1}$ for $\zeta^2 \leq 1.0$.

2.10 Draw the electrical analog circuit for the mechanical system with the foundation motion input shown in Figure 2.4. Determine the values of the analogous circuit parameters in terms of the mechanical parameters k, c, and m.

REFERENCES

1. Bendat, J. S., *Nonlinear System Techniques and Applications*, Wiley-Interscience, New York, 1998.
2. Stokey, W. F., "Vibrations of Systems Having Distributed Mass and Elasticity," Chapter 7 in *Shock and Vibration Handbook*, 4th ed. (C. M. Harris; Ed.), McGraw-Hill, New York, 1996.
3. Schaeffer, H. G., "Finite Element Methods," Chapter 28 Part II in *Shock and Vibration Handbook*, 4th ed. (C. M. Harris; Ed.), McGraw-Hill, New York, 1996.

CHAPTER 3

Probability Fundamentals

This chapter reviews the fundamental principles of probability theory that are needed as background for the concepts of random process theory developed in later chapters. The material covers random variables, probability distributions, expected values, change of variables, moment-generating functions, and characteristic functions for both single and multiple random variables. More detailed developments of probability theory from an engineering viewpoint are presented in Refs 1–3.

3.1 ONE RANDOM VARIABLE

The underlying concept in probability theory is that of a *set*, defined as a collection of objects (also called points or elements) about which it is possible to determine whether any particular object is a member of the set. In particular, the possible outcomes of an experiment (or a measurement) represent a set of *points* called the *sample space*. These points may be grouped together in various ways, called *events*, and under suitable conditions *probability functions* may be assigned to each. These probabilities always lie between zero and one, the probability of an impossible event being zero and the probability of the certain event being one. Sample spaces are either finite or infinite.

Consider a sample space of points representing the possible outcomes of a particular experiment (or measurement). A *random variable* $x(k)$ is a set function defined for points k from the sample space; that is, a random variable $x(k)$ is a real number between $-\infty$ and $+\infty$ that is associated to each sample point k that might occur. Stated another way, the random outcome of an experiment, indexed by k, can be represented by a real number $x(k)$, called the random variable. All possible experimental events that might occur constitute a completely additive class of sets, and a probability measure may be assigned to each event.

Random Data: Analysis and Measurement Procedures, Fourth Edition. By Julius S. Bendat and Allan G. Piersol
Copyright © 2010 John Wiley & Sons, Inc.

3.1.1 Probability Density and Distribution Functions

Let $x(k)$ denote a random variable of interest. Then for any fixed value of x, the random event $x(k) \leq x$ is defined as the set of possible outcomes k such that $x(k) \leq x$. In terms of the underlying probability measure in the sample space, one may define a *probability distribution function* $P(x)$ as the probability that is assigned to the set of points k satisfying the desired inequality $x(k) \leq x$. Observe that the set of points k satisfying $x(k) \leq x$ is a subset of the totality of all points k that satisfy $x(k) \leq \infty$. In notation form,

$$P(x) = \text{Prob}[x(k) \leq x] \tag{3.1}$$

Clearly,

$$P(a) \leq P(b) \quad \text{if } a \leq b \tag{3.2}$$

$$P(-\infty) = 0 \quad P(\infty) = 1 \tag{3.3}$$

If the random variable assumes a continuous range of values (which will be assumed hereafter), then a (first-order) *probability density function* $p(x)$ may be defined by the differential relation

$$p(x) = \lim_{\Delta x \to 0} \left[\frac{\text{Prob}[x < x(k) \leq x + \Delta x]}{\Delta x} \right] \tag{3.4}$$

It follows that

$$p(x) \geq 0 \tag{3.5}$$

$$\int_{-\infty}^{\infty} p(x) \, dx = 1 \tag{3.6}$$

$$P(x) = \int_{-\infty}^{x} p(\xi) \, d\xi \quad \frac{dP(x)}{dx} = p(x) \tag{3.7}$$

To handle discrete cases like Example 3.1, the probability density function $p(x)$ is permitted to include delta functions.

The probability density functions for common examples of both random and deterministic data are summarized in Table 3.1. Many of these functions are derived in this chapter.

Example 3.1. Discrete Distribution. Suppose an experiment consists of tossing a single coin where the two possible outcomes, called heads and tails, are assumed to occur with equal probability (1/2). The random variable $x(k)$ for this example takes on only two discrete values, x(heads) and x(tails), to which arbitrary real numbers may be assigned. Specifically, let x(heads) $= a$ and x(tails) $= b$, where a and b are real numbers with, say, $b > a$. With these choices for $x(k)$, it follows that the probability

ONE RANDOM VARIABLE

Table 3.1 Special Probability Density Functions

Type	Probability Density Function
Discrete	$p(x) = A\delta(x-a) + B\delta(x-b) + \cdots + N\delta(x-n)$ where $A + B + \cdots + N = 1$
Uniform (rectangular)	$p(x) = (b-a)^{-1}, a \leq x \leq b;$ otherwise zero
Sine wave	$p(x) = \left(\pi\sqrt{X^2 - x^2}\right)^{-1}, |x| < X;$ otherwise zero
Gaussian (normal)	$p(x) = \left(\sigma_x\sqrt{2\pi}\right)^{-1} e^{-(x-\mu_x)^2/2\sigma_x^2}$
Rayleigh	$p(x) = \dfrac{x}{c^2} e^{-x^2/2c^2}, \quad x \geq 0;$ otherwise zero
Maxwell	$p(x) = \dfrac{x^2}{c^3}\sqrt{\dfrac{2}{\pi}} e^{-x^2/2c^2}, \quad x \geq 0;$ otherwise zero
Truncated	Assume original $p_1(x)$ defined over $(-\infty, \infty)$. Truncated $p(x) = Cp_1(x), \quad a \leq x \leq b;$ otherwise zero where $\int_{-\infty}^{\infty} p(x)\,dx = C\int_a^b p_1(x)\,dx = 1$
Clipped	Assume original $p_1(x)$ defined over $(-\infty, \infty)$. Clipped $\begin{aligned} p(x) &= p_1(x) & a < x < b \\ &= A\delta(x-a) & x = a \\ &= B\delta(x-b) & x = b \\ &= 0 & x < a \text{ or } x > b \end{aligned}$ where $\int_{-\infty}^{\infty} p(x)\,dx = \int_a^b p_1(x)\,dx + A + B = 1$

distribution function is

$$P(x) = \begin{cases} 0 & x < a \\ \dfrac{1}{2} & a \leq x < b \\ 1 & x \geq b \end{cases}$$

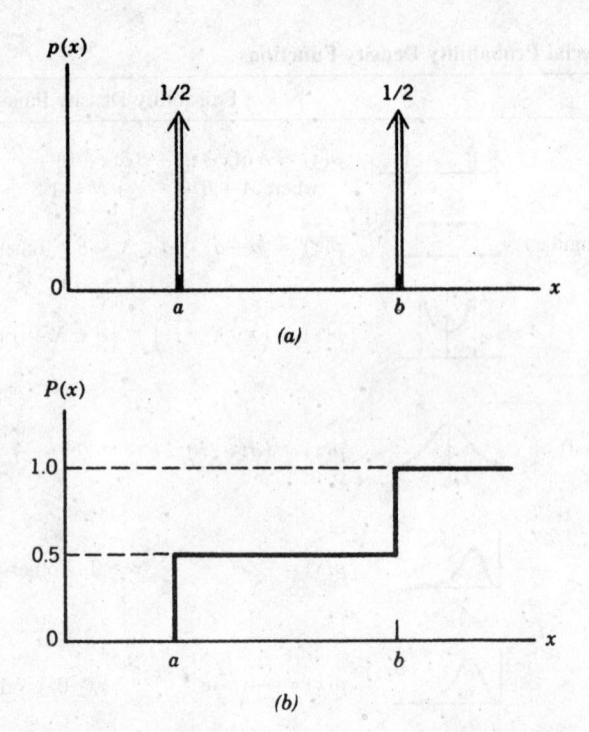

Figure 3.1 Discrete probability density and distribution functions. (*a*) Probability density function. (*b*) Probability distribution function.

and the probability density function is given by

$$p(x) = \frac{1}{2}\delta(x-a) + \frac{1}{2}\delta(x-b)$$

where $\delta(x-a)$ and $\delta(x-b)$ are delta functions, as shown in Figure 3.1.

Example 3.2. **Uniform (Rectangular) Distribution.** Suppose an experiment consists of choosing a point at random in the interval $[a, b]$, including the end points. A continuous random variable $x(k)$ for this example may be defined by the numerical value of the chosen point. The corresponding probability distribution function becomes

$$P(x) = \begin{cases} 0 & x < a \\ \dfrac{x-a}{b-a} & a \leq x \leq b \\ 1 & x > b \end{cases}$$

Hence, the probability density function is given by

$$p(x) = \begin{cases} (b-a)^{-1} & a \leq x \leq b \\ 0 & \text{otherwise} \end{cases}$$

ONE RANDOM VARIABLE

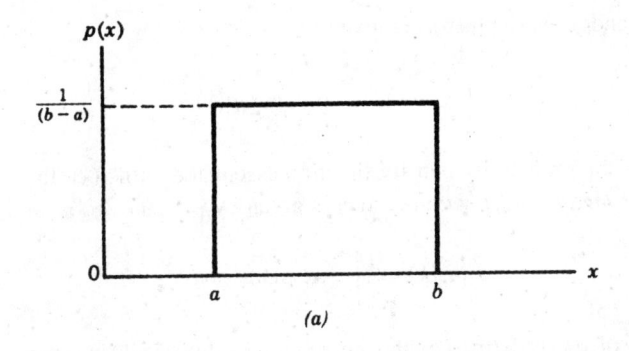

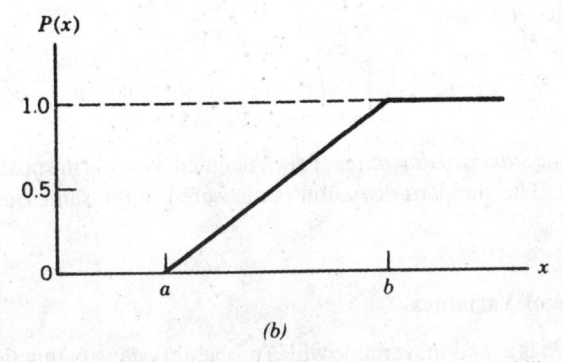

Figure 3.2 Uniform probability density and distribution functions. (*a*) Probability density function. (*b*) Probability distribution function.

For this example, from Equations (3.9) and (3.11) to follow, the mean value and the variance are given by

$$\mu_x = \frac{a+b}{2} \qquad \sigma_x^2 = \frac{(b-a)^2}{12}$$

Plots of $P(x)$ and $p(x)$ are shown in Figure 3.2.

3.1.2 Expected Values

Assume the random variable $x(k)$ may take on values in the range from $-\infty$ to $+\infty$. The *mean value* (also called *expected value* or *average value*) of $x(k)$ is obtained by an appropriate limiting operation when each value assumed by $x(k)$ is multiplied by its probability of occurrence. This gives

$$E[x(k)] = \int_{-\infty}^{\infty} xp(x)\,dx = \mu_x \qquad (3.8)$$

where $E[\,]$ represents the expected value over the index k of the term inside the brackets. Similarly, the expected value of any real single-valued continuous function

$g(x)$ of the random variable $x(k)$ is given by

$$E[g(x(k))] = \int_{-\infty}^{\infty} g(x)p(x)\,dx \tag{3.9}$$

where $p(x)$ is the probability density function associated with $x(k)$. In particular, for $g(x) = x^2$, the *mean square value* of $x(k)$ is given by

$$E[x^2(k)] = \int_{-\infty}^{\infty} x^2 p(x)\,dx = \psi_x^2 \tag{3.10}$$

The *variance* of $x(k)$ is defined by the mean square value of $x(k)$ about its mean value. Here, $g(x) = (x-\mu_x)^2$ and

$$E[(x(k)-\mu_x)^2] = \int_{-\infty}^{\infty} (x-\mu_x)^2 p(x)\,dx = \psi_x^2 - \mu_x^2 = \sigma_x^2 \tag{3.11}$$

By definition, the *standard deviation* of $x(k)$, denoted by σ_x, is the positive square root of the variance. The standard deviation is measured in the same units as the mean value.

3.1.3 Change of Variables

Suppose that $x(k)$ is a random variable with a probability density function $p(x)$ and that $y = g(x)$ is any real single-valued continuous function of x. Consider first the case where the inverse function $x(y)$ is also a real single-valued continuous function of y. The probability density function $p(y)$ associated with the random variable $y(k) = g[x(k)]$ will be a different functional form from $p(x)$ and is not obtained by merely replacing x by y. This different $p(y)$ can be determined from $p(x)$ by noting that x and y have the same probability of falling in associated small intervals. Thus, for small Δx and Δy, Equation (3.4) shows that

$$p(y)\Delta y \approx \text{Prob}[y < y(k) \le y+\Delta y] = \text{Prob}[x < x(k) \le x+\Delta x] \approx p(x)\Delta x$$

Hence, in the limit when Δx and Δy approach zero, one obtains the result

$$p(y) = \frac{p(x)}{|dy/dx|} \tag{3.12}$$

assuming the derivative exists and is not zero. The absolute value is required because probability density functions are nonnegative quantities. In Equation (3.12), it is necessary to replace the variable x on the right-hand side by its equivalent y so as to obtain $p(y)$ as a function of y.

For the case when the inverse function $x(y)$ is a real n-valued function of y, where n is an integer and all of the n values have equal probability, we have

$$p(y) = \frac{np(x)}{|dy/dx|} \tag{3.13}$$

ONE RANDOM VARIABLE

For various zero-memory nonlinear transformations of random data, many applications of Equations (3.12) and (3.13) are contained in Chapter 2 of Ref. 4 to predict different non-Gaussian output probability density functions $p(y)$ from Gaussian input probability density functions $p(x)$.

Example 3.3. **Sine Wave Distribution with Fixed Amplitude.** A sine wave of fixed amplitude A and fixed frequency f_0 can be considered a random variable if its initial phase angle $\theta = \theta(k)$ is a random variable. Let the sine wave random variable be represented by

$$x(k) = A \sin[2\pi f_0 t + \theta(k)] \tag{3.14}$$

The probability density function $p(k)$ of $x(k)$ will be determined assuming that $\theta(k)$ has a uniform probability density function $p(\theta)$ given by

$$p(\theta) = (1/2\pi) \quad 0 \leq \theta \leq 2\pi, \quad \text{otherwise zero}$$

For this example, the direct function $y(\theta)$ is single valued, but the inverse function $\theta(y)$ is double valued. From Equation (3.13), with θ replacing x and x replacing y, we have

$$p(x) = \frac{2p(\theta)}{|dx/d\theta|}$$

where

$$|dx/d\theta| = A \cos[2\pi f_0 t + \theta(k)] = \sqrt{A^2 - x^2}$$

Thus, the sine wave probability density function is

$$p(x) = \frac{1}{\pi\sqrt{A^2 - x^2}} \quad |x| < A, \quad \text{otherwise zero} \tag{3.15}$$

From Equations (3.8) and (3.11), the mean value and variance for this sine wave example are given by

$$\mu_x = 0 \quad \sigma_x^2 = (A^2/2)$$

The associated sine wave probability distribution function from Equation (3.7) is

$$\begin{aligned} P(x) &= 0 & x &< -A \\ P(x) &= \int_{-A}^{x} p(x)\, dx = \frac{1}{\pi}\left(\frac{\pi}{2} + \sin^{-1}\frac{x}{A}\right) & -A &\leq x \leq A \\ P(x) &= 1 & x &> A \end{aligned} \tag{3.16}$$

Plots of $p(x)$ and $P(x)$ from Equations (3.15) and (3.16) as a function of (x/σ_x) are shown in Figure 3.3. Note that (x/σ_x) is the same as $(x\sqrt{2}/A)$ so that $x = A$ when $(x/\sigma_x) = \sqrt{2}$.

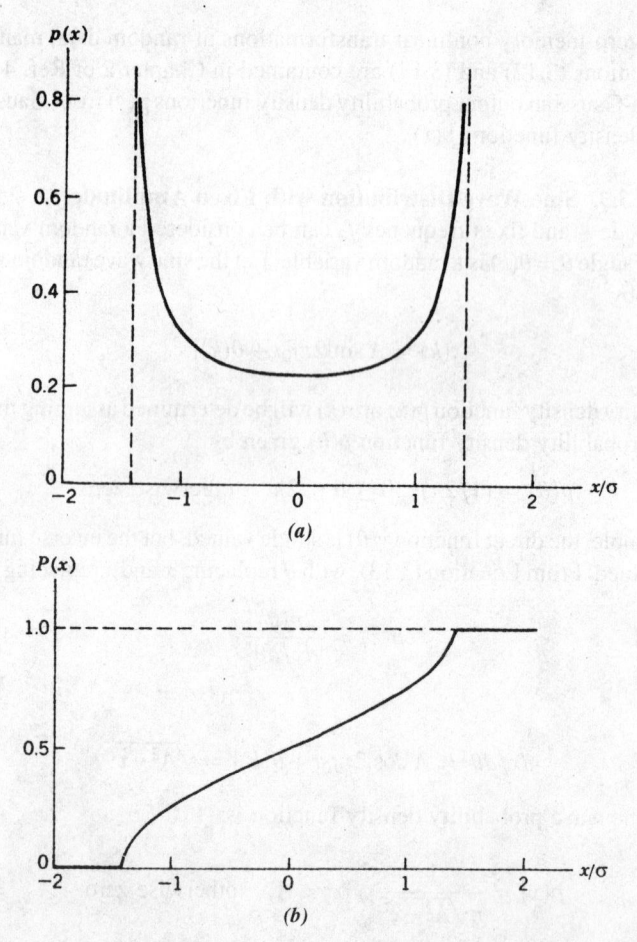

Figure 3.3 Sine wave probability density and distribution functions. (*a*) Probability density function. (*b*) Probability distribution function.

3.1.4 Moment-Generating and Characteristic Functions

The *moment-generating function* $m(s)$ of $x(k)$ is defined by letting $g(x) = \exp(sx)$ in Equation (3.9), namely,

$$m(s) = E[e^{sx}] = \int_{-\infty}^{\infty} e^{sx} p(x)\, dx \tag{3.17}$$

Now

$$m(0) = \int_{-\infty}^{\infty} p(x)\, dx = 1$$

ONE RANDOM VARIABLE

Assuming all derivatives exist, then

$$m'(s) = \frac{dm(s)}{ds} = \int_{-\infty}^{\infty} x e^{sx} p(x)\, dx$$

$$m''(s) = \frac{d^2 m(s)}{ds^2} = \int_{-\infty}^{\infty} x^2 e^{sx} p(x)\, dx$$

and so on. Hence at $s = 0$,

$$E[x] = \int_{-\infty}^{\infty} x p(x)\, dx = m'(0)$$

$$E[x^2] = \int_{-\infty}^{\infty} x^2 p(x)\, dx = m''(0)$$

and so on. For any integer n, the *moments* are given by

$$E[x^n] = \int_{-\infty}^{\infty} x^n p(x)\, dx = m^{(n)}(0) \qquad (3.18)$$

where $m^{(n)}$ denotes the nth derivative of $m(s)$.

The *characteristic function* $C(f)$ of $x(k)$ is defined by letting $g(x) = \exp(j2\pi f x)$ in Equation (3.9), namely,

$$C(f) = E[e^{j2\pi f x}] = \int_{-\infty}^{\infty} p(x) e^{j2\pi f x}\, dx \qquad (3.19)$$

Thus $C(f)$ has the form of an inverse Fourier transform, where $p(x)$ is the Fourier transform of $C(f)$. Assuming all integrals exist,

$$p(x) = \int_{-\infty}^{\infty} C(f) e^{-j2\pi f x}\, df \qquad (3.20)$$

If $p(x) = \delta(x)$, a delta function, then

$$C(f) = \int_{-\infty}^{\infty} \delta(x) e^{j2\pi f x}\, dx = 1$$

$$\delta(x) = \int_{-\infty}^{\infty} e^{-j2\pi f x}\, df \qquad (3.21)$$

Note that $C(f)$ is the same as $m(s)$ when $s = j2\pi f$, namely,

$$C(f) = m(j2\pi f) \qquad (3.22)$$

3.1.5 Chebyshev's Inequality

Suppose that $x(k)$ is an arbitrary random variable with a mean value μ_x, a mean square value ψ_x^2, and a variance σ_x^2. Suppose that its probability density function, which may be unknown, is $p(x)$. Then

$$\psi_x^2 = \int_{-\infty}^{\infty} x^2 p(x)\, dx \geq \int_{|x| \geq \varepsilon} x^2 p(x)\, dx \geq \varepsilon^2 \int_{|x| \geq \varepsilon} p(x)\, dx$$

because the integrand is nonnegative and because $x^2 \geq \varepsilon^2$ at every point in the right-hand region of integration. This proves that

$$\text{Prob}[|x(k)| \geq \varepsilon] = \int_{|x| \geq \varepsilon} p(x)\, dx \leq \frac{\psi_x^2}{\varepsilon^2} \tag{3.23}$$

Now replace $x(k)$ by $x(k) - \mu_x$. Then ψ_x^2 is replaced by σ_x^2 and Equation (3.23) becomes

$$\text{Prob}[|x(k) - \mu_x| \geq \varepsilon] \leq \frac{\sigma_x^2}{\varepsilon^2} \tag{3.23a}$$

In particular, if $\varepsilon = c\sigma_x$, then

$$\text{Prob}[|x(k) - \mu_x| \geq c\sigma_x] \leq \frac{1}{c^2} \tag{3.23b}$$

which is equivalent to

$$\text{Prob}[|x(k) - \mu_x| \leq c\sigma_x] \geq 1 - \frac{1}{c^2} \tag{3.23c}$$

Any of the forms of Equation (3.23) is known as *Chebyshev's inequality*.

Example 3.4. **Illustration of Probability Intervals.** Consider a random variable $x(k)$ with an unknown probability density function. Using the Chebyshev inequality in Equation (3.22)b with $c = 2$ and $c = 3$, the following probability statements apply:

$$\text{Prob}[|x(k) - \mu_x| \geq 2\sigma_x] \leq 0.250$$

$$\text{Prob}[|x(k) - \mu_x| \geq 3\sigma_x] \leq 0.111$$

These relatively weak results should be compared to situations where $x(k)$ follows a Gaussian distribution. From Table A.2 for Gaussian data, one obtains the stronger results

$$\text{Prob}[|x(k) - \mu_x| \geq 2\sigma_x] < 0.050$$

$$\text{Prob}[|x(k) - \mu_x| \geq 3\sigma_x] < 0.003$$

Here, one can state that 95% of the values will lie within $\pm 2\sigma$ of the mean value, whereas for an arbitrary distribution one can state that this will occur for only 75% of the values.

3.2 TWO RANDOM VARIABLES

Consider next two random variables $x(k)$ and $y(k)$, where k represents points in a suitable sample space. Let $P(x)$ and $P(y)$ be two distinct probability distribution functions associated with $x(k)$ and $y(k)$, respectively. The *joint probability distribution function* $P(x, y)$ is defined to be the probability that is associated with the subset of points k in the sample space satisfying simultaneously both of the inequalities

TWO RANDOM VARIABLES

$x(k) \leq x$ and $y(k) \leq y$. The totality of all points k satisfies the inequalities $x(k) \leq \infty$ and $y(k) \leq \infty$. In notation form,

$$P(x,y) = \text{Prob}[x(k) \leq x \text{ and } y(k) \leq y] \tag{3.24}$$

Clearly,

$$P(-\infty, y) = 0 = P(x, -\infty) \quad P(\infty, \infty) = 1 \tag{3.25}$$

As before, assuming the random variables to be continuous, the *joint probability density function* $p(x, y)$ is defined by

$$P(x,y) = \lim_{\substack{\Delta x \to 0 \\ \Delta y \to 0}} \left[\frac{\text{Prob}[x < x(k) \leq x + \Delta x \text{ and } y < y(k) \leq y + \Delta y]}{\Delta x \Delta y} \right] \tag{3.26}$$

It follows that

$$p(x,y) \geq 0 \tag{3.27}$$

$$\iint_{-\infty}^{\infty} p(x,y) \, dx \, dy = 1 \tag{3.28}$$

$$P(x,y) = \int_{-\infty}^{y} \int_{-\infty}^{x} p(\xi, \eta) \, d\xi \, d\eta \quad \frac{\partial}{\partial y}\left[\frac{\partial P(x,y)}{\partial x}\right] = p(x,y) \tag{3.29}$$

The probability density functions of $x(k)$ and $y(k)$ individually are obtained from the joint probability density function by

$$p(x) = \int_{-\infty}^{\infty} p(x,y) \, dy$$

$$p(y) = \int_{-\infty}^{\infty} p(x,y) \, dx \tag{3.30}$$

Now if

$$p(x,y) = p(x) \, p(y) \tag{3.31}$$

then the two random variables $x(k)$ and $y(k)$ are said to be *statistically independent*. It follows for statistically independent variables that

$$P(x,y) = P(x) \, P(y) \tag{3.32}$$

3.2.1 Expected Values and Correlation Coefficient

The *expected value* of any real single-valued continuous function $g(x, y)$ of the two random variables $x(k)$ and $y(k)$ is given by

$$E[g(x,y)] = \iint_{-\infty}^{\infty} g(x,y) \, p(x,y) \, dx \, dy \tag{3.33}$$

For example, if $g(x, y) = (x(k) - \mu_x)(y(k) - \mu_y)$, where μ_x and μ_y are the mean values of $x(k)$ and $y(k)$, respectively, this defines the *covariance* C_{xy} between $x(k)$ and $y(k)$. That is,

$$C_{xy} = E[x(k) - \mu_x)(y(k) - \mu_y)] = E[x(k)y(k)] - E[x(k)]E[y(k)]$$
$$= \iint_{-\infty}^{\infty} (x - \mu_x)(y - \mu_y)p(x, y)\, dx\, dy \qquad (3.34)$$

Note that $C_{xx} = \sigma_x^2$, the variance of $x(k)$, as defined in Equation (3.11).

A simple relation exists between the covariance of $x(k)$ and $y(k)$ and the standard deviations of $x(k)$ and $y(k)$ as expressed by the inequality

$$|C_{xy}| \leq \sigma_x \sigma_y \qquad (3.35)$$

Thus the magnitude of the covariance between $x(k)$ and $y(k)$ is less than or equal to the product of the standard deviation of $x(k)$ multiplied by the standard deviation of $y(k)$. This is proved later in Section 5.1.3.

It follows from the above result that the normalized quantity

$$\rho_{xy} = \frac{C_{xy}}{\sigma_x \sigma_y} \qquad (3.36)$$

known as the *correlation coefficient*, will lie between -1 and $+1$. Random variables $x(k)$ and $y(k)$ whose correlation coefficient is zero are said to be *uncorrelated*. This concept is quite distinct from the previous definition of *independent* random variables. Note that if $x(k)$ and $y(k)$ are independent random variables, then, from Equations (3.31) and (3.33),

$$E[x(k)y(k)] = \iint_{-\infty}^{\infty} xy p(x, y)\, dx\, dy$$
$$= \int_{-\infty}^{\infty} xp(x)\, dx \int_{-\infty}^{\infty} yp(y)\, dy = E[x(k)]E[y(k)] \qquad (3.37)$$

Hence C_{xy} and, in turn, ρ_{xy} equal zero so that *independent random variables are also uncorrelated*. The converse statement is not true in general; that is, *uncorrelated random variables are not necessarily independent*. For physically important situations involving two or more normally (Gaussian) distributed random variables, however, being mutually uncorrelated does imply independence. This is proved later in Section 3.3.4.

3.2.2 Distribution for Sum of Two Random Variables

Suppose $x(k)$ and $y(k)$ are two random variables with a joint probability density function $p(x, y)$. Determine the probability density function $p(z)$ of the sum of random variable

$$z(k) = x(k) + y(k)$$

For each fixed value of x, the corresponding $y = z - x$. This gives

$$p(x, y) = p(x, z - x)$$

For each fixed value of z, the values of x may range from $-\infty$ to ∞. Hence,

$$p(z) = \int_{-\infty}^{\infty} p(x, z - x)\, dx \qquad (3.38)$$

which shows that the desired sum probability density function requires knowledge of the joint probability density function. If $x(k)$ and $y(k)$ are independent random variables with probability density functions $p_1(x)$ and $p_2(x)$, respectively, then $p(x, y) = p_1(x)p_2(y) = p_1(x)p_2(z - x)$, and $p(z)$ is given by the convolution integral

$$p(z) = \int_{-\infty}^{\infty} p_1(x)\, p_2(z - x)\, dx \qquad (3.39)$$

Example 3.5. Sum of Two Independent Uniformly Distributed Variables. Suppose two independent random variables x and y satisfy

$$p_1(x) = \frac{1}{a} \quad 0 \leq x \leq a \quad \text{otherwise zero}$$

$$p_2(y) = \frac{1}{a} \quad 0 \leq y \leq a \quad \text{otherwise zero}$$

Find the probability density function $p(z)$ for their sum $z = x + y$.

The probability density function $p_2(y) = p_2(z - x)$ for $0 \leq z - x \leq a$, which may be written as $z - a \leq x \leq z$. Hence x cannot exceed z. Also, $p_1(x)$ requires $0 \leq x \leq a$. It follows from Equation (3.39) that

$$p(z) = \begin{cases} \int_0^z \left(\frac{1}{a}\right)^2 dx = \dfrac{z}{a^2} & 0 \leq z \leq a \\ \int_{z-a}^{a} \left(\frac{1}{a}\right)^2 dx = \dfrac{2a - z}{a^2} & a \leq z \leq 2a \\ 0 & \text{otherwise} \end{cases}$$

Plots of $p_1(x)$, $p_2(y)$, and $p(z)$ are shown in Figure 3.4. Observe that the sum of two independent random variables with uniform probability density functions will have a triangular probability density function. It is straightforward to verify that the probability density function for the sum of four independent random variables, each with uniform probability density function, will begin to resemble a Gaussian form, as predicted by the central limit theorem in Section 3.3.1.

3.2.3 Joint Moment-Generating and Characteristic Functions

The *joint moment-generating function* $m(s, t)$ of $x(k)$ and $y(k)$ is defined by letting $g(x, y) = \exp(sx + ty)$ in Equation (3.33), namely,

$$m(s, t) = E[e^{sx + ty}] = \iint_{-\infty}^{\infty} e^{sx + ty} p(x, y)\, dx\, dy \qquad (3.40)$$

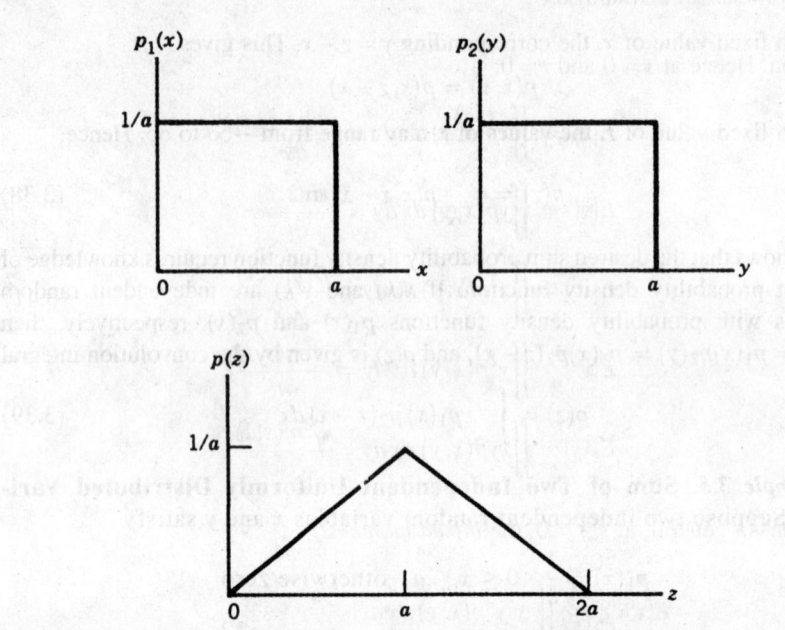

Figure 3.4 Probability density function for sum of two independent uniformly distributed variables.

Now

$$m(0,0) = \iint\limits_{-\infty}^{\infty} p(x,y)\,dx\,dy = 1$$

Assuming all partial derivatives exist, it follows that

$$\frac{\partial m(s,t)}{\partial s} = \iint xe^{sx+ty}p(x,y)\,dx\,dy$$

$$\frac{\partial m(s,t)}{\partial t} = \iint ye^{sx+ty}p(x,y)\,dx\,dy$$

$$\frac{\partial^2 m(s,t)}{\partial s^2} = \iint x^2 e^{sx+ty}p(x,y)\,dx\,dy$$

$$\frac{\partial^2 m(s,t)}{\partial t^2} = \iint y^2 e^{sx+ty}p(x,y)\,dx\,dy$$

$$\frac{\partial^2 m(s,t)}{\partial s \partial s} = \iint xye^{sx+ty}p(x,y)\,dx\,dy$$

and so on. Hence at $s=0$ and $t=0$,

$$E[x] = \iint xp(x,y)\,dx\,dy = \frac{\partial m(s,t)}{\partial s}$$

$$E[y] = \iint yp(x,y)\,dx\,dy = \frac{\partial m(s,t)}{\partial t}$$

$$E[x^2] = \iint x^2 p(x,y)\,dx\,dy = \frac{\partial^2 m(s,t)}{\partial s^2} \quad (3.41)$$

$$E[y^2] = \iint y^2 p(x,y)\,dx\,dy = \frac{\partial^2 m(s,t)}{\partial t^2}$$

$$E[xy] = \iint xyp(x,y)\,dx\,dy = \frac{\partial^2 m(s,t)}{\partial s\,\partial t}$$

and so on. In general, at $s, t = 0$, the *mixed moments* are

$$E[x^r y^n] = \iint_{-\infty}^{\infty} x^r y^n p(x,y)\,dx\,dy = \frac{\partial^{r+n} m(s,t)}{\partial s^r \partial t^n} \quad (3.42)$$

The *joint characteristic function* $C(f,g)$ of $x(k)$ and $y(k)$ is defined by letting $g(x,y) = \exp[j2\pi(fx + gy)]$ in Equation (3.33), namely,

$$C(f,g) = E[e^{j2\pi(fx+gy)}] = \iint_{-\infty}^{\infty} p(x,y) e^{j2\pi(fx+gy)}\,dx\,dy \quad (3.43)$$

Thus, $C(f,g)$ has the form of an inverse double Fourier transform, where $p(x,y)$ is the double Fourier transform of $C(f,g)$. Assuming all integrals exists,

$$p(x,y) = \iint_{-\infty}^{\infty} C(f,g) e^{-j2\pi(fx+gy)}\,df\,dg \quad (3.44)$$

Note that $C(f,g)$ is the same as $m(s,t)$ when $s = j2\pi f$ and $t = j2\pi g$, namely,

$$C(f,g) = m(j2\pi f, j2\pi g) \quad (3.45)$$

3.3 GAUSSIAN (NORMAL) DISTRIBUTION

A random variable $x(k)$ is said to follow a *Gaussian* (or *normal*) distribution if its probability density function is given by

$$p(x) = (b\sqrt{2\pi})^{-1} \exp\left[-\frac{(x-a)^2}{2b^2}\right] \quad (3.46)$$

where a is any real constant and b is any positive constant. It may be verified that a and b constitute the mean value and standard deviation of the random variable $x(k)$ because

$$E[x(k)] = \int_{-\infty}^{\infty} xp(x)\,dx = a = \mu_x$$

$$E[(x(k) - a)^2] = \int_{-\infty}^{\infty} (x - a)^2 p(x)\,dx = b^2 = \sigma_x^2$$

Thus, the Gaussian probability density function should be expressed by

$$p(x) = (\sigma_x \sqrt{2\pi})^{-1} \exp\left[-\frac{(x - \mu_x)^2}{2\sigma_x^2}\right] \quad (3.47)$$

The Gaussian probability distribution function is, by definition,

$$P(x) = (\sigma_x \sqrt{2\pi})^{-1} \int_{-\infty}^{x} \exp\left[-\frac{(\xi - \mu_x)^2}{2\sigma_x^2}\right] d\xi \quad (3.48)$$

For the purposes of plotting and tabulation of values, it is convenient to present the Gaussian probability density and distribution functions in terms of the standardized variable z defined as

$$z = \frac{x - \mu_x}{\sigma_x} \quad (3.49)$$

The Gaussian probability density and distribution functions are then given in standardized form by

$$p(z) = (\sqrt{2\pi})^{-1} \exp\left(\frac{-z^2}{2}\right) \quad (3.50)$$

and

$$P(z) = (\sqrt{2\pi})^{-1} \int_{-\infty}^{z} \exp\left(\frac{-\xi^2}{2}\right) d\xi \quad (3.51)$$

Plots of the standardized Gaussian (normal) probability density and distribution functions are shown in Figure 3.5. The values of $p(z)$ and $1 - P(z)$ are tabulated in Tables A.1 and A.2, respectively. These tables can be used for any normally distributed random variable x using Equation (3.49), that is, $x = z\sigma_x + \mu_x$. Applications of the normal distribution to statistical data analysis problems are outlined in Chapter 4. Further discussions of the normal distribution and its history are available from Ref. 5.

3.3.1 Central Limit Theorem

The importance of the normal distribution in physical problems may be attributed in part to the *central limit theorem,* [1], which asserts this distribution will result quite generally from the sum of a large number of independence, random variables acting

GAUSSIAN (NORMAL) DISTRIBUTION **61**

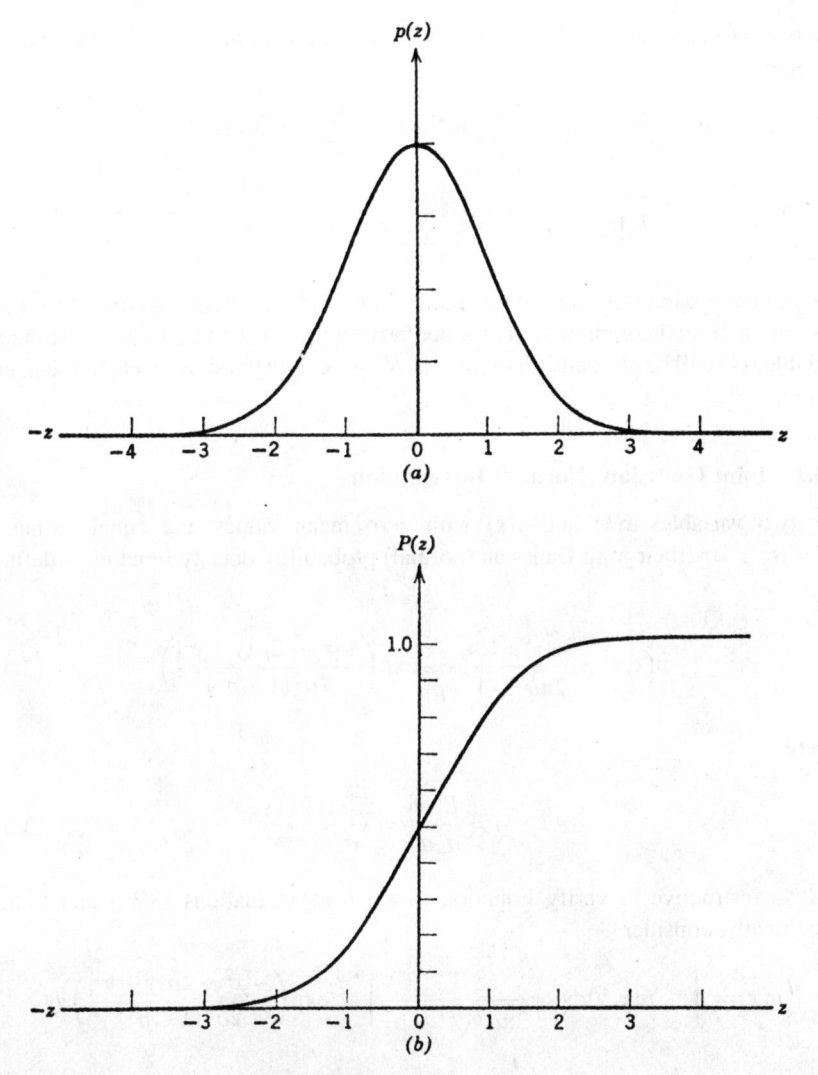

Figure 3.5 Standardized Gaussian (normal) probability density and distribution functions. (*a*) Probability density function. (*b*) Probability distribution function.

together. To be a bit more specific, let $x_1(k), x_2(k), \ldots, x_N(k)$ be N mutually independent random variables whose individual distributions are not specified and may be different. Let μ_i and σ_i^2 be the mean value and variance of each random variable $x_i(k)$, $i = 1, 2, \ldots, N$. Consider the sum random variable

$$x(k) = \sum_{i=1}^{N} a_i x_i(k) \tag{3.52}$$

where a_i are arbitrary fixed constants. Now, the mean value μ_x and the variance σ_x^2 become

$$\mu_x = E[x(k)] = E\left[\sum_{i=1}^{N} a_i x_i(k)\right] = \sum_{i=1}^{N} a_i E[x_i(k)] = \sum_{i=1}^{N} a_i \mu_i$$

$$\sigma_x^2 = E[(x(k)-\mu_x)^2] = E\left[\sum_{i=1}^{N} a_i(x_i(k)-\mu_i)\right]^2 = \sum_{i=1}^{N} a_i^2 \sigma_i^2$$

The last expression is a result of the mutual independence of $x_i(k)$ with $x_j(k)$ for $i \neq j$. The central limit theorem states that under fairly common conditions, the sum random variable $x(k)$ will be normally distributed as $N \to \infty$ with the above mean value μ_x and variance σ_x^2.

3.3.2 Joint Gaussian (Normal) Distribution

For two variables $x(k)$ and $y(k)$ with zero mean values and equal variances $\sigma_1^2 = \sigma_2^2 = \sigma^2$, their joint Gaussian (normal) probability density function is defined by

$$p(x,y) = \frac{1}{2\pi\sigma^2\sqrt{1-\rho^2}} \exp\left(\frac{-[x^2 - 2\rho xy + y^2]}{2\sigma^2(1-\rho^2)}\right) \qquad (3.53)$$

where

$$\rho = \frac{E[xy]}{\sigma_1 \sigma_2} = \frac{E[xy]}{\sigma^2} \qquad (3.54)$$

It is instructive to verify Equation (3.47) using Equations (3.30) and (3.53). Specifically, consider

$$p(x) = \int_{-\infty}^{\infty} p(x,y) dy = \frac{1}{2\pi\sigma^2\sqrt{1-\rho^2}} \int_{-\infty}^{\infty} \exp\left(\frac{-[x^2 - 2\rho xy + y^2]}{2\sigma^2(1-\rho^2)}\right) dy$$

Now

$$x^2 - 2\rho xy + y^2 = (1-\rho^2)x^2 + (y-\rho x)^2$$

so the exponential term can be written as

$$\exp\left(\frac{-[x^2 - 2\rho xy + y^2]}{2\sigma^2(1-\rho^2)}\right) = \exp\left(-\frac{x^2}{2\sigma^2}\right) \exp\left(\frac{-(y-\rho x)^2}{2\sigma^2(1-\rho^2)}\right)$$

Hence

$$p(x) = \frac{\exp(-x^2/2\sigma^2)}{2\pi\sigma^2\sqrt{1-\rho^2}} \int_{-\infty}^{\infty} \exp\left[\frac{-(y-\rho x)^2}{2\sigma^2(1-\rho^2)}\right] dy$$

GAUSSIAN (NORMAL) DISTRIBUTION

Now let

$$u = \frac{y - \rho x}{\sigma\sqrt{2(1-\rho^2)}} \qquad du = \frac{dy}{\sigma\sqrt{2(1-\rho^2)}}$$

Then

$$p(x) = \frac{\exp(-x^2/2\sigma^2)}{\sigma\pi\sqrt{2}} \int_{-\infty}^{\infty} \exp(-u^2)\,du = \frac{\exp(-x^2/2\sigma^2)}{\sigma\sqrt{2\pi}}$$

in agreement with Equation (3.47).

3.3.3 Moment-Generating and Characteristic Functions

From Equations (3.17) and (3.47), the moment-generating function for the zero mean value Gaussian variable is

$$m(s) = \exp(\sigma^2 s^2/2) \tag{3.55}$$

One can now verify from Equation (3.18) that

$$\begin{aligned} E[x^{2n-1}] &= 0 \\ E[x^{2n}] &= 1 \cdot 3 \cdot 5 \cdots (2n-1)\sigma^{2n} \end{aligned} \qquad n = 1, 2, 3 \ldots \tag{3.56}$$

Thus, all odd-order moments are zero while even-order moments become

$$\begin{aligned} E[x^2] &= \sigma^2 & E[x^4] &= 3\sigma^4 \\ E[x^6] &= 15\sigma^6 & E[x^8] &= 105\sigma^8 \end{aligned} \tag{3.57}$$

and so on.

From Equations (3.22) and (3.55), the characteristic function for the zero mean value Gaussian variable is

$$C(f) = \exp(-2\pi^2 \sigma^2 f^2) \tag{3.58}$$

The joint moment-generating function from Equation (3.40) for the two zero mean value Gaussian variables satisfying Equation (3.53) is

$$m(s,t) = \exp\left[\frac{\sigma^2}{2}(s^2 + 2\rho st + t^2)\right] \tag{3.59}$$

It follows directly from Equation (3.42) that

$$\begin{aligned} E[x^r y^n] &= 0 & &\text{if } r + n \text{ is odd} \\ E[x^2] &= E[y^2] = \sigma^2 & E[xy] &= \rho\sigma^2 \\ E[x^3 y] &= E[xy^3] = 3\rho\sigma^4 \\ E[x^2 y^2] &= \sigma^4(1 + 2\rho^2) \end{aligned} \tag{3.60}$$

and so on. The joint characteristic function from Equation (3.45) for the two zero mean value Gaussian variables satisfying Equation (3.58) is

$$C(f,g) = \exp\{-2\pi^2\sigma^2[f^2 + 2\rho fg + g^2]\} \tag{3.61}$$

3.3.4 N-Dimensional Gaussian (Normal) Distribution

Consider now N random variables $x_1(k), x_2(k), \ldots, x_N(k)$, which may be correlated. Denote their respective mean values, variances, and covariances by

$$\begin{aligned}
\mu_i &= E[x_i(k)] \\
\sigma_i^2 &= E[(x_i(k)-\mu_i)^2] \\
C_{ij} &= E[(x_i(k)-\mu_i)(x_j(k)-\mu_j)] \quad C_{ii} = \sigma_i^2
\end{aligned} \tag{3.62}$$

Their joint distribution is said to follow an *N-dimensional Gaussian* (*normal*) *distribution* if the associated N-fold probability density function is given by

$$p(x_1, x_2, \ldots, x_N) = \frac{\exp[(-1/2|\mathbf{C}|)\sum_{i,j=1}^{N} |\mathbf{C}_{ij}|(x_i-\mu_i)(x_j-\mu_j)]}{(2\pi)^{N/2}|\mathbf{C}|^{1/2}} \tag{3.63}$$

where $\mathbf{C}$ is the covariance matrix of the C_{ij} defined below, $|\mathbf{C}|$ is the determinant of $\mathbf{C}$, and $|\mathbf{C}_{ij}|$ is the cofactor of C_{ij} in determinant $|\mathbf{C}|$. To be explicit,

$$\mathbf{C} = \begin{bmatrix} C_{11} & C_{12} & \cdots & C_{1N} \\ C_{21} & C_{22} & \cdots & C_{2N} \\ \vdots & \vdots & & \vdots \\ C_{N1} & C_{N2} & \cdots & C_{NN} \end{bmatrix} \tag{3.64}$$

and the cofactor $|\mathbf{C}_{ij}|$ of any element C_{ij} is defined to be the determinant of order $N-1$ formed by omitting the ith row and jth column of $\mathbf{C}$, multiplied by $(-1)^{i+j}$.

The outstanding feature of the N-dimensional Gaussian distribution is that all of its properties are determined solely from a knowledge of the various mean values μ_i and covariances C_{ij}. For $N=1$, this function reduces to

$$p(x_1) = (\sigma_1\sqrt{2\pi})^{-1}\exp\left[-\frac{(x_1-\mu_1)^2}{2\sigma_1^2}\right] \tag{3.65}$$

which is the Gaussian probability density function denned previously in Equation (3.47). For $N=2$, the joint normal probability density function becomes

$$p(x_1, x_2) = \frac{\exp\left\{\left[\frac{-1}{2(1-\rho_{12}^2)}\right]\left[\left(\frac{x_1-\mu_1}{\sigma_1}\right)^2 - 2\rho_{12}\left(\frac{x_1-\mu_1}{\sigma_1}\right)\left(\frac{x_2-\mu_2}{\sigma_2}\right) + \left(\frac{x_2-\mu_2}{\sigma_2}\right)^2\right]\right\}}{2\pi\sigma_1\sigma_2\sqrt{1-\rho_{12}^2}} \tag{3.66}$$

where $\rho_{12} = c_{12}/\sigma_1\sigma_2$ is the correlation coefficient between $x_1(k)$ and $x_2(k)$. Observe that when $x_1(k)$ and $x_2(k)$ are uncorrelated so that $\rho_{12} = 0$, Equation (3.66) becomes

$$p(x_1, x_2) = p(x_1)p(x_2) \tag{3.67}$$

which shows that $x_1(k)$ and $x_2(k)$ are also independent. This result is not true for arbitrary distributions.

Similar formulas may be written for higher order cases where $N = 3, 4, 5, \ldots$. For arbitrary N, it follows quite easily that if all different pairs of Gaussian distributed random variables are mutually uncorrelated (that is, $\rho_{ij} = 0$ whenever $i \neq j$), then these random variables are mutually independent in the probability sense. That is,

$$p(x_1, x_2, \ldots, x_N) = p(x_1)p(x_2) \cdots p(x_N) \tag{3.68}$$

The importance of the N-dimensional Gaussian distribution in physical problems, analogous to the common one-dimensional Gaussian distribution, is due in part to the *multidimensional central limit theorem*, [6]. This theorem yields the result that the vector sum of a large number of mutually independent N-dimensional random variables approaches an N-dimensional Gaussian distribution under fairly general conditions.

For any N-dimensional Gaussian probability density function represented by Equation (3.63), it follows that

$$\int\!\!\int_{-\infty}^{\infty}\!\!\cdots\!\int p(x_1, x_2, \ldots x_N)\, dx_1\, dx_2 \cdots dx_N = 1 \tag{3.69}$$

Also, the expected value of any real single-valued continuous function $g(x_1, x_2, \ldots, x_N)$ of the N random variables involved is given by

$$E[g(x_1, x_2, \ldots, x_N)] = \int\!\!\int_{-\infty}^{\infty}\!\!\cdots\!\int g(x_1, x_2, \ldots, x_N)\,p(x_1, x_2, \ldots, x_N) \\ \times dx_1\, dx_2 \cdots dx_N \tag{3.70}$$

When $g(x_1, x_2, \ldots, x_N) = \exp(s_1 x_1 + s_2 x_2 + \cdots + s_N x_N)$, this defines from Equation (3.63) that the Nth-*order moment-generating function*, namely,

$$m(s_1, s_2, \ldots, s_N) = E[\exp(s_1 x_1 + s_2 x_2 + \cdots + s_N x_N)] \tag{3.71}$$

Consider the case of four Gaussian random variables, x_1, x_2, x_3, and x_4, with *zero mean values* and equal variances $\sigma_i^2 = \sigma^2$. Their respective covariances C_{ij} now satisfy $C_{ij} = \rho_{ij}\sigma^2$ where

$$\begin{aligned} C_{12} &= E[x_1 x_2] & C_{23} &= E[x_2 x_3] \\ C_{13} &= E[x_1 x_3] & C_{24} &= E[x_2 x_4] \\ C_{14} &= E[x_1 x_4] & C_{34} &= E[x_3 x_4] \end{aligned} \tag{3.72}$$

Let $p(x_1 x_2, x_3, x_4)$ be given by Equation (3.63). Then the *fourth-order moment-generating function* becomes

$$m(s_1, s_2, s_3, s_4) = E[\exp(s_1 x_1 + s_2 x_2 + s_3 x_3 + s_4 x_4)]$$

$$= \exp\left[\frac{\sigma^2}{2}(s_1^2 + s_2^2 + s_3^2 + s_4^2 + 2\rho_{12} s_1 s_2 + 2\rho_{13} s_1 s_3 \right.$$

$$\left. + 2\rho_{14} s_1 s_4 + 2\rho_{23} s_2 s_3 + 2\rho_{24} s_2 s_4 + 2\rho_{34} s_3 s_4)\right]$$

One can directly verify that the fourth-order moment is given by the fourth partial derivative

$$E[x_1 x_2 x_3 x_4] = \left. \frac{\partial^4 m(s_1, s_2, s_3, s_4)}{\partial s_1 \partial s_2 \partial s_3 \partial s_4} \right|_{s_1 = s_2 = s_3 = s_4 = 0}$$

It is now straightforward but tedious to perform the partial derivatives and to set $s_1 = s_2 = s_3 = s_4 = 0$ so as to derive

$$E[x_1 x_2 x_3 x_4] = C_{12} C_{34} + C_{13} C_{24} + C_{14} C_{23} \qquad (3.73)$$

This shows that the fourth-order moment is the sum of $3 = (3 \cdot 1)$ different pairs of second-order moments (covariances) contained therein.

A similar derivation for the sixth-order moment of zero mean value Gaussian data gives the result that the sixth-order moment is the product of $15 = (5 \cdot 3 \cdot 1)$ different triplets of second-order moments contained therein, namely,

$$\begin{aligned} E[x_1 x_2 x_3 x_4 x_5 x_6] &= C_{12}[C_{34} C_{56} + C_{35} C_{46} + C_{36} C_{45}] \\ &\quad + C_{13}[C_{24} C_{56} + C_{25} C_{46} + C_{26} C_{45}] \\ &\quad + C_{14}[C_{23} C_{56} + C_{25} C_{36} + C_{26} C_{35}] \qquad (3.74) \\ &\quad + C_{15}[C_{23} C_{46} + C_{24} C_{36} + C_{26} C_{34}] \\ &\quad + C_{16}[C_{23} C_{45} + C_{24} C_{35} + C_{25} C_{34}] \end{aligned}$$

In general, if n is an even integer, then $E[x_1 x_2 \cdots x_N]$ consists of $(N-1)(N-3)\cdots(3)(1)$ different products of all possible C_{ij} terms. On the other hand, all odd-order moments of Gaussian random variables with zero mean values will be zero, that is,

$$E[x_1 x_2 \cdots x_N] = 0 \quad \text{if } N \text{ is odd} \qquad (3.75)$$

All of these relations apply not only to the original random variables x_i, but also to any linear transformations, such as their Fourier transforms.

More complicated expressions occur when mean values are not zero. For example, consider four Gaussian random variables x_1, x_2, x_3, x_4 with equal *nonzero mean value* $\mu \neq 0$ and equal variances σ^2. Now, in place of Equation (3.72), the covariances C_{ij} for $i \neq j$ are given by

$$C_{ij} = E[(x_i - \mu)(x_j - \mu)] \qquad (3.76)$$

When $i=j$,

$$C_{ii} = E[(x_i-\mu)^2] = \sigma^2 = \psi^2 - \mu^2 \tag{3.77}$$

The result in Equation (3.73) applies to the four variables $(x_1 - \mu)$, $(x_2 - \mu)$, $(x_3 - \mu)$, and $(x_4 - \mu)$. Hence, from Equations (3.73) and (3.75), it follows that

$$\begin{aligned} E[x_1 x_2 x_3 x_4] &= C_{12}C_{34} + C_{13}C_{24} + C_{14}C_{23} + \mu^4 \\ &+ \mu^2[C_{12} + C_{13} + C_{14} + C_{23} + C_{24} + C_{34}] \end{aligned} \tag{3.78}$$

As a special case,

$$E[x_1^2 x_2^2] = \psi^4 + 2C_{12}^2 + 4\mu^4 C_{12} \tag{3.79}$$

The covariance term

$$\begin{aligned} C_{12} &= E[(x_1-\mu)(x_2-\mu)] = E[x_1 x_2] - \mu^2 \\ &= R_{12} - \mu^2 \end{aligned} \tag{3.80}$$

where

$$R_{12} = E[x_1 x_2] \tag{3.81}$$

Thus, Equation (3.79) can also be written

$$E[x_1^2 x_2^2] = \psi^4 + 2[R_{12}^2 - \mu^4] \tag{3.82}$$

3.4 RAYLEIGH DISTRIBUTION

Another important distribution that evolves from the Gaussian distribution is called the *Rayleigh distribution*. In Section 4.2.2, it is noted that the Rayleigh distribution is the square root of the chi-square distribution with two degrees of freedom. However, beyond its applications in classical statistics discussed in Chapter 4, the Rayleigh distribution has an important relationship to narrow bandwidth random data; specifically, it describes the probability density function of the envelope for such random data, as will now be proved. Further applications of the Rayleigh distribution to the peak values in narrow bandwidth Gaussian data are covered later in Section 5.5.2.

3.4.1 Distribution of Envelope and Phase for Narrow Bandwidth Data

Consider some statistical properties about the envelope and phase of an output random data record after passage through a narrow bandpass filter. The frequency spread of the output record is assumed to be small compared to the center frequency of the filter. Figure 3.6 pictures a typical narrow bandwidth output record with its output

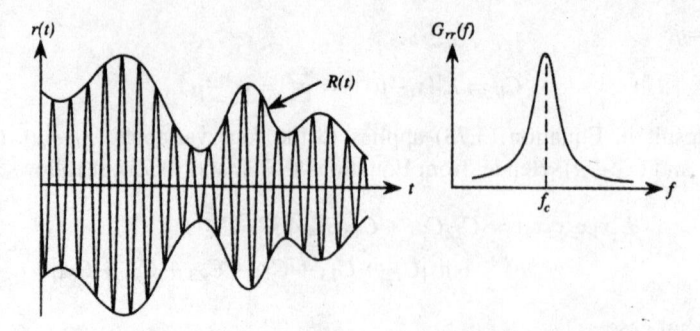

Figure 3.6 Time history and autospectrum for narrow bandwidth data.

autospectrum. The output record $r(t)$ depicted in Figure 3.6 can be expressed as

$$r(t) = R(t) \cos[2\pi f_c t + \theta(t)] \quad (3.83)$$

where the envelope $R(t)$ and the phase angle $\theta(t)$ are slowly varying functions of time relative to the oscillations at the center frequency f_c. An equivalent representation for $r(t)$ is

$$r(t) = x(t) \cos 2\pi f_c t - y(t) \sin 2\pi f_c t \quad (3.84)$$

where

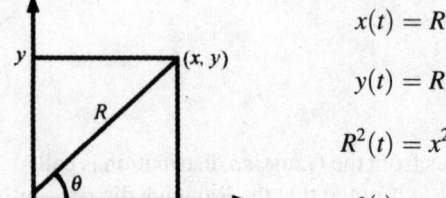

$$x(t) = R(t) \cos \theta(t) \quad (3.85a)$$

$$y(t) = R(t) \sin \theta(t) \quad (3.85b)$$

$$R^2(t) = x^2(t) + y^2(t) \quad (3.85c)$$

$$\theta(t) = \tan^{-1}[y(t)/x(t)] \quad (3.85d)$$

If $\{x\}$ and $\{y\}$ are thought of as an ensemble of possible rectangular errors in measuring the location of an object in an x, y coordinate system, then $\{R\}$ and $\{\theta\}$ can be considered as the corresponding range and phase angle errors in an R, θ coordinate system.

Suppose that the joint probability density function $p(x, y)$ is known. Then the joint probability density function $p(R, \theta)$ can be found from

$$p(x, y) \, dx \, dy = p(R \cos \theta, R \sin \theta) R \, dR \, d\theta \quad (3.86)$$

because the element of area $dx \, dy$ in the x, y plane corresponds to the element of area $R \, dR \, d\theta$ in the R, θ plane. Let

$$q(R, \theta) = Rp(R \cos \theta, R \sin \theta) \quad (3.87)$$

RAYLEIGH DISTRIBUTION

Then
$$p(x,y)\,dx\,dy = q(R,\theta)\,dR\,d\theta \tag{3.88}$$

Now, the probability density function of the envelopes $R(t)$ alone can be obtained by summing over all possible phase angles $\theta(t)$ from $(0, 2\pi)$ and is given by

$$q_1(R) = \int_0^{2\pi} q(R,\theta)\,d\theta \quad R \geq 0 \tag{3.89}$$

while the probability density function of the phase angles $\theta(t)$ alone can be obtained by summing over all possible envelopes $R(t)$ from $(0, \infty)$ and is given by

$$q_2(\theta) = \int_0^{\infty} q(R,\theta)\,dr \quad 0 \leq \theta \leq 2\pi \tag{3.90}$$

The above relations show that the problem of determining the statistical nature of the envelope function $R(t)$ and the phase function $\theta(t)$ is reduced to finding their joint probability density function $p(x, y)$. To this objective, assume that $r(t)$ is a narrow bandwidth Gaussian data record with a zero mean value and a variance σ_r^2. Because $x(t)$ and $y(t)$ are each of the same form as $r(t)$, consisting of $R(t)$ multiplied by sine and cosine functions, it follows that they are also Gaussian distributed with zero mean values and the same variance as $r(t)$, namely,

$$\sigma_r^2 = E[r^2(t)] = E[x^2(t)] = E[y^2(t)] \tag{3.91}$$

Also, $x(t)$ and $y(t)$ are independent random variables such that

$$E[x(t)\,y(t)] = 0 \tag{3.92}$$

because the product $x(t)\,y(t)$ is an odd function of t. Hence, the joint probability density function for $x(t)$ and $y(t)$ will be a two-dimensional Gaussian function of the form

$$p(x,y) = p(x)\,p(y) = \frac{1}{2\pi\sigma_r^2} \exp\left[-\frac{(x^2+y^2)}{2\sigma_r^2}\right] \tag{3.93}$$

From Equations (3.87) and (3.89), it now follows that

$$q(R,\theta) = \frac{R}{2\pi\sigma_r^2} \exp\left(-\frac{R^2}{2\sigma_r^2}\right) \tag{3.94}$$

$$q_1(R) = \frac{R}{\sigma_r^2} \exp\left(-\frac{R^2}{2\sigma_r^2}\right) \quad R \geq 0 \tag{3.95}$$

The probability density function $q_1(R)$ governing the distribution of the envelope $R(t)$ is the *Rayleigh probability density function*. Note that the parameter R in this function is restricted to nonnegative values. The probability distribution function for $R(t)$ is computed by integrating Equation (3.95) from zero to R. The result is

$$Q_1(R) = \text{Prob}[R(t) < R] = \int_0^R q_1(\xi)\,d\xi = 1 - \exp\left(-\frac{R^2}{2\sigma_r^2}\right) \tag{3.96}$$

Note that the Rayleigh probability density and distribution functions in Equations (3.95) and (3.96), respectively, are independent of the original center frequency f_c and a function only of the variance σ_r^2. This allows the Rayleigh probability density and distribution functions to be standardized on the variable (R/σ_r) to obtain

$$p\left(\frac{R}{\sigma_r}\right) = \left(\frac{R}{\sigma_r}\right) \exp\left[-\frac{(R/\sigma_r)^2}{2}\right] \quad R \geq 0 \tag{3.97}$$

$$P\left(\frac{R}{\sigma_r}\right) = 1 - \exp\left[-\frac{(R/\sigma_r)^2}{2}\right] \tag{3.98}$$

where Equation (3.97) is determined by taking the derivative of Equation (3.98) with respect to (R/σ_r). These standardized functions are pictured in Figure 3.7.

From Equation (3.95), the mean value of $R(t)$ over the set of all possible envelopes is

$$\mu_R = \int_0^\infty R q_1(R) \, dR = (\pi/2)^{1/2} \sigma_r \approx 1.25 \sigma_r \tag{3.99}$$

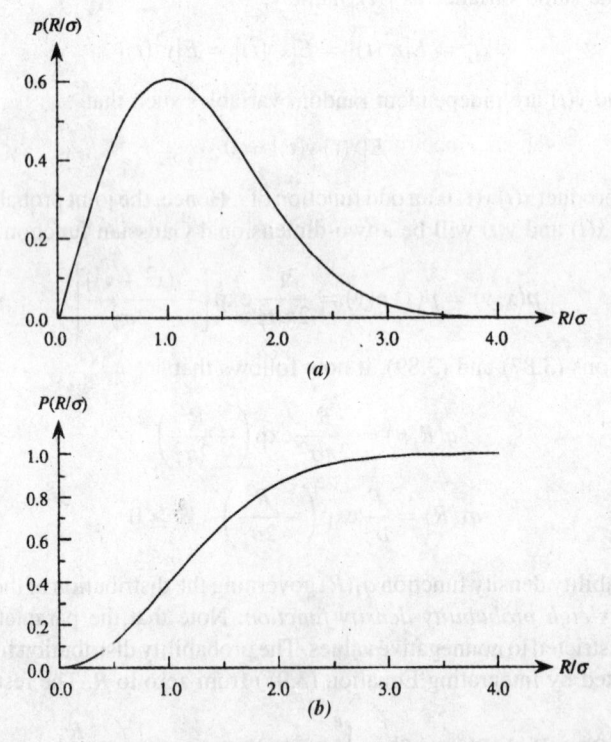

Figure 3.7 Standardized Rayleigh probability density and distribution functions. (*a*) Probability density function. (*b*) Probability distribution function.

RAYLEIGH DISTRIBUTION

and the mean square value is

$$\psi_R^2 = \int_0^\infty R^2 q_1(R)\,dR = 2\sigma_r^2 \qquad (3.100)$$

From Equations (3.90) and (3.94), the probability density function for $\theta(t)$ is

$$q_2(\theta) = \frac{1}{2\pi} \quad 0 \le \theta \le 2\pi \qquad (3.101)$$

showing that the phase angles $\theta(t)$ are uniformly distributed over $(0, 2\pi)$.

3.4.2 Distribution of Output Record for Narrow Bandwidth Data

In the derivation just conducted for the distribution of the envelope $R(t)$ and phase angle $\theta(t)$ of a narrow bandwidth output record $r(t)$, this record $r(t)$ was assumed to be a sample member of a normally distributed random process. It was then shown that the envelope function follows a Rayleigh distribution and the phase angle follows a uniform distribution. The *converse result* will now be proved: Specifically, the narrow bandwidth output record $r(t)$ has a normal distribution if the noise envelope $R(t)$ follows a Rayleigh distribution and the phase angle $\theta(t)$ follows a uniform distribution.

To prove this converse result, let the narrow bandwidth output record $r(t)$ be represented as before by

$$r(t) = R(t)\cos[2\pi f_c t + \theta(t)] \qquad (3.102)$$

Assume here that the envelope function $R(t)$ is governed by the Rayleigh probability density function

$$q_1(R) = \frac{R}{\sigma_r^2}\exp\left(-\frac{R^2}{2\sigma_r^2}\right) \quad R \ge 0 \qquad (3.103)$$

Assume also that the phase angle $\theta(t)$ is governed by the uniform probability density function

$$q_2(\theta) = \frac{1}{2\pi} \quad 0 \le \theta \le 2\pi \qquad (3.104)$$

The probability density function $p(r)$ can now be found from Equation (3.116) in Section 3.5 by replacing the variable x by r and the amplitude A by the envelope R. This gives

$$p(r) = \int_r^\infty \frac{q_1(R)}{\pi\sqrt{R^2 - r^2}}\,dR \qquad (3.105)$$

where $q_1(R)$ is represented by Equation (3.103). Substitution of this $q_1(R)$ into Equation (3.105) yields

$$p(r) = \frac{1}{\pi\sigma_r^2}\int_r^\infty \frac{R\exp(-R^2/2\sigma_r^2)}{\sqrt{R^2 - r^2}}\,dR \qquad (3.106)$$

The variable of integration can now be changed by letting $u = R^2 - r^2$ and $du = 2R\,dR$ to obtain

$$p(r) = \frac{\exp(-r^2/2\sigma_r^2)}{2\pi\sigma_r^2} \int_0^\infty \frac{\exp(-u/2\sigma_r^2)}{\sqrt{u}} du = \frac{1}{\sigma_r\sqrt{2\pi}} \exp\left(-\frac{r^2}{2\sigma_r^2}\right) \quad (3.107)$$

where the following formula from integral tables is used:

$$\int_0^\infty \frac{\exp(-u/2\sigma_r^2)}{\sqrt{u}} du = \sigma_r\sqrt{2\pi} \quad (3.108)$$

Equation (3.107) shows that the narrow bandwidth output data record $r(t)$ is normally distributed with a mean value of zero and a variance of σ_r^2, completing the desired proof.

3.5 HIGHER ORDER CHANGES OF VARIABLES

Consider two single-valued continuous random variables with continuous partial derivatives defined by

$$u = u(x, y) \qquad v = v(x, y) \quad (3.109)$$

where the inverse functions are also single valued. Let $p(x, y)$ be the joint probability density function of x and y and let $p(u, v)$ be the joint probability density function of u and v. Then, as x and y move about some probability area in the x, y plane, the corresponding u and v move about the same probability area in the u, v plane. Hence,

$$p(u, v)\,du\,dv = p(x, y)\,dx\,dy$$

The relation between the areas in the two planes can be determined by the mathematical expression for the Jacobian transformation of coordinates in Ref. 7, namely,

$$du\,dv = J\,dx\,dy$$

where

$$J = \left[\frac{\partial(u, v)}{\partial(x, y)}\right] = \begin{bmatrix} \partial u/\partial x & \partial u/\partial y \\ \partial v/\partial x & \partial v/\partial y \end{bmatrix} = (\partial u/\partial x)(\partial v/\partial y) - (\partial u/\partial y)(\partial v/\partial x)$$

$$(3.110)$$

It follows that

$$p(u, v) = \frac{p(x, y)}{|J|} \quad (3.111)$$

In using this formula, the variables x and y on the right-hand side must be replaced by their appropriate u and v so as to obtain $p(u, v)$ as a function of u and v. Also, the absolute value of J should be used because the joint probability density functions are nonnegative quantities.

HIGHER ORDER CHANGES OF VARIABLES

For the case of a three-variable change where

$$u = u(x,y,z) \quad v = v(x,y,z) \quad w = w(x,y,z) \tag{3.112}$$

the Jacobian is given by the determinant

$$J = \left[\frac{\partial(u,v,w)}{\partial(x,y,z)}\right] = \begin{bmatrix} \partial u/\partial x & \partial u/\partial y & \partial u/\partial z \\ \partial v/\partial x & \partial v/\partial y & \partial v/\partial z \\ \partial w/\partial x & \partial w/\partial y & \partial w/\partial z \end{bmatrix} \tag{3.113}$$

This indicates the change in probability expressions according to the relations

$$p(u,v,w)\,du\,dv\,dw = p(x,y,z)\,dx\,dy\,dz$$

with

$$du\,dv\,dw = J\,dx\,dy\,dz$$

Thus, for a three-variable change, we have

$$p(u,v,w) = \frac{p(x,y,z)}{|J|} \tag{3.114}$$

Similar formulas can be written down for changes of four or more variables.

Example 3.6. **Sine Wave Distribution with Random Amplitudes.** Consider a sine wave with random phase angles and random amplitudes represented by the variable

$$x(k) = A(k)\sin[2\pi f_0 t + \theta(k)] \tag{3.115}$$

where $A(k)$ and $\theta(k)$ are independent random variables. The random angle $\theta(k)$ is assumed to be uniformly distributed over $(0, 2\pi)$, and the random amplitude $A(k)$ is assumed to be governed by a probability density function $p(A)$. The problem of determining the probability density function $p(x)$ is more difficult here than in Example 3.3 because two events must be considered. To accomplish this goal, let $B(k) = \sin[2\pi f_0 t + \theta(k)]$ and introduce a second variable $u(k) = A(k)$. From Equations (3.110) and (3.111), the change of variables from $A(k)$ to $u(k)$ and $B(k)$ to $x(k)$ is given by the formula

$$p(u,x) = \frac{p(A,B)}{J}$$

where the Jacobian is defined as

$$J = \begin{bmatrix} \partial u/\partial A & \partial u/\partial B \\ \partial x/\partial A & \partial x/\partial B \end{bmatrix} = \begin{bmatrix} 1 & 0 \\ B & A \end{bmatrix} = A$$

Because $A(k)$ and $B(k)$ are independent random variables with $B = (x/A)$, the joint probability density function is expressed as

$$p(A,B) = p(A)p(B) = P(A)p(x/A)$$

Thus,

$$p(u, x) = \frac{p(A) p(x/A)}{A}$$

Finally, from Equation (3.30), the first-order probability density function $p(x)$ is given by

$$p(x) = \int_{-\infty}^{\infty} p(u, x) du = \int_{-\infty}^{\infty} \frac{p(A) p(x/A)}{A} dA$$

As shown in Example 3.3, for $B(k) = \sin[2\pi f_0 t + \theta(k)]$, the probability density function

$$p(B) = \frac{1}{\pi \sqrt{1 - B^2}} \qquad |B| < 1, \quad \text{otherwise zero}$$

Because $B = (x/A)$, this is the same as

$$p(x/A) = \frac{A}{\pi \sqrt{A^2 - x^2}} \qquad |x| < A, \quad \text{otherwise zero}$$

Substitution now yields the general result for any probability density function $p(A)$ of the random amplitudes in Equation (3.115), namely,

$$p(x) = \int_x^{\infty} \frac{p(A)}{\pi \sqrt{A^2 - x^2}} dA \qquad (3.116)$$

A special case of the random processes being discussed in this example is the ensemble of time functions $\{A(k) \sin[2\pi f_0 t + \theta(k)]\}$, where $\theta(k)$ is uniformly distributed over $(0, 2\pi)$ and $A(k)$ is governed by a Gaussian distribution. This offers a nontrivial example of a stationary random process that is not ergodic. If $A(k)$ reduces to a fixed constant amplitude A, then the random process becomes ergodic.

Example 3.7. Sine Wave in Gaussian Noise. Consider a single fixed sine wave plus normal (Gaussian) noise defined by

$$z(t) = A \sin(2\pi f_0 t + \theta) + n(t) \qquad (3.117)$$

where A and θ are constants and $n(t)$ is Gaussian noise with a mean value of zero and a variance of σ_n^2. The mean value of the sine wave is also zero and its variance is $(A^2/2)$. For this type of data, it is proved in Ref. 8 that the probability density function $p(z)$ of $z(t)$ over all time, as defined by

$$p(z) \, dz = \text{Prob}[z < z(t) \leq z + dz] \qquad (3.118)$$

is given by

$$p(z) = \frac{1}{\pi \sigma_n} \int_0^{\pi} \psi \left[\frac{z - A \cos \phi}{\sigma_n} \right] d\phi \qquad (3.119)$$

HIGHER ORDER CHANGES OF VARIABLES 75

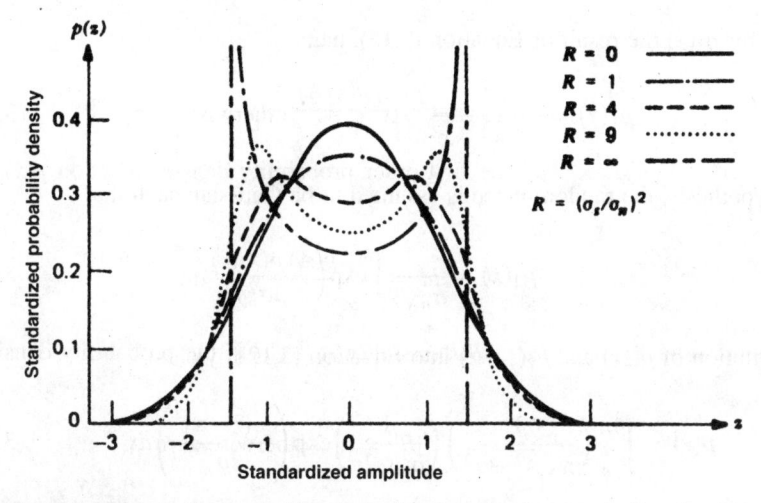

Figure 3.8 Standardized probability density functions of a sine wave in Gaussian noise.

where

$$\psi(x) = \frac{1}{\sqrt{2\pi}} \exp\left(\frac{-x^2}{2}\right) \qquad (3.120)$$

is the normal probability density function with a mean value of zero and a variance of unity.

Equation (3.119) is derived below by assuming, as in Section 5.3.2, that sufficient conditions for ergodicity exist so that the time average on one representative record over all time is equivalent to an ensemble average over the collection of records at a fixed time. Plots of the standardized $p(z)$ of Equation (3.119) as a function of z are shown in Figure 3.8 for different values of the variance ratio $R = (\sigma_s/\sigma_n)^2$, where $\sigma_s^2 = (A^2/2)$ is the variance of the sine wave and σ_n^2 is the variance of the noise.

The proof of Equation (3.119) is as follows. By the convolution property of Equation (3.39), the probability density function for the sum of the two independent random variables in Equation (3.117) is given by

$$p(z) = \int_{-\infty}^{\infty} p_1(x) p_2(z-x)\, dx \qquad (3.121)$$

where $p_1(x)$ is the probability density function of $A \sin(2\pi f_0 t + \theta)$ and $p_2(x)$ is the probability density function of $n(t)$. To be specific,

$$\begin{aligned} p_1(x)dx &\approx \text{Prob}[x < A \sin(2\pi f_0 t + \theta) \leq x + dx] \\ p_2(x)dx &\approx \text{Prob}[x < n(t) \leq x + dx] \end{aligned} \qquad (3.122)$$

To determine $p_1(x)$, instead of keeping the phase angle θ fixed and letting t vary over all time, one can hold t fixed and let the phase angles vary uniformly over $(0, 2\pi)$. This gives for $p_1(x)$ the result of Equation (3.15), namely,

$$p_1(x) = \frac{1}{\pi\sqrt{A^2 - x^2}} \quad |x| < A, \quad \text{otherwise zero} \quad (3.123)$$

By hypothesis, the random noise is assumed to be Gaussian such that

$$p_2(x) = \frac{1}{\sigma_n\sqrt{2\pi}} \exp\left(-\frac{x^2}{2\sigma_n^2}\right) \quad (3.124)$$

Substitution of $p_1(x)$ and $p_2(z-x)$ into Equation (3.121) yields

$$p(z) = \int_{-A}^{A} \left(\frac{1}{\pi\sqrt{A^2 - x^2}}\right)\left(\frac{1}{\sigma_n\sqrt{2\pi}}\right) \exp\left(\frac{-(z-x)^2}{2\sigma_n^2}\right) dx \quad (3.125)$$

Now, let $x = A\cos\phi$ and $dx = -A\sin\phi\, d\phi = -\sqrt{A^2 - x^2}\, d\phi$. With this change of variables, Equation (3.125) becomes

$$p(z) = \frac{1}{\pi\sigma_n} \int_0^\pi \psi\left(\frac{z - A\cos\phi}{\sigma_n}\right) d\phi \quad (3.126)$$

where $\psi(x)$ is given by Equation (3.120). This completes the proof of Equation (3.119) for the probability density function of a sine wave in Gaussian noise.

PROBLEMS

3.1 A manufacturer produces shafts and bearings that are ultimately assembled by placing a shaft into a bearing. The shafts are produced with an outside diameter s that is normally distributed with a mean value of $\mu_s = 1.0$ cm and a standard deviation of $\sigma_s = 0.003$ cm. The inside diameter b of the manufactured bearings is also normally distributed with a mean value of $\mu_b = 1.01$ cm and a standard deviation of $\sigma_b = 0.004$ cm. If the assembler selects a shaft and a bearing at random, what is the probability that a selected shaft will not fit inside the bearing? (Assume the shafts and bearings are perfectly circular and a fit occurs if $s < b$.)

3.2 A manufacturer produces washers with a thickness d that has a mean value of $\mu_d = 1.0$ mm and a standard deviation of $\sigma_d = 0.1$ mm. If $N = 25$ washers are selected at random and stacked on top of one another determine the probability that the height of the stack will be between 24 and 26 mm, assuming
 (a) the thickness d is normally distributed.
 (b) the thickness d has an unknown distribution function.

3.3 Consider a random variable x with a probability density function given by

$$p(x) = \begin{cases} 4x^3 & 0 < x < 1 \\ 0 & \text{otherwise} \end{cases}$$

(a) Determine the probability distribution function $P(x)$.
(b) Determine the mean value and the variance of x.

3.4 Consider a random variable x with a probability distribution function given by

$$P(x) = \begin{cases} 0 & x \leq 0 \\ x^n & 0 < x \leq 1 \\ 1 & x > 1 \end{cases}$$

(a) Determine the probability density function $p(x)$.
(b) Determine the mean value and variance of x.

3.5 Assume a computer generates random digits (0, 1, 2, 3, 4, 5, 6, 7, 8, 9) with equal probabilities. Let T be a random variable representing the sum of N digits. Determine the mean value and variance of T.

3.6 A random variable x is uniformly distributed such that the probability density function is given by

$$p(x) = \begin{cases} 1 & 0 < x < 1 \\ 0 & \text{elsewhere} \end{cases}$$

Find the probability density function of the random variable $y = 2x + 1$.

3.7 Assume a random variable x is normally distributed with a mean value of zero and a variance of unity. Determine the probability density function of the random variable $y = x^2$.

3.8 Gaussian random noise is passed through a narrow bandpass filter to produce a narrow bandwidth output $r(t)$ with an envelope $R(t)$. Assume the envelope $R(t)$ has a mean value of $\mu_R = 2.50$. What is the probability that the envelope at any instant will exceed a value of $R = 5$.

3.9 Consider a random variable x with a Poisson distribution defined by $p(x) = \mu^x e^{-\mu}/x!$. Determine the mean value and variance of x using the moment generating function.

3.10 Two independent random variables x and y have probability density functions given by

$$p(x) = \frac{1}{2\sqrt{\pi}} e^{-x(-1)2/4} \qquad p(y) = \frac{1}{2\sqrt{\pi}} e^{-(y+1)2/4}$$

Determine the probability density functions of the random variables
(a) $u = x - y$.
(b) $v = x + y$.

REFERENCES

1. Papoulis, A., *Probability, Random Variables, and Stochastic Processes*, 3rd ed., McGraw-Hill, New York, 1991.
2. Hines, W. W., and Montgomery, D. C., *Probability and Statistics in Engineering and Management Science*, 3rd ed., Wiley, New York, 1990.
3. Ross, S. M., *Introduction to Probability and Statistics for Engineers and Scientists*, Wiley, New York, 1987.
4. Bendat, J. S., *Nonlinear System Techniques and Applications*, Wiley–Intersrience, New York, 1998.
5. Patel, J. K., and Read, C. B., *Handbook of the Normal Distribution*, Dekker, New York, 1982.
6. Loeve, M. M., *Probability Theory*, 4th ed., Springer-Verlag, New York, 1977.
7. Miller, K. S., *Engineering Mathematics*, Reinhart, New York, 1957.
8. Rice, S. O., "Statistical Properties of a Sine Wave plus Random Noise," *Bell System Technical Journal*, Vol. 27, p. 109, 1948.

CHAPTER 4

Statistical Principles

Beyond the basic ideas of probability theory discussed in Chapter 3, the measurement and the analysis of random data involve uncertainties and estimation errors that must be evaluated by statistical techniques. This chapter reviews and illustrates various statistical ideas that have wide applications to commonly occurring data evaluation problems. The intent is to provide the reader with a minimum background in terminology and certain techniques of engineering statistics that are relevant to discussions in later chapters. More detailed treatments of applied statistics with engineering applications are available from Refs 1–3.

4.1 SAMPLE VALUES AND PARAMETER ESTIMATION

Consider a random variable x, as defined in Section 3.1, where the index k of the sample space is omitted for simplicity in notation. Further consider the two basic parameters of x that specify its central tendency and dispersion, namely the mean value and variance, respectively. From Equations (3.8) and (3.11), the mean value and variance are given by

$$\mu_x = E[x] = \int_{-\infty}^{\infty} x p(x) dx \qquad (4.1)$$

$$\sigma_x^2 = E[(x-\mu_x)^2] = \int_{-\infty}^{\infty} (x-\mu_x)^2 p(x) dx \qquad (4.2)$$

where $p(x)$ is the probability density function of the variable x. These two parameters of x cannot, of course, be precisely determined in practice because an exact knowledge of the probability density function will not generally be available. Hence, one must be content with estimates of the mean value and variance based on a finite number of observed values.

Random Data: Analysis and Measurement Procedures, Fourth Edition. By Julius S. Bendat and Allan G. Piersol
Copyright © 2010 John Wiley & Sons, Inc.

One possible method (there are others) for estimating the mean value and variance of x based on N independent observations would be as follows:

$$\bar{x} = \hat{\mu}_x = \frac{1}{N}\sum_{i=1}^{N} x_i \qquad (4.3)$$

$$s_b^2 = \hat{\sigma}_x^2 = \frac{1}{N}\sum_{i=1}^{N} (x-\bar{x})^2 \qquad (4.4)$$

Here, $\bar{x}$ and s_b^2 are the *sample mean* and *sample variance*, respectively. The hats (^) over $\hat{\mu}_x$ and $\hat{\sigma}_x^2$ indicate that these sample values are being used as *estimators* for the mean value and variance of x. The subscript on s_b^2 means that this is a *biased* variance estimate (to be discussed later). The number of observations used to compute the estimates (sample values) is called the *sample size*.

The specific sample values in Equations (4.3) and (4.4) are not the only quantities that might be used to estimate the mean value and variance of a random variable x. For example, reasonable estimates of the mean value and the variance would also be obtained by dividing the summations in Equations (4.3) and (4.4) by $N-1$ instead of N. Estimators are never clearly right or wrong since they are defined somewhat arbitrarily. Nevertheless, certain estimators can be judged as being "good" estimators or "better" estimators than others.

Three principal factors can be used to establish the quality or "goodness" of an estimator. First, it is desirable that the expected value of the estimator be equal to the parameter being established. That is,

$$E[\hat{\phi}] = \phi \qquad (4.5)$$

where $\hat{\phi}$ is an estimator for the parameter ϕ. If this is true, the estimator is said to be *unbiased*. Second, it is desirable that the mean square error of the estimator be smaller than for other possible estimators. That is,

$$E[(\hat{\phi}_1-\phi)^2] \leq E[(\hat{\phi}_i-\phi)^2] \qquad (4.6)$$

where $\hat{\phi}_1$ is the estimator of interest and $\hat{\phi}_i$ is any other possible estimator. If this is true, the estimator is said to be more *efficient* than other possible estimators. Third, it is desirable that the estimator approach the parameter being estimated with a probability approaching unity as the sample size becomes large. That is, for any $\varepsilon > 0$,

$$\lim_{N \to \infty} \text{Prob}[|\hat{\phi}-\phi| \geq \varepsilon] = 0 \qquad (4.7a)$$

If this is true, the estimator is said to be *consistent*. It follows from the Chebyshev inequality of Equation (3.23) that a sufficient (but not necessary) condition to meet the requirements of Equation (4.7a) is given by

$$\lim_{N \to \infty} E[(\hat{\phi}-\phi)^2] = 0 \qquad (4.7b)$$

SAMPLE VALUES AND PARAMETER ESTIMATION

Note that the requirements stated in Equation (4.7) are simply convergence requirements in (a) the probability and (b) the mean square sense, as defined later in Section 5.3.4.

Consider the example of the mean value estimator given by Equation (4.3). The expected value of the sample mean $\bar{x}$ is

$$E[\bar{x}] = E\left[\frac{1}{N}\sum_{i=1}^{N} x_i\right] = \frac{1}{N}E\left[\sum_{i=1}^{N} x_i\right] = \frac{1}{N}(N\mu_x) = \mu_x \qquad (4.8)$$

Hence, from Equation (4.5), the estimator $\hat{\mu}_x = \bar{x}$ is unbiased. The mean square error of the sample mean $\bar{x}$ is given by

$$E\left[(\bar{x}-\mu_x)^2\right] = E\left[\left(\frac{1}{N}\sum_{i=1}^{N} x_i - \mu_x\right)^2\right] = \frac{1}{N^2}E\left[\left(\sum_{i=1}^{N}(x_i-\mu_x)\right)^2\right]$$

From Section 3.2.1, since the observations x_i are independent, the cross product terms in the last expression will have an expected value of zero. It then follows that

$$E\left[(\bar{x}-\mu_x)^2\right] = \frac{1}{N^2}E\left[\sum_{i=1}^{N}(x_i-\mu_x)^2\right] = \frac{1}{N^2}(N\sigma_x^2) = \frac{\sigma_x^2}{N} \qquad (4.9)$$

Hence, from Equation (4.7b), the estimator $\hat{\mu}_x = \bar{x}$ is consistent. It can be shown that the estimator is also efficient.

Now consider the example of the variance estimator given by Equation (4.4). The expected value of the sample variance s_b^2 is

$$E[s_b^2] = E\left[\frac{1}{N}\sum_{i=1}^{N}(x_i-\bar{x})^2\right] = \frac{1}{N}E\left[\sum_{i=1}^{N}(x_i-\bar{x})^2\right]$$

However,

$$\sum_{i=1}^{N}(x_i-\bar{x})^2 = \sum_{i=1}^{N}(x_i-\mu_x+\mu_x-\bar{x})^2$$

$$= \sum_{i=1}^{N}(x_i-\mu_x)^2 - 2(\bar{x}-\mu_x)\sum_{i=1}^{N}(x_i-\mu_x) + \sum_{i=1}^{N}(\bar{x}-\mu_x)^2 \qquad (4.10)$$

$$= \sum_{i=1}^{N}(x_i-\mu_x)^2 - 2(\bar{x}-\mu_x)N(\bar{x}-\mu_x) + N(\bar{x}-\mu_x)^2$$

$$= \sum_{i=1}^{N}(x_i-\mu_x)^2 - N(\bar{x}-\mu_x)^2$$

Because $E[(x_i-\mu_x)^2] = \sigma_x^2$ and $E[(\bar{x}-\mu_x)^2] = \sigma_x^2/N$, it follows that

$$E[s_b^2] = \frac{1}{N}(N\sigma_x^2 - \sigma_x^2) = \frac{(N-1)}{N}\sigma_x^2 \qquad (4.11)$$

Hence, the estimator $\hat{\sigma}_x^2 = s_b^2$ is *biased*. Although the sample variance s_b^2 is a biased estimator for σ_x^2, it is a consistent and an efficient estimator.

From the results in Equation (4.11), it is clear that an unbiased estimator for σ_x^2 may be obtained by computing a slightly different sample variance as follows:

$$s^2 = \hat{\sigma}_x^2 = \frac{1}{N-1} \sum_{i=1}^{N} (x_i - \bar{x})^2 \qquad (4.12)$$

The quantity defined in Equation (4.12) is an *unbiased* estimator for σ_x^2. For this reason, the sample variance defined in Equation (4.12) is often considered a "better" estimator than the sample variance given by Equation (4.4). The sample variance defined in Equation (4.12) will be used henceforth as an estimator for the variance of a random variable.

4.2 IMPORTANT PROBABILITY DISTRIBUTION FUNCTIONS

Examples of several theoretical probability distribution functions are given in Chapter 3. The most important of these distribution functions from the viewpoint of applied statistics is the Gaussian (*normal*) distribution. There are three other distribution functions associated with normally distributed random variables that have wide applications as statistical tools. These are the χ^2 distribution, the t distribution, and the F distribution. Each of these three, along with the normal distribution, will now be defined and discussed. Applications for each as an analysis tool will be covered in later sections.

4.2.1 Gaussian (Normal) Distribution

The probability density and distribution functions of a Gaussian distributed random variable x are defined by Equations (3.47) and (3.48) in Section 3.3. As noted in that section, a more convenient form of the Gaussian distribution is obtained by using the standardized variable z given by

$$z = \frac{x - \mu_x}{\sigma_x} \qquad (4.13)$$

When Equation (4.13) is substituted into Equations (3.47) and (3.48), standardized Gaussian density and distribution functions with zero mean and unit variance ($\mu_z = 0$; $\sigma_x^2 = 1$) are obtained as given by

$$p(z) = \frac{1}{\sqrt{2\pi}} e^{-z^2/2} \qquad (4.14a)$$

$$P(z) = \frac{1}{\sqrt{2\pi}} \int_{-\infty}^{z} e^{-\xi^2/2} d\xi \qquad (4.14b)$$

The standardized Gaussian (normal) probability density and distribution functions in Equation (4.14) are plotted in Figure 3.5.

It is desirable for later applications to denote the value of z that corresponds to a specific probability distribution function value of $P(z) = 1 - \alpha$ by z_α. That is,

$$P(z_\alpha) = \int_{-\infty}^{z_\alpha} p(z)dz = \text{Prob}[z \leq z_\alpha] = 1-\alpha \qquad (4.15a)$$

or

$$1 - P(z_\alpha) = \int_{z_\alpha}^{\infty} p(z)dz = \text{Prob}[z > z_\alpha] = \alpha \qquad (4.15b)$$

The value of z_α that satisfies Equation (4.15) is called the *100α percentage point* of the normal distribution. A limited tabulation of percentage points for the normal distribution is presented in Table A.2.

4.2.2 Chi-Square Distribution

Let $z_1, z_2, z_3, \ldots, z_n$ be n independent random variables, each of which has a Gaussian distribution with zero mean and unit variance. Let a new random variable be defined as

$$\chi_n^2 = z_1^2 + z_2^2 + z_3^2 + \cdots + z_n^2 \qquad (4.16)$$

The random variable χ_n^2 is the chi-square variable with n degrees of freedom. The number of *degrees of freedom* n represents the number of independent or "free" squares entering into the expression. From Ref. 3, the probability density function of χ_n^2 is given by

$$p(\chi^2) = [2^{n/2}\Gamma(n/2)]^{-1} e^{-\chi^2/2} (\chi^2)^{(n/2)-1} \quad \chi^2 \geq 0 \qquad (4.17)$$

where $\Gamma(n/2)$ is the gamma function. The corresponding distribution function of χ_n^2, given by the integral of Equation (4.17) from $-\infty$ to a specific value of χ_n^2, is called the *chi-square distribution with n degrees of freedom*. The 100α percentage point of the χ^2 distribution will be denoted by $\chi_{n;\alpha}^2$. That is,

$$\int_{\chi_{n;\alpha}^2}^{\infty} p(\chi^2)d\chi^2 = \text{Prob}[\chi_n^2 > \chi_{n;\alpha}^2] = \alpha \qquad (4.18)$$

The mean value and variance of the variable χ_n^2 are

$$E[\chi_n^2] = \mu_{\chi^2} = n \qquad (4.19)$$

$$E[(\chi_n^2 - \mu_{\chi^2})^2] = \sigma_{\chi^2}^2 = 2n \qquad (4.20)$$

A limited tabulation of percentage points for the chi-square distribution function is presented in Table A.3.

Several features of the chi-square distribution should be noted. First, the chi-square distribution is a special case of the more general gamma function [2]. Second, the square root of chi-square with two degrees of freedom ($\sqrt{\chi_2^2}$) constitutes an important case called the *Rayleigh distribution function* [3]. The Rayleigh distribution has wide applications to two-dimensional target problems and is also the limiting distribution function of both the envelope (see Section 3.4) and the peak values (see Section 5.5) for narrow bandwidth Gaussian random data as the bandwidth approaches zero. Third, a chi-square distribution approaches a Gaussian distribution as the number of degrees of freedom becomes large. Specifically, for $n > 100$, the quantity $\sqrt{2\chi_n^2}$ is distributed approximately as a Gaussian variable with a mean of $\mu = \sqrt{2n-1}$ and a variance of $\sigma^2 = 1$ [Ref. 1].

4.2.3 The *t* Distribution

Let y and z be independent random variables such that y has a χ_n^2 distribution function and z has a Gaussian distribution function with zero mean and unit variance. Let a new random variable be defined as

$$t_n = \frac{z}{\sqrt{y/n}} \qquad (4.21)$$

The random variable t_n is Student's *t* variable with *n* degrees of freedom. From Ref. 2, the probability density function of t_n is given by

$$p(t) = \frac{\Gamma[(n+1)/2]}{\sqrt{\pi n}\,\Gamma(n/2)}\left[1 + \frac{t^2}{n}\right]^{-(n+1)/2} \qquad (4.22)$$

The corresponding distribution function of t_n, given by the integral of Equation (4.22) from $-\infty$ to a specific value of t_n, is called the *t distribution with n degrees of freedom*. The 100α percentage point of the *t* distribution will be denoted by $t_{n;\alpha}$. That is,

$$\int_{t_{n;\alpha}}^{\infty} p(t)\,dt = \text{Prob}[t_n > t_{n;\alpha}] = \alpha \qquad (4.23)$$

The mean value and variance of the variable t_n are

$$E[t_n] = \mu_t = 0 \quad \text{for } n > 1 \qquad (4.24)$$

$$E\left[(t_n - \mu_t)^2\right] = \sigma_t^2 = \frac{n}{n-2} \quad \text{for } n > 2 \qquad (4.25)$$

A limited tabulation of percentage points for the *t* distribution function is presented in Table A.4. It should be noted that the *t* distribution approaches a standardized Gaussian distribution as the number of degrees of freedom *n* becomes large.

4.2.4 The *F* Distribution

Let y_1 and y_2 be independent random variables such that y_1 has a χ^2 distribution function with n_1 degrees of freedom and y_2 has a χ^2 distribution function with n_2 degrees of freedom. Let a new random variable be defined as

$$F_{n_1,n_2} = \frac{y_1/n_1}{y_2/n_2} = \frac{y_1 n_2}{y_2 n_1} \qquad (4.26)$$

SAMPLING DISTRIBUTIONS AND ILLUSTRATIONS

The random variable F_{n_1,n_2} is the F variable with n_1 and n_2 degrees of freedom From Ref. 3, the probability density function of F_{n_1,n_2} is given by

$$p(F) = \frac{\Gamma[(n_1+n_2)/2](n_1/n_2)^{n_1/2} F^{(n_1/2)-1}}{\Gamma(n_1/2)\Gamma(n_2/2)[1+(n_1F/n_2)]^{(n_1+n_2)/2}} \quad F \geq 0 \quad (4.27)$$

The corresponding distribution function of F_{n_1,n_2}, given by the integral of Equation (4.27) from $-\infty$ to a specific value of F_{n_1,n_2}, is called the *F distribution with n_1 and n_2 degrees of freedom*. The 100α percentage point of the F distribution will be denoted by $F_{n_1,n_2;\alpha}$. That is,

$$\int_{F_{n_1,n_2;\alpha}}^{\infty} p(F)dF = \text{Prob}[F_{n_1,n_2} > F_{n_1,n_2;\alpha}] = \alpha \quad (4.28)$$

The mean value and variance of F_{n_1,n_2} are

$$E[F_{n_1,n_2}] = \mu_F = \frac{n_2}{n_2-2} \quad \text{for } n_2 > 2 \quad (4.29)$$

$$E[(F_{n_1,n_2}-\mu_F)^2] = \sigma_F^2 = \frac{2n_2^2(n_1+n_2-2)}{n_1(n_2-2)^2(n_2-4)} \quad \text{for } n_2 > 4 \quad (4.30)$$

A limited tabulation of percentage point for the F distribution function is presented in Tables A.5(a), A.5(b), and A.5(c). It should be noted that the statistic t_n^2, the square of the variable defined in Equation (4.21), has an F distribution with $n_1 = 1$ and $n_2 = n$ degrees of freedom.

4.3 SAMPLING DISTRIBUTIONS AND ILLUSTRATIONS

Consider a random variable x with a probability distribution function $P(x)$. Let $x_1, x_2, \ldots, x_N$ be a sample of N observed values of x. Any quantity computed from these sample values will also be a random variable. For example, consider the mean value $\bar{x}$ of the sample. If a series of different samples of size N were selected from the same random variable x, the value of $\bar{x}$ computed from each sample would generally be different. Hence, $\bar{x}$ is also a random variable with a probability distribution function $P(\bar{x})$. This probability distribution function is called the *sampling distribution* of $\bar{x}$.

Some of the more common sampling distributions that often arise in practice will now be considered. These involve the probability distribution functions defined and discussed in Section 4.2. The use of these sampling distributions to establish confidence intervals and perform hypothesis tests is illustrated in Sections 4.4–4.8.

4.3.1 Distribution of Sample Mean with Known Variance

Consider the mean value of a sample of N independent observations from a random variable x as follows:

$$\bar{x} = \frac{1}{N}\sum_{i=1}^{N} x_i \quad (4.31)$$

First, consider the case where the random variable x is normally distributed with a mean value of μ_x and a known variance of σ_x^2. From Section 3.3.1, the sampling distribution of the sample mean $\bar{x}$ will also be normally distributed. From Equation (4.8), the mean value of the sampling distribution of $\bar{x}$ is

$$\mu_{\bar{x}} = \mu_x \tag{4.32}$$

and from Equation (4.9), the variance of the sampling distribution of $\bar{x}$ is

$$\sigma_{\bar{x}}^2 = \frac{\sigma_x^2}{N} \tag{4.33}$$

Hence, from Equation (4.13), the following sampling distribution applies for the sample mean $\bar{x}$:

$$\frac{(\bar{x} - \mu_x)\sqrt{N}}{\sigma_x} = z \tag{4.34}$$

where z has a standardized normal distribution, as defined in Section 4.2.1. It follows that a probability statement concerning future values of the sample mean may be made as follows.

$$\operatorname{Prob}\left[\bar{x} > \left(\frac{\sigma_x z_\alpha}{\sqrt{N}} + \mu_x\right)\right] = \alpha \tag{4.35}$$

Now, consider the case where the random variable x is not normally distributed. From the practical implications of the central limit theorem (see Section 3.1.1), the following result occurs. As the sample size N becomes large, the *sampling distribution of the sample mean $\bar{x}$ approaches a normal distribution regardless of the distribution of the original variable x*. In practical terms, a normality assumption for the sampling distribution of $\bar{x}$ becomes reasonable in many cases for $N > 4$ and quite accurate in most cases for $N > 10$. Hence, for reasonably large sample sizes, Equation (4.34) applies to the sampling distribution of $\bar{x}$ computed for any random variable x, regardless of its probability distribution function.

4.3.2 Distribution of Sample Variance

Consider the variance of a sample of N independent observations from a random variable x as follows:

$$s^2 = \frac{1}{N-1} \sum_{i=1}^{N} (x_i - \bar{x})^2 \tag{4.36}$$

If the variable x is normally distributed with a mean of μ_x and a variance of σ_x^2, it is shown in Ref. 1 that

$$\sum_{i=1}^{N} (x_i - \bar{x})^2 = \sigma_n^2 \chi_n^2 \quad n = N-1$$

SAMPLING DISTRIBUTIONS AND ILLUSTRATIONS

where χ_n^2 has a chi-square distribution with $n = N - 1$ degrees of freedom, as defined in Section 4.2.2. Hence, the sampling distribution of the sample variance s^2 is given by

$$\frac{ns^2}{\sigma_x^2} = \chi_n^2 \quad n = N-1 \tag{4.37}$$

It follows that a probability statement concerning future values of the sample variance s^2 may be made as follows:

$$\text{Prob}\left[s^2 > \frac{\sigma_x^2 \chi_{n;\alpha}^2}{n}\right] = \alpha \tag{4.38}$$

4.3.3 Distribution of Sample Mean with Unknown Variance

Consider the mean value of a sample of N independent observations from a random variable x, as given by Equation (4.31). If the variable x is normally distributed with a mean value of μ_x and an unknown variance, it is seen from Equations (4.21) and (4.37) that

$$\frac{(\bar{x} - \mu_x)}{s/\sqrt{N}} = \frac{\sigma_x z/\sqrt{N}}{\sqrt{\sigma_x^2 \chi_n^2/n}/\sqrt{N}} = \frac{z}{\sqrt{\chi_n^2/n}} = t_n$$

where t_n has a t distribution with $n = N - 1$ degrees of freedom, as defined in Section 4.2.3. Hence, the sampling distribution of the sample mean $\bar{x}$ when σ_x^2 is unknown is given by

$$\frac{(\bar{x} - \mu_x)\sqrt{N}}{s} = t_n \quad n = N-1 \tag{4.39}$$

It follows that a probability statement concerning future values of the sample mean $\bar{x}$ may be made as follows:

$$\text{Prob}\left[\bar{x} > \left(\frac{s t_{n;\alpha}}{\sqrt{N}} + \mu_x\right)\right] = \alpha \tag{4.40}$$

4.3.4 Distribution of Ratio of Two Sample Variances

Consider the variances of two samples: One consists of N_x independent observations of a random variable x, and the other consists of N_y independent observations of a random variable y, as given by Equation (4.36). If the variable x is normally distributed with a mean value of μ_x and a variance of σ_x^2, and the variable y is normally distributed with a mean value of μ_y and a variance σ_y^2, it is seen from Equations (4.26) and (4.37) that

$$\frac{s_x^2/\sigma_x^2}{s_y^2/\sigma_y^2} = \frac{\sigma_x^2 \chi_n^2/n_x \sigma_x^2}{\sigma_y^2 \chi_n^2/n_y \sigma_y^2} = F_{n_x, n_y}$$

where F_{n_x,n_y} has an F distribution with $n_x = N_x - 1$ and $n_y = N_y - 1$ degrees of freedom, as defined in Section 4.2.4. Hence, the sampling distribution of the ratio of the sample variances s_x^2 and s_y^2 is given by

$$\frac{s_x^2/\sigma_x^2}{s_y^2/\sigma_y^2} = F_{n_x,n_y} \qquad \begin{array}{l} n_x = N_x - 1 \\ n_y = N_y - 1 \end{array} \qquad (4.41)$$

It follows that a probability statement concerning future values of the ratio of the sample variances s_x^2 and s_y^2 may be made as follows:

$$\text{Prob}\left[\frac{s_x^2}{s_y^2} > \frac{\sigma_x^2}{\sigma_y^2} F_{n_x,n_y;\alpha}\right] = \alpha \qquad (4.42)$$

Note that if the two samples are obtained from the same random variable $x = y$, then Equation (4.41) reduces to

$$\frac{s_1^2}{s_2^2} = F_{n_1,n_2} \qquad \begin{array}{l} n_1 = N_1 - 1 \\ n_2 = N_2 - 1 \end{array} \qquad (4.43)$$

4.4 CONFIDENCE INTERVALS

The use of sample values as estimators for parameters of random variables is discussed in Section 4.1. However, those procedures result only in point estimates for a parameter of interest: no indication is provided as to how closely a sample value estimates the parameter. A more meaningful procedure for estimating parameters of random variables involves the estimation of an interval, as opposed to a single point value, which will include the parameter being estimated with a known degree of uncertainty. For example, consider the case where the sample mean $\bar{x}$ computed from N independent observations of a random variable x is being used as an estimator for the mean value μ_x. It is usually more desirable to estimate μ_x in terms of some interval, such as $\bar{x} \pm d$, where there is a specified uncertainty that μ_x falls within that interval. Such intervals can be established if the sampling distributions of the estimator in question is known.

Continuing with the example of a mean value estimate, it is shown in Section 4.3 that probability statements can be made concerning the value of a sample mean $\bar{x}$ as follows:

$$\text{Prob}\left[z_{1-\alpha/2} < \frac{(\bar{x} - \mu_x)\sqrt{N}}{\sigma_x} \leq z_{\alpha/2}\right] = 1 - \alpha \qquad (4.44)$$

The above probability statement is technically correct *before* the sample has been collected and $\bar{x}$ has been computed. After the sample has been collected, however, the

CONFIDENCE INTERVALS

value of $\bar{x}$ is a fixed number rather than a random variable. Hence, it can be argued that the probability statement in Equation (4.44) no longer applies since the quantity $(\bar{x}-\mu_x)\sqrt{N}/\sigma_x$ either *does* or *does not* fall within the indicated limits. In other words, after a sample has been collected, a technically correct probability statement would be as follows:

$$\text{Prob}\left[z_{1-\alpha/2} < \frac{(\bar{x}-\mu_x)\sqrt{N}}{\sigma_x} \leq z_{\alpha/2}\right] = \begin{cases} 0 \\ 1 \end{cases} \quad (4.45)$$

Whether the correct probability is zero or unity is usually not known. As the value of α becomes small (as the interval between $z_{1-\alpha/2}$ and $z_{\alpha/2}$ becomes wide), however, one would tend to guess that the probability is more likely to be unity than zero. In slightly different terms, if many different samples were repeatedly collected and a value of $\bar{x}$ were computed for each sample, one would tend to expect the quantity in Equation (4.45) to fall within the noted interval for about $1 - \alpha$ of the samples. In this context, a statement can be made about an interval within which one would expect to find the quantity $(\bar{x}-\mu_x)\sqrt{N}/\sigma_x$ with a small degree of uncertainty. Such statements are called *confidence statements*. The interval associated with a confidence statement is called a *confidence interval*. The degree of trust associated with the confidence statement is called the *confidence coefficient*.

For the case of the mean value estimate, a confidence interval can be established for the mean value μ_x based on the sample value $\bar{x}$ by rearranging terms in Equation (4.45) as follows:

$$\left[\bar{x} - \frac{\sigma_x z_{\alpha/2}}{\sqrt{N}} \leq \mu_x < \bar{x} + \frac{\sigma_x z_{\alpha/2}}{\sqrt{N}}\right] \quad (4.46a)$$

Furthermore, if σ_x is unknown, a confidence interval can still be established for the mean value μ_x based on the sample values $\bar{x}$ and s by rearranging terms in Equation (4.39) as follows:

$$\left[\bar{x} - \frac{s t_{n;\alpha/2}}{\sqrt{N}} \leq \mu_x < \bar{x} + \frac{s t_{n;\alpha/2}}{\sqrt{N}}\right] \quad n = N-1 \quad (4.46b)$$

Equation (4.46) uses the fact that $z_{1-\alpha/2} = -z_{\alpha/2}$ and $t_{n;1-\alpha/2} = -t_{n;\alpha/2}$. The confidence coefficient associated with the intervals is $1 - \alpha$. Hence, the confidence statement would be as follows: The true mean value μ_x falls within the noted interval with a confidence coefficient of $1 - \alpha$, or, in more common terminology, with a confidence of $100(1 - \alpha)\%$. Similar confidence statements can be established for any parameter estimates where proper sampling distributions are known. For example, from Equation (4.37), a $1 - \alpha$ confidence interval for the variance σ_x^2 based on a sample variance s^2 from a sample of size N is

$$\left[\frac{ns^2}{\chi^2_{n;\alpha/2}} \leq \sigma_x^2 < \frac{ns^2}{\chi^2_{n;1-\alpha/2}}\right] \quad n = N-1 \quad (4.47)$$

Example 4.1. **Illustration of Confidence Intervals.** Assume a sample of $N=31$ independent observations are collected from a normally distributed random variable x with the following results:

$$\begin{array}{cccccc}
60 & 61 & 47 & 56 & 61 & 63 \\
65 & 69 & 54 & 59 & 43 & 61 \\
55 & 61 & 56 & 48 & 67 & 65 \\
60 & 58 & 57 & 62 & 57 & 58 \\
53 & 59 & 58 & 61 & 67 & 62 \\
54
\end{array}$$

Determine a 90% confidence interval for the mean value and variance of the random variable x.

From Equation (4.46b), a $1-\alpha$ confidence interval for the mean value μ_x based on the sample mean $\bar{x}$ and the sample variance s^2 for a sample size of $N=31$ is given by

$$\left[\left(\bar{x}-\frac{st_{30;\alpha/2}}{\sqrt{31}}\right) \leq \mu_x < \left(\bar{x}+\frac{st_{30;\alpha/2}}{\sqrt{31}}\right)\right]$$

From Table A.4, for $\alpha=0.10$, $t_{30;\alpha/2}=t_{30;0.05}=1.697$, so the interval reduces to

$$[(\bar{x}-0.3048s) \leq \mu_x < (\bar{x}+0.3048s)]$$

From Equation (4.47), a $1-\alpha$ confidence interval for the variance σ_x^2 based on the sample variance s^2 for a sample size of $N=31$ is given by

$$\left[\frac{30s^2}{\chi^2_{30;\alpha/2}} \leq \sigma_x^2 < \frac{30s^2}{\chi^2_{30;1-\alpha/2}}\right]$$

From Table A.3, for $\alpha=0.10$, $\chi^2_{30;\alpha/2}=\chi^2_{30;0.05}=43.77$ and $\chi^2_{30;1-\alpha/2}=\chi^2_{30;0.95}=18.49$, so the interval reduces to

$$[0.6854s^2 \leq \sigma_x^2 < 1.622s^2]$$

It now remains to calculate the sample mean and the variance, and substitute these values into the interval statements. From Equation (4.3), the sample mean is

$$\bar{x} = \frac{1}{N}\sum_{i=1}^{N} x_i = 58.61$$

From Equation (4.12), the sample variance is

$$s^2 = \frac{1}{N-1}\sum_{i=1}^{N}(x_i-\bar{x})^2 = \frac{1}{N-1}\left\{\sum_{i=1}^{N}x_i^2 - N(\bar{x})^2\right\} = 33.43$$

Hence, the 90% confidence intervals for the mean value and variance of the random variable x are as follows:

$$[56.85 \leq \mu_x < 60.37]$$
$$[22.91 \leq \sigma_x^2 < 54.22]$$

4.5 HYPOTHESIS TESTS

Consider the case where a given estimator $\hat{\phi}$ is computed from a sample of N independent observations of a random variable x. Assume there is reason to believe that the true parameter ϕ being estimated has a specific value ϕ_0. Now, even if $\phi = \phi_0$, the sample value $\hat{\phi}$ will probably not come out exactly equal to ϕ_0 because of the sampling variability associated with $\hat{\phi}$. Hence, the following question arises. If it is hypothesized that $\phi = \phi_0$, how much difference between $\hat{\phi}$ and ϕ_0 must occur before the hypothesis should be rejected as being invalid? This question can be answered in statistical terms by considering the probability of any noted difference between $\hat{\phi}$ and ϕ_0 based upon the sampling distribution of $\hat{\phi}$. If the probability of a given difference is small, the difference would be considered significant and the hypothesis that $\phi = \phi_0$ would be rejected. If the probability of a given difference is not small, the difference would be accepted as normal statistical variability and the hypothesis that $\phi = \phi_0$ would be accepted.

The preceding discussion outlines the simplest form of a statistical procedure called hypothesis testing. To clarify the general technique, assume that a sample value $\hat{\phi}$, which is an estimate of a parameter ϕ, has a probability density function of $p(\hat{\phi})$. Now, if a hypothesis that $\phi = \phi_0$ is true, then $p(\hat{\phi})$ would have a mean value of ϕ_0 as illustrated in Figure 4.1. The probability that $\hat{\phi}$ would fall below the lower level $\phi_{1-\alpha/2}$ is

$$\text{Prob}\left[\hat{\phi} \leq \phi_{1-\alpha/2}\right] = \int_{-\infty}^{\phi_{1-\alpha/2}} p(\hat{\phi})d\hat{\phi} = \frac{\alpha}{2} \qquad (4.48a)$$

The probability that $\hat{\phi}$ would fall above the upper value $\phi_{\alpha/2}$ is

$$\text{Prob}\left[\hat{\phi} > \phi_{\alpha/2}\right] = \int_{\phi_{\alpha/2}}^{\infty} p(\hat{\phi})d\hat{\phi} = \frac{\alpha}{2} \qquad (4.48b)$$

Hence, the probability that $\hat{\phi}$ would be outside the range between $\phi_{1-\alpha/2}$ and $\phi_{\alpha/2}$ is α. Now let α be small so that it is very unlikely that $\hat{\phi}$ would fall outside the range

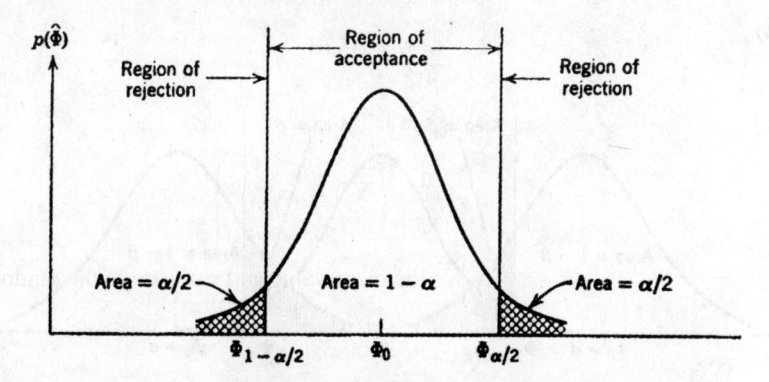

Figure 4.1 Acceptance and rejection regions for hypothesis tests.

between $\phi_{1-\alpha/2}$ and $\phi_{\alpha/2}$. If a sample were collected and a value of $\hat{\phi}$ were computed that in fact fell outside the range between $\phi_{1-\alpha/2}$ and $\phi_{\alpha/2}$, there would be a strong reason to question the original hypothesis that $\phi = \phi_0$ because such a value for $\hat{\phi}$ would be very unlikely if the hypothesis were true. Hence the hypothesis that $\phi = \phi_0$ would be rejected. On the other hand, if the value for $\hat{\phi}$ fell within the range between $\phi_{1-\alpha/2}$ and $\phi_{\alpha/2}$, there would be no strong reason to question the original hypothesis. Hence the hypothesis that $\phi = \phi_0$ would be accepted.

The small probability α used for the hypothesis test is called the *level of significance* of the test. The range of values of $\hat{\phi}$ for which the hypothesis will be rejected is called the *region of rejection* or *critical region*. The range of values of $\hat{\phi}$ for which the hypothesis will be accepted is called the *region of acceptance*. The simple hypothesis test outlined above is called a *two-sided test* because, if the hypothesis is not true, the value of ϕ could be either greater or less than ϕ_0. Hence, it is necessary to test for significant differences between ϕ and ϕ_0 in both directions. In other cases, a *one-sided test* might be sufficient. For example, let it be hypothesized that $\phi \geq \phi_0$. For this case, the hypothesis would be false only if ϕ were less than ϕ_0. Thus, the test would be performed using the lower side of the probability density function $p(\hat{\phi})$.

Two possible errors can occur when a hypothesis test is performed. First, the hypothesis might be rejected when in fact it is true. This possible error is called a *Type I error*. Second, the hypothesis might be accepted when in fact it is false. This possible error is called a *Type II error*. From Figure 4.1, a Type I error would occur if the hypothesis were true and $\hat{\phi}$ fell in the region of rejection. It follows that the probability of a Type I error is equal to α, the level of significance of the test.

In order to establish the probability of a Type II error, it is necessary to specify some deviation of the true parameter ϕ from the hypothesized parameter ϕ_0 that one desires to detect. For example, assume that the true parameter actually has a value of either $\phi = \phi_0 + d$ or $\phi = \phi_0 - d$, as illustrated in Figure 4.2. If it is hypothesized that $\phi = \phi_0$ when in fact $\phi = \phi_0 \pm d$, the probability that $\hat{\phi}$ would fall inside the acceptance region between $\phi_{1-\alpha/2}$ and $\phi_{\alpha/2}$ is β. Hence, the probability of a Type II error is β for detecting a difference of $\pm d$ from the hypothesized value ϕ_0.

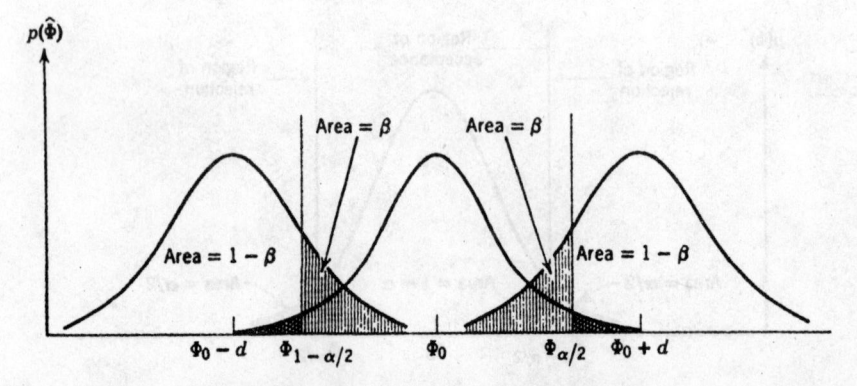

Figure 4.2 Type II error regions for hypothesis tests.

The probability $1 - \beta$ is called the *power of the test*. Clearly, for any given sample size N, the probability of a Type I error can be reduced by reducing the level of significance α. However, this will increase the probability β of a Type II error (reduce the power of the test). The only way to reduce both α and β is to increase the sample size N for the estimate $\hat{\phi}$. These ideas form the basis for selecting the necessary sample sizes for statistical experiments.

Example 4.2. Illustration of Hypothesis Test Design. Assume there is reason to believe that the mean value of a random variable x is $\mu_x = 10$. Further assume that the variance of x is known to be $\sigma_x^2 = 4$. Determine the proper sample size to test the hypothesis that $\mu_x = 10$ at the 5% level of significance, where the probability of a Type II error is to be 5% for detecting a difference of 10% from the hypothesized value. Determine the region of acceptance to be used for the test.

An unbiased estimate for μ_x is given by the sample mean value $\bar{x}$ as defined in Equation (4.3). The appropriate sampling distribution of $\bar{x}$ is given by Equation (4.34) as

$$\bar{x} = \frac{\sigma_x}{\sqrt{N}} z + \mu_x$$

where z is normally distributed with zero mean and unit variance. Note that this sampling distribution of $\bar{x}$ is precise if x is normally distributed and is still a good approximation if x is not normally distributed.

The upper and lower limits of the acceptance region for the hypothesis test are as follows:

$$\text{Upper limit} = \frac{\sigma_x}{\sqrt{N}} z_{\alpha/2} + \mu_x$$

$$\text{Lower limit} = \frac{\sigma_x}{\sqrt{N}} z_{1-\alpha/2} + \mu_x$$

Now if the true mean value were in fact $\mu'_x = \mu_x \pm d$, a Type II error would occur with probability β if the sample value $\bar{x}$ fell below the upper limit or above the lower limit. In terms of the sampling distributions of $\bar{x}$ with a mean value $\mu'_x = \mu_x + d$ or $\mu'_x = \mu_x - d$,

$$\text{Upper limit} = \frac{\sigma_x}{\sqrt{N}} z_{1-\beta} + \mu_x + d$$

$$\text{Lower limit} = \frac{\sigma_x}{\sqrt{N}} z_\beta + \mu_x - d$$

Hence the following equalities apply:

$$\frac{\sigma_x}{\sqrt{N}} z_{\alpha/2} + \mu_x = \frac{\sigma_x}{\sqrt{N}} z_{1-\beta} + \mu_x + d$$

$$\frac{\sigma_x}{\sqrt{N}} z_{1-\alpha/2} + \mu_x = \frac{\sigma_x}{\sqrt{N}} z_\beta + \mu_x - d$$

These relationships both reduce to

$$z_{\alpha/2} = z_{1-\beta} + \frac{\sqrt{N}}{\sigma_x}d = -z_\beta + \frac{\sqrt{N}}{\sigma_x}d$$

It follows that the required sample size is given by

$$N = \left[\frac{\sigma_x(z_{\alpha/2} + z_\beta)}{d}\right]^2$$

For the specific values in this example ($\sigma_x = 2$, $z_{\alpha/2} = 1.96$, $z_\beta = 1.645$, $d = 0.1(10) = 1$), the required sample size is

$$N = 52$$

The region of acceptance for the hypothesis test will be

$$\text{Upper limit} = \frac{\sigma_x}{\sqrt{N}} z_{\alpha/2} + \mu_x = 10.54$$

$$\text{Lower limit} = \frac{\sigma_x}{\sqrt{N}} z_{1-\alpha/2} + \mu_x = 9.46$$

4.5.1 Chi-Square Goodness-of-Fit Test

A special type of hypothesis test that is often used to test the equivalence of a probability density function of sampled data to some theoretical density function is called the chi-square goodness-of-fit test. The general procedure involves the use of a statistic with an approximate chi-square distribution as a measure of the discrepancy between an observed probability density function and the theoretical probability density function. A hypothesis of equivalence is then tested by studying the sampling distribution of this statistic.

To be more specific, consider a sample of N independent observations from a random variable x with a probability density function of $p(x)$. Let the N observations be grouped into K intervals, called *class intervals*, which together form a *frequency histogram*. The number of observations falling within the ith class interval is called the *observed frequency* in the ith class and will be denoted by f_i. The number of observations that would be expected to fall within the ith class interval if the true probability density function of x were $p_0(x)$ is called the *expected frequency* in the ith class interval and will be denoted by F_i. Now, the discrepancy between the observed frequency and the expected frequency within each class interval is given by $f_i - F_i$. To measure the total discrepancy for all class intervals, the squares of the discrepancies in each interval are normalized by the associated expected frequencies and summed to obtain the sample statistic

$$X^2 = \sum_{i=1}^{K} \frac{(f_i - F_i)^2}{F_i} \qquad (4.49)$$

It is shown in Ref. 2 that the distribution of X^2 in Equation (4.49) is approximately the same as for χ_n^2 discussed in Section 4.2.2. The number of degrees of freedom n in this case is equal to K minus the number of different independent linear restrictions imposed on the observations. There is one such restriction due to the fact that the frequency in the last class interval is determined once the frequencies in the first $K-1$ class intervals are known. If the comparison is made by fitting the expected theoretical density function to the frequency histogram for the observed data, then one additional constraint results from each independent parameter of the theoretical density function that must be computed to make the fit. For example, if the expected theoretical density function is a normal density function with unknown mean and variance, then two additional constraints are involved, because two parameters (a mean and a variance) must be computed to fit a normal density function. Hence, for the common case where the chi-square goodness-of-fit test is used as a test for normality, the number of degrees of freedom for X^2 in Equation (4.49) is $n = K - 3$.

Having established the proper degrees of freedom for X^2, a hypothesis test may be performed as follows. Let it be hypothesized that the variable x has a probability density function of $p(x) = p_0(x)$. After grouping the sampled observations into K class intervals and computing the expected frequency for each interval assuming $p(x) = p_0(x)$, compute X^2 as indicated in Equation (4.49). Because any deviation of $p(x)$ from $p_0(x)$ will cause X^2 to increase, an one-sided (upper tail) test is used. The region of acceptance is

$$X^2 \leq \chi_{n;\alpha}^2 \qquad (4.50)$$

where the value of $\chi_{n;\alpha}^2$ is available from Table A.3. If the sample value X^2 is greater than $\chi_{n;\alpha}^2$, the hypothesis that $p(x) = p_0(x)$ is rejected at the α level of significance. If X^2 is less than or equal to $\chi_{n;\alpha}^2$, the hypothesis is accepted at the α level of significance.

There are two basic ways to apply the chi-square goodness-of-fit test. The first way is to select class intervals in a manner that will provide equal expected frequencies within each interval. Excluding a uniform distribution hypothesis, this procedure will result in different interval widths from one class interval to another. The second way is to select class intervals of equal width. Again, except for the uniform distribution hypothesis, this procedure will result in different expected frequencies from one class interval to another. Chi-square tests for normality are usually performed using the constant interval width approach. Given sample data with a standard deviation of s, a class interval width of $\Delta x \simeq 0.4s$ is often used. A more fundamental requirement is that the expected frequencies in all class intervals must be sufficiently large to make Equation (4.49) an acceptable approximation to χ_n^2. A common recommendation is that $F_i > 3$ in all intervals. In a normality test where the expected frequencies diminish on the tails of the distribution, this requirement is complied with by letting the first and last intervals extend to $-\infty$ and $+\infty$, respectively, such that $F_1, F_K > 3$.

Table 4.1 Sample Observations Arranged in Increasing Order

−7.6	−3.8	−2.5	−1.6	−0.7	0.2	1.1	2.0	3.4	4.6
−6.9	−3.8	−2.5	−1.6	−0.7	0.2	1.1	2.1	3.5	4.8
−6.6	−3.7	−2.4	−1.6	−0.6	0.2	1.2	2.3	3.5	4.8
−6.4	−3.6	−2.3	−1.5	−0.6	0.3	1.2	2.3	3.6	4.9
−6.2	−3.5	−2.3	−1.5	−0.5	0.3	1.3	2.3	3.6	5.0
−6.1	−3.4	−2.3	−1.4	−0.5	0.3	1.3	2.4	3.6	5.2
−6.0	−3.4	−2.2	−1.4	−0.4	0.4	1.3	2.4	3.7	5.3
−5.7	−3.4	−2.2	−1.2	−0.4	0.4	1.4	2.5	3.7	5.4
−5.6	−3.3	−2.1	−1.2	−0.4	0.5	1.5	2.5	3.7	5.6
−5.5	−3.2	−2.1	−1.2	−0.3	0.5	1.5	2.6	3.7	5.9
−5.4	−3.2	−2.0	−1.1	−0.3	0.6	1.6	2.6	3.8	6.1
−5.2	−3.1	−2.0	−1.1	−0.2	0.6	1.6	2.6	3.8	6.3
−4.8	−3.0	−1.9	−1.0	−0.2	0.7	1.6	2.7	3.9	6.3
−4.6	−3.0	−1.9	−1.0	−0.2	0.8	1.7	2.8	4.0	6.5
−4.4	−2.9	−1.8	−1.0	−0.1	0.9	1.8	2.8	4.2	6.9
−4.4	−2.9	−1.8	−0.9	−0.0	0.9	1.8	2.9	4.2	7.1
−4.3	−2.9	−1.8	−0.9	0.0	1.0	1.8	3.1	4.3	7.2
−4.1	−2.7	−1.7	−0.8	0.1	1.0	1.9	3.2	4.3	7.4
−4.0	−2.6	−1.7	−0.8	0.1	1.1	1.9	3.2	4.4	7.9
−3.8	−2.6	−1.6	−0.7	0.2	1.1	2.0	3.3	4.4	9.0

Example 4.3. **Illustration of Test for Normality.** A sample of $N = 200$ independent observations of the digitized output of a thermal noise generator are presented in Table 4.1. The sample values have been rank ordered from the smallest to largest value for convenience. Test the noise generator output for normality by performing a chi-square goodness-of-fit test at the $\alpha = 0.05$ level of significance.

The calculations required to perform the test are summarized in Table 4.2. For an interval width of $\Delta x = 0.4s$, the standardized values of the normal distribution that define the class interval boundaries are as shown under z_α in the table. These interval boundaries are converted to volts in the next column. From Table A.2, the probability P that a sample value will fall in each class interval is determined using the z_α values. The product of P and the sample size N yields the expected frequency in each interval as listed under F in Table 4.2. Note that the first and last class intervals are selected so that $F > 3$. A total of 12 class intervals result. The observed frequencies are now counted using the interval boundaries in volts as indicated in Table 4.1. The normalized squared discrepancies between the expected and observed frequencies are then calculated and summed to obtain $X^2 = 2.43$. Note that the appropriate degrees of freedom is $n = K - 3 = 9$. The acceptance region for the test is found in Table A.3 to be $X^2 \leq \chi^2_{9;0.05} = 16.92$. Hence, the hypothesis of normality is accepted at the $\alpha = 0.05$ level of significance.

4.5.2 Nonparametric Trend Test

Situations often arise in data analysis where it is desired to establish if a sequence of observations or parameter estimates include an underlying trend. This is partiularly

HYPOTHESIS TESTS

Table 4.2 Calculations for Goodness-of-Fit Test

Interval Number	Upper Limit of Interval z_α	Upper Limit of Interval $x = sz + \bar{x}$	P	$F = NP$	f	$\|F - f\|$	$\frac{(F-f)^2}{F}$
1	−2.0	−6.36	0.0228	4.5	4	0.5	0.06
2	−1.6	−5.04	0.0320	6.4	8	1.6	0.40
3	−1.2	−3.72	0.0603	12.1	10	2.1	0.36
4	−0.8	−2.40	0.0968	19.4	21	1.6	0.13
5	−0.4	−1.08	0.1327	26.5	29	2.5	0.24
6	0	0.24	0.1554	31.1	31	0.1	0.00
7	0.4	1.56	0.1554	31.1	27	4.1	0.54
8	0.8	2.88	0.1327	26.5	25	1.5	0.08
9	1.2	4.20	0.0968	19.4	20	0.6	0.02
10	1.6	5.52	0.0603	12.1	13	0.9	0.07
11	2.0	6.84	0.0320	6.4	6	0.4	0.03
12	∞	∞	0.0228	4.5	6	1.5	0.50
			1.000	200	200		2.43
$N = 200$		$\bar{x} = 0.24$	$s = 3.30$		$n = K - 3 = 9$		$X^2 = 2.43$

true in the analysis of nonstationary data discussed later in Chapter 12. Because the observations or parameter estimates of interest may have a wide range of probability distribution functions, it is convenient to perform such evaluations with *distribution-free* or *nonparametric* procedures, where no assumption is made concerning the probability distribution of the data being evaluated. One such procedure that is easy to apply and useful for detecting underlying trends in random data records is the *reverse arrangement test*.

Consider a sequence of N observations of a random variable x, where the observations are denoted by x_i, $i = 1, 2, 3, \ldots, N$. Now, count the number of times that $x_i > x_j$ for $i < j$. Each such inequality is called a reverse arrangement. The total number of reverse arrangements is denoted by A.

A general definition for A is as follows. From the set of observations $x_1, x_2, \ldots, x_N$, define

$$h_{ij} = \begin{cases} 1 & \text{if } x_i > x_j \\ 0 & \text{otherwise} \end{cases} \quad (4.51)$$

Then

$$A = \sum_{i=1}^{N-1} A_i \quad (4.52)$$

where

$$A_i = \sum_{j=i+1}^{N} h_{ij} \quad (4.53)$$

For example,

$$A_1 = \sum_{j=2}^{N} h_{1j} \qquad A_2 = \sum_{j=3}^{N} h_{2j} \qquad A_3 = \sum_{j=4}^{N} h_{3j} \quad \text{etc.}$$

To help clarify the meaning of reverse arrangements, consider the following sequence of $N=8$ observations:

$$x_1 = 5, \quad x_2 = 3, \quad x_3 = 8, \quad x_4 = 9, \quad x_5 = 4, \quad x_6 = 1, \quad x_7 = 7, \quad x_8 = 5$$

In the above sequence $x_1 > x_2$, $x_1 > x_5$, and $x_1 > x_6$, which gives $A_1 = 3$ reverse arrangements for x_1. Now, choosing x_2 and comparing it against subsequent observations (i.e., for $i = 2$ and $i < j = 3, 4, \ldots, 8$), one notes $x_2 > x_6$ only, so that the number of reverse arrangements for x_2 is $A_2 = 1$. Continuing on, it is seen that $A_3 = 4$, $A_4 = 4$, $A_5 = 1$, $A_6 = 0$, and $A_7 = 1$. The total number of reverse arrangements is, therefore,

$$A = A_1 + A_2 + \cdots + A_7 = 3 + 1 + 4 + 4 + 1 + 0 + 1 = 14$$

If the sequence of N observations is independent observations of the same random variable, then the number of reverse arrangements is a random variable A, with a mean variable and a variance as follows [Ref. 4]:

$$\mu_A = \frac{N(N-1)}{4} \tag{4.54}$$

$$\sigma_A^2 = \frac{2N^3 + 3N^2 - 5N}{72} = \frac{N(2N+5)(N-1)}{72} \tag{4.55}$$

A limited tabulation of 100α percentage points for the distribution function of A is presented in Table A.6.

Example 4.4. Illustration of Reverse Arrangement Test. Assume a sequence of $N=20$ observations of a random variable produces results as noted below:

(1) 5.2	(6) 4.0	(11) 5.9	(16) 5.6
(2) 6.2	(7) 3.9	(12) 6.5	(17) 5.2
(3) 3.7	(8) 5.3	(13) 4.3	(18) 3.9
(4) 6.4	(9) 4.0	(14) 5.7	(19) 6.2
(5) 3.9	(10) 4.6	(15) 3.1	(20) 5.0

Test the sequence of $N=20$ observations for a trend at the $\alpha = 0.05$ level of significance. The number of reverse arrangements in the observations is as follows:

$A_1 = 10$	$A_6 = 3$	$A_{11} = 7$	$A_{16} = 3$
$A_2 = 15$	$A_7 = 1$	$A_{12} = 8$	$A_{17} = 2$
$A_3 = 1$	$A_8 = 7$	$A_{13} = 2$	$A_{18} = 0$
$A_4 = 15$	$A_9 = 2$	$A_{14} = 5$	$A_{19} = 1$
$A_5 = 1$	$A_{10} = 3$	$A_{15} = 0$	

The total number of reverse arrangements is $A = 86$.

Let it be hypothesized that the observations are independent observations of a random variable x, where there is no trend. The acceptance region for this hypothesis is

$$[A_{20;1-\alpha/2} < A \leq A_{20;\alpha/2}]$$

From Table A.6, for $\alpha = 0.05$, $A_{20;1-\alpha/2} = A_{20;0.975} = 64$ and $A_{20;\alpha/2} = A_{20;0.025} = 125$. Hence, the hypothesis is accepted at the 5% level of significance because $A = 86$ falls within the range between 64 and 125.

4.6 CORRELATION AND REGRESSION PROCEDURES

Techniques of correlation and regression analysis are fundamental to much of the material developed in this book. The concept of correlation between two random variables has already been introduced in Chapter 3 and will be expanded on in Chapter 5. The concept of linear regression is basic to the techniques of frequency response function estimation from input/output data, as formulated in Chapters 6 and 7. The material in these chapters, however, is developed in a frequency domain context that may obscure associations with more familiar classical presentations. Hence, a brief review of correlation and regression concepts from the viewpoint of elementary statistics may be helpful as an introduction to this later material.

4.6.1 Linear Correlation Analysis

For a wide class of problems, a matter of primary interest is whether or not two or more random variables are interrelated. For example, is there a relationship between cigarette smoking and life expectancy, or between measured aptitude and academic success? In an engineering context, such problems often reduce to detecting a relationship between some assumed excitation and an observed response of a physical system of interest. The existence of such interrelationships and their relative strength can be measured in terms of a correlation coefficient ρ as defined in Section 3.2.1. For the simple case of two random variables x and y, the correlation coefficient is given by Equation (3.36) as

$$\rho_{xy} = \frac{C_{xy}}{\sigma_x \sigma_y} \tag{4.56}$$

where C_{xy} is the covariance of x and y as defined in Equation (3.34).

Now assume the random variables x and y are sampled to obtain N pairs of observed values. The correlation coefficient may be estimated from the sample data by

$$\begin{aligned} r_{xy} = \hat{\rho}_{xy} &= \frac{s_{xy}}{s_x s_y} = \frac{\sum_{j=1}^{N}(x_i-\bar{x})(y_i-\bar{y})}{\left[\sum_{i=1}^{N}(x_i-\bar{x})^2 \sum_{i=1}^{N}(y_i-\bar{y})^2\right]^{1/2}} \\ &= \frac{\sum_{i=1}^{N} x_i y_i - N\bar{x}\bar{y}}{\left[\left(\sum_{i=1}^{N} x_i^2 - N\bar{x}^2\right)\left(\sum_{i=1}^{N} y_i^2 - N\bar{y}^2\right)\right]^{1/2}} \end{aligned} \tag{4.57}$$

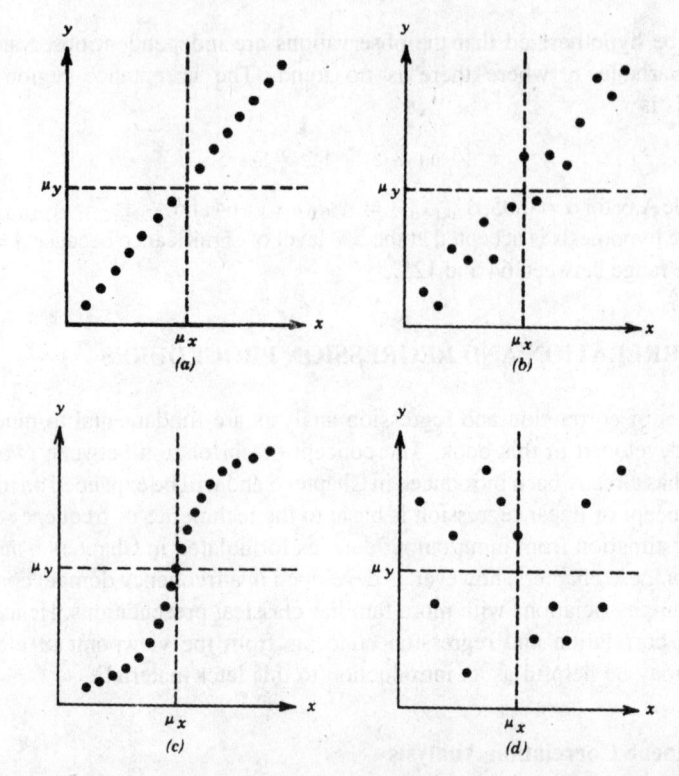

Figure 4.3 Illustration of varying degrees of correlation, (a) Perfect linear correlation, (b) Moderate linear correlation, (c) Nonlinear correlation, (d) No correlation.

Like ρ_{xy}, the sample correlation coefficient r_{xy} will lie between -1 and $+1$, and will have a bounding value only when the observations display a perfect linear relationship. A nonlinear relationship and/or data scatter, whether it be due to measurement errors or imperfect correlation of the variables, will force the value of r_{xy} toward zero, as illustrated in Figure 4.3.

To evaluate the accuracy of the estimate r_{xy}, it is convenient to work with a particular function of r_{xy} given by

$$w = \frac{1}{2}\ln\left[\frac{1+r_{xy}}{1-r_{xy}}\right] \quad (4.58)$$

From Ref. 1, the random variable w has an approximately normal distribution with a mean and a variance of

$$\mu_w = \frac{1}{2}\ln\left[\frac{1+\rho_{xy}}{1-\rho_{xy}}\right] \quad (4.59)$$

$$\sigma_w^2 = \frac{1}{N-3} \quad (4.60)$$

Using the above relationships, confidence intervals for ρ_{xy} based on a sample estimate r_{xy} may be readily established as outlined in Section 4.4.

Because of the variability of correlation estimates, it is usually desirable to verify that a nonzero value of the sample correlation coefficient indeed reflects the existence of a statistically significant correlation between the variables of interest. This may be accomplished by testing the hypothesis that $\rho_{xy}=0$, where a significant correlation is indicated if the hypothesis is rejected. From Equations (4.59) and (4.60), the sampling distribution of w given $\rho_{xy}=0$ is normal with a mean of $\mu_w=0$ and a variance of $\sigma_w^2 = 1/(N-3)$. Hence the acceptance region for the hypothesis of zero correlation is given by

$$\left[-z_{\alpha/2} \leq \frac{\sqrt{N-3}}{2} \ln\left[\frac{1+r_{xy}}{1-r_{xy}}\right] < z_{\alpha/2}\right] \tag{4.61}$$

where z is the standardized normal variable. Values outside the above interval would constitute evidence of statistical correlation at the α level of significance.

Example 4.5. Illustration of Linear Correlation Analysis. The heights and weights of $N=25$ male university students selected at random are presented in Table 4.3. Is there reason to believe that the height and weight of male students are correlated at the $\alpha=0.05$ level of significance?

Let x be height and y be weight. From the data in Table 4.3, the following values needed in Equation (4.61) are calculated:

$$\sum_{i=1}^{N} x_i y_i = 299,056 \qquad \sum_{i=1}^{N} x_i^2 = 124,986 \qquad \sum_{i=1}^{N} y_i^2 = 723,604$$

$$\bar{x} = \frac{1}{N}\sum_{i=1}^{N} x_i = \frac{1766}{25} = 70.64 \qquad \bar{y} = \frac{1}{N}\sum_{i=1}^{N} y_i = \frac{4224}{25} = 168.96$$

Substituting the above values into Equation (4.57) yields the estimated correlation coefficient as follows:

$$r_{xy} = \frac{299,056-(25)(70.64)(168.96)}{[(124,986-25(70.64)^2)(723,604-25(168.96)^2)]^{1/2}}$$
$$= 0.44$$

Table 4.3 Height and Weight Data for Male Students

	\multicolumn{5}{c}{x = height in inches}	\multicolumn{5}{c}{y = weight in pounds}
x	70	74	70	65	69	73	72	69	72	76	74	72
y	140	210	148	145	182	165	155	170	174	155	185	185
x	68	70	71	68	73	65	73	74	64	72	72	67	73
y	165	220	185	180	170	135	175	180	150	170	165	145	170

From Equation (4.58), the quantity $w = 0.472$; thus $\sqrt{N-3}\,w = 2.21$. Now using Equation (4.61), the hypothesis that $\rho_{xy} = 0$ is rejected at the 5% level of significance since $\sqrt{N-3}\,w = 2.21$ falls outside the acceptance region bounded by $\pm z_{\alpha/2} = \pm 1.96$. Hence, there is reason to believe that significant correlation exists between the height and weight of male students.

4.6.2 Linear Regression Analysis

Correlation analysis can establish the degree to which two or more random variables are interrelated. Beyond this, however, a model for the relationship may be desired so that predictions can be made for one variable based on specific values of other variables. For instance, a significant linear relationship between the height and weight of male university students is indicated by the correlation analysis of data presented in Example 4.5. A logical second step would be to evaluate the relationship further so that the weight of students can be predicted for any given height. Procedures for dealing with problems of this type come under the heading of regression analysis.

Consider the simple case of two correlated random variables x and y. Referring again to Example 4.5, x might be student height and y student weight. A linear relationship between the two variables would suggest that for a given value of x, a value of y would be predicted by

$$\tilde{y} = A + Bx \tag{4.62}$$

where A and B are the intercept and slope, respectively, of a straight line. For the case of data that display perfect linear correlation ($r_{xy} = 1$), the predicted value $\tilde{y}_i$ would always equal the observed value y_i for any given x_i. In practice, however, data usually do not display a perfect linear relationship. There generally is some scatter due to extraneous random effects, and perhaps distortion due to nonlinearities, as illustrated in Figure 4.3. Nevertheless, if a linear relationship is assumed and unlimited data are available, appropriate values of A and B can be determined that will predict the expected value of y_i for any given x_i. That is, $\tilde{y}_i$ will not necessarily equal the observed value y_i associated with the corresponding x_i, but it will be an average for all such values that might have been observed.

The accepted procedure for determining the coefficients in Equation (4.62) is to select those values of A and B that minimize the sum of the squared deviations of the observed values from the predicted values of y. This procedure is called a *least squares fit*. Specifically, noting that the deviation of the observed values from the predicted values is

$$y_i - \tilde{y}_i = y_i - (A + Bx_i) \tag{4.63}$$

it follows that the sum of this squared deviations is given by

$$Q = \sum_{i=1}^{N} (y_i - A - Bx_i)^2 \tag{4.64}$$

Hence, a least squares fit is provided by those values of A and B that make

$$\frac{\partial Q}{\partial A} = \frac{\partial Q}{\partial B} = 0 \qquad (4.65)$$

In practice, the available data will be limited to a sample of N pairs of observed values for x and y. This means that Equation (4.65) will yield only estimates of A and B, to be denoted by a and b, respectively. Substituting Equation (4.64) into Equation (4.65) and solving for the estimates of A and B yields

$$a = \bar{y} - b\bar{x} \qquad (4.66a)$$

$$b = \frac{\sum_{i=1}^{N}(x_i-\bar{x})y_i}{\sum_{i=1}^{N}(x_i-\bar{x})^2} = \frac{\sum_{i=1}^{N} x_i y_i - N\bar{x}\bar{y}}{\sum_{i=1}^{N} x_i^2 - N\bar{x}^2} \qquad (4.66b)$$

These estimates can now be used to write a prediction model for y given x as follows:

$$\hat{y} = a + bx = (\bar{y} - b\bar{x}) + bx = \bar{y} + b(x - \bar{x}) \qquad (4.67)$$

The straight line defined by Equation (4.67) is called the *linear regression line for y on x*. By switching the dependent and independent variables in Equation (4.66), a regression line for x on y could also be calculated. Specifically,

$$\hat{x} = \bar{x} + b'(y - \bar{y}) \qquad (4.68)$$

where

$$b' = \frac{\sum_{i=1}^{N} x_i y_i - N\bar{x}\bar{y}}{\sum_{i=1}^{N} y_i^2 - N\bar{y}^2} \qquad (4.69)$$

Comparing the product of Equations (4.66b) and (4.69) to Equation (4.57), it is seen that the slopes of the regression lines for y on x and x on y are related to the sample correlation coefficient of x and y by

$$r_{xy} = [bb']^{1/2} \qquad (4.70)$$

Now consider the accuracy of the estimates a and b given by Equation (4.66). Assuming a normal distribution of y given x, it is shown in Ref. 1 that a and b are unbiased estimates of A and B, respectively, with sampling distributions related to the t distribution as follows:

$$\frac{a-A}{\left(\frac{1}{N} + \frac{\bar{x}^2}{\sum_{i=1}^{N}(x_i-\bar{x})^2}\right)^{1/2}} = s_{y|x} t_{N-2} \qquad (4.71)$$

$$\frac{b-B}{\left(\frac{1}{\sum_{i=1}^{N}(x_i-\bar{x})^2}\right)^{1/2}} = s_{y|x} t_{N-2} \qquad (4.72)$$

Of particular interest is the sampling distribution of $\hat{y}$ associated with a specific value of $x = x_0$. This is given by

$$\frac{\hat{y}-\tilde{y}}{\left(\frac{1}{N} + \frac{(x_0-\bar{x})^2}{\sum_{i=1}^{N}(x_i-\bar{x})^2}\right)^{1/2}} = s_{y|x} t_{N-2} \qquad (4.73)$$

In Equations (4.71)–(4.73), the term $s_{y|x}$ is the sample standard deviation of the observed values of y_i about the prediction $\hat{y}_i = a + bx_i$ and is given by

$$s_{y|x} = \left[\frac{\sum_{i=1}^{N}(y_i-\hat{y}_i)^2}{N-2}\right]^{1/2} = \left[\left(\frac{n-1}{n-2}\right)s_y^2(1-r_{xy}^2)\right]^{1/2} \qquad (4.74)$$

The above relationships provide a basis for establishing confidence intervals for A, B, and $\tilde{y}$ based on the estimates a, b, and $\hat{y}$.

Example 4.6. Illustration of Linear Regression Analysis. Using the data presented in Table 4.3 for Example 4.5, determine a regression line that will provide a linear prediction for the average weight of male university students as a function of their height. Determining a 95% confidence interval for the average weight of male students who are 70 in. tall.
As in Example 4.5, let x be height and y be weight. The values needed to determine the slope and intercept of the regression line for y on x have already been calculated in Example 4.5. Substituting these values into Equation (4.66) yields the estimated slope and the intercept as follows:

$$b = \frac{299,056 - (25)(70.64)(168.96)}{168.96 - (25)(70.64)^2} = 2.85$$

$$a = 168.96 - (2.85)(70.64) = -32.6$$

Hence, the regression line estimating the average weight of male university students given height is

$$\hat{y} = -32.6 + 2.85x$$

which yields an estimated weight of $\hat{y} = 167.1$ lb for a height of $x = 70$ in.
To establish a confidence interval for the average weight $\tilde{y}$ based on the estimate $\hat{y} = 167.1$ lb, it is necessary to calculate $s_{y|x}$ given by Equation (4.74). A more convenient equation for $s_{y|x}$ from the computational viewpoint is

$$s_{y|x} = \left[\frac{1}{N-2}\left(\sum_{i=1}^{N}(y_i-\bar{y})^2 - \frac{[\sum_{i=1}^{N}(x_i-\bar{x})(y_i-\bar{y})]^2}{\sum_{i=1}^{N}(x_i-\bar{x})^2}\right)\right]^{1/2}$$

where the terms in the above expression are further simplified for computational purposes by noting that

$$\sum_{i=1}^{N}(v_i-\bar{v})^2 = \sum_{i=1}^{N}v_i^2 - N\bar{v}^2 \qquad \sum_{i=1}^{N}(x_i-\bar{x})(y_i-\bar{y}) = \sum_{i=1}^{N}x_i y_i - N\bar{x}\bar{y}$$

Substitution of the appropriate values into these expressions yields

$$s_{y|x} = \left[\frac{1}{23}\left(9917 - \frac{(673)^2}{236}\right)\right]^{1/2} = 18.65$$

Then, from Equation (4.73), a 95% confidence interval for the average weight of male university students with a height of 70 in. is

$$\hat{y} \pm s_{y|x} t_{N-2;\alpha/2}\left[\frac{1}{N} + \frac{(x_0-\bar{x})^2}{\sum_{i=1}^{N}(x_i-\bar{x})^2}\right]^{1/2}$$

$$= 167.2 \pm (18.65)t_{23;0.025}\left[\frac{1}{25} + \frac{(70-70.64)^2}{236}\right]^{1/2}$$

$$= 167.2 \pm 7.9 = 159.3 \text{ to } 175.1 \text{ lb}$$

This concludes Example 4.6.

The techniques of correlation and regression analysis are readily extended for applications involving more than two random variables. As noted earlier, such extensions are fundamental to the analysis of multiple-input/output problems developed in Chapter 7. Hence, further discussions of this subject are deferred to that chapter.

PROBLEMS

4.1 Given the random variable $y = cx$ where c is a constant and x is a random variable with a mean value and a variance of μ_x and σ_x^2, respectively, prove that the following relationships are true.
 (a) $\mu_y = c\mu_x$.
 (b) $\sigma_y^2 = c^2\sigma_x^2$.

4.2 Given a random variable x with a probability density function of

$$p(x) = \frac{1}{2\sqrt{2\pi}}e^{-(x-1)^2/8}$$

What are the mean value and variance of x?

4.3 Given two independent random variables, x and y, with mean values of μ_x and μ_y, and variances of σ_x^2 and σ_y^2, determine the
(a) mean value of the product xy.
(b) variance of the difference $x - y$.

4.4 The normalized random error (coefficient of variation) ε_r of an unbiased parameter estimate $\hat{\phi}$ is defined as the ratio of the standard deviation of the estimate to the expected value of the estimate, that is, $\varepsilon_r = \sigma_{\hat{\phi}}/\mu_{\hat{\phi}}$. Determine the normalized random error of a variance estimate s^2 computed from $N = 200$ sample observations using Equation (4.12).

4.5 Given four independent standardized normally distributed random variables, $z_1, z_2, z_3,$ and z_4, define the distribution functions of the following combinations of these variables. For each case, specify the associated degrees of freedom or mean value and variance, as appropriate.
(a) $z_1^2 + z_2^2 + z_3^2 + z_4^2$.
(b) $z_1 + z_2 - z_3 - z_4$.
(c) $\dfrac{z_4}{\{[z_1^2 + z_2^2 + z_3^2]/3\}^{1/2}}$.
(d) $\dfrac{[z_1^2 + z_2^2 + z_3^2]/3}{z_4^2}$.

4.6 What distribution function would be used to establish confidence intervals for the following parameters of two independent normally distributed random variables, x and y?
(a) Interval for μ_x based on a sample mean $\bar{x}$ and known variance σ_x^2.
(b) Interval for σ_x^2/σ_y^2 based on a ratio of sample variances s_x^2/s_y^2.
(c) Interval for σ_x^2 based on a sample variance s_x^2.
(d) Interval for μ_x based on a sample mean $\bar{x}$ and sample variance s_x^2.

4.7 A correlation study is performed using a sample of $N = 7$ pairs of observations $(x_1 y_1, x_2 y_2, \ldots, x_7 y_7)$. A sample correlation coefficient of $r_{xy} = 0.77$ is calculated. Test the hypothesis that ρ_{xy} is greater than zero at the $\alpha = 0.01$ level of significance.

4.8 Assume the sample mean values of two correlated random variables are $\bar{x} = 1$ and $\bar{y} = 2$. Further assume that the sample correlation coefficient is $r_{xy} = 0.5$. If the regression line for y on x is given by $\hat{y} = 1 + x$,
(a) what is the slope b' of the regression line for x on y?
(b) what is the equation for the regression line for x on $y (\hat{x} = a' + b'y)$?

4.9 Given a sample of N independent observations of a random variable x with a known mean value of zero, an *efficient* estimator for the variance of x is

$$s^2 = \frac{1}{N} \sum_{i=1}^{N} x_i^2$$

(a) Prove the above estimator is unbiased.

(b) Write an expression relating the above estimator to a chi-square variable with the appropriate degrees of freedom specified.

(c) What is the variance of the above estimator? (*Hint:* The variance of χ_n^2 is $2n$.)

4.10 Assume a time sequence of $N = 20$ measurements are made of a normally distributed random variable x with the following results:

Time	Value	Time	Value	Time	Value	Time	Value
1	10.1	6	10.6	11	10.9	16	11.4
2	10.4	7	11.3	12	10.1	17	10.1
3	9.9	8	9.7	13	10.5	18	11.5
4	10.0	9	10.2	14	10.7	19	10.3
5	10.0	10	11.2	15	10.8	20	10.9

Test the time sequence of measurements for a trend at the 5% level of significance in two ways, namely,

(a) by computing the reverse arrangements and performing a nonparametric test.

(b) by comparing the slope b of the linear regression line and testing the hypothesis that $B = 0$.

REFERENCES

1. Guttman, I., Wilks, S. S., and Hunter, J. S., *Introductory Engineering Statistics*, 3rd ed., Wiley, New York, 1982.
2. Ross, S. M., *Introduction to Probability and Statistics for Engineers and Scientists*, Wiley, New York, 1987.
3. Hines, W. H., and Montgomery, D. C., *Probability and Statistics in Engineering and Management Sciences*, 3rd ed., Wiley, New York, 1990.
4. Kendall, M. G., and Stuart, A., *The Advanced Theory of Statistics*, Vol. 2, *Inference and Relationships*, Hafner, New York, 1961.

CHAPTER 5

Stationary Random Processes

This chapter discusses elementary and advanced concepts from stationary random processes theory to form a foundation for applications to analysis and measurement problems as contained in later chapters and in Refs 1–3. Material includes theoretical definitions for stationary random processes together with basic properties for correlation and spectral density functions. Results are stated for ergodic random processes, Gaussian random processes, and derivative random processes. Nonstationary random processes are covered in Chapter 12.

5.1 BASIC CONCEPTS

A *random process* $\{x_k(t)\}$, $-\infty < t < \infty$ (also called a *time series* or *stochastic process*), denoted by the symbol { }, is an ensemble of real-valued (or complex-valued) functions that can be characterized through its probability structure. For convenience, the variable t will be interpreted as time in the following discussion. Each particular function $x_k(t)$, where t is variable and k is fixed, is called a *sample function*. In practice, a sample function (or some time history record of finite length from a sample function) may be thought of as the observed result of a single experiment. The possible number of experiments represents a sample space of index k, which may be countable or uncountable. For any number N and any fixed times $t_1, t_2, \ldots, t_N$, the quantities $x_k(t_1), x_k(t_2), \ldots, x_k(t_N)$, represent N random variables over the index k. It is required that there exist a well-defined N-dimensional probability distribution function for every N. An ensemble of sample functions forming a random process is illustrated in Figure 1.10.

A particular sample function $x_k(t)$, in general, would not be suitable for representing the entire random process $\{x_k(t)\}$ to which it belongs. Under certain conditions to be described later, however, it turns out that for the special class of ergodic random processes, it is possible to derive desired statistical information about the entire

---

Random Data: Analysis and Measurement Procedures, Fourth Edition. By Julius S. Bendat and Allan G. Piersol
Copyright © 2010 John Wiley & Sons, Inc.

random process from an appropriate analysis of a single arbitrary sample function. For the situation of a pair of random processes $\{x_k(t)\}$ and $\{y_k(t)\}$, the corresponding problem is to estimate joint statistical properties of the two random processes from a proper analysis of an arbitrary pair of sample functions $x_k(t)$ and $y_k(t)$.

Consider two arbitrary random processes $\{x_k(t)\}$ and $\{y_k(t)\}$. The first statistical quantities of interest are the ensemble *mean values* at arbitrary fixed values of t, where $x_k(t)$ and $y_k(t)$ are random variables over the index k. These are defined as in Equation (3.8) by

$$\mu_x(t) = E[x_k(t)]$$
$$\mu_y(t) = E[y_k(t)] \qquad (5.1)$$

In general, these mean values are different at different times and must be calculated separately for every t of interest. That is,

$$\mu_x(t_1) \neq \mu_x(t_2) \quad \text{if } t_1 \neq t_2$$
$$\mu_y(t_1) \neq \mu_y(t_2) \quad \text{if } t_1 \neq t_2 \qquad (5.2)$$

The next statistical quantities of interest are the *covariance functions* at arbitrary fixed values of $t_1 = t$ and $t_2 = t + \tau$. These are defined by

$$C_{xx}(t, t+\tau) = E[(x_k(t) - \mu_x(t))(x_k(t+\tau) - \mu_x(t+\tau))]$$
$$C_{yy}(t, t+\tau) = E[(y_k(t) - \mu_y(t))(y_k(t+\tau) - \mu_y(t+\tau))] \qquad (5.3)$$
$$C_{xy}(t, t+\tau) = E[(x_k(t) - \mu_x(t))(y_k(t+\tau) - \mu_y(t+\tau))]$$

In general, these quantities are different for different combinations of t_1 and t_2. Observe that at $\tau = 0$ ($t_1 = t_2 = t$),

$$C_{xx}(t, t) = E[(x_k(t) - \mu_x(t))^2] = \sigma_x^2(t)$$
$$C_{yy}(t, t) = E[(y_k(t) - \mu_y(t))^2] = \sigma_y^2(t) \qquad (5.4)$$
$$C_{xy}(t, t) = E[(x_k(t) - \mu_x(t))(y_k(t) - \mu_y(t))] = C_{xy}(t)$$

Thus, the covariance functions $C_{xx}(t, t)$ and $C_{yy}(t, t)$ represent the ordinary variances of $\{x_k(t)\}$ and $\{y_k(t)\}$ at a fixed value of t, whereas $C_{xy}(t, t)$ represents the covariance between $\{x_k(t)\}$ and $\{y_k(t)\}$. As before, different results would generally be obtained for different values of t.

Other statistical quantities can be defined over the ensemble that involve fixing three or more times. The probability structure of the random processes is thus described in finer and finer detail. If $\{x_k(t)\}$ and $\{y_k(t)\}$ form a two-dimensional Gaussian distribution at a fixed value of t, however, then $\{x_k(t)\}$ and $\{y_k(t)\}$ are separately Gaussian. The mean values and covariance functions listed above then provide a complete description of the underlying probability structure. For this reason, the main emphasis in this chapter is on only these two statistical quantities and their relationships to spectral density functions.

If the mean values $\mu_x(t)$ and $\mu_y(t)$, together with the covariance functions $C_{xx}(t, t + \tau)$, $C_{yy}(t, t + \tau)$, and $C_{xy}(t, t + \tau)$, yield the same results for all fixed values of t

(that is, are independent of time translations), then the random processes $\{x_x(t)\}$ and $\{y_k(t)\}$ are said to be *weakly stationary*. If all possible probability distributions involving $\{x_k(t)\}$ and $\{y_k(t)\}$ are independent of time translations, then the random processes are said to be *strongly stationary*. Because the mean values and covariance functions are consequences of only the first- and second-order probability distributions, it follows that the class of strongly stationary random processes is a subclass of the class of weakly stationary random processes. For Gaussian random processes, however, weak stationarity implies strong stationarity because all possible probability distributions may be derived from the mean values and covariance functions. Thus, for Gaussian random processes, these two stationary concepts coincide.

5.1.1 Correlation (Covariance) Functions

For stationary random processes $\{x_x(t)\}$ and $\{y_k(t)\}$, which will be considered henceforth in this chapter, the mean values become constants independent of t. That is, for all t,

$$\mu_x = E[x_k(t)] = \int_{-\infty}^{\infty} xp(x)\,dx$$
$$\mu_y = E[y_k(t)] = \int_{-\infty}^{\infty} yp(y)\,dy \tag{5.5}$$

where $p(x)$ and $p(y)$ are the probability density functions associated with the random variables $x_k(t)$ and $y_k(t)$, respectively. The covariance functions of stationary random processes are also independent of t.

For arbitrary fixed t and τ, define

$$R_{xx}(\tau) = E[x_k(t)x_k(t+\tau)]$$
$$R_{yy}(\tau) = E[y_k(t)y_k(t+\tau)] \tag{5.6}$$
$$R_{xy}(\tau) = E[x_k(t)y_k(t+\tau)]$$

where R is introduced instead of C to distinguish these expressions from the covariance functions defined in Equation (5.3). For nonzero mean values, R is different from C. The quantities $R_{xx}(\tau)$ and $R_{yy}(\tau)$ are called the *autocorrelations functions* of $\{x_k(t)\}$ and $\{y_k(t)\}$, respectively, whereas $R_{xy}(\tau)$ is called the *cross-correlation function* between $\{x_k(t)\}$ and $\{y_k(t)\}$.

A necessary and sufficient condition that $R_{xx}(\tau)$ be the autocorrelation function of a weakly stationary random process $\{x_k(t)\}$ is that $R_{xx}(\tau) = R_{xx}(-\tau)$, and that $R_{xx}(\tau)$ be a nonnegative definite function. One can also prove that $R_{xx}(\tau)$ will be a continuous function of τ if it is continuous at the origin. Similarly the cross-correlation function $R_{xy}(\tau)$ will be continuous for all τ if $R_{xx}(\tau)$ or $R_{yy}(\tau)$ is continuous at the origin [Ref. 4].

For a pair of stationary random processes $\{x_k(t)\}$ and $\{y_k(t)\}$, the joint probability density function $p(x_1, x_2)$ of the pair of random variables $x_1 = x_k(t)$ and $x_2 = x_k(t+\tau)$ is independent of t, and the joint probability density function $p(y_1, y_2)$ associated with the pair of random variables $y_1 = y_k(t)$ and $y_2 = y_k(t+\tau)$ is independent of t. This is also true for the joint probability density function $p(x_1, y_2)$ associated with the pair of random variables $x_1 = x_k(t)$ and $y_2 = y_k(t + \tau)$. In terms of these probability density functions,

$$R_{xx}(\tau) = \iint_{-\infty}^{\infty} x_1 x_2 p(x_1, x_2) \, dx_1 dx_2$$

$$R_{yy}(\tau) = \iint_{-\infty}^{\infty} y_1 y_2 p(y_1, y_2) \, dy_1 dy_2 \qquad (5.7)$$

$$R_{xy}(\tau) = \iint_{-\infty}^{\infty} x_1 y_2 p(x_1, y_2) \, dx_1 dy_2$$

For arbitrary values of μ_x and μ_y, the covariance functions are related to the correlation functions by the equations

$$\begin{aligned} C_{xx}(\tau) &= R_{xx}(\tau) - \mu_x^2 \\ C_{yy}(\tau) &= R_{yy}(\tau) - \mu_y^2 \\ C_{xy}(\tau) &= R_{xy}(\tau) - \mu_x \mu_y \end{aligned} \qquad (5.8)$$

Thus, correlation functions are identical with covariance functions when the mean values are zero. Note that, by definition, two stationary random processes are uncorrelated if $C_{xy}(\tau) = 0$ for all τ. This occurs, from Equation (5.8), whenever $R_{xy}(\tau) = \mu_x \mu_y$ for all τ. Hence, the two processes will be uncorrelated when $R_{xy}(\tau) = 0$ for all τ only if also either μ_x or μ_y equals zero.

From the stationary hypothesis, it follows that the autocorrelation functions $R_{xx}(\tau)$ and $R_{yy}(\tau)$ are even functions of τ. That is,

$$\begin{aligned} R_{xx}(-\tau) &= R_{xx}(\tau) \\ R_{yy}(-\tau) &= R_{yy}(\tau) \end{aligned} \qquad (5.9)$$

while the cross-correlation function is neither odd nor even, but satisfies the relation

$$R_{xy}(-\tau) = R_{yx}(\tau) \qquad (5.10)$$

Equation (5.10) can be proved as follows. By definition,

$$R_{xy}(-\tau) = E[x(t)y(t-\tau)]$$

where the dependence on k is omitted to simplify the notation. Since results are invariant with respect to translations in time, one can replace t by $t + \tau$ wherever t appears prior to taking the expected value. Hence,

$$\begin{aligned} R_{xy}(-\tau) &= E[x(t+\tau)y(t+\tau-\tau)] \\ &= E[y(t)x(t+\tau)] = R_{yx}(\tau) \end{aligned}$$

which completes the proof. When $x = y$, one obtains

$$R_{xx}(-\tau) = R_{xx}(\tau) \qquad R_{yy}(-\tau) = R_{yy}(\tau)$$

showing that Equation (5.9) is a special case of Equation (5.10).

BASIC CONCEPTS   113

The correlation properties of stationary random processes $\{x_k(t)\}$ and $\{y_k(t)\}$, which are described by the four functions $R_{xx}(\tau)$, $R_{yy}(\tau)$, $R_{xy}(\tau)$, and $R_{yx}(\tau)$, need be calculated only for values of $\tau \geq 0$, because the relations of Equations (5.9) and (5.10) yield results for $\tau < 0$.

5.1.2 Examples of Autocorrelation Functions

Examples of special autocorrelation functions that are useful in theoretical studies will now be derived.

***Example 5.1.* Autocorrelation Function of Sine Wave Process.** Suppose $\{x_k(t)\} = \{X \sin[2\pi f_0 t + \theta(k)]\}$ is a sine wave process in which X and f_0 are constants and $\theta(k)$ is a random variable with a uniform probability density function $p(\theta)$ over $(0, 2\pi)$. Determine the autocorrelation function $R_{xx}(\tau)$.

Here, for any fixed value of t, the random variable

$$x_k(t) = X \sin[2\pi f_0 + \theta(k)] = x_1(\theta)$$
$$x_k(t+\tau) = X \sin[2\pi f_0(t+\tau) + \theta(k)] = x_2(\theta)$$

From Equation (5.6),

$$R_{xx}(\tau) = E[x_k(t)x_k(t+\tau)] = E[x_1(\theta)x_2(\theta)]$$

with

$$p(\theta) = (2\pi)^{-1} \quad 0 \leq \theta \leq 2\pi \quad \text{otherwise zero}$$

Hence,

$$R_{xx}(\tau) = \frac{X^2}{2\pi} \int_0^{2\pi} \sin(2\pi f_0 t + \theta) \sin[2\pi f_0(t+\tau) + \theta]\, d\theta$$
$$= \frac{X^2}{2} \cos 2\pi f_0 \tau$$

giving the autocorrelation function of a sine wave stationary random process as pictured in Table 5.1.

***Example 5.2.* Autocorrelation Function of Rectangular Wave Process.** Consider a physical situation where a sample function $x_k(t)$ from a random rectangular wave process $\{x_k(t)\}$ is restricted so as to assume only values of c or $-c$, where the number of changes of sign in an interval $(t, t+\tau)$ occurs at random and independent times with an average density of λ. Assume also that what happens inside an interval $(t, t+\tau)$ is independent of what happens outside the interval. Define

$$A_n = \text{Event[exactly } n \text{ changes of sign fall inside } (t, t+\tau)]$$

This type of physical situation follows a Poisson distribution [Ref. 1], where the probability of event A_n is

$$P(A_n) = \frac{(\lambda|\tau|)^n}{n!} e^{-\lambda|\tau|}$$

Determine the autocorrelation function of $\{x_k(t)\}$.

The autocorrelation function may be calculated as follows. An individual product term $x_k(t)x_k(t+\tau)$ equals c^2 if $x_k(t)$ and $x_k(t+\tau)$ are of the same sign, and it equals $-c^2$ if they are of opposite sign. The total probability for c^2 is given by the sum $P(A_0) + P(A_2) + P(A_4) + \cdots$, and the total probability for $-c^2$ is given by the sum $P(A_1) + P(A_3) + P(A_5) + \cdots$. Hence,

$$R_{xx}(\tau) = E[x_k(t)x_k(t+\tau)] = c^2 \sum_{n=0}^{\infty} (-1)^n P(A_n)$$

$$= c^2 e^{-\lambda|\tau|} \sum_{n=1}^{\infty} (-1)^n \frac{(\lambda|\tau|)^n}{n!} = c^2 e^{-2\lambda|\tau|}$$

This exponential function is pictured in Table 5.1 with $a = 2\lambda$ and $c^2 = 1$.

***Example 5.3.* Autocorrelation Function of Sum of Two Processes.** Assume that a random process $\{y_k(t)\}$ is the sum of two stationary processes $\{x_{1,k}(t)\}$ and $\{x_{2,k}(t)\}$ such that each sample function

$$y_k(t) = a_1 x_{1,k}(t) + a_2 x_{2,k}(t)$$

where a_1 and a_2 are constants. Assume also that $\{x_{1,k}(t)\}$ and $\{x_{2,k}(t)\}$ may be correlated. Determine the autocorrelation function $R_{yy}(\tau)$.

From Equation (5.6), one obtains

$$\begin{aligned} R_{yy}(\tau) &= E[y_k(t)y_k(t+\tau)] \\ &= E[(a_1 x_{1,k}(t) + a_2 x_{2,k}(t))(a_1 x_{1,k}(t+\tau) + a_2 x_{2,k}(t+\tau))] \\ &= a_1^2 E[x_{1,k}(t)x_{1,k}(t+\tau)] + a_1 a_2 E[x_{1,k}(t)x_{2,k}(t+\tau)] \\ &\quad + a_1 a_2 E[x_{2,k}(t)x_{1,k}(t+\tau)] + a_2^2 E[x_{2,k}(t)x_{2,k}(t+\tau)] \\ &= a_1^2 R_{x_1 x_1}(\tau) + a_1 a_2 [R_{x_1 x_2}(\tau) + R_{x_2 x_1}(\tau)] + a_2^2 R_{x_2 x_2}(\tau) \end{aligned}$$

Thus, the sum autocorrelation function requires knowledge of the input cross-correlation functions as well as their autocorrelation functions.

***Example 5.4.* Uncorrelated-Dependent Random Variables.** Assume that two random variables x and y are such that $x = \cos\phi$ and $y = \sin\phi$, where ϕ is uniformly distributed from 0 to 2π. Here, x and y are related because

$$y = \sqrt{1 - x^2}$$

It follows that

$$p(x, y) \neq p(x)p(y)$$

BASIC CONCEPTS

showing that x and y are statistically dependent. However, the covariance between x and y is

$$\begin{aligned} C_{xy} &= E[xy] - E[x]E[y] \\ &= E[\cos\phi \sin\phi] - E[\cos\phi]E[\sin\phi] \\ &= \tfrac{1}{2}E[\sin 2\phi] = 0 \end{aligned}$$

Hence x and y are uncorrelated.

5.1.3 Correlation Coefficient Functions

The cross-correlation function is bounded by the *cross-correlation inequality*

$$|R_{xy}(\tau)|^2 \leq R_{xx}(0)R_{yy}(0) \tag{5.11}$$

which may be proved as follows. For any real constants a and b, the expected value

$$E[(ax(t) + by(t+\tau))^2] \geq 0$$

since only nonnegative quantities are being considered. This is equivalent to

$$a^2 R_{xx}(0) + 2ab R_{xy}(\tau) + b^2 R_{yy}(0) \geq 0$$

Hence, assuming $b \neq 0$,

$$\left(\frac{a}{b}\right)^2 R_{xx}(0) + 2\left(\frac{a}{b}\right) R_{xy}(\tau) + R_{yy}(0) \geq 0$$

This is a quadratic equation in a/b without real different roots since one side is nonnegative. Therefore, the discriminant of this quadratic equation in a/b must be nonpositive. That is,

$$\text{Discriminant} = 4R_{xy}^2(\tau) - 4R_{xx}(0)R_{yy}(0) \leq 0$$

Thus

$$R_{xy}^2(\tau) = |R_{xy}(\tau)|^2 \leq R_{xx}(0)R_{yy}(0)$$

This completes the proof.

By considering $x(t) - \mu_x$ and $y(t+\tau) - \mu_y$ instead of $x(t)$ and $y(t+\tau)$, the same proof gives the cross-covariance inequality

$$|C_{xy}(\tau)|^2 \leq C_{xx}(0)C_{yy}(0) \tag{5.12}$$

Noting that

$$|R_{xx}(\tau)| \leq R_{xx}(0) \qquad |C_{xx}(\tau)| \leq C_{xx}(0) \tag{5.13}$$

it follows that the maximum possible values of $R_{xx}(\tau)$ and $C_{xx}(\tau)$ occur at $\tau = 0$ and correspond to the mean square value and variance, respectively, of the data.

That is,

$$R_{xx}(0) = E[x_k^2(t)] = \psi_x^2 \quad C_{xx}(0) = \sigma_x^2$$
$$R_{yy}(0) = E[y_k^2(t)] = \psi_y^2 \quad C_{yy}(0) = \sigma_y^2 \tag{5.14}$$

Hence, Equation (5.12) takes the form

$$|C_{xy}(\tau)|^2 \leq \sigma_x^2 \sigma_y^2 \tag{5.15}$$

The *correlation coefficient function (normalized cross-covariance function)* may now be defined by

$$\rho_{xy}(\tau) = \frac{C_{xy}(\tau)}{\sigma_x \sigma_y} \tag{5.16}$$

and satisfies for all τ

$$-1 \leq \rho_{xy}(\tau) \leq 1 \tag{5.17}$$

If either u_x or u_y is equal to zero, then $\rho_{xy}(\tau)$ becomes

$$\rho_{xy}(\tau) = \frac{R_{xy}(\tau)}{\sigma_x \sigma_y} \tag{5.18}$$

because $C_{xy}(\tau) = R_{xy}(\tau)$ in these cases. The function $\rho_{xy}(\tau)$ measures the degree of linear dependence between $\{x_k(t)\}$ and $\{y_k(t)\}$ for a displacement of τ in $\{y_k(t)\}$ relative to $\{x_k(t)\}$. It is essentially a generalization of the correlation coefficient used in classical statistics as discussed earlier in Sections 3.2.1 and 4.6.1.

5.1.4 Cross-Correlation Function for Time Delay

Assume a transmitted signal is represented by a zero mean value stationary random signal $x(t)$. Let the received signal be represented by another zero mean value stationary random signal $y(t)$ such that

$$y(t) = \alpha x(t-\tau_0) + n(t) \tag{5.19}$$

The quantity α is a constant attenuation factor, the quantity $\tau_0 = (d/c)$ is a constant time delay equal to a distance d divided by a velocity of propagation c, and $n(t)$ represents uncorrelated zero mean value noise at the output, as illustrated in Figure 5.1.

For this problem, the cross-correlation function between $x(t)$ and $y(t)$ is given by

$$R_{xy}(\tau) = E[x(t)y(t+\tau)] = E[x(t)\{\alpha x(t+\tau-\tau_0) + n(t+\tau)\}]$$
$$= \alpha E[x(t)x(t+\tau-\tau_0)] = \alpha R_{xx}(\tau-\tau_0) \tag{5.20}$$

Thus, $R_{xy}(\tau)$ is merely the autocorrelation function $R_{xx}(\tau)$ displaced by the time delay τ_0 and multiplied by the attenuation factor α. The peak value of $R_{xy}(\tau)$ occurs at $\tau = \tau_0$, namely,

BASIC CONCEPTS

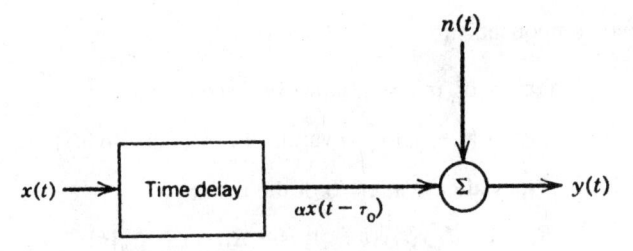

Figure 5.1 Model for time-delay problem.

$$R_{xy}(\tau)_{\text{peak}} = R_{xy}(\tau_0) = \alpha R_{xx}(0) = \alpha \sigma_x^2 \quad . \tag{5.21}$$

This result is pictured in Figure 5.2. Note that measurement of the value τ_0 where the peak occurs plus knowledge of either the distance d or the velocity of propagation c will yield the other quantity because $d = c\tau_0$. See Ref. 2 for physical illustrations of time-delay measurement problems.

Again assuming $x(t)$ and $n(t)$ have zero mean values, the correlation coefficient function at $\tau = \tau_0$ from Equation (5.18) is given by

$$\rho_{xy}(\tau_0) = \frac{R_{xy}(\tau_0)}{\sigma_x \sigma_y} = \alpha \frac{\sigma_x}{\sigma_y} \tag{5.22}$$

Thus, measurement of $\rho_{xy}(\tau_0)$ yields the attenuation factor α by

$$\alpha = \rho_{xy}(\tau_0)[\sigma_y/\sigma_x] \tag{5.23}$$

Also, the variance in $y(t)$, for uncorrelated $x(t)$ and $n(t)$, is

$$\sigma_y^2 = E[y^2(t)] = \alpha^2 \sigma_x^2 + \sigma_n^2 \tag{5.24}$$

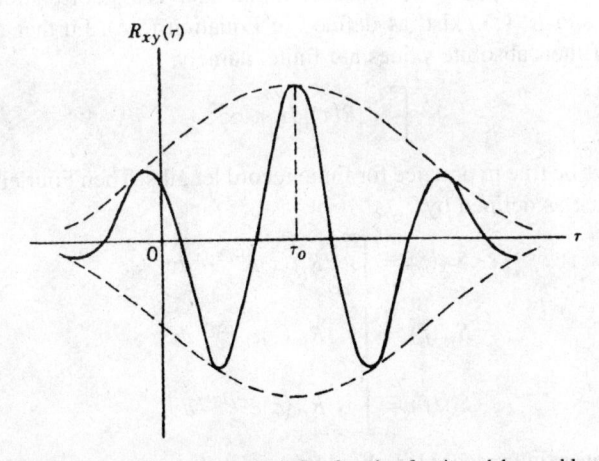

Figure 5.2 Typical cross-correlation function for time-delay problem.

where the two components are

$$\alpha^2 \sigma_x^2 = \rho_{xy}^2 \sigma_y^2 = \text{variance in } y(t) \text{ due to } x(t)$$
$$\sigma_n^2 = (1-\rho_{xy}^2)\sigma_y^2 = \text{variance in } y(t) \text{ due to } n(t) \qquad (5.25)$$

Equation (5.24) is a special case at $\tau = 0$ of the result

$$R_{yy}(\tau) = E[y(t)y(t+\tau)] = \alpha^2 R_{xx}(\tau) + R_{nn}(\tau) \qquad (5.26)$$

5.2 SPECTRAL DENSITY FUNCTIONS

Spectral density functions can be defined in three different equivalent ways as will be proved in later sections:

a. Via correlation functions
b. Via finite Fourier transforms
c. Via filtering–squaring–averaging operations

Important relations will also be developed for these functions that are needed for many applications.

5.2.1 Spectra via Correlation Functions

The first way to define spectral density functions is a (historical) mathematical method where a single Fourier transform is taken of a previously calculated correlation function. When mean values are removed, this (infinite) Fourier transform will usually exist even though the (infinite) Fourier transform of the original stationary random data does not exist. This approach yields *two-sided* spectral density functions, denoted by $S(f)$, which are defined for f over $(-\infty, \infty)$.

Specifically, assume that the autocorrelation and cross-correlation functions $R_{xx}(\tau)$, $R_{yy}(\tau)$, and $R_{xy}(\tau)$ exist, as defined in Equation (5.6). Further assume that the integrals of their absolute values are finite, namely,

$$\int_{-\infty}^{\infty} |R(\tau)| d\tau < \infty$$

This will always be true in practice for finite record lengths. Then Fourier transforms of $R(\tau)$ will exist as defined by

$$S_{xx}(f) = \int_{-\infty}^{\infty} R_{xx}(\tau) e^{-j2\pi f \tau} d\tau$$
$$S_{yy}(f) = \int_{-\infty}^{\infty} R_{yy}(\tau) e^{-j2\pi f \tau} d\tau \qquad (5.27)$$
$$S_{xy}(f) = \int_{-\infty}^{\infty} R_{xy}(\tau) e^{-j2\pi f \tau} d\tau$$

Such integrals over finite record lengths always exist. The quantities $S_{xx}(f)$ and $S_{yy}(f)$ are called the *autospectral density functions* of $\{x_k(t)\}$ and $\{y_k(t)\}$, respectively,

SPECTRAL DENSITY FUNCTIONS

whereas $S_{xy}(f)$ is called the *cross-spectral density function* between $\{x_k(t)\}$ and $\{y_k(t)\}$.

Inverse Fourier transforms of Equation (5.27) yield

$$R_{xx}(\tau) = \int_{-\infty}^{\infty} S_{xx}(f)e^{j2\pi f\tau} df$$

$$R_{yy}(\tau) = \int_{-\infty}^{\infty} S_{yy}(f)e^{j2\pi f\tau} df \quad (5.28)$$

$$R_{xy}(\tau) = \int_{-\infty}^{\infty} S_{xy}(f)e^{j2\pi f\tau} df$$

To handle practical problems, both $R(\tau)$ and $S(f)$ are permitted to include delta functions. The results in Equations (5.27) and (5.28) are often called the *Wiener–Khinchine relations* in honor of the two mathematicians, N. Wiener of the United States and A. I. Khinchine of the USSR, who independently proved the Fourier transform relationship between correlation functions and spectral density functions in the early 1930s.

From the symmetry properties of stationary correlation functions given in Equations (5.9) and (5.10), it follows that

$$S_{xx}(-f) = S_{xx}^*(f) = S_{xx}(f)$$
$$S_{yy}(-f) = S_{yy}^*(f) = S_{yy}(f) \quad (5.29)$$
$$S_{xy}(-f) = S_{xy}^*(f) = S_{yx}(f) \quad (5.30)$$

Thus, the autospectral density functions $S_{xx}(f)$ and $S_{yy}(f)$ are real-valued even functions of f, whereas the cross-spectral density function is a complex-valued function of f. It is also true that both $S_{xx}(f)$ and $S_{yy}(f)$ are nonnegative for all f, to be proved later.

Equation (5.30) can be proved as follows. By definition,

$$S_{xy}(-f) = \int_{-\infty}^{\infty} R_{xy}(\tau)e^{j2\pi f\tau} d\tau$$

$$S_{xy}^*(f) = \int_{-\infty}^{\infty} R_{xy}(\tau)e^{j2\pi f\tau} d\tau$$

$$S_{yx}(f) = \int_{-\infty}^{\infty} R_{yx}(\tau)e^{-j2\pi f\tau} d\tau$$

It is immediately obvious that $S_{xy}(-f) = S_{xy}^*(f)$. Now make a change of variable in the first integral by letting $\tau = -u$, $d\tau = -du$. Then

$$S_{xy}(-f) = \int_{-\infty}^{\infty} R_{xy}(-u)e^{-j2\pi fu} du$$

But $R_{xy}(-u) = R_{yx}(u)$ from Equation (5.10). Hence,

$$S_{xy}(-f) = \int_{-\infty}^{\infty} R_{yx}(u)e^{-j2\pi fu} du = S_{yx}(f)$$

This completes the proof. Results in Equation (5.29) are special cases of Equation (5.30) when $x(t) = y(t)$.

The autospectral relations in Equation (5.27) may be simplified to

$$S_{xx}(f) = \int_{-\infty}^{\infty} R_{xx}(\tau) \cos 2\pi f\tau \, d\tau = 2 \int_{0}^{\infty} R_{xx}(\tau) \cos 2\pi f\tau \, d\tau$$
$$S_{yy}(f) = \int_{-\infty}^{\infty} R_{yy}(\tau) \cos 2\pi f\tau \, d\tau = 2 \int_{0}^{\infty} R_{yy}(\tau) \cos 2\pi f\tau \, d\tau$$
(5.31)

Conversely,

$$R_{xx}(\tau) = 2 \int_{0}^{\infty} S_{xx}(f) \cos 2\pi f\tau \, df$$
$$R_{yy}(\tau) = 2 \int_{0}^{\infty} S_{yy}(f) \cos 2\pi f\tau \, df$$
(5.32)

The *one-sided* autospectral density functions, $G_{xx}(f)$ and $G_{yy}(f)$, where f varies only over $(0, \infty)$, are defined by

$$G_{xx}(f) = 2S_{xx}(f) \quad 0 < f < \infty \quad \text{otherwise zero}$$
$$G_{yy}(f) = 2S_{yy}(f) \quad 0 < f < \infty \quad \text{otherwise zero}$$
(5.33)

Theoretically, at the exact frequency $f = 0$, $G_{xx}(0) = S_{xx}(0)$, and $G_{yy}(0) = S_{yy}(0)$. However, this rigorous relationship between one-sided and two-sided spectral density functions at zero frequency will be omitted in all equations henceforth for simplicity. The one-sided spectral density functions defined in Equation (5.33) are the quantities measured by direct filtering procedures in practice. For mathematical calculations, however, the use of $S_{xx}(f)$ and $S_{yy}(f)$ defined over $(-\infty, \infty)$ and exponentials with imaginary exponents often simplifies the analysis. It is important to be able to deal properly with both of these representations, and both will be used in this book. See Figure 5.3 for a graphical illustration of the relationship.

In terms of the one-sided autospectral density functions $G_{xx}(f)$ and $G_{yy}(f)$, the correspondence with the stationary correlation functions $R_{xx}(\tau)$ and $R_{yy}(\tau)$ becomes

$$G_{xx}(f) = 4 \int_{0}^{\infty} R_{xx}(\tau) \cos 2\pi f\tau \, d\tau \quad 0 < f < \infty$$
$$G_{yy}(f) = 4 \int_{0}^{\infty} R_{xx}(\tau) \cos 2\pi f\tau \, d\tau \quad 0 < f < \infty$$
(5.34)

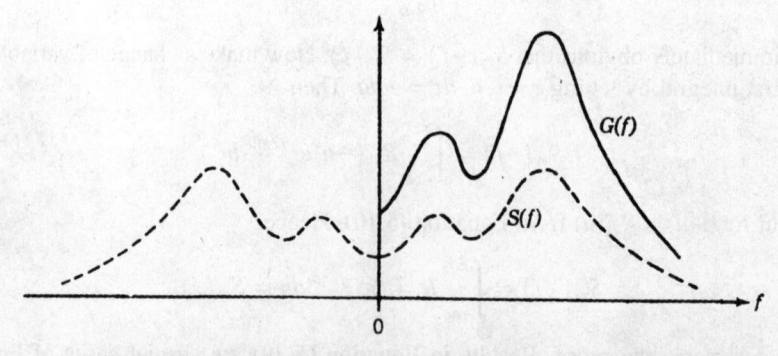

Figure 5.3 One-sided and two-sided autospectral density functions.

Conversely,

$$R_{xx}(\tau) = \int_0^\infty G_{xx}(f) \cos 2\pi f\tau \, df$$
$$R_{yy}(\tau) = \int_0^\infty G_{yy}(f) \cos 2\pi f\tau \, df$$
(5.35)

In particular, at $\tau = 0$, one obtains

$$R_{xx}(0) = E[x^2(t)] = \psi_x^2 = \int_0^\infty G_{xx}(f) df$$
$$R_{yy}(0) = E[y^2(t)] = \psi_y^2 = \int_0^\infty G_{yy}(f) df$$
(5.36)

The *one-sided* cross-spectral density function $G_{xy}(f)$, where f varies only over $(0, \infty)$, is defined by

$$G_{xy}(f) = 2S_{xy}(f) \quad 0 < f < \infty \quad \text{otherwise zero} \tag{5.37}$$

From Equation (5.27)

$$G_{xy}(f) = 2\int_{-\infty}^\infty R_{xy}(\tau) e^{-j2\pi f\tau} d\tau = C_{xy}(f) - jQ_{xy}(f) \tag{5.38}$$

where $C_{xy}(f)$ is called the *coincident spectral density function (co-spectrum)*, and $Q_{xy}(f)$ is called the *quadrature spectral density function (quad-spectrum)*. In terms of $C_{xy}(f)$ and $Q_{xy}(f)$, the cross-correlation function is given by

$$R_{xy}(\tau) = \int_0^\infty [C_{xy}(f) \cos 2\pi f\tau + Q_{xy}(f) \sin 2\pi f\tau] df \tag{5.39}$$

Observe that $C_{xy}(f)$ and $Q_{xy}(f)$ are defined in terms of $G_{xy}(f)$ rather than $S_{xy}(f)$. Note also that $\tau = 0$ yields the result

$$R_{xy}(0) = E[x(t)y(t)] = \int_0^\infty C_{xy}(f) df \tag{5.40}$$

The one-sided cross-spectral density function may be presented in complex polar notation as

$$G_{xy}(f) = |G_{xy}(f)| e^{-j\theta_{xy}(f)} \quad 0 < f < \infty \tag{5.41}$$

where the *absolute value (magnitude)* and *phase angle* are determined by

$$|G_{xy}(f)| = \sqrt{C_{xy}^2(f) + Q_{xy}^2(f)} \tag{5.42}$$

$$\theta_{xy}(f) = \tan^{-1} \frac{Q_{xy}(f)}{C_{xy}(f)} \tag{5.43}$$

The signs of the terms $C_{xy}(f)$ and $Q_{xy}(f)$ may be positive or negative and give the quadrant for the phase angle. These signs also determine at each frequency f whether $y(t)$ leads $x(t)$ or $x(t)$ leads $y(t)$. When the record $y(t)$ leads $x(t)$, this means $y(t) = x(t - \tau_0)$, where $\tau_0 > 0$ and $\theta_{xy}(f) = 2\pi f\tau_0$. The relation of the phase angle to $C_{xy}(f)$

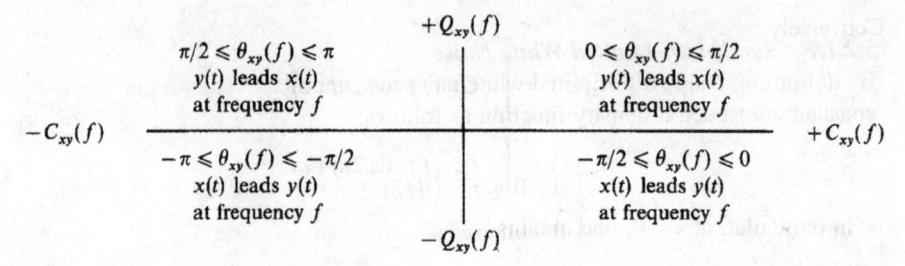

```
                          +Q_xy(f)
      π/2 ≤ θ_xy(f) ≤ π    |    0 ≤ θ_xy(f) ≤ π/2
        y(t) leads x(t)    |     y(t) leads x(t)
         at frequency f    |      at frequency f
-C_xy(f) ─────────────────────────────────────── +C_xy(f)
     -π ≤ θ_xy(f) ≤ -π/2   |   -π/2 ≤ θ_xy(f) ≤ 0
        x(t) leads y(t)    |     x(t) leads y(t)
         at frequency f    |      at frequency f
                          -Q_xy(f)
```

Figure 5.4 Relation of phase angle to cross-spectral terms.

and $Q_{xy}(f)$ is illustrated in Figure 5.4. Similarly, the two-sided cross-spectral density function in complex polar notation is

$$S_{xy}(f) = |S_{xy}(f)|e^{-j\theta_{xy}(f)} \tag{5.44}$$

where $|S_{xy}(f)| = \tfrac{1}{2}|G_{xy}(f)|$ and $\theta_{xy}(f)$ is the same as in Equations (5.41) and (5.43). Referring now to Equation (5.33), it follows that

$$C_{xy}(f) = 2\int_0^\infty [R_{xy}(\tau) + R_{yx}(\tau)]\cos 2\pi f\tau\, d\tau = C_{xy}(-f)$$
$$Q_{xy}(f) = 2\int_0^\infty [R_{xy}(\tau) - R_{yx}(\tau)]\sin 2\pi f\tau\, d\tau = -Q_{xy}(-f) \tag{5.45}$$

Thus $C_{xy}(f)$ is a real-valued even function of f, whereas $Q_{xy}(f)$ is a real-valued odd function of f. Also,

$$C_{xy}(f) = \tfrac{1}{2}[G_{xy}(f) + G_{yx}(f)] = |G_{xy}(f)|\cos\theta_{xy}(f)$$
$$Q_{xy}(f) = (j/2)[G_{xy}(f) - G_{yx}(f)] = |G_{xy}(f)|\sin\theta_{xy}(f) \tag{5.46}$$

The spectral properties of stationary random processes $\{x_k(t)\}$ and $\{y_k(t)\}$, which are described by the three functions $S_{xx}(f)$, $S_{yy}(f)$, and $S_{xy}(f)$, or by the four functions $S_{xx}(f)$, $S_{yy}(f)$, $C_{xy}(f)$, and $Q_{xy}(f)$, need be calculated only for values of $f \geq 0$, since the relations of Equations (5.29), (5.30) and (5.45) yield results for $f < 0$. Of course, corresponding G functions should be calculated only for $f \geq 0$.

When dealing with spectral functions involving delta functions at $f = 0$, it is convenient to let the lower limit of integration, zero, be approached from below. In particular, for $R(\tau) = c^2$, this allows the corresponding $G(f)$ to be $G(f) = c^2\delta(f)$. For this situation, $S(f)$ is also given by $S(f) = c^2\delta(f)$, showing that the factor of 2 in Equation (5.37) should not be applied to delta functions at $f = 0$. This consideration does not exist for correlation functions involving delta functions at $\tau = 0$, because correlation functions are defined for all τ. Thus, $R(\tau) = (a/2)\delta(\tau)$ corresponds to $S(f) = (a/2)$ for all f and $G(f) = a$ for $f \geq 0$.

Examples of special autospectral density functions that are useful in theoretical studies are given in Table 5.2.

5.2.1.1 Bandwidth-Limited White Noise

By definition, bandwidth-limited white noise is a stationary random process with a constant autospectral density function as follows:

$$G_{xx}(f) = \begin{cases} a & 0 \leq f_c - (B/2) \leq f \leq f_c + (B/2) \\ 0 & \text{otherwise} \end{cases} \quad (5.47)$$

Here, f_c is the center frequency of a rectangular filter of bandwidth B. This case is also called *bandpass white noise*. From Equation (5.35), it follows that the associated autocorrelation function is

$$R_{xx}(\tau) = \int_{f_c-(B/2)}^{f_c+(B/2)} a \cos 2\pi f \tau \, df = aB \left(\frac{\sin \pi B \tau}{\pi B \tau} \right) \cos 2\pi f_c \tau \quad (5.48)$$

For the special case where $f_c = (B/2)$, this case becomes *low-pass white noise* defined as follows:

$$G_{xx}(f) = \begin{cases} a & 0 \leq f \leq B \\ 0 & \text{otherwise} \end{cases} \quad (5.49)$$

with

$$R_{xx}(\tau) = aB \left(\frac{\sin 2\pi B \tau}{2\pi B \cdot} \right) \quad (5.50)$$

These results are pictured in Tables 5.1 and 5.2. For either bandpass white noise or low-pass white noise, the data have a finite mean square value given by

$$\int_0^\infty G_{xx}(f) df = aB = R_{xx}(0) \quad (5.51)$$

It is theoretically possible to approximate such cases with real data.

An extreme version of low-pass white noise, called *white noise*, is defined by a $G_{xx}(f)$ that is assumed to be a constant over all frequencies. This case never occurs for real data. Specifically, for white noise,

$$G_{xx}(f) = a \quad f \geq 0 \text{ only} \quad (5.52)$$

Hence,

$$S_{xx}(f) = (a/2) \quad \text{all } f \quad (5.53)$$

$$R_{xx}(\tau) = (a/2)\delta(\tau) \quad (5.54)$$

$$\int_0^\infty G_{xx}(f) df = \infty = R_{xx}(0) \quad (5.55)$$

showing that white noise has an infinite mean square value. Such theoretical white noise *cannot* be Gaussian because a Gaussian process must have a finite mean square value in order to be well defined.

Table 5.1 Special Autocorrelation Functions

Type		Autocorrelation Function
Constant		$R_{xx}(\tau)\, c^2$
Sine wave		$R_{xx}(\tau) = \dfrac{X^2}{2} \cos 2\pi f_0 \tau$
White noise		$R_{xx}(\tau) = a\, \delta(\tau)$
Low-pass, white noise		$R_{xx}(\tau) = aB \left(\dfrac{\sin 2\pi B\tau}{2\pi B\tau} \right)$
Bandpass white noise		$R_{xx}(\tau) = aB \left(\dfrac{\sin \pi B\tau}{\pi B\tau} \right) \cos 2\pi f_0 \tau$
Exponential		$R_{xx}(\tau) = e^{-a|\tau|}$
Exponential cosine		$R_{xx}(\tau) = e^{-a|\tau|} \cos 2\pi f_0 \tau$
Exponential cosine, exponential sine		$R_{xx}(\tau) = e^{-a|\tau|}(b \cos 2\pi f_0 \tau + c \sin 2\pi f_0 |\tau|)$

Example 5.5. **Autospectral Density Function of Sine Wave Process.** The sine wave process described in Example 5.1 has an autocorrelation function given by

$$R_{xx}(\tau) = \frac{X^2}{2} \cos 2\pi f_0 \tau$$

Substitution into Equation (5.27) yields the two-sided result

$$S_{xx}(f) = \frac{X^2}{4} [\delta(f-f_0) + \delta(f+f_0)]$$

SPECTRAL DENSITY FUNCTIONS

Table 5.2 Special Autospectral Density Functions

Type		(One-Sided) Autospectral Function
Constant		$G_{xx}(f) = c^2 \delta(f)$
Sine wave		$G_{xx}(f) = \dfrac{X^2}{2}\delta(f-f_0)$
White noise		$G_{xx}(f) = 2a,\ f \geq 0;\quad \text{otherwise zero}$
Low-pass, white noise		$G_{xx}(f) = a,\ 0 \leq f \leq B;\quad \text{otherwise zero}$
Bandpass white noise		$G_{xx}(f) = a,\quad 0 \leq f_c - (B/2) \leq f \leq f_c + (B/2);$ otherwise zero
Exponential		$G_{xx}(f) = \dfrac{4a}{a^2 + 4\pi^2 f^2}$
Exponential cosine		$G_{xx}(f) = 2a\left[\dfrac{1}{a^2 + 4\pi^2(f+f_0)^2} + \dfrac{1}{a^2 + 4\pi^2(f-f_0)^2}\right]$
Exponential cosine, exponential sine		$G_{xx}(f) = \dfrac{2ab + 4\pi c(f+f_0)}{a^2 + 4\pi^2(f+f_0)^2} + \dfrac{2ab - 4\pi c(f-f_0)}{a^2 + 4\pi^2(f-f_0)^2}$

which consists of two delta functions at $f = f_0$ and $f = -f_0$. Then, the one-sided autospectral density function is

$$G_{xx}(f) = \frac{X^2}{2}\delta(f-f_0)$$

as pictured in Table 5.2. Note that

$$\int_0^\infty G_{xx}(f)\,df = \frac{X^2}{2} = R_{xx}(0)$$

Example 5.6. **Autospectral Density Function of Rectangular Wave Process.**
The rectangular wave process described in Example 5.2 has an exponential autocorrelation function given by

$$R_{xx}(\tau) = c^2 e^{-2\lambda|\tau|}$$

Substitution into Equation (5.27) yields the two-sided result

$$S_{xx}(f) = \frac{\lambda c^2}{\lambda^2 + \pi^2 f^2}$$

Then, the one-sided autospectral density function is

$$G_{xx}(f) = \frac{2\lambda c^2}{\lambda^2 + \pi^2 f^2}$$

as pictured in Table 5.2, where $a = 2\lambda$ and $c^2 = 1$. Note that

$$\int_0^\infty G_{xx}(f)df = c^2 = R_{xx}(0)$$

Example 5.7. **Autospectral Density Function of Sum of Two Processes.** The autocorrelation function of the sum of two stationary random processes described in Example 5.3 is

$$R_{yy}(\tau) = a_1^2 R_{x_1 x_1}(\tau) + a_1 a_2 [R_{x_1 x_2}(\tau) + R_{x_2 x_1}(\tau)] + a_2^2 R_{x_2 x_2}(\tau)$$

Substitution into Equation (5.27) yields the two-sided result

$$S_{yy}(f) = a_1^2 S_{x_1 x_1}(f) + a_1 a_2 [S_{x_1 x_2}(f) + S_{x_2 x_1}(f)] + a_2^2 S_{x_2 x_2}(f)$$

But

$$S_{x_2 x_1}(f) = S_{x_1 x_2}^*(f)$$

Hence,

$$S_{x_1 x_2}(f) + S_{x_2 x_1}(f) = 2\text{Re}[S_{x_1 x_2}(f)] = C_{x_1 x_2}(f)$$

Thus $S_{yy}(f)$ is real valued and may be expressed as

$$S_{yy}(f) = a_1^2 S_{x_1 x_1}(f) + a_1 a_2 C_{x_1 x_2}(f) + a_2^2 S_{x_2 x_2}(f)$$

The corresponding one-sided result is

$$G_{yy}(f) = a_1^2 G_{x_1 x_1}(f) + 2a_1 a_2 C_{x_1 x_2}(f) + a_2^2 G_{x_2 x_2}(f)$$

5.2.2 Spectra via Finite Fourier Transforms

The second method to define spectral density functions is also mathematical. It is based on finite Fourier transforms of the original data records and represents the procedure that is followed in present spectral density calculations.

Consider a pair of associated sample records $x_k(t)$ and $y_k(t)$ from stationary random processes $\{x_k(t)\}$ and $\{y_k(t)\}$. For a finite time interval $0 \leq t \leq T$, define

SPECTRAL DENSITY FUNCTIONS

$$S_{xy}(f, T, k) = \frac{1}{T} X_k^*(f, T) Y_k(f, T) \tag{5.56}$$

where

$$\begin{aligned} X_k(f, T) &= \int_0^T x_k(t) e^{-j2\pi ft} dt \\ Y_k(f, T) &= \int_0^T y_k(t) e^{-j2\pi ft} dt \end{aligned} \tag{5.57}$$

The quantities $X_k(f, T)$ and $Y_k(f, T)$ represent finite Fourier transforms of $x_k(t)$ and $y_k(t)$, respectively, and $X_k^*(f, T)$ is the complex conjugate of $X_k(f, T)$. These finite-range Fourier transforms will exist for general stationary records, whereas their infinite-range Fourier transforms would not exist, because the stationary data theoretically persist forever.

A common mistake made by many people is now to use analogies from periodic data to define the cross-spectral density function by

$$S_{xy}(f, k) = \lim_{T \to \infty} S_{xy}(f, T, k) \tag{5.58}$$

This is an *unsatisfactory* definition for general stationary random data because the estimate of $S_{xy}(f, k)$ by $S_{xy}(f, T, k)$ does not improve in the statistical sense of consistency (defined in Section 4.1) as T tends to infinity. Also, observe that the left-hand side is still a function of the index k. The correct way to define $S_{xy}(f)$ is by the expression

$$S_{xy}(f) = \lim_{T \to \infty} E[S_{xy}(f, T, k)] \tag{5.59}$$

where $E[S_{xy}(f, T, k)]$ is, of course, the expected value operation over the ensemble index k in question. The autospectral density functions $S_{xx}(f)$ and $S_{yy}(f)$ are merely special cases of Equation (5.59). The equivalence of the result in Equation (5.59) with that previously given in Equation (5.27) will now be proved.

Using different variables of integration to avoid confusion, Equation (5.56) becomes

$$\begin{aligned} S_{xy}(f, T, k) &= \frac{1}{T} \int_0^T x_k(\alpha) e^{-j2\pi f\alpha} d\alpha \int_0^T y_k(\beta) e^{-j2\pi f\beta} d\beta \\ &= \frac{1}{T} \int_0^T \int_0^T x_k(\alpha) y_k(\beta) e^{-j2\pi f(\beta - \alpha)} d\alpha \, d\beta \end{aligned} \tag{5.60}$$

Now, change the region of integration from (α, β) to (α, τ), where $\tau = \beta - \alpha$, $d\tau = d\beta$. This changes the limits of integration as shown in the sketch below.

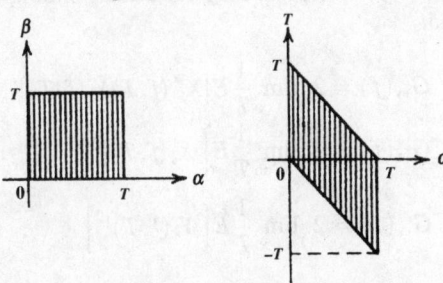

Proceed by integrating in the order (α, τ) instead of the order (α, β). This leads to

$$\int_0^T \int_0^T d\alpha\, d\beta = \int_{-T}^0 \int_{-\tau}^T d\alpha\, d\tau + \int_0^T \int_0^{T-\tau} d\alpha\, d\tau \tag{5.61}$$

As a check, it is readily verified that both sides of Equation (5.61) yield the value T^2. Hence, this change of the region of integration allows Equation (5.60) to take the form

$$\begin{aligned} S_{xy}(f, T, k) &= \int_{-T}^0 \left[\frac{1}{T} \int_{-\tau}^T x_k(\alpha) y_k(\alpha + \tau) d\alpha \right] e^{-j2\pi f \tau} d\tau \\ &+ \int_0^T \left[\frac{1}{T} \int_0^{T-\tau} x_k(\alpha) y_k(\alpha + \tau) d\alpha \right] e^{-j2\pi f \tau} d\tau \end{aligned} \tag{5.62}$$

By definition, the cross-correlation function $R_{xy}(\tau)$ is given by the expected value

$$R_{xy}(\tau) = E[x_k(\alpha) y_k(\alpha + \tau)] \tag{5.63}$$

The expected value of both sides of Equation (5.62) then gives

$$\begin{aligned} E[S_{xy}(f, T, k)] &= \int_{-T}^0 \left[\frac{1}{T} \int_{-\tau}^T R_{xy}(\tau) d\alpha \right] e^{-j2\pi f \tau} d\tau \\ &+ \int_0^T \left[\frac{1}{T} \int_0^{T-\tau} R_{xy}(\tau) d\alpha \right] e^{-j2\pi f \tau} d\tau \\ &= \int_{-T}^T \left(1 - \frac{|\tau|}{T} \right) R_{xy}(\tau) e^{-j2\pi f \tau} d\tau \end{aligned} \tag{5.64}$$

In the limit as T tends to infinity, it follows that

$$\lim_{T \to \infty} E[S_{xy}(f, T, k)] = \int_{-\infty}^{\infty} R_{xy}(\tau) e^{-j2\pi f \tau} d\tau \tag{5.65}$$

This is the desired result of Equation (5.59) since the right-hand side of Equation (5.65) is $S_{xy}(f)$, as previously defined in Equation (5.27).

Observe that when $S(f)$ is replaced by its corresponding $G(f)$, the following formulas are obtained:

$$G_{xy}(f) = 2 \lim_{T \to \infty} \frac{1}{T} E[X_k^*(f, T) Y_k(f, T)] \tag{5.66}$$

$$\begin{aligned} G_{xx}(f) &= 2 \lim_{T \to \infty} \frac{1}{T} E\left[|X_k(f, T)|^2 \right] \\ G_{yy}(f) &= 2 \lim_{T \to \infty} \frac{1}{T} E\left[|Y_k(f, T)|^2 \right] \end{aligned} \tag{5.67}$$

These formulas are estimated in fast finite Fourier transform digital computer procedures discussed later in Chapter 11. In practice, the record length T will always be finite since the limiting operation $T \to \infty$ can never be performed. The expected value operation E[ ] will also always be taken over only a finite number of ensemble elements because an infinite ensemble is impossible to obtain with real data.

5.2.3 Spectra via Filtering–Squaring–Averaging

The third way to compute autospectral density functions consists of the following operations, as pictured in Figure 5.5.

1. Frequency filtering of the signal $x(t)$ by a narrow bandpass filter of bandwidth B_e and center frequency f to obtain $x(f, B_e, t)$.
2. Squaring of the instantaneous value of the filtered signal.
3. Averaging of the squared instantaneous value over the record length T to obtain a mean square value estimate of the filtered signal.
4. Division by the filter bandwidth B_e to obtain an estimate of the rate of change of mean square value with frequency at the center frequency f.

The autospectral density function estimate is then

$$\hat{G}_{xx}(f) = \frac{1}{(B_e)T} \int_0^T x^2(f, B_e, t)\, dt \qquad (5.68)$$

Computation of the cross-spectral density function is a direct extension of this procedure using two different signals $x(t)$ and $y(t)$ with the following operations:

1. Individual frequency filtering of the two signals $x(t)$ and $y(t)$ by narrow bandpass filters having identical bandwidths B_e and the same center frequency f to obtain $x(f, B_e, t)$ and $y(f, B_e, t)$.
2. Multiplying the instantaneous values of the two filtered signals with no phase shift to obtain the in-phase terms, needed for the co-spectrum.
3. Multiplying the instantaneous values of the two filtered signals with $y(f, B_e, t)$ shifted 90° out of phase compared with $x(f, B_e, t)$ to obtain the out-of-phase terms, needed for the quad-spectrum.
4. Averaging each of the above instantaneous product values over the record length T to obtain mean product value estimates of the in-phase and out-of-phase terms.

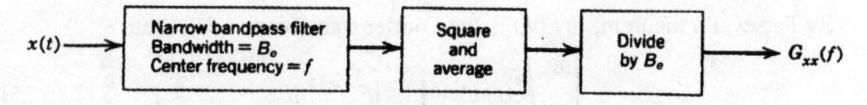

Figure 5.5 Autospectrum estimate by filtering–squaring–averaging.

5. Division of each of the two mean product value estimates by the filter bandwidth B_e to obtain estimates of $\hat{C}_{xy}(f)$ and $\hat{Q}_{xy}(f)$.

The cross-spectral density function estimate is then

$$\hat{G}_{xy}(f) = \hat{C}_{xy}(f) - j\hat{Q}_{xy}(f) \tag{5.69}$$

where

$$\hat{C}_{xy}(f) = \frac{1}{(B_e)T} \int_0^T x(f, B_e, t) y(f, B_e, t) dt$$

$$\hat{Q}_{xy}(f) = \frac{1}{(B_e)T} \int_0^T x(f, B_e, t) y^0(f, B_e, t) dt \tag{5.70}$$

The symbol $y^0(f, B_e, t)$ denotes a 90° phase shift from the filtered signal $y(f, B_e, t)$.

The equivalence of this third definition of spectral density functions with the previous two definitions in Sections 5.2.1 and 5.2.2 is not obvious and requires a proof. This will now be done for the autospectral computation. A similar proof applies for the cross-spectral computation.

Consider the autospectral formula of Equation (5.67) where

$$G_{xx}(f) = 2 \lim_{T \to \infty} \frac{1}{T} E\left[|X_k(f, T)|^2\right] \tag{5.71}$$

Although not obvious, the term

$$|X_k(f, T)|^2 = \left[\int_0^T x_k(t) \cos 2\pi f t \, dt\right]^2 + \left[\int_0^T x_k(t) \sin 2\pi f t \, dt\right]^2 \tag{5.72}$$

acts as a filter to help obtain the mean square value in any $x_k(t)$ associated with a narrow frequency band around the center frequency f. To derive this result, define for each $x_k(t)$ in $\{x_k(t)\}$

$$x_k(t, T) = \begin{cases} x_k(t) & 0 \leq t \leq T \\ 0 & \text{otherwise} \end{cases} \tag{5.73}$$

Then the mean square value of a particular $x_k(t)$ may be determined by

$$\psi_x^2(k) = \lim_{T \to \infty} \frac{1}{T} \int_0^T x_k^2(t) dt = \lim_{T \to \infty} \frac{1}{T} \int_{-\infty}^{\infty} x_k^2(t, T) dt \tag{5.74}$$

By Parseval's theorem, if $F(f)$ is the Fourier transform of $f(t)$, then

$$\int_{-\infty}^{\infty} f^2(t) dt = \int_{-\infty}^{\infty} |F(f)|^2 df \tag{5.75}$$

a relation proved in Equation (5.83). Hence, since $X_k(f, T)$ is the Fourier transform for $x_k(t, T)$, namely,

$$X_k(f, T) = \int_0^T x_k(t)e^{-j2\pi ft}dt = \int_{-\infty}^{\infty} x_k(t, T)e^{-j2\pi ft}dt \qquad (5.76)$$

it follows that

$$\psi_x^2(k) = \lim_{T\to\infty}\frac{1}{T}\int_{-\infty}^{\infty}|X_k(f,T)|^2 df = 2\lim_{T\to\infty}\frac{1}{T}\int_0^{\infty}|X_k(f,T)|^2 df \qquad (5.77)$$

Now, the expected value of $\psi_x^2(k)$ over all possible records $x_k(t)$ in $\{x_k(t)\}$ yields the familiar formula

$$\psi_x^2 = E[\psi_x^2(k)] = \int_0^{\infty} G_{xx}(f)df \qquad (5.78)$$

where $G_{xx}(f)$ is defined by Equation (5.71).

Next, suppose that $x_k(t)$ is passed through a narrow bandpass filter with a center frequency f_c and a bandwidth B_e such that the frequency response function $H(f)$ of the filter is

$$H(f) = \begin{cases} 1 & 0 \leq f_c - (B_e/2) \leq f \leq f_c + (B_e/2) \\ 0 & \text{otherwise} \end{cases} \qquad (5.79)$$

Then, the Fourier transform of the filter output is given by $H(f)X_k(f, T)$ instead of by $X_k(f, T)$. Hence in place of Equation (5.77), the mean square value of a particular filtered $x_k(t)$ becomes

$$\psi_x^2(f_c, B_e, k) = 2\lim_{T\to\infty}\frac{1}{T}\int_0^{\infty}|H(f)|^2|X_k(f,T)|^2 df \qquad (5.80)$$

The expected value of both sides of Equation (5.80) gives

$$\psi_x^2(f_c, B_e) = \int_0^{\infty}|H(f)|^2 G_{xx}(f)df = \int_{f_c-(B_e/2)}^{f_c+(B_e/2)} G_{xx}(f)df. \qquad (5.81)$$

In words, Equation (5.81) states that $G_{xx}(f)$ is *the rate of change of mean square value with frequency*. Furthermore, the term $|X_k(f, T)|^2$ must be acting as a filter on $x_k(t)$, which passes only a narrow band of frequency components in a certain range, and then squares these outputs prior to the final desired averaging operations. This is precisely how early analog spectral density analyzers operated and is the basis for the computation of time-varying spectral density functions using digital filters, as discussed in Chapter 11.

Parseval's Theorem. Let $X_1(f)$ and $X_2(f)$ be the Fourier transforms of real functions $x_1(t)$ and $x_2(t)$, respectively. The general Parseval's theorem states that

$$\int_{-\infty}^{\infty} x_1(t)x_2(t)dt = \int_{-\infty}^{\infty} X_1^*(f)X_2(f)df \qquad (5.82)$$

where $X_1^*(f)$ is the complex conjugate of $X_1(f)$.

Proof

$$x_1(t)x_2(t) = x_1(t)\int_{-\infty}^{\infty} X_2(f)\exp(j2\pi ft)df$$

$$\int_{-\infty}^{\infty} x_1(t)x_2(t)dt = \int_{-\infty}^{\infty} x_1(t)\left[\int_{-\infty}^{\infty} X_2(f)\exp(j2\pi ft)df\right]dt$$

$$= \int_{-\infty}^{\infty} X_2(f)\left[\int_{-\infty}^{\infty} x_1(t)\exp(j2\pi ft)df\right]df$$

$$= \int_{-\infty}^{\infty} X_1^*(f)X_2(f)df$$

This proves the general result. As a special case, if

$$x_1(t) = x_2(t) = x(t) \quad \text{and} \quad X_1(f) = X_2(f) = X(f)$$

then

$$X_1^*(f)X_2(f) = X^*(f)X(f) = |X(f)|^2$$

This gives the form of Parseval's theorem used in Equation (7.75), namely,

$$\int_{-\infty}^{\infty} x^2(t)dt = \int_{-\infty}^{\infty} |X(f)|^2 df \qquad (5.83)$$

5.2.4 Wavenumber Spectra

The random data considered in this book are generally defined as a function of time, denoted by t in seconds (s). However, any other parameter can replace time as the independent variable if warranted by the application of the data. In particular, some phenomena that produce random data are more conveniently described as a function of distance, denoted by δ in meters (m), rather than time. Examples include road roughness data, which are commonly measured in terms of the elevation of a road surface versus distance along the road, and atmospheric turbulence data, which are usually presented as particle velocity versus distance through the turbulence path. If such spatial random data have average properties that are invariant with distance, the data are said to be *homogeneous*, which is analogous to being stationary in time. Given two associated sample records $x_k(\delta)$ and $y_k(\delta)$ from homogeneous spatial random processes $\{x_k(\delta)\}$ and $\{y_k(\delta)\}$, the spatial Fourier transforms over a total distance D are

$$X_k(\kappa, D) = \int_0^D x_k(\delta)e^{-j2\pi\kappa\delta}d\delta \qquad Y_k(\kappa, D) = \int_0^D y_k(\delta)e^{-j2\pi\kappa\delta}d\delta \qquad (5.84)$$

where κ is called *wavenumber*, which has the units of cycles/m. The reciprocal of wavenumber is *wavelength* $\lambda = (1/\kappa)$, which has the units of m. If the units of $x(\delta)$ and

$y(\delta)$ are magnitudes V_a and V_b, respectively, versus m, then the units of $X_k(\kappa, D)$ and $Y_k(\kappa, D)$ are V_am and V_bm, respectively, versus cycles/m.

Analogous to the frequency spectral density functions for time history data defined in Equations (5.66) and (5.67), *wavenumber spectral density functions* (usually called wavenumber spectra) are defined as

$$G_{xy}(\kappa) = 2 \lim_{D \to \infty} \frac{1}{D} E\left[X_k^*(\kappa, D) Y_k(\kappa, D)\right] \quad (5.85)$$

$$G_{xx}(\kappa) = 2 \lim_{D \to \infty} \frac{1}{D} E\left[|X_k(\kappa, D)|^2\right]$$
$$G_{yy}(\kappa) = 2 \lim_{D \to \infty} \frac{1}{D} E\left[|Y_k(\kappa, D)|^2\right] \quad (5.86)$$

where all the approximations and errors discussed for frequency spectral density functions in Chapters 8 and 9 apply with time replaced by distance. If the units of $x(\delta)$ and $y(\delta)$ are magnitudes in V_a and V_b, respectively, the wavenumber cross-spectrum $G_{xy}(\kappa)$ in Equation (5.85) is generally a complex-valued function whose real and imaginary parts have the units of $V_a V_b$/(cycles/m) versus cycles/m, while the wavenumber autospectra $G_{xx}(\kappa)$ and $G_{yy}(\kappa)$ in Equation (5.86) are always real-valued functions that have the units of V_a^2/(cycles/m) and V_b^2/(cycles/m) versus cycles/m. Various related quantities and typical units for the wave-number and frequency domains are shown in Table 5.3, where the unit volts (V) represents the measured quantity, for example, height in m, velocity in m/s^2, force in N, pressure in Pa, and so on.

It should be mentioned that, when the measured quantities V_1 and V_2 are heights in meters, it is common to label the ordinate axis of a wavenumber spectrum plot as m^3 rather than m^2/(cycles/m). Also, if a spatial input load such as a road with a wavenumber spectrum of $G_{xx}(\kappa)$ in m^2/(cycles/m) versus cycles/m is transversed by a vehicle moving with a constant velocity of v in m/s, the temporal input load seen by the vehicle can be described by a frequency autospectrum $G_{xx}(f)$ in m^2/Hz, where

$$f = kv; G_{xx}(f) = G_{xx}(k)/v \quad (5.87)$$

Table 5.3 Related Quantities for Wavenumber and Frequency

Quantity	Units	Quantity	Units
Data record, $x(\delta)$	Volts (V)	Data record, $x(t)$	Volts (V)
Distance, δ	Meters (m)	Time, t	Seconds (s)
Wavenumber, κ	Cycles/m	Frequency, f	Cycles/s (Hz)
Wavelength, $\lambda = 1/\kappa$	m	Period, $P = 1/f$	s
Wavenumber spectra $G_{xx}(\kappa)$	V^2/cycles/m	Frequency spectra, $G_{xx}(f)$	V^2/cycles/s (V^2/Hz)

5.2.5 Coherence Functions

A simple, direct mathematical proof will now be carried out to show that the cross-spectral density function is bounded by the *cross-spectrum inequality*

$$|G_{xx}(f)|^2 \leq G_{xx}(f)G_{yy}(f) \tag{5.88}$$

This result is much more powerful than the corresponding cross-correlation inequality of Equation (5.11), which bounds $|R_{xy}(\tau)|^2$ in terms of the product $R_{xx}(0)R_{yy}(0)$ using values of $R_{xx}(\tau)$ and $R_{yy}(\tau)$ at $\tau = 0$.

For any value of f, the function $G_{xy}(f)$ can be expressed as

$$G_{xy}(f) = |G_{xy}(f)|e^{-j\theta_{xy}(f)}$$

using the magnitude factor $|G_{xy}(f)|$ and the phase factor $\theta_{xy}(f)$. It is also known that

$$G_{yx}(f) = G_{xy}^*(f) = |G_{xy}(f)|e^{j\theta_{xy}(f)}$$

Consider now the quantities $X_k(f)$ and $Y_k(f)e^{j\theta_{xy}(f)}$, where $X_k(f)$ and $Y_k(f)$ are finite Fourier transforms of records $x_k(t)$ and $y_k(t)$, respectively. For any real constants a and b, the absolute value quantity shown below will be greater than or equal to zero, namely,

$$|aX_k(f) + bY_k(f)e^{j\theta_{xy}(f)}|^2 \geq 0$$

This is the same as

$$a^2|X_k(f)|^2 + ab[X_k^*(f)Y_k(f)e^{j\theta_{xy}(f)} + X_k(f)Y_k^*(f)e^{-j\theta_{xy}(f)}] + b^2|Y_k(f)|^2 \geq 0$$

By taking the expectation of this equation over the index k, multiplying by $(2/T)$, and letting T increase without bound, one obtains

$$a^2 G_{xx}(f) + ab[G_{xy}(f)e^{j\theta_{xy}(f)} + G_{yx}(f)e^{-j\theta_{xy}(f)}] + b^2 G_{yy}(f) \geq 0$$

Use has been made here of the autospectra and cross-spectra formulas of Equations (5.66) and (5.67). From Equation (5.41),

$$G_{xy}(f)e^{j\theta_{xy}(f)} + G_{yx}(f)e^{-j\theta_{xy}(f)} = 2|G_{xy}(f)|$$

Hence,

$$a^2 G_{xx}(f) + 2ab|G_{xy}(f)| + b^2 G_{yy}(f) \geq 0$$

It now follows exactly as in the earlier proof for the cross-correlation inequality that Equation (5.88) is true, namely,

$$|G_{xy}(f)|^2 \leq G_{xx}(f)G_{yy}(f) \tag{5.89a}$$

SPECTRAL DENSITY FUNCTIONS

This also proves that for any f, the two-sided quantities satisfy

$$|S_{xy}(f)|^2 \leq S_{xx}(f)S_{yy}(f) \qquad (5.89b)$$

The *coherence function* (sometimes called the coherence squared function) may now be defined by

$$\gamma_{xy}^2(f) = \frac{|G_{xy}(f)|^2}{G_{xx}(f)G_{yy}(f)} = \frac{|S_{xy}(f)|^2}{S_{xx}(f)S_{yy}(f)} \qquad (5.90)$$

and satisfies for all f,

$$0 \leq \gamma_{xy}^2(f) \leq 1 \qquad (5.91)$$

A *complex coherence function* $\gamma_{xy}(f)$ may be defined by

$$\gamma_{xy}(f) = |\gamma_{xy}(f)|e^{-j\theta_{xy}(f)} \qquad (5.92)$$

where

$$|\gamma_{xy}(f)| = +\sqrt{\gamma_{xy}^2(f)} \qquad (5.93)$$

and $\theta_{xy}(f)$ is the phase angle of $G_{xy}(f)$. Throughout this book, the coherence function will always stand for the real-valued squared function of Equation (5.90) with $|\gamma_{xy}(f)|$ as the positive square root of $\gamma_{xy}^2(f)$.

5.2.6 Cross-Spectrum for Time Delay

From Equation (5.20), the cross-correlation function for the time-delay problem illustrated in Figure 5.1 is

$$R_{xy}(\tau) = \alpha R_{xx}(\tau - \tau_0) \qquad (5.94)$$

Substitution into Equation (5.27) yields the two-sided cross-spectral density function

$$S_{xy}(f) = \alpha S_{xx}(f)e^{-j2\pi f \tau_0} \qquad (5.95a)$$

The corresponding one-sided cross-spectral density function is

$$G_{xy}(f) = \alpha G_{xx}(f)e^{-j2\pi f \tau_0} \qquad (5.95b)$$

Hence, from Equation (5.41),

$$|G_{xy}(f)| = \alpha G_{xx}(f) \qquad (5.96)$$
$$\theta_{xy}(f) = 2\pi f \tau_0 \qquad (5.97)$$

Thus, the time delay τ_0 appears only in the phase angle $\theta_{xy}(f)$. Measurement of $\theta_{xy}(f)$ enables one to determine the time delay by noting that $\theta_{xy}(f)$ is a linear function of f with a slope equal to $2\pi\tau_0$, as illustrated in Figure 5.6. The attenuation factor α is

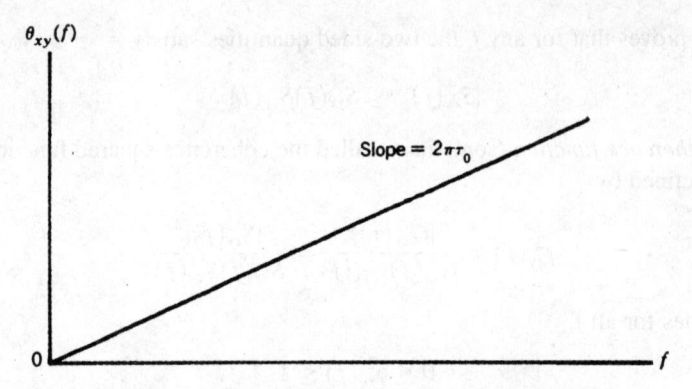

Figure 5.6 Typical phase angle plot for time-delay problem.

given at any frequency f by

$$\alpha = [|G_{xy}(f)|/G_{xx}(f)] \tag{5.98}$$

The one-sided autospectral density functions for the transmitted signal $x(t)$ and the received signal $y(t)$ in Figure 5.1 are given by $G_{xx}(f)$ and $G_{yy}(f)$, respectively, where

$$G_{yy}(f) = \alpha^2 G_{xx}(f) + G_{nn}(f) \tag{5.99}$$

This result also follows directly from Equation (5.26). The coherence function at any value of f from Equations (5.90) and (5.98) is given by

$$\gamma_{xy}^2(f) = \frac{|G_{xy}(f)|^2}{G_{xx}(f)G_{yy}(f)} = \alpha^2 \left[\frac{G_{xx}(f)}{G_{yy}(f)}\right] \tag{5.100a}$$

Observe also that the two components in $G_{yy}(f)$ are

$$\alpha^2 G_{xx}(f) = \gamma_{xy}^2(f) G_{yy}(f) = \text{spectrum in } y(t) \text{ due to } x(t)$$
$$G_{nn}(f) = [1 - \gamma_{xy}^2(f)] G_{yy}(f) = \text{spectrum in } y(t) \text{ due to } n(t)$$

These results are more significant than their integrated values over all frequencies as shown in Equation (5.25) where there is no frequency discrimination.

The coherence function of Equation (5.100) using Equation (5.99) for $G_{yy}(f)$ takes the form

$$\gamma_{xy}^2(f) = \frac{\alpha^2 G_{xx}(f)}{\alpha^2 G_{xx}(f) + G_{nn}(f)} \tag{5.100b}$$

where the terms on the right-hand side are nonnegative. For all values of f, it is clear that $\gamma_{xy}^2(f) \leq 1$ because the denominator is larger than the numerator. This result is equivalent to

$$\gamma_{xy}^2(f) = \frac{[\alpha^2 G_{xx}(f) + G_{nn}(f)] - G_{nn}(f)}{\alpha^2 G_{xx}(f) + G_{nn}(f)} = \frac{G_{yy}(f) - G_{nn}(f)}{G_{yy}(f)}$$
$$= 1 - [G_{nn}(f)/G_{yy}(f)]$$

SPECTRAL DENSITY FUNCTIONS

Again, it is clear that $\gamma_{xy}^2(f) \leq 1$ for all f since $G_{nn}(f) \leq G_{yy}(f)$. When $G_{nn}(f) = 0$, then $\gamma_{xy}^2(f) = 1$. When $G_{nn}(f) = G_{yy}(f)$, then $\gamma_{xy}^2(f) = 0$.

5.2.7 Location of Peak Value

From Equations (5.21) and (5.28), the peak value of $R_{xy}(\tau)$ is given by

$$R_{xy}(\tau)_{peak} = R_{xy}(\tau_0) = \int_{-\infty}^{\infty} S_{xy}(f) e^{j2\pi f \tau_0} df$$

Let estimates of $R_{xy}(\tau_0)$ and $S_{xy}(f)$ be denoted by $\hat{R}_{xy}(\tau_0)$ and $\hat{S}_{xy}(f)$, respectively. Then

$$\hat{S}_{xy}(f) = |\hat{S}_{xy}(f)| e^{-j\hat{\theta}_{xy}(f)}$$

gives the estimate

$$\hat{R}_{xy}(\tau_0) = \int_{-\infty}^{\infty} |\hat{S}_{xy}(f)| e^{j[2\pi f \tau_0 - \hat{\theta}_{xy}(f)]} df$$

$$= \int_{-\infty}^{\infty} |\hat{S}_{xy}(f)| \cos[2\pi f \tau_0 - \hat{\theta}_{xy}(f)] df$$

because $\hat{R}_{xy}(\tau_0)$ is real valued. At the peak location τ_0,

$$\frac{\partial \hat{R}_{xy}(\tau_0)}{\partial \tau_0} = 0 = \int_{-\infty}^{\infty} (-2\pi f) |\hat{S}_{xy}(f)| \sin[2\pi f \tau_0 - \hat{\theta}_{xy}(f)] df$$

From Equation (5.97), the estimate

$$\hat{\theta}_{xy}(f) \simeq 2\pi f \tau_0$$

so that

$$\sin[2\pi f \tau_0 - \hat{\theta}_{xy}(f)] \simeq 2\pi f \tau_0 - \hat{\theta}_{xy}(f)$$

Hence, one obtains the approximate formula

$$\int_{-\infty}^{\infty} (-2\pi f) |\hat{S}_{xy}(f)| [2\pi f \tau_0 - \hat{\theta}_{xy}(f)] df \simeq 0$$

This can be solved for τ_0 to yield the result

$$\tau_0 \simeq \frac{\int_{-\infty}^{\infty} (2\pi f) |\hat{S}_{xy}(f)| \hat{\theta}_{xy}(f) df}{\int_{-\infty}^{\infty} (2\pi f)^2 |\hat{S}_{xy}(f)| df} \quad (5.101a)$$

The use of one-sided cross-spectral density function estimates $\hat{G}_{xy}(f)$ instead of the two-sided $\hat{S}_{xy}(f)$ gives the equivalent result

$$\tau_0 \simeq \frac{\int_{0}^{\infty} (2\pi f) |\hat{G}_{xy}(f)| \hat{\theta}_{xy}(f) df}{\int_{0}^{\infty} (2\pi f)^2 |\hat{G}_{xy}(f)| df} \quad (5.101b)$$

5.2.8 Uncertainty Relation

Consider a zero mean value stationary random process $\{y(t)\}$ with an autocorrelation function $R_{yy}(\tau)$ and an associated two-sided spectral density function $S_{yy}(f)$ as defined in Equations (5.6) and (5.27), where

$$S_{yy}(f) = \int_{-\infty}^{\infty} R_{yy}(\tau) e^{-j2\pi f\tau} d\tau = 2 \int_{0}^{\infty} R_{yy}(\tau) \cos 2\pi f\tau \, d\tau$$
$$R_{yy}(\tau) = \int_{-\infty}^{\infty} S_{yy}(f) e^{j2\pi f\tau} df = 2 \int_{0}^{\infty} S_{yy}(f) \cos 2\pi f\tau \, df$$
(5.102)

It is known also that

$$R_{yy}(0) \geq R_{yy}(\tau) \qquad \text{for all } \tau$$
$$S_{yy}(f) \geq 0 \qquad \text{for all } f$$
(5.103)

In place of $S_{yy}(f)$, a one-sided spectral density function $G_{yy}(f)$ can be denoted by

$$G_{yy}(f) = \begin{cases} 2S_{yy}(f) & f > 0 \\ 0 & f < 0 \end{cases}$$
(5.104)

Thus,

$$G_{yy}(f) = 4 \int_{0}^{\infty} R_{yy}(\tau) \cos 2\pi f\tau \, d\tau \qquad R_{yy}(\tau) = \int_{0}^{\infty} G_{yy}(f) \cos 2\pi f\tau \, df \qquad (5.105)$$

Definitions can now be given for equivalent noise spectral bandwidth and equivalent noise correlation duration. A useful uncertainty relation can be proved for the product of these two quantities.

The *noise spectral bandwidth* is defined by

$$B_n = \int_{0}^{\infty} G_{yy}(f) df / G_{yy}(f)|_{\max} = R_{yy}(0) / G_{yy}(f)|_{\max} \qquad (5.106)$$

The *noise correlation duration* is denned by

$$T_n = \int_{-\infty}^{\infty} |R_{yy}(\tau)| d\tau / R_{yy}(\tau)|_{\max} = 2 \int_{0}^{\infty} |R_{yy}(\tau)| d\tau / R_{yy}(0) \qquad (5.107)$$

From these definitions, it follows that

$$B_n T_n = 2 \int_{0}^{\infty} |R_{yy}(\tau)| d\tau / G_{yy}(f)|_{\max} \qquad (5.108)$$

and estimation of this product leads to the *uncertainty relation:* for an arbitrary $R_{yy}(\tau)$ and the associated $G_{yy}(f)$, the product of B_n and T_n satisfies the inequality

$$B_n T_n \geq \frac{1}{2} \qquad (5.109)$$

Hence, as B_n becomes small, T_n must become large and, conversely, as T_n becomes small, B_n must become large.

SPECTRAL DENSITY FUNCTIONS

The uncertainty relation can be proved as follows. From Equation (5.105), for any f,

$$G_{yy}(f) \leq 4 \int_0^\infty |R_{yy}(\tau)\cos 2\pi f\tau| d\tau \leq 4 \int_0^\infty |R_{yy}(\tau)| d\tau \qquad (5.110)$$

Hence,

$$G_{yy}(f)|_{\max} \leq 4 \int_0^\infty |R_{yy}(\tau)| d\tau \qquad (5.111)$$

Substitution of Equation (5.111) into Equation (5.108) leads immediately to the result stated in Equation (5.109). Note that this simple proof does *not* require use of the Schwartz inequality of Equation (5.116).

Example 5.8. Low-Pass White Noise. For low-pass white noise, one has

$$S_{yy}(f) = a/2 \qquad -B \leq f \leq B \qquad \text{otherwise zero}$$
$$G_{yy}(f) = a \qquad 0 \leq f \leq B \qquad \text{otherwise zero}$$
$$R_{yy}(\tau) = aB\{\sin(2\pi B\tau)/(2\pi B\tau)\}$$

The noise spectral bandwidth is given here by

$$B_n = R_{yy}(0)/G_{yy}(f)|_{\max} = B$$

However, the noise correlation duration becomes

$$T_n = \frac{2\int_0^\infty |R_{yy}(\tau)| d\tau}{R_{yy}(0)} = \frac{1}{\pi B}\int_0^\infty \left|\frac{\sin u}{u}\right| du = \infty$$

Thus $B_n T_n = \infty$, which clearly satisfies the uncertainty relation of Equation (5.109). Because of the shape of $R_{yy}(\tau)$, it would appear to be appropriate here to define T_n as the width of the main lobe that represents most of the energy, namely,

$$T_n = 1/B$$

This gives $B_n T_n = 1$, which still satisfies the uncertainty relation.

Example 5.9. Gaussian Spectrum Noise. For such noise, one has

$$R_{yy}(\tau) = ae^{-2\pi\sigma^2\tau^2}$$
$$S_{yy}(f) = (a/\sigma\sqrt{2\pi})e^{-f^2/2\sigma^2} \qquad -\infty < f < \infty$$
$$G_{yy}(f) = (a\sqrt{2}/\sigma\sqrt{\pi})e^{-f^2/2\sigma^2} \qquad f \geq 0 \text{ only}$$
$$\int_0^\infty |R_{yy}(\tau)| d\tau = \frac{a}{2\sigma\sqrt{2\pi}} = \frac{G_{yy}(0)}{4}.$$

Here, the noise spectral bandwidth is

$$B_n = \frac{\sigma\sqrt{\pi}}{\sqrt{2}} \approx 1.25\sigma$$

Now

$$G_{yy}(B_n) = G_{yy}(0)e^{-\pi/4} \approx 0.456\, G_{yy}(0)$$

The noise correlation duration is

$$T_n = \frac{1}{\sigma\sqrt{2\pi}} \approx \frac{0.40}{\sigma}$$

Then

$$R_{yy}(T_n) = R_{yy}(0)e^{-\pi} \approx 0.043 R_{yy}(0)$$

Note that Gaussian noise achieves the minimum uncertainty value

$$B_n T_n = \tfrac{1}{2}$$

Example 5.10. Exponential Autocorrelation Function Noise. For noise with an exponential autocorrelation function, one has

$$R_{yy}(\tau) = Ae^{-a|\tau|} \quad a > 0$$
$$S_{yy}(f) = 2Aa/\{a^2 + (2\pi f)^2\} \quad -\infty < f < \infty$$
$$G_{yy}(f) = 4Aa/\{a^2 + (2\pi f)^2\} \quad f \geq 0 \text{ only}$$
$$\int_0^\infty |R_{yy}(\tau)|d\tau = \frac{A}{a} = \frac{G_{yy}(0)}{4}$$

The noise spectral bandwidth is given by

$$B_n = \frac{a}{4}$$

Then

$$G_{yy}(B_n) = G_{yy}(0)[1/\{1 + (\pi/2)^2\}] \approx 0.288 G_{yy}(0)$$

The noise correlation duration is

$$T_n = \frac{2}{a}$$

Thus,

$$R_{yy}(T_n) = R_{yy}(0)e^{-2} \approx 0.10 R_{yy}(0)$$

In this case also the minimum uncertainty value is achieved, that is,

$$B_n T_n = \tfrac{1}{2}$$

Other illustrations of the uncertainty relation can be seen from corresponding $R_{xx}(\tau)$ and $G_{xx}(f)$ functions in Tables 5.1 and 5.2.

5.2.9 Uncertainty Principle and Schwartz Inequality

A more general *uncertainty principle* will now be derived using the Schwartz inequality of Equation (5.116). This result applies to an arbitrary function $y(t)$ and

SPECTRAL DENSITY FUNCTIONS

its Fourier transform $Y(f)$. The function $y(t)$ should be standardized so that by the Parseval Theorem of Equation (5.83),

$$\int_{-\infty}^{\infty} y^2(t)dt = \int_{-\infty}^{\infty} |Y(f)|^2 df = 1 \tag{5.112}$$

A measure of the spread of $y(t)$ on the timescale is given by

$$T_0 = \left[\int_{-\infty}^{\infty} t^2 y^2(t)dt\right]^{1/2} \tag{5.113}$$

A corresponding measure of the spread of $Y(f)$ on the frequency scale is given by

$$B_0 = \left[\int_{-\infty}^{\infty} f^2 |Y(f)|^2 df\right]^{1/2} \tag{5.114}$$

The *uncertainty principle* states that the product

$$T_0 B_0 \geq (1/4\pi) \tag{5.115}$$

Thus, a small value for T_0 implies a large value for B_0, and conversely. The physical implication of this result is that it is impossible to localize $y(t)$ within a small region in the timescale and simultaneously to localize $Y(f)$ within a narrow band in the frequency scale. To derive the *uncertainty principle*, note that

$$j(2\pi f)Y(f) = \text{Fourier transform of } \dot{y}(t)$$

It follows by Parseval's theorem and Equation (5.114) that

$$\int_{-\infty}^{\infty} \dot{y}^2(t)dt = \int_{-\infty}^{\infty} (2\pi f)^2 |Y(f)|^2 df = (2\pi)^2 B_0^2$$

Hence, the product $T_0 B_0$ is the same as

$$T_0 B_0 = (1/2\pi)\left[\int_{-\infty}^{\infty} t^2 y^2(t)dt\right]^{1/2} \left[\int_{-\infty}^{\infty} \dot{y}^2(t)dt\right]^{1/2}$$

The Schwartz inequality of Equation (5.116) should now be applied by letting $f(t) = ty(t)$ and $g(t) = \dot{y}(t)$. This gives the result that

$$T_0 B_0 \geq (1/2\pi) \int_{-\infty}^{\infty} ty(t)\dot{y}(t)dt$$

One should next integrate by parts with the formula $\int u\, dv = uv - \int v\, du$ by setting $u = t$ and $dv = y(t)\dot{y}(t)$. Then $du = dt$ and $v = [y^2(t)/2]$. Assuming the integrated portion goes to zero as t approaches $\pm$ infinity,

$$T_0 B_0 \geq (1/4\pi) \int_{-\infty}^{\infty} y^2(t)dt = (1/4\pi)$$

because $y(t)$ is standardized. This completes the proof.

5.2.9.1 Schwartz Inequality

The Schwartz inequality states that for two functions $f(t)$ and $g(t)$ with arbitrary integral limits, under quite general conditions,

$$\int |f(t)|^2 dt \int |g(t)|^2 dt \geq \left[\int f(t)g(t)dt\right]^2 \qquad (5.116)$$

The equality occurs only when $f(t)/g(t)$ equals a constant. A simple proof of Schwartz's inequality comes from the observation that the integral $\int |af(t) + bg(t)|^2 dt > 0$ for all real values of a and b unless $af(t) + bg(t) = 0$. This implies that the discriminant of the resulting quadratic equation in (a/b) must be negative. Setting this discrimination less than zero proves the Schwartz inequality.

5.3 ERGODIC AND GAUSSIAN RANDOM PROCESSES

The most important stationary random processes in practice are those considered to be

a. Ergodic with arbitrary probability structure.
b. Gaussian whether ergodic or not.

Various cases will now be examined, including linear transformations of random processes.

5.3.1 Ergodic Random Processes

Consider two weakly stationary random processes $\{x_k(t)\}$ and $\{y_k(t)\}$ with two arbitrary sample functions $x_k(t)$ and $y_k(t)$. These stationary random processes are said to be *weakly ergodic* if the mean values and covariance (correlation) functions, which are defined by certain *ensemble averages* in Section 5.1.1, may be calculated by performing corresponding *time averages* on the arbitrary pair of sample functions. In this way, the underlying statistical structure of the weakly stationary random processes may be determined quite simply from an available sample pair without the need for collecting a considerable amount of data.

To be more specific, the mean values of the individual sample functions $x_k(t)$ and $y_k(t)$, when computed by a time average, may be represented by

$$\mu_x(k) = \lim_{T \to \infty} \frac{1}{T} \int_0^T x_k(t)dt$$

$$\mu_y(k) = \lim_{T \to \infty} \frac{1}{T} \int_0^T y_k(t)dt \qquad (5.117)$$

Observe that the answer is no longer a function of t, because t has been averaged out. In general, however, the answer is a function of the particular sample function chosen, denoted by the index k.

ERGODIC AND GAUSSIAN RANDOM PROCESSES

The cross-covariance function and cross-correlation function between $x_k(t)$ and $y_k(t + \tau)$, when computed by a time average, are defined by the expression

$$\begin{aligned}
C_{xy}(\tau, k) &= \lim_{T \to \infty} \frac{1}{T} \int_0^T [x_k(t) - \mu_x(k)][y_k(t+\tau) - \mu_y(k)] dt \\
&= \lim_{T \to \infty} \frac{1}{T} \int_0^T x_k(t) y_k(t+\tau) dt - \mu_x(k) \mu_y(k) \\
&= R_{xy}(\tau, k) - \mu_x(k) \mu_y(k)
\end{aligned} \quad (5.118)$$

The autocovariance functions and autocorrelation functions are defined by

$$\begin{aligned}
C_{xx}(\tau, k) &= \lim_{T \to \infty} \frac{1}{T} \int_0^T [x_k(t) - \mu_x(k)][x_k(t+\tau) - \mu_x(k)] dt \\
&= R_{xx}(\tau, k) - \mu_x^2(k) \\
C_{yy}(\tau, k) &= \lim_{T \to \infty} \frac{1}{T} \int_0^T [y_k(t) - \mu_y(k)][y_k(t+\tau) - \mu_y(k)] dt \\
&= R_{yy}(\tau, k) - \mu_y^2(k)
\end{aligned} \quad (5.119)$$

These quantities should now be compared with the previously defined ensemble mean values μ_x, μ_y, and ensemble covariance functions $C_{xx}(\tau)$, $C_{yy}(\tau)$, and $C_{xy}(\tau)$ for stationary random processes developed in Section 5.1.1. If it turns out that, independent of k,

$$\begin{aligned}
\mu_x(k) &= \mu_x \\
\mu_y(k) &= \mu_y \\
C_{xx}(\tau, k) &= C_{xx}(\tau) \\
C_{yy}(\tau, k) &= C_{yy}(\tau) \\
C_{xy}(\tau, k) &= C_{xy}(\tau)
\end{aligned} \quad (5.120)$$

then the random processes $\{x_k(t)\}$ and $\{y_k(t)\}$ are said to be *weakly ergodic*. If all ensemble-averaged statistical properties of $\{x_k(t)\}$ and $\{y_k(t)\}$, not just the means and covariances, are deducible from corresponding time averages, then the random processes are said to be *strongly ergodic*. Thus strong ergodicity implies weak ergodicity, but not conversely. No distinction between these concepts exists for Gaussian random processes.

For an arbitrary random process to be ergodic, it must first be stationary. Each sample function must then be representative of all the others in the sense described above so that it does not matter which particular sample function is used in the time-averaging calculations. With arbitrary ergodic processes $\{x(t)\}$ and $\{y(t)\}$, in place of Equation (5.6), their autocorrelation and cross-correlation functions are defined by

$$\begin{aligned}
R_{xx}(\tau) &= \lim_{T \to \infty} \frac{1}{T} \int_0^T x(t) x(t+\tau) dt \\
R_{yy}(\tau) &= \lim_{T \to \infty} \frac{1}{T} \int_0^T y(t) y(t+\tau) dt \\
R_{xy}(\tau) &= \lim_{T \to \infty} \frac{1}{T} \int_0^T x(t) y(t+\tau) dt
\end{aligned} \quad (5.121)$$

Example 5.11. **Nonergodic Stationary Random Process.** A simple example of a nonergodic stationary random process follows. Consider a hypothetical random process $\{x_k(t)\}$ composed of sinusoidal sample functions such that

$$\{x_k(t)\} = \{X_k \sin[2\pi ft + \theta_k]\}$$

Let the amplitude X_k and the phase angle θ_k be random variables that take on a different set of values for each sample function, as illustrated in Figure 5.7. If θ_k is uniformly distributed, the properties of the process computed over the ensemble at specific times will be independent of time; hence the process is stationary. The properties computed by time averaging over individual sample functions are not always the same, however. For example, the autocovariance (or autocorrelation) function for each sample function is given here by

$$C_{xx}(\tau, k) = \frac{X_k^2}{2} \sin 2\pi f \tau$$

Because X_k is a function of k, $C_{xx}(\tau, k) \neq C_x(\tau)$. Hence, the random process is nonergodic.

Instead of having random amplitudes $\{X_k\}$, suppose each amplitude is the same X independent of k. Now the random process consists of sinusoidal sample functions such that

$$\{x_k(t)\} = \{X \sin(2\pi ft + \theta_k)\}$$

Note: Different initial phase angles, *different* amplitude, same frequency

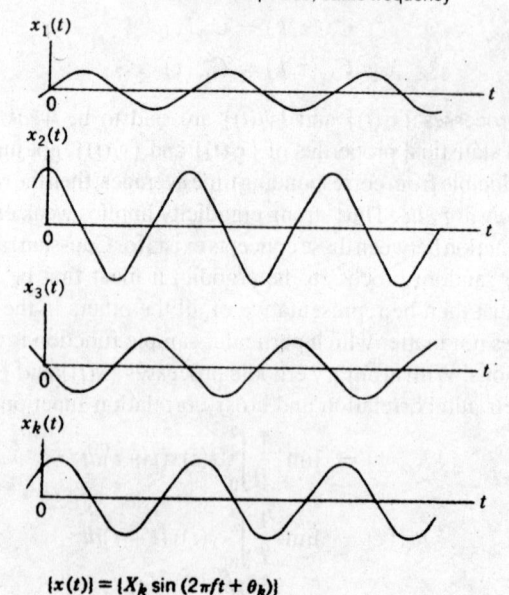

$\{x(t)\} = \{X_k \sin(2\pi ft + \theta_k)\}$

Figure 5.7 Illustration of nonergodic stationary sine wave process.

Note: Different initial phase angles, same amplitude, same frequency

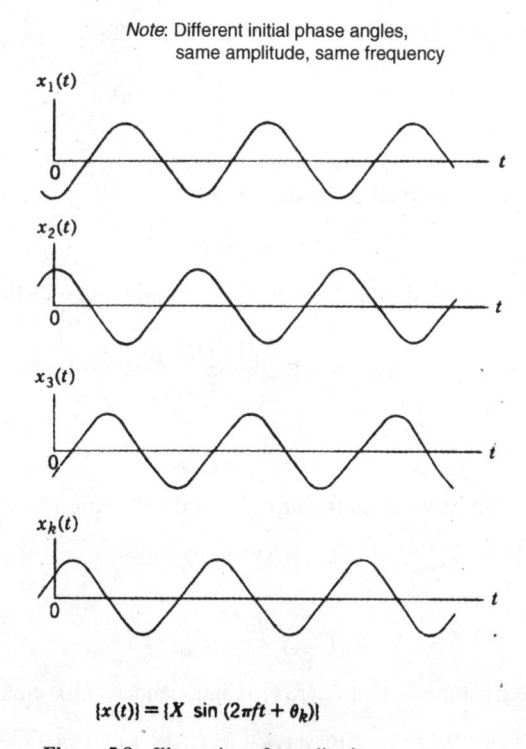

$\{x(t)\} = \{X \sin(2\pi ft + \theta_k)\}$

Figure 5.8 Illustration of ergodic sine wave process.

For this case, the random process is ergodic, with each record statistically equivalent to every other record for any time-averaging results, as illustrated in Figure 5.8. This concludes Example 5.11.

5.3.2 Sufficient Condition for Ergodicity

There are two important classes of random processes that one can state in advance will be ergodic. The first ergodic class is the class of stationary Gaussian random processes whose autospectral density functions are absolutely continuous; that is, no delta functions appear in the autospectra corresponding to infinite spectral densities at discrete frequencies. The second ergodic class (a special case of the first class) is the class of stationary Gaussian Markov processes; a Markov process is one whose relationship to the past does not extend beyond the immediately preceding observation. The autocorrelation function of a stationary Gaussian Markov process may be shown to be of a simple exponential form [Ref. 4].

Sufficient conditions for a random process to be ergodic are as follows:

> I. A sufficient condition for an arbitrary random process to be weakly ergodic is that it be weakly stationary and that the time averages $\mu_x(k)$ and $C_{xx}(\tau, k)$ be the same for all sample functions k.

The proof of this result is as follows. By definition,

$$\mu_x(k) = \lim_{T \to \infty} \frac{1}{T} \int_0^T x_k(t) dt$$

By hypothesis, $\mu_x(k)$ is independent of k. Hence, the expected value over k is the same as an individual estimate, namely,

$$E[\mu_x(k)] = \mu_x(k)$$

Also, as will be proved later, expected values commute with linear operations. Hence,

$$E[\mu_x(k)] = \lim_{T \to \infty} \frac{1}{T} \int_0^T E[x_k(t)] dt$$

$$= \lim_{T \to \infty} \frac{1}{T} \int_0^T \mu_x dt = \mu_x$$

The assumption of weak stationarity is used in setting $E[x_k(t)] = \mu_x$. Thus,

$$\mu_x(k) = \mu_x$$

Similarly,

$$C_{xx}(\tau, k) = C_{xx}(\tau)$$

because the hypothesis that $C_x(\tau, k)$ is independent of k yields

$$E[C_{xx}(\tau, k)] = C_{xx}(\tau, k)$$

whereas the stationary hypothesis yields

$$E[C_{xx}(\tau, k)] = C_{xx}(\tau)$$

This completes the proof.

II. A sufficient condition for a Gaussian random process to be ergodic is that it be weakly stationary, and the autocovariance function $C_{xx}(\tau)$ has the following four integrable properties.

$$\int_{-\infty}^{\infty} |C_{xx}(\tau)| d\tau < \infty \quad \int_{-\infty}^{\infty} C_{xx}^2(\tau) d\tau < \infty$$

$$\int_{-\infty}^{\infty} |\tau C_{xx}(\tau)| d\tau < \infty \quad \int_{-\infty}^{\infty} |\tau| C_{xx}^2(\tau) d\tau < \infty$$
(5.122)

The four conditions of Equation (5.122) can be replaced by the single requirement that

$$\frac{1}{T} \int_{-T}^{T} |C_{xx}(\tau)| d\tau \to 0 \quad \text{as } T \to \infty \qquad (5.123)$$

The proof of this result is in Sections 8.2.1 and 8.2.2, where it is shown that mean value and autocorrelation function estimates produced by time averages are independent of the particular sample record when Equation (5.122) is satisfied. Result II then follows from Result I. In practice, these conditions are usually satisfied, justifying the assumption of ergodicity.

5.3.3 Gaussian Random Processes

The formal definition of a Gaussian random process is as follows. A random process $\{x_k(t)\}$ is said to be a Gaussian random process if, for every set of fixed times $\{t_n\}$, the random variables $x_k(t_n)$ follow a multidimensional normal distribution as defined by Equation (3.63). Gaussian random processes are quite prevalent in physical problems and often may be mathematically predicted by the multidimensional central limit theorem. Also, it can be shown that if a Gaussian process undergoes a linear transformation, then the output will still be a Gaussian process. This property is quite important in various theoretical and practical applications of random process theory.

Consider a time history $x(t)$, which is a sample function from an ergodic Gaussian random process with a zero mean value. Note that the index k is no longer needed because the properties of any one sample function will be representative of all other sample functions. From the ergodic property, the behavior of $x(t)$ over a long period of time will exhibit the same statistical characteristics as corresponding ensemble averages at various fixed times. As a consequence, it follows that the probability density function associated with the instantaneous values of $x(t)$ that will occur over a long time interval is given by the Gaussian probability density function with zero mean value, as follows:

$$p(x) = (\sigma_x \sqrt{2\pi})^{-1} e^{-x^2/2\sigma_x^2} \tag{5.124}$$

The variance σ_x^2 when $x(t)$ has a zero mean is determined by

$$\sigma_x^2 = E[x^2(t)] = \int_{-\infty}^{\infty} x^2 p(x) dx \quad \text{independent of } t$$

$$\approx \frac{1}{T} \int_0^T x^2(t) dt \quad \text{for large } T \tag{5.125}$$

$$= \int_{-\infty}^{\infty} S_{xx}(f) df = 2 \int_0^{\infty} S_{xx}(f) df = \int_0^{\infty} G_{xx}(f) df$$

Thus, the Gaussian probability density function $p(x)$ is completely characterized through a knowledge of $S_{xx}(f)$ or $G_{xx}(f)$ since they alone determine σ_x. This important result places a knowledge of $S_{xx}(f)$ or $G_{xx}(f)$ at the forefront of much work in the analysis of random records. It should be noted that no restriction is placed on the shape of the autospectral density function or its associated autocorrelation function.

If the mean value of $x(t)$ is not zero, then the underlying probability density function is given by the general Gaussian formula

$$p(x) = (\sigma_x \sqrt{2\pi})^{-1} e^{-(x-\mu_x)^2/2\sigma_x^2} \tag{5.126}$$

where the mean value

$$\mu_x = E[x(t)] = \int_{-\infty}^{\infty} x p(x) dx \quad \text{independent of } t$$

$$\approx \frac{1}{T} \int_0^T x(t) dt \quad \text{for large } T \tag{5.127}$$

and the variance

$$\sigma_x^2 = E[(x(t)-\mu_x)^2] = E[x^2(t)]-\mu_x^2 \tag{5.128}$$

Assume that $\{x(t)\}$ is a stationary Gaussian random process where the index k is omitted for simplicity in notation. Consider the two random variables $x_1 = x(t)$ and $x_2 = x(t + \tau)$ at an arbitrary pair of fixed times t and $t + \tau$. Assume that x_1 and x_2 follow a two-dimensional (joint) Gaussian distribution with *zero means* and *equal variances* σ_x^2. By definition, then

$$\sigma_x^2 = E[x^2(t)] = E[x^2(t+\tau)] = \int_{-\infty}^{\infty} x^2 p(x)dx \tag{5.129}$$

$$R_{xx}(\tau) = E[x(t)x(t+\tau)] = \rho_{xx}(\tau)\sigma_x^2 = \iint_{-\infty}^{\infty} x_1 x_2 p(x_1,x_2) dx_1 dx_2 \tag{5.130}$$

The quantity $\rho_{xx}(\tau)$ is the correlation coefficient function of Equation (5.16) for $C_{x_1 x_2}(\tau) = R_{xx}(\tau)$ and $\sigma_{x_1} = \sigma_{x_2} = \sigma_x$, namely,

$$\rho_{xx}(\tau) = \frac{R_{xx}(\tau)}{\sigma_x^2} \tag{5.131}$$

Letting $\rho = \rho_{xx}(\tau)$ and $\mu = 0$, the joint Gaussian probability density function is given by

$$p(x_1,x_2) = (2\pi\sigma_x^2\sqrt{1-\rho^2})^{-1}\exp\left[\frac{-1}{2\sigma_x^2(1-\rho^2)}(x_1^2 - 2\rho x_1 x_2 + x_2^2)\right] \tag{5.132}$$

All properties developed in Section 3.3 apply to joint Gaussian random processes at any set of fixed times.

Consider four random variables x_1, x_2, x_3, x_4, with zero mean values, which follow a four-dimensional Gaussian distribution. From Equation (3.73),

$$E[x_1 x_2 x_3 x_4] = E[x_1 x_2]E[x_3 x_4] + E[x_1 x_3]E[x_2 x_4] + E[x_1 x_4]E[x_2 x_3] \tag{5.133}$$

In particular, let $x_1 = x(u), x_2 = y(u + \tau), x_3 = x(v), x_4 = y(v + \tau)$, and let $R_{xy}(\tau)$ be the stationary cross-correlation function given by

$$R_{xy}(\tau) = E[x(t)y(t+\tau)] \tag{5.134}$$

It now follows from Equation (5.133) that

$$\begin{aligned} E[x(u)y(u+\tau)x(v)y(v+\tau)] &= R_{xy}^2(\tau) + R_{xx}(v-u)R_{yy}(v-u) \\ &\quad + R_{xy}(v-u+\tau)R_{yx}(v-u-\tau) \end{aligned} \tag{5.135}$$

This result will be used later in Equation (8.99).

5.3.4 Linear Transformations of Random Processes

The dynamic behavior of representative linear physical systems has been discussed in practical terms in Chapter 2. It will be helpful at this time to consider very briefly the mathematical properties of linear transformations of random processes. This background will be assumed in Chapters 6 and 7 to develop important input/output relationships for linear systems subjected to random inputs.

Consider an arbitrary random process $\{x_k(t)\}$. An operator A that transforms a sample function $x_k(t)$ into another function $y_k(v)$ may be written as

$$y_k(v) = A[x_k(t)] \qquad (5.136)$$

where A denotes a functional operation on the term inside the brackets [ ]. The argument v may or may not be the same as t. For example, if the operation in question is differentiation, then $v = t$ and $y_k(t)$ will be a sample function from the derivative random process $\{\dot{x}_k(t)\}$, assuming of course that the derivative exists. A different example is when the operation in question is integration between definite limits. Here, $v \neq t$, and $y_k(v)$ will be a random variable over the index k, determined by $x_k(t)$ and the definite limits. The operator A can take many different forms. In the following, the sample space index k will be omitted for simplicity in notation.

The operator A is said to be *linear* if, for any set of admissible values $x_1, x_2, \ldots, x_N$ and constants $a_1, a_2, \ldots, a_N$, it follows that

$$A\left[\sum_{i=1}^{N} a_i x_i\right] = \sum_{i=1}^{N} a_i A[x_i] \qquad (5.137)$$

In words, the operation is both additive and homogeneous. The admissible values here may be different sample functions at the same t, or they may be different values from the same sample function at different t.

The operator A is said to be *time invariant* if any shift t_0 of the input $x(t)$ to $x(t + t_0)$ causes a similar shift of the output $y(t)$ to $y(t + t_0)$. In equation form,

$$y(t + t_0) = A[x(t + t_0)] \quad \text{for any } t_0 \qquad (5.138)$$

Unless stated otherwise, all linear systems will henceforth be assumed to be time invariant. Such systems are the constant-parameter linear systems of Chapter 2.

For any linear operation where all quantities exist, the procedure of taking expected values of random variables is commutative with the linear operation. That is, for fixed t and v,

$$E[y(v)] = E[A[x(t)]] = A[E[x(t)]] \qquad (5.139)$$

This result is proved easily, as follows. Assume $x(t)$ takes on N discrete values $x_1, x_2, \ldots, x_N$, and $y(v)$ takes on N corresponding discrete values $y_1, y_2, \ldots, y_N$, where $y_i = A[x_i]$. Then

$$E[y(v)] = \frac{1}{N}\sum_{i=1}^{N} y_i = \frac{1}{N}\sum_{i=1}^{N} A[x_i] \quad \text{and} \quad E[x(t)] = \frac{1}{N}\sum_{i=1}^{N} x_i$$

Now, because A is a linear operator,

$$\frac{1}{N}\sum_{i=1}^{N} A[x_i] = A\left[\frac{1}{N}\sum_{i=1}^{N} x_i\right] = A[E[x(t)]]$$

Hence

$$E[y(v)] = A[E[x(t)]] \tag{5.140}$$

The continuous case follows by letting N approach infinity and using an appropriate convergence criterion, such as Equation (5.143) to follow. This completes the proof.

A basic result whose proof evolves directly from definitions is as follows. *If $x(t)$ is from a weakly (strongly) stationary random process and if the operator A is linear and time invariant, then $y(v) = A[x(t)]$ will form a weakly (strongly) stationary random process.* Another result of special significance, proved in Ref. 5, is as follows. *If $x(t)$ follows a Gaussian distribution and the operator A is linear, then $y(v) = A[x(t)]$ will also follow a Gaussian distribution.*

An integral transformation of any particular sample function $x(t)$ from an arbitrary random process $\{x(t)\}$ is defined by

$$I = \int_a^b x(t)\phi(t)\, dt \tag{5.141}$$

where $\phi(t)$ is an arbitrary given function for which the integral exists. For any given $\phi(t)$ and limits (a, b), the quantity I is a random variable that depends on the particular sample function $x(t)$. To investigate statistical properties of the random variable I, it is customary to break up the integration interval (a, b) into subintervals Δt and consider the approximation linear sum

$$I_N = \sum_{i=1}^{N} x(i\Delta t)\phi(i\Delta t)\,\Delta t \tag{5.142}$$

Convergence of I_N to I may be defined by two different criteria. Specifically, the sequence $\{I_N\}$ is said to converge to I

1. In the *mean square sense* if

$$\lim_{N\to\infty} E[|I_N - I|^2] = 0 \tag{5.143}$$

2. In *probability* if for every $\varepsilon > 0$

$$\lim_{N\to\infty} \text{Prob}[|I_N - I| \geq \varepsilon] = 0$$

From the Chebyshev inequality of Equation (3.23), it follows directly that convergence in the mean square sense implies convergence in probability. In practice, most integral expressions involving random variables exist by assuming convergence in the mean square sense.

5.4 DERIVATIVE RANDOM PROCESSES

The derivative of any particular sample function $x(t)$ from an arbitrary random process $\{x(t)\}$ is defined by

$$\dot{x}(t) = \frac{dx(t)}{dt} = \lim_{\varepsilon \to 0} \left[\frac{x(t+\varepsilon) - x(t)}{\varepsilon} \right] \quad (5.144)$$

Existence of this limit may occur in different ways. The derivative $\dot{x}(t)$ is said to exist

1. In the *usual sense* if the limit exists for all functions $x(t)$ in $\{x(t)\}$.
2. In the *mean square sense* if

$$\lim_{\varepsilon \to 0} E\left[\left| \frac{x(t+\varepsilon) - x(t)}{\varepsilon} - \dot{x}(t) \right|^2 \right] = 0 \quad (5.145)$$

For a stationary random process, a necessary and sufficient condition for $\dot{x}(t)$ to exist in the mean square sense is that its autocorrelation function $R_{xx}(\tau)$ should have derivatives of order up to 2; that is, $R'_{xx}(\tau)$ and R''_{xx} must exist [Ref. 5].

5.4.1 Correlation Functions

Consider the following derivative functions, which are assumed to be well defined:

$$R'_{xx}(\tau) = \frac{dR_{xx}(\tau)}{d\tau} \quad R''_{xx}(\tau) = \frac{d^2 R_{xx}(\tau)}{d\tau^2}$$
$$\dot{x}(t) = \frac{dx(t)}{dt} \quad \ddot{x}(t) = \frac{d^2 x(t)}{dt^2} \quad (5.146)$$

By definition, for stationary random data,

$$R_{xx}(\tau) = E[x(t)x(t+\tau)] = E[x(t-\tau)x(t)]$$
$$R_{x\dot{x}}(\tau) = E[x(t)\dot{x}(t+\tau)] = E[x(t-\tau)\dot{x}(t)] \quad (5.147)$$
$$R_{\dot{x}\dot{x}}(\tau) = E[\dot{x}(t)\dot{x}(t+\tau)] = E[\dot{x}(t-\tau)\dot{x}(t)]$$

Now

$$R'_{xx}(\tau) = \frac{d}{d\tau} E[x(t)x(t+\tau)] = E[x(t)\dot{x}(t+\tau)] = R_{x\dot{x}}(\tau) \quad (5.148)$$

Also,

$$R'_{xx}(\tau) = \frac{d}{d\tau} E[x(t-\tau)x(t)] = -E[\dot{x}(t-\tau)x(t)] = -R_{\dot{x}x}(\tau)$$

Hence,

$$R'_{xx}(0) = R_{x\dot{x}}(0) = -R_{\dot{x}x}(0) = 0 \quad (5.149)$$

since $R'_{xx}(0)$ equals the positive and negative of the same quantity. The corresponding $R_{xx}(0)$ is a maximum value of $R_{xx}(\tau)$. This proves that for stationary random data

$$E[x(t)\dot{x}(t)] = 0 \qquad (5.150)$$

In words, at any t, Equation (5.150) indicates that the derivative $\{\dot{x}(t)\}$ for stationary random data $\{x(t)\}$ is equally likely to be positive or negative. Equation (5.148) states that the derivative $R'_{xx}(\tau)$ of the autocorrelation function $R_{xx}(\tau)$ with respect to τ is the same as the cross-correlation function between $\{x(t)\}$ and $\{\dot{x}(t)\}$. A maximum value for the autocorrelation function $R_{xx}(\tau)$ corresponds to a zero crossing for its derivative $R'_{xx}(t)$, which becomes a zero crossing for the cross-correlation function between $\{x(t)\}$ and $\{\dot{x}(t)\}$. This crossing of zero by $R'_{xx}(\tau)$ will be with *negative* slope, that is

$$R'_{xx}(0-) > 0 \quad \text{and} \quad R'_{xx}(0+) < 0 \qquad (5.151)$$

as can be seen from the picture in Figure 5.9. In practice, determining the location where zero crossings will occur is usually easier than determining the location of maximum values.

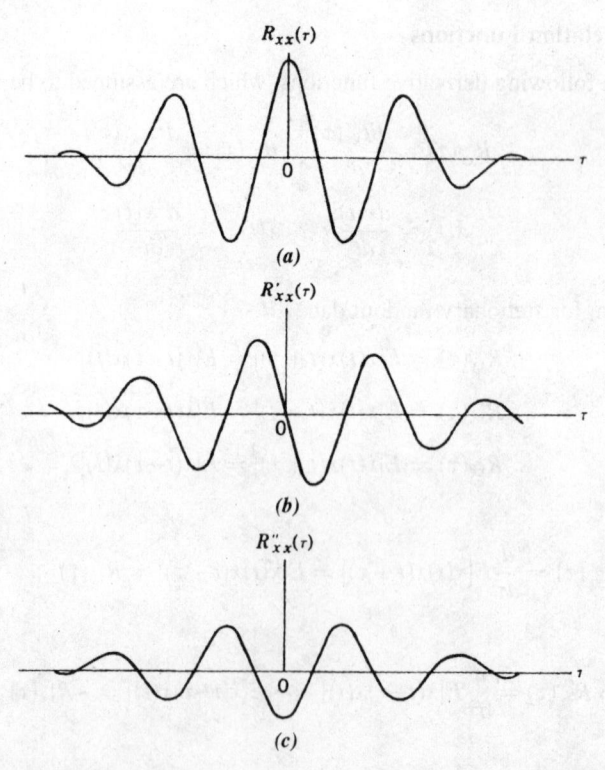

Figure 5.9 Illustration of derivatives of autocorrelation functions. (*a*) Original function. (*b*) First derivative. (*c*) Second derivative.

DERIVATIVE RANDOM PROCESSES

It will now be shown that $R'_{xx}(\tau)$ is an odd function of τ corresponding to $R_{xx}(\tau)$ being an even function of τ. By definition

$$R_{xx}(-\tau) = E[x(t)x(t-\tau)] = E[x(t+\tau)x(t)] \tag{5.152}$$

Hence,

$$R'_{xx}(-\tau) = \frac{d}{d\tau}E[x(t+\tau)x(t)] = E[\dot{x}(t+\tau)x(t)] = R_{\dot{x}x}(\tau) \tag{5.153}$$

But, as shown earlier, $R_{\dot{x}x}(\tau) = -R'_{xx}(\tau)$. Hence Equation (5.153) becomes

$$R'_{xx}(-\tau) = -R'_{xx}(\tau) \tag{5.154}$$

This proves that $R'_{xx}(\tau)$ is an odd function of τ.

The second derivative gives

$$\begin{aligned}R''_{xx}(\tau) &= \frac{d}{d\tau}R'_{xx}(\tau) = \frac{d}{d\tau}R_{x\dot{x}}(\tau) = \frac{d}{d\tau}E[x(t-\tau)\dot{x}(t)] \\ &= -E[\dot{x}(t-\tau)\dot{x}(t)] = -R_{\dot{x}\dot{x}}(\tau)\end{aligned} \tag{5.155}$$

Also,

$$\begin{aligned}R''_{xx}(\tau) &= \frac{d}{d\tau}R'_{xx}(\tau) = \frac{d}{d\tau}R_{x\dot{x}}(\tau) = \frac{d}{d\tau}E[x(t)\dot{x}(t+\tau)] \\ &= E[x(t)\ddot{x}(t+\tau)] = R_{x\ddot{x}}(\tau)\end{aligned} \tag{5.156}$$

One can also verify directly that $R''_{xx}(\tau)$ is an even function of τ, namely,

$$R''_{xx}(-\tau) = R''_{xx}(\tau) \tag{5.157}$$

At $\tau = 0$, one obtains

$$E[\dot{x}^2(t)] = R_{\dot{x}\dot{x}}(0) = -R_{\dot{x}\dot{x}}(0) - R''_{xx}(0) \tag{5.158}$$

As shown earlier,

$$R_{x\dot{x}}(\tau) = \frac{d}{d\tau}R_{xx}(\tau) = R'_{xx}(\tau) \tag{5.159}$$

Typical plots for $R_{xx}(\tau)$, $R'_{xx}(\tau)$, and $R''_{xx}(\tau)$ are drawn in Figure 5.9, based on a sine wave process where

$$\begin{aligned}R_{xx}(\tau) &= X \cos 2\pi f_0 \tau \\ R'_{xx}(\tau) &= -X(2\pi f_0)\sin 2\pi f_0 \tau \\ R''_{xx}(\tau) &= -X(2\pi f_0)^2 \cos 2\pi f_0 \tau\end{aligned} \tag{5.160}$$

The results given above can be extended to higher order derivatives. For example,

$$R_{x\ddot{x}}(\tau) = \frac{d}{d\tau} R_{\dot{x}\dot{x}}(\tau) = -R_{xx}'''(\tau) \tag{5.161}$$

$$R_{\dot{x}\ddot{x}}(\tau) = -\frac{d}{d\tau} R_{\ddot{x}\ddot{x}}(\tau) = R_{xx}'''(\tau) \tag{5.162}$$

At $\tau = 0$, one obtains

$$E[\ddot{x}^2(t)] = R_{\ddot{x}\ddot{x}}(0) = R_{xx}''''(0) \tag{5.163}$$

Thus, knowledge of $R_{xx}(\tau)$ and its successive derivatives can enable one to state the properties for autocorrelation and cross-correlation functions between $\{x(t)\}$ and its successive derivatives $\{\dot{x}(t)\}$, $\{\ddot{x}(t)\}$ and so on.

5.4.2 Spectral Density Functions

It is easy to derive corresponding properties for the autospectral and cross-spectral density functions between $\{x(t)\}$ and its successive derivatives $\{\dot{x}(t)\}$ and $\{\ddot{x}(t)\}$. Let

$$X(f) = \mathscr{F}[x(t)] = \text{Fourier transform}[x(t)] \tag{5.164}$$

Then

$$\mathscr{F}[\dot{x}(t)] = (j2\pi f)X(f) \tag{5.165}$$

$$\mathscr{F}[\ddot{x}(t)] = -(2\pi f)^2 X(f) \tag{5.166}$$

From Equations (5.66) and (5.67), it follows directly that

$$G_{x\dot{x}}(f) = j(2\pi f) G_{xx}(f) \tag{5.167}$$

$$G_{\dot{x}\dot{x}}(f) = (2\pi f)^2 G_{xx}(f) \tag{5.168}$$

$$G_{x\ddot{x}}(f) = j(2\pi f)^3 G_{xx}(f) \tag{5.169}$$

$$G_{\ddot{x}\ddot{x}}(f) = (2\pi f)^4 G_{xx}(f) \tag{5.170}$$

and so on. These formulas are the same with one-sided G's replaced by the corresponding two-sided S's.

These results can also be derived from the Wiener–Khincnine relations of Equation (5.28). Start with the basic relation

$$R_{xx}(\tau) = \int_{-\infty}^{\infty} S_{xx}(f) e^{j2\pi f \tau} df \tag{5.171}$$

Then successive derivatives will be

$$R_{xx}'(\tau) = j \int_{-\infty}^{\infty} (2\pi f) S_{xx}(f) e^{j2\pi f \tau} df \tag{5.172}$$

$$R_{xx}''(\tau) = -\int_{-\infty}^{\infty} (2\pi f)^2 S_{xx}(f) e^{j2\pi f \tau} df \tag{5.173}$$

LEVEL CROSSINGS AND PEAK VALUES

$$R'''_{xx}(\tau) = -j \int_{-\infty}^{\infty} (2\pi f)^3 S_{xx}(f) e^{j2\pi f \tau} df \qquad (5.174)$$

$$R''''_{xx}(\tau) = \int_{-\infty}^{\infty} (2\pi f)^4 S_{xx}(f) e^{j2\pi f \tau} df \qquad (5.175)$$

The Wiener-Khinchine relations, together with previous formulas in Section 5.4.1, show that these four derivative expressions are the same as

$$R'_{xx}(\tau) = R_{x\dot{x}}(\tau) = \int_{-\infty}^{\infty} S_{x\dot{x}}(f) e^{j2\pi f \tau} df \qquad (5.176)$$

$$R''_{xx}(\tau) = -R_{\dot{x}\dot{x}}(\tau) = -\int_{-\infty}^{\infty} S_{\dot{x}\dot{x}}(f) e^{j2\pi f \tau} df \qquad (5.177)$$

$$R'''_{xx}(\tau) = -R_{\ddot{x}\dot{x}}(\tau) = -\int_{-\infty}^{\infty} S_{\ddot{x}\dot{x}}(f) e^{j2\pi f \tau} df \qquad (5.178)$$

$$R''''_{xx}(\tau) = R_{\ddot{x}\ddot{x}}(\tau) = \int_{-\infty}^{\infty} S_{\ddot{x}\ddot{x}}(f) e^{j2\pi f \tau} df \qquad (5.179)$$

Corresponding terms in the last eight formulas yield Equations (5.167)–(5.170).

5.5 LEVEL CROSSINGS AND PEAK VALUES

This section addresses the probability functions for certain characteristics of random data including

1. Expected number of level crossings per unit time
2. Peak probability functions for narrow bandwidth data
3. Expected number and spacing of positive peaks
4. Peak probability functions for wide bandwidth data

Most of these results were originally derived by Rice in Ref. 6, and various extensions of these matters are presented in Refs 6–10.

5.5.1 Expected Number of Level Crossings per Unit Time

Consider a stationary random record $x(t)$ that has the time derivative $v(t) = \dot{x}(t)$. Let $p(\alpha, \beta)$ represent the joint probability density function of $x(t)$ and $v(t)$ at $x(t) = \alpha$ and $v(t) = \beta$. By definition, for all t,

$$p(\alpha, \beta) \Delta\alpha\Delta\beta \approx \text{Prob}[\alpha < x(t) \le \alpha + \Delta\alpha \text{ and } \beta < v(t) \le \beta + \Delta\beta] \qquad (5.180)$$

In words, $p(\alpha, \beta) \Delta\alpha\Delta\beta$ estimates the probability over all time that $x(t)$ lies in the interval $[\alpha, \alpha + \Delta\alpha]$ when its derivative $v(t)$ is in the interval $[\beta, \beta + \Delta\beta]$. For unit total time, when $\Delta\beta$ is negligible compared to β, the value of $v(t)$ is essentially β.

To find the expected number of crossings of $x(t)$ through the interval $[\alpha, \alpha + \Delta\alpha]$, the amount of time that $x(t)$ is inside the interval should be divided by the time required to cross the interval. If t_β is the crossing time for a particular derivative β, then

$$t_\beta = \frac{\Delta\alpha}{|\beta|} \qquad (5.181)$$

where the absolute value of β is used because the crossing time must be a positive quantity. Hence, the expected number of passages of $x(t)$ per unit time through the interval $[\alpha, \alpha + \Delta\alpha]$ for a given value of $v(t) = \beta$ is

$$\frac{p(\alpha,\beta)\Delta\alpha\Delta\beta}{t_\beta} = |\beta|p(\alpha,\beta)\Delta\beta \qquad (5.182)$$

In the limit as $\Delta\beta \to 0$, the total expected number of crossings of $x(t)$ per unit time through the level $x(t) = \alpha$ for all possible values of β is found by

$$N_\alpha = \int_{-\infty}^{\infty} |\beta|p(\alpha,\beta)d\beta \qquad (5.183)$$

This represents the expected number of crossings of the level α with both positive and negative slopes as shown in Figure 5.10.

The expected number of zeros of $x(t)$ per unit time is found by the number of crossings of the level $x(t) = 0$ with both positive and negative slopes. This is given by N_α when $\alpha = 0$, namely,

$$N_0 = \int_{-\infty}^{\infty} |\beta|p(0,\beta)d\beta \qquad (5.184)$$

This value of N_0 can be interpreted as twice the "apparent frequency" of the record. For example, if the record were a sine wave of frequency f_0 Hz, then N_0 would be $2f_0$ zeros per second (e.g., a 60 Hz sine wave has 120 zeros per second). For random data, the situation is more complicated, but still a knowledge of N_0, together with other quantities, helps to characterize the particular random data. The above formulas apply to arbitrary Gaussian or non-Gaussian random data.

For an arbitrary random record $x(t)$ and its derivative $v(t) = \dot{x}(t)$ from a zero mean value stationary random process, it follows from Equations (5.147), (5.150) and (5.158)

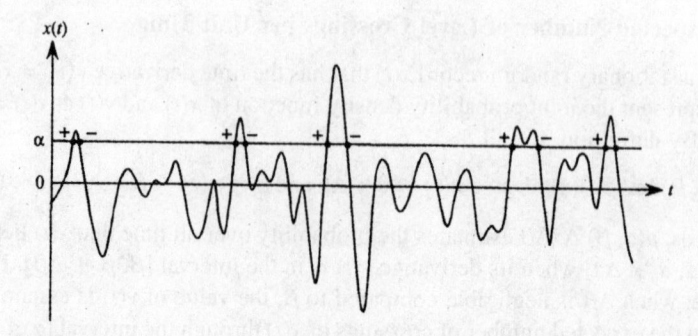

Figure 5.10 Illustration of crossings of level α with positive and negative slopes.

that the variances and covariance are

$$\sigma_x^2 = E[x^2(t)] = R_{xx}(0) \tag{5.185}$$

$$\sigma_v^2 = E[v^2(t)] = R_{vv}(0) = -R_{xx}''(0) \tag{5.186}$$

$$\sigma_{xv} = E[x(t)v(t)] = 0 \tag{5.187}$$

From Equations (5.171) and (5.173), it also follows that

$$\sigma_x^2 = \int_{-\infty}^{\infty} S_{xx}(f)df = \int_{0}^{\infty} G_{xx}(f)df \tag{5.188}$$

$$\sigma_v^2 = \int_{-\infty}^{\infty} (2\pi f)^2 S_{xx}(f)df = \int_{0}^{\infty} (2\pi f)^2 G_{xx}(f)df \tag{5.189}$$

If $x(t)$ and $v(t)$ are statistically independent with $p(\alpha, \beta) = p(\alpha)q(\beta)$, then Equations (5.183) and (5.184) show that

$$\frac{N_\alpha}{N_0} = \frac{p(\alpha)}{p(0)} \tag{5.190}$$

regardless of the nature of $p(\alpha)$ or $q(\beta)$. The formulas in Equations (5.18)–(5.19) apply to stationary random data with any joint probability density function.

5.5.1.1 Gaussian Data
Assume now that $x(t)$ and its derivative $v(t) = \dot{x}(t)$ have zero mean values and form a joint Gaussian distribution with the above variances and zero covariance. Then, the joint probability density function

$$p(\alpha, \beta) = p(\alpha)q(\beta) \tag{5.191}$$

with

$$p(\alpha) = \left(\frac{1}{\sigma_x\sqrt{2\pi}}\right)\exp\left(-\frac{\alpha^2}{2\sigma_x^2}\right) \tag{5.192}$$

$$q(\beta) = \left(\frac{1}{\sigma_v\sqrt{2\pi}}\right)\exp\left(-\frac{\beta^2}{2\sigma_v^2}\right) \tag{5.193}$$

Substitution of Equation (5.190) into (5.183) now shows for Gaussian data that

$$N_\alpha = \frac{\exp(-\alpha^2/2\sigma_x^2)}{2\pi\sigma_x\sigma_v}\int_{-\infty}^{\infty}|\beta|\exp\left(-\frac{\beta^2}{2\sigma_v^2}\right)d\beta = \frac{1}{\pi}\left(\frac{\sigma_v}{\sigma_x}\right)\exp\left(-\frac{\alpha^2}{2\sigma_x^2}\right) \tag{5.194}$$

In particular, for $\alpha = 0$, one obtains the simple formula

$$N_0 = \frac{1}{\pi}\left(\frac{\sigma_v}{\sigma_x}\right) \tag{5.195}$$

Thus, for Gaussian data, the expected number of level crossings per unit time at level α is given by

$$N_\alpha = N_0 \exp\left(-\frac{\alpha^2}{2\sigma_x^2}\right) \quad (5.196)$$

These simple results for N_α and N_0 were derived originally in a different way in Ref. 6.

Non-Gaussian data do not satisfy Equations (5.195) and (5.196), and different types of non-Gaussian data will produce different results. This fact can be used to help detect and identify the properties of nonlinear systems when Gaussian data pass through these systems.

Example 5.12. Zero Crossings of Low-Pass Gaussian White Noise. To illustrate the above formulas, consider the case of low-pass white noise where

$$G_{xx}(f) = K \quad 0 \leq f \leq B \quad \text{otherwise zero}$$

Here,

$$\sigma_x^2 = \int_0^B K\, df = KB$$

$$\sigma_v^2 = \int_0^B (2\pi f)^2 K\, df = \left(\frac{4\pi^2}{3}\right) KB^3$$

From Equation (5.195),

$$N_0 = \frac{1}{\pi}\left(\frac{\sigma_v}{\sigma_x}\right) = \left(\frac{2}{\sqrt{3}}\right) B \approx 2(0.58B)$$

This shows for low-pass Gaussian white noise cutting off at B Hz that the apparent frequency of the noise is about 0.58 of the cutoff frequency.

Example 5.13. Zero Crossings of Bandwidth-Limited Gaussian White Noise. As in Equation (5.47), the autospectral density function of bandwidth-limited white noise is

$$G_{xx}(f) = K \quad 0 \leq f_c - (B/2) \leq f \leq f_c + (B/2) \quad \text{otherwise zero}$$

Here,

$$\sigma_x^2 = \int_{f_c-(B/2)}^{f_c+(B/2)} K\, df = KB$$

$$\sigma_v^2 = \int_{f_c-(B/2)}^{f_c+(B/2)} (2\pi f)^2 K\, df = \left(\frac{4\pi^2}{3}\right) KB \left[3f_c^2 + \left(\frac{B}{2}\right)^2\right]$$

From Equation (5.195),

$$N_0 = \frac{1}{\pi}\left(\frac{\sigma_v}{\sigma_x}\right) = 2\left[\frac{3f_c^2 + (B/2)^2}{3}\right]^{1/2}$$

LEVEL CROSSINGS AND PEAK VALUES

This shows for bandwidth-limited Gaussian white noise with a center frequency f_c and bandwidth B that the apparent frequency of the noise is greater than $2f_c$ for any B greater than zero.

5.5.2 Peak Probability Functions for Narrow Bandwidth Data

The *peak probability density function* $p_p(\alpha)$ describes the probability of positive peaks falling inside the interval $(\alpha, \alpha + d\alpha)$. To be specific,

$$p_p(\alpha)d\alpha \approx \text{Prob}[\alpha < \text{positive peak} \leq \alpha + d\alpha] \tag{5.197}$$

The *peak probability distribution function* that a positive peak is less than α is given by the formula

$$P_p(\alpha) = \text{Prob}[\text{positive peak} < \alpha] = \int_{-\infty}^{\alpha} p_p(\zeta)d\zeta \tag{5.198}$$

Because $p_p(\alpha)$ is a probability density function over $(-\infty, \infty)$, it must satisfy

$$P_p(\infty) = \int_{-\infty}^{\infty} p_p(\alpha)\,d\alpha = 1 \tag{5.199}$$

From Equation (5.198),

$$\frac{dP_p(\alpha)}{d\alpha} = p_p(\alpha) \tag{5.200}$$

Note that the probability that a positive peak is greater than α is

$$\text{Prob}[\text{positive peak} > \alpha] = \int_{\alpha}^{\infty} p_p(\zeta)d\zeta = 1 - P_p(\alpha) \tag{5.201}$$

The above formulas apply to arbitrary Gaussian or non-Gaussian random data.

If each cycle of the random data leads to a single positive peak as occurs for narrow bandwidth random data, then $N_\alpha^+ = (1/2)N_\alpha$ estimates the expected number of crossings of $x(t)$ per unit time with positive peaks above the level $x(t) = \alpha$. Thus, for such narrow bandwidth random data, an estimate of the fraction of the crossings having peaks greater than $x(t) = \alpha$ is given by

$$1 - P_p(\alpha) = \text{Prob}[\text{positive peak} > \alpha] = \frac{N_\alpha^+}{N_0^+} = \frac{N_\alpha}{N_0} \tag{5.202}$$

From Equation (5.190), when $x(t)$ and $v(t) = \dot{x}(t)$ are statistically independent, one obtains

$$1 - P_p(\alpha) = \text{Prob}[\text{positive peak} > \alpha] = \frac{p(\alpha)}{p(0)} \tag{5.203}$$

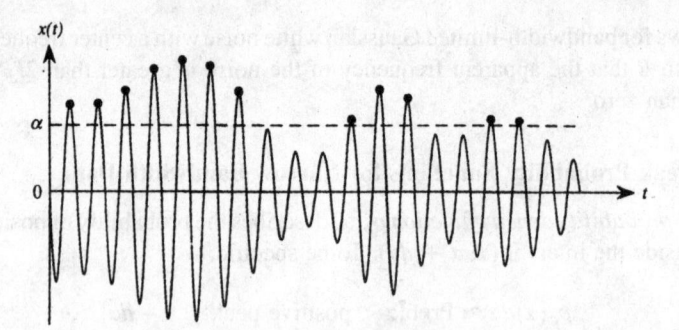

Figure 5.11 Illustration of positive peaks above level α.

Hence, for narrow bandwidth random data, from Equation (5.200), a reasonable approximation for the peak probability density function is

$$p_p(\alpha) = \frac{-\dot{p}(\alpha)}{p(0)} \qquad (5.204)$$

Equations (5.202)–(5.204) apply to positive peaks above a level α as shown in Figure 5.11.

5.5.2.1 Gaussian Data

Now consider the case where $x(t)$ is Gaussian with a mean value of zero and a variance of σ_x^2 such that the probability density function is

$$p(x) = \left(\frac{1}{\sigma_x \sqrt{2\pi}}\right) \exp\left(-\frac{x^2}{2\sigma_x^2}\right) \qquad (5.205)$$

Here, from Equation (5.203), the probability of $x(t)$ having positive peaks greater than α is simply

$$1 - P_p(\alpha) = \text{Prob}[\text{positive peak} > \alpha] = \exp\left(-\frac{\alpha^2}{2\sigma_x^2}\right) \qquad (5.206)$$

This simple exponential result for Gaussian data is plotted in Figure 5.12. The associated peak probability density function from Equations (5.204) and (5.205) is

$$p_p(\alpha) = (\alpha/\sigma_x^2) \exp\left(-\frac{\alpha^2}{2\sigma_x^2}\right) \qquad (5.207)$$

Thus, for narrow bandwidth Gaussian random data, the resulting peak probability density function $p_p(\alpha)$ will have the Rayleigh probability density function of Equation (3.95). A generalization of this result that applies to wide bandwidth Gaussian random data is derived in Section 5.5.5.

Example 5.14. **Peak Probability for Narrow Bandwidth Gaussian Data.** Consider a narrow bandwidth Gaussian random signal with a zero mean value and a root-mean-square (rms) amplitude of $\sigma_x = 1$ V. What is the probability of a positive peak occurring with an amplitude greater than 4 V? From Equation (5.206),

LEVEL CROSSINGS AND PEAK VALUES

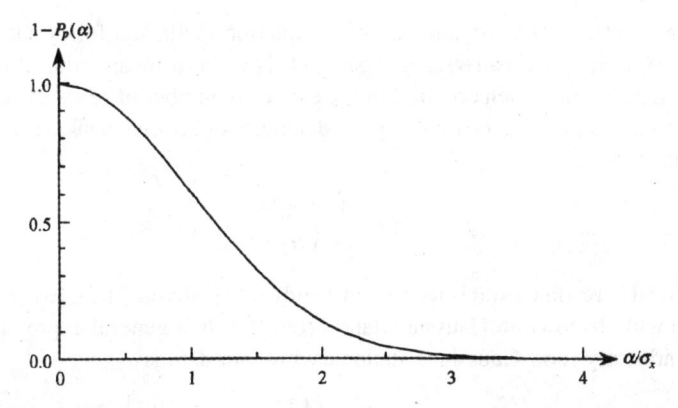

Figure 5.12 Probability (positive peak $> \alpha$) for narrow bandwidth Gaussian data.

the answer is

$$\text{Prob}[\text{positive peak} > 4] = \exp(-8) = 0.00033$$

Hence, there is only about one chance in 3000 that any given positive peak will have an amplitude greater than 4 V.

5.5.3 Expected Number and Spacing of Positive Peaks

Let M denote the total expected number of positive peaks of $x(t)$ per unit time and let M_α denote the expected number of positive peaks of $x(t)$ per unit time above the level $x(t) = \alpha$. Then

$$M_\alpha = M[1 - P_p(\alpha)] \tag{5.208}$$

where $[1 - P_p(\alpha)]$ is the probability that a positive peak exceeds α, as given by Equation (5.203). Hence, if T is the total time during which $x(t)$ is observed, the expected number of positive peaks that exceeds the level α in time T is given by

$$M_\alpha T = M[1 - P_p(\alpha)]T \tag{5.209}$$

The average time (spacing) between positive peaks above the level α, denoted by T_α, is equal to the reciprocal of the expected number of positive peaks per unit time above that level, that is

$$T_\alpha = \frac{1}{M_\alpha} \tag{5.210}$$

Consider the special case where $x(t)$ is a narrow bandwidth random record. For this case, each peak above the level α is associated with a crossing of this level. Then, the average time between crossings (with positive slope) of the level α is T_α as given by Equation (5.210). Also, for this case, the total expected number of positive peaks of $x(t)$ per unit time, denoted by M, is equal to one-half of the expected number of zeros of $v(t) = \dot{x}(t)$ per unit time—that is, the number of crossings by $v(t)$ of the level $v(t) = 0$. The factor of one-half comes from the observation that, on the average, half of the zeros of $v(t)$ represent negative peaks.

Let $a(t) = \dot{v}(t) = \ddot{x}(t)$. By analogy with Equation (5.195), it follows that if $[x(t), v(t)]$ and $[v(t), a(t)]$ are pairwise independent, have zero mean values, and follow Gaussian distributions, then one-half of the expected number of zeros of $v(t)$ per unit time, which is the same as the total expected number of positive peaks of $x(t)$ per unit time, is given by

$$M = \frac{1}{2\pi}\left(\frac{\sigma_a}{\sigma_v}\right) \qquad (5.211)$$

As derived here, this result is for narrow bandwidth Gaussian data. However, it also applies to wide bandwidth Gaussian data. From Ref. 6, a general expression that is valid for arbitrary (non-Gaussian) stationary random data is

$$M = \int_\alpha^\infty g(\alpha)d\alpha = \int_{-\infty}^\infty \left[\int_0^{-\infty} \gamma p(\alpha, 0, \gamma) d\gamma\right] d\alpha \qquad (5.212)$$

where $p(\alpha, 0, \gamma)$ is the third-order probability density function associated with $x(t) = \alpha$, $v(t) = 0$, and $a(t) = \gamma$. Equations (5.211) and (5.212) for wide bandwidth Gaussian random data and for arbitrary random data are derived in Section 5.5.5.

Example 5.15. Expected Number of Positive Peaks for Narrow Bandwidth Gaussian Data. Consider a narrow bandwidth Gaussian random signal, as in Example 5.14, where the total expected number of positive peaks per second is $M = 100$. What is the expected number of positive peaks per second with an amplitude greater than $\alpha = 4$ V and what is the average time between such peaks? In Example 5.14, the probability of a positive peak occurring with an amplitude greater than 4 V is 0.00033. It follows from Equations (5.209) and (5.210) that the expected number of positive peaks per second above 4 V is $M_4 = M(0.00033) = 0.033$, and the average time between such positive peaks is given by $T_4 = (1/M_4) = 30$ s.

5.5.4 Peak Probability Functions for Wide Bandwidth Data

Assume that $x(t)$ is a sample record from a stationary Gaussian random process with a zero mean value and variance σ_x^2. Let N_0 denote the expected number of zero crossing per unit time and let M denote the expected number of positive peaks (maxima) per unit time. Then $2M$ is the expected number of both positive and negative peaks per unit time. As derived in Sections 5.5.1 and 5.5.5, the quantities N_0 and M are given by

$$N_0 = \frac{1}{\pi}\left(\frac{\sigma_v}{\sigma_x}\right) \quad \text{and} \quad M = \frac{1}{2\pi}\left(\frac{\sigma_a}{\sigma_v}\right) \qquad (5.213)$$

where $v(t) = \dot{x}(t)$, $a(t) = \dot{v}(t) = \ddot{x}(t)$, and

$$\sigma_x^2 = E[x^2(t)] = \int_0^\infty G_{xx}(f)df \qquad (5.214)$$

$$\sigma_v^2 = E[v^2(t)] = \int_0^\infty (2\pi f)^2 G_{xx}(f)df \qquad (5.215)$$

LEVEL CROSSINGS AND PEAK VALUES

$$\sigma_a^2 = E[a^2(t)] = \int_0^\infty (2\pi f)^4 G_{xx}(f) df \qquad (5.216)$$

The peak probability density function represents the probability that a positive peak will be found among the population of all positive peaks. In terms of a standardized variable z with zero mean value and unit variance where $z = (\alpha/\sigma_x)$ with $\sigma_z^2 = 1$, the peak probability density function $p_p(\alpha)$ is replaced by $w(z)$, where $w(z)$ describes the probability that a positive peak will fall between z and $z + dz$. This *peak probability density function* $w(z)$ is expressed in Ref. 6 by

$$w(z) = \left(\frac{k_1}{\sqrt{2\pi}}\right)\exp\left(-\frac{z^2}{2k_1^2}\right) + \left(\frac{N_0}{2M}\right) z \exp\left(-\frac{z^2}{2}\right)\left[1 - Q_n\left(\frac{z}{k_2}\right)\right] \qquad (5.217)$$

where

$$k_1^2 = 1 - \left(\frac{N_0}{2M}\right)^2 \quad k_2 = k_1 \Big/ \left(\frac{N_0}{2M}\right) \quad \left(\frac{N_0}{2M}\right) = \left(\frac{\sigma_v^2}{\sigma_x \sigma_a}\right) \qquad (5.218)$$

$$Q_n\left(\frac{z}{k_2}\right) = \frac{1}{\sqrt{2\pi}} \int_{z/k_2}^\infty \exp\left(-\frac{u^2}{2}\right) du \qquad (5.219)$$

The function $Q_n(z/k_2)$ is the probability for a standardized Gaussian density function with a zero mean value and a unit variance that the value (z/k_2) will be exceeded. Equation (5.217) is derived in Section 5.5.5.

The shape and nature of $w(z)$ is determined by the dimensionless parameter $(N_0/2M)$. It is verified in Section 5.5.5 that $(N_0/2M)$ always falls between zero and unity, namely,

$$0 \le \left(\frac{N_0}{2M}\right) = \left(\frac{\sigma_v^2}{\sigma_x \sigma_a}\right) \le 1 \qquad (5.220)$$

If $(N_0/2M) = 0$, then $w(z)$ reduces to the standardized *Gaussian probability density function*

$$w(z) = \left(\frac{1}{\sqrt{2\pi}}\right) \exp\left(-\frac{z^2}{2}\right) \qquad (5.221)$$

This case occurs in practice for wide bandwidth random data where the expected number of maxima and minima per second, $2M$, is much larger than the expected number of zero crossings per second, N_0, so that $(N_0/2M)$ approaches zero. If $(N_0/2M) = 1$, then $w(z)$ becomes the standardized *Rayleigh probability density function*,

$$w(z) = z \exp\left(-\frac{z^2}{2}\right) \qquad (5.222)$$

This case occurs in practice for narrow bandwidth random data where the expected number of maxima and minima per second, $2M$, is approximately equal to the expected number of zero crossings per second N_0, so that $(N_0/2M)$ approaches unity. The general form of $w(z)$ from Equation (5.217) is thus something between a Gaussian

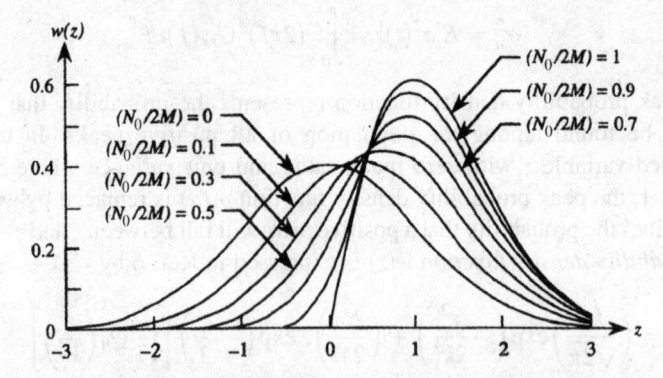

Figure 5.13 Probability density functions for peak values of Gaussian random data.

and a Rayleigh probability density function. Figure 5.13 shows plots of $w(z)$ as a function of z for various values of the dimensionless parameter $(N_0/2M)$.

In terms of $w(z)$, the probability that a positive peak chosen at random from among all the possible positive peaks will exceed the value $z = (\alpha/\sigma_x)$ is

$$\text{Prob[positive peak} > z] = \int_z^\infty w(\zeta)d\zeta = 1 - W(z)$$

$$= Q_n\left(\frac{z}{k_1}\right) + \left(\frac{N_0}{2M}\right)\exp\left(-\frac{z^2}{2}\right)\left[1 - Q_n\left(\frac{z}{k_2}\right)\right]$$

(5.223)

where Equation (5.219) is used to compute the Q_n terms. The function $W(z)$ is the *peak probability distribution function* for the standardized variable z, which defines the probability that a positive peak will not exceed the value z. Equation (5.223) is derived in Section 5.5.5.

5.5.5 Derivations

Detailed mathematical derivations will now be carried out for the main formulas in Sections 5.5.1–5.5.4. Readers not interested in these matters should proceed to Chapter 6.

Assume that $x(t)$ is a random record from an ergodic stationary random process with an arbitrary probability density function $p(x)$. By definition, the third-order probability density function of $x(t)$, $v(t) = \dot{x}(t)$, and $a(t) = \dot{v}(t) = \ddot{x}(t)$ is given by $p(\alpha, \beta, \gamma)$, where

$$p(\alpha, \beta, \gamma)d\alpha d\beta d\gamma \approx \text{Prob}[\alpha < x(t) < \alpha + d\alpha, \beta < v(t) < \beta + d\beta,$$
$$\gamma < a(t) < \gamma + d\gamma]$$

(5.224)

This represents the probability over all time that $x(t)$ lies in the interval $(\alpha, \alpha + d\alpha)$ when $v(t)$ is in the interval $(\beta, \beta + d\beta)$ and $a(t)$ is in the interval $(\gamma, \gamma + d\gamma)$. For unit total time, when $d\beta$ and $d\gamma$ are small, this represents the probability that $x(t)$ is in the interval $(\alpha, \alpha + d\alpha)$ with a velocity that is essentially β and an acceleration that is

LEVEL CROSSINGS AND PEAK VALUES

essentially γ. If $v(t) = \beta = 0$ and also if $a(t) = \gamma < 0$, this can be related to the probability that $x(t)$ has maxima (peaks) in $(\alpha, \alpha + d\alpha)$ with the given negative value of $a(t)$.

The amount of time that $v(t) = \beta$ spends in the interval $(\beta, \beta + d\beta)$ with a given $a(t) = \gamma < 0$ can be expressed by the formula

$$\tau = \frac{-d\beta}{\gamma} \tag{5.225}$$

where the negative sign is required because the crossing time must be positive. Hence, the expected number of maxima (peaks) of $x(t)$ per unit time when $x(t)$ is in $(\alpha, \alpha + d\alpha)$ for fixed values of $\beta = 0$ and $\gamma < 0$ is

$$\frac{p(\alpha, 0, \gamma) d\alpha\, d\beta\, d\gamma}{\tau} = -\gamma p(\alpha, 0, \gamma) d\gamma\, d\alpha \tag{5.226}$$

Then, the expected number of maxima (peaks) of $x(t)$ per unit time for all possible values of $\gamma < 0$ can be obtained by summing from $\gamma = -\infty$ to $\gamma = 0$. This gives the formula

$$\int_{-\infty}^{0} -\gamma p(\alpha, 0, \gamma) d\gamma\, d\alpha = \int_{0}^{-\infty} \gamma p(\alpha, 0, \gamma) d\gamma\, d\alpha = g(\alpha) d\alpha \tag{5.227}$$

where

$$g(\alpha) = \int_{0}^{-\infty} \gamma p(\alpha, 0, \gamma) d\gamma \tag{5.228}$$

The above result is for $x(t)$ lying in the interval $(\alpha, \alpha + d\alpha)$. It follows that the expected number of maxima (peaks) of $x(t)$ per unit time for all possible values of α over the range $(-\infty, \infty)$ is given by

$$M = \int_{-\infty}^{\infty} g(\alpha) d\alpha \tag{5.229}$$

and the expected number of maxima (peaks) of $x(t)$ lying above the line where $x(t) = \alpha$ can be computed by

$$M_\alpha = \int_{\alpha}^{\infty} g(\alpha) d\alpha \tag{5.230}$$

This result is the same as

$$M_\alpha = M \int_{\alpha}^{\infty} p_p(\alpha) d\alpha \tag{5.231}$$

where $p_p(\alpha)$ is the *peak probability density function* that a positive peak falls inside $(\alpha, \alpha + d\alpha)$. Note that

$$p_p(\alpha) = (1/M) g(\alpha) \tag{5.232}$$

These formulas apply to arbitrary stationary random data.

5.5.5.1 Special Results for Gaussian Data

Assume now that $x(t)$, $v(t) = \dot{x}(t)$, and $a(t) = \ddot{x}(t)$ have zero mean values and form a three-dimensional Gaussian distribution. The threefold probability density function $p(\alpha, 0, \gamma)$ from Equation (3.63) is

$$p(\alpha, 0, \gamma) = \frac{\exp[(1/2|\mathbf{C}|)(\sigma_v^2\sigma_a^2\alpha^2 + 2\sigma_v^4\alpha\gamma + \sigma_x^2\sigma_v^2\gamma^2)]}{(2\pi)^{3/2}|\mathbf{C}|^{1/2}} \quad (5.233)$$

where the covariance matrix is

$$\mathbf{C} = \begin{bmatrix} \sigma_x^2 & 0 & -\sigma_v^2 \\ 0 & \sigma_v^2 & 0 \\ -\sigma_v^2 & 0 & \sigma_a^2 \end{bmatrix} \quad (5.234)$$

The determinant $|\mathbf{C}|$ is

$$|\mathbf{C}| = \sigma_v^2(\sigma_x^2\sigma_a^2 - \sigma_v^4) \quad (5.235)$$

with the variance terms

$$\sigma_x^2 = E[x^2(t)] = \int_0^\infty G_{xx}(f)df \quad (5.236)$$

$$\sigma_v^2 = E[v^2(t)] = \int_0^\infty (2\pi f)^2 G_{xx}(f)df \quad (5.237)$$

$$\sigma_a^2 = E[a^2(t)] = \int_0^\infty (2\pi f)^4 G_{xx}(f)df \quad (5.238)$$

It follows from Equation (5.235) and the Schwartz inequality of Equation (5.116) that $|\mathbf{C}| > 0$ because $\sigma_x^2\sigma_a^2 > \sigma_v^4$ for any $G_{xx}(f) > 0$. To apply the Schwartz inequality here, one should choose

$$A(f) = [G_{xx}(f)]^{1/2} \quad \text{and} \quad B(f) = (2\pi f)^2[G_{xx}(f)]^{1/2} \quad (5.239)$$

and use the formula

$$\int_0^\infty [A(f)]^2 df \int_0^\infty [B(f)]^2 df > \left[\int_0^\infty A(f)B(f)df\right]^2 \quad (5.240)$$

This result that $|\mathbf{C}| > 0$ proves Equation (5.220).

5.5.5.2 Expected Number of Maxima per Unit Time

Equation (5.211) will now be derived for M, the expected number of maxima of $x(t)$ per unit time. This formula applies to any Gaussian stationary random data, narrow or wide bandwidth.

From Equation (5.233), the term $p(\alpha, 0, \gamma)$ can be represented by

$$p(\alpha, 0, \gamma) = \frac{\exp(-\gamma^2/2\sigma_a^2)\exp\{-(\sigma_v^2\sigma_a^2/2|\mathbf{C}|)[\alpha + (\sigma_v/\sigma_a)^2\gamma]^2\}}{(2\pi)^{3/2}|\mathbf{C}|^{1/2}} \quad (5.241)$$

LEVEL CROSSINGS AND PEAK VALUES 167

using the relation

$$\sigma_v^2\sigma_a^2\alpha^2 + 2\sigma_v^4\alpha\gamma + \sigma_x^2\sigma_v^2\gamma^2 = \sigma_v^2\sigma_a^2\left[\alpha + \left(\frac{\sigma_v}{\sigma_a}\right)^2\gamma\right]2 + \left(\frac{|\mathbf{C}|\gamma^2}{\sigma_a^2}\right) \tag{5.242}$$

From Equations (5.228), (5.229) and (5.241), the quantity M can be computed by

$$M = \int_{-\infty}^{\infty}\left[\int_0^{-\infty}\gamma p(\alpha,0,\gamma)d\gamma\right]d\alpha = \int_0^{-\infty}\gamma\left[\int_{-\infty}^{\infty}p(\alpha,0,\gamma)d\alpha\right]d\gamma$$

$$= \frac{1}{2\pi\sigma_v\sigma_a}\int_0^{-\infty}\gamma\exp(\gamma^2/2\sigma_a^2)d\gamma = \frac{1}{2\pi}\left(\frac{\sigma_a}{\sigma_v}\right) \tag{5.243}$$

The strong similarity of this result to N_0 in Equation (5.195) should be noted.

5.5.5.3 Peak Probability Density and Distribution Functions
Formulas will now be derived for the standardized peak probability density and distribution functions in Equations (5.217) and (5.223). To compute these results, use the relation

$$\sigma_v^2\sigma_a^2\alpha^2 + 2\sigma_v^4\alpha\gamma + \sigma_x^2\sigma_v^2\gamma^2 = \sigma_x^2\upsilon_v^2[\gamma + (\sigma_v/\sigma_x)^2\alpha]^2 + (|\mathbf{C}|\alpha^2/\sigma_x^2) \tag{5.244}$$

This changes Equation (5.233) to

$$p(\alpha,0,\gamma) = \frac{\exp(-\alpha^2/2\sigma_x^2)\exp\{-(\sigma_x^2\sigma_v^2/2|\mathbf{C}|)[\gamma + (\sigma_v/\sigma_x)^2\alpha]^2\}}{(2\pi)^{3/2}|\mathbf{C}|^{1/2}} \tag{5.245}$$

By making the substitutions

$$x = \gamma + (\sigma_v/\sigma_x)^2\alpha \quad \text{and} \quad dx = d\gamma \tag{5.246}$$

the formula for the $g(\alpha)$ of Equation (5.228) can be written as

$$g(\alpha) = A(\alpha) + B(\alpha) \tag{5.247}$$

where

$$A(\alpha) = \frac{\exp(-\alpha^2/2\sigma_x^2)}{(2\pi)^{3/2}|\mathbf{C}|^{1/2}}\int_{(\sigma_v/\sigma_x)^2\alpha}^{-\infty}x\exp\left[-\left(\frac{\sigma_x^2\sigma_v^2}{2|\mathbf{C}|}\right)x^2\right]dx$$

$$= \frac{|\mathbf{C}|^{1/2}}{(2\pi)^{3/2}\sigma_x^2\sigma_v^2}\exp\left[-\left(\frac{\sigma_v^2\sigma_a^2}{2|\mathbf{C}|}\right)\alpha^2\right] \tag{5.248}$$

$$B(\alpha) = \frac{(\sigma_v/\sigma_x)^2 \alpha \exp(-\alpha^2/2\sigma_x^2)}{(2\pi)^{3/2}|C|^{1/2}} \int_{-\infty}^{(\sigma_v/\sigma_x)^2\alpha} \exp\left[-\left(\frac{\sigma_x^2 \sigma_v^2}{2|C|}\right)x^2\right]dx$$
$$= \frac{\sigma_v \alpha \exp(-\alpha^2/2\sigma_x^2)}{(2\pi)\sigma_x^3}\left[1-Q_n\left(\frac{\sigma_v^3 \alpha}{\sigma_x|C|^{1/2}}\right)\right] \quad (5.249)$$

In $B(\alpha)$, like in Equation (5.219), the function

$$Q_n(x) = \frac{1}{\sqrt{2\pi}} \int_x^\infty \exp\left(-\frac{u^2}{2}\right) du \quad (5.250)$$

is the probability under the standardized normal density function that x will be exceeded. This function is listed in Table A.2.

From the above results, the peak probability density function of Equation (5.232) is given by

$$p_p(\alpha) = \left(\frac{1}{M}\right)g(\alpha) = 2\pi\left(\frac{\sigma_v}{\sigma_a}\right)g(\alpha) = 2\pi\left(\frac{\sigma_v}{\sigma_a}\right)[A(\alpha)+B(\alpha)] \quad (5.251)$$

One should now change the variable α to the variable z, where z is the standardized normal variable with zero mean value and unit variance, by setting $\alpha = \sigma_x z$. Then $p_p(\alpha)$ is replaced by $w(z)$, where

$$w(z) = \sigma_x p_p(\sigma_x z) = 2\pi\left(\frac{\sigma_x \sigma_v}{\sigma_a}\right)[A(\sigma_x z)+B(\sigma_x z)] \quad (5.252)$$

satisfies the requirement that

$$\int_{-\infty}^\infty w(z)dz = \int_{-\infty}^\infty p_p(\alpha)d\alpha = 1 \quad (5.253)$$

Substituting for $A(\sigma_x z)$ and $B(\sigma_x z)$ in Equation (5.252) gives the formula

$$w(z) = \frac{|C|^{1/2}}{\sqrt{2\pi}\sigma_x \sigma_v \sigma_a} \exp\left[-\left(\frac{\sigma_x^2 \sigma_v^2 \sigma_a^2}{2|C|}\right)z^2\right]$$
$$+ \frac{\sigma_v^2 z \exp(-z^2/2)}{\sigma_x \sigma_a}\left[1-Q_n\left(\frac{\sigma_v^3 z}{|C|^{1/2}}\right)\right] \quad (5.254)$$
$$= \left(\frac{k_1}{\sqrt{2\pi}}\right)\exp\left(-\frac{z^2}{2k_1^2}\right) + \left(\frac{N_0}{2M}\right)z\exp\left(-\frac{z^2}{2}\right)\left[1-Q_n\left(\frac{z}{k_2}\right)\right]$$

where the terms

$$k_1^2 = \frac{|C|}{(\sigma_x \sigma_v \sigma_a)^2} = 1-\left(\frac{\sigma_v^2}{\sigma_x \sigma_a}\right)^2 = 1-\left(\frac{N_0}{2M}\right)^2 \quad (5.255)$$

$$k_2 = \frac{|C|^{1/2}}{\sigma_v^3} = \frac{k_1 \sigma_x \sigma_v \sigma_a}{\sigma_v^3} = k_1 \bigg/ \left(\frac{N_0}{2M}\right) \quad (5.256)$$

use the relations that

$$N_0 = \frac{1}{\pi}\left(\frac{\sigma_v}{\sigma_x}\right) \quad \text{and} \quad M = \frac{1}{2\pi}\left(\frac{\sigma_a}{\sigma_v}\right) \quad (5.257)$$

This proves the desired result for the peak probability density function $w(z)$ stated in Equation (5.217).

The formula for the peak probability distribution function $W(z)$ can be obtained by computing

$$1 - W(z) = \int_z^\infty w(z)\,dz = f_1(z) + f_2(z) + f_3(z) \quad (5.258)$$

where the functions

$$f_1(z) = \left(\frac{k_1}{\sqrt{2\pi}}\right)\int_z^\infty \exp\left(-\frac{z^2}{2k_1^2}\right)dz = \left[1 - \left(\frac{N_0}{2M}\right)^2\right]Q_n\left(\frac{z}{k_1}\right) \quad (5.259)$$

$$f_2(z) = \left(\frac{N_0}{2M}\right)\int_z^\infty z\exp\left(-\frac{z^2}{2}\right)dz = \left(\frac{N_0}{2M}\right)\exp\left(-\frac{z^2}{2}\right) \quad (5.260)$$

$$f_3(z) = -\left(\frac{N_0}{2M}\right)\int_z^\infty z\exp\left(-\frac{z^2}{2}\right)Q_n\left(\frac{z}{k_2}\right)dz$$

$$= -\left(\frac{N_0}{2M}\right)\exp\left(-\frac{z^2}{2}\right)Q_n\left(\frac{z}{k_2}\right) + \left(\frac{N_0}{2M}\right)^2 Q_n\left(\frac{z}{k_1}\right) \quad (5.261)$$

The sum of these three functions shows that

$$1 - W(z) = Q_n\left(\frac{z}{k_1}\right) + \left(\frac{N_0}{2M}\right)\exp\left(-\frac{z^2}{2}\right)\left[1 - Q_n\left(\frac{z}{k_2}\right)\right] \quad (5.262)$$

This proves the desired result for $W(z)$ stated in Equation (5.223). A different method of proof was used in Ref. 6 to obtain these important special formulas.

PROBLEMS

5.1 Which of the following properties are always true of autocorrelation functions of stationary data?
  (a) must be an even function.
  (b) must be nonnegative.
  (c) must be bounded by its value at zero.

(d) can determine the mean value of the data.
(e) can determine the variance of the data.

5.2 Which of the properties in Problem 5.1 are always true of cross-correlation functions of stationary data?

5.3 Which of the properties in Problem 5.1 are always true of the two-sided
   (a) autospectral density functions?
   (b) cross-spectral density functions?

5.4 Which of the following properties are always true for two ergodic random processes?
   (a) $R_{xy}(\infty) = \mu_x \mu_y$.
   (b) $R_{xy}(0) = 0$ when $\mu_x = 0$ or $\mu_y = 0$.
   (c) $R_{xy}(\tau) = 0$ when $R_{xx}(\tau) = 0$ or $R_{yy}(\tau) = 0$.
   (d) $|R_{xy}(\tau)|^2 \leq R_{xx}(\tau) R_{yy}(\tau)$.
   (e) $G_{xy}(0) = 0$ when $\mu_x = 0$ or $\mu_y = 0$.
   (f) $|G_{xy}(f)|^2 \leq G_{xx}(0) G_{yy}(0)$.
   (g) $G_{xy}(f) = 0$ when $G_{xx}(f) = 0$ or $G_{yy}(f) = 0$.

5.5 Given data with an autocorrelation function defined by $R_{xx}(\tau) = 25e^{-4|\tau|} \cos 4\pi\tau + 16$, determine
   (a) the mean value and the variance.
   (b) the associated one-sided autospectral density function.

5.6 Given data with a two-sided autospectral density function defined by

$$S_{xx}(f) = \begin{cases} 16\delta(f) + 20\left(1 - \dfrac{|f|}{10}\right) & f \leq 10 \\ 0 & |f| > 10 \end{cases}$$

determine for the data
   (a) the mean value and the variance.
   (b) the associated autocorrelation function.

5.7 Assume a record $x(t)$ from an ergodic random process has a one-sided autospectral spectral density function given by

$$G_{xx}(f) = \frac{1}{25 + f^2} \quad 0 \leq f \leq 25 \quad \text{otherwise zero}$$

Determine the average number of zero crossings per second in the record $x(t)$.

5.8 For the random record $x(t)$ in Problem 5.7 determine the average number of positive peaks (maxima) per second.

5.9 Assume data have an one-sided cross-spectral density function given by $G_{xy}(f) = (6/f^2) + j(8/f^3)$. Determine the two-sided cross-spectral density function $S_{xy}(f)$ for all frequencies in terms of

(a) real and imaginary functions.

(b) gain and phase functions.

5.10 If a record $x(t)$ from an ergodic Gaussian random process has an autocorrelation function given by $R_{xx}(\tau) = e^{-a|\tau|}\cos 2\pi f_0 \tau$ with $a > 0$, determine the autocorrelation function for the first time derivative of the data $\dot{x}(t)$.

REFERENCES

1. Bendat, J. S., *Principles and Applications of Random Noise Theory*, Wiley, New York, 1958. Reprinted by Krieger, Melbourne, Florida, 1977.
2. Bendat, J. S., and Piersol, A. G., *Engineering Applications of Correlation and Spectral Analysis*, 2nd ed., Wiley–Interscience, New York, 1993.
3. Bendat, J. S., *Nonlinear System Techniques and Applications*, Wiley–Interscience, New York, 1998.
4. Doob, J. L., *Stochastic Processes*, Wiley, New York, 1953.
5. Papoulis, A., *Probability, Random Variables and Stochastic Processes*, 3rd ed., McGraw-Hill, New York, 1991.
6. Rice, S. O., "Mathematical Analysis of Random Noise," in *Selected Papers on Noise and Stochastic Processes* (N. Wax; Ed.), Dover, New York, 1954.
7. Crandall, S. H., and Mark, W, D., *Random Vibration in Mechanical Systems*, Academic Press, New York, 1963.
8. Yang, C, Y., *Random Vibration of Structures*, Wiley–Interscience, New York, 1986.
9. Ochi, M. K., *Applied Probability and Stochastic Processes*, Wiley–Interscience, New York, 1990.
10. Wirsching, P. H., Paez, T. L., and Ortiz, H., *Random Vibrations: Theory and Practice*, Wiley–Interscience, New York, 1995.

CHAPTER 6

Single-Input/Output Relationships

This chapter is concerned with the theory and applications of input/output relationships for single-input problems. It is assumed that records are from stationary random processes with zero mean values and that systems are constant-parameter linear systems. Single-input/single-output (SI/SO) models and single-input/multiple-output (SI/MO) models are discussed. Ordinary coherence functions and optimum frequency response functions are defined for these models. Multiple-input problems are covered in Chapter 7.

6.1 SINGLE-INPUT/SINGLE-OUTPUT MODELS

Consider a constant-parameter linear system with a weighting function $h(\tau)$ and frequency response function $H(f)$ as defined and discussed in Chapter 2. Assume the system is subjected to a well-defined single input $x(t)$ from a stationary random process $\{x(t)\}$ and produces a well-defined output $y(t)$, as illustrated in Figure 6.1. This output will belong to a stationary random process $\{y(t)\}$.

6.1.1 Correlation and Spectral Relations

Under ideal conditions, the output $y(t)$ for the system in Figure 6.1 is given by the convolution integral

$$y(t) = \int_0^\infty h(\tau)x(t-\tau)d\tau \qquad (6.1)$$

where $h(\tau) = 0$ for $\tau < 0$ when the system is physically realizable. The product $y(t)y(t + \tau)$ is given by

---

Random Data: Analysis and Measurement Procedures, Fourth Edition. By Julius S. Bendat and Allan G. Piersol
Copyright © 2010 John Wiley & Sons, Inc.

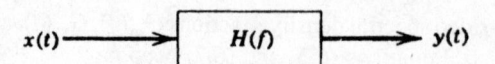

$$y(t)y(t+\tau) = \iint_0^\infty h(\alpha)h(\beta)x(t-\beta)x(t+\tau-\alpha)\,d\alpha\,d\beta) \qquad (6.2)$$

Taking expected values of both sides yields the *input/output autocorrelation relation*

$$R_{yy}(\tau) = \iint_0^\infty h(\alpha)h(\beta)R_{xx}(\tau+\beta-\alpha)\,d\alpha\,d\beta \qquad (6.3)$$

Similarly, the product $x(t)y(t+\tau)$ is given by

$$x(t)y(t+\tau) = \int_0^\infty h(\alpha)x(t)x(t+\tau-\alpha)\,d\alpha \qquad (6.4)$$

Here, expected values of both sides yields the *input/output cross-correlation relation*

$$R_{xy}(\tau) = \int_0^\infty h(\alpha)R_{xx}(\tau-\alpha)\,d\alpha \qquad (6.5)$$

Note that Equation (6.5) is a convolution integral of the same form as Equation (6.1).

Direct Fourier transforms of Equations (6.3) and (6.5) after various algebraic steps yield two-sided spectral density functions $S_{xx}(f)$, $S_{yy}(f)$, and $S_{xy}(f)$, which satisfy the important formulas

$$S_{yy}(f) = |H(f)|^2 S_{xx}(f) \qquad (6.6)$$

$$S_{xy}(f) = H(f)S_{xx}(f) \qquad (6.7)$$

Here f may be either positive or negative. Note that Equation (6.6) is a real-valued relation containing only the gain factor $|H(f)|$ of the system. Equation (6.7) is a complex-valued relation, which can be broken down into a pair of equations to give both the gain factor $|H(f)|$ and the phase factor $\phi(f)$ of the system. Equation (6.6) is called the *input/output autospectrum relation*, while Equation (6.7) is called the *input/output cross-spectrum relation*. These results apply only to ideal situations where no extraneous noise exists at input or output points, and the systems have no time-varying or nonlinear characteristics. Interpretation of these spectral relations in the frequency domain is much easier than their corresponding correlation relations in the time domain.

SINGLE-INPUT/SINGLE-OUTPUT MODELS

In terms of one-sided spectral density functions $G_{xx}(f)$, $G_{yy}(f)$, and $G_{xy}(f)$, where $G(f) = 2S(f)$ for $f > 0$, Equations (6.6) and (6.7) become

$$G_{yy}(f) = |H(f)|^2 G_{xx}(f) \qquad (6.8)$$

$$G_{xy}(f) = H(f) G_{xx}(f) \qquad (6.9)$$

Let

$$G_{xy}(f) = |G_{xy}(f)| e^{-j\theta_{xy}(f)} \qquad (6.10)$$

$$H(f) = |H(f)| e^{-j\phi(f)} \qquad (6.11)$$

Then Equation (6.9) is equivalent to the pair of relations

$$|G_{xy}(f)| = |H(f)| G_{xx}(f) \qquad (6.12)$$

$$\theta_{xy}(f) = \phi(f) \qquad (6.13)$$

These results provide the basis for many engineering applications of spectral density functions. See Ref. 1 for physical illustrations. Figure 6.2 shows how an input spectrum $G_{xx}(f)$ is modified in passing through a linear system described by $H(f)$.

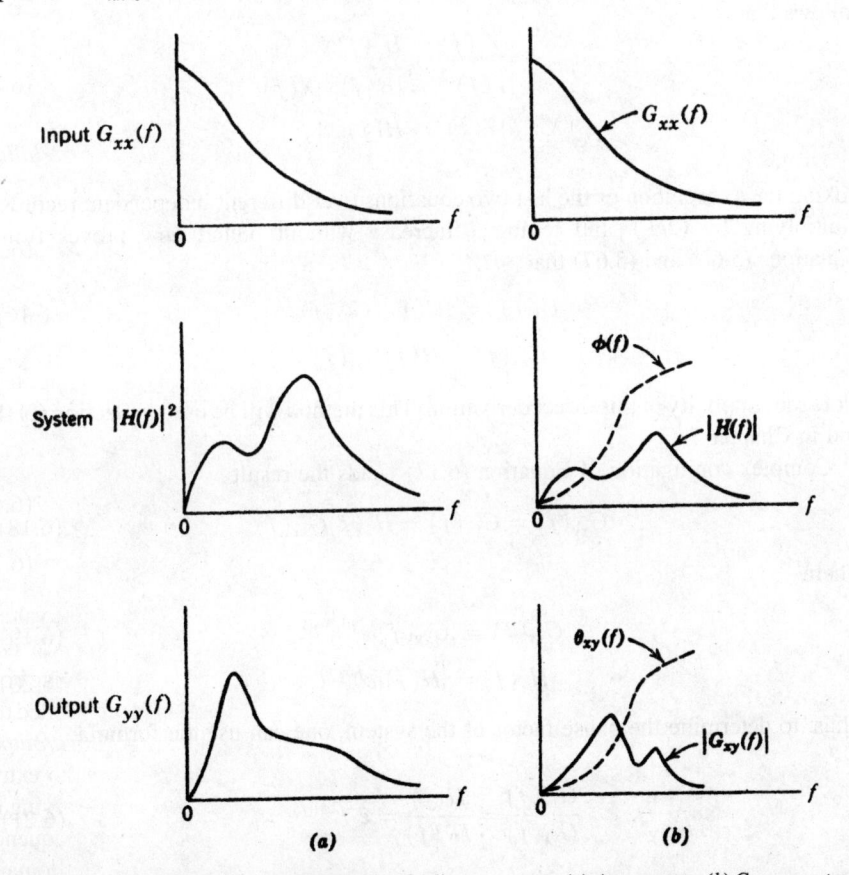

Figure 6.2 Input/output spectral relationships for linear systems, (a) Autospectra. (b) Cross-spectra.

From Equation (6.8), the output mean square value is given by

$$\psi_y^2 = \int_0^\infty G_{yy}(f)df = \int_0^\infty |H(f)|^2 G_{xx}(f)df \tag{6.14}$$

Equation (6.8) also permits the determination of $G_{xx}(f)$ from a knowledge of $G_{yy}(f)$ and $|H(f)|$, or the determination of $|H(f)|$ from a knowledge of $G_{xx}(f)$ and $G_{yy}(f)$. Equation (6.8) does not yield the complete frequency response function $H(f)$ of the system, however, since it contains no phase information. The complete frequency response function in both gain and phase can only be obtained from Equations (6.9)–(6.13) when both $G_{xy}(f)$ and $G_{xx}(f)$ are known.

An alternative direct transform is available to derive Equations (6.8) and (6.9) without first computing the correlation expressions of Equations (6.3) and (6.5). For any pair of long but finite records of length T, Equation (6.1) is equivalent to

$$Y(f) = H(f)X(f) \tag{6.15}$$

where $X(f)$ and $Y(f)$ are finite Fourier transforms of $x(t)$ and $y(t)$, respectively. It follows that

$$Y^*(f) = H^*(f)X^*(f)$$
$$|Y(f)|^2 = |H(f)|^2|X(f)|^2$$
$$X^*(f)Y(f) = H(f)|X(f)|^2$$

Taking the expectation of the last two equations over different independent records, multiplying by $(2/T)$, and letting T increase without bound now proves from Equations (5.66) and (5.67) that

$$G_{yy}(f) = |H(f)|^2 G_{xx}(f) \tag{6.16}$$

$$G_{xy}(f) = H(f) G_{xx}(f) \tag{6.17}$$

Note the simplicity of this direct derivation. This method will be used in Section 6.1.4 and in Chapter 7.

Complex conjugation of Equation (6.17) yields the result

$$G_{xy}^*(f) = G_{yx}(f) = H^*(f) G_{xx}(f) \tag{6.18}$$

where

$$G_{yx}(f) = |G_{xy}(f)| e^{j\theta_{xy}(f)} \tag{6.19}$$

$$H^*(f) = |H(f)| e^{j\phi(f)} \tag{6.20}$$

Thus, to determine the phase factor of the system, one can use the formula

$$\frac{G_{xy}(f)}{G_{yx}(f)} = \frac{H(f)}{H^*(f)} = e^{-j2\phi(f)} \tag{6.21}$$

SINGLE-INPUT/SINGLE-OUTPUT MODELS

To determine the complete frequency response function of the system, Equations (6.16) and (6.18) show that

$$G_{yy}(f) = H(f)[H^*(f)G_{xx}(f)] = H(f)G_{yx}(f) \tag{6.22}$$

Hence, for the ideal single-input/single-output model, one can determine $H(f)$ using Equation (6.17) to yield

$$H(f) = \frac{G_{xy}(f)}{G_{xx}(f)} \tag{6.23}$$

while Equation (6.22) gives

$$H(f) = \frac{G_{yy}(f)}{G_{yx}(f)} \tag{6.24}$$

Thus,

$$\frac{G_{xy}(f)}{G_{xx}(f)} = \frac{G_{yy}(f)}{G_{yx}(f)} \tag{6.25}$$

which is equivalent to

$$|G_{xy}(f)|^2 = G_{xx}(f)G_{yy}(f) \tag{6.26}$$

For transient data, discussed in Chapter 12, "energy" spectral density functions are used instead of "power"-type spectral density functions defined in Chapters 5 and 6. These are related by $\mathcal{G}_{xy}(f) = TG_{xy}(f)$ where $\mathcal{G}_{xy}(f)$ represents the "energy" cross-spectral density function. The transients $x(t)$ and $y(t)$ are assumed to exist only in the range $0 \leq t \leq T$. Input/output formulas derived in this chapter and Chapter 7 apply to such transient data by merely replacing "power" spectral density functions by corresponding "energy" spectral density functions.

Example 6.1. **Response Properties of Low-Pass Filter to White Noise.** Assume white noise is applied to the input of a low-pass RC filter with a time constant $K = RC$. Determine the output autospectral density function, the output mean square value, and the output autocorrelation function.

The frequency response function of the low-pass filter is

$$H(f) = (1 + j2\pi Kf)^{-1} = |H(f)|e^{-j\phi(f)}$$

corresponding to a weighting function of

$$h(\tau) = \begin{cases} \frac{1}{k}e^{-\tau/K} & \tau \geq 0 \\ 0 & \tau < 0 \end{cases}$$

Here

$$|H(f)| = [1 + (2\pi Kf)^2]^{-1/2}$$

$$\phi(f) = \tan^{-1}(2\pi Kf)$$

If $G_{xx}(f)$ is white noise where $G_{xx}(f) = A$, a constant for all $f \geq 0$, then

$$G_{yy}(f) = |H(f)|^2 G_{xx}(f) = \frac{A}{1+(2\pi K f)^2}$$

$$\psi_y^2 = \int_0^\infty G_{yy}(f) df = \int_0^\infty \frac{A}{1+(2\pi K f)^2} df = \frac{A}{4K}$$

$$R_{yy}(\tau) = \int_0^\infty G_{yy}(f) \cos 2\pi f \tau \, df = \frac{A}{4K} e^{-|\tau|/K}$$

Example 6.2. Response Properties of Low-Pass Filter to Sine Wave. Assume a sine wave with an autospectral density function

$$G_{xx}(f) = \{X^2/2\} \delta(f - f_0)$$

is applied to the low-pass RC filter in Example 6.1. Determine the output autospectral density function, the output mean square value, and the output autocorrelation function.

For this problem,

$$G_{yy}(f) = |H(f)|^2 G_{xx}(f) = \frac{(X^2/2)\delta(f-f_0)}{1+(2\pi K f)^2}$$

$$\psi_y^2 = \int_0^\infty G_{yy}(f) df = \frac{X^2/2}{1+(2\pi K f)^2}$$

$$R_{yy}(\tau) = \int_0^\infty G_{yy}(f) \cos 2\pi f \tau \, df = \frac{X^2/2}{1+(2\pi K f_0)^2} \cos 2\pi f_0 \tau$$

Example 6.3. Force-Input/Displacement-Output System. Determine the output autospectral density function, the output autocorrelation function, and the output mean square value when the input is white noise for the force-input/displacement-output system in Figure 2.2. These results apply also to other analogous systems, as discussed in Chapter 2.

Assume $G_{xx}(f) = G$, a constant. Then, from Equation (2.24a) or Table 2.1, when the force is expressed in displacement units, that is $x(t) = F(t)/k$, the output autospectral density function becomes

$$G_{yy}(f) = |H(f)|^2_{f-d} G = \frac{G}{[1-(f/f_n)^2]^2 + 2\zeta f/f_n)^2} \quad 0 \leq f < \infty$$

The corresponding output autocorrelation function is given by

$$R_{yy}(\tau) = \frac{G\pi f_n e^{-2\pi f_n \zeta |\tau|}}{4\zeta} \left[\cos\left(2\pi f_n \sqrt{1-\zeta^2}|\tau|\right) + \frac{\zeta}{\sqrt{1-\zeta^2}} \sin\left(2\pi f_n \sqrt{1-\zeta^2}|\tau|\right) \right]$$

SINGLE-INPUT/SINGLE-OUTPUT MODELS

The output mean square value is

$$\psi_y^2 = \int_0^\infty G_{yy}(f)df = R_{yy}(0) = \frac{G\pi f_n}{4\zeta}$$

Thus, for a white noise input, the output mean square value ψ_y^2 is inversely proportional to ζ.

For a sine wave input, it will now be shown that the maximum value of ψ_y^2 is inversely proportional to ζ^2. Consider

$$F(t) = kx(t) = kX \sin 2\pi f_0 t \quad f_0 = (1/T)$$

passing through a force-input/displacement-output system specified by the $H(f)$ in Figure 2.2. Here, the output $y(t)$ from Equation (2.28) becomes

$$y(t) = kX|H(f_0)|\sin[2\pi f_0 t - \phi(f_0)]$$

with

$$\psi_y^2 = \frac{1}{T}\int_0^T y^2(t)dt = k^2(X^2/2)|H(f_0)|^2$$

From Equation (2.26), for small ζ,

$$\max|H(f_0)| = |H(f_r)| \approx \frac{1}{2k\zeta}$$

Hence

$$\max \psi_y^2 \approx \frac{X^2}{8\zeta^2}$$

proving the stated result.

Example 6.4. Displacement-Input/Displacement-Output System. Determine the output autospectral density function, the output autocorrelation function, and the output mean square value when the input is white noise for the displacement-input/displacement-output system in Figure 2.4. These results apply also to other analogous systems, as discussed in Chapter 2.

Assume $G_x(f) = G$, a constant. Then, from Equation (2.38a) or Table 2.1, the output autospectral density function becomes

$$G_{yy}(f) = |H(f)|_{d-d}^2 G = \frac{G[1+(2\zeta f/f_n)^2]}{[1-(f/f_n)^2]^2 + (2\zeta f/f_n)^2}$$

The corresponding output autocorrelation function is given by

$$R_{yy}(\tau) = \frac{G\pi f_n(1+4\zeta^2)}{4\zeta}e^{-2f_n\zeta|\tau|}\left[\cos\left(2\pi f_n\sqrt{1-\zeta^2}|\tau|\right)\right.$$

$$\left. + \frac{\zeta(1-4\zeta^2)}{\sqrt{1-\zeta^2(1+4\zeta^2)}}\sin\left(2\pi f_n\sqrt{1-\zeta^2}|\tau|\right)\right]$$

The output mean square value is

$$\psi_y^2 = \int_0^\infty G_{yy}(f)df = R_{yy}(0) = \frac{G\pi f_n(1+4\zeta^2)}{4\zeta}$$

The importance of exponential-cosine and exponential-sine autocorrelation functions for many physical problems is apparent from the last two examples. In cases where $\zeta \ll 1$, results can be approximated using only exponential-cosine functions.

6.1.2 Ordinary Coherence Functions

Assuming $G_{xx}(f)$ and $G_{yy}(f)$ are both different from zero and do not contain delta functions, the coherence function between the input $x(t)$ and the output $y(t)$ is a real-valued quantity defined by

$$\gamma_{xy}^2(f) = \frac{|G_{xy}(f)|^2}{G_{xx}(f)G_{yy}(f)} = \frac{|S_{xy}(f)|^2}{S_{xx}(f)S_{yy}(f)} \qquad (6.27)$$

where the G's are the one-sided spectra and the S's are the two-sided theoretical spectra defined previously. From Equation (5.91), it follows that the coherence function satisfies for all f

$$0 \le \gamma_{xy}^2(f) \le 1 \qquad (6.28)$$

To eliminate delta functions at the origin, mean values different from zero should be removed from the data before applying these last two results. Note that the coherence function is analogous to the square of the correlation function coefficient $\rho_{xy}^2(\tau)$ defined by Equation (5.16).

For a constant-parameter linear system, Equations (6.16) and (6.17) apply and may be substituted into Equations (6.27) to obtain

$$\gamma_{xy}^2(f) = \frac{|H(f)|^2 G_{xx}^2(f)}{G_{xx}(f)|H(f)|^2 G_{xx}(f)} = 1 \qquad (6.29)$$

Hence, for the ideal case of a constant-parameter linear system with a single clearly defined input and output, the coherence function will be unity. If $x(t)$ and $y(t)$ are completely unrelated, the coherence function will be zero. If the coherence function is greater than zero but less than unity, one or more of three possible physical situations exist.

a. Extraneous noise is present in the measurements.
b. The system relating $x(t)$ and $y(t)$ is not linear.
c. $y(t)$ is an output due to an input $x(t)$ as well as to other inputs.

For linear systems, the coherence function $\gamma_{xy}^2(f)$ can be interpreted as the fractional portion of the mean square value at the output $y(t)$ that is contributed by the input $x(t)$ at frequency f. Conversely, the quantity $[1-\gamma_{xy}^2(f)]$ is a measure of the mean square value of $y(t)$ not accounted for by $x(t)$ at frequency f.

SINGLE-INPUT/SINGLE-OUTPUT MODELS

Ouput $y(t)$ = vertical C.G. acceleration

Input $x(t)$ = vertical gust velocity

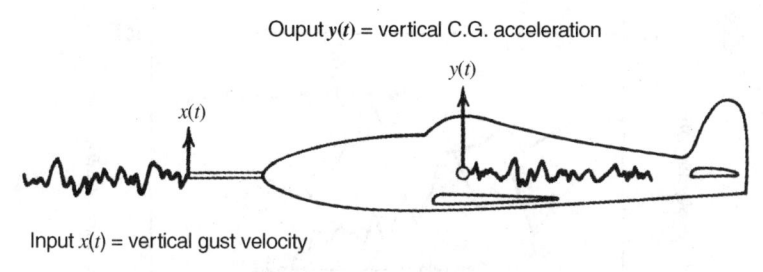

Figure 6.3 Airplane flying through atmospheric turbulence.

Example 6.5. Physical Illustration of Coherence Measurement. Consider an airplane flying through a patch of atmospheric turbulence, as illustrated in Figure 6.3. Let the input $x(t)$ be vertical gust velocity in meters/second (m/s) as measured with a probe extending forward of the airplane, and the output $y(t)$ be vertical acceleration in G's measured with an accelerometer at the center of gravity of the airplane. The resulting coherence function and autospectra for actual data of this type are presented in Figures 6.4 and 6.5. In this problem, the spectral data were computed over a frequency range from 0.1 to 4.0 Hz with a resolution bandwidth of 0.05 Hz and a record length of about 10 min.

From Figure 6.4, it is seen that the input gust velocity and output airplane acceleration display a relatively strong coherence of 0.8–0.9 over the frequency range from about 0.4 to about 2.0 Hz. Below and above this range, however, the

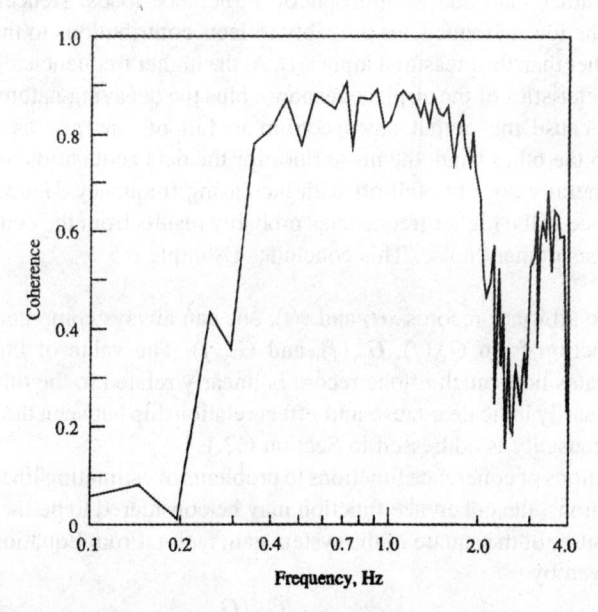

Figure 6.4 Coherence function between gust velocity and response acceleration of airplane. These data resulted from studies funded by the NASA Langley Research Center, Hampton, Virginia, under Contract NAS 1-8538.

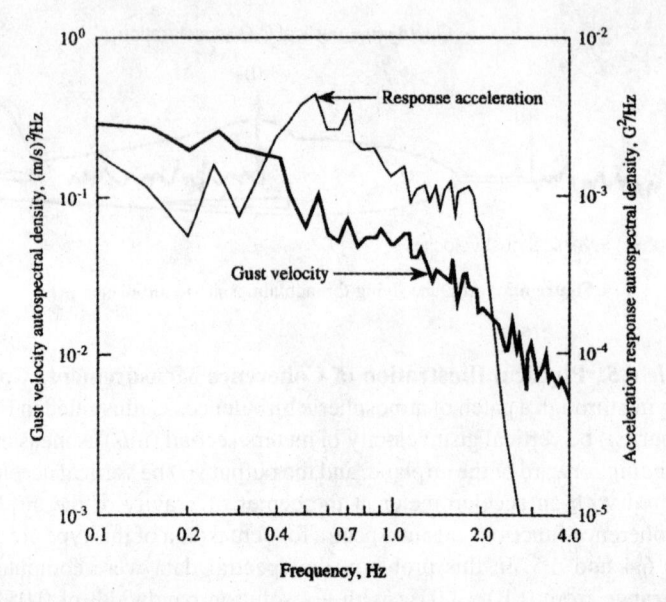

Figure 6.5 Autospectra of gust velocity and response acceleration of airplane. These data resulted from studies funded by the NASA Langley Research Center, Hampton, Virginia, under Contract NAS 1-8538.

coherence function diminishes. At the lower frequencies, the vertical acceleration of the airplane is increasingly due to maneuver loads induced through the control system by the pilot, rather than due to atmospheric turbulence loads. Hence, the loss of coherence at the lower frequencies probably reflects contributions to the output $y(t)$ from inputs other than the measured input $x(t)$. At the higher frequencies, the low-pass filtering characteristics of the airplane response plus the decaying nature of the input autospectrum cause the output autospectrum to fall off sharply, as indicated in Figure 6.5. On the other hand, the noise floor for the data acquisition and recording equipment generally does not fall off with increasing frequency. Hence, the diminishing coherence at the higher frequencies probably results from the contributions of extraneous measurement noise. This concludes Example 6.5.

For any two arbitrary records $x(t)$ and $y(t)$, one can always compute the ordinary coherence function from $G_{xx}(f)$, $G_{yy}(f)$, and $G_{xy}(f)$. The value of this coherence function indicates how much of one record is linearly related to the other record. It does not necessarily indicate a cause-and-effect relationship between the two records. The issue of causality is addressed in Section 6.2.1.

For applications of coherence functions to problems of estimating linear frequency response functions, the coherence function may be considered to be the ratio of two different measures of the square of the system gain factor. From Equation (6.16), one measure is given by

$$|H(f)|_1^2 = \frac{G_{yy}(f)}{G_{xx}(f)} \tag{6.30}$$

SINGLE-INPUT/SINGLE-OUTPUT MODELS

From Equation (6.17), the second measure is given by

$$|H(f)|_2^2 = \frac{|G_{yy}(f)|^2}{G_{xx}^2(f)} \tag{6.31}$$

Now, their ratio gives the coherence function

$$\frac{|H(f)|_2^2}{|H(f)|_1^2} = \frac{|G_{xy}(f)|^2}{G_{xx}(f)G_{yy}(f)} = \gamma_{xy}^2(f) \tag{6.32}$$

In practice, measured values of Equation (6.32) will be between zero and unity. The gain factor estimate of Equation (6.30), based on autospectra calculations of input and output, will be a biased estimate for all cases except when the coherence function equals unity. The gain factor estimate of Equation (6.31), however, based on the input autospectrum and the cross-spectrum between input and output, will be a biased estimate for cases where extraneous noise is present at the input, but will be an unbiased estimate for cases where extraneous noise is present at the output only. In particular, Equation (6.31) provides an unbiased estimate of the frequency response function gain factors in multiple-input problems when the inputs are uncorrelated. These matters are discussed further in Chapter 9, where it is shown how the accuracy of frequency response function estimate increases as the coherence function approaches unity.

Coherence functions are preserved under linear transformations. To be specific, suppose one desires the coherence function between $x(t)$ and $y(t)$ where these two quantities cannot be easily measured. Assume, however, that one can measure two other quantities $x_1(t)$ and $y_1(t)$, where, from physical considerations, it can be stated that $x_1(t)$ has a perfect linear relationship to $x(t)$ and $y_1(t)$ has a perfect linear relationship to $y_1(t)$. Then the coherence function between $x_1(t)$ and $y_1(t)$ will give the desired coherence function between $x(t)$ and $y(t)$. The proof is as follows.

Perfect linear relationships mean that there exist hypothetical frequency response functions $A(f)$ and $B(f)$, which do not have to be computed, such that

$$X_1(f) = A(f)X(f) \qquad Y_1(f) = B(f)Y(f)$$

Then, at any value of f,

$$G_{x_1x_1} = |A|^2 G_{xx} \quad G_{y_1y_1} = |B|^2 G_{yy} \quad G_{x_1y_1} = A^*B G_{xy}$$

Hence,

$$\gamma_{x_1y_1}^2 = \frac{|G_{x_1y_1}|^2}{G_{x_1x_1}G_{y_1y_1}} = \frac{|A^*B|^2 |G_{xy}|^2}{|A|^2 G_{xx}|B|^2 G_{yy}} = \frac{|G_{xy}|^2}{G_{xx}G_{yy}} = \gamma_{xy}^2$$

This result is important for many applications discussed in Ref. 1.

6.1.3 Models with Extraneous Noise

Consider models where extraneous noise is measured at the input and output points to a linear system $H(f)$. Let the true signals be $u(t)$ and $v(t)$ and the extraneous noise be $m(t)$

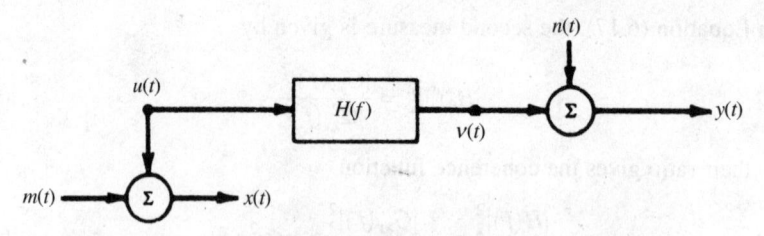

Figure 6.6 Single-input/single-output system with extraneous noise.

and $n(t)$ respectively, as shown in Figure 6.6. Assume that only $u(t)$ passes through the system to produce the true output $v(t)$, but that the measured input and output records are

$$x(t) = u(t) + m(t)$$
$$y(t) = v(t) + n(t) \tag{6.33}$$

For arbitrary correlations between the signal and noise terms, autospectral and cross-spectral density functions for $x(t)$ and $y(t)$ will be

$$G_{xx}(f) = G_{uu}(f) + G_{mm}(f) + G_{um}(f) + G_{mu}(f)$$
$$G_{yy}(f) = G_{vv}(f) + G_{nn}(f) + G_{nv}(f) + G_{nv}(f) \tag{6.34}$$
$$G_{xy}(f) = G_{uv}(f) + G_{un}(f) + G_{mv}(f) + G_{mn}(f)$$

where

$$G_{vv}(f) = |H(f)|^2 G_{uu}(f) \tag{6.35}$$
$$G_{uv}(f) = H(f) G_{uu}(f) \tag{6.36}$$

Various cases occur, depending on the correlation properties of $m(t)$ and $n(t)$ to each other and to the signals. Three cases of interest are

Case 1. No input noise; uncorrelated output noise
Case 2. No output noise; uncorrelated input noise
Case 3. Both noises present; uncorrelated with each other and with the signals

CASE 1. *No Input Noise; Uncorrelated Output Noise*

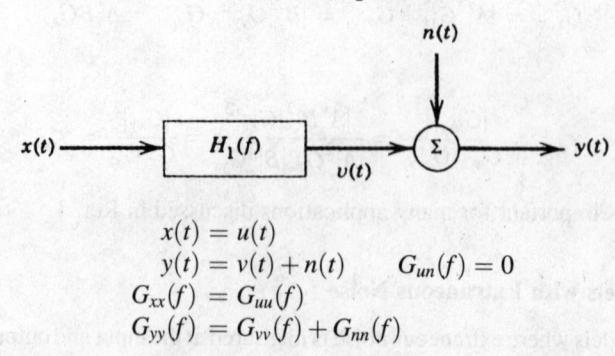

$$x(t) = u(t)$$
$$y(t) = v(t) + n(t) \qquad G_{un}(f) = 0$$
$$G_{xx}(f) = G_{uu}(f)$$
$$G_{yy}(f) = G_{vv}(f) + G_{nn}(f)$$

SINGLE-INPUT/SINGLE-OUTPUT MODELS

$$G_{xy}(f) = G_{uv}(f) = H_1(f)G_{xx}(f)$$
$$H_1(f) = \frac{G_{xy}(f)}{G_{xx}(f)} \qquad (6.37)$$
$$G_{vv}(f) = |H_1(f)|^2 G_{uu}(f) = \frac{|G_{xy}(f)|^2}{G_{xx}(f)} \qquad (6.38)$$

Note that $G_{vv}(f)$ can be calculated from $x(t)$ and $y(t)$ even though $v(t)$ cannot be measured. Also, $G_{nn}(f)$ can be calculated without measuring $n(t)$. For applications in practice, this is by far the most important case because one can often define inputs and minimize input noise. However, one will have no control over the output noise, which is due to nonlinear operations or the contributions from other unmeasured inputs.

For Case 1, the ordinary coherence function is

$$\gamma_{xy}^2(f) = \frac{|G_{xy}(f)|^2}{G_{xx}(f)G_{yy}(f)} = \frac{|G_{uv}(f)|^2}{G_{uu}(f)[G_{vv}(f)+G_{nn}(f)]} = \frac{1}{1+G_{nn}(f)/G_{vv}(f)} \qquad (6.39)$$

because

$$\gamma_{uv}^2(f) = \frac{|G_{uv}(f)|^2}{G_{uu}(f)G_{vv}(f)} = 1$$

Note that $\gamma_{xy}^2(f) < 1$ when $G_{nn}(f) > 0$ with

$$G_{vv}(f) = \gamma_{xy}^2(f)G_{yy}(f) \qquad (6.40)$$

This product of γ_{xy}^2 with $G_{yy}(f)$ is called the *coherent output spectrum*. Note also that the *noise output spectrum* is

$$G_{nn}(f) = [1-\gamma_{xy}^2(f)]G_{yy}(f) \qquad (6.41)$$

Thus, $\gamma_{xy}^2(f)$ can be interpreted here as the portion of $G_{yy}(f)$ that is due to $x(t)$ at frequency f, while $[1-\gamma_{xy}^2(f)]$ is a measure of the portion of $G_{yy}(f)$ not due to $x(t)$ at frequency f. Here, the ordinary coherence function decomposes the measured *output* spectrum into its uncorrelated components due to the input signal and extraneous noise. Equation (6.40) is the basis for solving many source identification problems using ordinary coherence functions, as illustrated in Ref. 1.

CASE 2. *No Output Noise; Uncorrelated Input Noise*

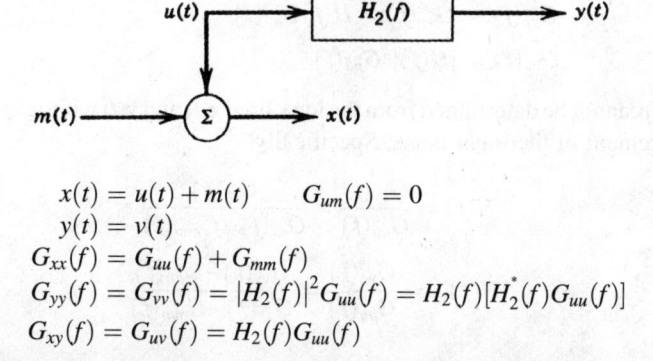

$$x(t) = u(t) + m(t) \qquad G_{um}(f) = 0$$
$$y(t) = v(t)$$
$$G_{xx}(f) = G_{uu}(f) + G_{mm}(f)$$
$$G_{yy}(f) = G_{vv}(f) = |H_2(f)|^2 G_{uu}(f) = H_2(f)[H_2^*(f)G_{uu}(f)]$$
$$G_{xy}(f) = G_{uv}(f) = H_2(f)G_{uu}(f)$$

$$G_{yx}(f) = H_2^*(f)G_{uu}(f)$$

$$H_2(f) = \frac{G_{yy}(f)}{G_{yx}(f)} \tag{6.42}$$

$$G_{uu}(f) = \frac{G_{vv}(f)}{|H_2(f)|^2} = \frac{|G_{xy}(f)|^2}{G_{yy}(f)} = \frac{|G_{xy}(f)|^2}{G_{yy}(f)} \tag{6.43}$$

Here $G_{uu}(f)$ and $G_{mm}(f)$ can be determined from $x(t)$ and $y(t)$. This case is useful for special applications where extraneous noise contamination of the input measurement only is anticipated. It should not be applied when output noise is expected because of possible nonlinear operations, the contributions from other inputs, and/or output measurement instrumentation noise. Case 1 is always preferred in these situations.

For Case 2, the ordinary coherence function is

$$\gamma_{xy}^2(f) = \frac{|G_{xy}(f)|^2}{G_{xx}(f)G_{yy}(f)} = \frac{|G_{uv}(f)|^2}{[G_{uu}(f)+G_{mm}(f)]G_{vv}(f)} = \frac{1}{1+[G_{mm}(f)/G_{uu}(f)]} \tag{6.44}$$

It follows that $\gamma_{xy}^2(f) < 1$ when $G_{mm}(f) > 0$ with

$$G_{uu}(f) = \gamma_{xy}^2(f)G_{xx}(f) \tag{6.45}$$

$$G_{mm}(f) = [1-\gamma_{xy}^2(f)]G_{xx}(f) \tag{6.46}$$

Thus, for Case 2, the ordinary coherence function can decompose a measured *input* spectrum into its uncorrelated signal and noise components.

If one divides the frequency response function $H_1(f)$ for Case 1 as given by Equation (6.37) by the frequency response function $H_2(f)$ for Case 2 as given by Equation (6.42), the result is the coherence function, namely,

$$\frac{H_1(f)}{H_2(f)} = \frac{G_{xy}(f)/G_{xx}(f)}{G_{yy}(f)/G_{yx}(f)} = \gamma_{xy}^2(f) \tag{6.47}$$

CASE 3. *Both Noises Present; Uncorrelated with Each Other and with the Signals*

$$x(t) = u(t)+m(t) \quad G_{um}(f) = G_{un}(f) = 0$$
$$y(t) = v(t)+n(t) \quad G_{mn}(f) = 0$$
$$G_{xx}(f) = G_{uu}(f)+G_{mm}(f)$$
$$G_{yy}(f) = G_{vv}(f)+G_{nn}(f)$$
$$G_{xy}(f) = G_{uv}(f) = H(f)G_{uu}(f)$$
$$G_{vv}(f) = |H(f)|^2 G_{uu}(f) \tag{6.48}$$

Here, $H(f)$ cannot be determined from the measured $x(t)$ and $y(t)$ without a knowledge or measurement of the input noise. Specifically,

$$H(f) = \frac{G_{xy}(f)}{G_{uu}(f)} = \frac{G_{xy}(f)}{G_{xx}(f)-G_{mm}(f)} \tag{6.49}$$

$$|H(f)|^2 = \frac{G_{vv}(f)}{G_{uu}(f)} = \frac{G_{yy}(f)-G_{nn}(f)}{G_{xx}(f)-G_{mm}(f)} \tag{6.50}$$

SINGLE-INPUT/SINGLE-OUTPUT MODELS

Note that $H(f)$ is a function of $G_{mm}(f)$, but is independent of $G_{nn}(f)$ by Equation (6.49). Using Equation (6.50) to calculate $|H(f)|^2$ shows that $|H(f)|^2$ is a function of both $G_{mm}(f)$ and $G_{nn}(f)$.

For Case 3, the ordinary coherence function is

$$\gamma_{xy}^2(f) = \frac{|G_{xy}(f)|^2}{G_{xx}(f)G_{yy}(f)} = \frac{|G_{uv}(f)|^2}{[G_{uu}(f)+G_{mm}(f)][G_{vv}(f)+G_{nn}(f)]} \qquad (6.51)$$

$$= \frac{1}{1+c_1(f)+c_2(f)+c_1(f)c_2(f)}$$

where $c_1(f)$ and $c_2(f)$ are the noise-to-signal ratios given by

$$\begin{aligned} c_1(f) &= [G_{mm}(f)/G_{uu}(f)] \\ c_2(f) &= [G_{nn}(f)/G_{vv}(f)] \end{aligned} \qquad (6.52)$$

Clearly, $\gamma_{xy}^2(f) < 1$ whenever $c_1(f) > 0$ or $c_2(f) > 0$. Here, using only $x(t)$ and $y(t)$, it is *not* possible to decompose $G_{xx}(f)$ or $G_{yy}(f)$ into their separate signal and noise components.

6.1.4 Optimum Frequency Response Functions

Return now to the basic single-input/single-output system with output noise only (Case 1), as illustrated in Figure 6.7. Without assuming that $n(t)$ is uncorrelated with $v(t)$, let $H(f)$ be *any* linear frequency response function acting on $x(t)$. Of interest is the specific $H(f)$ that will minimize the noise at the output; that is, the optimum estimate of $H(f)$ in the least squares sense. Note that if there is any correlation between the output signal and the noise, as would occur if the output included signal-dependent instrumentation noise or the contributions of other inputs that are correlated with the measured $x(t)$, then the resulting optimum $H(f)$ will not represent the physical direct path between the points where $x(t)$ and $y(t)$ are measured. Also, there may be nonlinear operations between the measured input and output data. In any case, the optimum $H(f)$ will simply constitute a mathematical function that defines the best linear relationship between $x(t)$ and $y(t)$ in the least squares sense.

For any set of long records of finite length T in Figure 6.7, the governing relation is

$$Y(f) = H(f)X(f) + N(f) \qquad (6.53)$$

where capital letters are finite Fourier transforms of associated time-domain records. Solving for $N(f)$ and $N^*(f)$ gives

$$N(f) = Y(f) - H(f)X(f) \qquad N^*(f) = Y^*(f) - H^*(f)X^*(f)$$

It follows that

$$|N(f)|^2 = |Y(f)|^2 - H(f)Y^*(f)X(f) - H^*(f)X^*(f)Y(f) + H(f)H^*(f)|X(f)|^2 \qquad (6.54)$$

Taking the expectation of Equation (6.54), multiplying by $(2/T)$, and letting T increase to infinity yields

$$G_{nn}(f) = G_{yy}(f) - H(f)G_{xy}(f) - H^*(f)G_{xy}(f) + H(f)H^*(f)G_{xx}(f) \qquad (6.55)$$

This is the form of $G_{nn}(f)$ for *any* $H(f)$. By definition, the *optimum* $H(f)$ will now be defined as that $H(f)$ that minimizes $G_{nn}(f)$ at any f over all possible choices of $H(f)$. This is called the *least squares estimate*.

The minimization of $G_{nn}(f)$ as a function of $H(f)$ will now be carried out. To simplify the derivation, the dependence on f will be omitted. Thus,

$$G_{nn} = G_{yy} - HG_{yx} - H^*G_{xy} + HH^*G_{xx} \qquad (6.56)$$

Now let the complex numbers be expressed in terms of their real and imaginary parts as follows:

$$H = H_R - jH_I \qquad H^* = H_R + jH_I$$
$$G_{xy} = G_R - jG_I \qquad G_{yx} = G_R + jG_I$$

Then

$$G_{nn} = G_{yy} - (H_R - jH_I)G_{yx} - (H_R + jH_I)G_{xy} + (H_R^2 + H_I^2)G_{xx}$$

To find the form of H that will minimize G_{nn}, one should now set the partial derivatives of G_{nn} with respect to H_R and H_I equal to zero and solve the resulting pair of equations. This gives

$$\frac{\partial G_{nn}}{\partial H_R} = -G_{yx} - G_{xy} + 2H_R G_{xx} = 0$$

$$\frac{\partial G_{nn}}{\partial H_I} = jG_{yx} - jG_{xy} + 2H_I G_{xx} = 0$$

which leads to

$$H_R = \frac{G_{xy} + G_{yx}}{2G_{xx}} = \frac{G_R}{G_{xx}}$$

$$H_I = \frac{j(G_{xy} - G_{yx})}{2G_{xx}} = \frac{G_I}{G_{xx}}$$

Hence, the optimum H is

$$H = H_R - jH_I = \frac{G_R - jG_I}{G_{xx}} = \frac{G_{xy}}{G_{xx}} \qquad (6.57)$$

Again, the optimum H calculated by Equation (6.57), using arbitrary measured records, does not have to be physically realizable; it may be only a theoretically computed result.

Another important property satisfied by the optimum $H(f)$ is revealed by substitution of the optimum system satisfying Equation (6.57) into Equation (6.55). This gives the noise output spectrum

$$G_{nn}(f) = [1 - \gamma_{xy}^2(f)]G_{yy}(f) \qquad (6.58)$$

SINGLE-INPUT/SINGLE-OUTPUT MODELS

which leads to the coherent output spectrum

$$G_{vv}(f) = G_{yy}(f) - G_{nn}(f) = \gamma_{xy}^2(f) G_{yy}(f) \tag{6.59}$$

Moreover, using the optimum $H(f)$ shows that

$$G_{xv}(f) = H(f) G_{xx}(f)$$

and

$$G_{xn}(f) = G_{xy}(f) - H(f) G_{xx}(f) = 0 \tag{6.60}$$

It follows that

$$G_{vn}(f) = H^*(f) G_{xn}(f) = 0 \tag{6.61}$$

Thus, $n(t)$ and $v(t)$ will *automatically be uncorrelated* when the optimum $H(f)$ is used to estimate the linear system in Figure 6.7.

It should also be noted here that because of the special form of Equation (6.56), a simple way to derive the same optimum H can be obtained by setting either the partial derivative of G_{nn} with respect to H equal to zero (holding H^* fixed) or setting the partial derivative of G_{nn} with respect to H^* equal to zero (holding H fixed). By this alternative method,

$$\frac{\partial G_{nn}}{\partial H} = -G_{yx} + H^* G_{xx} = 0$$

$$H^* = \frac{G_{yx}}{G_{xx}} \qquad H = \frac{G_{xy}}{G_{xx}} \tag{6.62}$$

The following steps justify this method. Equation (6.56) shows that G_{nn} is a real-valued functions of (H_R, H_I) or of (H, H^*) denoted by

$$G_{nn} = f(H_R, H_I) = g(H, H^*)$$

which has the structure

$$g(H, H^*) = AH + A^* H^* + BHH^* + C \tag{6.63}$$

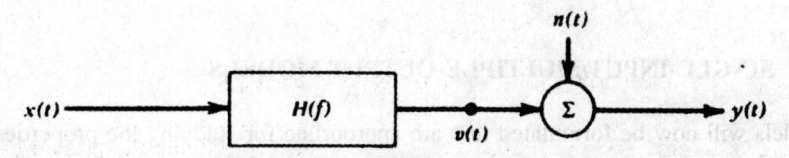

Figure 6.7 Single-input/single-output system with output noise.

where A is complex valued and B, C are real valued. The quantity $H_R(f)$ is the real part of $H(f)$, while $H_I(f)$ is the imaginary part of $H(f)$ satisfying $H = H_R - jH_I$, and $H^* = H_R + jH_I$. Now

$$\frac{\partial G_{nn}}{\partial H_R} = \frac{\partial g}{\partial H}\frac{\partial H}{\partial H_R} + \frac{\partial g}{\partial H^*}\frac{\partial H^*}{\partial H_R} = \frac{\partial g}{\partial H} + \frac{\partial g}{\partial H^*}$$

$$\frac{\partial G_{nn}}{\partial H_I} = \frac{\partial g}{\partial H}\frac{\partial H}{\partial H_I} + \frac{\partial g}{\partial H^*}\frac{\partial H^*}{\partial H_I} = -j\left(\frac{\partial g}{\partial H} - \frac{\partial g}{\partial H^*}\right)$$

(6.64)

Hence, minimization requirements that both

$$\frac{\partial G_{nn}}{\partial H_R} = 0 \quad \text{and} \quad \frac{\partial G_{nn}}{\partial H_I} = 0 \tag{6.65}$$

are equivalent to setting both

$$\frac{\partial g}{\partial H} = A + BH^* = 0 \quad \text{and} \quad \frac{\partial g}{\partial H^*} = 0 \tag{6.66}$$

From Equation (6.63), this will occur when

$$\frac{\partial g}{\partial H} = A + BH^* = 0 \quad \text{giving } H^* = -\frac{A}{B}$$

$$\frac{\partial g}{\partial H^*} = A^* + BH = 0 \quad \text{giving } H = -\frac{A^*}{B}$$

(6.67)

Thus, both of the conditions of Equation (6.66) hold when

$$H = -\frac{A^*}{B} \tag{6.68}$$

Note that this solution is obtained by setting either $\partial g/\partial H = 0$ (holding H^* fixed) or setting $\partial g/\partial H^* = 0$ (holding H fixed) without going back to H_R and H_I. From Equation (6.56), $A = -G_{yx}(f)$ and $B = G_{xx}(f)$. Hence,

$$H(f) = \frac{G_{xy}(f)}{G_{xx}(f)} \tag{6.69}$$

which is the same as Equation (6.57).

6.2 SINGLE-INPUT/MULTIPLE-OUTPUT MODELS

Models will now be formulated that are appropriate for studying the properties of multiple transmission paths between a single source and different output points. It will

SINGLE-INPUT/MULTIPLE-OUTPUT MODELS

be assumed that constant-parameter linear systems can be used to describe these different possible paths and that all unknown deviations from ideal cases can be included in uncorrelated extraneous output noise terms.

6.2.1 Single-Input/Two-Output Model

Consider the special case of a single-input/two-output system, as pictured in Figure 6.8. The following frequency domain equations apply to this situation assuming that the noise terms $n_1(t)$ and $n_2(t)$ are incoherent (uncorrelated) with each other and with the input signal $x(t)$. The dependence on frequency f will be omitted here to simplify the notation.

$$G_{xn_1} = G_{v_1 n_1} = G_{xn_2} = G_{v_2 n_2} = G_{n_1 n_2} = 0$$

$$G_{y_1 y_1} = G_{v_1 v_1} + G_{n_1 n_1} = |H_1|^2 G_{xx} + G_{n_1 n_1} \qquad (6.70)$$

$$G_{y_2 y_2} = G_{v_2 v_2} + G_{n_2 n_2} = |H_2|^2 G_{xx} + G_{n_2 n_2}$$

$$G_{xy_1} = G_{xv_1} = H_1 G_{xx} \qquad G_{xy_2} = G_{xv_2} = H_2 G_{xx} \qquad (6.71)$$

$$G_{y_1 y_2} = G_{v_1 v_2} = H_1^* H_2 G_{xx} \qquad (6.72)$$

For this model, the coherence function between the output records is given by

$$\gamma_{y_1 y_2}^2 = \frac{|G_{y_1 y_2}|^2}{G_{y_1 y_1} G_{y_2 y_2}} = \frac{|G_{v_1 v_2}|^2}{G_{y_1 y_1} G_{y_2 y_2}} = \gamma_{xy_1}^2 \gamma_{xy_2}^2 \qquad (6.73)$$

where the last equality occurs because

$$|G_{v_1 v_2}|^2 = |H_1^* H_2 G_{xx}|^2 = (|H_1|^2 G_{xx})(|H_2|^2 G_{xx}) = G_{v_1 v_1} G_{v_2 v_2}$$

$$\gamma_{xy_1}^2 = \frac{|G_{xy_1}|^2}{G_{xx} G_{y_1 y_1}} = \frac{|H_1 G_{xx}|^2}{G_{xx} G_{y_1 y_1}} = \frac{G_{v_1 v_1}}{G_{y_1 y_1}}$$

$$\gamma_{xy_2}^2 = \frac{|G_{xy_2}|^2}{G_{xx} G_{y_2 y_2}} = \frac{|H_2 G_{xx}|^2}{G_{xx} G_{y_2 y_2}} = \frac{G_{v_2 v_2}}{G_{y_2 y_2}} \qquad (6.74)$$

A number of applications exist for these results, depending on whether or not the input signal $x(t)$ can be measured along with the two output records $y_1(t)$ and $y_2(t)$.

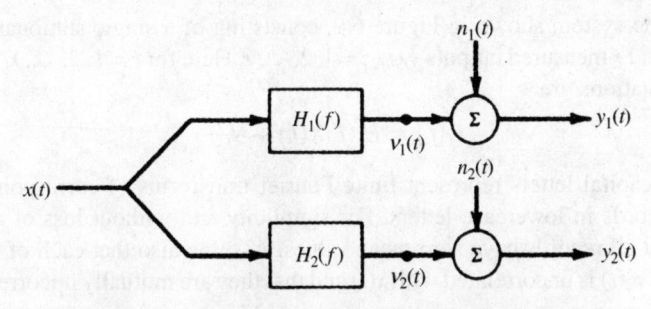

Figure 6.8 Single-input/two-output system with output noise.

CASE 1. *x(t)*, *y₁(t)*, and *y₂(t)* Can Be Measured Simultaneously

For this case, Equation (6.71) yields H_1 and H_2 by

$$H_1 = \frac{G_{xy_1}}{G_{xx}} \qquad H_2 = \frac{G_{xy_2}}{G_{xx}}$$

Then one can determine from Equations (6.70) and (6.74),

$$G_{v_1 v_1} = |H_1|^2 G_{xx} = \gamma_{xy_1}^2 G_{y_1 y_1} \qquad G_{n_1 n_1} = (1 - \gamma_{xy_1}^2) G_{y_1 y_1}$$

$$G_{v_2 v_2} = |H_2|^2 G_{xx} = \gamma_{xy_2}^2 G_{y_2 y_2} \qquad G_{n_2 n_2} = (1 - \gamma_{xy_2}^2) G_{y_2 y_2}$$

Thus all quantities in Equations (6.70)–(6.74) can be found.

CASE 2. Only *y₁(t)* and *y₂(t)* Can Be Measured Simultaneously

For this case, H_1 and H_2 *cannot* be determined using Equation (6.71). If, however, H_1 and H_2 are known from other considerations, such as theoretical ideas, then Equation (6.72) can be used to obtain G_{xx} by

$$G_{xx} = \frac{G_{y_1 y_2}}{H_1^* H_2}$$

The assumed H_1 and H_2 together with the computed G_{xx} will give all the remaining quantities in Equations (6.70)–(6.74) .

If H_1 and H_2 are not known from other considerations, one can still compute $G_{y_1 y_1}$, $G_{y_2 y_2}$, and $G_{y_1 y_2}$. One can then use Equation (6.73) to determine the coherence function $\gamma_{y_1 y_2}^2$. A high value for $\gamma_{y_1 y_2}^2$ indicates that $y_1(t)$ and $y_2(t)$ can come from an unmeasured common source $x(t)$ via unknown linear transformations and that extraneous output noise is small compared to the signal terms. It should be noted here that *a high coherence value does not indicate a causal relationship between* $y_1(t)$ *and* $y_2(t)$. In fact, there is no causal relationship between them in this model. Applications of two output models in energy source location problems are detailed in Ref. 1.

6.2.2 Single-Input/Multiple-Output Model

Consider the system shown in Figure 6.9, consisting of a single stationary random input $x(t)$ and r measured outputs $y_i(t)$, $i = 1, 2, \ldots, r$. Here for $i = 1, 2, \ldots, r$, frequency domain equations are

$$Y_i(f) = H_i(f) X(f) + N_i(f) \tag{6.75}$$

where the capital letters represent finite Fourier transforms of corresponding time domain records in lowercase letters. For simplicity and without loss of generality, assume that all records have zero mean values. Assume also that each of the output noise terms $n_i(t)$ is uncorrelated with $x(t)$ and that they are mutually uncorrelated with each other.

SINGLE-INPUT/MULTIPLE-OUTPUT MODELS

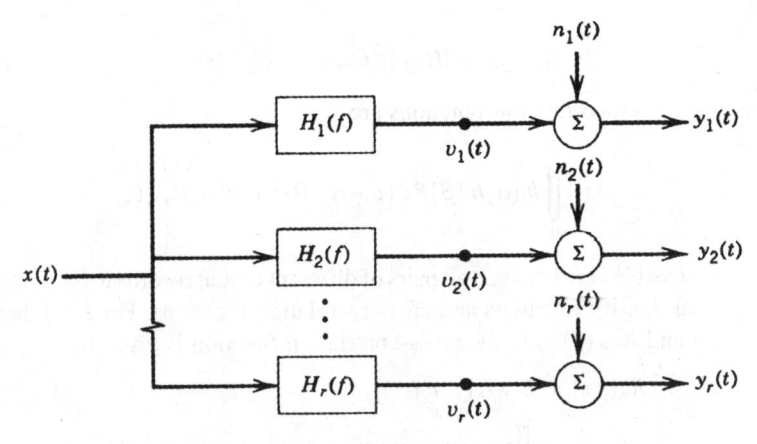

Figure 6.9 Single-input/multiple-output system with output noise.

CASE 1. *Input Plus Output Measurements*

From simultaneous measurements of $x(t)$ with each of the outputs $y_i(t)$, $i = 1, 2, \ldots, r$, one can compute

$$G_{xy_i}(f) = H_i(f)G_{xx}(f) \qquad (6.76)$$

These equations are the same as for earlier single-input/single-output models. Each $H_i(f)$ is then given by the formula

$$H_i(f) = \frac{G_{xy_i}(f)}{G_{xx}(f)} \qquad (6.77)$$

In words, the frequency response function $H_i(f)$ is the cross-spectral density function between the input $x(t)$ and the particular output $y_i(t)$, divided by the autospectral density function of the input. The ordinary coherence function between $x(t)$ and $y_i(t)$ is

$$\gamma_{xy_i}^2(f) = \frac{|G_{xy_i}(f)|^2}{G_{xx}(f)G_{y_iy_i}(f)} \qquad (6.78)$$

Each output can be easily decomposed into its separate signal and noise components. In the time domain, the cross-correlation function between $x(t)$ and $y_i(t)$ is given by

$$R_{xy_i}(\tau) = \int_0^\infty h_i(\tau)R_{xx}(\tau - \alpha)d\alpha \qquad (6.79)$$

where $h_i(\tau)$ is the inverse Fourier transform of $H_i(f)$—that is, the unit impulse response function of the ith path.

CASE 2. *Output Measurements Only*

Consider cases where only the outputs $y_i(t)$ can be measured. For each $i = 1, 2, \ldots, r$, one can compute the autospectral density functions

$$G_{y_iy_i}(f) = |H_i(f)|^2 G_{xx}(f) + G_{n_in_i}(f) \tag{6.80}$$

The associated autocorrelation functions are

$$R_{y_iy_i}(\tau) \iint_0^\infty h_i(\alpha)h_i(\beta)R_{xx}(\tau+\alpha-\beta)d\alpha\, d\beta + R_{n_in_i}(\tau) \tag{6.81}$$

It is also possible here between all pairs of different output records to compute their cross-spectral density functions and cross-correlation functions. For $i \neq j$, because $R_{n_in_j}(\tau) = 0$ and $R_{n_in_j}(f) = 0$, the cross-correlation function is given by

$$\begin{aligned}R_{y_iy_j}(\tau) &= E[y_i(t)y_j(t+\tau)] \\ &= \iint_0^\infty h_i(\alpha)h_j(\beta)E[x(t-\alpha)x(t+\tau-\beta)]d\alpha\, d\beta \\ &= \iint_0^\infty h_i(\alpha)h_j(\beta)R_{xx}(\tau+\alpha-\beta)]d\alpha\, d\beta\end{aligned} \tag{6.82}$$

with other terms that average to zero. On the other hand, the cross-spectral density function between any two of the output records is the simple expression

$$G_{y_iy_j}(f) = H_i^*(f)H_j(f)G_{xx}(f) \tag{6.83}$$

Algebraic operations are now involved to interpret this result easily. Measurement of $G_{y_iy_j}(f)$ plus separate knowledge of $H_i(f)$ and $H_j(f)$ enables one to estimate $G_{xx}(f)$ when $G_{xx}(f)$ cannot be measured directly.

From Equations (6.80) and (6.83), the coherence function between any two of the output records is given by

$$\begin{aligned}\gamma^2_{y_iy_j}(f) &= \frac{|G_{y_iy_j}(f)|^2}{G_{y_iy_i}(f)G_{y_jy_j}(f)} \\ &= \frac{|H_i(f)|^2|H_j(f)|^2 G_{xx}(f)}{[|H_i(f)|^2 G_{xx}(f) + G_{n_in_i}(f)][|H_j(f)|^2 G_{xx}(f) + G_{n_jn_j}(f)]}\end{aligned} \tag{6.84}$$

Various special cases of Equation (6.84) of physical interest are discussed in Chapter 7 of Ref. 1.

6.2.3 Removal of Extraneous Noise

Assume that three or more output measurements, say, $y_1(t)$, $y_2(t)$, and $y_3(t)$, are noisy measurements of the desired output signals $v_1(t)$, $v_2(t)$, and $v_3(t)$, as shown in Figure 6.9. The noise terms $n_1(t)$, $n_2(t)$ and $n_3(t)$ are assumed to be mutually

SINGLE-INPUT/MULTIPLE-OUTPUT MODELS

uncorrelated with each other and with $v_1(t)$, $v_2(t)$ and $v_3(t)$. It will now be shown how to determine the autospectral density function properties of the true output signals $v_i(t)$ from an analysis of the measured $y_i(t)$.

The following equations are all functions of frequency f, which is omitted to simply the notation. The measured output autospectra are

$$G_{11} = G_{y_1 y_1} = G_{v_1 v_1} + G_{n_1 n_1} = G_{v_1 v_1}(1 + c_1)$$
$$G_{22} = G_{y_2 y_2} = G_{v_2 v_2} + G_{n_2 n_2} = G_{v_2 v_2}(1 + c_2) \qquad (6.85)$$
$$G_{33} = G_{y_3 y_3} = G_{v_3 v_3} + G_{n_3 n_3} = G_{v_3 v_3}(1 + c_3)$$

where the $c_i \geq 0$, $i = 1, 2, 3$, represent

$$c_1 = G_{n_1 n_1}/G_{v_1 v_1} = \text{noise-to-signal ratio at output 1}$$
$$c_2 = G_{n_2 n_2}/G_{v_2 v_2} = \text{noise-to-signal ratio at output 2} \qquad (6.86)$$
$$c_3 = G_{n_3 n_3}/G_{v_3 v_3} = \text{noise-to-signal ratio at output 3}$$

The measured cross-spectra between pairs of outputs are

$$G_{12} = G_{y_1 y_2} = G_{v_1 v_2}$$
$$G_{13} = G_{y_1 y_3} = G_{v_1 v_3} \qquad (6.87)$$
$$G_{23} = G_{y_2 y_3} = G_{v_2 v_3}$$

In Figure 6.9, it is assumed that $v_1(t)$, $v_2(t)$, and $v_3(t)$ are due to a common single unmeasured source $x(t)$. Hence, the ordinary coherence functions between pairs of $v_i(t)$ must be unity, namely,

$$\gamma^2_{v_1 v_2} = \frac{|G_{v_1 v_2}|^2}{G_{v_1 v_1} G_{v_2 v_2}} = 1$$

$$\gamma^2_{v_1 v_3} = \frac{|G_{v_1 v_3}|^2}{G_{v_1 v_1} G_{v_3 v_3}} = 1 \qquad (6.88)$$

$$\gamma^2_{v_2 v_3} = \frac{|G_{v_2 v_3}|^2}{G_{v_2 v_2} G_{v_3 v_3}} = 1$$

Thus

$$|G_{12}|^2 = |G_{v_1 v_2}|^2 = G_{v_1 v_1} G_{v_2 v_2}$$
$$|G_{13}|^2 = |G_{v_1 v_3}|^2 = G_{v_1 v_1} G_{v_3 v_3} \qquad (6.89)$$
$$|G_{23}|^2 = |G_{v_3 v_3}|^2 = G_{v_2 v_2} G_{v_3 v_3}$$

From Equations (6.85) and (6.89), it follows that

$$\gamma_{12}^2 = \frac{|G_{12}|^2}{G_{11}G_{22}} = \frac{1}{(1+c_1)(1+c_2)}$$

$$\gamma_{13}^2 = \frac{|G_{13}|^2}{G_{11}G_{33}} = \frac{1}{(1+c_1)(1+c_3)} \qquad (6.90)$$

$$\gamma_{23}^2 = \frac{|G_{23}|^2}{G_{22}G_{33}} = \frac{1}{(1+c_2)(1+c_3)}$$

It is reasonable to assume that none of the measured coherence functions in Equation (6.90) will be zero to obtain

$$(1+c_1) = \frac{1}{\gamma_{12}^2(1+c_2)}$$

$$(1+c_2) = \frac{1}{\gamma_{23}^2(1+c_3)} \qquad (6.91)$$

$$(1+c_3) = \frac{1}{\gamma_{13}^2(1+c_1)}$$

This yields

$$(1+c_1) = \frac{\gamma_{23}^2(1+c_3)}{\gamma_{12}^2} = \frac{\gamma_{23}^2}{\gamma_{12}^2\gamma_{13}^2(1+c_1)} \qquad (6.92)$$

with similar formulas for $(1 + c_2)$ and $(1 + c_3)$. Hence,

$$(1+c_1) = \frac{|\gamma_{23}|}{|\gamma_{12}|\,|\gamma_{13}|}$$

$$(1+c_2) = \frac{|\gamma_{13}|}{|\gamma_{12}|\,|\gamma_{23}|} \qquad (6.93)$$

$$(1+c_3) = \frac{|\gamma_{12}|}{|\gamma_{13}|\,|\gamma_{23}|}$$

From Equation (6.85), one now obtains the desired results

$$G_{v_1v_1} = \frac{G_{11}}{(1+c_1)} = \frac{|\gamma_{12}|\,|\gamma_{13}|}{|\gamma_{23}|}G_{11} = \frac{|G_{12}|\,|G_{13}|}{|G_{23}|}$$

$$G_{v_2v_2} = \frac{G_{22}}{(1+c_2)} = \frac{|\gamma_{12}|\,|\gamma_{13}|}{|\gamma_{13}|}G_{22} = \frac{|G_{12}|\,|G_{23}|}{|G_{13}|} \qquad (6.94)$$

$$G_{v_3v_3} = \frac{G_{33}}{(1+c_3)} = \frac{|\gamma_{13}|\,|\gamma_{23}|}{|\gamma_{12}|}G_{33} = \frac{|G_{13}|\,|G_{23}|}{|G_{12}|}$$

Because $G_{v_1v_1} \leq G_{11}, G_{v_2v_2} \leq G_{22}$, and $G_{v_3v_3} \leq G_{33}$, the coherence functions must satisfy

$$\gamma_{12}^2\gamma_{13}^2 \leq \gamma_{23}^2 \qquad \gamma_{12}^2\gamma_{23}^2 \leq \gamma_{13}^2 \qquad \gamma_{13}^2\gamma_{23}^2 \leq \gamma_{12}^2 \qquad (6.95)$$

One can also solve for the noise autospectra $G_{n_1n_1}, G_{n_2n_2}$, and $G_{n_3n_3}$ using Equations (6.85) and (6.94).

Example 6.6. Illustration of Noisy Measurements. The spectral densities of three output measurements are computed to be $G_{11}(f) = G_{22}(f) = G_{33}(f) = G$, a constant, and the coherence values among the output measurements are computed to be $\gamma_{12}^2 = 0.25$, $\gamma_{13}^2 = 0.25$, and $\gamma_{23}^2 = 0.16$. Determine the signal-to-noise ratios and the spectral densities of the signals in the three output measurements.

From Equation (6.93), the noise-to-signal ratios are given by

$$c_1 = \frac{0.4}{(0.5)(0.5)} - 1 = 0.60$$

$$c_2 = \frac{0.5}{(0.5)(0.4)} - 1 = 1.50$$

$$c_3 = \frac{0.5}{(0.5)(0.4)} - 1 = 1.50$$

Hence the *signal-to-noise ratios*, given by $SNR = 1/c$ (see Section 10.1.4), at the output measurements are

$$SNR_1 = 1.67 \qquad SNR_2 = 0.67 \qquad SNR_3 = 0.67$$

and the spectral densities of the signals in the output measurements are

$$G_{v_1v_1} = 0.625G \qquad G_{v_2v_2} = 0.40G \qquad G_{v_3v_3} = 0.40G$$

PROBLEMS

6.1 The input to a physical system has an autospectral density function given by $G_{xx}(f) = 2/f^2$. The cross-spectral density function between the input and output is $G_{xy}(f) = (4/f^3) - j(4/f^2)$. Determine
   (a) the gain factor of the system.
   (b) the phase factor of the system.
   (c) the time delay through the system.

6.2 Assume that three identical physical systems with uniform gain factors of $|H(f)| = 10$ have statistically independent white noise inputs with spectral densities of $G_{x_1x_1}(f) = 1$, $G_{x_2x_2}(f) = 2$, and $G_{x_3x_3}(f) = 3$. Further assume that the systems produce a common output with extraneous noise having a spectral density of $G_{nn}(f) = 100$. Determine the coherence function between each input and output.

6.3 Consider the simple mechanical system shown in Figure 2.2, where the frequency response function between the input force in displacement units $x(t) = F(t)/k$ and the output displacement $y(t)$ is given by

$$H(f) = \frac{1}{1-(f/f_n)^2 + j2\zeta f/f_n}$$

Assuming $f_n = 10$ Hz and $\zeta = 0.01$, determine the rms value of the response displacement to a white noise excitation with a mean value of zero and a spectral density of $G_{xx}(f) = 0.1$ at all frequencies.

6.4 For the mechanical system in Problem 6.3, determine the maximum rms; value of the response displacement to a sinusoidal excitation given by $x(t) = 2 \sin 20\pi t$.

6.5 In Problem 6.3, assume there is extraneous noise in the output measurement with a spectral density of $G_{nn}(f) = 0.1$ at all frequencies. Determine the coherence function between $x(t)$ and $y(t)$ at

(a) $f = 0$ Hz.
(b) $f = 10$ Hz.
(c) $f = 100$ Hz.

6.6 In Problem 6.3, assume there is extraneous noise in the input measurement with a spectral density of $G_{mm}(f) = 0.1$ at all frequencies. Determine the frequency response function that would be computed (ignoring estimation errors) using the equations

(a) $H_1(f) = G_{xy}(f)/G_{xx}(f)$
(b) $H_2(f) = G_{yy}(f)/G_{yx}(f)$

6.7 Consider two physical systems with frequency response functions given by

$$H_1(f) = 1(1+j4f)^{-1} \qquad H_2(f) = (1+j8f)^{-1}$$

Assume the two systems have a common input with a spectral density of $G_{xx}(f) = 10$ and that the outputs of the two systems are contaminated by extraneous noise signals with identical spectral densities of $G_{n_1 n_1}(f) = G_{n_2 n_2}(f) = 0.1$. At a frequency of 1 Hz, determine

(a) the coherence function between the input and each output.
(b) the coherence function between the two outputs.

6.8 In Problem 6.9, assume the common input signal, rather than the output signals, is contaminated by extraneous noise with a spectral density of $G_{mm}(f) = 10$. Again, at a frequency of 1 Hz, determine

(a) the coherence function between the input and each output.
(b) the coherence function between the two outputs.

6.9 Consider the simple mechanical system shown in Figure 2.4, where the frequency response function between an input acceleration $\ddot{x}(t)$ and the output acceleration $\ddot{y}(t)$ is given by

$$H(f) = \frac{1 + j2\zeta f/f_n}{1 - (f/f_n)^2 + j2\zeta f/f_n}$$

Assuming $f_n = 100$ Hz and $\zeta = 0.7$, determine the rms value of the response acceleration to a white noise acceleration input with a mean value of zero and a spectral density of $G_{\ddot{x}\ddot{x}}(f) = 0.01$.

6.10 In Problem 6.9, determine the rms value of the relative displacement response $[y(t) - x(t)]$ of the system to the white noise acceleration input $\ddot{x}(t)$. (*Hint:* See Table 2.1.)

REFERENCES

1. Bendat, J. S. and Piersol, A. G., *Engineering Applications of Correlation and Spectral Analysis*, 2nd ed. Wiley–Interscience, New York, 1993.

CHAPTER 7

Multiple-Input/Output Relationships

Material contained in Chapter 6 is now extended to multiple-input problems. As before, all data are assumed to be from stationary random processes with zero mean values, and all systems are constant-parameter linear systems. Section 7.1 describes multiple-input/single-output (MI/SO) models for general cases of arbitrary inputs and for special cases of mutually uncorrelated inputs. These ideas are discussed for special cases of two-input/one-output models in Section 7.2. Optimum frequency response functions, and partial and multiple coherence functions are defined for these models. Iterative computational procedures to decompose MI/SO models into physically meaningful ways are presented in Section 7.3, based upon original ideas in Refs 1 and 2. A practical modified procedure with simpler notation is recommended in Section 7.4, with details given for cases of three-input/single-output models. Results for multiple-input/multiple-output (MI/MO) models are stated in Section 7.5 using a matrix formulation. Many engineering applications of Ml/SO procedures for different fields are in Refs 2 and 3.

7.1 MULTIPLE-INPUT/SINGLE-OUTPUT MODELS

Consider q constant-parameter linear systems $H_i(f)$, $i = 1, 2, \ldots, q$, with q clearly defined and measurable inputs $x_i(t)$, $i = 1, 2, \ldots, q$, and one measured output $y(t)$, as illustrated in Figure 7.1. There is *no* requirement that the inputs be mutually uncorrelated. The output noise term $n(t)$ accounts for all deviations from the ideal model, which may be due to unmeasured inputs, nonlinear operations, and instrument noise. Measured records are assumed to be realizations of stationary (ergodic) random processes, where nonzero mean values and any periodicities have been removed prior to this analysis. Multiple-input/multiple-output models are direct extensions of these techniques by merely considering such models to be combinations of the multiple-input single-output cases of Figure 7.1.

Random Data: Analysis and Measurement Procedures, Fourth Edition. By Julius S. Bendat and Allan G. Piersol
Copyright © 2010 John Wiley & Sons, Inc.

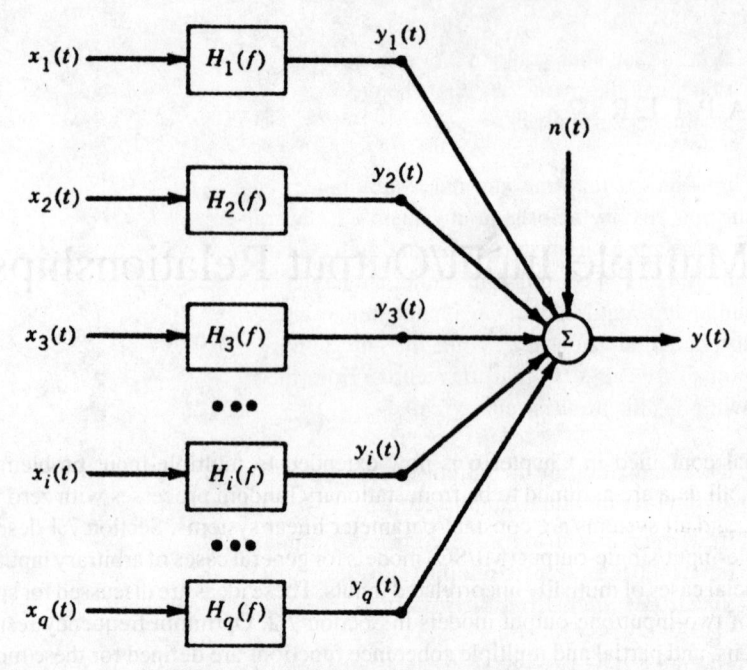

Figure 7.1 Multiple-input/single-output model.

7.1.1 General Relationships

Referring to the multiple-input model in Figure 7.1, four conditions are required for this model to be well defined.

1. None of the ordinary coherence functions between any pair of input records should equal unity. If this occurs, these two inputs contain redundant information and one of the inputs should be eliminated from the model. This consideration allows distributed input systems to be studied as discrete inputs.
2. None of the ordinary coherence functions between any input and the total output should equal unity. If this occurs, then the other inputs are not contributing to this output and the model should be considered as simply a single-input/single-output model.
3. The multiple coherence function (defined later) between any input and other inputs, excluding the given input, should not equal unity. If this occurs, then this input can be obtained by linear operations from the other inputs. This input is not providing any new information to the output and should be eliminated from the model.
4. The multiple coherence function between the output and the given inputs, in a practical situation, should be sufficiently high, say above 0.50, for the theoretical assumptions and later conclusions to be reasonable. Otherwise, some important inputs are probably being omitted, or nonlinear effects should be

considered. This value of 0.50 is not precise but is a matter of engineering and statistical judgment, based on the physical environment and the amount of data available for analysis.

It is assumed that one can make simultaneous measurements of the input and output time history records in any specified multiple-input/output model. It is also assumed that possible system errors and statistical errors in computed quantities have been minimized by careful calibration and choice of data processing parameters. In particular, it is required that one obtain good estimates of the real-valued autospectral density functions of each record and the complex-valued cross-spectral density functions between every pair of records. From these stored spectral quantities, the following results are desired:

1. Decomposition of the output spectra into physically meaningful components due to the measured input records.
2. Determination of optimum constant-parameter linear systems between each input and the output to minimize any noise spectra at the output that is not due to linear operations from the measured input records.

The output $y(t)$ may be considered to be the sum of the unmeasured q outputs $y_i(t)$, $i = 1, 2, \ldots, q$, plus the noise term $n(t)$ namely,

$$y(t) = \sum_{i=1}^{q} y_i(t) + n(t) \tag{7.1}$$

with the corresponding finite Fourier transforms

$$Y(f) = \sum_{i=1}^{q} Y_i(f) + (f) \tag{7.2}$$

Each output term $Y_i(f)$ for $i = 1, 2, \ldots, q$ satisfies

$$Y_i(f) = H_i(f) X_i(f) \tag{7.3}$$

Thus, the basic frequency-domain equation for Figure 7.1 is

$$Y(f) = \sum_{i=1}^{q} H_i(f) X_i(f) + N(f) \tag{7.4}$$

where each $X_i(f)$ and $Y(f)$ can be computed from the measured $x_i(t)$ and $y(t)$. From this information, it is required to determine the systems $H_i(f)$ and other quantities of interest where all results are functions of frequency.

Finite Fourier transforms $X_i(f)$ and $Y(f)$ for single records $x_i(t)$ and $y(t)$ of length T are

$$X_i(f) = \int_0^T x_i(t) e^{-j2\pi ft} dt \qquad Y(f) = \int_0^T y(t) e^{-j2\pi ft} dt \tag{7.5}$$

As per Equations (5.66) and (5.67), one-sided autospectral and cross-spectral density functions are defined by

$$G_{ii}(f) = G_{x_i x_i}(f) = \lim_{T \to \infty} \frac{2}{T} E\left[|X_i(f)|^2\right]$$

$$G_{ij}(f) = G_{x_i x_j}(f) = \lim_{T \to \infty} \frac{2}{T} E[X_i^*(f) X_j(f)]$$

(7.6)

$$G_{yy}(f) = \lim_{T \to \infty} \frac{2}{T} E\left[|Y(f)|^2\right]$$

$$G_{iy}(f) = G_{x_i y}(f) = \lim_{T \to \infty} \frac{2}{T} E[X_i^*(f) Y(f)]$$

(7.7)

These one-sided functions where $G(f) = 0$ for $f < 0$ can be replaced by theoretical two-sided functions $S(f)$, as discussed in Section 5.2.1. All formulas in this chapter can be stated in terms of either $G(f)$ or $S(f)$ quantities on both sides of the equations. The ratio of two $G(f)$ quantities is the same as the ratio of the corresponding two $S(f)$ quantities. Further work here, as in Chapter 6, will use the one-sided $G(f)$ quantities.

In practice, one obtains only estimates of Equations (7.6) and (7.7) because T will be finite and the expected value operation $E[\ ]$ can be taken only over a finite number of sample records. Also, when records are digitized, as discussed in Chapters 10 and 11, results will be obtained only at selected discrete frequencies. At any such frequency f, an estimate of $G_{xy}(f)$, denoted by $\hat{G}_{xy}(f)$, is usually obtained by

$$\hat{G}_{xy}(f) = \frac{2}{n_d T} \sum_{k=1}^{n_d} X_k^*(f) Y_k(f)$$

(7.8)

where n_d is the number of different (disjoint) sample records of $x(t)$ and $y(t)$, each of length T, so that the total record length $T_r = n_d T$. It is proved in Chapter 8 that to reduce bias errors, T should be made as large as possible, while to reduce random errors, n_d should be as large as possible. Hence, compromise choices are necessary when T_r is fixed.

If desired, corresponding time-domain equations can be written involving convolution integrals of the respective weighting functions $h_i(\tau)$, $i = 1, 2, \ldots, q$, associated with the $H_i(f)$. In place of Equation (7.3), one would have

$$y_i(t) = \int_0^\infty h_i(\tau) x_i(t - \tau) d\tau$$

(7.9)

where the lower limit of integration is zero only when the systems are physically realizable. Such convolution integrals and their extensions to correlation functions are much more complicated than the associated Fourier transform spectral relations and will not be used in the further development here. These correlation relations do not show how results vary as a function of frequency. That such information is hidden within the correlation functions is no justifiction for computing them when it is unnecessary and more efficient to compute spectral quantities directly.

7.1.2 General Case of Arbitrary Inputs

Consider the general case of arbitrary inputs. From Equation (7.4), with a different index of summation j instead of i,

$$Y(f) = \sum_{j=1}^{q} H_j(f) X_j(f) + N(f) \qquad (7.10)$$

Multiplication of both sides by $X_i^*(f)$ for any fixed $i = 1, 2, \ldots, q$ yields

$$X_i^*(f) Y(f) = \sum_{j=1}^{q} H_j(f) X_i^*(f) X_j(f) + X_i^*(f) N(f)$$

Expected values of both sides show that

$$E[X_i^*(f) Y(f)] = \sum_{j=1}^{q} H_j(f) E[X_i^*(f) X_j(f)] + E[X_i^*(f) N(f)]$$

Equations (7.6) and (7.7), with a scale factor of $(2/T)$ to obtain one-sided results, now prove at any f that

$$G_{iy}(f) = \sum_{j=1}^{q} H_j(f) G_{ij}(f) + G_{in}(f) \quad i = 1, 2, \ldots, q$$

where the cross-spectral terms $G_{in}(f)$ will be zero if $n(t)$ is uncorrelated with each $x_i(t)$. Making this assumption gives the set of equations

$$G_{iy}(f) = \sum_{j=1}^{q} H_j(f) G_{ij}(f) \quad i = 1, 2, \ldots, q \qquad (7.11)$$

This is a set of q equations with q unknowns, namely, $H_i(f)$ for $i = 1, 2, \ldots, q$, where all the spectral terms shown are computed from the measured input and output records. If the model is well defined, one can solve for the $H_i(f)$ by matrix techniques using Cramer's rule or the equivalent.

In terms of the computed $H_i(f)$, as found by solving Equation (7.11), the total output autospectral density function $G_{yy}(f)$ is

$$G_{yy}(f) = \sum_{i=1}^{q} \sum_{j=1}^{q} H_i^*(f) H_j(f) G_{ij}(f) + G_{nn}(f) \qquad (7.12)$$

assuming, as before, that $n(t)$ is uncorrelated with each $x_i(t)$. Equation (7.12) is derived from

$$Y^*(f) = \sum_{i=1}^{q} H_i^*(f) X_i^*(f) + N^*(f)$$

$$Y^*(f) Y(f) = \left[\sum_{i=1}^{q} H_i^*(f) X_i^*(f) + N^*(f) \right] \left[\sum_{j=1}^{q} H_j(f) X_j(f) + N(f) \right]$$

$$= \sum_{i=1}^{q} \sum_{j=1}^{q} H_i^*(f) H_j(f) X_i^*(f) X_j(f) + N^*(f) N(f)$$

$$= \sum_{i=1}^{q} H_i^*(f) X_i^*(f) N(f) + \sum_{j=1}^{q} H_j(f) N^*(f) X_j(f)$$

Expected values of both sides, multiplication of both sides by the scale factor $(2/T)$, and passage to the limit give the result

$$G_{yy}(f) = \sum_{i=1}^{q}\sum_{j=1}^{q} H_i^*(f)H_j(f)G_{ij}(f) + G_{nn} + \sum_{i=1}^{q} H_i^*(f)G_{in}(f) + \sum_{j=1}^{q} H_j(f)G_{nj}(f)$$

This reduces to Equation (7.12) when the cross-spectral terms $G_{in}(f) = 0$ for all f and all i. For q different inputs and for terms $G_{ij}(f) \neq 0$ when $i \neq j$, the output $G_{yy}(f)$ of Equation (7.12) contains $(q^2 + 1)$ parts. Decomposing $G_{yy}(f)$ into each of these parts and interpreting their meaning can be a very involved exercise.

7.1.3 Special Case of Mutually Uncorrelated Inputs

Consider the important special case when not only is $n(t)$ uncorrelated with each of the $x(t)$, but the inputs are mutually uncorrelated with each other. For this special case, Equations (7.11) and (7.12) become

$$G_{iy}(f) = H_i(f)G_{ii}(f) \quad i = 1, 2, \ldots, q \qquad (7.13)$$

$$G_{yy}(f) = \sum_{i=1}^{q} |H_i(f)|^2 G_{ii}(f) + G_{nn}(f) \qquad (7.14)$$

These relations have a very simple interpretation as a collection of distinct single-input/single-output models. No system of equations is required to solve for the $H_i(f)$. From Equation (7.13), each $H_i(f)$ is given by the ratio

$$H_i(f) = \frac{G_{iy}(f)}{G_{ii}(f)} \quad i = 1, 2, \ldots, q \qquad (7.15)$$

The output $G_{yy}(f)$ of Equation (7.14), unlike the output of Equation (7.12), now contains only $(q + 1)$ parts. Each of the q parts is the coherent output spectrum result for single-input/single-output models, namely,

$$|H_i(f)|^2 G_{ii}(f) = \gamma_{iy}^2(f) G_{yy}(f) \qquad (7.16)$$

These quantities represent the input record $x_i(t)$ passing only through its particular $H_i(f)$ to reach $y(t)$. No leakage of $x_i(t)$ occurs through any other system $H_j(f)$ because $x_i(t)$ is uncorrelated with $x_j(t)$ for $i \neq j$.

For general cases of multiple-input records, with arbitrary correlations between the inputs, any input record $x_i(t)$ can reach $y(t)$ by passage through any of the systems $H_i(f)$ for all $i = 1, 2, \ldots, q$. It can now be quite difficult to decompose $G_{yy}(f)$ into its respective contributions from each of the input records if one attempts to solve the general multiple-input/output problem by the usual "brute force" matrix techniques. These matrix techniques also give no physical insight into how models should be formulated to provide good agreements between mathematical results and physical situations. Better methods are required to solve many problems, as explained in this chapter.

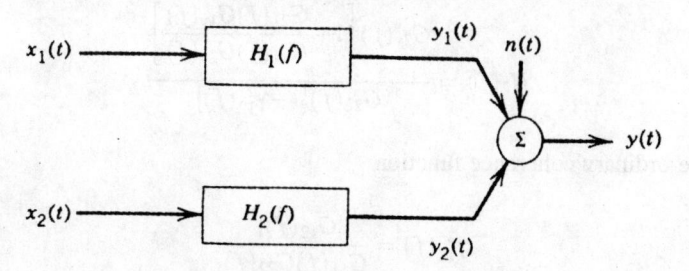

7.2 TWO-INPUT/ONE-OUTPUT MODELS

For an understanding of the methodology to solve general multiple-input/output problems, one should consider special cases of two-input/one-output models and three-input/one-output models. The general case is then merely more of the same features encountered in these special cases. This will now be done in detail for the two-input/one-output model. Equations for the three-input/one-output model are given in Sections 7.3 and 7.4.

7.2.1 Basic Relationships

Consider a two-input/one-output model as pictured in Figure 7.2, where the two inputs may be correlated. Assume that $x_1(t)$, $x_2(t)$, and $y(t)$ can be measured. This system is defined by the basic transform relation

$$Y(f) = H_1(f)X_1(f) + H_2(f)X_2(f) + N(f) \qquad (7.17)$$

For arbitrary $n(t)$, which may be correlated with $x_1(t)$ and/or $x_2(t)$, the one-sided autospectral density function of $y(t)$ from Equations (7.5–7.8), for a very long but finite record length T, is given by

$$G_{yy}(f) = G_{yy} = \frac{2}{T}E[Y^*Y]$$
$$= \frac{2}{T}E[\{H_1^*X_1^* + H_2^*X_2^* + N^*\}\{H_1X_1 + H_2X_2 + N\}] \qquad (7.18)$$

where the dependence on f and the limiting operation on T have been omitted to simplify the notation. Equation (7.18) becomes

$$G_{yy} = |H_1|^2 G_{11} + H_1^* H_2 G_{12} + H_1 H_2^* G_{21} + |H_2|^2 G_{22} + G_{nn}$$
$$+ H_1^* G_{1n} + H_1 G_{n1} + H_2^* G_{2n} + H_2 G_{n2} \qquad (7.19)$$

where the last four terms occur only when $n(t)$ is correlated with $x_1(t)$ and $x_2(t)$.

For arbitrary $n(t)$, the cross-spectral density functions between $x_1(t)$ and $y(t)$, and between $x_2(t)$ and $y(t)$, are given in a similar way by

Figure 7.2 Two-input/one-output model.

$$G_{1y} = \frac{2}{T}E[X_1^* Y] = \frac{2}{T}E[X_1^*(H_1 X_1 + H_2 X_2 + N)]$$
$$= H_1 G_{11} + H_2 G_{12} + G_{1n} \qquad (7.20)$$

$$G_{2y} = \frac{2}{T}E[X_2^* Y] = \frac{2}{T}E[X_2^*(H_1 X_1 + H_2 X_2 + N)]$$
$$= H_1 G_{21} + H_2 G_{22} + G_{1n} \qquad (7.21)$$

where, again, the dependence on f and the limiting operation on T have been omitted to simplify the notation. The terms G_{1n} and G_{2n} occur only when $n(t)$ is correlated with $x_1(t)$ and $x_2(t)$.

From a knowledge of $x_1(t)$, $x_2(t)$, and $y(t)$ the one-sided spectral quantities will be

$G_{11} = G_{11}(f) =$ autospectrum of $x_1(t)$
$G_{22} = G_{22}(f) =$ autospectrum of $x_2(t)$
$G_{yy} = G_{yy}(f) =$ autospectrum of $y(t)$
$G_{12} = G_{12}(f) =$ cross-spectrum between $x_1(t)$ and $x_2(t)$
$G_{1y} = G_{1y}(f) =$ cross-spectrum between $x_1(t)$ and $y(t)$
$G_{2y} = G_{2y}(f) =$ cross-spectrum between $x_2(t)$ and $y(t)$
$G_{21} = G_{12}^*(f) =$ complex conjugate of G_{12}

All spectral quantities involving $n(t)$ will be unknown. In particular, Equations (7.20) and (7.21) cannot be solved for H_1 and H_2 unless the terms $G_{1n} = 0$ and $G_{2n} = 0$, where

$G_{1n} = G_{1n}(f) =$ cross-spectrum between $x_1(t)$ and $n(t)$
$G_{2n} = G_{2n}(f) =$ cross-spectrum between $x_2(t)$ and $n(t)$

When $n(t)$ is uncorrelated with $x_1(t)$ and $x_2(t)$, Equations (7.20) and (7.21) become

$$G_{1y}(f) = H_{1n}(f)G_{11}(f) + H_2(f)G_{12}(f)$$
$$G_{2y}(f) = H_{1n}(f)G_{21}(f) + H_2(f)G_{22}(f) \qquad (7.22)$$

The solutions for $H_1(f)$ and $H_2(f)$, assuming $\gamma_{12}^2(f) \neq 1$, are

$$H_1(f) = \frac{G_{1y}(f)\left[1 - \dfrac{G_{12}(f)G_{2y}(f)}{G_{22}(f)G_{1y}(f)}\right]}{G_{11}(f)[1 - \gamma_{12}^2(f)]}$$

$$H_2(f) = \frac{G_{2y}(f)\left[1 - \dfrac{G_{21}(f)G_{1y}(f)}{G_{11}(f)G_{2y}(f)}\right]}{G_{22}(f)[1 - \gamma_{12}^2(f)]} \qquad (7.23)$$

where the ordinary coherence function

$$\gamma_{12}^2(f) = \frac{|G_{12}(f)|^2}{G_{11}(f)G_{22}(f)} \qquad (7.24)$$

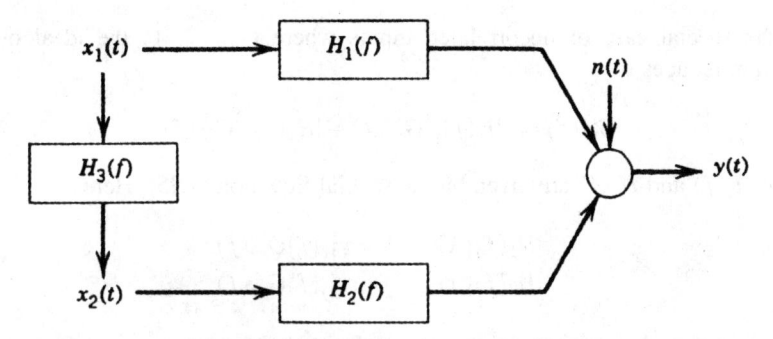

Figure 7.3 Illustration of fully coherent inputs.

For the special case of uncorrelated inputs when $\gamma_{12}^2(f) = 0$ terms $G_{12}(f)$ and $G_{21}(f)$ are also zero, and Equation (7.23) reduces to the usual relations for single-input/single-output models

$$H_1(f) = \frac{G_{1y}(f)}{G_{11}(f)} \qquad H_2(f) = \frac{G_{2y}(f)}{G_{22}(f)} \qquad (7.25)$$

The case in which $\gamma_{12}^2(f) = 1$ must be handled separately. A coherence function of unity between $x_1(t)$ and $x_2(t)$ implies complete linear dependence. Hence, one would consider a linear system existing between them, as illustrated in Figure 7.3. The implication is that the first input $x_1(t)$ is actually taking two different paths to arrive at the output $y(t)$. For this situation, a single frequency response function $H(f)$ will relate $y(t)$ to $x_1(t)$, namely,

$$H(f) = H_1(f) + H_2(f)H_3(f)$$

When $n(t)$ is uncorrelated with $x_1(t)$ and $x_2(t)$, but $G_{12}(f) \neq 0$, Equation (7.19) becomes

$$\begin{aligned}G_{yy}(f) = &|H_1(f)|^2 G_{11}(f) + H_1^*(f)H_2(f)G_{12}(f) \\ &+ H_2^*(f)H_1(f)G_{21}(f) + |H_2(f)|^2 G_{22}(f) + G_{nn}(f)\end{aligned} \qquad (7.26)$$

This can be written as

$$G_{yy}(f) = G_{vv}(f) + G_{nn}(f) = G_{y:x}(f) + G_{y:n}(f) \qquad (7.27)$$

where $G_{nn}(f) = G_{y:n}(f)$ is the output spectrum due to the noise, and $G_{vv}(f) = G_{y:x}(f)$ represents the ideal output spectrum due to the two inputs, as computed by the first four terms in Equation (7.26). To be explicit, $G_{vv}(f)$ comes from a knowledge of the terms $G_{11}(f)$, $G_{12}(f)$, and $G_{22}(f)$ plus the computed $H_1(f)$ and $H_2(f)$ by the general Equation (7.23). Finally, even though $n(t)$ is unmeasured, the autospectral density function $G_{nn}(f)$ can be computed by the formula

$$G_{nn}(f) = G_{yy}(f) - G_{vv}(f) \qquad (7.28)$$

For the special case of uncorrelated inputs where $G_{12}(f) = 0$, the ideal output spectrum reduces to

$$G_{vv}(f) = |H_1(f)|^2 G_{11}(f) + |H_2(f)|^2 G_{22}(f) \qquad (7.29)$$

where $H_2(f)$ and $H_2(f)$ are given by the special Equation (7.25). Here

$$\begin{aligned}|H_1(f)|^2 G_{11}(f) &= \gamma_{1y}^2(f) G_{yy}(f) \\ |H_2(f)|^2 G_{21}(f) &= \gamma_{2y}^2(f) G_{yy}(f)\end{aligned} \qquad (7.30)$$

where $\gamma_{1y}^2(f)$ and $\gamma_{2y}^2(f)$ are the ordinary coherence functions

$$\gamma_{1y}^2(f) = \frac{|G_{1y}(f)|^2}{G_{11}(f) G_{yy}(f)} \qquad \gamma_{2y}^2(f) = \frac{|G_{2y}(f)|^2}{G_{22}(f) G_{yy}(f)} \qquad (7.31)$$

It follows for uncorrelated inputs that

$$G_{vv}(f) = [\gamma_{1y}^2(f) + \gamma_{2y}^2(f)] G_{yy}(f) \qquad (7.32)$$

and

$$G_{nn}(f) = [1 - \gamma_{1y}^2(f) - \gamma_{2y}^2(f)] G_{yy}(f) \qquad (7.33)$$

The quantity $|H_1|^2 G_{11}$ represents the spectral output of x_1 through the H_1 system only. Similarly, $|H_2|^2 G_{22}$ represents the spectral output of x_2 through the H_2 system only. These two results are the ordinary coherent output spectra $\gamma_{1y}^2 G_{yy}$ and $\gamma_{2y}^2 G_{yy}$, respectively, between input x_1 and the output y, and between input x_2 and the output y.

7.2.2 Optimum Frequency Response Functions

Equations (7.22) and (7.26) are based on the assumption that $n(t)$ is uncorrelated with $x_1(t)$ and $x_2(t)$. Without making this assumption, when $x_1(t)$ and $x_2(t)$ pass through any pair of constant-parameter linear systems $H_1(f)$ and $H_2(f)$, respectively, Equation (7.17) states that

$$N(f) = Y(f) - H_1(f) X_1(f) - H_2(f) X_2(f)$$

Hence, for any $H_1(f)$ and $H_2(f)$, the noise output spectrum is

$$\begin{aligned}G_{nn}(f) &= \frac{2}{T} E[N^*(f) N(f)] \\ &= G_{yy}(f) - H_1(f) G_{y1}(f) - H_2(f) G_{y2}(f) \\ &\quad - H_1^*(f) G_{1y}(f) + H_1^*(f) H_1(f) G_{11}(f) + H_1^*(f) H_2(f) G_{12}(f) \\ &\quad - H_2^*(f) G_{2y}(f) + H_1(f) H_2^*(f) G_{21}(f) + H_2(f) H_2^*(f) G_{22}(f)\end{aligned}$$

The *optimum frequency response functions* are now defined as the particular $H_1(f)$ and $H_2(f)$ that minimize $G_{nn}(f)$ at any f over all possible choices of $H_1(f)$ and $H_2(f)$. They yield the least squares estimate of $y(t)$ from $x_1(t)$ and $x_2(t)$.

To derive the optimum $H_1(f)$ and $H_2(f)$, as explained previously in Chapter 6, it is sufficient to set the following partial derivatives equal to zero:

$$\frac{\partial G_{nn}(f)}{\partial H_1^*(f)} = 0 \quad \text{holding } H_1(f) \text{ fixed}$$

$$\frac{\partial G_{nn}(f)}{\partial H_2^*(f)} = 0 \quad \text{holding } H_2(f) \text{ fixed}$$

This leads to the pair of equations

$$-G_{1y}(f) + H_1(f)G_{11}(f) + H_2(f)G_{12}(f) = 0$$
$$-G_{2y}(f) + H_1(f)G_{21}(f) + H_2(f)G_{12}(f) = 0$$

which are identical to Equation (7.22).

For any pair, $H_1(f)$ and $H_2(f)$, the cross-spectral density functions $G_{1n}(f)$ and $G_{2n}(f)$ are given by

$$G_{1n}(f) = \frac{2}{T} E[X_1^*(f)N(f)]$$
$$= G_{1y}(f) - H_1(f)G_{11}(f) - H_2(f)G_{12}(f)$$
$$G_{2n}(f) = \frac{2}{T} E[X_2^*(f)N(f)]$$
$$= G_{2y}(f) - H_1(f)G_{21}(f) - H_2(f)G_{22}(f)$$

When $H_1(f)$ and $H_2(f)$ are the optimum results that satisfy the relations of Equation (7.22), these two cross-spectra will be identically zero for all f. Thus, computation of the optimum $H_1(f)$ and $H_2(f)$ to minimize $G_{nn}(f)$ automatically makes $n(t)$ uncorrelated with $x_1(t)$ and $x_2(t)$, namely,

$$G_{1n}(f) = 0 \qquad G_{2n}(f) = 0$$

It should be pointed out here that the optimum computed $H_1(f)$ and $H_2(f)$ satisfying Equation (7.22) do not have to be physically realizable. That is, their associated weighting functions $h_1(\tau)$ and $h_2(\tau)$ may not be zero for τ less than zero. In fact, if the actual systems are nonlinear, these results will only represent optimum linear approximations as done by the computer and could never be the true nonlinear systems. Of course, if the actual systems are physically realizable constant-parameter linear systems where the model includes all the inputs producing the output, then these computed results would represent the true conditions provided the output noise is uncorrelated with all the inputs and there is negligible input noise. Henceforth, it will be assumed that $H_1(f)$ and $H_2(f)$ are computed by Equation (7.23). These results come from either (a) assuming in advance that $n(t)$ is uncorrelated with $x_1(t)$ and $x_2(t)$, or (b) requiring $H_1(f)$ and $H_2(f)$ to be the optimum constant-parameter linear systems to minimize $G_{nn}(f)$, whereupon the $n(t)$ in the model will become uncorrelated with $x_1(t)$ and $x_2(t)$.

7.2.3 Ordinary and Multiple Coherence Functions

Return to the general case of correlated inputs where $\gamma_{12}^2(f)$ is any positive value less than unity. The ordinary coherence functions between each input and the output are

$$\gamma_{1y}^2(f) = \frac{|H_1(f)G_{11}(f) + H_2(f)G_{12}(f)|^2}{G_{11}(f)G_{yy}(f)}$$
$$\gamma_{2y}^2(f) = \frac{|H_1(f)G_{21}(f) + H_2(f)G_{22}(f)|^2}{G_{22}(f)G_{yy}(f)}$$
(7.34)

where the numerators represent $|G_{1y}(f)|^2$ and $|G_{2y}(f)|^2$ as computed using Equation (7.22). The product $\gamma_{1y}^2 G_{yy}$ still represents the ordinary coherent output spectrum between the input x_1 and the output y. However, x_1 does not now get to the output via the H_1 system only. Instead because $\gamma_{12}^2 \neq 0$, part of x_1 also gets to the output y via the H_2 system. Similarly, x_2 gets to the output via both H_1 and H_2 when $\gamma_{12}^2 \neq 0$, and the ordinary coherent output spectrum $\gamma_{2y}^2 G_{yy}$ represents all the ways x_2 can get to the output y. In general, for small $G_{nn}(f)$ the sum of $\gamma_{1y}^2(f)$ with $\gamma_{2y}^2(f)$ will be greater than unity when the inputs are correlated.

The *multiple coherence function* is a relatively simple concept and is a direct extension of the ordinary coherence function. By definition, the multiple coherence function is the ratio of the ideal output spectrum due to the measured inputs in the absence of noise to the total output spectrum, which includes the noise. In equation form, the multiple coherence function is

$$\gamma_{y:x}^2(f) = \frac{G_{vv}(f)}{G_{yy}(f)} = 1 - \left[\frac{G_{nn}(f)}{G_{yy}(f)}\right]$$
(7.35)

because $G_{vv}(f) = G_{yy}(f) - G_{nn}(f)$. For the general two-input case, $G_{vv}(f)$ is shown in Equation (7.26). The *multiple coherent output spectrum* is defined by the product of the multiple coherence function and the output spectrum, namely,

$$G_{vv}(f) = \gamma_{y:x}^2(f) G_{yy}(f)$$
(7.36)

Clearly, for all values of f, Equation (7.35) shows

$$0 \leq \gamma_{y:x}^2(f) \leq 1$$
(7.37)

The value of unity occurs when $G_{nn}(f) = 0$, indicating a perfect linear model, and the value of zero occurs when $G_{yy}(f) = G_{nn}(f)$, indicating that none of the output record comes from linear operations on the measured input records.

For a single-input/single-output model where $x_2(t) = 0$ and $H_2(f) = 0$, the ideal output spectrum as previously derived in Equation (6.59) is

$$G_{vv}(f) = |H(f)|^2 G_{xx}(f) = \gamma_{xy}^2(f) G_{yy}(f)$$
(7.38)

MULTIPLE-INPUT/OUTPUT RELATIONSHIPS

where $x_1(t) = x(t)$ and $H(f) = [(G_{xy}(f)/G_{xx}(f)]$. It follows that

$$\gamma^2_{y:x}(f) = \frac{G_{vv}(f)}{G_{yy}(f)} = \gamma^2_{xy}(f) \tag{7.39}$$

In words, the multiple coherence function is the same here as the ordinary coherence function.

For a two-input/one-output model with uncorrelated inputs, the ideal output spectrum as previously derived in Equation (7.32) is

$$G_{vv}(f) = [\gamma^2_{1y}(f) + \gamma^2_{2y}(f)]G_{yy}(f)$$

Here, the multiple coherence function is

$$\gamma^2_{y:x}(f) = \gamma^2_{1y}(f) + \gamma^2_{2y}(f) \tag{7.40}$$

In words, for uncorrelated inputs, the multiple coherence function is the sum of the ordinary coherence functions between each input and the output. No such simple relation exists for correlated inputs.

Example 7.1. **Multiple Coherence Function for Two Uncorrelated Inputs.** Consider the example of an uncorrelated two-input/one-output system with negligible output noise and assume that the two inputs produce equal output spectra. For this example,

$$\gamma^2_{y:x}(f) = \gamma^2_{1y}(f) + \gamma^2_{2y}(f) = 1.0$$

with

$$\gamma^2_{1y}(f) = \gamma^2_{2y}(f) = 0.50$$

Here, there are ideal constant-parameter linear systems $H_1(f)$ and $H_2(f)$ between each input and the output. The fact that $\gamma^2_{1y}(f) = 0.50$ is due to the second input. If this was not known and one assumed a single-input/single output model, erroneous conclusions would be drawn.

7.2.4 Conditioned Spectral Density Functions

When correlation exists between any pair of input records, to make mathematical results agree with the physical situation, wherever possible one should try to determine if one record causes part or all of the second record. If this can be determined, then turning off the first record will remove the correlated parts from the second record and leave only the part of the second record that is not due to the first record. To be precise, if engineering considerations state that any correlation between $x_1(t)$ and $x_2(t)$ comes from $x_1(t)$, then the optimum linear effects of $x_1(t)$ to $x_2(t)$ should be found, as denoted by $x_{2 \cdot 1}(t)$. This should be subtracted from $x_2(t)$ to yield the *conditioned record* (also called the *residual record*) $x_{2 \cdot 1}(t)$ representing the part of $x_2(t)$ not due to $x_1(t)$. In equation form, $x_2(t)$ is decomposed into the sum of two

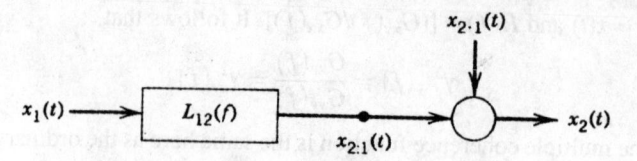

Figure 7.4 Decomposition of $x_2(t)$ from $x_1(t)$.

uncorrelated term shown in Figure 7.4, where

$$x_2(t) = x_{2:1}(t) + x_{2\cdot 1}(t) \tag{7.41}$$

Fourier transforms yield

$$X_2(f) = X_{2:1}(f) + X_{2\cdot 1}(f) \tag{7.42}$$

where

$$X_{2:1}(f) = L_{12}(f)X_1(f) \tag{7.43}$$

This defines the optimum linear least squares prediction of $x_2(t)$ from $x_1(t)$. The Fourier transform of $x_{2\cdot 1}(t)$ is

$$X_{x\cdot 1}(f) = X_2(f) - L_{12}(f)X_1(f) \tag{7.44}$$

The constant-parameter linear system $L_{12}(f)$ represents the optimum linear system to predict $x_2(t)$ from $x_1(t)$ taken in that order. As proved in Chapter 6, $L_{12}(f)$ is given by the ratio of the cross-spectrum from input to output divided by the autospectrum of the input, namely,

$$L_{12}(f) = \frac{G_{12}(f)}{G_{11}(f)} \tag{7.45}$$

It is also known from Equation (6.60) that this makes $x_{2\cdot 1}(t)$ uncorrelated with $x_1(t)$ and decomposes the spectrum of $x_2(t)$ into

$$G_{22}(f) = G_{22:1}(f) + G_{22\cdot 1}(f) \tag{7.46}$$

where $G_{22:1}(f)$ is the coherent output spectrum

$$G_{22:1}(f) = |L_{12}(f)|^2 G_{11}(f) = \gamma_{12}^2(f) G_{22}(f) \tag{7.47}$$

and $G_{22\cdot 1}(f)$ is the noise output spectrum

$$G_{22\cdot 1}(f) = [1 - \gamma_{12}^2(f)] G_{22}(f) \tag{7.48}$$

Note carefully the destinction between the indices 22:1 and 22·1.

Example 7.2. Illustration of Erroneous High Coherence. An example of erroneous high ordinary coherence is shown in Figure 7.5. Assume that a coherence function value near unity is computed between the two variables $x_1(t)$ and $y(t)$. One would be inclined to believe that there is a physical linear system relating these two

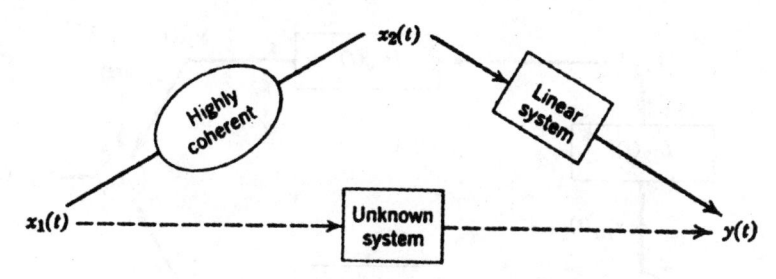

Figure 7.5 Illustration of erroneous high coherence.

variables as input and output. But suppose there is a third variable $x_2(t)$, which is highly coherent with $x_1(t)$ and also passes through a linear system to make up $y(t)$. In this type of situation, the high coherence computed between $x_1(t)$ and $y(t)$ might be only a reflection of the fact that $x_2(t)$ is highly coherent with $x_1(t)$, and $x_2(t)$ is related via a linear system to $y(t)$. In reality, there may be no direct physical system between $x_1(t)$ and $y(t)$ at all. If the partial coherence function (to be defined) were computed between $x_1(t)$ and $y(t)$ in this situation, it would be a very small number near zero. This concludes Example 7.2.

For cases where cause-and-effect matters are not clear between the input records, one might compute the cross-correlation function between the two records to see if there is a relative time delay to indicate which record precedes the other record. As noted in Section 6.2.1, a strong cross-correlation can exist between any pair of records that come from a common source, even when neither record is the cause of the other.

When no physical basis exists for ordering the records and when the relative time delay from a cross-correlation function is insignificant, a recommended approach is to compute the ordinary coherence function between each input record and the output record. At special frequencies of interest, such as peaks in the output spectrum where most of the power or energy is being transmitted, the records should be ordered according to their ordinary coherence functions. For example, at a selected frequency f_1, that input $x_1(t)$ or $x_2(t)$ giving the highest ordinary coherence function $\gamma^2_{1y}(f_1)$ or $\gamma^2_{2y}(f_1)$ should be selected as the first record. At a different selected frequency f_2, a similar examination of the ordinary coherence functions $\gamma^2_{1y}(f_2)$ and $\gamma^2_{2y}(f_2)$ may result in choosing a different ordering of the input records. Thus, different models may be appropriate at different frequencies.

For definiteness in this discussion, assume that $x_1(t)$ should precede $x_2(t)$. In place of Figure 7.2, one can now draw the equivalent Figure 7.6, where $H_1 = H_{1y}$ and $H_2 = H_{2y}$. Figure 7.6 shows that the input $x_1(t)$ reaches the output via two parallel paths, whereas the conditioned input $x_{2\cdot 1}(t)$ goes via only one path. This is drawn explicitly in Figure 7.7.

In the original Figure 7.2, the two measured inputs $x_1(t)$ and $x_2(t)$ are correlated, with linear outputs $y_1(t)$ and $y_2(t)$ that are also correlated. In the equivalent Figure 7.7, the two inputs $x_1(t)$ and $x_{2\cdot 1}(t)$ will be uncorrelated as accomplished by the data processing. The linear outputs $v_1(t)$ and $v_2(t)$ will also be uncorrelated. Figure 7.7 is

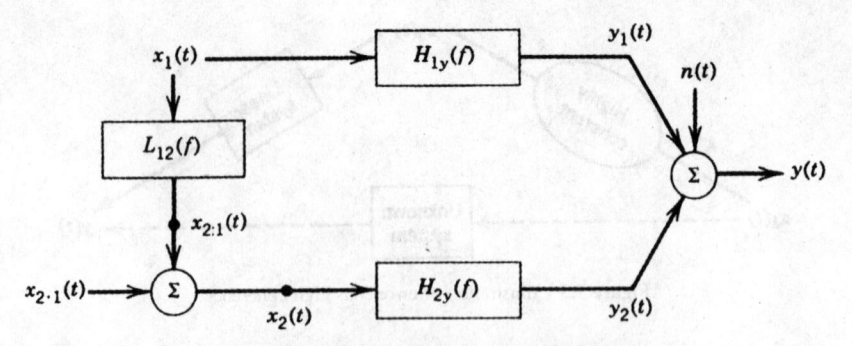

Figure 7.6 Model equivalent to Figure 7.2.

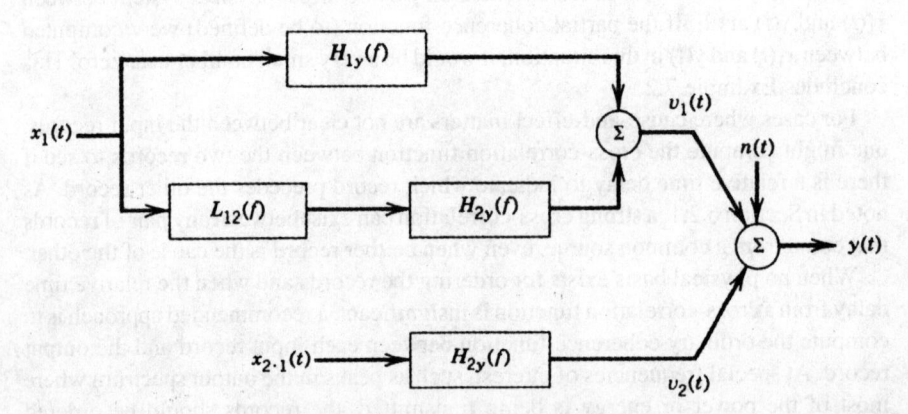

Figure 7.7 Model equivalent to Figure 7.6.

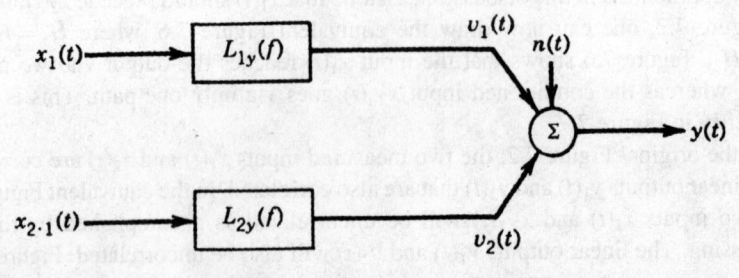

Figure 7.8 Model equivalent to Figure 7.7.

MULTIPLE-INPUT/OUTPUT RELATIONSHIPS

equivalent to Figure 7.8 using different systems $L_{1y}(f)$ and $L_{2y}(f)$, where

$$L_{1y}(f) = H_{1y}(f) + L_{12}(f)H_{2y}(f)$$
$$L_{2y}(f) = H_{2y}(f) \qquad (7.49)$$

Figure 7.8 represents a two-input/one-output model, where the output $y(t)$ and the noise $n(t)$ are the same as in Figure 7.2. The inputs are now mutually uncorrelated, however, so that Figure 7.8 is equivalent to two separate single-input/single-output models whose nature will now be described. The constant-parameter linear system L_{1y} is the optimum linear system to predict $y(t)$ from $x_1(t)$, whereas the constant-parameter linear system L_{2y} is the optimum linear system to predict $y(t)$ from $x_{2\cdot1}(t)$. In equation form, for stationary random data, the basic frequency domain relation for Figure 7.8 is

$$Y(f) = L_{1y}(f)X_1(f) + L_{2y}(f)X_{2\cdot1}(f) + N(f) \qquad (7.50)$$

where

$$L_{1y}(f) = \frac{G_{1y}(f)}{G_{11}(f)}$$
$$L_{2y}(f) = \frac{G_{2y\cdot1}(f)}{G_{22\cdot1}(f)} \qquad (7.51)$$

The quantities

$G_{1y}(f)$ = cross-spectrum between $x_1(t)$ and $y(t)$
$G_{11}(f)$ = autospectrum of $x_1(t)$
$G_{2y\cdot1}(f)$ = cross-spectrum between $x_{2\cdot1}(t)$ and $y(t)$
$G_{22\cdot1}(f)$ = autospectrum of $x_{2\cdot1}(t)$

The quantity $G_{2y\cdot1}(f)$ is called a *conditioned (residual) cross-spectral density function*, and $G_{22\cdot1}(f)$ is called a *conditioned (residual) autospectral density function*.

Computation of these conditioned spectral density functions can be done by algebraic operations on previously computed basic spectral density functions of the original measured records. It is *not* necessary to do any averaging of conditioned Fourier transforms except as a way to derive the desired algebraic formula. By definition, if averaging were performed, for finite T,

$$G_{2y\cdot1}(f) = \frac{2}{T}E[X_{2\cdot1}^*(f)Y(f)]$$

$$G_{22\cdot1}(f) = \frac{2}{T}E[X_{2\cdot1}^*(f)X_{2\cdot1}(f)]$$

From Equations (7.43) and (7.45),

$$X_{2\cdot1}(f) = X_2(f) - L_{12}(f)X_1(f)$$

where $L_{12}(f) = [G_{12}(f)/G_{11}(f)]$. Hence, for any three records $x_1(t)$, $x_2(t)$, and $y(t)$,

$$G_{2y \cdot 1}(f) = \frac{2}{T} E\left[\{X_2^*(f) - L_{12}^*(f)X_1^*(f)\}Y(f)\right]$$

$$= \frac{2}{T} E[X_2^*(f)Y(f)] - L_{12}^*(f)\left\{\frac{1}{T} E[X_1^*(f)Y(f)]\right\}$$

$$= G_{2y}(f) - [G_{21}(f)/G_{11}(f)]G_{1y}(f) \qquad (7.52)$$

As a special case, replacing $y(t)$ by $x_2(t)$, we obtain

$$\begin{aligned} G_{22 \cdot 1}(f) &= G_{22}(f) - [G_{21}(f)/G_{11}(f)]G_{12}(f) \\ &= [1 - \gamma_{12}^2(f)]G_{22}(f) \end{aligned} \qquad (7.53)$$

showing that $G_{22 \cdot 1}(f)$ is the noise output spectrum for a single-input/single-output model with $x_1(t)$ as the input and $x_2(t)$ as the output as in Figure 7.4. Similarly, replacing $x_2(t)$ by $y(t)$ yields

$$G_{yy \cdot 1}(f) = [1 - \gamma_{1y}^2(f)]G_{yy}(f) \qquad (7.54)$$

which is the noise output spectrum for a single-input/single-output model with $x_1(t)$ as the input and $y(t)$ as the output. Equations (7.52)–(7.54) are algebraic equations to compute conditioned cross-spectra and conditioned autospectra from the original computed spectra.

The result in Equation (7.54) applies to the model pictured in Figure 7.9 showing how $y(t)$ can be decomposed into the sum of two uncorrelated terms representing the part of $y(t)$ due to $x_1(t)$ via optimum linear operations and the part of $y(t)$ not due to $x_1(t)$. This model is described in the frequency domain by the Fourier transforms

$$Y(f) = Y_{y:1}(f) + Y_{y \cdot 1}(f) \qquad (7.55)$$

where

$$Y_{y:1}(f) = L_{1y}(f)X_1(f) \qquad (7.56)$$

$$L_{1y}(f) = [G_{1y}(f)/G_{11}(f)] \qquad (7.57)$$

$$Y_{y \cdot 1}(f) = Y(f) - L_{1y}(f)X_1(f) \qquad (7.58)$$

Note that results here are of the same nature as Equations (7.42)–(7.45).

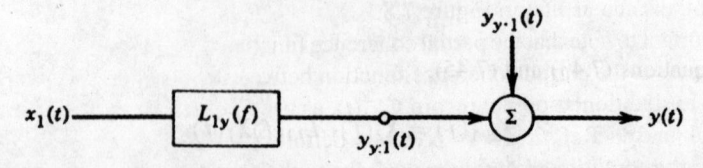

Figure 7.9 Decomposition of $y(t)$ from $x_1(t)$.

7.2.5 Partial Coherence Functions

Return now to Figure 7.8. Because the output terms $v_1(t)$, $v_2(t)$, and $n(t)$ are mutually uncorrelated, the measured output autospectrum $G_{yy}(f)$ is the sum of three autospectra terms with no cross-spectra terms, namely,

$$G_{yy}(f) = G_{v_1 v_1}(f) + G_{v_2 v_2}(f) + G_{nn}(f) \qquad (7.59)$$

where

$$G_{v_1 v_1}(f) = |L_{1y}(f)|^2 G_{11}(f) \qquad (7.60)$$
$$G_{v_2 v_2}(f) = |L_{2y}(f)|^2 G_{22 \cdot 1}(f) \qquad (7.61)$$
$$G_{nn}(f) = G_{yy \cdot 1,2}(f) \qquad (7.62)$$

The notation $G_{yy \cdot 1,2}(f)$ indicates the autospectrum of $y(t)$ not due to either $x_1(t)$ or $x_2(t)$. Observe also that the first output $v_1(t)$ in Figure 7.8 is the same as the output $y_{y \cdot 1}(t)$ in Figure 7.9. The first autospectrum term

$$G_{v_1 v_1}(f) = \left|\frac{G_{1y}(f)}{G_{11}(f)}\right|^2 G_{11}(f) = \gamma_{1y}^2(f) G_{yy}(f) \qquad (7.63)$$

is the ordinary coherent output spectrum associated with a single-input/single-output model with $x_1(t)$ as the input and $y(t)$ as the output as in Figure 7.9. Here,

$$\gamma_{1y}^2(f) = \frac{|G_{1y}(f)|^2}{G_{11}(f) G_{yy}(f)} \qquad (7.64)$$

is the ordinary coherence function between $x_1(t)$ and $y(t)$.

The second autospectrum term

$$G_{v_2 v_2}(f) = \left|\frac{G_{2y \cdot 1}(f)}{G_{22 \cdot 1}(f)}\right|^2 G_{22 \cdot 1}(f) = \gamma_{2y \cdot 1}^2(f) G_{yy}(f) \qquad (7.65)$$

where

$$\gamma_{2y \cdot 1}^2(f) = \frac{|G_{2y \cdot 1}(f)|^2}{G_{22 \cdot 1}(f) G_{yy}(f)} \qquad (7.66)$$

is, by definition, the *partial coherence function* between the conditioned record $x_{2 \cdot 1}(t)$ and $y(t)$. It follows that $G_{v_2 v_2}(f)$ is the *partial coherent output spectrum* associated with a conditioned-input/output model with $x_{2 \cdot 1}(t)$ as the input and $y(t)$ as the output as shown in Figure 7.10. The uncorrelated noise term in Figure 7.10, which is denoted $y_{y \cdot 1,2}(t)$, is the same as $n(t)$ in Figure 7.8.

It is important to note that the partial coherence function defined by Equation (7.66) is *not* the same as the partial coherence function between a conditioned-input record $x_{2 \cdot 1}(t)$ and a conditioned-output record $y_{y \cdot 1}(t)$, as used previously in earlier editions of this book and in Ref. 2. These previous definitions give the percentage of the spectrum of the *conditioned-output record* due to the conditioned-input record. This

```
                           y_{y·1,2}(t)
                                ↓
x_{2·1}(t) ──── [ L_{2y}(f) ] ──────→(Σ)────→ y(t)
                              v_2(t)
```

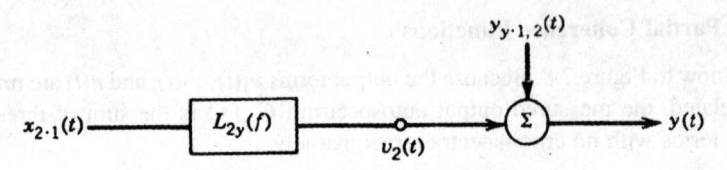

Figure 7.10 Decomposition of $y(t)$ from $x_{2·1}(t)$.

is a mathematical result rather than a physical result. The present definition by Equation (7.66) gives the percentage of the spectrum of the *total output record* $y(t)$ due to the conditioned input record $x_{2·1}(t)$. This is a much more meaningful physically significant result.

Examination of Figure 7.10 shows that it is precisely the same form as Figure 7.9 except that

1. The input record $x_1(t)$ is replaced by the uncorrelated conditioned-input record $x_{2·1}(t)$.
2. The optimum linear system $L_{1y}(f)$ is replaced by the optimum linear system $L_{2y}(f)$.
3. Original spectral quantities $G_{11}(f)$ and $G_{1y}(f)$ are replaced by conditioned-spectral quantities $G_{22·1}(f)$ and $G_{2y·1}(f)$.
4. The ordinary coherence function between $x_1(t)$ and $y(t)$ is replaced by the partial coherence function between $x_{2·1}(t)$ and $y(t)$.

From this viewpoint, it is clear that partial coherence functions play the same role as ordinary coherence functions, except that they apply to conditioned-input records instead of to the original records. For all values of f, by the cross-spectrum inequality of Equation (5.88), it follows that

$$0 \leq \gamma^2_{2y·1}(f) \leq 1 \tag{7.67}$$

A formula is still needed for the noise output spectrum in Figure 7.8. From Equations (7.59), (7.63), and (7.65), this is given by

$$G_{nn}(f) = [1 - \gamma^2_{1y}(f) - \gamma^2_{2y·1}(f)] G_{yy}(f) \tag{7.68}$$

The multiple coherence function for Figure 7.8 from Equation (7.35) is now the simple sum

$$\gamma^2_{y:x}(f) = \gamma^2_{1y}(f) + \gamma^2_{2y·1}(f) \tag{7.69}$$

This formula shows how the multiple coherence function is related to associated ordinary and partial coherence functions for the special ordering of the two-input records where $x_1(t)$ precedes $x_2(t)$. Equations (7.64) and (7.66) give the maximum percentage of the output spectrum of $y(t)$ that is due to $x_1(t)$ and the minimum percentage of the output spectrum of $y(t)$ that is due to $x_{2·1}(t)$.

MULTIPLE-INPUT/OUTPUT RELATIONSHIPS

For the reverse ordering of the two-input records in Figure 7.8 where $x_2(t)$ precedes $x_1(t)$, one would have the ordinary and partial coherence functions

$$\gamma_{2y}^2(f) = \frac{|G_{2y}(f)|^2}{G_{22}(f)G_{yy}(f)}$$

$$\gamma_{1y\cdot2}^2(f) = \frac{|G_{1y\cdot2}(f)|^2}{G_{11\cdot2}(f)G_{yy}(f)}$$ (7.70)

with the multiple coherence function given by

$$\gamma_{y:x}^2(f) = \gamma_{2y}^2(f) + \gamma_{1y\cdot2}^2(f)$$ (7.71)

Here, Equation (7.70) gives the maximum percentage of the output spectrum of $y(t)$ that is due to $x_2(t)$ and the minimum percentage that is due to $x_{1\cdot2}(t)$. Thus, upper and lower bounds can be found for the response effects of $y(t)$ in two-input/one-output models depending upon the ordering of the two inputs.

7.3 GENERAL AND CONDITIONED MULTIPLE-INPUT MODELS

The general multiple-input/output model for arbitrary inputs is illustrated in Figure 7.11, where the terms $X_i(f)$, $i = 1, 2, \ldots, q$, represent computed finite Fourier transforms of the input records $x_i(t)$. The finite Fourier transform of the computed output record $y(t)$ is represented by $Y(f) = X_{q+1}(f)$. Constant-parameter linear frequency response functions to be determined are represented by $H_{iy}(f)$,

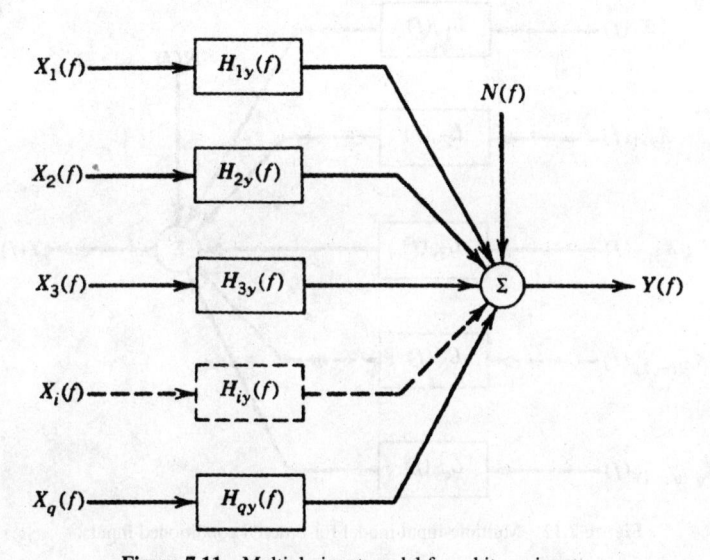

Figure 7.11 Multiple-input model for arbitrary inputs.

$i = 1, 2, \ldots, q$, where the input index *precedes* the output index. All possible deviations from the ideal overall model are accounted for in the finite Fourier transform $N(f)$ of the unknown extraneous output noise. Similar models can be formulated by interchanging the order of the input records or by selecting different output records. It is assumed that the input and output records are measured simultaneously using a common time base. It is also assumed that nonzero mean values are removed and that possible bias errors due to propagation time delays are corrected prior to computing $X_i(f)$ and $Y(f)$.

An alternative conditioned multiple-input/output model is shown in Figure 7.12 by replacing the original given input records of Figure 7.11 by an ordered set of conditioned-input records. No change is made in $Y(f)$ or $N(f)$. One can then compute the finite Fourier transforms $X_{i \cdot (i-1)!}(f)$, $i = 1, 2, \ldots, q$, selected in the order as shown in Figure 7.12. For any i, the subscript notation $i \cdot (i-1)!$ represents the ith record conditioned on the previous $(i-1)$ records, that is, when the linear effects of $x_1(t)$, $x_2(t)$, up to $x_{i-1}(t)$ have been removed from $x_i(t)$ by optimum linear least squares prediction techniques. These ordered conditioned-input records will be mutually uncorrelated, a property not generally satisfied by the original arbitrary records. Constant-parameter linear frequency response functions to be determined are represented by $L_{iy}(f)$, $i = 1, 2, \ldots, q$, where again the input index *precedes* the output index.

For the q input records, one can formulate a total of $q!$ different ordered conditioned multiple-input/output models since any of the original q records could be the first record, any of the remaining $(q-1)$ records could be the second record, any of the remaining $(q-2)$ records could be the third record, and so on. No one wants to or should analyze $q!$ models when q is a large number. For example, $q = 5$ could conceivably involve 120 different models. Fortunately, in practice, the number of

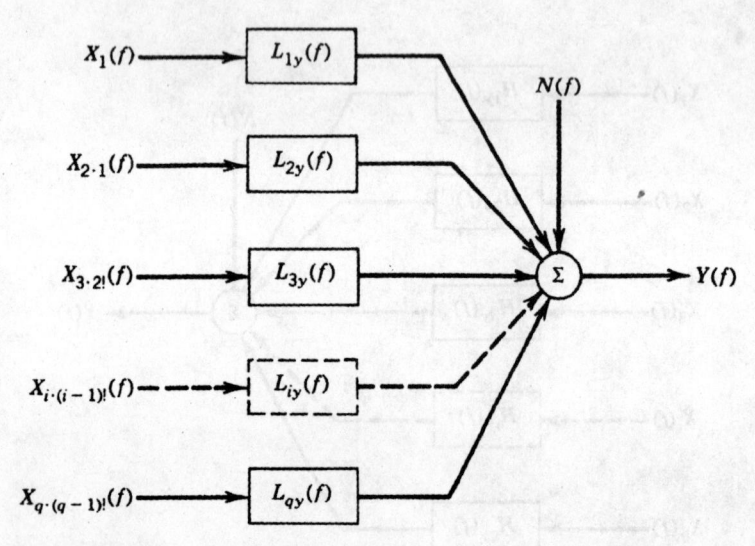

Figure 7.12 Multiple-input model for ordered conditioned inputs.

orders is often limited to only a few that make physical sense. However, as discussed in Section 7.2.4, in the absence of clear physical reasons to establish an order, it is recommended that the input records be ranked in terms of the magnitude of the ordinary coherence functions computed between each input record and the output record. Specifically, the input record with the highest ordinary coherence function would be first, the input record with the second highest ordinary coherence function would be second, and so on. Note that this procedure may result in a different ordering of the input records for different frequency ranges. See Ref. 2 for a detailed illustration.

From the previous discussion in Section 7.1, it is clear that solutions for the $\{H_{iy}\}$ systems in Figure 7.11 will be considerably more difficult than solutions for the $\{L_{iy}\}$ systems in Figure 7.12. It is also clear from Equations (7.12) and (7.14) that the output autospectrum $G_{yy}(f)$ in Figure 7.11 will contain $(q^2 + 1)$ terms, whereas this same output autospectrum $G_{yy}(f)$ in Figure 7.12 will contain only $(q + 1)$ terms.

Henceforth, Fourier transforms of original records and of conditional records will be denoted by capital letters where the dependence on frequency f will be omitted. Optimum systems $\{H_{iy}\}$ and optimum systems $\{L_{iy}\}$ will be calculated for both Figures 7.11 and 7.12, as well as the relationship between these optimum systems. To this end, one must know how to computed conditioned Fourier transforms and conditioned spectral density functions, as will be explained in succeeding sections.

7.3.1 Conditioned Fourier Transforms

For Figure 7.12, the defining Fourier transform equation is

$$Y = \sum_{i=1}^{q} L_{iy} X_{i \cdot (i-1)!} + N \tag{7.72}$$

If the output Y is considered to be a $(q + 1)$th record $X_{(q+1)}$ and if the noise N is considered to be this $(q + 1)$th record conditioned on the previous q records, then $N = X_{(q + 1) \cdot q!}$ and Equation (7.72) becomes

$$X_{(q+1)} = \sum_{i=1}^{q} L_{i(q+1)} X_{i \cdot (i-1)!} + X_{(q+1) \cdot q!} \tag{7.73}$$

Here, $X_{(q+1) \cdot q!}$ is considered to be the $(q + 1)$th record conditioned on *all* of the preceding q records.

Various subsets are of interest. For the first r conditioned-input records only where $r \leq q$, one can write

$$X_{(q+1)} = \sum_{i=1}^{r} L_{i(q+1)} X_{i \cdot (i-1)!} + X_{(q+1) \cdot r!} \tag{7.74}$$

Here, $X_{(q+1) \cdot r!}$ is considered to be the $(q + 1)$th record conditioned on the first r records, where $r = 1, 2, \ldots, q$. Substitution of any jth record X_j for $X_{(q+1)}$, where $j > r$, yields the more general relation

$$X_j = \sum_{i=1}^{r} L_{ij} X_{i \cdot (i-1)!} + X_{j \cdot r!} \qquad (7.75)$$

Here, the $\{L_{ij}\}$ systems replace the previous $\{L_{i(q+1)}\}$ systems. If r is now changed to $(r-1)$, then Equation (7.75) becomes

$$X_j = \sum_{i=1}^{r-1} L_{ij} X_{i \cdot (i-1)!} + X_{j \cdot (r-1)!} \qquad (7.76)$$

These last two results yield the conditioned Fourier transform algorithm

$$X_{j \cdot r!} = X_{j \cdot (r-1)!} - L_{rj} X_{r \cdot (r-1)!} \qquad (7.77)$$

Thus, $\{X_{j \cdot r!}\}$ can be computed from a knowledge of $\{X_{j \cdot (r-1)!}\}$ and the $\{L_{rj}\}$ systems for all $j > r$. In particular, Equation (7.77) shows that the $\{X_{j \cdot 1}\}$ terms follow from a knowledge of the $\{X_j\}$ terms and the $\{L_{1i}\}$ systems. Then the $\{X_{j \cdot 2!}\}$ terms follow from a knowledge of the $\{X_{j \cdot 1}\}$ terms and the $\{L_{2j}\}$ systems, and so on.

7.3.2 Conditioned Spectral Density Functions

For the original records $\{X_i\}$, $i = 1, 2, \ldots, q$, and $Y = X_{q+1}$, their original autospectra and cross-spectra can be defined by the expressions

$$G_{ii} = \frac{2}{T} E[X_i^* X_i] \quad G_{ij} = \frac{2}{T} E[X_i^* X_j]$$
$$G_{iy} = \frac{2}{T} E[X_i^* Y] \quad G_{yy} = \frac{2}{T} E[Y^* Y] \qquad (7.78)$$

Similarly, for conditioned records $X_{j \cdot r!}$, where $j > r$, their *conditioned autospectral density functions* are defined by

$$G_{jj \cdot r!} = \frac{2}{T} E\left[X_{j \cdot r!}^* X_{j \cdot r!}\right] \qquad (7.79)$$

Conditioned cross-spectral density functions between $X_{i \cdot r!}$ and $X_{j \cdot r!}$, when $i \neq j$ with both $i > r$ and $j > r$, are defined by

$$G_{ij \cdot r!} = \frac{2}{T} E\left[X_{i \cdot r!}^* X_{j \cdot r!}\right] \qquad (7.80)$$

The results in Equation (7.78) are special cases of Equations (7.79) and (7.80) when $r = 0$. Note also that

$$G_{ij \cdot r!} = \frac{2}{T} E\left[X_{i \cdot r!}^* X_j\right] = \frac{2}{T} E\left[X_i^* X_{j \cdot r!}\right] \qquad (7.81)$$

To compute conditioned spectral density functions from the original spectral density functions, one uses the transform algorithm of Equation (7.77). Specifically multiply both sides by X_i^*, take expected values, and multiply by the scale factor $(2/T)$.

MULTIPLE-INPUT/OUTPUT RELATIONSHIPS

This gives the conditioned spectra algorithm

$$G_{ij \cdot r!} = G_{ij \cdot (r-1)!} - L_{rj} G_{ir \cdot (r-1)!} \qquad (7.82)$$

Thus $\{G_{ij \cdot r!}\}$ can be computed from a knowledge of $\{G_{ij \cdot (r-1)!}\}$ and the $\{L_{rj}\}$ systems for all $i > r$ and $j > r$.

Equation (7.82) is the basic algorithm required to solve multiple-input/output problems. In particular, Equation (7.82) shows that the $\{G_{ij \cdot 1}\}$ terms follow from a knowledge of the $\{G_{ij}\}$ terms and the $\{L_{1j}\}$ systems. Then the $\{G_{ij \cdot 2!}\}$ terms follow from a knowledge of the $\{G_{ij \cdot 1}\}$ terms and the $\{L_{2j}\}$ systems, and so on. The key to using this algorithm is to determine the $\{L_{rj}\}$ systems for all $r = 1, 2, \ldots, q$, and all $j > r$. This will now be developed.

7.3.3 Optimum Systems for Conditioned Inputs

The systems $\{L_{iy}\}$, $i = 1, 2, \ldots, q$, in Figure 7.12 are optimum linear systems for a collection of single-input/single-output systems because the inputs in Figure 7.12 are mutually uncorrelated. Consequently, as proved in Chapter 6, each system L_{iy} is defined by the ratio of the cross-spectral density function between its input and the output divided by the autospectral density function of its input. Without assuming it, the noise $n(t)$ will be automatically uncorrelated with each input in Figure 7.12 when L_{iy} is computed in this fashion. Thus, because conditioned inputs are present, one obtains the result

$$L_{iy} = \frac{G_{iy \cdot (i-1)!}}{G_{ii \cdot (i-1)!}} \qquad i = 1, 2, \ldots, q \qquad (7.83)$$

Equation (7.83) can also be proved directly from Equation (7.72) if one assumes in advance that $n(t)$ is uncorrelated with each input in Figure 7.12. To derive this result, write Equation (7.72) with a different index of summation as

$$Y = \sum_{j=1}^{q} L_{jy} X_{j \cdot (j-1)!} + N$$

Multiply through both sides by $X^*_{i \cdot (i-1)!}$, where $i = 1, 2, \ldots, q$. This gives

$$X^*_{i \cdot (i-1)!} Y = \sum_{j=1}^{q} L_{jy} X^*_{i \cdot (i-1)!} X_{j \cdot (j-1)!} + X^*_{i \cdot (i-1)!} N$$

Now, taking expected values of both sides and multipling by the factor $(2/T)$ yields Equation (7.83), namely,

$$G_{iy \cdot (i-1)!} = L_{iy} G_{ii \cdot (i-1)!}$$

because

$$E[X^*_{i \cdot (i-1)!} X_{j \cdot (j-1)!}] = 0 \quad \text{for } i \neq j$$
$$E[X^*_{i \cdot (i-1)!} N] = 0 \quad \text{for all } i$$

As special cases of Equation (7.83), note that

$$i = 1 \quad L_{1y} = \frac{G_{1y}}{G_{11}}$$

$$i = 2 \quad L_{2y} = \frac{G_{2y \cdot 1}}{G_{22 \cdot 1}} \tag{7.84}$$

$$i = 3 \quad L_{3y} = \frac{G_{3y \cdot 2!}}{G_{33 \cdot 2!}}$$

and so on. The last system where $i = q$ is

$$L_{qy} = \frac{G_{qy \cdot (q-1)!}}{G_{qq \cdot (q-1)!}} \tag{7.85}$$

The separate uncorrelated optimum conditioned single-input/single-output systems contained in Figure 7.12 are shown in Figure 7.13. For any $i = 1, 2, \ldots, q$, the coherent output spectrum from the passage of the conditioned-input $X_{i \cdot (i-1)!}$ through L_{iy} is given by

$$|L_{iy}|^2 G_{ii \cdot (i-1)!} = \gamma^2_{iy \cdot (i-1)!} G_{yy} \tag{7.86}$$

where $G_{ii \cdot (i-1)!}$ is the conditioned-input spectrum and where

$$\gamma^2_{iy,(i-1)!} = \frac{|G_{iy \cdot (i-1)!}|^2}{G_{ii \cdot (i-1)!} G_{yy}} \tag{7.87}$$

is the *partial coherence function* between $X_{i \cdot (i-1)!}$ and the output Y in Figure 7.13.

The output autospectrum in Figure 7.13 for any $i = 1, 2, \ldots, q$ is given by

$$G_{yy} = |L_{iy}|^2 G_{ii \cdot (i-1)!} + G_{n_i n_i} \tag{7.88}$$

where the separate noise spectrum terms are

$$G_{n_i n_i} = \left[1 - \gamma^2_{iy \cdot (i-1)!}\right] G_{yy} \tag{7.89}$$

These separate noise terms should not be confused with the total output noise spectrum $G_{nn}(f)$ in Figure 7.12, as given later in Equation (7.121).

7.3.4 Algorithm for Conditioned Spectra

The algorithm to compute conditioned spectral density functions is contained in Equation (7.82), where the $\{L_{rj}\}$ systems must still be defined. This will now be done

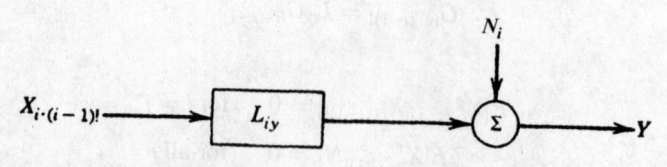

Figure 7.13 General conditioned-input/output model.

MULTIPLE-INPUT/OUTPUT RELATIONSHIPS

by extending the interpretation of the optimum $\{L_{iy}\}$ systems of Equation (7.83) for the inputs $X_1, X_{2\cdot 1}, X_{3\cdot 2!}$ up to $X_{q\cdot(q-1)!}$ with the output Y. In place of Y, consider any output X_j, where $j = 1, 2, \ldots, (q+1)$. Let the inputs be $X_1, X_{2\cdot 1}, X_{3\cdot 2!}$ up to $X_{r\cdot(r-1)!}$, where r can be any integer $r < j$, that is, $r = 1, 2, \ldots, (j-1)$. Conceptually, this creates new conditioned multiple-input/single-output models where the associated optimum linear systems $\{L_{rj}\}$ per the derivation of the optimum $\{L_{iy}\}$ systems must be such that j replaces y and r replaces i to give the result

$$L_{rj} = \frac{G_{rj\cdot(r-1)!}}{G_{rr\cdot(r-1)!}} \quad \begin{array}{l} r = 1, 2, \ldots, (j-1) \\ j = 1, 2, \ldots, (q+1) \end{array} \tag{7.90}$$

Note that L_{rj} involves conditioned records of order $(r-1)!$ In particular, for $r = 1, 2, 3$, one obtains

$$r = 1 \quad L_{1j} = \frac{G_{1j}}{G_{11}} \quad j = 2, 3, \ldots, q, q+1 \tag{7.91}$$

$$r = 2 \quad L_{2j} = \frac{G_{2j\cdot 1}}{G_{22\cdot 1}} \quad j = 3, 4, \ldots, q, q+1 \tag{7.92}$$

$$r = 3 \quad L_{3j} = \frac{G_{3j\cdot 2!}}{G_{33\cdot 2!}} \quad j = 4, 5, \ldots, q, q+1 \tag{7.93}$$

and so on. The case where $r = q$ and $j = (q+1)$ yields the system $L_q = L_{qy}$, as in Equation (7.85).

Return now to the previous iterative spectrum algorithm of Equation (7.82) and substitute Equation (7.90) for L_{rj}. This yields the final desired formula

$$G_{ij\cdot r!} = G_{ij\cdot(r-1)!} - \left[\frac{G_{rj\cdot(r-1)!}}{G_{rr\cdot(r-1)!}}\right] G_{ir\cdot(r-1)!} \tag{7.94}$$

which shows exactly how conditioned spectral quantities of order $r!$ can be computed from previously known conditioned spectral quantities of order $(r-1)!$ for any $r = 1, 2, \ldots, q$ and any i, j up to $(q+1)$, where $i > r$ and $j > r$.

To make this result as explicit as possible, consider special cases where $r = 1, 2, 3$. For $r = 1$, Equation (7.94) states

$$G_{ij\cdot 1} = G_{ij} - \left[\frac{G_{1j}}{G_{11}}\right] G_{i1} \tag{7.95}$$

All terms on the right-hand side are original autospectra and cross-spectra from the collected input and output records. The conditioned spectral quantities $G_{ij\cdot 1}$ are obtained by the algebraic operations in Equation (7.95) without choosing any bandwidth resolution or performing any averaging. These quantities are real-valued conditioned autospectra $G_{ii\cdot 1}$ when $i = j$ and complex-valued conditioned cross-spectra $G_{ij\cdot 1}$ when $i \neq j$. The indices i and j must be greater than 1.

For $r = 2$, Equation (7.94) states

$$G_{ij \cdot 2!} = G_{ij \cdot 1} - \frac{G_{2j \cdot 1}}{G_{22 \cdot 1}} G_{i2 \cdot 1} \qquad (7.96)$$

Now, all terms on the right-hand side are the computed conditioned spectra $\{G_{ij \cdot 1}\}$ from the previous step. The algebraic operations in Equation (7.96) yield the conditioned spectra $\{G_{ij \cdot 2!}\}$ without choosing any bandwidth resolution or performing any averaging. These quantities are real-valued conditioned autospectra $G_{ii \cdot 2!}$ when $i = j$ and are complex-valued conditioned cross-spectra when $i \ne j$. The indices i and j must now be greater than 2.

For $r = 3$, Equation (7.94) becomes an equation where the conditioned spectra $\{G_{ij \cdot 3!}\}$ can be calculated algebraically from the previously computed conditioned spectra $\{G_{ij \cdot 2!}\}$ and so on. This iterative procedure is displayed in Figure 7.14 using the L_{rj} of Equation (7.90), where one goes from the first inner loop to the next inner loop successively. The results in Figure 7.14 apply to both conditioned autospectra where $i = j$ and conditioned cross-spectra where $i \ne j$. An alternative special algorithm, however, can be used for conditioned autospectra. When $i = j$, Equation (7.94) becomes

$$G_{jj \cdot r!} = G_{jj \cdot (r-1)!} - |L_{rj}|^2 G_{rr \cdot (r-1)!} \qquad (7.97)$$

This procedure is displayed in Figure 7.15.

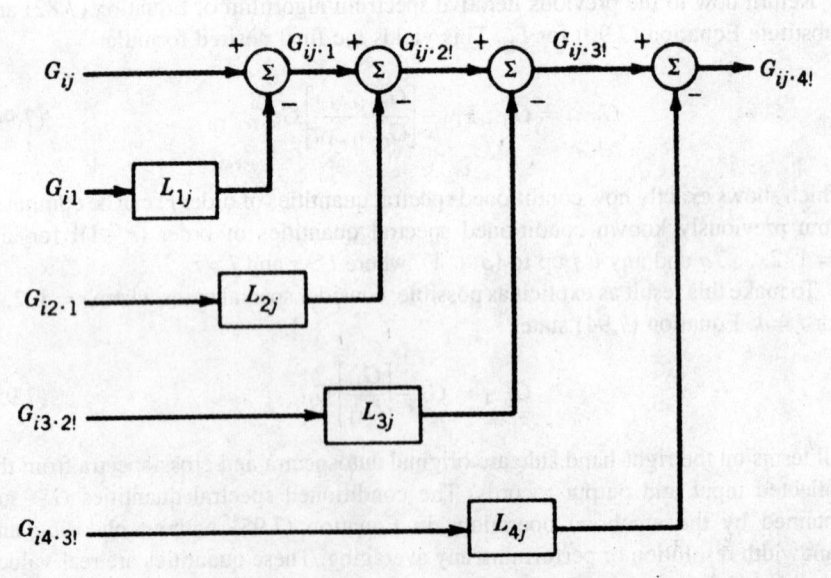

Figure 7.14 Algorithm to compute conditioned spectral density functions. (Results extend to any number of inputs.)

MULTIPLE-INPUT/OUTPUT RELATIONSHIPS

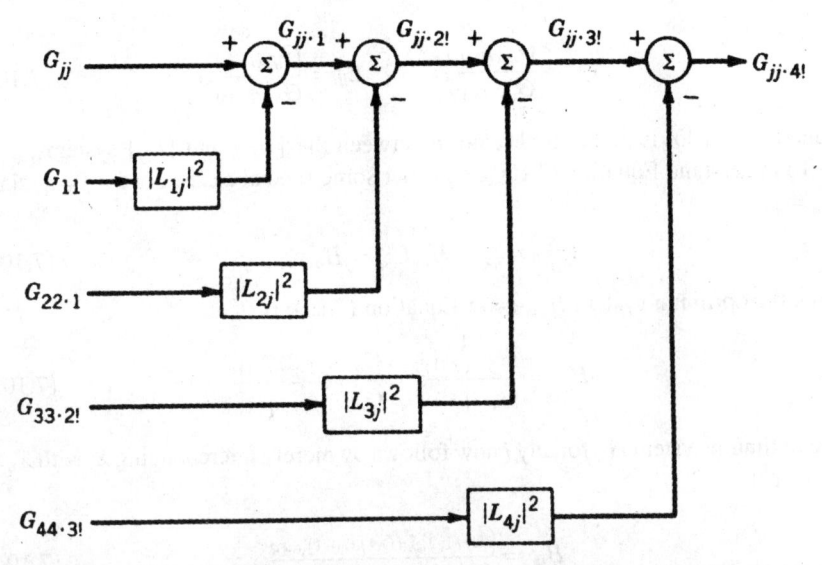

Figure 7.15 Special algorithm to compute conditioned autospectral density functions. (Results extend to any number of inputs.)

7.3.5 Optimum Systems for Original Inputs

For the original inputs in Figure 7.11, the optimum linear systems $\{H_{iy}\}$, $i = 1, 2, \ldots, q$, are more complicated to compute than the optimum $\{L_{iy}\}$ systems in Figure 7.12. These $\{H_{iy}\}$ systems must satisfy the various q equations in q unknowns specified in Equation (7.11). It is not difficult, however, to derive relations that must exist between the $\{H_{iy}\}$ and $\{L_{iy}\}$ systems, as will now be demonstrated.

The governing equation for Figure 7.11 is

$$Y = \sum_{j=1}^{q} H_{jy} + N \tag{7.98}$$

Multiply through by $X^*_{i \cdot (i-1)!}$, where $i = 1, 2, \ldots, q$, and take expected values of both sides. A scale factor of $(2/T)$ then proves

$$G_{iy \cdot (i-1)!} = \sum_{j=1}^{q} H_{jy} G_{ij \cdot (i-1)!} \tag{7.99}$$

where the index j starts at $j = i$ since $G_{ij \cdot (i-1)!} = 0$ for $j < i$. Divide both sides by $G_{ii \cdot (i-1)!}$ to obtain the result

$$L_{iy} = \sum_{j=1}^{q} H_{jy} L_{ij} \quad i = 1, 2, \ldots, q \quad j \geq i \tag{7.100}$$

where, from Equation (7.83)

$$L_{iy} = \frac{G_{iy \cdot (i-1)!}}{G_{ii \cdot (i-1)!}} \qquad L_{ij} = \frac{G_{ij \cdot (i-1)!}}{G_{ii \cdot (i-1)!}} \qquad (7.101)$$

Equation (7.100) is the desired relation between the $\{H_{iy}\}$ and $\{L_{iy}\}$ systems.

To understand Equation (7.100), consider some special cases. For $i=j=q$, since $L_{qq}=1$,

$$L_{qy} = H_{qy}L_{qq} = H_{qy} \qquad (7.102)$$

Thus the optimum system H_{qy}, as in Equation (7.85), is

$$H_{qy} = \frac{G_{qy \cdot (q-1)!}}{G_{qq \cdot (q-1)!}} = \frac{G_{qy \cdot 1,2,\ldots,(q-1)}}{G_{qq \cdot 1,2,\ldots,(q-1)}} \qquad (7.103)$$

The optimum system H_{iy} for any i now follows by merely interchanging X_i with X_q to show that

$$H_{iy} = \frac{G_{iy \cdot 1,2,\ldots,(i-1),(i+1),\ldots,q}}{G_{ii \cdot 1,2,\ldots,(i-1),(i+1),\ldots,q}} \qquad (7.104)$$

As special cases,

$$H_{1y} = \frac{G_{1y \cdot 2,3,\ldots,q}}{G_{11 \cdot 2,3,\ldots,q}}$$

$$H_{2y} = \frac{G_{2y \cdot 1,3,4,\ldots,q}}{G_{22 \cdot 1,3,4,\ldots,q}} \qquad (7.105)$$

$$H_{3y} = \frac{G_{3y \cdot 1,2,4,5,\ldots,q}}{G_{33 \cdot 1,2,4,5,\ldots,q}}$$

and so on. Comparison of Equation (7.84) with Equation (7.105) shows that the $\{L_{iy}\}$ systems are always simpler than the corresponding $\{H_{iy}\}$ systems for every $i=1, 2, \ldots, (q-1)$, except for $i=q$, where $L_{qy}=H_{qy}$.

For the two-input/single-output system of Figure 7.2, where H_{1y} and H_{2y} are given by Equation (7.23), one now sees from Equation (7.105) that a shorthand way to describe these answers is

$$H_{1y} = \frac{G_{1y \cdot 2}}{G_{11 \cdot 2}}$$

$$H_{2y} = \frac{G_{2y \cdot 1}}{G_{22 \cdot 1}} \qquad (7.106)$$

Corresponding L_{1y} and L_{2y} systems are given in Equation (7.51). Note that relationships between these L and H systems are shown in Equation (7.49), in agreement with Equation (7.100).

Equation (7.100) provides a general procedure to determine the $\{H_{iy}\}$ systems from the $\{L_{iy}\}$ systems by working backward, as follows:

$$H_{qy} = L_{qy}$$
$$H_{ij} = L_{iy} - \sum_{j=i+1}^{q} L_{ij}H_{jy} \quad (7.107)$$

where $i = (q-1), (q-2), \ldots, 2, 1$. For example, if $q = 3$,

$$\begin{aligned} H_{3y} &= L_{3y} \\ H_{2y} &= L_{2y} - L_{23}H_{3y} \\ H_{1y} &= L_{1y} - L_{12}H_{2y} - L_{13}H_{3y} \end{aligned} \quad (7.108)$$

In practice, to solve for the possible $\{H_{jy}\}$ systems, rather than finding them directly, a simpler two-step method is to compute the $\{L_{ij}\}$ systems first and then use Equation (7.107) to obtain the associated $\{H_{iy}\}$ systems.

7.3.6 Partial and Multiple Coherence Functions

Ordinary coherence functions between any input X_i for $i = 1, 2, \ldots, q$ and the total output Y are defined by

$$\gamma_{iy}^2 = \frac{|G_{iy}|^2}{G_{ii}G_{yy}} \quad (7.109)$$

Partial coherence functions between any conditioned-input $X_{i \cdot 1}$ for $i = 2, 3, \ldots, q$ and the total output Y are defined by

$$\gamma_{iy \cdot 1}^2 = \frac{|G_{iy \cdot 1}|^2}{G_{ii \cdot 1}G_{yy}} \quad (7.110)$$

Partial coherence functions between any conditioned input $X_{i \cdot 2!}$ for $i = 3, 4, \ldots, q$ and the total output Y are defined by

$$\gamma_{iy \cdot 2!}^2 = \frac{|G_{iy \cdot 2!}|^2}{G_{ii \cdot 2!}G_{yy}} \quad (7.111)$$

and so on up to

$$\gamma_{qy \cdot (q-1)!}^2 = \frac{|G_{qy \cdot (q-1)!}|^2}{G_{qq \cdot (q-1)!}G_{yy}} \quad (7.112)$$

It is now easy to define multiple coherence functions for any ordered multiple-input/single-output model like Figure 7.12, where the conditioned inputs are mutually uncorrelated. For a single-input/single output model,

$$\gamma_{y:1}^2 = \gamma_{1y}^2 \quad (7.113)$$

For a two-input/single-output model,

$$\gamma_{y:2!}^2 = \gamma_{1y}^2 + \gamma_{2y \cdot 1}^2 \quad (7.114)$$

For a three-input/single-output model,

$$\gamma^2_{y:3!} = \gamma^2_{1y} + \gamma^2_{2y \cdot 1} + \gamma^2_{3y \cdot 2!} \qquad (7.115)$$

and so on. For a general q-input/single-output model like Figure 7.12, the multiple coherence function is given by

$$\gamma^2_{y:q!} = \sum_{i=1}^{q} \gamma^2_{iy \cdot (i-1)!} \qquad (7.116)$$

Equations (7.13)–(7.16) are easy formulas to apply in practice where the physical interpretation of these formulas depends upon the ordering of the input records.

For the special case where the q original input records in Figure 7.11 are mutually uncorrelated, the multiple coherence function becomes

$$\gamma^2_{y:q!} = \sum_{i=1}^{q} \gamma^2_{iy} \qquad (7.117)$$

In words, the multiple coherence function is now the sum of the ordinary coherence functions between each input and the total output.

The noise output spectrum in a single-input/single-output model is

$$G_{yy \cdot 1} = [1 - \gamma^2_{1y}] G_{yy} \qquad (7.118)$$

For a conditioned two-input/single-output model,

$$G_{yy \cdot 2!} = [1 - \gamma^2_{y:2!}] G_{yy} \qquad (7.119)$$

For a conditioned three-input/single-output model,

$$G_{yy \cdot 3!} = [1 - \gamma^2_{y:3!}] G_{yy} \qquad (7.120)$$

and so on. For a general conditioned q-input/single-output model as shown in Figure 7.12, the noise output spectrum is

$$G_{nn} = G_{yy \cdot q!} = [1 - \gamma^2_{y:q!}] G_{yy} \qquad (7.121)$$

where $\gamma^2_{y:q!}$ is the multiple coherence function.

7.4 MODIFIED PROCEDURE TO SOLVE MULTIPLE-INPUT/SINGLE-OUTPUT MODELS

An alternative modified procedure, described and applied in Refs 2 and 3, will now be outlined to solve general multiple-input/single-output (MI/SO) linear models. Like the previous material in this chapter, this modified procedure applies to stationary random data with arbitrary probability and spectral properties. The advantages of this modified procedure are as follows:

MULTIPLE-INPUT/OUTPUT RELATIONSHIPS

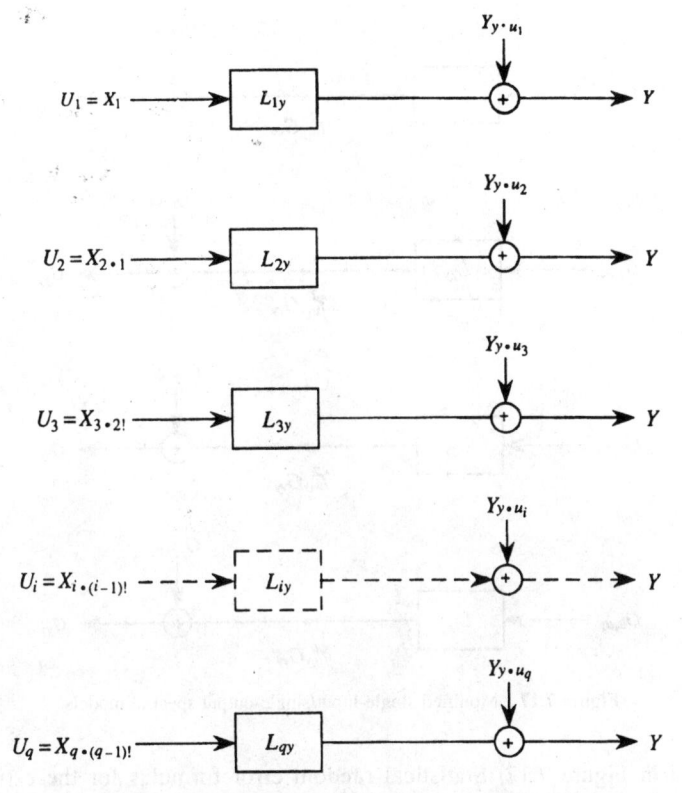

Figure 7.16 Modified single-input/single-output models.

1. The set of mutually uncorrelated conditioned-input records in Figure 7.12 are denoted by the simpler notation $U_i = U_i(f) = X_{i \cdot (i-1)!}(f)$ for $i = 1, 2, \ldots, q$.
2. The set of conditioned single-input/single-output (SI/SO) models in Figure 7.12 can be replaced by the simpler set of modified SI/SO models shown in Figure 7.16, where now each of the mutually uncorrelated inputs goes to the total output $Y = Y(f)$.
3. Ordinary coherence functions can be computed between each of the uncorrelated inputs and the total output to determine the percentage of the output spectrum due to each input. This makes it relatively easy to interpret the computed results because there is now no need to interpret partial coherence functions as defined by Equation (7.87).
4. The complicated multiple coherence function formula of Equation (7.116) can now be replaced by the simple additive formula of Equation (7.117) using the set of ordinary coherence functions between each of the uncorrelated inputs and the total output.

By computing the autospectra and cross-spectra of the input/output terms in Figure 7.16, an associated new set of modified SI/SO spectral models is obtained as

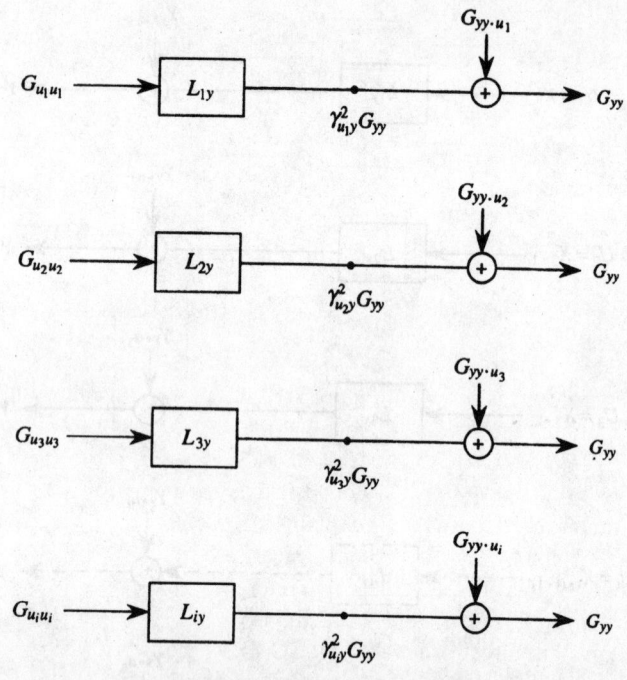

Figure 7.17 Modified single-input/single-output spectral models.

illustrated in Figure 7.17. Statistical random error formulas for the estimates of various terms in Figure 7.17 are listed in Section 9.3.8.

Formulas to solve the modified models in Figures 7.16 and 7.17 will now be discussed in some detail for the special case of a three-input/single-output linear model. The notation and procedure used here extend directly to analyzing general multiple-input/single-output cases.

7.4.1 Three-Input/Single-Output Models

The special case of a three-input/single-output linear model is shown in Figure 7.18 where the three-input records, $X_i(f)$, $i = 1, 2, 3$, can be correlated. The revised model

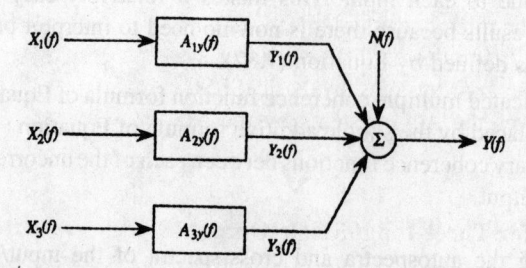

Figure 7.18 Three-input/single-output linear model where the inputs can be correlated.

MULTIPLE-INPUT/OUTPUT RELATIONSHIPS

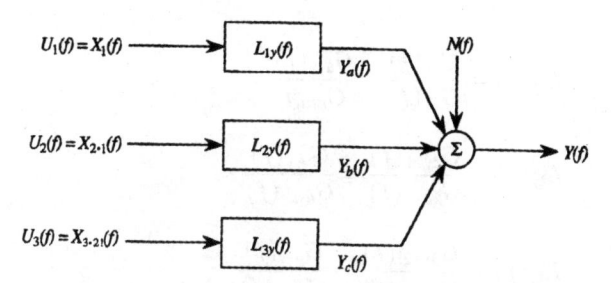

Figure 7.19 Revised three-input/single-output linear model equivalent to Figure 7.18 where the inputs are mutually uncorrelated.

equivalent to Figure 7.18 is shown in Figure 7.19 where the three new inputs, $U_i(f)$, $i = 1, 2, 3$, are mutually uncorrelated. Note that the linear systems in Figure 7.18 are denoted here by $A_{iy}(f)$, $i = 1,2,3$, instead of by $H_{iy}(f)$, $i = 1, 2, 3$, as shown in Figure 7.11. These two sets of linear systems are exactly the same. The reason for this change in notation from $H(f)$ to $A(f)$ is explained in Chapter 13 of Ref. 2 and Chapter 4 of Ref. 3. In Chapter 14, $A(f)$ represents linear systems that are "after" specified nonlinear operations. It is proved in these two references that the key to solving many important types of nonlinear system problems is to change their nonlinear system models into equivalent direct or reverse MI/SO linear models. These MI/SO linear models can then be replaced with a set of mutually uncorrelated SI/SO linear models where the desired $A(f)$ systems can be identified by the techniques in this chapter. Thus, the material developed here is not only applicable to identifying the various systems and response properties in general MI/SO linear models, but is also applicable to the determination of various systems and response properties for a large class of nonlinear system problems, as detailed in Refs 2 and 3.

The basis of the MI/SO procedure for identifying the $A(f)$ systems in Figure 7.18 is to use conditioned spectral density techniques to change the generally correlated input records, $X_i(f)$, $i = 1, 2, 3$, into the mutually uncorrelated input records, $U_i(f)$, $i = 1, 2, 3$, so the first input record is $U_1(f) = X_1(f)$, the second input record is $U_2(f) = X_{2 \cdot 1}(f)$, and the third input record is $U_3(f) = X_{3 \cdot 2!}(f)$. These mutually uncorrelated conditioned input records, $U_i(f)$, $i = 1, 2, 3$, are the inputs to the revised model in Figure 7.19. The noise output record $N(f)$ and the total output record $Y(f)$ are exactly the same in Figures 7.18 and 7.19. However, the correlated output records, $Y_1(f), Y_2(f)$, and $Y_3(f)$, in Figure 7.18 are now replaced in Figure 7.19 by three new mutually uncorrelated output records, $Y_a(f)$, $Y_b(f)$, and $Y_c(f)$. The three linear systems, $A_{iy}(f)$, $i = 1, 2, 3$, in Figure 7.18 are now replaced in Figure 7.19 by three different linear systems, namely, $L_{iy}(f)$, $i = 1,2,3$. Identification of the $L(f)$ systems by basic SI/SO linear system spectral density techniques then gives the $A(f)$ systems by the algebraic operations developed in Section 7.3.5.

7.4.2 Formulas for Three-Input/Single-Output Models

General formulas for the $L(f)$ and $A(f)$ systems in the three-input/single-output models of Figures 7.18 and 7.19 are as follows:

$$L_{1y}(f) = \frac{G_{1y}(f)}{G_{11}(f)} = \frac{G_{u_1y}(f)}{G_{u_1u_1}f} \qquad (7.122)$$

$$L_{2y}(f) = \frac{G_{2y\cdot 1}(f)}{G_{22\cdot 1}(f)} = \frac{G_{u_2y}(f)}{G_{u_2u_2}(f)} \qquad (7.123)$$

$$L_{3y}(f) = \frac{G_{3y\cdot 2!}(f)}{G_{33\cdot 2!}(f)} = \frac{G_{u_3y}(f)}{G_{u_3u_3}(f)} \qquad (7.124)$$

$$A_{3y}(f) = L_{3y}(f) \qquad (7.125)$$

$$A_{2y}(f) = L_{2y}(f) - \frac{G_{23\cdot 1}(f)}{G_{22\cdot 1}(f)} A_{3y}(f) \qquad (7.126)$$

$$A_{1y}(f) = L_{1y}(f) - \frac{G_{12}(f)}{G_{11}(f)} A_{2y}(f) - \frac{G_{13}(f)}{G_{11}(f)} A_{3y}(f) \qquad (7.127)$$

Equations (7.125)–(7.127) show that the computed linear system $A_{3y}(f)$ is the same as $L_{3y}(f)$, the computed linear system $A_{2y}(f)$ is a function of $L_{2y}(f)$ and $L_{3y}(f)$, and the computed linear system $A_{1y}(f)$ is a function of $L_{1y}(f)$, $A_{2y}(f)$, and $A_{3y}(f)$. Note that, in general, $L_{1y}(f)$ is not the same as $A_{1y}(f)$, and $L_{2y}(f)$ is not the same as $L_{2y}(f)$.

The coherent output spectral density functions in Figures 7.17 and 7.19 are given by the formulas

$$G_{y_ay_a}(f) = |L_{1y}(f)|^2 G_{u_1u_1}(f) = \gamma_{u_1y}^2(f) G_{yy}(f) \qquad (7.128)$$

$$G_{y_by_b}(f) = |L_{2y}(f)|^2 G_{u_2u_2}(f) = \gamma_{u_2y}^2(f) G_{yy}(f) \qquad (7.129)$$

$$G_{y_cy_c}(f) = |L_{3y}(f)|^2 G_{u_3u_3}(f) = \gamma_{u_3y}^2(f) G_{yy}(f) \qquad (7.130)$$

The total output spectral density function in Figure 7.19 is

$$G_{yy}(f) = G_{y_ay_a}(f) + G_{y_by_b}(f) + G_{y_cy_c}(f) + G_{nn}(f) \qquad (7.131)$$

where $G_{nn}(f)$ is the output noise spectrum. The total coherent output spectral density function in Figure 7.19 is

$$G_{vv}(f) = G_{yy}(f) - G_{nn}(f) = \gamma_{y:x}^2(f) G_{yy}(f) \qquad (7.132)$$

The various terms in Equations (7.128) through (7.132) can be interpreted as follows:

1. The first ordinary coherence function given by

$$\gamma_{u_1y}^2(f) = \frac{|G_{u_1y}(f)|^2}{G_{u_1u_1}(f) G_{yy}(f)} \qquad (7.133)$$

is the ordinary coherence between the input $U_1(f) = X_1(f)$ and the total output $Y(f)$. It states the proportion of the output spectrum $G_{yy}(f)$ that is due to $U_1(f)$ passing through the linear system $L_1(f)$, which represents all of the possible ways that $U_1(f)$ can reach $Y(f)$.

2. The second ordinary coherence function given by

$$\gamma_{u_2 y}^2(f) = \frac{|G_{u_2 y}(f)|^2}{G_{u_2 u_2}(f) G_{yy}(f)} \qquad (7.134)$$

is the ordinary coherence between the input $U_2(f) = X_{2 \cdot 1}(f)$ and the total output $Y(f)$. It states the proportion of the output spectrum $G_{yy}(f)$ that is due to $U_2(f)$ passing through the linear system $L_2(f)$, which represents all of the possible ways that $U_2(f)$ can reach $Y(f)$.

3. The third ordinary coherence function given by

$$\gamma_{u_3 y}^2(f) = \frac{|G_{u_3 y}(f)|^2}{G_{u_3 u_3}(f) G_{yy}(f)} \qquad (7.135)$$

is the ordinary coherence between the input $U_3(f) = X_{3 \cdot 2!}(f)$ and the total output $Y(f)$. It states the proportion of the output spectrum $G_{yy}(f)$ that is due to $U_3(f)$ passing through the linear system $L_3(f)$, which represents all of the possible ways that $U_3(f)$ can reach $Y(f)$.

4. The multiple coherence function for the model in Figure 7.19 is the additive sum of the three ordinary coherence functions in Equations (7.133)–(7.135)—that is,

$$\gamma_{y:x}^2(f) = \gamma_{u_1 y}^2(f) + \gamma_{u_2 y}^2(f) + \gamma_{u_3 y}^2(f) \qquad (7.136)$$

It defines the goodness-of-fit of the model at each frequency. Note that Equation (7.136) does not involve any partial coherence function. Good models occur at those frequencies where the multiple coherence function is close to unity.

5. The associated uncorrelated noise output spectrum in Figure 7.19 that represents all possible deviations from the model is given by

$$G_{nn}(f) = [1 - \gamma_{y:x}^2(f)] G_{yy}(f) \qquad (7.137)$$

Good models occur at those frequencies where $G_{nn}(f)$ is negligible compared to the total output spectrum $G_{yy}(f)$.

7.5 MATRIX FORMULAS FOR MULTIPLE-INPUT/MULTIPLE-OUTPUT MODELS

General cases will now be considered as represented in multiple-input/multiple-output models, where the number of output records is the same as the number of input records. It is straightforward to extend these results to cases of uneven numbers of input and output records. For the greatest physical insight into these problems, it is recommended that they be broken down into multiple-input/single-output problems and solved by the algebraic procedures outlined in Sections 7.2–7.4. If one desires to solve these multiple-input/multiple-output models by employing matrix techniques, however, a consistent set of definitions and matrix formulas are stated in this section. Different but equivalent sets of definitions and matrix formulas are presented in Ref. 4. These matrix results provide no useful decomposition of measured output spectra into their components from measured input records. Also, error analysis criteria for these matrix results are considerably more complicated than error analysis criteria for the results computed in Sections 7.2–7.4, where a multiple-input/single-output model is changed into a set of single-input/single-output models. Relatively simple error analysis criteria are developed in Chapter 9 for such single-input/single-output linear models.

7.5.1 Multiple-Input/Multiple-Output Model

Let $\mathbf{X}$ be a column vector representing the Fourier transforms of the q input records $X_i = X_i(f)$, $i = 1, 2, \ldots, q$, and $\mathbf{Y}$ be a column vector representing the Fourier transforms of the q output records $Y_k = Y_k(f)$, $k = 1, 2, \ldots, q$;

$$\mathbf{X} = \begin{bmatrix} X_1 \\ X_2 \\ \vdots \\ X_q \end{bmatrix} \quad \mathbf{Y} = \begin{bmatrix} Y_1 \\ Y_2 \\ \vdots \\ Y_q \end{bmatrix} \tag{7.138}$$

$\mathbf{X}^*, \mathbf{Y}^* = $ complex conjugate (column) vectors of $\mathbf{X}, \mathbf{Y}$

$\mathbf{X}', \mathbf{Y}' = $ transpose (row) vectors of $\mathbf{X}, \mathbf{Y}$

$$\mathbf{G}_{xx} = \frac{2}{T} E\{\mathbf{X}^* \mathbf{X}'\} = \text{input spectral density matrix} \tag{7.139}$$

$$\mathbf{G}_{yy} = \frac{2}{T} E\{\mathbf{Y}^* \mathbf{Y}'\} = \text{output spectral density matrix} \tag{7.140}$$

$$\mathbf{G}_{xy} = \frac{2}{T} E\{\mathbf{X}^* \mathbf{Y}'\} = \text{input/output cross-spectral density matrix} \tag{7.141}$$

Ideally, Equations (7.139)–(7.141) involve a limit as $T \to \infty$, but the limit notation, like the frequency dependence notation, is omitted for clarity. In practice, with finite records, the limiting operation is never performed.

The basic matrix terms are defined as follows:

$$G_{ij} = \frac{2}{T} E[X_i^* X_j] \tag{7.142}$$

$$G_{y_i y_j} = \frac{2}{T} E[Y_i^* Y_j] \tag{7.143}$$

$$G_{x_i y_j} = \frac{2}{T} E[X_i^* Y_j] \tag{7.144}$$

$$\mathbf{G}_{xx} = \frac{2}{T} E \left\{ \begin{bmatrix} X_1^* \\ X_2^* \\ \vdots \\ X_q^* \end{bmatrix} \begin{bmatrix} X_1 & X_2 & \cdots & X_q \end{bmatrix} \right\}$$

$$= \begin{bmatrix} G_{11} & G_{12} & \cdots & G_{1q} \\ G_{21} & G_{22} & \cdots & G_{2q} \\ \vdots & \vdots & & \vdots \\ G_{q1} & G_{q2} & \cdots & G_{qq} \end{bmatrix} \quad (7.145)$$

$$\mathbf{G}_{yy} = \frac{2}{T} E \left\{ \begin{bmatrix} Y_1^* \\ Y_2^* \\ \vdots \\ Y_q^* \end{bmatrix} \begin{bmatrix} Y_1 & Y_2 & \cdots & Y_q \end{bmatrix} \right\}$$

$$= \begin{bmatrix} G_{y_1 y_1} & G_{y_1 y_2} & \cdots & G_{y_1 y_q} \\ G_{y_2 y_1} & G_{y_2 y_2} & \cdots & G_{y_2 y_q} \\ \vdots & & & \\ G_{y_q y_1} & G_{y_q y_2} & \cdots & G_{y_q y_q} \end{bmatrix} \quad (7.146)$$

Observe that $\mathbf{G}_{xx}$ and $\mathbf{G}_{yy}$ are Hermitian matrices, namely, $G_{ij} = G_{ji}^*$ for all i and j. For these Hermitian matrices, $\mathbf{G}_{xx}^* = \mathbf{G}'_{xx}$ and $\mathbf{G}_{yy}^* = \mathbf{G}'_{yy}$.

$$\mathbf{G}_{xy} = \frac{2}{T} E \left\{ \begin{bmatrix} X_1^* \\ X_2^* \\ \vdots \\ X_q^* \end{bmatrix} \begin{bmatrix} Y_1 & Y_2 & \cdots & Y_q \end{bmatrix} \right\}$$

$$= \begin{bmatrix} G_{1 y_1} & G_{1 y_2} & \cdots & G_{1 y_q} \\ G_{2 y_1} & G_{2 y_2} & \cdots & G_{2 y_q} \\ \vdots & \vdots & & \vdots \\ G_{q y_1} & G_{q y_2} & \cdots & G_{q y_q} \end{bmatrix} \quad (7.147)$$

In all these terms, $G_{i y_j} = G_{x_i y_j}(f)$, where the input precedes the output.

Define the system matrix between $\mathbf{X}$ and $\mathbf{Y}$ by $\mathbf{H}_{xy} = \mathbf{H}_{xy}(f)$, where, as above, input always precedes output. The matrix terms $H_{i y_k} = H_{x_i y_k}$. Then

$$\mathbf{H}_{xy} = \begin{bmatrix} H_{1 y_1} & H_{1 y_2} & \cdots & H_{1 y_q} \\ H_{2 y_1} & H_{2 y_2} & \cdots & H_{2 y_q} \\ \vdots & \vdots & & \vdots \\ H_{q y_1} & H_{q y_2} & \cdots & H_{q y_q} \end{bmatrix} \quad (7.148)$$

From this definition, it follows that

$$\mathbf{Y} = \mathbf{H}'_{xy} \mathbf{X} \quad (7.149)$$

where $\mathbf{H}'_{xy}$ is the transpose matrix to $\mathbf{H}_{xy}$. Thus

$$\begin{bmatrix} Y_1 \\ Y_2 \\ \vdots \\ Y_q \end{bmatrix} = \begin{bmatrix} H_{1y_1} & H_{2y_1} & \cdots & H_{qy_1} \\ H_{1y_2} & H_{2y_2} & \cdots & H_{qy_2} \\ \vdots & \vdots & & \vdots \\ H_{1y_q} & H_{2y_q} & \cdots & H_{qy_q} \end{bmatrix} \begin{bmatrix} X_1 \\ X_2 \\ \vdots \\ X_q \end{bmatrix} \quad (7.150)$$

Note that this gives the algebraic results

$$Y_k = \sum_{i=1}^{q} H_{iy_k} X_i \quad k = 1, 2, \ldots, q \quad (7.151)$$

This is the logical way to relate any Y_k to the inputs $\{X_i\}$, where X_1 passes through H_{1y_k}, X_2 passes through H_{2y_k}, and so on, until X_q passes through H_{qy_k} (see Figure 7.11).

The consequences of these definitions will now be developed that provide matrix solutions for general multiple-input/multiple-output linear models when the number of outputs is the same as the number of inputs. It is assumed that all inverse matrix operations can be performed.

Determination of $\mathbf{G}_{xy}$ and $\mathbf{H}_{xy}$:

$$\mathbf{Y} = \mathbf{H}'_{xy}\mathbf{X} \quad (7.152)$$
$$\mathbf{Y}' = (\mathbf{H}'_{xy}\mathbf{X})' = \mathbf{X}'\mathbf{H}'_{xy} \quad (7.153)$$
$$\mathbf{X}^*\mathbf{Y}' = \mathbf{X}^*\mathbf{X}'\mathbf{H}_{xy} \quad (7.154)$$

Taking expected values of both sides and multiplying by $(2/T)$ gives

$$\mathbf{G}_{xy} = \mathbf{G}_{xx}\mathbf{H}_{xy} \quad (7.155)$$

This shows how to obtain $\mathbf{G}_{xy}$ from $\mathbf{G}_{xx}$ and $\mathbf{H}_{xy}$. Multiply both sides of Equation (7.155) by $\mathbf{G}_{xx}^{-1}$ to obtain

$$\mathbf{G}_{xx}^{-1}\mathbf{G}_{xy} = \mathbf{G}_{xx}^{-1}(\mathbf{G}_{xx}\mathbf{H}_{xy}) \quad (7.156)$$

where

$$\mathbf{G}_{xx}^{-1} \text{ is the } \textit{inverse} \text{ matrix of } \mathbf{G}_{xx} \quad (7.157)$$

Equation (7.156) is the same as

$$\mathbf{H}_{xy} = \mathbf{G}_{xx}^{-1}\mathbf{G}_{xy} \quad (7.158)$$

This shows how to obtain $\mathbf{H}_{xy}$ from $\mathbf{G}_{xx}$ and $\mathbf{G}_{xy}$. The result of Equation (7.155) is easily pictured as the product of two $q \times q$ matrices $\mathbf{G}_{xx}$ and $\mathbf{H}_{xy}$ to give $\mathbf{G}_{xy}$.

Determination of $\mathbf{G}_{yy}$ and $\mathbf{G}_{xx}$:

$$\mathbf{Y} = \mathbf{H}'_{xy}\mathbf{X} \quad (7.159)$$
$$\mathbf{Y}' = (\mathbf{H}'_{xy}\mathbf{X})' = \mathbf{X}'\mathbf{H}_{txy} \quad (7.160)$$
$$\mathbf{Y}^* = (\mathbf{H}'_{xy}\mathbf{X})^* = \mathbf{H}'^*_{xy}\mathbf{X}^* \quad (7.161)$$

MULTIPLE-INPUT/OUTPUT RELATIONSHIPS

$$\mathbf{Y}^*\mathbf{Y}' = (\mathbf{H}'^{*}_{xy}\mathbf{X}^*)(\mathbf{X}'\mathbf{H}_{xy}) \tag{7.162}$$

Taking expected values of both sides and multiplying by $(2/T)$ gives

$$\mathbf{G}_{yy} = \mathbf{H}'^{*}_{xy}\mathbf{G}_{xx}\mathbf{H}_{xy} \tag{7.163}$$

It follows that

$$\mathbf{G}_{xx} = (\mathbf{H}'^{*}_{xy})^{-1}\mathbf{G}_{yy}(\mathbf{H}_{xy})^{-1} \tag{7.164}$$

assuming the required inverse matrices exist. The result of Equation (7.163) is easily pictured as the product of three $q \times q$ matrices, $\mathbf{H}'^{*}_{xy}$, $\mathbf{G}_{xx}$, and $\mathbf{H}_{xy}$, to give $\mathbf{G}_{yy}$. The complex conjugate transpose matrix is as follows:

$$\mathbf{H}'^{*}_{xy} = \begin{bmatrix} H^*_{1y_1} & H^*_{2y_1} & \cdots & H^*_{qy_1} \\ H^*_{1y_2} & H^*_{2y_2} & \cdots & H^*_{qy_2} \\ \vdots & \vdots & & \vdots \\ H^*_{1y_q} & H^*_{2y_q} & \cdots & H^*_{qy_q} \end{bmatrix} \tag{7.165}$$

Equations (7.155), (7.158), (7.163), and (7.164) are the main matrix formulas to solve multiple-input/multiple-output problems.

Matrix formulas will next be stated for a general multiple-input/single-output model. As before, the input records are not ordered or conditioned in any way.

7.5.2 Multiple-Input/Single-Output Model

$$\mathbf{X} = \begin{bmatrix} X_1 \\ X_2 \\ \vdots \\ X_q \end{bmatrix} \quad \mathbf{H}_{xy} = \begin{bmatrix} H_{1y} \\ H_{2y} \\ \vdots \\ H_{qy} \end{bmatrix} \quad \mathbf{Y} = Y \tag{7.166}$$

$$Y = \mathbf{H}'_{xy}\mathbf{X} = \begin{bmatrix} H_{1y} & H_{2y} & \cdots & H_{qy} \end{bmatrix} \begin{bmatrix} X_1 \\ X_2 \\ \vdots \\ X_q \end{bmatrix} \tag{7.167}$$

$$Y' = Y = \mathbf{X}'\mathbf{H}_{xy} = \begin{bmatrix} X_1 & X_2 & \cdots & X_q \end{bmatrix} \begin{bmatrix} H_{1y} \\ H_{2y} \\ \vdots \\ H_{qy} \end{bmatrix} \tag{7.168}$$

$$\mathbf{X}^* = \begin{bmatrix} X^*_1 \\ X^*_2 \\ \vdots \\ X^*_q \end{bmatrix} \quad \mathbf{X}' = \begin{bmatrix} X_1 & X_2 & \cdots & X_q \end{bmatrix} \tag{7.169}$$

The input spectral density matrix is here

$$\mathbf{G}_{xx} = \frac{2}{T} E\{\mathbf{X}^*\mathbf{X}'\} = \begin{bmatrix} G_{11} & G_{12} & \cdots & G_{1q} \\ G_{21} & G_{22} & \cdots & G_{2q} \\ \vdots & \vdots & & \vdots \\ G_{q1} & G_{q2} & \cdots & G_{qq} \end{bmatrix} \qquad (7.170)$$

The input/output column vector is

$$\mathbf{G}_{xy} = \frac{2}{T} E\{\mathbf{X}^*\mathbf{Y}\} = \begin{bmatrix} G_{1y} \\ G_{2y} \\ \vdots \\ G_{qy} \end{bmatrix} \qquad (7.171)$$

The output spectral density function is

$$G_{yy} = \frac{2}{T} E\{Y^*Y'\} = \frac{2}{T} E\{\mathbf{H}_{xy}'^* \mathbf{X}^* \mathbf{X}' \mathbf{H}_{xy}\} = \mathbf{H}_{xy}'^* \mathbf{G}_{xx} \mathbf{H}_{xy} \qquad (7.172)$$

Equation (7.172) is equivalent to writing

$$G_{yy} = [H_{1y}^* \quad H_{2y}^* \quad \cdots \quad H_{qy}^*] \begin{bmatrix} G_{11} & G_{12} & \cdots & G_{1q} \\ G_{21} & G_{22} & \cdots & G_{2q} \\ \vdots & \vdots & & \vdots \\ G_{q1} & G_{q2} & \cdots & G_{qq} \end{bmatrix} \begin{bmatrix} H_{1y} \\ H_{2y} \\ \vdots \\ H_{qy} \end{bmatrix} \qquad (7.173)$$

Also,

$$G_{yy}^* = \mathbf{H}_{xx}' \mathbf{G}_{xx}^* \mathbf{H}_{xy}^* \qquad (7.174)$$

$$\mathbf{G}_{xx}^* = \mathbf{G}_{xx}' \qquad (7.175)$$

For the multiple-input/single-output model

$$G_{yy} = G_{yy}^* = G_{yy}' \qquad (7.176)$$

$$\mathbf{G}_{xx}^* = (\mathbf{H}_{xy}')^{-1} G_{yy} (\mathbf{H}_{xy}^*)^{-1} \qquad (7.177)$$

$$\mathbf{G}_{xx} = (\mathbf{H}_{xy}'^*)^{-1} G_{yy} (\mathbf{H}_{xy})^{-1} \qquad (7.178)$$

$$\mathbf{G}_{xy} = \mathbf{G}_{xx} \mathbf{H}_{xy} \qquad (7.179)$$

Equation (7.179) is equivalent to writing

$$\begin{bmatrix} G_{1y} \\ G_{2y} \\ \vdots \\ G_{qy} \end{bmatrix} = \begin{bmatrix} G_{11} & G_{12} & \cdots & G_{1q} \\ G_{21} & G_{22} & \cdots & G_{2q} \\ \vdots & \vdots & & \vdots \\ G_{q1} & G_{q2} & \cdots & G_{qq} \end{bmatrix} \begin{bmatrix} H_{1y} \\ H_{2y} \\ \vdots \\ H_{qy} \end{bmatrix} \qquad (7.180)$$

Note also that

$$\mathbf{H}_{xy} = \mathbf{G}_{xx}^{-1} \mathbf{G}_{xy} \qquad (7.181)$$

follows directly from Equation (7.179), where $\mathbf{G}_{xx}^{-1}$ is the inverse matrix of $\mathbf{G}_{xx}$. It is assumed here that the model is well defined and that all inverse matrices exist.

7.5.3 Model with Output Noise

Consider now a more realistic multiple-input/single-output model where extraneous uncorrelated output noise can occur. Instead of the ideal Equation (7.167), Y is given by

$$Y = \mathbf{H}'_{xy}\mathbf{X} + N \qquad (7.182)$$

where $N = N(f)$ is the finite Fourier transform of the output noise $n(t)$. In place of Equation (7.172), one now obtains

$$G_{yy} = \mathbf{H}'^{*}_{xy}\mathbf{G}_{xx}\mathbf{H}_{xy} + G_{nn} \qquad (7.183)$$

No change occurs in Equations (7.179), so that $\mathbf{G}_{xy}$ with extraneous noise present is still

$$\mathbf{G}_{xy} = \mathbf{G}_{xx}\mathbf{H}_{xy} \qquad (7.184)$$

Thus, G_{yy} can be expressed as

$$G_{yy} = \mathbf{H}'^{*}_{xy}\mathbf{G}_{xy} + G_{nn} \qquad (7.185)$$

The input spectral density matrix $\mathbf{G}_{xx}$ of Equation (7.170) is a $q \times q$ Hermitian matrix. Define an augmented spectral density matrix of the output $y(t)$ with the inputs $x_i(t)$ by the $(q+1) \times (q+1)$ Hermitian matrix

$$\mathbf{G}_{yxx} = \begin{bmatrix} G_{yy} & G_{y1} & G_{y2} & \cdots & G_{yq} \\ G_{1y} & G_{11} & G_{12} & \cdots & G_{1q} \\ G_{2y} & G_{21} & G_{22} & \cdots & G_{2q} \\ \vdots & \vdots & \vdots & & \vdots \\ G_{qy} & G_{q1} & G_{q2} & \cdots & G_{qq} \end{bmatrix} \qquad (7.186)$$

The determinant $|\mathbf{G}_{yxx}|$ of this augmented matrix will now be shown to be zero for all f in an ideal noise-free situation, where $G_{nn} = 0$ in Equation (7.185).

The G_{iy} terms for $i = 1, 2, \ldots, q$ in the first column of $\mathbf{G}_{yxx}$ (below the G_{yy} term) are linear combinations of the G_{ij} terms that appear in the columns of its row. That is, from Equation (7.170),

$$G_{iy} = \sum_{j=1}^{q} H_{jy}G_{ij} \qquad i = 1, 2, \ldots, q \qquad (7.187)$$

For the ideal noise-free case, the output spectrum is

$$G_{yy} = \mathbf{H}'^{*}_{xy}\mathbf{G}_{xy} = \mathbf{H}'_{xy}\mathbf{G}_{yx} \qquad (7.188)$$

where the last relation occurs because $G_{yy} = G_{yy}^*$ and $\mathbf{G}_{xy}^* = \mathbf{G}_{yx}$. Equation (7.188) is the same as

$$G_{yy} = \sum_{i=1}^{q} H_{iy} G_{yi} \tag{7.189}$$

Thus, G_{yy} is a linear combination of the G_{yi} terms that appear in the columns of the first row of $\mathbf{G}_{yxx}$. It follows that the matrix $\mathbf{G}_{yxx}$ is such that its entire first column is the result of linear combinations from corresponding terms in the other columns. By a theorem proved in Ref. 5, the determinant of this matrix must then be zero, that is

$$|\mathbf{G}_{yxx}| = 0 \quad \text{when } G_{nn} = 0 \tag{7.190}$$

Return to the noise model where G_{yy} is given by Equation (7.185) with $G_{nn} \neq 0$. As noted earlier, no change occurs in Equation (7.179) whether or not extraneous output noise is present. Hence, by using the results derived for the noise-free case, the determinant $|\mathbf{G}_{yxx}|$ of the matrix $\mathbf{G}_{yxx}$ can be computed at any f by the formula

$$|\mathbf{G}_{yxx}| = G_{nn} |\mathbf{G}_{xx}| \tag{7.191}$$

where $|\mathbf{G}_{xx}|$ is the determinant of the matrix G_{xx}. Note that this equation gives $|\mathbf{G}_{yxx}| = 0$ when $G_{nn} = 0$.

From Equation (7.35), it follows that the multiple coherence function is given by the determinant formula

$$\gamma_{y:x}^2 = 1 - \left(\frac{|\mathbf{G}_{yxx}|}{G_{yy} |\mathbf{G}_{xx}|} \right) \tag{7.192}$$

As a check on this formula, when $q = 1$, corresponding to a single-input/single-output model,

$$\mathbf{G}_{yxx} = \begin{bmatrix} G_{yy} & G_{yx} \\ G_{xy} & G_{xx} \end{bmatrix} \tag{7.193}$$

Here, the determinants

$$|\mathbf{G}_{yxx}| = G_{xx} G_{yy} - |G_{xy}|^2 \quad |\mathbf{G}_{xx}| = G_{xx} \tag{7.194}$$

Substitution into Equation (7.192) yields

$$\gamma_{y:x}^2 = 1 - \left(\frac{G_{xx} G_{yy} - |G_{xy}|^2}{G_{xx} G_{yy}} \right) = \frac{|G_{xy}|^2}{G_{xx} G_{yy}} \tag{7.195}$$

which is the required ordinary coherence function for this situation.

7.5.4 Single-Input/Single-Output Model

$$\mathbf{X} = \mathbf{X}' = X \quad \mathbf{Y} = \mathbf{Y}' = Y \tag{7.196}$$

$$\mathbf{H}_{xy} = \mathbf{H}'_{xy} = H \tag{7.197}$$

$$Y = HX \tag{7.198}$$

$$G_{xx} = \frac{2}{T} E[X^*X] = G^*_{xx} \tag{7.199}$$

$$G_{yy} = \frac{2}{T} E[Y^*Y] = G^*_{yy} \tag{7.200}$$

$$G_{xy} = \frac{2}{T} E[X^*Y] \quad G^*_{xy} = G_{yx} \tag{7.201}$$

From Equations (7.198)–(7.201), it follows that

$$G_{xy} = HG_{xx} \tag{7.202}$$

with

$$H = \frac{G_{xy}}{G_{xx}} \tag{7.203}$$

$$G_{yy} = H^* G_{xx} H = |H|^2 G_{xx} \tag{7.204}$$

and

$$G_{xx} = \frac{G_{yy}}{|H|^2} \tag{7.205}$$

The relations given above are well-known results from Chapter 6 for single-input/single-output problems. They are special cases of previously derived matrix formulas in Sections 7.5.1 and 7.5.2, and show that definitions used there are appropriate for multiple-input/multiple-output problems and multiple-input/single-output problems.

PROBLEMS

7.1 Consider a multiple-input linear system where the q inputs are mutually uncorrelated except for nonzero mean values. Determine the equations for
  (a) the cross-spectrum between the ith input and the output that replaces Equation (7.13).
  (b) the autospectrum of the output that replaces Equation (7.14).

7.2 Consider a two-input/single-output system where the following spectral density functions are measured at a frequency of interest

$$G_{11} = 3 \quad G_{22} = 2 \quad G_{yy} = 10$$
$$G_{12} = 1 + j1 \quad G_{1y} = 4 + j1 \quad G_{2y} = 3 - j1$$

Determine the conditioned spectral density functions

(a) $G_{22 \cdot 1}$
(b) $G_{2y \cdot 1}$
(c) $G_{yy \cdot 1}$

Also, determine the estimated frequency response function H_2.

7.3 Using the data in Problem 7.2, determine the multiple coherence function between the two inputs and the output.

7.4 Consider a two-input/single-output system with uncorrelated output noise as shown below.

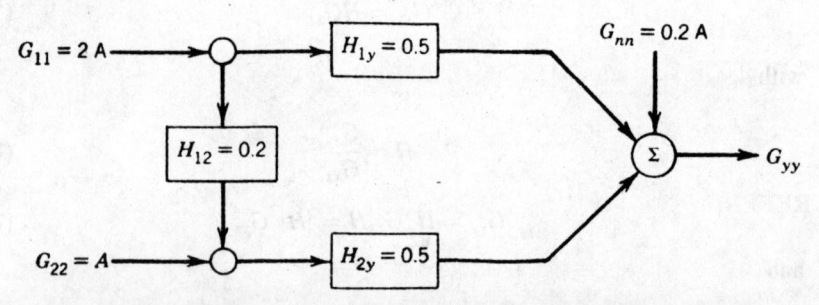

Determine the output spectral density G_{yy}. What would be the output spectral density if the two inputs were uncorrelated ($H_{12} = 0$)?

7.5 In Problem 7.1, determine the coherence γ_{12}^2 between the two inputs as well as the coherence γ_{1y}^2 and γ_{2y}^2 between each input and the output.

7.6 In Problem 7.1, determine the multiple coherence function between the two inputs and the output.

7.7 Using the data in Problem 7.4, determine the systems L_{1y} and L_{2y} that relate the uncorrelated inputs with autospectra G_{11} and $G_{22 \cdot 1}$ to the output, as defined in Equation (7.51).

7.8 In a three-input/single-output model, the following input quantities are measured at a frequency of interest:

$$G_{11} = 10 \quad G_{22} = 8 \quad G_{33} = 6$$
$$G_{12} = 2 + j1 \quad G_{32} = 1 - j2 \quad G_{13} = 3 + j3$$

Determine an appropriate order for the three input records that would provide the most physically meaningful results from a conditioned analysis using the model in Figure 7.12.

7.9 Consider an ideal two-input/single-output system where the frequency response functions are defined by

$$H_1(f) = \frac{2}{5+jf} \qquad H_2(f) = \frac{3}{5+jf}$$

Assume the inputs satisfy

$$R_{11}(\tau) = 3\delta(\tau) \quad G_{22}(f) = 12 \quad G_{12}(f) = 8$$

Determine the following quantities:
(a) $\gamma_{12}^2(f)$
(b) $R_{yy}(\tau)$ and $G_{yy}(f)$
(c) $R_{1y}(\tau)$ and $G_{1y}(f)$
(d) $\gamma_{1y}^2(f)$

7.10 Verify Equations (7.125)–(7.127) and explain physically why $L_{1y}(f)$ is not the same as $A_{1y}(f)$.

REFERENCES

1. Dodds, C. J., and Robson, J. D., "Partial Coherence in Multivariate Random Processes," *Journal of Sound and Vibration*, Vol. 42, p. 243, 1975.
2. Bendat, J. S., and Piersol, A. G., *Engineering Applications of Correlations and Spectral Analysis*, 2nd ed., Wiley–Interscience, New York, 1993.
3. Bendat, J. S., *Nonlinear System Techniques and Applications*, Wiley–Interscience, New York, 1998.
4. Smallwood, D. G., "Using Singular Value Decomposition to Compute the Conditioned Cross-Spectral Density Matrix and Coherence Functions," *Proceedings of the 66th Shock and Vibration Symposium*, Vol. 1, p. 109, November 1995.
5. Liebeck, H., *Algebra for Scientists and Engineers*, Wiley, New York, 1969.

CHAPTER 8

Statistical Errors in Basic Estimates

As noted in Chapter 4, the descriptive properties of a random variable cannot be precisely determined from sample data. Only estimates of the parameters of interest can be obtained from a finite sample of observations. The accuracy of certain basic parameter estimates is discussed in Chapter 4 for the case of data in the form of discrete independent observations of sample size N. In this chapter, the accuracy of parameter estimates is developed for data in the form of continuous time history records of record length T. It is assumed that the data are single sample records from continuous stationary (ergodic) random processes with arbitrary mean values. Statistical error formulas are developed for

- Mean value estimates
- Mean square value estimates
- Probability density function estimates
- Correlation function estimates
- Autospectral density function estimates

Attention in this chapter and the next chapter is restricted to those errors that are due solely to statistical considerations. Other errors associated with data acquisition and processing are covered in Chapter 10.

8.1 DEFINITION OF ERRORS

Referring to Section 4.1, the accuracy of parameter estimates based on sample values can be described by a mean square error defined as

$$\text{Mean square error} = E[(\hat{\phi} - \phi)^2] \tag{8.1}$$

Random Data: Analysis and Measurement Procedures, Fourth Edition. By Julius S. Bendat and Allan G. Piersol
Copyright © 2010 John Wiley & Sons, Inc.

where $\hat{\phi}$ is an estimator for ϕ. Expanding Equation (8.1) yields

$$E[(\hat{\phi} - \phi)^2] = E[(\hat{\phi} - E[\hat{\phi}] + E[\hat{\phi}] - \phi)^2]$$
$$= E[(\hat{\phi} - E[\hat{\phi}])^2] + 2E[(\hat{\phi} - E[\hat{\phi}])(E[\hat{\phi}] - \phi)]$$
$$+ E[(E[\hat{\phi}] - \phi)^2]$$

Note that the middle term in the above expression has a factor equal to zero, namely,

$$E[\hat{\phi} - E[\hat{\phi}]] = E[\hat{\phi}] - E[\hat{\phi}] = 0$$

Hence, the mean square error reduces to

$$\text{Mean square error} = E[(\hat{\phi} - E[\hat{\phi}])^2] + E[(E[\hat{\phi}] - \phi)^2] \quad (8.2)$$

In words, the mean square error is the sum of two parts. The first part is a variance term that describes the random portion of the error,

$$\text{Var}[\hat{\phi}] = E[(\hat{\phi} - E[\hat{\phi}])^2] = E[\hat{\phi}^2] - E^2[\hat{\phi}] \quad (8.3)$$

and the second part is the square of a bias term that describes the systematic portion of the error,

$$b^2[\hat{\phi}] = E[b^2[\hat{\phi}]] = E[(E[\hat{\phi}] - \phi)^2] \quad (8.4)$$

Thus, the mean square error is the sum of the variance of the estimate plus the square of the bias of the estimate, that is,

$$E[(\hat{\phi} - \phi)^2] = \text{Var}[\hat{\phi}] + b^2[\hat{\phi}] \quad (8.5)$$

It is generally more convenient to describe the error of an estimate in terms that have the same engineering units as the parameter being estimated. This can be achieved by taking the positive square roots of the error terms in Equations (8.3)–(8.5). The square root of Equation (8.3) yields the standard deviation for the estimate, called the *standard error* or *random error*, as follows:

$$\text{Random error} = \sigma[\hat{\phi}] = \sqrt{E[\hat{\phi}^2] - E^2[\hat{\phi}]} \quad (8.6)$$

The square root of Equation (8.4) gives the *bias error* directly as

$$\text{Bias error} = b[\hat{\phi}] = E[\hat{\phi}] - \phi \quad (8.7)$$

The square root of the sum of the squared errors, as given by Equation (8.5), defines the *root-mean-square* (rms) error as

$$\text{rms error} = \sqrt{E[(\hat{\phi} - \phi)^2]} = \sqrt{\sigma^2[\hat{\phi}] + b^2[\hat{\phi}]} \quad (8.8)$$

As a further convenience, it is often desirable to define the error of an estimate in terms of a fractional portion of the quantity being estimated. This is done by dividing the error by the quantity being estimated to obtain a *normalized error*. For $\phi \neq 0$, the

DEFINITION OF ERRORS

normalized random, bias, and rms errors are given by

$$\text{Normalized random error} = \varepsilon_r = \frac{\sigma[\hat{\phi}]}{\phi} = \frac{\sqrt{E[\hat{\phi}^2] - E^2[\hat{\phi}]}}{\phi} \quad (8.9a)$$

$$\text{Normalized bias error} = \varepsilon_b = \frac{b[\hat{\phi}]}{\phi} = \frac{E[\hat{\phi}]}{\phi} - 1 \quad (8.9b)$$

$$\text{Normalized rms error} = \varepsilon = \frac{\sqrt{\sigma^2[\hat{\phi}] + b^2[\hat{\phi}]}}{\phi} = \sqrt{\frac{E[(\hat{\phi} - \phi)^2]}{\phi}} \quad (8.9c)$$

Note that the normalized random error ε_r is often called the *coefficient of variation*. For situations where ε_r is small, if one sets

$$\hat{\phi}^2 = \phi^2(1 \pm \varepsilon_r)$$

then

$$\hat{\phi} = \phi(1 \pm \varepsilon_r)^{1/2} \approx \phi\left(1 \pm \frac{\varepsilon_r}{2}\right)$$

Thus

$$\varepsilon_r[\hat{\phi}^2] \approx 2\varepsilon_r[\hat{\phi}] \quad (8.10)$$

In words, when ε_r is small, the normalized random error for squared estimates $\hat{\phi}^2$ is approximately twice the normalized random error for unsquared estimates $\hat{\phi}$.

When estimates $\hat{\phi}$ have a negligible bias error $b[\hat{\phi}] \approx 0$ and a small normalized rms error $\varepsilon = \varepsilon[\hat{\phi}] = \sigma[\hat{\phi}]/\phi$, say $\varepsilon \le 0.10$, then the probability density function $p(\hat{\phi})$ for these estimates can be approximated by a Gaussian distribution, where the mean value $E[\hat{\phi}] \approx \phi$ and the standard deviation $\sigma[\hat{\phi}] = \varepsilon\phi$, as follows:

$$p(\hat{\phi}) \approx \frac{1}{\varepsilon\phi\sqrt{2\pi}} \exp\left[\frac{-(\hat{\phi} - \phi)^2}{2(\varepsilon\phi)^2}\right] \quad (8.11)$$

This gives probability statements for future values of the estimates $\hat{\phi}$, such as

$$\text{Prob}[\phi(1 - \varepsilon) \le \hat{\phi} \le \phi(1 - \varepsilon)] \approx 0.68$$
$$\text{Prob}[\phi(1 - 2\varepsilon) \le \hat{\phi} \le \phi(1 + 2\varepsilon)] \approx 0.95 \quad (8.12)$$

A confidence interval for the unknown true value ϕ based on any single estimate $\hat{\phi}$ then becomes

$$\left[\frac{\hat{\phi}}{1+\varepsilon} \le \phi \le \frac{\hat{\phi}}{1-\varepsilon}\right] \text{ with 68\% confidence}$$

$$\left[\frac{\hat{\phi}}{1+2\varepsilon} \le \phi \le \frac{\hat{\phi}}{1-2\varepsilon}\right] \text{ with 95\% confidence} \quad (8.13)$$

For small ε, say $\varepsilon \leq 0.10$, this simplifies to

$$[\hat{\phi}(1-\varepsilon) \leq \phi \leq \hat{\phi}(1+\varepsilon)] \quad \text{with 68\% confidence}$$
$$[\hat{\phi}(1-2\varepsilon) \leq \phi \leq \hat{\phi}(1+2\varepsilon)] \quad \text{with 95\% confidence} \quad (8.14)$$

These confidence claims can be made when ε is small even though the actual unknown sampling distribution for $\hat{\phi}$ is theoretically chi-square, F, or some other more complicated distribution detailed in Chapter 4.

For cases where normalized rms errors are not small, confidence interval statements can still be made, as described in Section 4.4. Such matters will be discussed for spectral density estimates later in this chapter. Along with the derivation of errors, the consistency of various estimates will also be noted, as defined by Equation (4.7).

Example 8.1. Approximate 95% Confidence Intervals for Mean Square and rms Value Estimates. Assume the mean square value of a signal $x(t)$ is estimated to be $\hat{\psi}_x^2 = 4$ with a normalized random error of $\varepsilon_r = 0.05$. Determine the approximate 95% confidence intervals for the mean square value ψ_x^2 and the rms value ψ_x of the signal.

From Equation (8.14), the approximate 95% confidence interval for ψ_x^2 is

$$[4(0.90) \leq \psi_x^2 \leq 4(1.10)] = [3.6 \leq \psi_x^2 \leq 4.4]$$

Using the result in Equation (8.10), $\varepsilon_r = 0.025$ for $\hat{\psi}_x = 2$, so the approximate 95% confidence interval for ψ_x is

$$[2(0.95) \leq \psi_x \leq 2(1.05)] = [1.9 \leq \psi_x \leq 2.1]$$

Note that the confidence interval for ψ_x is approximately the square root of the interval for ψ_x^2.

8.2 MEAN AND MEAN SQUARE VALUE ESTIMATES

8.2.1 Mean Value Estimates

Suppose that a single sample time history record $x(t)$ from a stationary (ergodic) random process $\{x(t)\}$ exists over a finite time T. The mean value of $\{x(t)\}$ can be estimated by

$$\hat{\mu}_x = \frac{1}{T} \int_0^T x(t)\, dt \quad (8.15)$$

The true mean value is

$$\mu_x = E[x(t)] \quad (8.16)$$

and is independent of t because $\{x(t)\}$ is stationary. The expected value of the estimate $\hat{\mu}_x$ is

$$E[\hat{\mu}_x] = E\left[\frac{1}{T} \int_0^T x(t)dt\right] = \frac{1}{T} \int_0^T E[x(t)]dt = \frac{1}{T} \int_0^T \mu_x\, dt = \mu_x \quad (8.17)$$

MEAN AND MEAN SQUARE VALUE ESTIMATES

because expected values commute with linear operations. Hence $\hat{\mu}_x$ is an *unbiased* estimate of μ_x, independent of T. Because $\hat{\mu}_x$ is unbiased, the mean square error of the estimate $\hat{\mu}_x$ is equal to the variance as follows:

$$\text{Var}[\hat{\mu}_x] = E[(\hat{\mu}_x - \mu_x)^2] = E[\hat{\mu}_x^2] - \mu_x^2 \qquad (8.18)$$

where from Equation (8.15),

$$E[\hat{\mu}_x^2] = \frac{1}{T^2} \int_0^T \int_0^T E[x(\xi)x(\eta)] d\eta d\xi \qquad (8.19)$$

Now the autocorrelation function $R_{xx}(\tau)$ of a stationary random process $\{x(t)\}$ is defined by Equation (5.6) as

$$R_{xx}(\tau) = E[x(t)x(t+\tau)] \qquad (8.20)$$

From the stationary hypothesis, $R_{xx}(\tau)$ is independent of t, and an even function of τ with a maximum at $\tau = 0$. It will be assumed that $R_{xx}(\tau)$ is continuous and finite for all values of τ and that all periodic components in $R_{xx}(\tau)$ have been removed at the onset. The autocovariance function $C_{xx}(\tau)$ is defined by Equation (5.8) as

$$C_{xx}(\tau) = R_{xx}(\tau) - \mu_x^2 \qquad (8.21)$$

It turns out that whenever $\mu_x \neq 0$, it is more convenient to work with $C_{xx}(\tau)$ than with $R_{xx}(\tau)$. It will be assumed that $C_{xx}(\tau)$ satisfies the integrable properties of Equation (5.122) so as to make $\{x(t)\}$ ergodic.

In terms of the autocovariance function $C_{xx}(\tau)$, the variance (mean square error) from Equations (8.18) and (8.19) becomes

$$\text{Var}[\hat{\mu}_x] = \frac{1}{T^2} \int_0^T \int_0^T C_{xx}(\eta - \xi) d\eta \, d\xi = \frac{1}{T^2} \int_0^T \int_{-\xi}^{T-\xi} C_{xx}(\tau) d\tau \, d\xi$$

$$= \frac{1}{T} \int_{-T}^T \left(1 - \frac{|\tau|}{T}\right) C_{xx}(\tau) d\tau \qquad (8.22)$$

The last expression occurs by reversing the orders of integration between τ and ξ and carrying out the ξ integration. This changes the limits of integration for τ and ξ as shown in the sketch below so that

$$\int_0^T \int_{-\xi}^{T-\xi} C_{xx}(\tau) d\tau \, d\xi = \int_{-T}^0 \int_{-\tau}^T C_{xx}(\tau) d\xi \, d\tau + \int_0^T \int_0^{T-\tau} C_{xx}(\tau) d\xi \, d\tau$$

$$= \int_{-T}^0 (T+\tau) C_{xx}(\tau) \, d\tau + \int_0^T (T-\tau) C_{xx}(\tau) \, d\tau$$

$$= \int_{-T}^T (T - |\tau|) C_{xx}(\tau) \, d\tau$$

Now on letting T tend to infinity, Equation (8.22) becomes

$$\lim_{T \to \infty} T \, \text{Var}[\hat{\mu}_x] = \int_{-\infty}^\infty C_{xx}(\tau) \, d\tau < \infty \qquad (8.23)$$

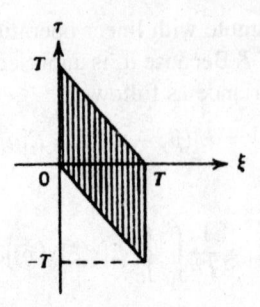

where Equation (5.122) is used, which provides that $C_{xx}(\tau)$ and $\tau C_{xx}(\tau)$ are absolutely integrable over $(-\infty, \infty)$ to justify passage to the limit inside the integral sign. In particular, Equation (8.23) shows that for large T, where $|\tau| \ll T$, the variance is given by

$$\text{Var}[\hat{\mu}_x] \approx \frac{1}{T}\int_{-\infty}^{\infty} C_{xx}(\tau)d\tau \qquad (8.24)$$

Hence, when the integral is finite valued, $\text{Var}[\hat{\mu}_x]$ approaches zero as T approaches infinity, proving that $\hat{\mu}_x$ is a *consistent* estimate of μ_x.

Consider the important special case where $\{x(t)\}$ is *bandwidth-limited white noise* with a mean value $\mu_x \neq 0$ and a variance σ_x^2. Its autospectral density function can be described by

$$G_{xx}(f) = \begin{cases} \dfrac{\sigma_x^2}{B} + \mu_x^2\delta(f) & 0 \le f \le B \\ 0 & f > B \end{cases} \qquad (8.25)$$

where B is the bandwidth. The associated autocovariance function is given by

$$\begin{aligned} C_{xx}(\tau) &= \int_0^{\infty} G_{xx}(f)\cos 2\pi f\tau\, df - \mu_x^2 \\ &= \sigma_x^2\left(\frac{\sin 2\pi B\tau}{2\pi B\tau}\right) \end{aligned} \qquad (8.26)$$

Note that $C_{xx}(0) = \sigma_x^2$ and $C_{xx}(\tau) = 0$ for $\tau = (n/2B)$, where n is an integer. Thus points $(1/2B)$ apart are uncorrelated. They will be statistically independent if $\{x(t)\}$ is also Gaussian. For this case, Equation (8.24) yields the approximate result when $BT \ge 5$ that

$$\text{Var}[\hat{\mu}_x] \approx \frac{\sigma_x^2}{2BT} \qquad (8.27)$$

When $\mu_x \neq 0$, the normalized rms error is

$$\varepsilon[\hat{\mu}_x] \approx \frac{1}{\sqrt{2BT}}\left(\frac{\sigma_x}{\mu_x}\right) \qquad (8.28)$$

MEAN AND MEAN SQUARE VALUE ESTIMATES

From Equation (8.3), note that

$$E[\hat{\mu}_x^2] = \text{Var}[\hat{\mu}_x] + \mu_x^2 \qquad (8.29)$$

Hence, using Equation (8.27),

$$E[\hat{\mu}_x^2] \approx \frac{\sigma_x^2}{2BT} + \mu_x^2 \qquad (8.30)$$

For Gaussian data, when $\mu_x \neq 0$, the fourth-order moment from Equation (3.82) becomes

$$E[\hat{\mu}_x^4] = 3\{E[\hat{\mu}_x^2]\}^2 - 2\mu_x^4 \qquad (8.31)$$

Then, neglecting terms of order $(1/BT)^2$,

$$\text{Var}[\hat{\mu}_x^2] = E[\hat{\mu}_x^4] - \{E[\hat{\mu}_x^2]\}^2 \approx \frac{2\mu_x^2 \sigma_x^2}{BT} \qquad (8.32)$$

Thus, the normalized mean square random error for bandwidth-limited Gaussian white noise is given by

$$\varepsilon_r^2[\hat{\mu}_x^2] = \frac{\text{Var}[\hat{\mu}_x^2]}{\mu_x^4} \approx \frac{2}{BT}\left(\frac{\sigma_x}{\mu_x}\right)^2$$

Now, comparing with Equation (8.28),

$$\varepsilon_r^2[\hat{\mu}_x^2] \approx 4\varepsilon^2[\hat{\mu}_x]$$

and

$$\varepsilon_r[\hat{\mu}_x^2] \approx 2\varepsilon[\hat{\mu}_x] \approx \frac{\sqrt{2}}{\sqrt{BT}}\left(\frac{\sigma_x}{\mu_x}\right) \qquad (8.33)$$

This agrees with the general relation of Equation (8.10).

Example 8.2. **Random Error in Mean Value Estimate.** Consider a bandwidth-limited white noise signal $x(t)$ with a bandwidth of $B = 100$ Hz, a mean value of $\mu_x = 0$, and a standard deviation of $\sigma_x = 2$. If the mean value of $x(t)$ is to be estimated by averaging over a record of length $T = 2$ s, determine an interval that will include the mean value estimate with a probability of approximately 95%.

From Equation (8.27), the random error of the estimate $\hat{\mu}_x$ will have a standard deviation of

$$\sigma[\hat{\mu}_x] = \frac{2}{\sqrt{2(100)(2)}} = 0.10$$

It then follows from Equation (8.12) that the probability is about 95% that an estimate $\hat{\mu}_x$ will fall within the interval

$$[-0.2 \leq \hat{\mu}_x \leq 0.2]$$

8.2.2 Mean Square Value Estimates

As in Section 8.2.1, let $x(t)$ be a single sample time history record from a stationary (ergodic) random process $\{x(t)\}$. The mean square value of $\{x(t)\}$ can be estimated by time averaging over a finite time interval T as follows:

$$\hat{\psi}_x^2 = \frac{1}{T} \int_0^T x^2(t)\, dt \tag{8.34}$$

The true mean square value is

$$\psi_x^2 = E[x^2(t)] \tag{8.35}$$

and is independent of t because $\{x(t)\}$ is stationary. The expected value of the estimate $\hat{\psi}_x^2$ is

$$E[\hat{\psi}_x^2] = \frac{1}{T} \int_0^T E[x^2(t)]\, dt = \frac{1}{T} \int_0^T \psi_x^2\, dt = \psi_x^2 \tag{8.36}$$

Hence $\hat{\psi}_x^2$ is an *unbiased* estimate of ψ_x^2, independent of T.

The mean square error here is given by the variance

$$\begin{aligned}
\operatorname{Var}[\hat{\psi}_x^2] &= E[(\hat{\psi}_x^2 - \psi_x^2)^2] = E[\hat{\psi}_x^4] - \psi_x^4 \\
&= \frac{1}{T^2} \int_0^T \int_0^T (E[x^2(\xi)x^2(\eta)] - \psi_x^4)\, d\eta\, d\xi
\end{aligned} \tag{8.37}$$

Assume now that $\{x(t)\}$ is a *Gaussian* random process with a mean value $\mu_x \neq 0$. Then the expected value in Equation (8.37) takes the special form, derived from Equation (3.82) as follows:

$$E[x^2(\xi)x^2(\eta)] = 2(R_{xx}^2(\eta - \xi) - \mu_x^4) + \psi_x^4 \tag{8.38}$$

From the basic relationship in Equation (8.21), we obtain

$$R_{xx}^2(\eta - \xi) - \mu_x^4 = C_{xx}^2(\eta - \xi) + 2\mu_x^2 C_{xx}(\eta - \xi) \tag{8.39}$$

Hence

$$\begin{aligned}
\operatorname{Var}[\hat{\psi}_x^2] &= \frac{2}{T^2} \int_0^T \int_0^T (R_{xx}^2(\eta - \xi) - \mu_x^4)\, d\eta\, d\xi \\
&= \frac{2}{T} \int_{-T}^T \left(1 - \frac{|\tau|}{T}\right)(R_{xx}^2(\tau) - \mu_x^4)\, d\tau \\
&= \frac{2}{T} \int_{-T}^T \left(1 - \frac{|\tau|}{T}\right)(C_{xx}^2(\tau) + 2\mu_x^2 C_{xx}(\tau))\, d\tau
\end{aligned} \tag{8.40}$$

For large T, where $|\tau| \ll T$, the variance becomes

$$\operatorname{Var}[\hat{\psi}_x^2] \approx \frac{2}{T} \int_{-\infty}^{\infty} (C_{xx}^2(\tau) + 2\mu_x^2 C_{xx}(\tau))\, d\tau \tag{8.41}$$

MEAN AND MEAN SQUARE VALUE ESTIMATES

Thus $\hat{\psi}_x^2$ is a *consistent* estimate of ψ_x^2 because $\text{Var}[\hat{\psi}_x^2]$ will approach zero as T approaches infinity, assuming that $C_{xx}^2(\tau)$ and $C_{xx}(\tau)$ are absolutely integrable over $(-\infty, \infty)$, as stated in Equation (5.122).

Consider the special case of bandwidth-limited Gaussian white noise as defined by Equation (8.25). From Equation (8.26).

$$C_{xx}(\tau) = \sigma_x^2 \left(\frac{\sin 2\pi B\tau}{2\pi B\tau} \right) \tag{8.42}$$

For this case, Equation (8.41) shows that

$$\text{Var}[\hat{\psi}_x^2] \approx \frac{\sigma_x^4}{BT} + \frac{2}{BT} \mu_x^2 \sigma_x^2 \tag{8.43}$$

This is the variance of mean square value estimates, where B is the *total* bandwidth of the data and T is the *total* record length of the data. In general, for $\mu_x \neq 0$, the normalized rms error is

$$\varepsilon[\hat{\psi}_x^2] = \frac{\text{s.d.}[\hat{\psi}_x^2]}{\psi_x^2} \approx \frac{1}{\sqrt{BT}} \left(\frac{\sigma_x}{\psi_x} \right)^2 + \frac{\sqrt{2}}{\sqrt{BT}} \left(\frac{\mu_x \sigma_x}{\psi_x^2} \right) \tag{8.44}$$

For those cases where $\mu_x = 0$, the quantity $\psi_x^2 = \sigma_x^2$ and results simplify to

$$\text{Var}[\hat{\psi}_x^2] \approx \frac{\psi_x^4}{BT} = \frac{R_{xx}^2(0)}{BT} \tag{8.45}$$

with

$$\varepsilon[\hat{\psi}_x^2] \approx \frac{1}{\sqrt{BT}} \tag{8.46}$$

Corresponding results for rms value estimates $\hat{\psi}_x$ instead of $\hat{\psi}_x^2$, when $\mu_x = 0$, are found from Equation (8.10) to be

$$\varepsilon[\hat{\psi}_x] \approx \frac{1}{2\sqrt{BT}} \tag{8.47}$$

Plots of Equations (8.46) and (8.47) versus the BT product are presented in Figure 8.1.

Again for cases where $\mu_x = 0$, the normalized random error for mean square value estimates, as given for bandwidth-limited white noise in Equation (8.46), can be generalized for Gaussian random data with any arbitrary autospectral density function as follows. From Parseval's theorem in Equation (5.75), because $S_{xx}(f)$ is the Fourier transform of $C_{xx}(\tau)$ and $G_{xx}(f) = 2S_{xx}(f)$ when $f > 0$, it follows that

$$\int_{-\infty}^{\infty} C_{xx}^2(\tau) d\tau = \int_{-\infty}^{\infty} S_{xx}^2(f) df = 2 \int_0^{\infty} S_{xx}^2(f) df = \frac{1}{2} \int_0^{\infty} G_{xx}^2(f) df \tag{8.48}$$

Substituting Equation (8.48) into Equation (8.41) with $\mu_x = 0$ yields

$$\text{Var}[\hat{\psi}_x^2] = \frac{1}{T} \int_0^{\infty} G_{xx}^2(f) df \tag{8.49}$$

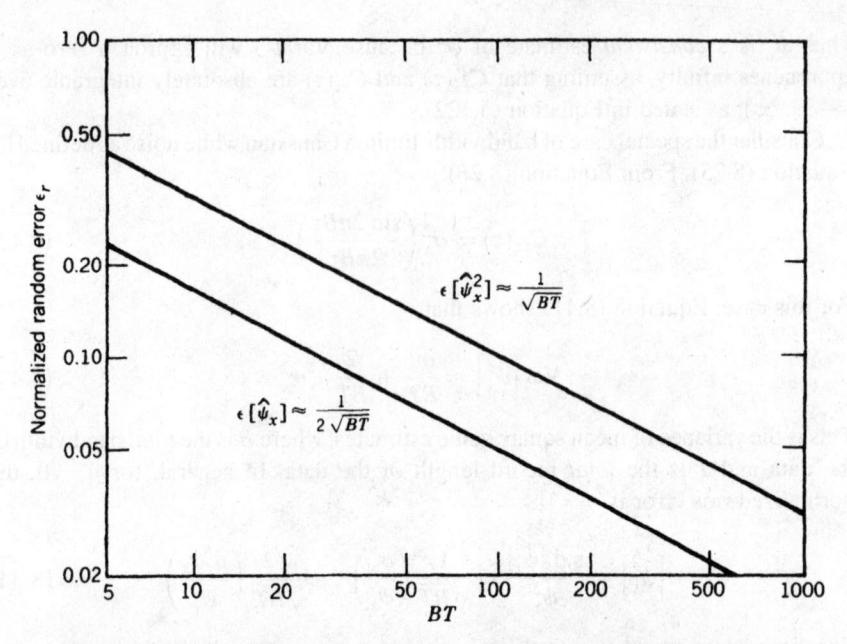

Figure 8.1 Normalized random error of mean square value and rms value estimates.

Hence, the normalized variance of the mean square value estimate becomes

$$\varepsilon_r^2\left[\hat{\psi}_x^2\right] = \frac{\mathrm{Var}[\hat{\psi}_x^2]}{\psi_x^4} = \frac{\frac{1}{T}\int_0^\infty G_{xx}^2(f)\,df}{\psi_x^4} \tag{8.50}$$

and the normalized random error may be written as

$$\varepsilon_r\left[\hat{\psi}_x^2\right] = \frac{1}{\sqrt{B_s T}} \tag{8.51}$$

where

$$B_s = \frac{\psi_x^4}{\int_0^\infty G_{xx}^2(f)\,df} = \frac{\left[\int_0^\infty G_{xx}(f)\,df\right]^2}{\int_0^\infty G_{xx}^2(f)\,df} \tag{8.52}$$

is called the *statistical bandwidth* of the data. The statistical bandwidth B_s should not be confused with the noise spectral bandwidth B_n defined in Equation (5.106), which is the bandwidth of a stationary random process with an arbitrary autospectral density function that has the same mean square value as white noise with a bandwidth $B = B_n$. Instead, the statistical bandwidth is the bandwidth of a stationary random process with an arbitrary autospectral density function where mean square value estimates have the same random error as the mean square value estimates of white noise with a bandwidth $B = B_s$. In other words, B_s is that value of bandwidth that makes Equations (8.46) and (8.47) correct for any Gaussian random data with an arbitrary autospectral density function of $G_{xx}(f)$.

Example 8.3. **Bandwidths for Random Noise with a Nonuniform Autospectrum.** Assume a random process $\{x(t)\}$ has an autospectral density function given by

$$G_{xx}(f) = \frac{a^2}{a^2+(f-f_r)^2} + \frac{a^2}{a^2+(f+f_r)^2} \quad a \ll f_r$$

A plot of this autospectrum for the special case where $a = 0.1 f_r$ is shown in Figure 8.2. It is seen from Figure 8.2 that the autospectrum has a single peak with a maximum value of $G_{xx}(f) \approx 1$ at the frequency $f = f_r$ and a spectral shape similar to the response of the resonant system shown in Figure 2.3 to a white noise input. For this random process, the noise bandwidth B_n defined in Equation (5.106) is given by

$$B_n = \int_0^\infty \left[\frac{a^2}{a^2+(f-f_r)^2} + \frac{a^2}{a^2+(f+f_r)^2} \right] df = \pi a$$

while the statistical bandwidth defined in Equation (8.52) is given by

$$B_s = \frac{\left\{ \int_0^\infty \left[\frac{a^2}{a^2+(f-f_r)^2} + \frac{a^2}{a^2+(f+f_r)^2} \right] df \right\}^2}{\int_0^\infty \left[\frac{a^2}{a^2+(f-f_r)^2} + \frac{a^2}{a^2+(f+f_r)^2} \right]^2 df} = \frac{(\pi a)^2}{\pi a/2} = 2\pi a$$

It follows that $B_s = 2B_n$ for this particular random process. It should be mentioned that these same bandwidth descriptions can be applied to filters or spectral windows by simply substituting the squared frequency response function magnitude $|H(f)|^2$ of the filter or window for the autospectral density function $G_{yy}(f)$ in Equation (5.106) and $G_{xx}(f)$ in Equation (8.52).

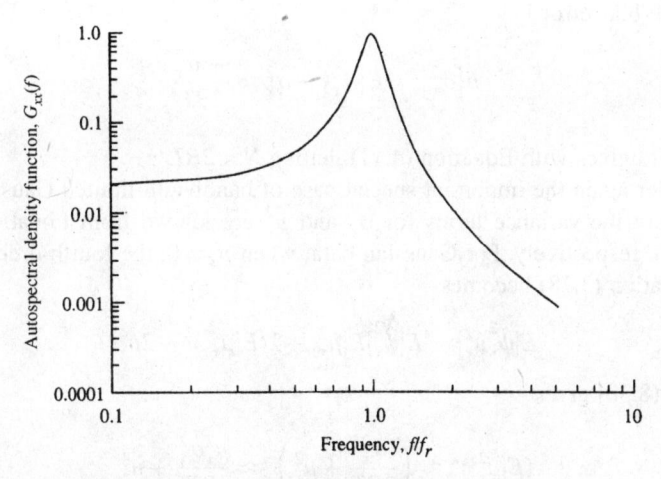

Figure 8.2 Autospectral density function of example random process.

8.2.3 Variance Estimates

Variance estimates can be obtained from

$$\hat{\sigma}_x^2 = \hat{\psi}_x^2 - \hat{\mu}_x^2 \qquad (8.53)$$

Now

$$\text{Var}[\hat{\sigma}_x^2] = E[\hat{\sigma}_x^4] - (E[\hat{\sigma}_x^2])^2 \qquad (8.54)$$

where

$$E[\hat{\sigma}_x^2] = E[\hat{\psi}_x^2] - E[\hat{\mu}_x^2] \qquad (8.55)$$

$$\begin{aligned} E[\hat{\sigma}_x^4] &= E[\hat{\psi}_x^4 - 2\hat{\psi}_x^2\hat{\mu}_x^2 + \hat{\mu}_x^4] \\ &= E[\hat{\psi}_x^4] - 2E[\hat{\psi}_x^2\hat{\mu}_x^2] + E[\hat{\mu}_x^4] \end{aligned} \qquad (8.56)$$

Hence

$$\text{Var}[\hat{\sigma}_x^2] = \text{Var}[\hat{\psi}_x^2] + \text{Var}[\hat{\mu}_x^2] - 2(E[\hat{\psi}_x^2\hat{\mu}_x^2] - E[\hat{\psi}_x^2]E[\hat{\mu}_x^2]) \qquad (8.57)$$

Unlike mean value and mean square value estimates, variance estimates based on Equation (8.53) will be *biased* estimates. Specifically, for bandwidth-limited Gaussian white noise, substitution of Equations (8.36) and (8.30) into Equation (8.55) shows that

$$\begin{aligned} E[\hat{\sigma}_x^2] &\approx \psi_x^2 - \left(\frac{\sigma_x^2}{2BT} + \mu_x^2 \right) \\ &\approx \sigma_x^2 \left(1 - \frac{1}{2BT} \right) \end{aligned} \qquad (8.58)$$

Hence, the bias error is

$$b[\hat{\sigma}_x^2] = E[\hat{\sigma}_x^2] - \sigma_x^2 \approx \frac{-\sigma_x^2}{2BT} \qquad (8.59)$$

This result agrees with Equation (4.11), letting $N = 2BT$.

Consider again the important special case of bandwidth-limited Gaussian white noise where the variance terms for $\hat{\psi}_x^2$ and $\hat{\mu}_x^2$ are known from Equations (8.43) and (8.32), respectively. For Gaussian data, when $\mu_x \neq 0$, the fourth-order moment from Equation (3.78) becomes

$$E[\hat{\psi}_x^2\hat{\mu}_x^2] = E[\hat{\psi}_x^2]E[\hat{\mu}_x^2] + 2(E[\mu_x^2])^2 - 2\mu_x^4 \qquad (8.60)$$

Equation (8.30) gives

$$(E[\hat{\mu}_x^2])^2 \approx \left(\frac{\sigma_x^2}{2BT} + \mu_x^2 \right)^2 \approx \frac{\mu_x^2\sigma_x^2}{BT} + \mu_x^4 \qquad (8.61)$$

neglecting terms of order $(1/BT)^2$. Hence

$$E\left[\hat{\psi}_x^2 \hat{\mu}_x^2\right] - E\left[\hat{\psi}_x^2\right] E\left[\hat{\mu}_x^2\right] \approx \frac{2\mu_x^2 \sigma_x^2}{BT} \tag{8.62}$$

Now, substitutions of Equations (8.32), (8.43), and (8.62) into Equation (8.57) yield

$$\text{Var}[\hat{\sigma}_x^2] \approx \frac{\sigma_x^4}{BT} \tag{8.63}$$

which is independent of μ_x. The normalized random error is then given by

$$\varepsilon_r[\hat{\sigma}_x^2] = \frac{\text{s.d.}[\hat{\sigma}_x^2]}{\sigma_x^2} = \frac{1}{\sqrt{BT}} \tag{8.64}$$

Note that the above result applies even if $\mu_x \neq 0$, whereas the result in Equation (8.46) for mean square value estimates should be used only when $\mu_x = 0$. In either case, the random error can be generalized for all Gaussian random data with an arbitrary autospectral density function $G_{xx}(f)$ by substituting the statistical bandwidth B_s defined in Equation (8.52) for B in Equation (8.64). From Equation (8.10), the normalized random error for the standard deviation estimate $\hat{\sigma}_x$ is given by

$$\varepsilon_r[\hat{\sigma}_x] = \frac{1}{2\sqrt{BT}} \tag{8.65}$$

The plots for the normalized random errors in mean square and rms value estimates in Figure 8.1 also apply to variance and standard deviation estimates with arbitrary mean values, as given in Equations (8.64) and (8.65).

8.3 PROBABILITY DENSITY FUNCTION ESTIMATES

Consider a probability density measurement of a single sample time history record $x(t)$ from a stationary (ergodic) random process $\{x(t)\}$. The probability that $x(t)$ assumes values between $x - (W/2)$ and $x + (W/2)$ during a time interval T may be estimated by

$$\hat{P}[x, W] = \text{Prob}\left[\left(x - \frac{W}{2}\right) \leq x(t) \leq \left(x + \frac{W}{2}\right)\right]$$
$$= \frac{1}{T} \sum_i \Delta t_i = \frac{T_x}{T} \tag{8.66}$$

where Δt_i is the time spent by $x(t)$ in this range during the ith entry into the range, and $T_x = \Sigma \Delta t_i$. The ratio T_x/T is the total fractional portion of the time spent by $x(t)$ in the range $[x - (W/2), x + (W/2)]$. It should be noted that T_x will usually be a function of the value x. The estimated probability $\hat{P}[x,W]$ will approach the true probability $P[x, W]$ as T approaches infinity. Moreover, this estimated probability is an unbiased estimate of the true probability. Hence

$$P[x, W] = E[\hat{P}[x, W]] = \lim_{T \to \infty} \hat{P}[x, W] = \lim_{T \to \infty} \frac{T_x}{T} \qquad (8.67)$$

The probability density function $p(x)$ is defined by

$$p(x) = \lim_{W \to 0} \frac{P[x, W]}{W} = \lim_{\substack{T \to \infty \\ W \to 0}} \frac{\hat{P}[x, W]}{W} = \lim_{\substack{T \to \infty \\ W \to 0}} \hat{p}(x) \qquad (8.68)$$

where

$$\hat{p}(x) = \frac{\hat{P}[x, W]}{W} = \frac{T_x}{TW} \qquad (8.69)$$

is a sample estimate of $p(x)$. In terms of the probability density function $p(x)$, the probability of the time history $x(t)$ falling between any two values x_1 and x_2 is given by

$$\text{Prob}[x_1 \leq x(t) \leq x_2] = \int_{x_1}^{x_2} p(x)dx \qquad (8.70)$$

In particular,

$$P[x, W] = \text{Prob}\left[x - \frac{W}{2} \leq x(t) \leq x + \frac{W}{2}\right] = \int_{x-(W/2)}^{x+(W/2)} p(\xi)\,d\xi \qquad (8.71)$$

Then, from Equation (8.69)

$$E[\hat{p}(x)] = \frac{E[\hat{P}[x, W]]}{W} = \frac{P[x, W]}{W} = \frac{1}{W}\int_{x-(W/2)}^{x+(W/2)} p(\xi)\,d\xi \qquad (8.72)$$

Thus for most $p(x)$,

$$E[\hat{p}(x)] \neq p(x) \qquad (8.73)$$

proving that $\hat{p}(x)$ is generally a *biased* estimate of $p(x)$.

The mean square error of the estimate $\hat{p}(x)$ is calculated from Equation (8.5) by

$$E[(\hat{p}(x) - p(x))^2] = \text{Var}[\hat{p}(x)] + b^2[\hat{p}(x)] \qquad (8.74)$$

where $\text{Var}[\hat{p}(x)]$ is the variance of the estimate as defined by

$$\text{Var}[\hat{p}(x)] = E[(\hat{p}(x) - E[\hat{p}(x)])^2] \qquad (8.75)$$

and $b[\hat{p}(x)]$ is the bias of the estimate as defined by

$$b[\hat{p}(x)] = E[\hat{p}(x)] - p(x) \qquad (8.76)$$

8.3.1 Bias of the Estimate

An expression will now be derived for the bias term of Equation (8.76). In terms of the true probability density function, Equation (8.72) shows that

$$E[\hat{p}(x)] = \frac{1}{W}\int_{x-(W/2)}^{x+(W/2)} p(\xi)\,d\xi \qquad (8.77)$$

By expanding $p(\xi)$ in a Taylor series about the point $\xi = x$, and retaining only the first three terms

$$p(\xi) \approx p(x) + (\xi - x)p'(x) + \frac{(\xi - x)^2}{2}p''(x) \qquad (8.78)$$

From the two relations

$$\int_{x-(W/2)}^{x+(W/2)} (\xi - x)\,d\xi = 0 \qquad (8.79)$$

and

$$\int_{x-(W/2)}^{x+(W/2)} \frac{(\xi - x)^2}{2}\,d\xi = \frac{W^3}{24} \qquad (8.80)$$

it follows that

$$E[\hat{p}(x)] \approx p(x) + \frac{W^2}{24}p''(x) \qquad (8.81)$$

Thus, a first-order approximation for the bias term is given by

$$b[\hat{p}(x)] \approx \frac{W^2}{24}p''(x) \qquad (8.82)$$

where $p''(x)$ is the second derivative of $p(x)$ with respect to x.

Example 8.4. **Bias in Probability Density Estimate of Gaussian Random Data.** Probability density estimates are generally made using a window width of $W \leq 0.2\sigma_x$. However, consider the case where a crude probability density estimate is made using a window width of $W = \sigma_x$. Assume the data being analyzed are Gaussian random noise with a mean value of zero and a variance of unity. From Equation (8.72), the expected value of the estimate is given by

$$E[\hat{p}(x)] = \frac{1}{\sqrt{2\pi}}\int_{x-0.5}^{x+0.5} e^{-x^2/2}\,dx$$

where solutions of the integral are available from Table A.2. For example, at the mean value ($x = 0$), $E[\hat{p}(0)] = 0.3830$. From Table A.1, however, $p(0) = 0.3989$. Hence, the actual bias error in the estimate of a Gaussian probability density function at its mean value is given by Equation (8.76) as

$$b[\hat{p}(0)] = 0.3830 - 0.3989 = -0.0159$$

where the minus sign means the estimate is less than the actual value.

Consider now the first-order approximation for the bias error given by Equation (8.82). For Gaussian data with zero mean value and unity variance,

$$p''(x) = \frac{-(1-x^2)}{\sqrt{2\pi}} e^{-x^2/2}$$

Hence, at $x=0$, the bias is approximated by

$$b[\hat{p}(0)] = \frac{-1}{24\sqrt{2\pi}} = -0.0166$$

which is within 5% of the actual bias error computed earlier.

8.3.2 Variance of the Estimate

To evaluate the variance of an estimate $\hat{p}(x)$ it is necessary to know the statistical properties of the time intervals Δt_i that constitute T_x. Unfortunately, such time statistics for a random process are very difficult to obtain. However, the general form of an appropriate variance expression for $\hat{p}(x)$ can be established by the following heuristic argument.

From Equation (8.69), the variance of $\hat{p}(x)$ is given by

$$\text{Var}[\hat{p}(x)] = \frac{1}{W^2} \text{Var}[\hat{P}(x, W)] \quad (8.83)$$

where $\hat{P}(x, W)$ is the estimate of a proportion $P(x, W)$. The variance for a proportion estimate based on N independent sample values is given by

$$\text{Var}[\hat{P}(x, W)] = \frac{P(x, W)[1 - P(x, W)]}{N} \quad (8.84)$$

Substituting Equation (8.84) into Equation (8.83), and assuming $P(x, W) \approx Wp(x) \ll 1$, the variance of probability density estimates may be approximated by

$$\text{Var}[\hat{p}(x)] = \frac{p(x)}{NW} \quad (8.85)$$

where N is still to be determined. Now from the time-domain sampling theorem derived in Section 10.3.1, a sample record $x(t)$ of bandwidth B and length T can be completely reproduced with $N = 2BT$ discrete values. Of course, the N discrete values will not necessarily be statistically independent. Nevertheless, for any given stationary (ergodic) random process, each sample record will represent $n = N/c^2$ independent sample values (degrees of freedom), where c is a constant. Hence from

PROBABILITY DENSITY FUNCTION ESTIMATES

Equation (8.85),

$$\text{Var}[\hat{p}(x)] \approx \frac{c^2 p(x)}{2BTW} \tag{8.86}$$

The constant c is dependent on the autocorrelation function of the data and the sampling rate. For continuous bandwidth-limited white noise, experimental studies indicate that $c \approx 0.3$. If the bandwidth-limited white noise is digitized to $N = 2BT$ discrete values, the experimental studies indicate that $c = 1.0$, as would be expected from the results of Equation (8.85).

8.3.3 Normalized rms Error

The total mean square error of the probability density estimate $\hat{p}(x)$ is the sum of the variance defined in Equation (8.86) and the square of the bias defined in Equation (8.82). That is,

$$E\left[(\hat{p}(x) - p(x))^2\right] = \frac{c^2 p(x)}{2BTW} + \left[\frac{W^2 p''(x)}{24}\right]^2 \tag{8.87}$$

Hence, the normalized mean square error is approximated by

$$\varepsilon^2[\hat{p}(x)] \approx \frac{c^2}{2BTWp(x)} + \frac{W^4}{576}\left[\frac{p''(x)}{p(x)}\right]^2 \tag{8.88}$$

The square root gives the normalized rms error.

It is clear from Equation (8.88) that there are conflicting requirements on the window width W in probability density measurements. On the one hand, a large value of W is desirable to reduce the random error. On the other hand, a small value of W is needed to suppress the bias error. However, the total error will approach zero as $T \to \infty$ if W is restricted so that $W \to \infty$ and $WT \to \infty$. In practice, values of $W \leq 0.2\sigma_x$ will usually limit the normalized bias error to less than 1%. This is true because of the $p''(x)$ term in the bias portion of the error given by Equation (8.88), Probability density functions of common (approximately Gaussian) random data do not display abrupt or sharp peaks, which are indicative of a large second derivative.

8.3.4 Joint Probability Density Function Estimates

Joint probability density function estimates for a pair of sample time history records $x(t)$ and $y(t)$ from two stationary (ergodic) random processes $\{x(t)\}$ and $\{y(t)\}$ may be defined as follows. Analogous to Equation (8.66), let

$$\hat{P}[x, W_x; y, W_y] = \frac{T_{x,y}}{T} \tag{8.89}$$

estimate the joint probability that $x(t)$ is inside the interval W_x centered at x, while simultaneously $y(t)$ is inside the interval W_y centered at y. This is measured by the ratio $T_{x,y}/T$, where $T_{x,y}$ represents the amount of time that these two events coincide in time

T. Clearly, $T_{x,y}$ will usually be a function of both x and y. This estimated joint probability will approach the true probability $P[x, W_x; y, W_y]$ as T approaches infinity, namely,

$$P[x, W_x; y, W_y] = \lim_{T \to \infty} \hat{P}[x, W_x; y, W_y] = \lim_{T \to \infty} \frac{T_{x,y}}{T} \qquad (8.90)$$

The joint probability density function $p(x, y)$ is now defined by

$$p(x,y) = \lim_{\substack{W_x \to 0 \\ W_y \to 0}} \frac{P[x, W_x; y, W_y]}{W_x W_y} = \lim_{\substack{T \to \infty \\ W_x \to 0 \\ W_y \to 0}} \frac{\hat{P}[x, W_x; y, W_y]}{W_x W_y} = \lim_{\substack{T \to \infty \\ W_x \to 0 \\ W_y \to 0}} \hat{p}(x,y) \qquad (8.91)$$

where

$$\hat{p}(x,y) = \frac{\hat{P}[x, W_x; y, W_y]}{W_x W_y} = \frac{T_{x,y}}{TW_x W_y} \qquad (8.92)$$

Assume that W_x and W_y are sufficiently small that the bias errors are negligible. Then the mean square error associated with the estimate $\hat{p}(x, y)$ will be given by the variance of the estimate. As for first-order probability density estimates, this quantity is difficult to determine precisely by theoretical arguments alone. However, by using the same heuristic arguments that produced Equation (8.86), a general form for the variance can be approximated. Specifically, for the special case where $x(t)$ and $y(t)$ are both bandwidth-limited white noise with identical bandwidths B,

$$\text{Var}[\hat{p}(x,y)] \approx \frac{c^2 p(x,y)}{2BTW_x W_y} \qquad (8.93)$$

where c is an unknown constant.

8.4 CORRELATION FUNCTION ESTIMATES

Consider now two sample time history records $x(t)$ and $y(t)$ from two stationary (ergodic) random processes $\{x(t)\}$ and $\{y(t)\}$. The next statistical quantities of interest are the stationary autocorrelation functions $R_{xx}(\tau)$ and $R_{yy}(\tau)$ and the cross-correlation function $R_{xy}(\tau)$. To simplify the following derivation, the mean values μ_x and μ_y will be assumed to be zero. For continuous data, $x(t)$ and $y(t)$, which exist only over a time interval T, the sample cross-correlation estimate $\hat{R}_{xy}(\tau)$ can be defined by

$$\hat{R}_{xy}(\tau) = \begin{cases} \dfrac{1}{T-\tau} \displaystyle\int_0^{T-\tau} x(t)y(t+\tau)\,dt & 0 \leq \tau < T \\ \dfrac{1}{T-|\tau|} \displaystyle\int_{|\tau|}^T x(t)y(t+\tau)\,dt & -T < \tau \leq 0 \end{cases} \qquad (8.94)$$

CORRELATION FUNCTION ESTIMATES

To avoid the use of absolute value signs, τ will be considered positive henceforth since a similar proof applies for negative τ. The sample autocorrelation function estimates $\hat{R}_{xx}(\tau)$ and $\hat{R}_{yy}(\tau)$ are merely special cases when the two records coincide. That is,

$$\hat{R}_{xx}(\tau) = \frac{1}{T-\tau} \int_0^{T-\tau} x(t)x(t+\tau)\,dt \quad 0 \le \tau < T$$
$$\hat{R}_{yy}(\tau) = \frac{1}{T-\tau} \int_0^{T-\tau} y(t)y(t+\tau)\,dt \quad 0 \le \tau < T$$
(8.95)

Thus by analyzing the cross-correlation function estimate, one derives results that are also applicable to the autocorrelation function estimates.

If the data exist for time $T + \tau$ instead of only for time T, then an alternative definition for $\hat{R}_{xy}(\tau)$ is

$$\hat{R}_{xy}(\tau) = \frac{1}{T} \int_0^T x(t)y(t+\tau)\,dt \quad 0 \le \tau < T \tag{8.96}$$

This formula has a fixed integration time T instead of a variable integration time as in Equation (8.94) and is the way the correlation functions have been defined previously. Note that for either Equation (8.94) or Equation (8.96), mean square estimates of $x(t)$ or $y(t)$ are merely special cases when $\tau = 0$. For simplicity in notation, Equation (8.96) will be used in the following development instead of Equation (8.94). The same final results are obtained for both definitions, assuming the data exist for time $T + \tau$.

The expected value of the estimate $\hat{R}_{xy}(\tau)$ is given by

$$E[\hat{R}_{xy}(\tau)] = \frac{1}{T} \int_0^T E[x(t)y(t+\tau)]\,dt$$
$$= \frac{1}{T} \int_0^T R_{xy}(\tau)\,dt = R_{xy}(\tau)$$
(8.97)

Hence, $\hat{R}_{xy}(\tau)$ is an *unbiased* estimate of $R_{xy}(\tau)$, independent of T. The mean square error is given by the variance

$$\mathrm{Var}[\hat{R}_{xy}(\tau)] = E[(\hat{R}_{xy}(\tau) - R_{xy}(\tau))^2] = E[\hat{R}_{xy}^2(\tau)] - R_{xy}^2(\tau)$$
$$= \frac{1}{T^2} \int_0^T \int_0^T (E[x(u)y(u+\tau)x(v)y(v+\tau)] - R_{xy}^2(r))\,dv\,du$$
(8.98)

At this point, in order to simplify the later mathematical analysis and to agree with many physical cases of interest, it will be assumed that the random processes $\{x(t)\}$ and $\{y(t)\}$ are jointly *Gaussian* for any set of fixed times. This restriction may be removed by substituting certain integrability conditions on the non-Gaussian parts of the random processes without altering in any essential way the results to be derived.

When $\{x(t)\}$ and $\{y(t)\}$ are jointly Gaussian, it follows that $\{x(t)\}$ and $\{y(t)\}$ are separately Gaussian.

For Gaussian stationary random processes with zero mean values, the fourth-order statistical expression is obtained from Equation (5.135) as follows:

$$E[x(u)y(u+\tau)x(v)y(v+\tau)] = R_{xy}^2(\tau) + R_{xx}(v-u)R_{yy}(v-u) \\ + R_{xy}(v-u+\tau)R_{yx}(v-u-\tau) \quad (8.99)$$

Hence, the variance expression may be written as

$$\mathrm{Var}[\hat{R}_{xy}(\tau)] = \frac{1}{T^2}\int_0^T\int_0^T (R_{xx}(v-u)R_{yy}(v-u) \\ + R_{xy}(v-u+\tau)R_{yx}(v-u-\tau))dv\,du \quad (8.100)$$

$$= \frac{1}{T}\int_{-T}^T \left(1 - \frac{|\xi|}{T}\right)(R_{xx}(\xi)R_{yy}(\xi) + R_{xy}(\xi+\tau)R_{yx}(\xi-\tau))\,d\xi$$

The second expression occurs from the first by letting $\xi = v - u$, $d\xi = dv$, and then reversing the order of integration between ξ and u. Now,

$$\lim_{T\to\infty} T\,\mathrm{Var}[\hat{R}_{xy}(\tau)] = \int_{-\infty}^\infty (R_{xx}(\xi)R_{yy}(\xi) + R_{xy}(\xi+\tau)R_{yx}(\xi-\tau))d\xi < \infty \quad (8.101)$$

assuming $R_{xx}(\xi)R_{yy}(\xi)$ and $R_{xy}(\xi)R_{yx}(\xi)$ are absolutely integrable over $(-\infty,\infty)$. This proves that $\hat{R}_{xy}(\tau)$ is a *consistent* estimate of $R_{xy}(\tau)$, and for large T, has a variance given by

$$\mathrm{Var}[\hat{R}_{xy}(\tau)] \approx \frac{1}{T}\int_{-\infty}^\infty (R_{xx}(\xi)R_{yy}(\xi) + R_{xy}(\xi+\tau)R_{yx}(\xi-\tau))d\xi \quad (8.102)$$

Several special cases of Equation (8.102) are worthy of note. For autocorrelation estimates, Equation (8.102) becomes

$$\mathrm{Var}[\hat{R}_{xx}(\tau)] \approx \frac{1}{T}\int_{-\infty}^\infty (R_{xx}^2(\xi) + R_{xx}(\xi+\tau)R_{xx}(\xi-\tau))d\xi \quad (8.103)$$

At the zero displacement point $\tau = 0$,

$$\mathrm{Var}[\hat{R}_{xx}(0)] \approx \frac{2}{T}\int_{-\infty}^\infty R_{xx}^2(\xi)d\xi \quad (8.104)$$

The assumption that $R_{xx}(\tau)$ approaches zero for large τ shows that

$$R_{xx}^2(\xi) \gg R_{xx}(\xi+\tau)R_{xx}(\xi-\tau) \quad \text{for } \tau \gg 0$$

CORRELATION FUNCTION ESTIMATES

Hence for large τ,

$$\text{Var}[\hat{R}_{xx}(\tau)] \approx \frac{1}{T}\int_{-\infty}^{\infty} R_{xx}^2(\xi)d\xi \tag{8.105}$$

which is one-half the value of Equation (8.104).

8.4.1 Bandwidth-Limited Gaussian White Noise

Consider the special case where $\{x(t)\}$ is bandwidth-limited Gaussian white noise with a mean value $\mu_x = 0$ and a bandwidth B as defined in Equations (8.25) and (8.26). For sample records $x(t)$ of length T, from Equation (8.103), the variance for $\hat{R}_{xx}(\tau)$ is given conservatively by

$$\text{Var}[\hat{R}_{xx}(\tau)] \approx \frac{1}{2BT}\left[R_{xx}^2(0) + R_{xx}^2(\tau)\right] \tag{8.106}$$

This reduces to Equation (8.45) at the point $\tau = 0$. Similarly, when both $x(t)$ and $y(t)$ are samples of length T from bandwidth-limited Gaussian white noise with mean values $\mu_x = \mu_y = 0$ and identical bandwidths B, it follows from Equation (8.102) that

$$\text{Var}[\hat{R}_{xy}(\tau)] \approx \frac{1}{2BT}\left[R_{xx}(0)R_{yy}(0) + R_{xy}^2(\tau)\right] \tag{8.107}$$

This result requires that T be sufficiently large that Equation (8.102) can replace Equation (8.100). Satisfactory conditions in practice are $T \geq 10|\tau|$ and $BT \geq 5$.

For $\mu_x = \mu_y = 0$ and $R_{xy}(\tau) \neq 0$, the normalized mean square error is given by

$$\varepsilon^2[\hat{R}_{xy}(\tau)] = \frac{\text{Var}[\hat{R}_{xy}(\tau)]}{R_{xy}^2(\tau)} \approx \frac{1}{2BT}\left[1 + \frac{R_{xx}(0)R_{yy}(0)}{R_{xy}^2(\tau)}\right] \tag{8.108}$$

The square root gives the normalized rms error ε, which includes only a random error term because the bias error is zero if the record length is longer than $T + \tau$. Thus, for cross-correlation function estimates,

$$\varepsilon[\hat{R}_{xy}(\tau)] \approx \frac{1}{\sqrt{2BT}}[1 + \rho_{xy}^{-2}(\tau)]^{1/2} \tag{8.109}$$

where

$$\rho_{xy}(\tau) = \frac{R_{xy}(\tau)}{\sqrt{R_{xx}(0)R_{yy}(0)}} \tag{8.110}$$

is the cross-correlation coefficient function. Note that $R_{xy}(\tau) = C_{xy}(\tau)$ when $\mu_x = \mu_y = 0$. When $x(t) = y(t)$, at the special point $\tau = 0$, the quantity $\hat{R}_{xx}(0) = \hat{\psi}_x^2$ and $\rho_{xx}(0) = 1$ so that one obtains

$$\varepsilon[\hat{R}_{xx}(0)] = \varepsilon[\hat{\psi}_x^2] \approx \frac{1}{\sqrt{BT}} \tag{8.111}$$

in agreement with Equation (8.46). In general, for autocorrelation function estimates,

$$\varepsilon[\hat{R}_{xx}(\tau)] \approx \frac{1}{\sqrt{2BT}}[1 + \rho_{xx}^{-2}(\tau)]^{1/2} \qquad (8.112)$$

where

$$\rho_{xx}(\tau) = \frac{R_{xx}(\tau)}{R_{xx}(0)} \qquad (8.113)$$

Equation (8.112) is plotted in Figure 8.3.

8.4.2 Noise-to-Signal Considerations

Some applications of Equation (8.109) are worthy of note. Suppose $x(t)$ and $y(t)$ are given by

$$\begin{aligned} x(t) &= s(t) + m(t) \\ y(t) &= s(t) + n(t) \end{aligned} \qquad (8.114)$$

where $s(t)$, $m(t)$, and $n(t)$ are mutually uncorrelated. Then

$$R_{xy}(\tau) = R_{ss}(\tau) = R_{ss}(0)\rho_{ss}(\tau) = S\rho_{ss}(\tau)$$

$$R_{xx}(0) = R_{ss}(0) + R_{mm}(0) = S + M \qquad (8.115)$$

$$R_{yy}(0) = R_{ss}(0) + R_{nn}(0) = S + N$$

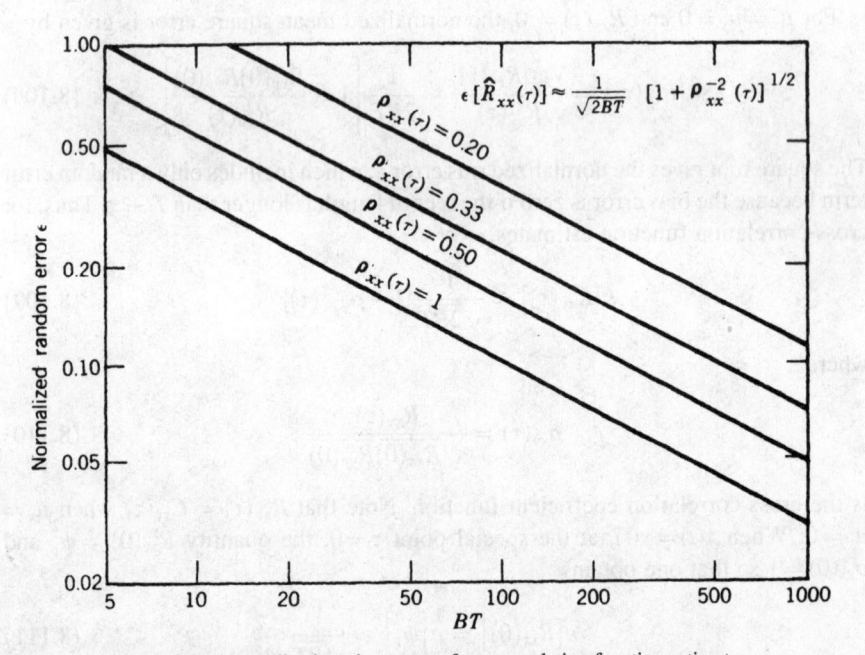

Figure 8.3 Normalized random error of autocorrelation function estimates.

CORRELATION FUNCTION ESTIMATES

It follows from Equation (8.108) that the normalized mean square error is

$$\varepsilon^2\left[\hat{R}_{xy}(\tau)\right] \approx \frac{1}{2BT}\left[1 + \frac{(S+M)(S+N)}{S^2\rho_{ss}^2(\tau)}\right] \quad (8.116)$$

At $\tau = 0$, where $\rho_{ss}(0) = 1$,

$$\varepsilon^2\left[\hat{R}_{xy}(0)\right] \approx \frac{1}{2BT}[2 + (M/S) + (N/S) + (M/S)(N/S)] \quad (8.117)$$

These relations are useful for two-detector systems where $x(t)$ and $y(t)$ of Equation (8.114) measure the outputs of the two detectors containing a common signal $s(t)$ but uncorrelated noises $m(t)$ and $n(t)$.

CASE 1. $M = 0$ where $(N/S) \gg 1$:

$$\varepsilon^2\left[\hat{R}_{xy}(0)\right] \approx \frac{1}{2BT}\left(\frac{N}{S}\right) \quad (8.118)$$

CASE 2. $M = N$ where $(N/S) \gg 1$:

$$\varepsilon^2\left[\hat{R}_{xy}(0)\right] \approx \frac{1}{2BT}\left(\frac{N}{S}\right)^2 \quad (8.119)$$

These two cases can represent important physical applications. For example, in Case 1, $x(t)$ might be a noise-free reference signal being cross-correlated against a corrupted received signal $y(t)$. In Case 2, a corrupted received signal $y(t)$ is being autocorrelated against itself. For any given value of $(N/S) \gg 1$, a much larger value of BT is required in Case 2 than in Case 1 to achieve a desired mean square error. Applications for these and other formulas in this chapter are given in Ref. 1.

8.4.3 Location Estimates of Peak Correlation Values

Previous results in this section give random error formulas that indicate how well one can estimate the magnitudes of peak values of $R_{xy}(\tau)$ and $R_{xx}(\tau)$. There remains the difficult related problem of determining the precise location where these peak correlation values occur. For definiteness, assume that $R_{xx}(\tau)$ has the form associated with bandwidth-limited white noise, namely,

$$R_{xx}(\tau) = R_{xx}(0)\left(\frac{\sin 2\pi B\tau}{2\pi B\tau}\right) \quad (8.120)$$

The maximum value of $R_{xx}(\tau)$ occurs at $\tau = 0$. Expansion of $\sin 2\pi B\tau$ near $\tau = 0$ yields

$$\sin 2\pi B\tau \approx (2\pi B\tau) - \frac{(2\pi B\tau)^3}{6} \quad (8.121)$$

Thus near $\tau = 0$, the estimate $\hat{R}_{xx}(\tau)$ is given by

$$\hat{R}_{xx}(\tau) \approx \left[1 - \frac{2(\pi B \tau)^2}{3}\right] R_{xx}(0) \qquad (8.122)$$

where the mean value is

$$E[\hat{R}_{xx}(0)] = R_{xx}(0) \qquad (8.123)$$

Hence, $\hat{R}_{xx}(0)$ is an unbiased estimate of $R_{xx}(0)$. The variance in these estimates is given by

$$\text{Var}[\hat{R}_{xx}(0)] = E\left[\{\hat{R}_{xx}(0) - R_{xx}(0)\}^2\right] \approx \frac{4}{9}(\pi B)^4 R_{xx}^2(0) E[\tau^4] \qquad (8.124)$$

The normalized mean square error is then

$$\varepsilon^2[\hat{R}_{xx}(0)] = \frac{\text{Var}[\hat{R}_{xx}(0)]}{R_{xx}^2(0)} \approx \frac{4}{9}(\pi B)^4 E[\tau^4] \qquad (8.125)$$

Assume next that these values of τ are such that τ follows a Gaussian distribution with zero mean value and variance $\sigma_1^2(\tau)$, namely,

$$\mu_1(\tau) = E(\tau) = 0$$
$$\sigma_1^2(\tau) = E[\tau^2] \qquad (8.126)$$

Then, the fourth-order moment in Equation (8.125) satisfies

$$E[\tau^4] = 3\sigma_1^4(\tau) \qquad (8.127)$$

It follows that

$$\varepsilon^2[\hat{R}_{xx}(0)] \approx \frac{4}{3}(\pi B)^4 \sigma_1^4(\tau) \qquad (8.128)$$

This proves that

$$\sigma_1(\tau) \approx \frac{0.93}{\pi B}\{\varepsilon[\hat{R}_{xx}(0)]\}^{1/2} \qquad (8.129)$$

The 95% confidence interval for determining the location where the peak value occurs is now

$$[-2\sigma_1(\tau) \leq \tau \leq 2\sigma_1(\tau)] \qquad (8.130)$$

Example 8.5. Time-Delay Estimate from Cross-Correlation Calculation. Assume that two received time history records, $x(t)$ and $y(t)$, contain a common signal $s(t)$ and uncorrelated noises, $m(t)$ and $n(t)$, such that

AUTOSPECTRAL DENSITY FUNCTION ESTIMATES

$$x(t) = s(t) + m(t)$$
$$y(t) = s(t - \tau_0) + n(t)$$

From the developments in Section 5.1.4, the maximum value in the cross-correlation function

$$R_{xy}(\tau) = R_{ss}(\tau - \tau_0)$$

will occur at $\tau = \tau_0$, which defines the time delay between the received signal $s(t)$ in $x(t)$ and $y(t)$. Now assume that $s(t)$ represents bandwidth-limited white noise with a bandwidth of $B = 100$ Hz, and the noise-to-signal ratios in $x(t)$ and $y(t)$ are given by $M/S = N/S = 10$. If the available record lengths for $x(t)$ and $y(t)$ are $T = 5$ s, determine the accuracy of the time-delay estimate τ_0 based on the time of the maximum value of the cross-correlation estimate $\hat{R}_{xy}(\tau)$.

From Equation (8.119), the normalized random error of the cross-correlation estimate at its maximum value is approximated by

$$\varepsilon[\hat{R}_{xy}(\tau_0)] \approx \varepsilon[\hat{R}_{ss}(0)] \approx \left[\frac{10^2}{(2)(100)(5)}\right]^{1/2} = 0.32$$

Note that a more exact error is given by Equation (8.117) as $\varepsilon = 0.35$. Now the standard deviation of the estimate τ_0 is approximated from Equation (8.129) by

$$\sigma_1(\tau) \approx \frac{0.93(0.35)^{1/2}}{\pi(100)} = 0.0017 \text{ s}$$

Hence, from Equation (8.130), an approximate 95% confidence interval for the time delay τ_0 in seconds is given by

$$[\hat{\tau}_0 - 0.0034 \leq \tau_0 \leq \hat{\tau}_0 + 0.0034]$$

It should be mentioned that more accurate time delay estimates can often be achieved using the Hilbert transform procedures discussed in Chapter 13 or the phase analysis procedures detailed in Ref. 2.

8.5 AUTOSPECTRAL DENSITY FUNCTION ESTIMATES

Assume the autospectral density function associated with a sample time history record $x(t)$ is estimated using the filtering–squaring–averaging procedure detailed in Section 5.2.3 and illustrated in Figure 5.5. From Equation (5.68), the autospectral density function estimate computed by this procedure is

$$\hat{G}_{xx}(f) = \frac{1}{B_e T} \int_0^T x^2(f, B_e, t) \, dt = \frac{\hat{\psi}_x^2(f, B_e)}{B_e} \tag{8.131}$$

where $x(f, B_e, t)$ is that portion of $x(t)$ passed by an ideal rectangular bandpass filter with a bandwidth of B_e centered at frequency f, and $\hat{\psi}_x^2(f, B_e)$ is an estimate of the mean square value of $x(f, B_e, t)$. The true mean square value that would be computed with an infinite averaging time is given by

$$\psi_x^2(f, B_e) = \int_{f-(B_e/2)}^{f+(B_e/2)} G_{xx}(\xi)\, d\xi \tag{8.132}$$

Equations (8.131) and (8.132) show that

$$E[\hat{G}_{xx}(f)] = \frac{\psi_x^2(f, B_e)}{B_e} = \frac{1}{B_e} \int_{f-(B_e/2)}^{f+(B_e/2)} G_{xx}(\xi)\, d\xi \tag{8.133}$$

Thus, for most $G_{xx}(f)$,

$$E[\hat{G}_{xx}(f)] \neq G_{xx}(f) \tag{8.134}$$

so that $\hat{G}_{xx}(f)$ is generally a *biased* estimate of $G_{xx}(f)$.

The mean square error of the estimate $\hat{G}_{xx}(f)$ is calculated from Equation (8.5) by

$$E[(\hat{G}_{xx}(f) - G_{xx}(f))^2] = \text{Var}[\hat{G}_{xx}(f)] + b^2[\hat{G}_{xx}(f)] \tag{8.135}$$

where $\text{Var}[\hat{G}_{xx}(f)]$ is the variance of the estimate as defined by

$$\text{Var}[\hat{G}_{xx}(f)] = E[(\hat{G}_{xx}(f) - E[\hat{G}_{xx}(f)])^2] \tag{8.136}$$

and $b[\hat{G}_{xx}(f)]$ is the bias of the estimate as defined by

$$b[\hat{G}_{xx}(f)] = E[\hat{G}_{xx}(f)] - G_{xx}(f) \tag{8.137}$$

8.5.1 Bias of the Estimate

An expression for the bias term of Equation (8.136) may be derived by the procedure used to derive the bias term for probability density estimates in Section 8.3.1. Specifically, by expanding $G_{xx}(\xi)$ in a Taylor series about the point $\xi = f$ and retaining only the first three terms, it follows from Equation (8.133) that

$$E[\hat{G}_{xx}(f)] \approx G_{xx}(f) + \frac{B_e^2}{24} G''_{xx}(f) \tag{8.138}$$

Thus, the bias term is approximated by

$$b[\hat{G}_{xx}(f)] \approx \frac{B_e^2}{24} G''_{xx}(f) \tag{8.139}$$

where $G''_{xx}(f)$ is the second derivative of $G_{xx}(f)$ with respect to f and is related to $R_{xx}(\tau)$ by the expression

$$G''_{xx}(f) = -8\pi^2 \int_{-\infty}^{\infty} \tau^2 R_{xx}(\tau) e^{-j2\pi f \tau}\, d\tau \tag{8.140}$$

It should be emphasized that Equation (8.139) is only a first-order approximation of the bias error, which is applicable for cases where $B_e^2 G''_{xx}(f) < G_{xx}(f)$. Because

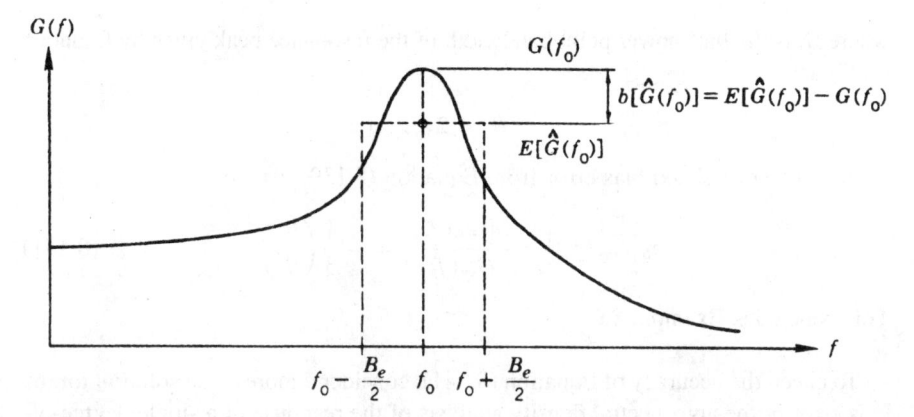

Figure 8.4 Illustration of bias error introduced by frequency smoothing of spectral density estimates.

autospectra in practice often display sharp peaks reflecting large second derivatives, this may provide an inadequate measure of the bias error in some cases. Generally speaking, Equation (8.139) will exaggerate the degree of bias in estimates where $B_e^2 G''_{xx}(f)$ is large.

The bias error in Equation (8.139) is derived assuming that the spectral estimation is accomplished using an ideal rectangular spectral window as defined in Equation (8.132) and illustrated in Figure 8.4. It will be seen in Section 11.5 that spectral estimation procedures in practice involve spectral windows that deviate widely from an ideal rectangular form. Nevertheless, Equation (8.139) constitutes a useful first-order approximation that correctly describes important qualitative results. In particular, the bias error increases as $G''(f)$ increases for a given B_e, or as B_e increases for a given $G''(f)$. Also, it is clear from Figure 8.4 that the bias error is always in the direction of reduced dynamic range; that is, spectral density peaks are underestimated and spectral density valleys are overestimated.

Example 8.6. Illustration of Bias Error in Autospectrum Estimate. Assume that white noise is applied to a single degree-of-freedom system defined in Section 2.4.1. From Example 6.3, the displacement response of the system will have an autospectral density function given by

$$G_{yy}(f) = \frac{G}{[1-(f/f_n)^2]^2 + [2\zeta f/f_n]^2}$$

where G is the spectral density of the excitation in displacement units, f_n is the undamped natural frequency of the system, and ζ is the damping ratio of the system. As pointed out in Equation (2.25), the peak value of $G_{yy}(f)$ occurs at the resonance frequency $f_r = f_n\sqrt{1-2\zeta^2}$. For the case where $\zeta \ll 1$ so that $f_r \approx f_n$, the second derivative of $G_{yy}(f)$ at the frequency f_r yields

$$G''_{yy}(f_r) \approx (-8/B_r^2)G_{yy}(f_r)$$

where B_r is the half-power point bandwidth of the resonance peak given by Equation (2.27) as

$$B_r \approx 2\zeta f_r$$

Hence, the normalized bias error from Equation (8.139) becomes

$$\varepsilon_b[\hat{G}_{yy}(f_r)] = \frac{b[\hat{G}_{yy}(f_r)]}{G_{yy}(f_r)} = -\frac{1}{3}\left(\frac{B_e}{B_r}\right)^2 \quad (8.141)$$

This concludes Example 8.6.

To check the accuracy of Equation (8.141), consider a more exact solution for the bias error in the autospectral density analysis of the response of a single degree-of-freedom system to white noise when $\zeta \ll 1$ so that $f_r \approx f_n$. Specifically, from Equation (8.133),

$$E[\hat{G}_{yy}(f_r)] = \frac{1}{B_e}\int_{f_r-(B_e/2)}^{f_r+(B_e/2)} G_{yy}(f)\,df = \frac{G}{B}\int_{f_r-(B_e/2)}^{f_r+(B_e/2)} \frac{df}{[1-(f/f_n)^2]^2 + [2\zeta f/f_n]^2}$$

Now

$$[1-(f/f_n)^2]^2 + [2\zeta f/f_n]^2 = \{[(f/f_n)-1][(f/f_n)+1]\}^2 + [2\zeta f/f_n]^2$$
$$\approx 4[(f/f_n)-1]^2 + 4\zeta^2 \quad \text{when } f \approx f_n$$

Hence,

$$E[\hat{G}_{yy}(f_r)] = \frac{G}{4B_e}\int_{f_r-(B_e/2)}^{f_r+(B_e/2)} \frac{df}{[(f/f_n)-1]^2 + \zeta^2}$$

Letting $x = (f/f_n) - 1$, it follows that $dx = df/f_n$ and

$$E[\hat{G}_{yy}(f_r)] = \frac{Gf_n}{4B_e}\int_{-B_e/2f_n}^{B_e/2f_n} \frac{dx}{x^2 + \zeta^2}$$

From integral tables,

$$\int \frac{dx}{x^2 + \zeta^2} = \frac{1}{\zeta}\tan^{-1}\left(\frac{x}{\zeta}\right)$$

Hence,

$$E[\hat{G}_{yy}(f_r)] = \frac{Gf_n}{4\zeta B_e}\left[\tan^{-1}\left(\frac{B_e}{2\zeta f_n}\right) - \tan^{-1}\left(\frac{B_e}{2\zeta f_n}\right)\right] = \frac{Gf_n}{2\zeta B_e}\tan^{-1}\left(\frac{B_e}{2\zeta f_n}\right)$$

Noting that the half-power bandwidth $B_r \approx 2\zeta f_r \approx 2\zeta f_n$ when $\zeta \ll 1$, it follows that

$$E[\hat{G}_{yy}(f_r)] = \frac{Gf_n}{2\zeta B_e}\tan^{-1}\left(\frac{B_e}{B_r}\right)$$

At $f=f_n$, the actual value of $G_{yy}(f)$ is

$$G_{yy}(f_n) = \frac{G}{4\zeta^2} = G_{yy}(f_r)$$

Thus,

$$\frac{E[\hat{G}_{yy}(f_r)]}{G_{yy}(f_r)} = \frac{B_r}{B_e}\tan^{-1}\left(\frac{B_e}{B_r}\right)$$

which is in agreement with a formula determined by different procedures in Ref. 3. In terms of the normalized bias error defined in Equation (8.9b),

$$\varepsilon_b[\hat{G}_{yy}(f_r)] = \frac{B_r}{B_e}\tan^{-1}\left(\frac{B_e}{B_r}\right) - 1 \qquad (8.142)$$

The normalized bias error results given by Equations (8.141) and (8.142) are compared in Figure 8.5. It is seen from this figure that the two results are in good agreement for resolution to half-power point bandwidth ratios of $B_e/B_r \leq 0.5$, which corresponds to a normalized bias error of about -9%. When adequate record lengths are available, it is common practice to choose $B_e = B_r/4$ so that a negligible bias error of $\varepsilon_b \approx -2\%$ is obtained. Even for relatively short record lengths where the resolution bandwidth might be selected using the minimum mean square error criterion in Section 8.5.3 to follow, it is unusual to choose a resolution bandwidth of greater than $B_e = B_r/2$. Hence, the simpler and more conservative result in Equation (8.141) is usually an acceptable approximation for the maximum bias error in autospectral density estimates of data representing the response of lightly damped mechanical and electrical systems. See Ref. 4 for further details on the bias errors in autospectral density analysis when the resolution filter has other than an ideal rectangular bandwidth.

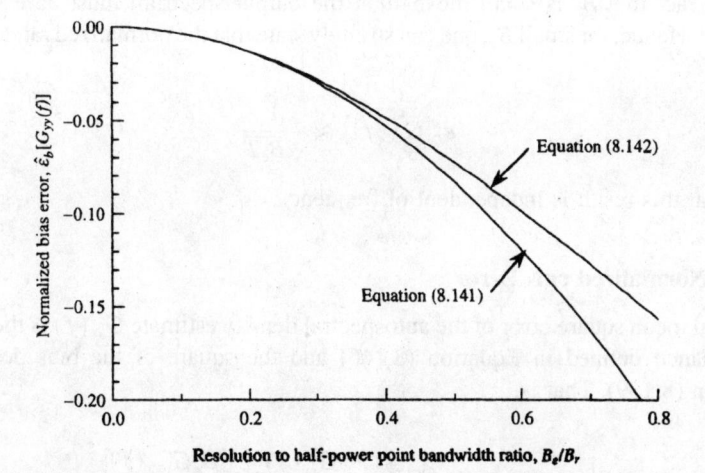

Figure 8.5 Normalized bias error for autospectral density estimates of single degree-of-freedom system response to white noise.

8.5.2 Variance of the Estimate

The most direct way to arrive at a variance expression for autospectral density estimates is to apply the results derived in Section 8.2.2 as follows. From Equation (8.131), the estimate

$$B_e \hat{G}_{xx}(f) = \hat{\psi}_x^2(f, B_e) \qquad (8.143)$$

is an unbiased estimate of the mean square value of $x(t)$ within the bandwidth B_e centered at f. The true value is given by $\psi_x^2(f, B_e) = B_e G_{xx}(f)$ when $G_{xx}(f)$ is constant over the bandwidth B_e. This will be approximately the case if B_e is sufficiently small. The result of Equation (8.45) applies to these estimates with $R_{xx}(0) = B_e G_{xx}(f)$. Hence

$$\text{Var}\left[B_e \hat{G}_{xx}(f)\right] \approx \frac{B_e^2 G_{xx}^2(f)}{B_e T} \qquad (8.144)$$

But, because B_e is a constant,

$$\text{Var}[B_e \hat{G}_{xx}(f)] = B_e^2 \text{Var}[G_{xx}^2(f)] \qquad (8.145)$$

This gives for the variance of the estimate

$$\text{Var}\left[\hat{G}_{xx}(f)\right] \approx \frac{G_{xx}^2(f)}{B_e T} \qquad (8.146)$$

The result in Equation (8.146) is based on the assumption that the filtered data behave like bandwidth-limited Gaussian white noise. This is an excellent assumption in practice when the filter resolution bandwidth B_e is small. The central limit theorem applies to indicate that the filtered data should be more Gaussian than the input data, and the fact that B_e is small means that the output spectrum must be essentially constant. Hence, for small B_e, one can strongly state that the normalized random error will be

$$\varepsilon_r\left[\hat{G}_{xx}(f)\right] \approx \frac{1}{\sqrt{B_e T}} \qquad (8.147)$$

Note that this result is independent of frequency.

8.5.3 Normalized rms Error

The total mean square error of the autospectral density estimate $\hat{G}_{xx}(f)$ is the sum of the variance defined in Equation (8.146) and the square of the bias defined in Equation (8.139). That is,

$$E\left[(\hat{G}_{xx}(f) - G_{xx}(f))^2\right] \approx \frac{G_{xx}^2(f)}{B_e T} + \left[\frac{B_e^2 G''_{xx}(f)}{24}\right]^2 \qquad (8.148)$$

Hence, the normalized mean square error is approximated by

$$\varepsilon^2[\hat{G}_{xx}(f)] = \frac{E[(\hat{G}_{xx}(f) - G_{xx}(f))^2]}{G_{xx}^2(f)} \approx \frac{1}{B_e T} + \frac{B_e^4}{576}\left[\frac{G''_{xx}(f)}{G_{xx}(f)}\right]^2 \quad (8.149)$$

The square root gives the normalized rms error.

Two important features of the error expression for autospectral density estimates should be noted. First, there are conflicting requirements on the resolution bandwidth B_e, namely, a small value of B_e is needed to suppress the bias portion of the error, while a large value of B_e is desired to reduce the random portion of the error. This is similar to the situation discussed in Section 8.3.3 for the window width W in probability density measurements. The problem here, however, is more critical since autospectra in practice often display sharp peaks (large second derivatives), which aggravate the bias error problem. Second, the random portion of the error includes only the resolution bandwidth B_e, and not the total data bandwidth B. Hence, the random portion of the error is a function primarily of analysis parameters rather than unknown data parameters. This greatly enhances the practical value of Equation (8.149) in experimental design and data analysis.

Example 8.7. Illustration of Optimum Resolution Bandwidth Selection. As in Example 8.6, consider the response of a single degree-of-freedom system to white noise. The maximum frequency resolution bias error in an autospectral density estimate of the response data for this case is given by Equation (8.141). Hence, the maximum normalized mean square error in an autospectral density estimate is given from Equation (8.149) by

$$\varepsilon^2[\hat{G}_{xx}(f)] \approx \frac{1}{B_e T} + \frac{1}{9}\left(\frac{B_e}{B_r}\right)^4$$

If one assumes that the system has light damping ($\zeta \ll 1$), then Equation (2.27) applies and

$$\varepsilon^2[\hat{G}_{xx}(f)] \approx \frac{1}{B_e T} + \frac{1}{9}\left(\frac{B_e}{2\zeta f_r}\right)^4$$

The resolution bandwidth that will minimize the normalized mean square error is obtained by taking the derivative of the error with respect to B_e, equating to zero, and solving for the *optimum resolution bandwidth* B_o. This yields

$$B_o \approx 2\frac{(\zeta f_r)^{4/5}}{T^{1/5}} \quad (8.150)$$

See Ref. 5 for further discussions of optimum resolution bandwidths for the computation of autospectral density estimates.

Two aspects of Equation (8.150) are important to note. First, the optimum resolution bandwidth is inversely proportional to the one-fifth power of the averaging time T, meaning that the optimum bandwidth is not very sensitive to the averaging time. For example, the value of B_o for $T = 1$ s is less than 60% greater than the B_o for $T = 10$.

Second, the optimum resolution bandwidth is a function of the four-fifths power of the system resonant frequency f_r, meaning that the optimum bandwidth is almost directly proportional to the resonance frequency assuming a constant damping ratio ζ. This explains why a resolution bandwidth that is proportional to the bandwidth center frequency (referred to as a *constant percentage resolution bandwidth*) is often recommended for the autospectral density analysis of random data representing the resonant response of lightly damped mechanical and electrical systems.

8.5.4 Estimates from Finite Fourier Transforms

In Section 8.5.2, an expression is derived for the variance of autospectral density estimates obtained by the filtering, squaring, and averaging operations illustrated in Figure 5.5. This approach evolves from the definition of the autospectral density function given in Section 5.2.3 and was implemented in the past by analog instruments, as well as currently on digital computers using computational procedures involving digital filters. However, as detailed in Chapter 11, most current digital data analysis procedures for the estimation of autospectral density functions use finite Fourier transform computations that evolve from the definition of the autospectral density function given in Section 5.2.2. The finite Fourier transforms are accomplished using a fast Fourier transform (FFT) algorithm and, hence, are commonly referred to as *FFT procedures*. The normalized random error for the spectral estimates obtained using FFT procedures is equivalent to that given in Equation (8.147), but the parameters in the error expression are different. The direct derivation of the normalized random error for autospectral density estimates using FFT procedures may add insight into the spectral density estimation error problem.

Consider the autospectral density function of a stationary (ergodic) Gaussian random process $\{x(t)\}$, as defined in Equation (5.67). Specifically, given a sample record $x(t)$ of unlimited length T, the autospectrum is

$$G_{xx}(f) = 2 \lim_{T \to \infty} \frac{1}{T} E\left[|X(f,T)|^2\right] \qquad (8.151)$$

where $X(f, T)$ is the finite Fourier transform of $x(t)$, that is,

$$X(f,T) = \int_0^T x(t)e^{-j2\pi ft}dt \qquad (8.152)$$

Now an estimate of $G_{xx}(f)$ can be obtained by simply omitting the limiting and expectation operations in Equation (8.151). This will yield the "raw" estimate

$$\tilde{G}_{xx}(f) = \frac{2}{T}|X(f,T)|^2 \qquad (8.153)$$

with the narrowest possible resolution $\Delta f = (1/T)$.

To determine the variance of this estimate, observe that the finite Fourier transform $X(f, T)$ is defined by a series of components at frequencies $f = k/T$, $k = 1,2,3, \ldots$. Further observe that $X(f, T)$ is a complex number where the real and imaginary parts, $X_R(f, T)$ and $X_I(f, T)$, can be shown to be uncorrelated random variables with zero

AUTOSPECTRAL DENSITY FUNCTION ESTIMATES

means and equal variances. Because a Fourier transformation is a linear operation, $X_R(f, T)$ and $X_I(f, T)$ will be Gaussian random variables if $x(t)$ is Gaussian. It follows that the quantity

$$|X(f,T)|^2 = X_R^2(f,T) + X_I^2(f,T) \qquad (8.154)$$

is the sum of the squares of two independent Gaussian variables. Hence, from the definition of Equation (4.16) as applied in Equation (4.37), each frequency component of the estimate $\tilde{G}_{xx}(f)$ will have a sampling distribution given by

$$\frac{\tilde{G}_{xx}(f)}{G_{xx}(f)} = \frac{\chi_2^2}{2} \qquad (8.155)$$

where χ_2^2 is the chi-square variable with $n = 2$ degrees-of-freedom.

Note that the result in Equation (8.155) is independent of the record length T; that is, increasing the record length does not alter the distribution function defining the random error of the estimate. It only increases the number of spectral components in the estimate. If the record length is interpreted as a measure of the sample size for the estimate, this implies that *Equation (8.153) produces an inconsistent estimate of autospectral density functions*, as previously stated in Section 5.2.2. Furthermore, the random error of the estimate is substantial. Referring to Equations (4.19) and (4.20), the mean and variance of the chi-square variable are n and $2n$, respectively. Then the normalized random error is

$$\varepsilon_r[\tilde{G}_{xx}(f)] = \frac{\sigma[\tilde{G}_{xx}(f)]}{G_{xx}(f)} = \frac{\sqrt{2n}}{n} = \sqrt{\frac{2}{n}} \qquad (8.156)$$

For the case at hand, $n = 2$, so $\varepsilon_r = 1$, which means that the standard deviation of the estimate is as great as the quantity being estimated. This would be an unacceptable random error for most applications.

In practice, the random error of autospectra estimates produced by Equation (8.153) is reduced by computing an ensemble of estimates from n_d different (distinct, disjoint) subrecords, each of length T, and averaging the results to obtain a final "smooth" estimate given by

$$\hat{G}_{xx}(f) = \frac{2}{n_d T} \sum_{i=1}^{n_d} |X_i(f,T)|^2 \qquad (8.157)$$

Since each spectral calculation in Equation (8.157) adds two statistical degrees-of-freedom to the estimate, it follows that

$$\varepsilon_r[\hat{G}_{xx}(f)] = \sqrt{\frac{2}{2n_d}} = \frac{1}{\sqrt{n_d}} \qquad (8.158)$$

The minimum total record length required to compute the autospectrum estimate is clearly

$$T_r = n_d T \qquad (8.159)$$

and the resolution bandwidth of the analysis is approximated by

$$B_e \approx \Delta f = 1/T \qquad (8.160)$$

Hence, $n_d = (T_r/T) \approx B_e T_r$, so Equation (8.158) is equivalent to

$$\varepsilon_r[\hat{G}_{xx}(f)] \approx \frac{1}{\sqrt{B_e T_r}} \qquad (8.161)$$

in agreement with Equation (8.147) where T_r replaces T.

Referring back to Equation (8.155), the sampling distribution for an autospectral density estimate may now be written as

$$\frac{\hat{G}_{xx}(f)}{G_{xx}(f)} = \frac{\chi_n^2}{n} \quad n = 2n_d \qquad (8.162)$$

From Equation (4.47), it follows that a $(1 - \alpha)$ confidence interval for $G_{xx}(f)$ based on an estimate $\hat{G}_{xx}(f)$ is given by

$$\left[\frac{n\hat{G}_{xx}(f)}{\chi^2_{n;\alpha/2}} \leq G_{xx}(f) \leq \frac{n\hat{G}_{xx}(f)}{\chi^2_{n;1-\alpha/2}} \right] \quad n = 2n_d \qquad (8.163)$$

As before, if the normalized random error is relatively small, say $\varepsilon_r \leq 0.10$, then 95% confidence intervals can be approximated from Equations (8.14) and (8.158) by

$$\left[\left(1 - \frac{2}{\sqrt{n_d}}\right) \hat{G}_{xx}(f) \leq G_{xx}(f) \leq \left(1 + \frac{2}{\sqrt{n_d}}\right) \hat{G}_{xx}(f) \right] \qquad (8.164)$$

It should be mentioned that the random errors in spectral density calculations might be somewhat greater than indicated in the foregoing equations, depending on the exact details of the calculations, as discussed in Section 11.5.2.

8.5.5 Test for Equivalence of Autospectra

An estimate $\hat{G}(f)$ of an autospectral density function $G(f)$ will have a sampling distribution that is approximately Gaussian if the number of averages n_d is large, say $n_d \geq 30$. It is shown in Section 8.5.4 that the mean value (assuming no bias) and variance of the estimate are given by

$$E[\hat{G}(f)] = G(f) \qquad (8.165)$$

$$\text{Var}[\hat{G}(f)] = \frac{1}{n_d} G^2(f) \qquad (8.166)$$

Hence, a $(1 - \alpha)$ confidence interval for $G(f)$ based on a measurement $\hat{G}(f)$ may be approximated by

$$\left[\hat{G}(f)\left(1 - z_{\alpha/2}\sqrt{\frac{1}{n_d}}\right) \leq G(f) \leq \hat{G}(f)\left(1 + z_{\alpha/2}\sqrt{\frac{1}{n_d}}\right) \right] \qquad (8.167)$$

where $z_{\alpha/2}$ is the $100\alpha/2$ percentage point of the standardized Gaussian distribution. To arrive at Equation (8.167), it is assumed that $z_{\alpha/2}\sqrt{1/n_d} \ll 1$, so that

$$\left(1 \pm z_{\alpha/2}\sqrt{\frac{1}{n_d}}\right)^{-1} \simeq \left(1 \pm z_{\alpha/2}\sqrt{\frac{1}{n_d}}\right) \tag{8.168}$$

A logarithmic transformation of the estimate $\hat{G}(f)$ to $\log \hat{G}(f)$ has the effect of producing a distribution that is closer to Gaussian than the original distribution. The sample mean value and variance of $\log \hat{G}(f)$ become

$$E[\log \hat{G}(f)] \simeq \log G(f) \tag{8.169}$$

$$\text{Var}[\log \hat{G}(f)] \simeq \frac{1}{n_d} \tag{8.170}$$

Thus the variance here is independent of frequency. Now, a $(1 - \alpha)$ confidence interval for $\log G(f)$ may be approximated by

$$\left[\log \hat{G}(f) - z_{\alpha/2}\sqrt{\frac{1}{n_d}}\right] \leq \log G(f) \leq \left[\log \hat{G}(f) + z_{\alpha/2}\sqrt{\frac{1}{n_d}}\right] \tag{8.171}$$

This result can be derived directly from Equation (8.167) to provide a heuristic explanation for Equations (8.169) and (8.170). This derivation uses the assumption that $z_{\alpha/2}\sqrt{1/n_d} \ll 1$, so that

$$\log\left(1 \pm z_{\alpha/2}\sqrt{\frac{1}{n_d}}\right) \simeq \pm z_{\alpha/2}\sqrt{\frac{1}{n_d}} \tag{8.172}$$

Consider now two different autospectral density function estimates $\hat{G}_1(f)$ and $\hat{G}_2(f)$ obtained under different conditions—for example, from two different sample records or from two different parts of the same sample record. The problem is to decide whether or not these two autospectra are statistically equivalent over some frequency interval (f_a, f_b) of bandwidth $B = f_b - f_a$.

Assume that each of the two autospectral density function estimates is based on a resolution bandwidth B_e, where N_f bandwidths are needed to cover the frequency range of interest. That is,

$$N_f = \frac{B}{B_e} \tag{8.173}$$

Further assume the number of averages for each estimate are n_{d1} and n_{d2}, respectively, meaning that the averaging time (record length) for each estimate may be different even though the resolution bandwidth is the same. From Equations (8.169) and (8.170), the sampling distributions of the logarithm of the estimates in the ith bandwidth are approximated by

$$\log \hat{G}_1(f_i) = y\left[\log G_1(f_i), \frac{1}{n_{d1}}\right]$$
$$\log \hat{G}_2(f_i) = y\left[\log G_2(f_i), \frac{1}{n_{d2}}\right] \quad (8.174)$$

where $y[\mu, \sigma^2]$ is a Gaussian distributed random variable with a mean of μ and a variance of σ^2. Now, if the two sample records in question have the same autospectral density function $G(f) = G_1(f) = G_2(f)$, it follows from Equations (8.174) that

$$\log \frac{\hat{G}_1(f_i)}{\hat{G}_2(f_i)} = y\left[0, \frac{1}{n_{d1}} + \frac{1}{n_{d2}}\right] \quad (8.175)$$

Hence, from Section 4.6, the statistic

$$X^2 = \left[\frac{1}{n_{d1}} + \frac{1}{n_{d2}}\right]^{-1} \sum_{i=1}^{n} \left[\log \frac{\hat{G}_1(f_i)}{\hat{G}_2(f_i)}\right]^2 \quad (8.176)$$

has a chi-square distribution with N_f degrees-of-freedom. That is,

$$X^2 \approx \chi_n^2 \quad n = N_f \quad (8.177)$$

The result in Equation (8.176) provides a basis for testing the hypothesis that $G_1(f) = G_2(f)$. The region of acceptance for the hypothesis test is

$$X^2 \leq \chi_{n;\alpha}^2 \quad n = N_f \quad (8.178)$$

where α is the level of significance for the test, as detailed in Section 4.5.1.

8.6 RECORD LENGTH REQUIREMENTS

The error expressions derived in Sections 8.2–8.5 provide ways to assess the statistical accuracy of various parameter estimates after an experiment has been completed. It would be desirable if these error expressions could also be used to predict the minimum record lengths required in future experiments to obtain data with a predetermined degree of accuracy. The error formulas do relate the total record length T_r to the random error ε_r for each parameter estimate. However, these relationships generally include other factors, primarily the autospectrum of the data, which are usually unknown prior to data collection. If one could assume that the data have an autospectrum that can be approximated by bandwidth-limited white noise, then the minimum total record length or minimum number of averages needed to achieve a desired accuracy, ignoring bias errors, would be as shown in Table 8.1. Unfortunately, such an assumption is rarely justified in practice so, in most cases, the relationships in Table 8.1 constitute only crude guidelines.

There is one important parameter estimate where reasonable assumptions often can be made that justify the direct use of a result in Table 8.1, namely, an autospectral density estimate. From Equation (8.147), under the assumptions that the autospectrum is relatively smooth over the resolution bandwidth B_e and the data are Gaussian, it is seen that the random portion of the normalized rms error of an estimate is a function only of the total record length T_r and the resolution bandwidth B_e, which are both analysis parameters and not parameters of the data. The only problem then is to select an appropriate value for the resolution bandwidth B_e. This often can be accomplished when the data represent the response of a lightly damped mechanical or electrical system, as detailed in Section 8.5.1. In this case, the potential bias error for a selected resolution bandwidth B_e can be predicted by either Equation (8.141) or (8.142). Specifically, using Equation (8.141), the resolution bandwidth required to achieve a desired maximum bias error ε_b can be predicted by $B_e = 2\zeta f_r (3\varepsilon_b)^{1/2}$, where ζ and f_r are the damping ratio and resonance frequency, respectively, of the lightly damped system. At least lower bound values for ζ and f_r commonly can be predicted based upon past experience to achieve a conservative estimate for B_e, which in turn can then be used to predict the minimum required record length from $T_r = (B_e \varepsilon_r^2)^{-1}$, as given in Table 8.1.

The foregoing discussions of record length selections for autospectral density function estimates are particularly important for two reasons. First, the spectrum is the single most important parameter of random data for many engineering applications. Second, spectral estimates are generally the most demanding of the various parameter estimates considered in this chapter from the viewpoint of required record length for a given error. This latter fact is easily verified by comparing the error expression for autospectra estimates to the error expressions for other parameter estimates. It is seen that the denominators of the error terms for other parameter estimates generally involve factors that are larger than the value B_e required for well resolved spectral estimates.

Table 8.1 Record Lengths and Averages for Basic Estimates

Estimate	Required Total Record Length	Required Number of Averages
$\hat{\mu}_x$	$T_r = \frac{1}{2B\varepsilon_r^2}\left(\frac{\sigma_x}{\mu_x}\right)^2$	$N = \frac{1}{\varepsilon_r^2}\left(\frac{\sigma_x}{\mu_x}\right)^2$
$\hat{\mu}_x^2$	$T_r = \frac{2}{B\varepsilon_r^2}\left(\frac{\sigma_x}{\mu_x}\right)^2$	$N = \frac{4}{\varepsilon_r^2}\left(\frac{\sigma_x}{\mu_x}\right)^2$
$\hat{\sigma}_x, \hat{\psi}_x$	$T_r = \frac{1}{4B\varepsilon_r^2}$	$N = \frac{1}{2\varepsilon_r^2}$
$\hat{\sigma}_x^2, \hat{\psi}_x^2$	$T_r = \frac{1}{B\varepsilon_r^2}$	$N = \frac{2}{\varepsilon_r^2}$
$\hat{p}(x)$	$T_r = \frac{1}{WBp(x)\varepsilon_r^2}$	$N = \frac{2}{Wp(x)\varepsilon_r^2}$
$\hat{R}_{xy}(\tau)$	$T_r = \frac{1}{2B\varepsilon_r^2}\left[1+\rho_{xy}^{-2}(\tau)\right]$	$N = \frac{1}{\varepsilon_r^2}\left[1+\rho_{xy}^{-2}(\tau)\right]$
$\hat{G}_{xx}(f)$	$T_r = \frac{1}{B_e\varepsilon_r^2}$	$n_d = \frac{1}{\varepsilon_r^2}$

PROBLEMS

8.1 The mean value of a bandwidth-limited Gaussian white noise random signal $x(t)$ is estimated from a sample record of length T. Assume the standard deviation of $x(t)$ is $\sigma_x = 1$ and the standard deviation of the estimate is $\sigma[\hat{\mu}_x] = 0.1$. Determine the normalized random error ε associated with estimates of the following parameters from the same sample record.
   (a) Mean square value.
   (b) rms value.
   (c) Standard deviation.

8.2 Assume $x(t)$ is a sample record of bandwidth-limited Gaussian white noise where $\mu_x = 0.10$, $\sigma_x = 0.20$, $B = 200$ Hz, and $T = 2$ s. Compute the normalized rms error for
   (a) mean value estimates.
   (b) mean square value estimates.

8.3 Which of the following parameter estimates usually involves a bias error as well as a random error?
   (a) Mean value.
   (b) Mean square value.
   (c) Probability density function.
   (d) Autocorrelation function.
   (e) Autospectral density function.

8.4 Consider two bandwidth-limited white noise records $x(t)$ and $y(t)$ of bandwidth B and length T where

$$x(t) = s(t) + n_1(t) \quad \text{and} \quad y(t) = s(t) + n_2(t)$$

Assume $s(t)$, $n_1(t)$, and $n_2(t)$ are mutually uncorrelated with zero mean values and mean square values of $\psi_s^2 = S$, $\psi_{n1}^2 = N_1$, and $\psi_{n2}^2 = N_2$. Determine
   (a) the normalized rms error of the autocorrelation estimates $\hat{R}_{xx}(\tau)$ and $\hat{R}_{yy}(\tau)$ at $\tau = 0$.
   (b) the normalized rms error of the cross-correlation estimate $\hat{R}_{xy}(\tau)$ at $\tau = 0$.
   (c) the result in (b) if $N_1 \gg S$ and $N_2 \gg S$.
   (d) the result in (b) if $N_1 = 0$ and $N_2 \gg S$.

8.5 Given the two bandwidth-limited white noise signals defined in Problem 8.4, determine an approximate 95% probability interval for the time delay $\hat{\tau}$ corresponding to the maximum value of the estimated cross-correlation function $\hat{R}_{xy}(\tau)$.

8.6 Assume the probability distribution (not density) function of a Gaussian random process $\{x(t)\}$ is estimated by ensemble-averaging procedures over

$N=100$ independent sample records. Determine the normalized random error of the estimate $\hat{P}(x)$ at $x=\mu$. Is there a bias error in this estimate?

8.7 Assume the probability density function of a Gaussian random signal $x(t)$ is estimated using a window width of $W=0.25\sigma_x$. Determine the bias error of the estimate $\hat{p}(x)$ at $x = \mu_x + 2.5\sigma_x$.
  (a) by exact calculations.
  (b) using the first-order approximation of Equation (8.82).

8.8 Assume a random process $\{x(t)\}$ has an autospectral density function given by

$$G_{xx}(f) = \frac{10}{[1-(f/100)^2]^2 + [0.1f/100]^2}$$

If the autospectrum is to be estimated from sample data, determine
  (a) the resolution bandwidth B_e and the total record length T_r required to limit the normalized bias error to $\varepsilon_b \leq 0.05$ and the normalized random error to $\varepsilon_r = 0.10$.
  (b) the resolution bandwidth B_e that will minimize the mean square error of the estimate at $f=100$ Hz, assuming that a total record length of $T_r=60$ s is collected.

8.9 Let $\lambda(f) = |G_{xx}(f)/G''_{xx}(f)|^{1/2}$ and define λ_m as the maximum value of $\lambda(f)$. Determine the requirements on B_e and T as a function of λ_m if the normalized bias error and the normalized random error of an autospectral density function estimate are each to be less than 5%.

8.10 Consider an autospectral density function estimate $\hat{G}_{xx}(f)$ computed from finite Fourier transform operations and the ensemble-averaging procedure described in Section 8.5.4. Suppose a sample record $x(t)$ of total length $T_r=60$ s is divided into 12 independent contiguous segments. Determine the 95% confidence interval for the true value $G_{xx}(f)$ when $\hat{G}_{xx}(f) = 0.30$ units^2/Hz. What is the normalized random error of the estimate?

REFERENCES

1. Bendat, J. S., and Piersol, A. G., *Engineering Applications of Correlation and Spectral Analysis*, 2nd ed., Wiley–Interscience, New York, 1993.
2. Piersol, A. G., "Time Delay Estimation using Phase Data," *IEEE Transactions on Acoustics, Speech, and Signal Processing*, Vol. ASSP-29, p. 471, June 1981.
3. Forlifer, W. R., "Effects of Filter Bandwidth in Spectrum Analysis of Random Vibration," *Shock and Vibration Bulletin*, No. 33, Part 2, p. 273, 1964.
4. Schmidt, H., "Resolution Bias Errors in Spectral Density, Frequency Response nd Coherence Function Measurements," *Journal of Sound and Vibration*, Vol. 101, No. 3, p. 347, 1985.
5. Piersol, A. G., "Optimum Resolution Bandwidth for Spectral Analysis of Stationary Random Vibration Data," *Shock and Vibration*, Vol. 1, p. 33, 1993/1994.

CHAPTER 9

Statistical Errors in Advanced Estimates

This chapter continues the development from Chapter 8 on statistical errors in random data analysis. Emphasis is now on frequency domain properties of joint sample records from two different stationary (ergodic) random processes. The advanced parameter estimates discussed in this chapter include magnitude and phase estimates of cross-spectral density functions, followed by various quantities contained in single-input/output problems and multiple-input/output problems, as covered in Chapters 6 and 7. In particular, statistical error formulas are developed for

Frequency response function estimates (gain and phase)
Coherence function estimates
Coherent output spectrum estimates
Multiple coherence function estimates
Partial coherence function estimates

9.1 CROSS-SPECTRAL DENSITY FUNCTION ESTIMATES

Consider the cross-spectral density function between two stationary (ergodic) Gaussian random processes $\{x(t)\}$ and $\{y(t)\}$, as defined in Equation (5.66). Specifically, given a pair of sample records $x(t)$ and $y(t)$ of unlimited length T, the one-sided cross-spectrum is given by

$$G_{xy}(f) = \lim_{T \to \infty} \frac{2}{T} E[X^*(f,T)Y(f,T)] \qquad (9.1)$$

Random Data: Analysis and Measurement Procedures, Fourth Edition. By Julius S. Bendat and Allan G. Piersol
Copyright © 2010 John Wiley & Sons, Inc.

where $X(f, T)$ and $Y(f, T)$ are the finite Fourier transforms of $x(t)$ and $y(t)$, respectively–that is,

$$X(f) = X(f,T) = \int_0^T x(t)e^{-j2\pi ft}dt$$
$$Y(f) = Y(f,T) = \int_0^T y(t)e^{-j2\pi ft}dt$$
(9.2)

It follows that a "raw" estimate (no averages) of the cross-spectrum for a finite record length T is given by

$$\tilde{G}_{xy} = \frac{2}{T}[X^*(f)Y(f)]$$
(9.3)

and will have a resolution bandwidth of

$$B_e \approx \Delta f = \frac{1}{T}$$
(9.4)

meaning that spectral components will be estimated *only* at the discrete frequencies

$$f_k = \frac{k}{T} \quad k = 0, 1, 2, \ldots$$
(9.5)

As discussed in Section 8.5.1, the resolution $B_e \approx (1/T)$ in Equation (9.4) establishes the potential resolution bias error in an analysis. It will be assumed in this chapter, however, that T is sufficiently long to make the resolution bias error of the cross-spectrum estimates negligible.

As for the autospectrum estimates discussed in Section 8.5.4, the "raw" cross-spectrum estimate given by Equation (9.3) will have an unacceptably large random error for most applications. In practice, the random error is reduced by computing an ensemble of estimates from n_d different (distinct, disjoint) subrecords, each of length T, and averaging the results to obtain a final "smooth" estimate given by

$$\hat{G}_{xy}(f) = \frac{2}{n_d T} \sum_{i=1}^{n_d} X_i^*(f) Y_i(f)$$
(9.6)

It follows that the minimum total record length required to compute the cross-spectrum estimate is $T_r = n_d T$. Special cases of Equation (9.6) produce the autospectra estimates $\hat{G}_{xx}(f)$ and $\hat{G}_{yy}(f)$ by letting $x(t) = y(t)$.

The quantities $X(f)$ and $Y(f)$ in Equation (9.2) can be broken down into real and imaginary parts as follows:

$$X(f) = X_R(f) - jX_I(f) \quad Y(f) = Y_R(f) - jY_I(f)$$
(9.7)

where

$$X_R(f) = \int_0^T x(t)\cos 2\pi ft\, dt \quad X_I(f) = \int_0^T x(t)\sin 2\pi ft\, dt$$
(9.8)

$$Y_R(f) = \int_0^T y(t)\cos 2\pi ft\, dt \quad Y_I(f) = \int_0^T y(t)\sin 2\pi ft\, dt$$
(9.9)

If $x(t)$ and $y(t)$ are normally distributed with zero mean values, the quantities in Equations (9.8) and (9.9) will be normally distributed with zero mean values. From

CROSS-SPECTRAL DENSITY FUNCTION ESTIMATES

Equation (9.3), omitting the frequency f to simplify the notation, "raw" estimates are then given by

$$\tilde{G}_{xx} = \frac{2}{T}(X_R^2 + X_I^2) \qquad \tilde{G}_{yy} = \frac{2}{T}(Y_R^2 + Y_I^2) \qquad (9.10)$$

$$\tilde{G}_{xy} = \tilde{C}_{xy} - j\tilde{Q}_{xy} = |\tilde{G}_{xy}|e^{-j\tilde{\theta}_{xy}} \qquad (9.11)$$

where

$$\tilde{C}_{xy} = \frac{2}{T}(X_R Y_R + X_I Y_I) \qquad \tilde{Q}_{xy} = \frac{2}{T}(X_R Y_I - X_I Y_R) \qquad (9.12)$$

$$|\tilde{G}_{xy}|^2 = \tilde{C}_{xy}^2 + \tilde{Q}_{xy}^2 \qquad \tan\tilde{\theta}_{xy} = \tilde{Q}_{xy}/\tilde{C}_{xy} \qquad (9.13)$$

For values computed only at $f = f_k$ defined in Equation (9.5), one can verify from Equations (9.8) and (9.9) that

$$E[X_R X_I] = E[Y_R Y_I] = 0$$

$$E[X_R^2] = E[X_I^2] = (T/4)G_{xx}$$

$$E[Y_R^2] = E[Y_I^2] = (T/4)G_{yy} \qquad (9.14)$$

$$E[X_R Y_R] = E[X_I Y_I] = (T/4)C_{xy}$$

$$E[X_R Y_I] = -E[X_I Y_R] = (T/4)Q_{xy}$$

Hence, $E[\tilde{C}_{xy}] = C_{xy}$ and $E[\tilde{Q}_{xy}] = Q_{xy}$ with

$$E[\tilde{G}_{xx}] = G_{xx} \qquad E[\tilde{G}_{yy}] = G_{yy} \qquad (9.15)$$

$$E[\tilde{G}_{xy}] = E[\tilde{C}_{xy}] - jE[\tilde{Q}_{xy}] = C_{xy} - jQ_{xy} = G_{xy} \qquad (9.16)$$

The Gaussian assumption for any four variables $a_1, a_2, a_3,$ and a_4 with zero mean values gives from Equation (3.73)

$$E[a_1 a_2 a_3 a_4] = E[a_1 a_2]E[a_3 a_4] + E[a_1 a_3]E[a_2 a_4] + E[a_1 a_4]E[a_2 a_3] \qquad (9.17)$$

Repeated application of this formula shows that

$$E[\tilde{G}_{xx}^2] = \frac{4}{T^2} E\left[(X_R^2 + X_I^2)^2\right]$$

$$= \frac{4}{T^2} E[X_R^4 + 2X_I^2 X_R^2 + X_I^4] = 2G_{xx}^2 \qquad (9.18)$$

where the following relationships are used:

$$E[X_R^4] = 3(E[X_R^2])^2 = 3(T/4)^2 G_{xx}^2$$

$$E[X_I^2 X_R^2] = E[X_I^2]E[X_R^2] = (T/4)^2 G_{xx}^2 \qquad (9.19)$$

$$E[X_I^4] = 3(E[X_I^2])^2 = 3(T/4)^2 G_{xx}^2$$

Similarly, one can verify that

$$E[\tilde{G}_{yy}^2] = 2G_{yy}^2 \tag{9.20}$$

$$E\left[\tilde{C}_{xy}^2\right] = \tfrac{1}{2}(G_{xx}G_{yy} + 3C_{xy}^2 - Q_{xy}^2) \tag{9.21}$$

$$E\left[\tilde{Q}_{xy}^2\right] = \tfrac{1}{2}(G_{xx}G_{yy} + 3Q_{xy}^2 - C_{xy}^2) \tag{9.22}$$

9.1.1 Variance Formulas

Basic variance error formulas will now be calculated. By definition, for any unbiased "raw" estimate $\tilde{A}$, where $E[\tilde{A}] = A$, its variance from Equation (8.3) is

$$\text{Var}[\tilde{A}] = E[\tilde{A}^2] - A^2 \tag{9.23}$$

Hence

$$\text{Var}[\tilde{G}_{xx}] = G_{xx}^2 \quad \text{Var}[\tilde{G}_{yy}] = G_{yy}^2 \tag{9.24}$$

$$\text{Var}[\tilde{C}_{xy}] = \tfrac{1}{2}(G_{xx}G_{yy} + C_{xy}^2 - Q_{xy}^2) \tag{9.25}$$

$$\text{Var}[\tilde{Q}_{xy}] = \tfrac{1}{2}(G_{xx}G_{yy} + Q_{xy}^2 - C_{xy}^2) \tag{9.26}$$

Observe also from Equations (9.13), (9.21) and (9.22) that

$$E[|\tilde{G}_{xy}|^2] = E[\tilde{C}_{xy}^2] + E[\tilde{Q}_{xy}^2] = G_{xx}G_{yy} + |G_{xy}|^2 \tag{9.27}$$

Hence

$$\text{Var}[|\tilde{G}_{xy}|] = G_{xx}G_{yy} = \frac{|G_{xy}|^2}{\gamma_{xy}^2} \tag{9.28}$$

where γ_{xy}^2 is the ordinary coherence function defined by

$$\gamma_{xy}^2 = \frac{|G_{xy}|^2}{G_{xx}G_{yy}} \tag{9.29}$$

In accordance with Equation (4.9), the corresponding variance errors for "smooth" estimates of all of the above "raw" estimates will be reduced by a factor of n_d when averages are taken over n_d statistically independent "raw" quantities. To be specific,

$$\text{Var}[\hat{G}_{xx}] = G_{xx}^2/n_d \quad \text{Var}[\hat{G}_{yy}] = G_{yy}^2/n_d \tag{9.30}$$

$$\text{Var}[|\hat{G}_{xy}|] = |G_{xy}|^2/\gamma_{xy}^2 n_d \tag{9.31}$$

Table 9.1 Normalized Random Errors for Spectral Estimates

Estimate	Normalized Random Error, ε
$\hat{G}_{xx}(f), \hat{G}_{yy}(f)$	$\dfrac{1}{\sqrt{n_d}}$
$\|\hat{G}_{xy}(f)\|$	$\dfrac{1}{\|\gamma_{xy}(f)\|\sqrt{n_d}}$
$\hat{C}_{xy}(f)$	$\dfrac{[G_{xx}(f)G_{yy}(f) + C_{xy}^2(f) - Q_{xy}^2(f)]^{1/2}}{C_{xy}(f)\sqrt{2n_d}}$
$\tilde{Q}_{xy}(f)$	$\dfrac{[G_{xx}(f)G_{yy}(f) + Q_{xy}^2(f) - C_{xy}^2(f)]^{1/2}}{Q_{xy}(f)\sqrt{2n_d}}$

From Equation (8.9), the normalized rms errors (which are here the same as the normalized random errors) become

$$\varepsilon[\hat{G}_{xx}] = \frac{1}{\sqrt{n_d}} \qquad \varepsilon[\hat{G}_{yy}] = \frac{1}{\sqrt{n_d}} \qquad (9.32)$$

$$\varepsilon[|\hat{G}_{xy}|] = \frac{1}{|\gamma_{xy}|\sqrt{n_d}} \qquad (9.33)$$

The quantity $|\gamma_{xy}|$ is the positive square root of γ_{xy}^2. Note that ε for the cross-spectrum magnitude estimate $|\hat{G}_{xy}|$ varies inversely with $|\gamma_{xy}|$ and approaches $(1/\sqrt{n_d})$ as γ_{xy}^2 approaches one.

A summary is given in Table 9.1 on the main normalized random error formulas for various spectral density estimates. The number of averages n_d represents n_d distinct (nonoverlapping) records, which are assumed to contain statistically different information from record to record. These records may occur by dividing a long stationary ergodic record into n_d parts, or they may occur by repeating an experiment n_d times under similar conditions. With the exception of autospectrum estimates, all error formulas are functions of frequency. Unknown true values of desired quantities are replaced by measured values when one applies these results to evaluate the random errors in actual measured data.

9.1.2 Covariance Formulas

A number of basic covariance error formulas will now be derived. By the definition in Equation (3.34), for two unbiased "raw" estimates $\tilde{A}$ and $\tilde{B}$, where $E[\tilde{A}] = A$ and $E[\tilde{B}] = B$, their covariance is

$$\text{Cov}(\tilde{A}, \tilde{B}) = E[(\Delta A)(\Delta B)] = E[(\tilde{A}-A)(\tilde{B}-B)] = E[\tilde{A}\tilde{B}] - AB \qquad (9.34)$$

where the increments $\Delta A = (\tilde{A} - A)$ and $\Delta B = (\tilde{B} - B)$. The estimates $\tilde{A}$ and $\tilde{B}$ are said to be *uncorrelated* when $\text{Cov}(\tilde{A}, \tilde{B}) = 0$.

The application of Equation (9.17) shows that

$$E[\tilde{C}_{xy}\tilde{Q}_{xy}] = \frac{4}{T^2}E[(X_RY_R+X_IY_I)(X_RY_I-X_IY_R)] = 2C_{xy}Q_{xy} \quad (9.35)$$

Hence, by Equation (9.34), at every frequency f_k

$$\text{Cov}(\tilde{C}_{xy}, \tilde{Q}_{xy}) = C_{xy}Q_{xy} \quad (9.36)$$

Similarly, one can verify that

$$\begin{array}{ll} \text{Cov}(\tilde{G}_{xx}, \tilde{C}_{xy}) = G_{xx}C_{xy} & \text{Cov}(\tilde{G}_{xx}, \tilde{Q}_{xy}) = G_{xx}Q_{xy} \\ \text{Cov}(\tilde{G}_{yy}, \tilde{C}_{xy}) = G_{yy}C_{xy} & \text{Cov}(\tilde{G}_{yy}, \tilde{Q}_{xy}) = G_{yy}\tilde{Q}_{xy} \end{array} \quad (9.37)$$

Also,

$$E[\tilde{G}_{xx}\tilde{G}_{xy}] = \frac{4}{T^2}E[(X_R^2+X_I^2)(Y_R^2+Y_I^2)] = G_{xx}G_{yy} + |G_{xy}|^2 \quad (9.38)$$

Hence,

$$\text{Cov}(\tilde{G}_{xx}, \tilde{G}_{yy}) = |G_{xy}|^2 = \gamma_{xy}^2 G_{xx}G_{yy} \quad (9.39)$$

The following covariance results will now be proved.

$$\begin{array}{ll} \text{Cov}(\tilde{G}_{xx}, \tilde{\theta}_{xy}) = 0 & \text{Cov}(\tilde{G}_{yy}, \tilde{\theta}_{xy}) = 0 \end{array} \quad (9.40)$$
$$\text{Cov}(|\tilde{G}_{xy}|, \tilde{\theta}_{xy}) = 0 \quad (9.41)$$

In words, $\tilde{\theta}_{xy}$ is uncorrelated with $\tilde{G}_{xx}$, $\tilde{G}_{yy}$, and $|\tilde{G}_{xy}|$ at every frequency f_k. To prove Equation (9.40), note that

$$\tan\theta_{xy} = \frac{Q_{xy}}{C_{xy}}$$

as illustrated below. Then, differential increments of both sides yield

$$\sec^2\theta_{xy}\Delta\theta_{xy} \approx \frac{C_{xy}\Delta Q_{xy} - Q_{xy}\Delta C_{xy}}{C_{xy}^2}$$

where

$$\sec^2\theta_{xy} = \frac{|G_{xy}|^2}{C_{xy}^2}$$

Thus

$$\Delta\theta_{xy} \approx \frac{C_{xy}\Delta Q_{xy} - Q_{xy}\Delta C_{xy}}{|G_{xy}|^2} \quad (9.42)$$

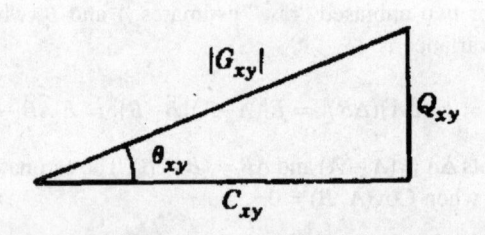

Now, one can set

$$\Delta\theta_{xy} = \tilde{\theta}_{xy} - \theta_{xy} \quad \Delta Q_{xy} = \tilde{Q}_{xy} - Q_{xy} \quad \Delta C_{xy} = \tilde{C}_{xy} - C_{xy}$$

Then, using Equation (9.37),

$$\text{Cov}(\tilde{G}_{xx}, \tilde{\theta}_{xy}) = E[(\Delta G_{xx})(\Delta\theta_{xy})]$$
$$\approx \frac{C_{xy}}{|G_{xy}|^2} \text{Cov}(\tilde{G}_{xx}, \tilde{Q}_{xy}) - \frac{Q_{xy}}{|G_{xy}|^2} \text{Cov}(\tilde{G}_{xx}, \tilde{C}_{xy}) = 0$$

Similarly

$$\text{Cov}(\tilde{G}_{yy}, \tilde{\theta}_{xy}) = 0$$

This proves Equation (9.40).

To prove Equation (9.41), note that

$$|G_{xy}|^2 = C_{xy}^2 + Q_{xy}^2$$

Taking differential increments of both sides yields

$$|G_{xy}|\Delta|G_{xy}| \approx C_{xy}\Delta C_{xy} + Q_{xy}\Delta Q_{xy}$$

Thus

$$\Delta|G_{xy}| \approx \frac{C_{xy}\Delta C_{xy} + Q_{xy}\Delta Q_{xy}}{|G_{xy}|} \tag{9.43}$$

Now, Equations (9.42) and (9.43) give

$$\text{Cov}(|\tilde{G}_{xy}|, \tilde{\theta}_{xy}) = E[(\Delta|G_{xy}|)(\Delta\theta_{xy})]$$
$$\approx \frac{1}{|G_{xy}|^3} E[(C_{xy}\Delta C_{xy} + Q_{xy}\Delta Q_{xy})(C_{xy}\Delta Q_{xy} - Q_{xy}\Delta C_{xy})]$$
$$\approx \frac{1}{|G_{xy}|^3} \left\{ (C_{xy}^2 - Q_{xy}^2) \text{Cov}(\tilde{C}_{xy}, \tilde{Q}_{xy}) \right.$$
$$\left. + C_{xy}Q_{xy}(\text{Var}[\tilde{Q}_{xy}] - \text{Var}[\tilde{C}_{xy}]) \right\} = 0$$

This proves Equation (9.41).

From Equation (9.43), one can also derive the following covariance results:

$$\text{Cov}(\tilde{G}_{xx}, |\tilde{G}_{xy}|) = E[(\Delta G_{xx})(\Delta|G_{xy}|)] \approx G_{xx}|G_{xy}| \tag{9.44}$$
$$\text{Cov}(\tilde{G}_{yy}, |\tilde{G}_{xy}|) = E[(\Delta G_{yy})(\Delta|G_{xy}|)] \approx G_{yy}|G_{xy}|$$

$$\text{Cov}(\tilde{C}_{xy}, |\tilde{G}_{xy}|) = E[(\Delta C_{xy})(\Delta|G_{xy}|)] \approx \frac{C_{xy}|G_{xy}|(1+\gamma_{xy}^2)}{2\gamma_{xy}^2}$$
$$\text{Cov}(\tilde{Q}_{xy}, |\tilde{G}_{xy}|) = E[(\Delta Q_{xy})(\Delta|G_{xy}|)] \approx \frac{Q_{xy}|G_{xy}|(1+\gamma_{xy}^2)}{2\gamma_{xy}^2} \tag{9.45}$$

Equation (9.43) offers a way to derive an approximate formula for $\text{Var}[|\tilde{G}_{xy}|]$ as follows:

$$\text{Var}[|\tilde{G}_{xy}|] = E\left[(\Delta|G_{xy}|)^2\right] \approx \frac{1}{|G_{xy}|^2} E\left[(C_{xy}\Delta C_{xy} + Q_{xy}\Delta Q_{xy})^2\right]$$

$$\approx \frac{1}{|G_{xy}|^2}\left\{C_{xy}^2\,\text{Var}(\tilde{C}_{xy}) + 2C_{xy}Q_{xy}\,\text{Cov}(\tilde{C}_{xy},\tilde{Q}_{xy}) + Q_{xy}^2\,\text{Var}(\tilde{Q}_{xy})\right\}$$

$$\approx \frac{1}{|G_{xy}|^2}\left\{\frac{|G_{xy}|^2}{2}G_{xx}G_{yy} + \frac{|G_{xy}|^4}{2}\right\} \approx \frac{|G_{xy}|^2(1+\gamma_{xy}^2)}{2\gamma_{xy}^2} \qquad (9.46)$$

This approximate formula from Ref. 1, based on differential increments, is inferior to the direct derivation producing the more exact formula of Equation (9.28), namely,

$$\text{Var}[|\tilde{G}_{xy}|] = \frac{|G_{xy}|^2}{\gamma_{xy}^2} \qquad (9.47)$$

Note that the variance from Equation (9.47) will always be greater than the variance from Equation (9.46) because

$$\frac{1}{\gamma_{xy}^2} > \frac{1+\gamma_{xy}^2}{2\gamma_{xy}^2} \quad \text{for all } \gamma_{xy}^2 < 1$$

Consider the coherence function defined by

$$\gamma_{xy}^2 = \frac{|G_{xy}|^2}{G_{xx}G_{yy}} \qquad (9.48)$$

Logarithms of both sides give

$$\log \gamma_{xy}^2 = 2\log|G_{xy}| - \log G_{xx} - \log G_{yy}$$

Then, differential increments of both sides show that

$$\frac{\Delta \gamma_{xy}^2}{\gamma_{xy}^2} \approx \frac{2\Delta|G_{xy}|}{|G_{xy}|} - \frac{\Delta G_{xx}}{G_{xx}} - \frac{\Delta G_{yy}}{G_{yy}}$$

where

$$\Delta \gamma_{xy}^2 = \tilde{\gamma}_{xy}^2 - \gamma_{xy}^2 \qquad \Delta|G_{xy}| = |\tilde{G}_{xy}| - G_{xy}$$
$$\Delta G_{xx} = \tilde{G}_{xx} - G_{xx} \qquad \Delta G_{yy} = \tilde{G}_{yy} - G_{yy}$$

Table 9.2 Covariance Formulas for Various Estimates

$$\mathrm{Cov}(\tilde{C}_{xy}, \tilde{Q}_{xy}) = C_{xy}Q_{xy}$$

$$\mathrm{Cov}(\tilde{G}_{xx}, \tilde{C}_{xy}) = G_{xx}G_{xy}$$

$$\mathrm{Cov}(\tilde{G}_{xx}, \tilde{Q}_{xy}) = G_{xx}Q_{xy}$$

$$\mathrm{Cov}(\tilde{G}_{xx}, \tilde{G}_{yy}) = |G_{xy}|^2 = \gamma_{xy}^2 G_{xx}G_{yy}$$

$$\mathrm{Cov}(\tilde{G}_{xx}, \tilde{\theta}_{xy}) = 0$$

$$\mathrm{Cov}(|\tilde{G}_{xy}|, \tilde{\theta}_{xy}) = 0$$

$$\mathrm{Cov}(\tilde{\gamma}_{xy}^2, \tilde{\theta}_{xy}) = 0$$

$$\mathrm{Cov}(\tilde{G}_{xx}, |\tilde{G}_{xy}|) = G_{xx}|G_{xy}|$$

$$\mathrm{Cov}(\tilde{C}_{xy}, |\tilde{G}_{xy}|) = \frac{C_{xy}|G_{xy}|(1+\gamma_{xy}^2)}{2\gamma_{xy}^2}$$

$$\mathrm{Cov}(\tilde{Q}_{xy}, |\tilde{G}_{xy}|) = \frac{Q_{xy}|G_{xy}|(1+\gamma_{xy}^2)}{2\gamma_{xy}^2}$$

Thus

$$\Delta\gamma_{xy}^2 \approx \gamma_{xy}^2 \left\{ \frac{2\Delta|G_{xy}|}{|G_{xy}|} - \frac{\Delta G_{xx}}{G_{xx}} - \frac{\Delta G_{yy}}{G_{yy}} \right\} \qquad (9.49)$$

Now, using Equations (9.40) and (9.41), it follows directly from Equation (9.49) that

$$\mathrm{Cov}(\tilde{\gamma}_{xy}^2, \tilde{\theta}_{xy}) = 0 \qquad (9.50)$$

In words, the estimates $\tilde{\gamma}_{xy}^2$ and $\tilde{\theta}_{xy}$ are uncorrelated at every frequency f_k.

A summary is given in Table 9.2 of some of the main covariance formulas derived in this section.

9.1.3 Phase Angle Estimates

A formula for the variance of "raw" phase estimates $\tilde{\theta}_{xy}$ (expressed in radians) can be derived from Equation (9.42) as follows:

$$\begin{aligned}
\mathrm{Var}[\tilde{\theta}_{xy}] &= E\left[(\Delta\theta_{xy})^2\right] \approx \frac{1}{|G_{xy}|^4} E\left[(C_{xy}\Delta Q_{xy} - Q_{xy}\Delta C_{xy})^2\right] \\
&= \frac{1}{|G_{xy}|^4}\left\{ C_{xy}^2 \mathrm{Var}(\tilde{Q}_{xy}) - 2C_{xy}Q_{xy}\mathrm{Cov}(\tilde{C}_{xy},\tilde{Q}_{xy}) + Q_{xy}^2 \mathrm{Var}(\tilde{C}_{xy}) \right\} \\
&= \frac{1}{|G_{xy}|^4}\left\{ \frac{|G_{xy}|^2}{2} G_{xx}G_{yy} - \frac{|G_{xy}|^4}{2} \right\} \approx \frac{1-\gamma_{xy}^2}{2\gamma_{xy}^2}
\end{aligned} \qquad (9.51)$$

For "smooth" estimates of $\hat{\theta}_{xy}$ from n_d averages, one obtains

$$\text{s.d.}\left[\hat{\theta}_{xy}\right] = \frac{\text{s.d.}[\tilde{\theta}_{xy}]}{\sqrt{n_d}} \approx \frac{(1-\gamma_{xy}^2)^{1/2}}{|\gamma_{xy}|\sqrt{2n_d}} \tag{9.52}$$

This gives the standard deviation of the phase estimate $\hat{\theta}_{xy}$. Here, one should not use the normalized random error because θ_{xy} may be zero. The result in Equation (9.52) for the cross-spectrum phase angle, like the result in Equation (9.33) for the cross-spectrum magnitude estimate, varies with frequency. Independent of n_d for any $n_d > 1$, note that s.d.$[\hat{\theta}_{xy}]$ approaches zero as γ_{xy}^2 approaches one.

Example 9.1. **Illustration of Random Errors in Cross-Spectral Density Estimate.** Consider a pair of sample records $x(t)$ and $y(t)$, which represent stationary Gaussian random processes with zero mean values. Assume that the coherence function between the two random processes at a frequency of interest is $\gamma_{xy}^2 = 0.25$. If the cross-spectral density function $\hat{G}_{xy}(f)$ is estimated using $n_d = 100$ averages, determine the normalized random error in the magnitude estimate and the standard deviation of the phase estimate at the frequency of interest.

From Equation (9.33), the normalized random error in the magnitude of the cross-spectral density function estimate will be

$$\varepsilon\left[|\tilde{G}_{xy}|\right] = \frac{1}{0.5\sqrt{100}} = 0.20$$

Note that this is twice as large as the normalized random errors in the autospectra estimates given by Equation (9.32). The standard deviation of the phase estimate is given by Equation (9.52) as

$$\text{s.d.}\left[\hat{\theta}_{xy}\right] = \frac{(0.75)^{1/2}}{(0.5)\sqrt{200}} = 0.12 \text{ rad}$$

or about 7°.

9.2 SINGLE-INPUT/OUTPUT MODEL ESTIMATES

Consider the single-input/single-output linear model of Figure 9.1 where

$X(f) =$ Fourier transform of measured input signal $x(t)$, assumed noise free
$Y(f) =$ Fourier transform of measured output signal $y(t) = v(t) + n(t)$

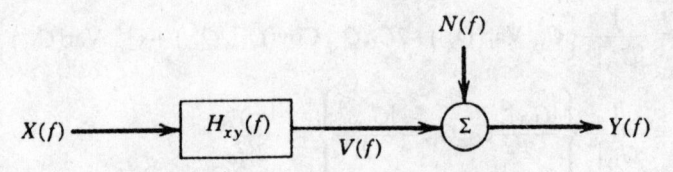

Figure 9.1 Single-input/single-output linear model.

SINGLE-INPUT/OUTPUT MODEL ESTIMATES

$V(f)$ = Fourier transform of computed output signal $v(t)$
$N(f)$ = Fourier transform of computed output noise $n(t)$
$H_{xy}(f)$ = frequency response function of optimum constant-parameter linear system estimating $y(t)$ from $x(t)$

Assume that $x(t)$ and $y(t)$ are the only records available for analysis and that they are representative members of zero mean value Gaussian random processes. Data can be either stationary random data or transient random data. For definiteness here, stationary data will be assumed and spectral results will be expressed using one-sided spectra. Normalized error formulas are the same for one-sided or two-sided spectra.

From Section 6.1.4, the following equations apply to this model in Figure 9.1 to estimate various quantities of interest. The optimum frequency response function estimate is

$$\hat{H}_{xy}(f) = \frac{\hat{G}_{xy}(f)}{\hat{G}_{xx}(f)} \tag{9.53}$$

where $\hat{G}_{xx}(f)$ and $\hat{G}_{xy}(f)$ are "smooth" estimates of the input autospectral density function and the input/output cross-spectral density function, respectively. The associated ordinary coherence function estimate is

$$\hat{\gamma}^2_{xy}(f) = \frac{|\hat{G}_{xy}(f)|^2}{\hat{G}_{xy}(f)\hat{G}_{yy}(f)} \tag{9.54}$$

where $\hat{G}_{yy}(f)$ is a "smooth" estimate of the output autospectral density function. The coherent output spectrum estimate is

$$\hat{G}_{vv}(f) = |\hat{H}_{xy}(f)|^2 \hat{G}_{xx}(f) = \hat{\gamma}^2_{xy}(f)\hat{G}_{yy}(f) \tag{9.55}$$

The noise output spectrum estimate is

$$\hat{G}_{nn}(f) = [1-\hat{\gamma}^2_{xy}(f)]\hat{G}_{yy}(f) \tag{9.56}$$

It is also known from Equation (6.61) that

$$\hat{G}_{yy}(f) = \hat{G}_{vv}(f) + \hat{G}_{nn}(f) \tag{9.57}$$

since $v(t)$ and $n(t)$ are uncorrelated with $G_{vn}(f) = 0$ when $\hat{H}_{xy}(f)$ is computed by Equation (9.53).

In polar form, the frequency response function can be expressed as

$$\hat{H}_{xy}(f) = |\hat{H}_{xy}(f)| e^{-j\hat{\phi}_{xy}(f)} \tag{9.58}$$

where

$$|\hat{H}_{xy}(f)| = \frac{|\hat{G}_{xy}(f)|}{\hat{G}_{xx}(f)} = \text{system gain factor estimate} \tag{9.59}$$

$$\hat{\phi}_{xy}(f) = \tan^{-1}\left[\frac{\hat{Q}_{xy}(f)}{\hat{C}_{xy}(f)}\right] = \text{system phase factor estimate} \tag{9.60}$$

This quantity $\hat{\phi}_{xy}(f)$ is the same as the phase angle $\hat{\theta}_{xy}(f)$ in $\hat{G}_{xy}(f)$, and it is also the phase that would be assigned to $\hat{\gamma}_{xy}(f)$ when $\hat{\gamma}_{xy}(f)$ is defined as the complex-valued function given by

$$\hat{\gamma}_{xy}(f) = |\hat{\gamma}_{xy}(f)| e^{-j\hat{\phi}_{xy}(f)} = +\sqrt{\hat{\gamma}_{xy}^2(f)}\, e^{-j\hat{\phi}_{xy}(f)} \tag{9.61}$$

Note that all of the above "smooth" estimates can be computed from the original computed "smooth" estimates of $\hat{G}_{xx}(f)$, $\hat{G}_{yy}(f)$ and $\hat{G}_{xy}(f)$.

Random error formulas for all of these quantities will be derived in terms of the unknown true coherence function $\gamma_{xy}^2(f)$ and the number of independent averages n_d. To apply these results to evaluate measured data, one should use the computed coherence function estimate $\hat{\gamma}_{xy}^2(f)$ with an appropriate number of independent averages n_d. This will give practical results, particularly if the resulting normalized random errors are less than 20%.

9.2.1 Bias in Frequency Response Function Estimates

Estimation of the frequency response function and coherence function will generally involve bias errors from a number of sources as follows:

1. Bias inherent in the estimation procedure
2. Bias due to propagation time delays
3. Nonlinear and/or time-varying system parameters
4. Bias in autospectral and cross-spectral density estimates
5. Measurement noise at the input point (no bias problem from uncorrelated noise at the output point)
6. Other inputs that are correlated with the measured input (no bias problem from other uncorrelated inputs, which merely act as uncorrelated output noise with respect to the measured input)

The first noted source of bias error results from the fact that, in general,

$$E[\hat{H}_{xy}] = E\left[\frac{\hat{G}_{xy}}{\hat{G}_{xx}}\right] \neq \frac{E[\hat{G}_{xy}]}{E[\hat{G}_{xx}]}$$

$$E[\hat{\gamma}_{xy}^2] = E\left[\frac{|\hat{G}_{xy}|^2}{\hat{G}_{xx}\hat{G}_{yy}}\right] \neq \frac{E[|\hat{G}_{xy}|^2]}{E[\hat{G}_{xx}]E[\hat{G}_{yy}]}$$

(9.62)

Hence $E[\hat{H}_{xy}] \neq \hat{H}_{xy}$ and $E[\hat{\gamma}_{xy}^2] \neq \gamma_{xy}^2$. These bias errors are usually negligible compared to other possible errors that occur in practice, and they can be ignored when combinations of n_d and $\hat{\gamma}_{xy}^2$ make associated normalized random errors small. As either $n_d \to \infty$ or $\gamma_{xy}^2 \to 1$, these inherent bias errors go to zero.

The second noted source of bias error occurs because it is required to measure $x(t)$ and $y(t)$ using a common time base and to correct for propagation time delays τ_1 that may occur between $x(t)$ and $y(t)$ if τ_1 is not negligible compared to the sample record lengths T. Assume

$$x(t) = x(t) \qquad 0 \leq t \leq T$$

$$y(t) = \begin{cases} \text{arbitrary} & 0 \leq t < \tau_1 \\ x(t-\tau_1) & \tau_1 \leq t \leq T \end{cases}$$

(9.63)

Then, to a first order of approximation, one can express the cross-correlation function estimate $\hat{R}_{xy}(\tau)$ by

$$\hat{R}_{xy}(\tau) \approx \left(1 - \frac{\tau_1}{T}\right) R_{xy}(\tau)$$

(9.64)

showing that $\hat{R}_{xy}(\tau)$ is a *biased* estimate of $R_{xy}(\tau)$ because $E[\hat{R}_{xy}(\tau)] \neq R_{xy}(\tau)$. It follows that

$$\hat{G}_{xy}(f) \approx \left(1 - \frac{\tau_1}{T}\right) G_{xy}(f)$$

$$\hat{H}_{xy}(f) \approx \left(1 - \frac{\tau_1}{T}\right) H_{xy}(f)$$

$$\hat{\gamma}_{xy}^2(f) \approx \left(1 - \frac{\tau_1}{T}\right)^2 \gamma_{xy}^2(f)$$

(9.65)

Thus $\hat{G}_{xy}(f)$, $\hat{H}_{xy}(f)$, and $\hat{\gamma}_{xy}^2(f)$ are also biased estimates. To remove these possible bias errors, the signal $y(t)$ should be shifted in time by the amount τ_1 so as to bring $x(t)$ and $y(t)$ into time coincidence. The time delay τ_1 can be estimated either from the physical geometry of the problem with a known velocity of propagation or from a separate measurement of $\hat{R}_{xy}(\tau)$ to determine where the first peak value occurs.

The third indicated source of bias results from violations of the basic assumptions that the system is a constant-parameter linear system. Even when the constant-parameter assumption is reasonably valid, the linearity assumption will often be violated if the operating range of interest is sufficiently wide. It should be noted, however, that the application of Equation (9.53) to nonlinear systems will produce the best linear approximation (in the least squares sense) for the frequency response function under the specified input and output conditions. This fact constitutes an important advantage to estimating frequency response functions from actual data rather than from laboratory or simulated data, which do not reproduce the actual input conditions.

The fourth source of bias occurs because of bias errors in spectral density estimates. As noted in Section 8.5.1, this error can be quite significant at frequencies where spectral peaks occur. These errors can be suppressed by obtaining properly resolved estimates of autospectra and cross-spectra, that is, by making B_e sufficiently narrow to accurately define peaks in the spectra. A quantitative formula is developed in Example 8.6 for spectra representing the response of a resonant system.

The fifth source of bias is measurement noise $m(t)$ at the input, where this noise does not actually pass through the system. Assuming the true input to be $u(t)$, the measured input autospectrum $\hat{G}_{xx} = \hat{G}_{uu} + \hat{G}_{mm}$. In place of Equations (9.53) and (9.54), one obtains

$$\hat{H}_{xy} = \frac{\hat{G}_{xy}}{\hat{G}_{uu} + \hat{G}_{mm}} \qquad \hat{\gamma}_{xy}^2 = \frac{|\hat{G}_{xy}|^2}{(\hat{G}_{uu} + \hat{G}_{mm})\hat{G}_{yy}} \qquad (9.66)$$

where the frequency f is omitted to simplify the notation. If all other bias errors are ignored, then $E[\hat{G}_{xy}] = \hat{G}_{uy}$ and

$$E[\hat{H}_{xy}] = \frac{G_{uy}}{G_{uu} + G_{mm}} = H_{uy}\left[\frac{G_{uu}}{G_{uu} + G_{mm}}\right] \qquad (9.67)$$

$$E[\hat{\gamma}_{xy}^2] = \frac{|G_{uy}|^2}{(G_{uu} + G_{mm})G_{yy}} = \gamma_{uy}^2\left[\frac{G_{uu}}{G_{uu} + G_{mm}}\right] \qquad (9.68)$$

Hence, because $G_{mm} > 0$, these expected values will be too low and the resulting bias errors will be negative. The normalized bias errors of Equation (8.9b) become here

$$\varepsilon_b[\hat{H}_{xy}] = \varepsilon_b[\hat{\gamma}_{xy}^2] = -\left[\frac{G_{mm}}{G_{uu} + G_{mm}}\right] \qquad (9.69)$$

For example, if $G_{mm} = 0.10\ G_{uu}$, then the resulting estimates would be biased downward by $(0.10/1.10) \approx 9\%$.

The sixth source of bias is due to the contributions of other inputs that are correlated with the measured input. This error is readily illustrated for the simple case of one additional correlated input by the developments in Section 7.2. Specifically, when the problem is treated properly, the correct frequency response function for $H_1(f)$ is stated in Equation (7.23). On the other hand, when treated as a single-input/single-output problem, the estimate $\hat{H}_1(f)$ is given by Equation (9.53). The expected value of this estimate does not yield the correct result, showing that it is biased. Also, the correct coherence function between x_1 and the output y when x_2 is present and correlated with x_1 is stated in Equation (7.34). When x_1 alone is assumed to be present, the estimate

$\hat{\gamma}_{xy}^2(f)$ is given by Equation (9.54). Again, the expected value of this estimate does not yield the correct result.

The types of bias errors discussed above also occur in general multiple-input/output problems, where more complicated expressions are needed to evaluate the bias errors.

9.2.2 Coherent Output Spectrum Estimates

From Equation (9.57), assuming $\hat{G}_{vv}$ and $\hat{G}_{nn}$ are statistically independent, it follows that

$$\text{Var}[\hat{G}_{yy}] = \text{Var}[\hat{G}_{vv}] + \text{Var}[\hat{G}_{nn}] \qquad (9.70)$$

where the frequency f is omitted to simplify the notation. From Equation (9.30), the variances are

$$\text{Var}[\hat{G}_{yy}] = \frac{G_{yy}^2}{n_d} \qquad \text{Var}[\hat{G}_{nn}] = \frac{G_{nn}^2}{n_d} \qquad (9.71)$$

Hence, by substituting $G_{nn} = (1 - \gamma_{xy}^2) G_{yy}$ and $G_{vv} = \gamma_{xy}^2 G_{yy}$,

$$\text{Var}[\hat{G}_{vv}] = \frac{G_{yy}^2 - G_{nn}^2}{n_d} = \frac{(2 - \gamma_{xy}^2) G_{vv}^2}{\gamma_{xy}^2 n_d} \qquad (9.72)$$

Finally, the normalized random error becomes

$$\varepsilon[\gamma_{xy}^2 \hat{G}_{yy}] = \varepsilon[\hat{G}_{vv}] = \frac{\text{s.d.}[\hat{G}_{vv}]}{G_{vv}} = \frac{[2 - \gamma_{xy}^2]^{1/2}}{|\gamma_{xy}| \sqrt{n_d}} \qquad (9.73)$$

This derivation does not use any differential increments. Note that $\varepsilon[\hat{G}_{vv}] = \varepsilon[\hat{G}_{yy}] = (1/\sqrt{n_d})$ as $\gamma_{xy}^2 \to 1$. Note also that

$$\varepsilon[\hat{G}_{vv}] > \varepsilon[\hat{G}_{yy}] \quad \text{for all } \gamma_{xy}^2 < 1 \qquad (9.74)$$

Figure 9.2 plots Equation (9.73) as a function of γ_{xy}^2 for the special case when $n_d = 100$. Figure 9.3 plots Equation (9.73) for arbitrary values of n_d and γ_{xy}^2. Table 9.3 contains appropriate values that must be satisfied between γ_{xy}^2 and n_d to achieve $\varepsilon[\hat{G}_{vv}] = 0.10$ using Equation (9.73).

Example 9.2. Illustration of Bias and Random Errors in Coherent Output Spectrum Estimate. Consider the case where a number of independent acoustic noise sources in air produce an acoustic pressure signal $y(t)$ at a receiver location of interest. A coherent output spectrum is estimated based on an input measurement $x(t)$ representing a source located about 30 m from the receiver. Assume that the analysis is performed using $n_d = 400$ averages and subrecord lengths of $T = 0.1$ s ($B_e \approx 10$ Hz). Further assume that $x(t)$ and $y(t)$ are measured and analyzed on a common time base; that is, no precomputational delay is used. If the true coherence and the output spectral density at a frequency of interest are $\gamma_{xy}^2 = 0.4$ and $G_{yy} = 10$, determine the primary bias and random errors in the coherent output spectrum estimate.

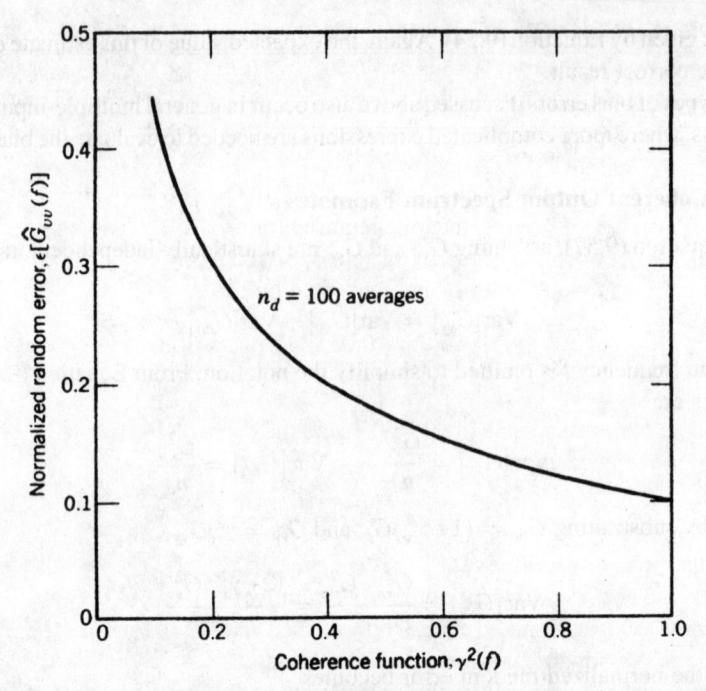

Figure 9.2 Normalized random error of coherent output spectral estimates when $n_d = 100$.

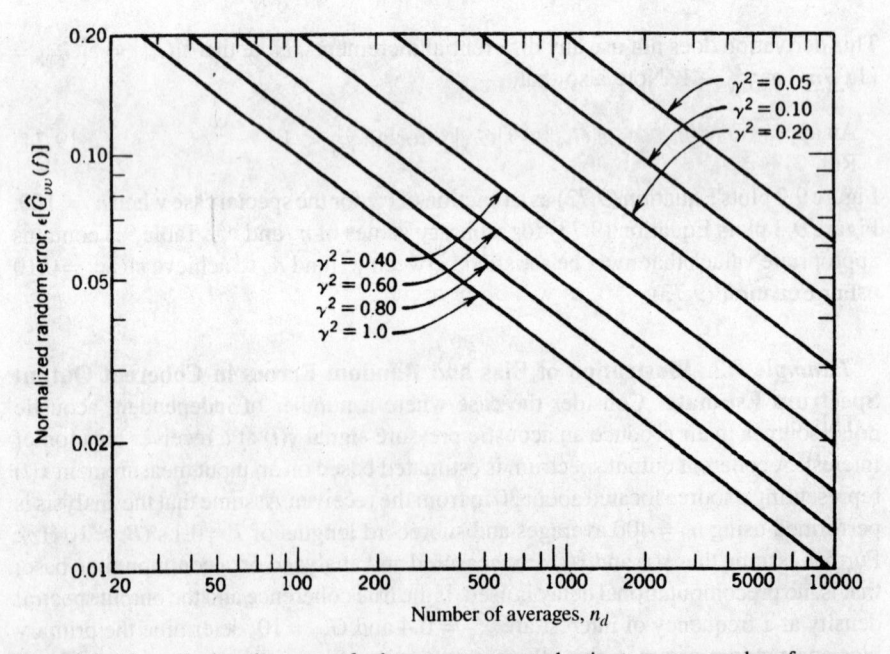

Figure 9.3 Normalized random error of coherent output spectral estimates versus number of averages.

SINGLE-INPUT/OUTPUT MODEL ESTIMATES

Table 9.3 Conditions for $\varepsilon[\hat{G}_{vv}]=0.10$

γ_{xy}^2	0.30	0.40	0.50	0.60	0.70	0.80	0.90	1.00
n_d	567	400	300	234	186	156	123	100

First considering bias errors, the time required for acoustic noise to propagate about 10 m in air ($c \approx 340$ m/s) is approximately $\tau_1 = 0.03$ s. Hence from Equation (9.65), the coherence estimate will be biased to yield on the average

$$\hat{\gamma}_{xy}^2 = \left(1 - \frac{0.03}{0.1}\right)^2 (0.4) = 0.2$$

rather than the correct value of $\gamma_{xy}^2 = 0.4$, and the coherent output spectrum estimate will be on the average

$$\hat{G}_{vv} = (0.2)10 = 2$$

rather than the correct value of $G_{vv} = 4$. The time delay bias error in this case causes an underestimate of the coherent output spectrum by 50% on the average.

Now considering the random error, it is the biased value of the coherence estimate that will control the random error. Hence, from Equation (9.73), the normalized random error of the coherent output spectrum estimate at the frequency of interest is

$$\varepsilon[\hat{G}_{vv}] = \frac{[2-0.2]^{1/2}}{(0.45)(20)} = 0.15$$

9.2.3 Coherence Function Estimates

An approximate result for the bias error in coherence function estimates is derived in Ref. 2. It is stated there that

$$b[\hat{\gamma}_{xy}^2] \approx \frac{1}{n_d}(1-\hat{\gamma}_{xy}^2)^2 \tag{9.75}$$

For example, if $n_d \geq 100$, as will often occur in practice, then for all $\hat{\gamma}_{xy}^2$,

$$b[\hat{\gamma}_{xy}^2] \leq 0.01$$

This bias error approaches zero as $n_d \to \infty$ or $\hat{\gamma}_{xy}^2 \to 1$.

To obtain a formula for the random error, start with the equation

$$G_{vv} = \gamma_{xy}^2 G_{yy} \tag{9.76}$$

Then, differential increments of both sides yield

$$\Delta G_{vv} \approx \gamma_{xy}^2 \Delta G_{yy} + G_{yy}\Delta \gamma_{xy}^2 \tag{9.77}$$

where, using "smooth" estimates,

$$\Delta G_{vv} = \hat{G}_{vv} - G_{vv} \qquad \Delta G_{yy} = \hat{G}_{yy} - G_{yy} \qquad \Delta \gamma_{xy}^2 = \hat{\gamma}_{xy}^2 - \gamma_{xy}^2 \qquad (9.78)$$

By definition, for unbiased estimates,

$$\text{Var}[\hat{G}_{vv}] = E[\Delta G_{vv} \Delta G_{vv}] \quad \text{Var}[\hat{G}_{yy}] = E[\Delta G_{yy} \Delta G_{yy}]$$
$$\text{Var}[\hat{\gamma}_{xy}^2] = E[\Delta \gamma_{xy}^2 \Delta \gamma_{xy}^2] \qquad (9.79)$$

Also,

$$\text{Cov}(\hat{G}_{vv}, \hat{G}_{yy}) = E[\Delta G_{vv} \Delta G_{yy}] = \text{Var}[\hat{G}_{vv}] \qquad (9.80)$$

because

$$\Delta G_{yy} = \Delta G_{vv} + \Delta G_{nn} \quad \text{and} \quad E[\Delta G_{vv} \Delta G_{nn}] = 0$$

Solving Equation (9.77) for $G_{yy} \Delta \gamma_{xy}^2$ gives

$$G_{yy} \Delta \gamma_{xy}^2 \approx \Delta G_{vv} - \gamma_{xy}^2 \Delta G_{yy}$$

Squaring both sides and taking expected values yields

$$G_{yy}^2 \text{Var}[\hat{\gamma}_{xy}^2] \approx \text{Var}[\hat{G}_{vv}] - 2\gamma_{xy}^2 \text{Cov}(\hat{G}_{vv}, \hat{G}_{yy}) + \gamma_{xy}^4 \text{Var}[\hat{G}_{yy}]$$

Substitutions from Equations (9.71), (9.72), and (9.80) then show

$$\text{Var}[\hat{\gamma}_{xy}^2] \approx \frac{2\gamma_{xy}^2 (1 - \gamma_{xy}^2)^2}{n_d} \qquad (9.81)$$

Finally

$$\varepsilon[\hat{\gamma}_{xy}^2] = \frac{\text{s.d.}[\hat{\gamma}_{xy}^2]}{\gamma_{xy}^2} \approx \frac{\sqrt{2}(1 - \gamma_{xy}^2)}{|\gamma_{xy}| \sqrt{n_d}} \qquad (9.82)$$

For small ε, Equation (9.82) agrees with results in Ref. 2. Note that $\varepsilon[\hat{\gamma}_{xy}^2]$ approaches zero as either $n_d \to \infty$ or $\gamma_{xy}^2 \to 1$. For any $n_d > 1$, the coherence function estimates can be more accurate than the autospectra and cross-spectra estimates used in their computation provided γ_{xy}^2 is close to unity. The restriction that $n_d > 1$ is of course needed because $\hat{\gamma}_{xy}^2 = 1$ at all f when $n_d = 1$ and gives a meaningless estimate for $\hat{\gamma}_{xy}^2$.

Figure 9.4 plots Equation (9.82) as a function of γ_{xy}^2 for the special case when $n_d = 100$. Figure 9.5 plots Equation (9.82) for arbitrary values of n_d and γ_{xy}^2. Table 9.4 contains appropriate values that must be satisfied between γ_{xy}^2 and n_d to achieve $\varepsilon[\hat{\gamma}_{xy}^2] = 0.10$ using Equation (9.82).

Example 9.3. Illustration of Confidence Interval for Coherence Function Estimate. Suppose the coherence function between two random signals $x(t)$ and $y(t)$ is estimated using $n_d = 100$ averages. Assume a value of $\hat{\gamma}_{xy}^2 = 0.5$ is estimated at a frequency of interest. Determine approximate 95% confidence intervals for the true value of γ_{xy}^2.

SINGLE-INPUT/OUTPUT MODEL ESTIMATES 307

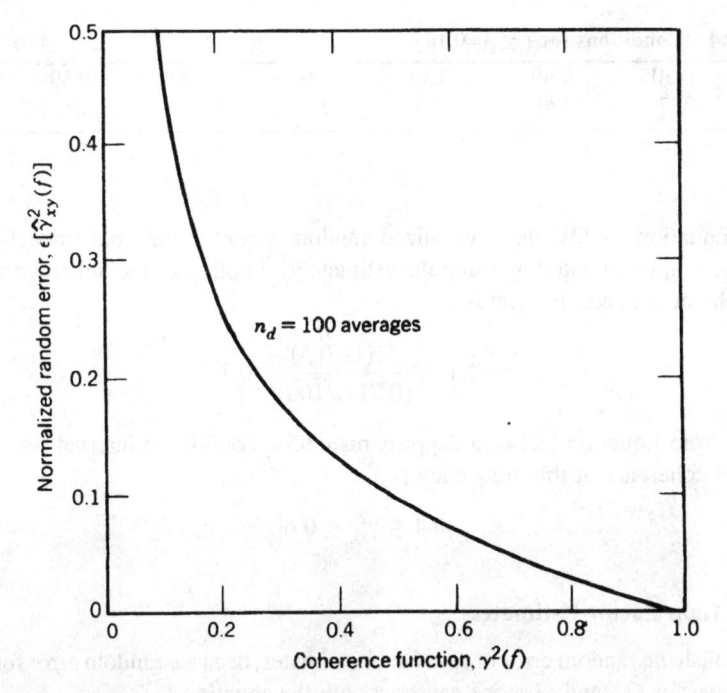

Figure 9.4 Normalized random errors of coherence function estimates when $n_d = 100$.

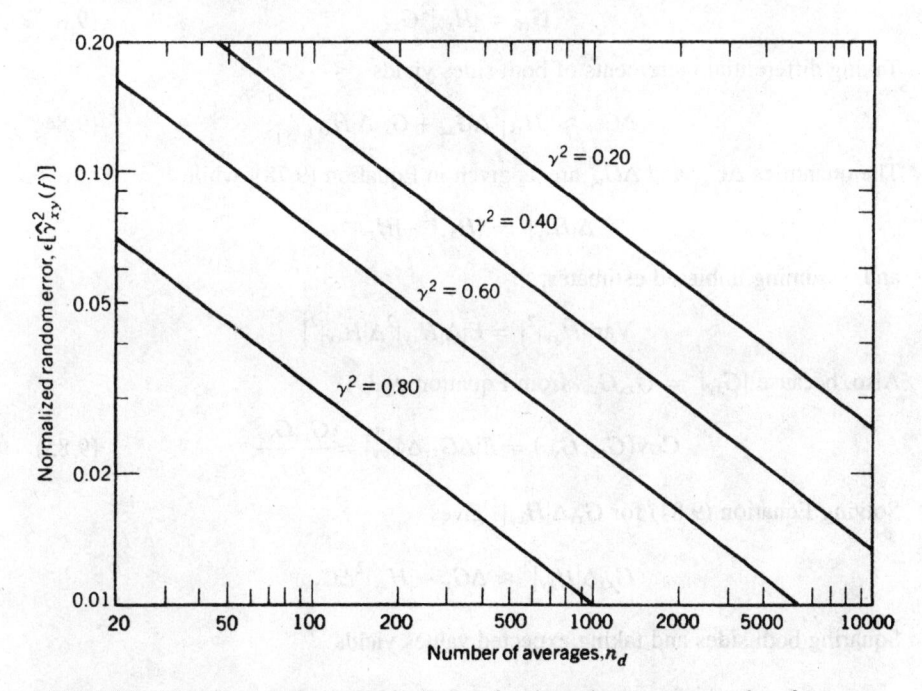

Figure 9.5 Normalized random error of coherence function estimates versus number of averages.

Table 9.4 Conditions for $\varepsilon[\hat{\gamma}_{xy}^2]=0.10$

γ_{xy}^2	0.30	0.40	0.50	0.60	0.70	0.80	0.90
n_d	327	180	100	54	26	10	3

From Equation (9.82), the normalized random error of the coherence function estimate is approximated by using the estimate $\hat{\gamma}_{xy}^2$ in place of the unknown γ_{xy}^2. For the problem at hand, this yields

$$\varepsilon\left[\hat{\gamma}_{xy}^2\right] = \frac{\sqrt{2}(1-0.5)}{(0.71)\sqrt{100}} = 0.1$$

Hence, from Equation (8.14), an approximate 95% confidence interval for the true value of coherence at this frequency is

$$[0.4 \leq \gamma_{xy}^2 \leq 0.6]$$

9.2.4 Gain Factor Estimates

To establish the random error in gain factor estimates, because random error formulas are known for G_{xx} and G_{vv}, one can start with the equation

$$G_{vv} = |H_{xy}|^2 G_{xx} \qquad (9.83)$$

Taking differential increments of both sides yields

$$\Delta G_{vv} \approx |H_{xy}|^2 \Delta G_{xx} + G_{xx}\Delta|H_{xy}|^2 \qquad (9.84)$$

The quantities ΔG_{xx} and ΔG_{vv} are as given in Equation (9.78), while

$$\Delta|H_{xy}|^2 = |\hat{H}_{xy}|^2 - |H_{xy}|^2$$

and, assuming unbiased estimates,

$$\text{Var}[|\hat{H}_{xy}|^2] = E[\Delta|H_{xy}|^2 \Delta|H_{xy}|^2]$$

Also, because $|G_{xv}|^2 = G_{xx}G_{vv}$, from Equation (9.39),

$$\text{Cov}(\hat{G}_{xx}, \hat{G}_{vv}) = E[\Delta G_{xx}\Delta G_{vv}] = \frac{G_{xx}G_{vv}}{n_d} \qquad (9.85)$$

Solving Equation (9.84) for $G_{xx}\Delta|H_{xy}|^2$ gives

$$G_{xx}\Delta|H_{xy}|^2 \approx \Delta G_{vv} - |H_{xy}|^2 \Delta G_{xx}$$

Squaring both sides and taking expected values yields

$$G_{xx}^2 \text{Var}[|\hat{H}_{xy}|^2] \approx \text{Var}[\hat{G}_{vv}] - 2|H_{xy}|^2 \text{Cov}(\hat{G}_{xy}, \hat{G}_{vv}) + |H_{xy}|^4 \text{Var}[\hat{G}_{xx}]$$

SINGLE-INPUT/OUTPUT MODEL ESTIMATES

Substitutions then show

$$\text{Var}\left[|\hat{H}_{xy}|^2\right] \approx \frac{2(1-\gamma_{xy}^2)|H_{xy}|^4}{\gamma_{xy}^2 n_d} \tag{9.86}$$

For any estimate $\hat{A}$, as a first order of approximation,

$$\Delta A^2 \approx 2A \Delta A$$

where

$$\Delta A = \hat{A} - A \qquad \Delta A^2 = \hat{A}^2 - A^2$$
$$E[\Delta A] = 0 \qquad E[\Delta A^2] = 0$$

Now

$$(\Delta A^2)^2 \approx 4A^2 (\Delta A)^2$$
$$E[\Delta A^2 \Delta A^2] \approx 4A^2 E[\Delta A \Delta A]$$

This is the same as

$$\text{Var}[\hat{A}^2] \approx 4A^2 \, \text{Var}[\hat{A}] \tag{9.87}$$

Dividing through by A^4 gives

$$\varepsilon^2\left[\hat{A}^2\right] = \frac{\text{Var}[\hat{A}^2]}{A^4} \approx \frac{4\text{Var}[\hat{A}]}{A^2} = 4\varepsilon^2\left[\hat{A}\right]$$

Hence

$$\varepsilon[\hat{A}^2] \approx 2\varepsilon[\hat{A}] \tag{9.88}$$

This useful result can compare random errors from mean square and rms estimates, as shown earlier in Equation (8.10).

Applying Equation (9.87) to Equation (9.86) gives the formula

$$\text{Var}\left[|\hat{H}_{xy}|\right] \approx \frac{(1-\gamma_{xy}^2)|H_{xy}|^2}{2\gamma_{xy}^2 n_d} \tag{9.89}$$

Finally

$$\varepsilon\left[|\hat{H}_{xy}|\right] = \frac{\text{s.d.}[|\hat{H}_{xy}|]}{|H_{xy}|} \approx \frac{(1-\gamma_{xy}^2)^{1/2}}{|\gamma_{xy}|\sqrt{2n_d}} \tag{9.90}$$

Note that this result is the same as Equation (9.52). It shows that $\varepsilon[|\hat{H}_{xy}|]$ approaches zero as γ_{xy}^2 approaches one, independent of the size of n_d, and also approaches zero as n_d becomes large, independent of the value of γ_{xy}^2. These results agree with the nature

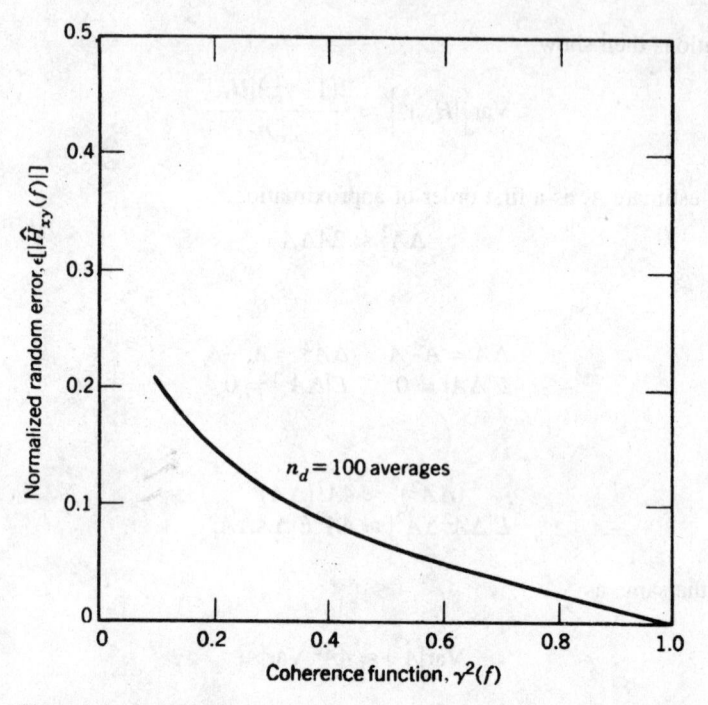

Figure 9.6 Normalized random error of gain factor estimates when $n_d = 100$.

of much more complicated formulas in Ref. 3, where error results were obtained using the F distribution.

Figure 9.6 plots Equation (9.90) as a function of γ_{xy}^2 for the special case when $n_d = 100$. Figure 9.7 plots Equation (9.90) for arbitrary values of n_d and γ_{xy}^2. Table 9.5 gives examples of values that must be satisfied between γ_{xy}^2 and n_d to achieve $\varepsilon[|\hat{H}_{xy}|] = 0.10$ using Equation (9.90).

9.2.5 Phase Factor Estimates

Phase factor estimates $\hat{\phi}_{xy}(f)$ from Equation (9.60) are the same as phase angle estimates $\hat{\theta}_{xy}(f)$ whose standard deviation is derived in Equation (9.52). Hence

$$\text{s.d.}[\hat{\phi}_{xy}] \approx \frac{(1-\gamma_{xy}^2)^{1/2}}{|\gamma_{xy}|\sqrt{2n_d}} \tag{9.91}$$

Equation (9.90) now shows that

$$\text{s.d.}[\hat{\phi}_{xy}] \approx \varepsilon[|\hat{H}_{xy}|] \tag{9.92}$$

In words, the standard deviation for the phase factor estimate $\hat{\phi}_{xy}$, measured in radians, is approximately the same as the normalized random error for the gain factor estimate $|\hat{H}_{xy}|$. This claim is reasonable whenever $\varepsilon[|\hat{H}_{xy}|]$ is small, say $\varepsilon \leq 0.20$, as

SINGLE-INPUT/OUTPUT MODEL ESTIMATES

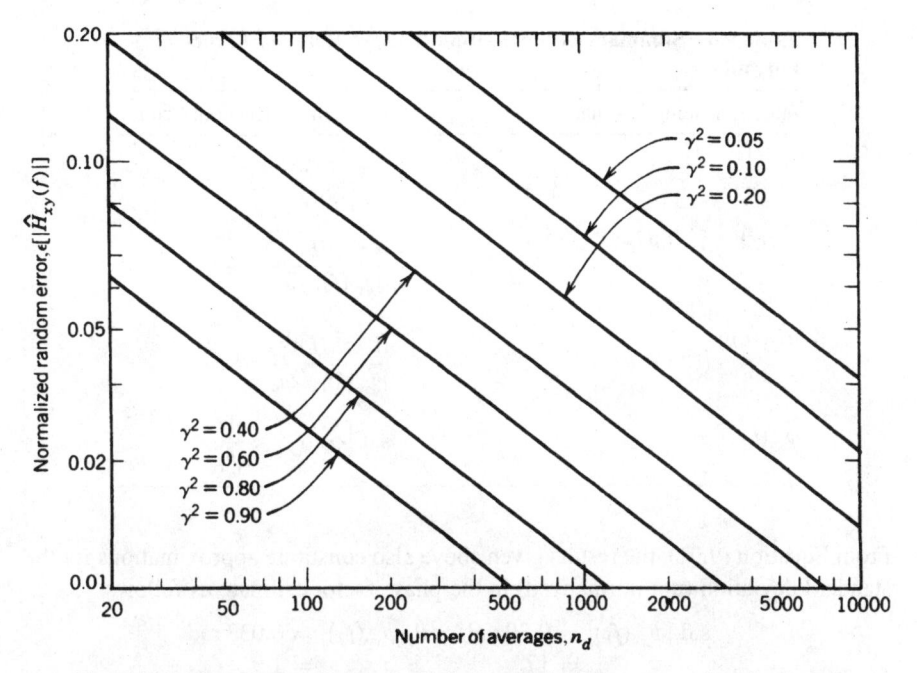

Figure 9.7 Normalized random error of gain factor estimates versus number of averages.

demonstrated in Ref. 4. Hence, one can state that Figure 9.6 plots the standard deviation s.d.$[\hat{\phi}_{xy}]$ in radians as a function of γ^2_{xy} for the special case when $n_d = 100$. Also, Table 9.5 gives examples of values that must be satisfied between γ^2_{xy} and n_d to achieve s.d.$[\hat{\phi}_{xy}] \approx 0.10$ radian.

Example 9.4. Illustration of Random Errors in Frequency Response Function Estimate. Suppose the frequency response function between two random signals $x(t)$ and $y(t)$ is estimated using $n_d = 50$ averages. Assume that the coherence function at one frequency of interest is $\gamma^2_{xy}(f_1) = 0.10$ and at a second frequency of interest is $\gamma^2_{xy}(f_2) = 0.90$. Determine the random errors in the frequency response function gain and phase estimates at the two frequencies of interest.

From Equation (9.90), the normalized random error in the gain factor estimates at frequencies f_1 and f_2 will be

$$\varepsilon[|\hat{H}_{xy}(f_1)|] = \frac{(1-0.10)^{1/2}}{(0.32)(10)} = 0.30$$

$$\varepsilon[|\hat{H}_{xy}(f_2)|] = \frac{(1-0.90)^{1/2}}{(0.95)(10)} = 0.033$$

Table 9.5 Conditions for $\varepsilon[|\hat{H}_{xy}|]=0.10$

γ^2_{xy}	0.30	0.40	0.50	0.60	0.70	0.80	0.90
n_d	117	75	50	34	22	13	6

Table 9.6 Summary of Single-Input/Output Random Error Formulas

Function Being Estimated	Normalized Random Error, ε
$\hat{\gamma}_{xy}^2(f)$	$\dfrac{\sqrt{2}[1-\gamma_{xy}^2(f)]}{|\gamma_{xy}(f)|\sqrt{n_d}}$
$\hat{G}_{vv}(f) = \hat{\gamma}_{xy}^2(f)\hat{G}_{yy}(f)$	$\dfrac{[2-\gamma_{xy}^2(f)]^{1/2}}{|\gamma_{xy}(f)|\sqrt{n_d}}$
$|\hat{H}_{xy}(f)|$	$\dfrac{[1-\gamma_{xy}^2(f)]^{1/2}}{|\gamma_{xy}(f)|\sqrt{2n_d}}$
$\hat{\phi}_{xy}(f)$	s.d.$\left[\hat{\phi}_{xy}(f)\right] \approx \dfrac{[1-\gamma_{xy}^2(f)]^{1/2}}{|\gamma_{xy}(f)|\sqrt{2n_d}}$

From Equation (9.91), the results given above also constitute approximations for the standard deviation (not normalized) in the phase factor estimate as follows:

$$\text{s.d.}[\hat{\phi}_{xy}(f_1)] = 0.30 \text{ rad} \quad \text{s.d.}[\hat{\phi}_{xy}(f_2)] = 0.033 \text{ rad}$$
$$= 17° \qquad\qquad\qquad = 1.9°$$

Hence, the estimates made with a coherence of $\gamma_{xy}^2(f_2) = 0.90$ are almost 10 times as accurate as those made with a coherence of $\gamma_{xy}^2(f_1) = 0.10$. This concludes the example.

A summary is given in Table 9.6 on the main normalized random error formulas for single-input/output model estimates. Some engineering measurements are shown in Ref. 4. A general theory for resolution bias errors is presented in Ref. 5.

9.3 MULTIPLE-INPUT/OUTPUT MODEL ESTIMATES

Consider the more general multiple-input/output model of Figure 7.11. All records should be measured simultaneously using a common time base. The first series of steps should be to replace this given model by the conditioned model of Figure 7.12 as defined in Chapter 7. Procedures for doing this are described by the iterative computational algorithms in Section 7.3. The only averaging required is in the computation of "smooth" estimates $\hat{G}_{ij}(f)$ of autospectra and cross-spectra from the original given data. All other quantities are then computed algebraically as follows (for simplicity in notation, the dependence on f will be omitted).

Compute first the initial set of conditioned estimates $\hat{G}_{ij\cdot 1}$ by the formula

$$\hat{G}_{ij\cdot 1} = \hat{G}_{ij} - \hat{L}_{1j}\hat{G}_{i1} \tag{9.93}$$

where

$$\hat{L}_{1j} = \frac{\hat{G}_{1j}}{\hat{G}_{11}} \tag{9.94}$$

This is the only step that uses the original $\hat{G}_{ij}$. From these results, compute next the second set of conditioned estimates $\hat{G}_{ij\cdot 2!}$ by exactly the same procedure as in Equations (9.93) and (9.94), namely,

$$\hat{G}_{ij\cdot 2!} = \hat{G}_{ij\cdot 1} - \hat{L}_{2j}\hat{G}_{i2\cdot 1} \qquad (9.95)$$

where

$$\hat{L}_{2j} = \frac{\hat{G}_{2j\cdot 1}}{\hat{G}_{22\cdot 1}} \qquad (9.96)$$

Compute next the third set of conditioned estimates $\hat{G}_{ij\cdot 3!}$ using the just obtained $\hat{G}_{ij\cdot 2!}$ by a similar procedure and so on to as many terms as required. Further algebraic operations on these results yield estimates for all of the partial coherence functions, the multiple coherence function, and related quantities.

The computation of the "smooth" conditioned spectral density estimates in Equation (9.93), where the first record is removed, followed by the computation of the "smooth" spectral density estimates in Equation (9.95), where the first two records are removed, and so on involves a subtraction of terms. This leads to reducing the number of records by one for each successive step. Thus, when the original autospectra and cross-spectra terms are computed using n_d averages, then the terms in Equation (9.93) will be associated with $(n_d - 1)$ averages, the terms in Equation (9.95) will be associated with $(n_d - 2)$ averages, and so on.

Figure 7.12 can be replaced by the set of modified uncorrelated conditioned single-input/single-output SI/SO models of Figure 7.16 where $U_i = X_{i\cdot(i-1)!}$ for $i = 1, 2, \ldots, q$. The first system in Figure 7.16 is the same as the basic single-input/single-output linear model of Figure 9.1. The succeeding systems in Figure 7.16 are direct extensions where it is obvious which terms should be related to terms in the first system. The top three systems in Figures 7.16 and 7.17 represent the three-input/single-output linear model discussed in Section 7.4.1 where Figure 7.19 replaces Figure 7.18.

Assume in Figure 7.16 that estimates of spectral functions that use the first input record $U_1 = X_1$ are computed with n_d averages. It follows that spectral estimates computed from the second input record $U_2 = X_{2\cdot 1}$ will have $(n_d - 1)$ averages, spectral estimates computed from the third input record $U_3 = X_{3\cdot 2!}$ will have $(n_d - 2)$ averages, and so on up to spectral estimates computed from the qth input record that will have $(n_d + 1 - q)$ averages.

Random error formulas are listed below for estimates of various functions in Figures 7.17 and 7.19. These results extend directly to general MI/SO cases. The top three ordinary coherence functions in Figure 7.17 can be computed by Equations (7.133) to (7.135). In place of Equation (9.82), normalized random errors for estimates of these three functions are given by

$$\varepsilon[\hat{\gamma}^2_{u_1 y}] \approx \frac{\sqrt{2}[1 - \gamma^2_{u_1 y}]}{|\gamma_{u_1 y}|\sqrt{n_d}}$$

$$\varepsilon[\hat{\gamma}^2_{u_2 y}] \approx \frac{\sqrt{2}[1 - \gamma^2_{u_2 y}]}{|\gamma_{u_2 y}|\sqrt{n_d - 1}} \qquad (9.97)$$

$$\varepsilon[\hat{\gamma}^2_{u_3 y}] \approx \frac{\sqrt{2}[1 - \gamma^2_{u_3 y}]}{|\gamma_{u_3 y}|\sqrt{n_d - 2}}$$

For the model in Figure 7.19 with the modified notation, the multiple coherence function can be computed by the simple additive formula of Equation (7.136). The normalized random error for this computed multiple coherence function is given by,

$$\varepsilon\left[\hat{\gamma}_{y:x}^2\right] \approx \frac{\sqrt{2}[1-\gamma_{y:x}^2]}{|\gamma_{y:x}|\sqrt{n_d-2}} \tag{9.98}$$

The normalized random error for the associated total coherent output spectrum estimate of Equation (7.132) is given by

$$\varepsilon\left[\hat{G}_{vv}\right] \approx \frac{[2-\gamma_{y:x}^2]^{1/2}}{|\gamma_{y:x}|\sqrt{n_d-2}} \tag{9.99}$$

The top three coherent output spectral density functions in Figure 7.17 can be computed by Equations (7.128)–(7.130). In place of Equation (9.73), the normalized random errors for estimates of these three functions are given by

$$\varepsilon[|\hat{L}_{1y}|^2 \hat{G}_{u_1 u_1}] = \varepsilon\left[\hat{\gamma}_{u_1 y}^2 \hat{G}_{yy}\right] \approx \frac{[2-\gamma_{u_1 y}^2]^{1/2}}{|\gamma_{u_1 y}|\sqrt{n_d}}$$

$$\varepsilon[|\hat{L}_{2y}|^2 \hat{G}_{u_2 u_2}] = \varepsilon\left[\hat{\gamma}_{u_2 y}^2 \hat{G}_{yy}\right] \approx \frac{[2-\gamma_{u_2 y}^2]^{1/2}}{|\gamma_{u_2 y}|\sqrt{n_d-1}} \tag{9.100}$$

$$\varepsilon[|\hat{L}_{3y}|^2 \hat{G}_{u_3 u_3}] = \varepsilon\left[\hat{\gamma}_{u_3 y}^2 \hat{G}_{yy}\right] \approx \frac{[2-\gamma_{u_3 y}^2]^{1/2}}{|\gamma_{u_3 y}|\sqrt{n_d-2}}$$

The top three L-systems in Figure 7.17 can be computed by Equations (7.122)–(7.124). In place of Equation (9.90), normalized random errors for estimates of the gain factors of these three L-systems are given by

$$\varepsilon[|\hat{L}_{1y}|] \approx \frac{[1-\gamma_{u_1 y}^2]^{1/2}}{|\gamma_{u_1 y}|\sqrt{2n_d}}$$

$$\varepsilon[|\hat{L}_{2y}|] \approx \frac{[1-\gamma_{u_2 y}^2]^{1/2}}{|\gamma_{u_2 y}|\sqrt{2(n_d-1)}} \tag{9.101}$$

$$\varepsilon[|\hat{L}_{3y}|] \approx \frac{[1-\gamma_{u_3 y}^2]^{1/2}}{|\gamma_{u_3 y}|\sqrt{2(n_d-2)}}$$

Error formulas for associated phase factor estimates of the three L-systems are the same as stated in Equation (9.92).

PROBLEMS

9.1 Consider a single-input/single-output system where the coherence function between the input $x(t)$ and the output $y(t)$ is $\gamma_{xy}^2 = 0.75$ at a frequency of interest. Suppose the autospectra of the input and output are $G_{xx} = 2.1$ and $G_{yy} = 0.8$, respectively. What should be the minimum number of averages n_d in a frequency response function estimate to ensure that the estimated gain factor $|\hat{H}_{xy}|$ is within $\pm 10\%$ of the true gain factor $|H_{xy}|$ with a probability of 95%?

9.2 For the single-input/single-output system in Problem 9.1, what value of coherence is needed to provide a gain factor estimate and autospectra estimates with the same normalized random error?

9.3 Consider two random signals $x(t)$ and $y(t)$ representing stationary random processes. Assume the autospectra of the two signals, as well as the cross-spectrum between the signals, is to be estimated using $n_d = 100$ averages. If the coherence function between $x(t)$ and $y(t)$ is $\gamma_{xy}^2 = 0.50$ at a frequency of interest, determine the normalized random error for

(a) the autospectra estimates $\hat{G}_{xx}$ and $\hat{G}_{yy}$.
(b) the cross-spectrum magnitude estimate $|\hat{G}_{xy}|$.

9.4 For two random signals $x(t)$ and $y(t)$, suppose that at the frequency of interest the autospectra values are $G_{xx} = G_{yy} = 1$ and the coincident and quadrature spectral values are $C_{xy} = Q_{xy} = 0.5$. Assuming $n_d = 100$ averages, determine the normalized random error for estimates of the coincident and quadrature spectral density values $\hat{C}_{xy}$ and $\hat{Q}_{xy}$.

9.5 For the two random signals in Problem 9.4, determine at the frequency of interest approximate 95% probability intervals for the estimated values of

(a) the coherence function $\hat{\gamma}_{xy}^2$.
(b) the coherent output spectrum $\hat{G}_{vv} = \hat{\gamma}_{xy}^2 \hat{G}_{yy}$.

9.6 For the two random signals in Problem 9.4 determine an approximate 95% probability interval for the estimated value of the phase factor $\hat{\theta}_{xy}$ at the frequency of interest.

9.7 Consider two bandwidth-limited white noise random signals defined by

$$x(t) = u(t) + m(t)$$
$$y(t) = 10u(t-\tau_1) + n(t)$$

where $m(t)$ and $n(t)$ are statistically independent noise signals. Assume the spectral density values of the input signal and noise at a frequency of interest are equal, that is, $G_{uu} = G_{mm}$, and the delay value $\tau_1 = 0.1$ s. If the frequency response function from $x(t)$ to $y(t)$ is estimated using a large number of averages and individual record lengths of $T = 0.5$ s, determine the primary sources of bias errors and the magnitude of the bias errors.

9.8 For the two bandwidth-limited white noise signals in Problem 9.7, assume $G_{mm}=0$ and $G_{nn}=100G_{uu}$ at a frequency of interest. If the output spectral density at the frequency of interest is $G_{yy}=1$, determine
  (a) the true value of the coherent output spectrum $G_{vv} = \gamma_{xy}^2 G_{yy}$.
  (b) the bias error in the estimate $\hat{G}_{vv}$.
  (c) the random error in the estimate $\hat{G}_{vv}$ assuming $n_d = 400$ averages.

9.9 Consider a two-input/one-output system as in Figure 7.2 where the inputs are $x_1(t)$ and $x_2(t)$ and the output is $y(t)$. Assume estimates are computed using $n_d = 100$ averages to obtain the following quantities at a frequency of interest $\hat{G}_{11} = 20$, $\hat{G}_{22} = 25$, $\hat{G}_{yy} = 40$, $\hat{G}_{12} = 15$, and $\hat{G}_{1y} = \hat{G}_{2y} = 16 - j12$. Determine the normalized random error and the standard deviation, respectively, for the gain and phase factors of the frequency response function H_{2y} between $x_2(t)$ and $y(t)$.

9.10 Using the data in Problem 9.9, determine the expected value and normalized random error for the multiple coherence function estimate $\hat{\gamma}_{y:x}^2$ between the two inputs and the output.

REFERENCES

1. Jenkins, G. M, and Watts, D. G., *Spectral Analysis and Its Applications*, Holden-Day, San Francisco, 1968.
2. Carter, G. C., Knapp, C. H., and Nutall, A. H., "Estimation of the Magnitude-Squared Coherence via Overlapped Fast Fourier Transform Processing," *IEEE Transactions on Audio and Electroacoustics*, Vol. **AU-21**, p. 337, August 1973.
3. Goodman, N. R., "Measurement of Matrix Frequency Response Functions and Multiple Coherence Functions," AFFDL TR 65-56, Air Force Flight Dynamics Laboratory, Wright-Patterson AFB, Ohio, February 1965.
4. Bendat, J. S., and Piersol, A. G., *Engineering Applications of Correlation and Spectral Analysis*, 2nd ed., Wiley–Interscience, New York, 1993.
5. Schmidt, H., "Resolution Bias Errors in Spectral Density, Frequency Response and Coherence Function Measurements," *Journal of Sound and Vibration*, Vol. **101**, p. 347, 1985.

CHAPTER 10

Data Acquisition and Processing

Some random time history data that might be of interest occur naturally in a digital format, for example, stock or commodity prices from one transaction to the next. In such cases, the data can be entered directly into a digital computer for analysis by the procedures detailed in Chapter 11. This chapter is concerned with those random data that represent continuous physical phenomena where specific data acquisition and processing procedures are required before an analysis of the data can be accomplished. The appropriate techniques for the acquisition and processing of continuous random data are heavily dependent on the physical phenomena represented by the data and the desired engineering goals of the processing. In broad terms, however, the required operations may be divided into four primary categories as follows:

Data acquisition
Data conversion
Data qualification
Data analysis

Each of these categories involves sequential steps as schematically illustrated in Figure 10.1. The purpose of this chapter is to summarize the basic considerations associated with each of these key steps. The emphasis throughout is on potential sources of error beyond the statistical errors inherent in the data sampling considerations developed in Chapters 8 and 9. The digital computations required for the analysis of stationary and nonstationary random data through linear and nonlinear systems are covered in Chapters 11 through 14.

Random Data: Analysis and Measurement Procedures, Fourth Edition. By Julius S. Bendat and Allan G. Piersol
Copyright © 2010 John Wiley & Sons, Inc.

```
In → Acquisition → Conversion → Qualification → Analysis → Out
                        (a) Data acquisition
→ Transducer → Signal conditioning → Transmission → Calibration →
                        (b) Data conversion
→ Analog-to-digital conversion → Sampling errors → Storage →
                        (c) Data qualification
→ Classification → Validation → Editing →
                        (d) Data analysis
→ Individual sample records → Multiple sample records →
```

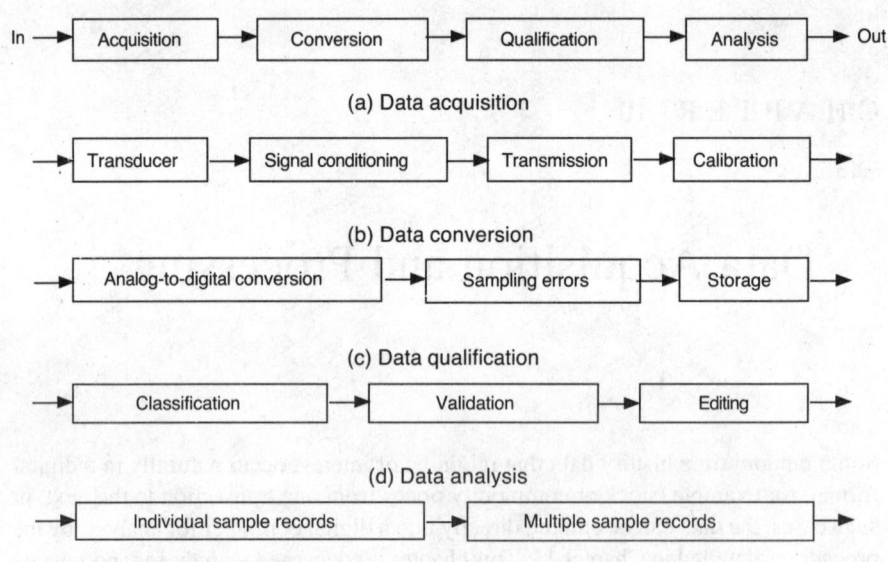

Figure 10.1 Key steps in data acquisition and processing.

10.1 DATA ACQUISITION

Referring to Figure 10.1, a data acquisition system usually involves a transducer with signal conditioning, transmission of the conditioned signal to an analog-to-digital converter (ADC), and a calibration of the data acquisition system (sometimes called *standardization*) to establish the relationship between the physical phenomena being measured arid the conditioned signal transmitted to the analog-to-digital converter. Each element of the data acquisition system must be carefully selected to provide the frequency range and dynamic range needed for the final engineering applications of the data, as discussed in Ref. 1.

10.1.1 Transducer and Signal Conditioning

The primary element in a data acquisition system is the instrumentation transducer. In general terms, a transducer is any device that translates power from one form to another. In an engineering context, this usually means the translation of a physical phenomenon being measured into an electrical signal. In some cases, the physical phenomenon being measured may be an electrical signal so that no transducer is required—for example, the voltage output of a power-generating device. In other cases, the transducer may be a simple device that directly translates the physical phenomenon being measured into an electrical signal without intermediate mechanical operations—for example, a thermocouple. In many data acquisition problems, however, the physical phenomenon being measured is a mechanical quantity such as force, pressure, or motion (displacement, velocity, or acceleration). In these situations, the transducer typically consists of a mechanical element that converts the physical phenomenon into a deformation of a sensing element, which in turn produces an electrical quantity that is proportional to the magnitude of the physical phenomenon. A signal conditioner then converts the generated electrical quantity into a voltage signal with a low source impedance (generally less than 100 Ω) and the desired magnitude and frequency range for transmission to the remainder of the data acquisition system.

Sensing elements for force, pressure, and motion transducers commonly employ piezoelectric or strain-sensitive materials. A piezoelectric material is one that produces an electrical charge when it is deformed. Examples include (a) naturally polarized single crystals such as quartz and (b) artificially polarized ferroelectric polycrystalline ceramics such as barium titanate. The basic signal conditioning element for a piezoelectric transducer is a charge amplifier. A strain-sensitive material is one that changes its electrical resistance when it is deformed. There are two basic types of strain-sensitive materials, namely, metallic and semiconductor. A common metallic strain-sensitive material is constantan. (a copper–nickel alloy), while a common semiconductor material for this application is nearly pure monocrystalline silicon. The basic signal conditioning element for strain-sensitive transducers is a power supply and a conventional Wheatstone bridge circuit. There are many other types of sensing elements for force, pressure, and motion transducers, including capacitance, electrodynamic, servo-control, and electro-optical devices, as detailed in Refs 2 and 3. In most cases, however, the transducer will have dynamic properties that limit its useful frequency range, as illustrated in Example 10.1 to follow.

Example 10.1. **Illustration of Piezoelectric Accelerometer.** Consider an idealized piezoelectric accelerometer, as schematically illustrated in Figure 10.2(*a*). The mechanical conversion in this transducer is achieved through a seismic mass supported by a flexible piezoelectric material, where an input acceleration at the base of the accelerometer is converted to a relative displacement of the mass. The piezoelectric material generates a charge that is proportional to its deformation—that is, the displacement of the mass relative to the base of the accelerometer. A signal conditioner in the form of a charge amplifier converts the charge produced by the piezoelectric material into a voltage signal with a low source impedance. In most cases, the charge amplifier is incorporated into the accelerometer, but in some cases all signal conditioning is accomplished by a separate instrument.

Again referring to Figure 10.2(*a*), the piezoelectric accelerometer is mechanically equivalent to the simple mechanical system shown in Figure 2.4, where the piezoelectric material is represented by the spring and the dashpot. From Table 2.1, the frequency response function of this system between the input acceleration and the output voltage is given by

$$H(f) = \frac{c}{4\pi^2 f_n^2 [1-(f/f_n)^2 + j2\zeta f/f_n]} \quad (10.1)$$

where c is a calibration constant, and ζ and f_n are the damping ratio and undamped natural frequency, respectively, of the system, as defined in Equation (2.22). The gain and phase factors for this system are plotted in Figure 10.2(*b*) and (*c*). Note that these gain and phase factors are identical in form to those for a simple mechanical system with force excitation, as plotted in Figure 2.3. Hence, the same gain and phase factors

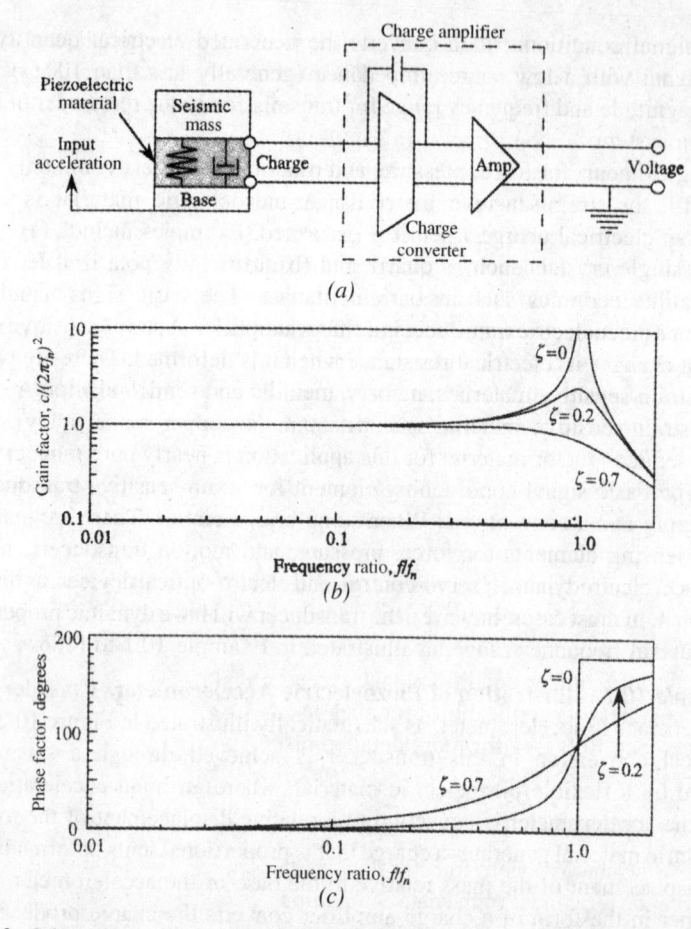

Figure 10.2 Schematic diagram and frequency response characteristics of piezoelectric accelerometer. (*a*) Schematic diagram, (*b*) Gain factor, (*c*) Phase factor.

apply to various types of force and pressure transducers, including microphones and hydrophones.

Consider first the gain factor given in Figure 10.2(*b*). It is seen that the widest frequency range with a near-uniform gain is obtained when the damping ratio is about $\zeta = 0.7$. It is for this reason that certain types of large, high-gain accelerometers are designed with added damping to achieve the $\zeta \approx 0.7$ damping ratio and, hence, maximize their useful frequency range. On the other hand, small piezoelectric accelerometers (as well as many other types of piezoelectric and piezoresistive transducers) are available that have a first natural frequency approaching 1 MHz—that is, many times higher than the highest frequency of normal interest. From Figure 10.2(*b*), it is seen that the gain factor is relatively uniform (within 2%) for frequencies up to about 20% of the undamped natural frequency of the transducer, independent of the damping ratio. Hence, it is common for the manufacturers to ignore the damping in such transducers, which is usually very small, and simply advertise a useful frequency range up to 20% of the first natural frequency of the transducer.

Now referring to the phase factor in Figure 10.2(c), the $\zeta \approx 0.7$ damping ratio produces a near-linear phase function (when viewed on a linear frequency scale) over the frequency range where the gain factor is near-uniform. A linear phase function corresponds to a simple time delay (see Figure 5.6) that does not distort the time history of the physical phenomenon being measured. However, any substantial deviation from the $\zeta \approx 0.7$ damping ratio will result in a phase distortion of the measured phenomenon. On the other hand, if the transducer has low damping but a high natural frequency so that the frequency range of the physical phenomenon being measured does not exceed 20% of the first natural frequency of the transducer, the phase factor is essential zero. This concludes Example 10.1.

In summary, considerable care is warranted in the selection and use of data acquisition transducers and signal conditioning equipment. When transducers are obtained from commercial sources, supporting literature is normally provided that specifies the limitations on their use. These specifications are generally accurate, but it must be remembered that commercial manufacturers are not inclined to be pessimistic in the claims they make for their products. Hence, it is unwise to use a commercially procured transducer under conditions that exceed the limits of the manufacturer's specifications unless its applicability for such use has been substantiated by appropriate studies. See Refs 2–4 for more detailed discussions of transducer systems.

10.1.2 Data Transmission

There are two primary ways to transfer data signals from the transducer and signal conditioner to the remainder of the data acquisition system, namely, (a) landlines and (b) radio frequency (RF) telemetry, also called *wireless*. Landlines include wires, coaxial cables, twisted shielded cables, and fiber-optic cables. Unshielded wire should be avoided for the transmission due to interchannel modulation (cross talk) and excessive background noise problems. To further surpass such problems, landlines should be kept as short as feasible. Coaxial cables are the most commonly used landlines for data transmission at this time, but the use of fiber-optic data links is rapidly increasing due to their ability to meet low noise and security requirements. See Ref. 2 for details on the selection of landlines for various data transmission requirements.

Landlines are usually the preferred mode of data transmission when their use is feasible. There are situations, however, where the use of landlines is not feasible. This occurs primarily when measurements must be made on an object that is moving relative to the reference frame for the remainder of the data acquisition system and, in particular, when the object carrying the transducer cannot be recovered. A common example is the measurement of various types of data on a missile or expendable space vehicle in flight. For these situations, RF telemetry is used to transmit the measured data to a receiver station in the same reference frame as the remainder of the data acquisition equipment. This usually involves an air-to-ground transmission, but could also be a ground-to-air, air-to-air, or even a ground-to-ground transmission in some situations. Details on RF telemetry are available from Refs 2 and 3.

10.1.3 Calibration

The calibration procedure for all elements of the data acquisition system may be divided into three separate categories: (a) laboratory calibration of individual instruments, (b) end-to-end electrical calibration of the data acquisition system excluding the transducer, and (c) end-to-end mechanical calibration of the entire data acquisition system. The calibration process should also include a determination of the dynamic range of the data acquisition system. This subject is addressed separately in Section 10.1.4.

10.1.3.1 Laboratory Calibration

Most organizations engaged in the acquisition of random data have a specific group or instrument laboratory that is responsible for providing the necessary instrumentation. Such groups commonly have a formal procedure and schedule for the routine maintenance and calibration of individual transducers and instruments. If such a group does not exist, it is recommended that it be created. The exact details of how the transducers and instruments are maintained and calibrated should be based upon the manufacturer's recommendations. For force, pressure, or motion transducers in particular, when they are newly purchased or recalibrated by a calibration service, a certificate should be provided that states the traceability to the National Institute of Standards and Technology (NIST), or an equivalent agency in countries other than the United States, through an identified transfer standard transducer. This certificate should clearly state which portion of the calibration is simply typical for the transducer type or model, and which is actually measured on the transducer being calibrated. Further details and recommendations on the laboratory calibration of random data acquisition instruments are provided in Refs 2 and 3.

10.1.3.2 End-to-End Electrical Calibration

An end-to-end electrical calibration means a full calibration of the data acquisition system from the electrical output of the transducer to the output of the data acquisition system where the data signal will be analyzed. It is recommended that an end-to-end electrical calibration be performed on all channels of the data acquisition system prior to each experiment for which the system is used. The calibration should be performed with the data acquisition system in its completed configuration, including all transducers mounted, cables installed, and all signal conditioner gains set as they will be for the actual measurements. If a different gain setting is used for the calibration, it should be recorded so that the calibration results can be later corrected for the gain used to make the actual measurements. In those cases where the acquired data are to be recorded and stored for later analysis, the calibration signals should be recorded and stored in exactly the same manner, and the calibration should be performed on the output signals from the storage device.

For most types of transducers (including piezoelectric transducers), a calibration signal can be applied across a resistor inserted in the circuit between the transducer and the signal conditioner; the transducer manufacturer usually provides such a voltage insertion circuit with the transducer. Various types of calibration signals might be used, but a broadband random signal with a nearly uniform autospectrum over a frequency range that exceeds the bandwidth of the data acquisition system is considered the most desirable calibration signal for random data acquisition systems. The recommended calibration procedure is as follows:

1. For each channel of the data acquisition system, insert a random calibration signal at the transducer with an accurately defined autospectrum and measure the output at that point where the data will be analyzed.
2. Compute the coherence function between the input calibration signal and the output (see Section 11.6.6). The coherence should be in excess of 0.99 at all frequencies of interest. If it is not, every effort should be made to identify the reasons for the lesser coherence and correct the problem. See Ref. 1 for details on the common sources of poor coherence in measurement systems.
3. Compute the frequency response function between the input calibration signal and the output (see Section 11.6.4). This frequency response function establishes the voltage gain and phase of each channel of the data acquisition system. Deviations from a uniform gain and linear phase should be recorded for later corrections of the data.
4. During the calibration of each channel, the cables in the data acquisition system for that channel should be moved about, and the output signal should be checked for noise spikes, power line pickup, and other evidence of faulty connectors, broken shields, multiple grounding points, and motion-induced problems (see Section 10.4.2).

For those channels of the data acquisition system where dual-channel analyses of the transducer signals is anticipated, the following additional calibration steps are recommended:

5. Insert a common random signal with an accurately defined autospectrum simultaneously into all channels of the data acquisition system and measure the simultaneous outputs of all channels at those points where the data will be analyzed.
6. Compute the coherence and phase functions between the output of each channel and the output of every other channel.
7. The coherence between the output of each channel and all other channels should be in excess of 0.99 at all frequencies of interest. If it is not, every effort should be made to identify the source of the inadequate coherence and correct the problem. See Ref. 1 for details on the common sources of poor coherence between channels in measurement systems.
8. The phase between the output of each channel and all other channels would ideally be zero over the entire frequency range of interest. However, due to differences in the instrumentation for the various channels, this

may not occur. If not, the phase versus frequency measured between the various channels should be recorded and used to make appropriate corrections to the phase data computed during later dual-channel analyses of the data signals.

10.1.3.3 End-to-End Mechanical Calibration

An end-to-end mechanical calibration means a full calibration of the data acquisition system from the actual physical input to the transducer to the output of the data acquisition system where the data signal will be analyzed. Mechanical calibrations are generally limited to data channels where the introduction of a known physical input is easily achieved. For example, calibration shakers are available that will apply a broadband random vibration with a known autospectrum to a motion transducer, such as an accelerometer, although this may require removing the accelerometer from its actual mounting location for calibration purposes.

When the insertion of a mechanical excitation to the transducer is feasible, end-to-end mechanical calibrations are recommended for all transducer channels in the data acquisition system prior to each test. An end-to-end mechanical calibration of a given transducer channel generally constitutes a final check on the calibration of that channel, and it may replace the end-to-end electrical calibration of that channel in most cases. The calibration procedure is essentially the same as described for end-to-end electrical calibration where the physical random excitation into the transducer replaces the electrical random signal inserted at the output of the transducer.

After completing the end-to-end electrical and/or mechanical calibration of the data acquisition system, it is desirable to compare the system calibration factor at all frequencies determined from the end-to-end calibration with the net system calibration factor computed from the laboratory calibrations of the individual instruments. If there is a significant discrepancy between these two sets of calibration factors, every effort should be made to identify the source of the discrepancy and correct the problem. If the source of the discrepancy cannot be identified, but no error can be found in the end-to-end calibration, then the results of the end-to-end calibration should be accepted and, after the measurements are complete, all instruments in the data acquisition system should be recalibrated in the laboratory. See Ref. 3 for further details on calibration procedures.

10.1.4 Dynamic Range

An important characteristic of any data acquisition system that should be determined during the calibration process is the *dynamic range* of the system, where dynamic range is generally defined as the ratio of the maximum to minimum data values the system can acquire without significant distortion. The dynamic range of a data acquisition system is commonly assessed in terms of a maximum allowable *signal-to-noise ratio* (*SNR*) defined as

$$SNR = \psi_s^2 / \psi_n^2 \qquad (10.2a)$$

or in decibels (dB) as

$$(S/N) = 10 \log_{10}(\psi_s^2/\psi_n^2) \qquad (10.2b)$$

where ψ_s is the maximum rms value of the signal that can be acquired without significant distortion and ψ_n is the rms value of the data acquisition system noise floor, which is commonly assumed to have a zero mean value so that $\psi_n = \sigma_n$. Note that a ratio of mean square values, rather than rms values, is used in Equation (10.2) because signal-to-noise ratios are traditionally defined as a ratio of power quantities.

The standard deviation of the data acquisition system noise floor can be directly measured during the calibration process by simply measuring the output of the system with no excitation applied to the transducer. As for the end-to-end calibration procedures, the noise floor measurement should be made with the data acquisition system in its completed configuration, including all transducers mounted, cables installed, and all signal conditioner gains set as they will be for the actual measurements. If a different gain setting is used for the noise floor measurement, it should be recorded so that the noise floor results can be later corrected for the gain used to make the actual measurements. The noise floor for data acquisition systems is due primarily to the electronic noise of analog instruments and/or the quantization noise (round-off error) of digital instruments discussed in Section 10.2.4. In either case, the noise commonly has a near-uniform autospectral density function. Nevertheless, the autospectral density function of the noise floor should be computed as part of the calibration process.

The maximum rms value of the signal that can be acquired without significant distortion is a function of the signal characteristics. For example, assume the linear range of the data acquisition system extends symmetrically about zero from $-L_{max}$ to $+L_{max}$. A static signal can be acquired without distortion up to $\psi_s = L_{max}$, because the rms value of a constant equals the absolute value of the constant. On the other hand, a sinusoidal signal with a zero mean value can be acquired without distortion up to only $\psi_s = (1/\sqrt{2})L_{max}$ because the peak value of a sine wave is $\sqrt{2}\psi_s$. For a Gaussian random signal, the peak value is theoretically undefined and, hence, some distortion must always be accepted. In practice, however, it is common to assume that a Gaussian random signal with a zero mean value can be clipped at ± 3 standard deviations without a significant error, meaning $\psi_s = (1/3)L_{max}$, to obtain a measure of the dynamic range of a data acquisition system that is not dependent on the detailed characteristics of the signal to be acquired. Ref. 3 suggests the determination of a *peak signal-to-noise ratio* (PSNR) given by

$$PSNR = L_{max}^2/\psi_n^2 \qquad (10.3a)$$

or in decibels as

$$(PS/N) = 10 \log_{10}(L_{max}^2/\psi_n^2) \qquad (10.3b)$$

where L_{max} can be determined during the calibration of the data acquisition system by the following steps:

1. With the data acquisition system in its completed configuration, including all transducers mounted, cables installed, and all signal conditioner gains set as

they were for the noise floor measurements, apply as an input to the system (either electrical or mechanical) a sine wave with a zero mean value.
2. Slowly increase the rms value of the sine wave input until a distortion of the sine wave output of the system is detected.
3. Compute $L_{max} = \sqrt{2}\psi_s$, where ψ_s is the rms value of the sine wave output just before a distortion is detected.
4. Although L_{max} will usually be independent of frequency, it is wise to perform the measurement at several frequencies within the frequency range of the data acquisition system.

Having determined the *PSNR* of the data acquisition system defined in Equation (10.3), the *SNR* defined in Equation (10.2) can be determined by reducing the value of *PSNR* as required to account for the anticipated peak-to-rms value of the data to be acquired. For example,

a. For static data, $SNR = PSNR$ or $(S/N) = (PS/N)$.
b. For sinusoidal data, $SNR = \frac{1}{2}PSNR$ or $(S/N) = (PS/N) - 3$ dB.
c. For Gaussian random data, $SNR \approx \frac{1}{9}PSNR$ or $(S/N) \approx (PS/N) - 10$ dB.

10.2 DATA CONVERSION

The conditioned signal from the transducer generally must be converted into a digital format for later data analysis operations. This digital conversion operation is accomplished by an *analog-to-digital converter*. The ADC may be incorporated into the front end of an applicable online data analysis instrument or be a separate item of equipment that delivers the digital data to storage for later analysis.

10.2.1 Analog-to-Digital Converters

An analog-to-digital converter is a device that translates a continuous analog signal, which represents an uncountable set, into a series of discrete values (often called a time series), which represents a countable set, There are numerous types of ADC designs (see Ref. 3), but due to the merits of very high sampling rates relative to the highest frequency of interest in the data (oversampling), perhaps the most common type of ADC in current use is that referred to as the sigma-delta ($\Sigma\Delta$) converter, which is schematically illustrated in Figure 10.3. The key features of a $\Sigma\Delta$ converter are

a. the input of the analog signal through an integrator to a clock-driven comparator, which essentially acts as a one binary digit (one-bit) ADC,
b. the feedback of the one-bit comparator output through a one-bit digital-to-analog converter (see Ref. 2), which is then subtracted from the input analog signal, and
c. an averaging operation by a low-pass digital filter, which essentially increases the number of bits forming a digital value (the word size) in the digital output (digital filters are discussed in Chapter 11).

DATA CONVERSION

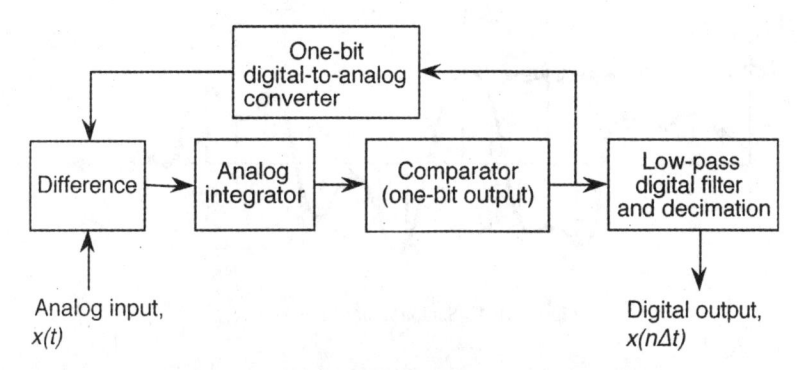

Figure 10.3 Schematic diagram of sigma-delta converter.

Since the basic comparator and DAC operations are accomplished using a one-bit resolution, a very high initial sampling rate (>10^7 sps) can be achieved. The digital filter is then set to provide an output sampling rate after decimation that is substantially less than the initial one-bit sampling rate, commonly by a ratio of 256 : 1 [2]. The frequency range of the final digital data can be varied by one of the two procedures. The first is to lock the cutoff frequency of the digital filter to the initial one-bit sampling rate of the comparator so that the final sampling rate is controlled by simply varying the comparator sampling rate. The second is to fix the initial sampling rate of the comparator and then control the frequency limit and sampling rate of the final digital data be varying the cutoff frequency of the digital filter and the degree of decimation. In either case, this process of oversampling followed by low-pass digital filtering and decimation can be interpreted as increasing the effective resolution of the digital output by suppressing the spectral density of the digital noise in the output.

Some of the important general considerations associated with the use of an ADC may be summarized as follows:

1. *Format.* Many ADCs are integrated into more general signal processing equipment where the natural binary output of the converter is easily accepted. However, some ADCs operate as independent instruments. In this case, the output of the instrument is usually in the ASCII (American Standard Code Information Interchange) format, which allows the ADC output to be read directly by any computer program written in a common language, such as C or FORTRAN, or to drive terminal and register displays directly.
2. *Resolution.* The output of an ADC is a series of digital words, each composed of w bits, which determine the number of discrete levels that can be used to define the magnitude of the input analog signal at discrete times. Hence, there is a round-off error introduced by the conversion, as detailed in Section 10.2.4.
3. *Sampling Interval.* In most cases, an ADC samples the input analog signal with a fixed sampling interval Δt, as illustrated in Figure 10.4. However, there are sometimes situations where a variable sampling interval might be desired, for example, the sampling of an otherwise sinusoidal signal with a time-varying

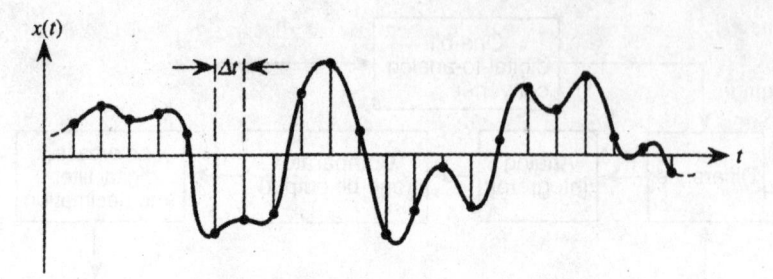

Figure 10.4 Sampling of analog signal.

frequency. To accommodate such situations, most ADCs allow the sampling rate to be varied continuously with time as desired.

4. *Sampling Rate.* At least two sample values per cycle are required to define the highest frequency in an analog signal. Hence, the sampling rate of the ADC, denoted by R_s, imposes an upper frequency limit on the digital data. More important, any frequency content in the analog signal above this upper frequency limit will fold back and sum with the digital data at frequencies below this limit to produce a serious error, called aliasing, to be discussed later.

10.2.2 Sampling Theorems for Random Records

Suppose a sample random time history record $x(t)$ from a random process $\{x_k(t)\}$ exists only for the time interval from 0 to T seconds and is zero at all other times. Its Fourier transform is

$$X(f) = \int_0^T x(t) e^{-j2\pi ft} dt \tag{10.4}$$

Assume that $x(t)$ is continually repeated to obtain a periodic time function with a period of T seconds. The fundamental frequency increments is $f = 1/T$. By a Fourier series expansion,

$$x(t) = \sum_{-\infty}^{\infty} A_n e^{j2\pi nt/T} \tag{10.5}$$

where

$$A_n = \frac{1}{T} \int_0^T x(t) e^{-j2\pi nt/T} dt \tag{10.6}$$

From Equation (10.4),

$$X\left(\frac{n}{T}\right) = \int_0^T x(t) e^{-j2\pi nt/T} dt = TA_n \tag{10.7}$$

DATA CONVERSION

Thus $X(n/T)$ determines A_n and, therefore, $x(t)$ at all t. In turn, this determines $X(f)$ for all f. This result is the *sampling theorem in the frequency domain*. The fundamental frequency increment $1/T$ is called a *Nyquist co-interval*.

Suppose that a Fourier transform $X(f)$ of some sample random time history record $x(t)$ exists only over a frequency interval from $-B$ to B Hz, and is zero at all other frequencies. The actual realizable frequency band ranges from 0 to B Hz. The inverse Fourier transform yields

$$x(t) = \int_{-B}^{B} X(f) e^{j2\pi ft} df \qquad (10.8)$$

Assume that $X(f)$ is continually repeated in frequency to obtain a periodic frequency function with a period of $2B$ Hz. The fundamental time increment is $t = 1/(2B)$. Now

$$X(f) = \sum_{-\infty}^{\infty} C_n e^{-j\pi nf/B} \qquad (10.9)$$

where

$$C_n = \frac{1}{2B} \int_{-B}^{B} X(f) e^{j\pi nf/B} df \qquad (10.10)$$

From Equation (10.8),

$$x\left(\frac{n}{2B}\right) = \int_{-B}^{B} X(f) e^{j\pi nf/B} df = 2BC_n \qquad (10.11)$$

Thus $x[n/(2B)]$ determines C_n and, hence, $X(f)$ at all f. In turn, this determines $x(t)$ for all t. Specifically, substituting Equations (10.9) and (10.10) into Equation (10.8) gives

$$\begin{aligned} x(t) &= \frac{1}{2B} \int_{-B}^{B} e^{j2\pi ft} \left[\sum_{-\infty}^{\infty} x[n/(2B)] e^{-j\pi nf/B} \right] df \\ &= \frac{1}{2B} \sum_{-\infty}^{\infty} x[n/(2B)] \int_{-B}^{B} e^{j2\pi f[t-n/(2B)]} df \qquad (10.12) \\ &= \sum_{-\infty}^{\infty} x[n/(2B)] \frac{\sin \pi (2Bt-n)}{\pi (2Bt-n)} \end{aligned}$$

which shows exactly how $x(t)$ should be reconstructed from the sample values taken $1/(2B)$ seconds apart. Note that at each sample point, $n/(2B)$, the function $x[n/(2B)]$ is multiplied by a $(\sin t)/t$ curve, which is centered at the sample point and is zero at all other sample points. This result is the *sampling theorem in the time domain*. The fundamental time increment $1/(2B)$ is called a *Nyquist interval*.

Now assume that the sample record $x(t)$ exists only for the time interval from 0 to T seconds and suppose also that its Fourier transform $X(f)$ exists only in a frequency interval from $-B$ to B Hz. This dual assumption is not theoretically possible because of an *uncertainty principle* (see Section 5.2.9). In practice, however, it may be closely approximated with finite time intervals and bandpass filters. Assuming $x(t)$ and $X(f)$ are so restricted in their time and frequency properties, only a finite number of discrete samples of $x(t)$ or $X(f)$ are required to describe $x(t)$ completely for all t. By sampling $X(f)$ at Nyquist co-interval points $1/T$ apart on the frequency scale from $-B$ to B, the number of discrete samples required to describe $x(t)$ is

$$N = \frac{2B}{1/T} = 2BT \qquad (10.13\text{a})$$

By sampling $x(t)$ at Nyquist interval points $1/2B$ apart on the timescale from 0 to T it follows that

$$N = \frac{T}{1/2B} = 2BT \qquad (10.13\text{b})$$

Thus, the same number of discrete samples are required when sampling the Nyquist co-intervals on the frequency scale, or when sampling the Nyquist intervals on the timescale.

10.2.3 Sampling Rates and Aliasing Errors

The sampling of analog signals for digital data analysis is usually performed at equally spaced time intervals, as shown in Figure 10.4. The problem then is to determine an appropriate sampling interval Δt. From Equation (10.13), the minimum number of discrete sample values required to describe a data record of length T and bandwidth B is $N = 2BT$. It follows that the maximum sampling interval for equally spaced samples is $\Delta t = 1/(2B)$. On the one hand, sampling at points that are more closely spaced than $1/(2B)$ will yield correlated and highly redundant sample values and, thus, unnecessarily increase later computations. On the other hand, sampling at points that are further apart than $1/(2B)$ will lead to confusion between the low- and high-frequency components in the original data. This latter problem is called *aliasing*. It constitutes a potential source of error that does not arise in direct analog data processing, but is inherent in all digital processing that is preceded by an analog-to-digital conversion. Those who have viewed a motion picture of the classic western vintage have undoubtedly observed the apparent reversal in the direction of rotation of the stage coach wheels as the coach slows down or speeds up. That observation is a simple illustration of an aliasing error caused by the analog-to-digital conversion operation performed by a motion picture camera.

To be more explicit on this matter of aliasing, consider a continuous analog record that is sampled such that the time interval between sample values is Δt seconds, as shown in Figure 10.4. The sampling rate is then $1/(\Delta t)$ sps. However, at least two samples per cycle are required to define a frequency component in the original data. This follows directly from the sampling theorems in Section 10.2.2. Hence, the highest frequency that can be defined by a sampling rate of $1/\Delta t$ sps is $1/(2\Delta t)$ Hz. Frequencies in the original data above $1/(2\Delta t)$ Hz will appear below $1/(2\Delta t)$ Hz and be

DATA CONVERSION 331

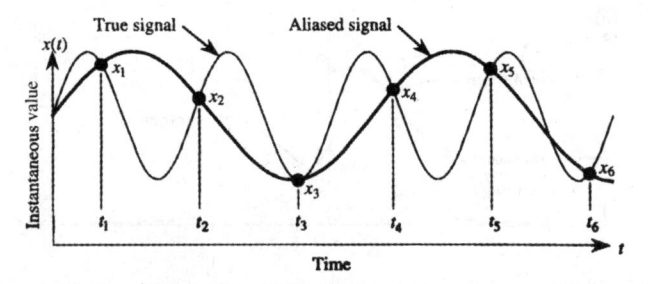

Figure 10.5 Frequency aliasing due to an inadequate digital sampling rate.

confused with the data in this lower frequency range, as illustrated in Figure 10.5. This aliasing frequency

$$f_A = \frac{1}{2\Delta t} \tag{10.14}$$

is called the *Nyquist frequency*, denoted by f_A. The folding of data frequencies into the frequency range from 0 to f_A occurs in an accordion-pleated fashion, as indicated in Figure 10.6. Specifically, for any frequency f in the range $0 \leq f \leq f_A$, the higher frequencies that are aliased with f are defined by

$$(2f_A \pm f), (4f_A \pm f), \ldots, (2nf_A \pm f), \ldots, \tag{10.15}$$

To prove this fact, observe that for $t = 1/(2f_A)$ we have

$$\cos 2\pi f t = \cos 2\pi (2nf_A \pm f)\frac{1}{2f_A} = \cos\left(2\pi n \pm \frac{\pi f}{f_A}\right) = \cos\frac{\pi f}{f_A} \quad n = 1, 2, 3, \ldots \tag{10.16}$$

Thus, all data at frequencies $2nf_A \pm f$ have the same cosine function as the data at frequency f when sampled at points $1/(2f_A)$ apart. For example, if $f_A = 100$ Hz, then data at $f = 30$ Hz would be aliased with the data at the frequencies 170, 230, 370, 430 Hz, and so forth. Similarly, the power at these higher confounding frequencies is aliased with the power in the lower frequencies. This occurs because for $t = 1/(2f_A)$,

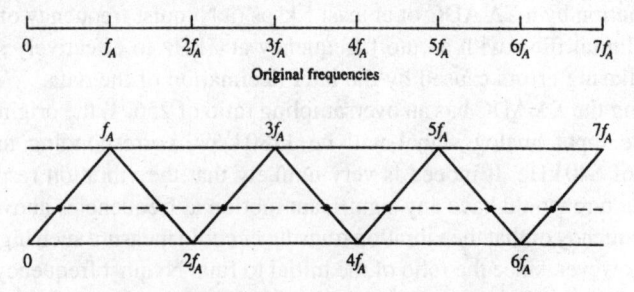

Figure 10.6 Folding about the Nyquist frequency.

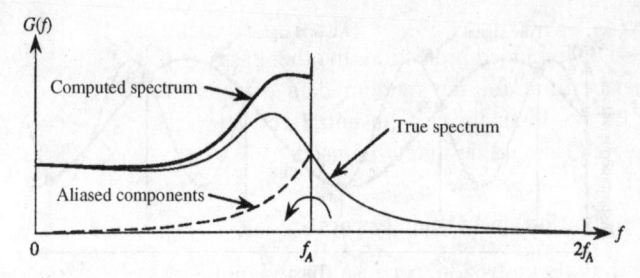

Figure 10.7 Illustration of aliasing error in the computation of an autospectral density function.

the power quantities $\sin^2(2\pi ft)$ and $\cos^2(2\pi ft)$ do not distinguish between a frequency f and the frequencies $2nf_A \pm f$; $n = 1,2,3,\ldots$ It follows that if a random signal has significant power at frequencies above the Nyquist frequency f_A, the true autospectral density function would be folded into an abased autospectral density function, as illustrated in Figure 10.7.

The only sure way to avoid aliasing errors in digital data analysis is to remove that information in the original analog data that might exist at frequencies above the Nyquist frequency f_A prior to the analog-to-digital conversion. This is done by restricting the frequency range of the original analog data with an analog low-pass filter prior to the analog-to-digital conversion. Such an analog filter on ADC equipment is commonly referred to as the *anti-aliasing filter*. Because no low-pass filter has an infinitely sharp rolloff, it is customary to set the anti-aliasing filter cutoff frequency, denoted by f_c, at 50–80% of f_A, depending on the rolloff rate of the filter. It should be emphasized that there is no way to recover meaningful information from digital data when an aliasing error occurs. Furthermore, an aliasing error is usually not apparent in digital data, meaning aliased data might be accepted as correct. Hence, it is recommended that anti-aliasing filters always be used before analog-to-digital conversion, even when it is believed there is no power in the data above the Nyquist frequency.

It should be mentioned that with the increasing use of very high sampling rate ADCs, such as the $\Sigma\Delta$ converter illustrated in Figure 10.3, it is often argued that an anti-aliasing filter on the original analog signal input to the ADC is not required. For example, assume that the vibration response of an aircraft structure during taketoff is to be analyzed to an upper frequency limit of 2 kHz. This requires a final sampling rate after decimation by a $\Sigma\Delta$ ADC of at least 5 ksps (a Nyquist frequency of 2.5 kHz) to allow the digital filter with a cutoff frequency at 2 kHz to effectively suppress the potential aliasing errors caused by the later decimation of the data.

Assuming the $\Sigma\Delta$ ADC has an oversampling ratio of 256:1, the original sampling rate for the input analog signal will be 1280 ksps, corresponding to a Nyquist frequency of 640 kHz. It indeed is very unlikely that the vibration response of the aircraft structure would have any significant motion at frequencies above this initial Nyquist frequency or that the vibration transducer could measure such high frequency motions. However, since the ratio of the initial to final Nyquist frequency is so large, any relatively simple low-pass filter (e.g., an RC filter) could be applied to the analog input to the ADC for added protection. In other cases, it may not be known what the upper frequency limit for the random data of interest and/or the measurement transducer may be. In such cases, an initial anti-aliasing filter on the input analog signal to the ADC should definitely be used.

10.2.4 Quantization and Other Errors

In analog-to-digital conversion, because the magnitude of each data value must be expressed by a binary word of finite size (a finite number of bits), only a finite set of levels are available for approximating the infinite number of values in the analog data. No matter how fine the scale, a choice between two consecutive levels separated by an interval Δx will be required, as illustrated in Figure 10.8. If the quantization is done properly, the true value at each sampling instant will be approximated by the quantized level closest to it. This results in a round-off error, referred to as the *quantization error*. To define this error, let $p(x)$ denote the probability density function of the error. For an ideal conversion, this probability density function will be uniform between the levels $x - 0.5\Delta x$ and $x + 0.5\Delta x$, that is

$$p(x) = \begin{cases} 1/\Delta x & -0.5\Delta x \leq x \leq 0.5\Delta x \\ 0 & \text{otherwise} \end{cases}$$

From Example 3.2, the mean value of the error is $\mu_x = 0$ and the variance is

$$\sigma_x^2 = \int_{-\infty}^{\infty} (x-\mu_x)^2 p(x) dx = \frac{1}{\Delta x} \int_{-0.5\Delta x}^{0.5\Delta x} x^2 dx = \frac{1}{12} \Delta x^2$$

Hence, the standard deviation of the error is given by

$$\sigma_x = \sqrt{\frac{1}{12}} \Delta x = 0.289 \Delta x \qquad (10.17)$$

The quantization error defined in Equation (10.17) can be interpreted as the digital noise floor of the ADC. A peak signal-to-noise ratio for the ADC can then be

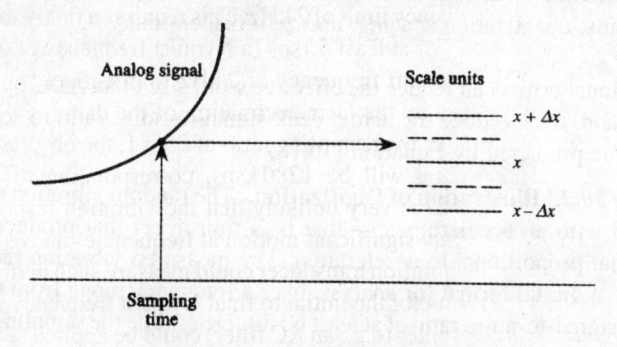

Figure 10.8 Illustration of quantization error.

determined using Equation (10.3). Specifically, for any binary system, the number of levels is 2^w, where w is the total word size (including a polarity bit). Letting the first level be zero and using one bit to define polarity, it follows that the maximum value, either positive or negative, that can be digitized by the ADC is $[2^{(w-1)} - 1]\Delta x$. Hence, using Equations (10.3) and (10.17), the peak signal-to-noise ratio is given by

$$PSNR = \{[2^{(w-1)} - 1]\Delta x\}^2 / (0.289\Delta x)^2 \approx 2^{2(w-1)}/(0.289)^2 = 12 \times 2^{2(w-1)} \tag{10.18a}$$

or in decibels by

$$(PS/N) = 10\log_{10}(PSNR) \approx 6(w-1) + 10.8 \text{ dB} \tag{10.18b}$$

For 8-, 12-, and 16-bit ADCs, the peak signal-to-noise ratios are $PS/N = 53$, 77, and 101 dB, respectively. To arrive at the available signal-to-noise ratio S/N, the PS/N in Equation (10.18b) should be reduced by the squared ratio of the peak to rms value of the signal in decibels, as discussed in Section 10.1.4.

In practice, if at least a 12-bit ADC is used, the quantization error is usually unimportant relative to other sources of error (noise) in the data acquisition and processing procedures. However, care must be exercised to ensure that the range of the continuous data is set to occupy as much of the available ADC range as possible. Otherwise, the resolution will be poor and the quantization error could become significant.

Beyond the potential sampling and quantization errors already discussed, other possible ADC errors of importance include the following:

1. *Aperture error*—arising from the fact that the data sample is taken over a finite period of time rather than instantaneously.
2. *Jitter*—arising from the fact that the time interval between samples can vary slightly in some random manner.
3. *Nonlinearities*—arising from many sources such as misalignment of parts, bit dropouts, quantization spacing, and zero discontinuity.

These additional errors can reduce the effective word size of an ADC by perhaps one or two bits and, thus, reduce the actual peak signal-to-noise ratio to somewhat less than the value predicted by Equation (10.18).

Example 10.2. Illustration of Digitization. The random vibration of a structure is measured with an accelerometer—that is, a transducer that produces an analog voltage signal proportional to acceleration. The measured vibration record is to be converted to a digital format for analysis over a frequency range from 0 to 2000 Hz with a peak signal-to-noise ratio of at least 60 dB, Determine the sampling rate and the word size required for the analog-to-digital conversion.

First, to obtain an accurate definition of the data up to 2000 Hz without aliasing, the data should be low-pass filtered with a cutoff frequency of $f_c = 2000$ Hz. Because the low-pass filter does not have an infinitely sharp rolloff, the Nyquist frequency should be set somewhat above 2000 Hz, say at $f_N = 2500$ Hz. Then from Equation (10.14), the required sampling interval is $\Delta t = 1/(2f_c) = 0.2$ ms, which gives a sampling rate of 5000 sps.

Second, to obtain a peak signal-to-noise ratio of 60 dB, it follows from Equation (10.18) that $w \geq 1 + (60 - 10.8)/6$, where w is the word size. Hence, $w = 10$ is the minimum word size required for the analog-to-digital conversion of the data. To allow for other errors that might reduce the effective word size, $w = 12$ would be recommended in this case.

10.2.5 Data Storage

For some applications, it is possible to perform all desired data analysis procedures directly on the measured data (conditioned transducer signals) in real time. For many applications, however, this may not be practical and some form of digital storage of the output of the analog-to-digital converter is required. For digital data that will be analyzed in the near future, the most common approaches are to input the data into the random access memory (RAM) or directly onto the hard disk (HD) of a digital computer. A direct input into RAM is generally the best approach if the number of data values is within the available RAM capacity. For those cases where the data analysis is to be performed at a later time, it is best to download the RAM into a HD, or record the data directly into a HD. The speed that a HD can accept data is steadily increasing with time, but is currently in excess of 40 MB/s. (for 16-bit sample values, 20 Msps). This is adequate to record the output of an ADC in real time for most digitized random signals. For long-term storage of digital data after the desired analyses have been performed, the data in RAM or HD can be downloaded into a removable storage medium such as a digital video disk (DVD) or a compact disk/read-only memory (CD/ROM).

10.3 DATA QUALIFICATION

Prior to detailed data analysis, it is important that all random data be qualified in three ways. First, those data with nonstationary characteristics, periodic components, and non-Gaussian properties should be identified because these various classifications of data may require different analysis procedures and/or interpretations from those appropriate for stationary Gaussian random data. Second, the data should be validated by a careful inspection of the data time history records for anomalies indicative of data acquisition errors. Third, if anomalies are identified during the validation, those data records should be edited to remove the identified anomalies when feasible. Of course, if the data are acquired and analyzed in real time, the recommended qualification steps may not be feasible. However, when data have been acquired and stored for later analysis, all data should be qualified prior to the data analysis, or as a preliminary step in the data analysis.

10.3.1 Data Classification

The correct procedures for analyzing random data, as well as interpreting the analyzed results, are strongly influenced by certain basic characteristics that may or may not be exhibited by the data. The three most important of these stationarity basic characteristics are (a) the stationary of the data, (b) the presence of periodic components in the data, and (c) the normality of the data. Stationarity is of concern because the analysis procedures for nonstationary and transient data (see Chapter 12) are generally more complicated than those that are appropriate for stationary data. Similarly, periodic data require different data analysis procedures and/or different interpretations than those appropriate for random data (see Refs 2–4). The validity of an assumption that the data (excluding periodicities) have a Gaussian probability density function should be investigated because the normality assumption is vital to many analytical applications for random data.

10.3.1.1 Test for Stationarity

Perhaps the simplest way to evaluate the stationary properties of sampled random data is to consider the physics of the phenomenon producing the data. If the basic physical factors that generate the phenomenon are time invariant, then stationarity of the resulting data generally can be accepted without further study. For example, consider the random data representing pressure fluctuations in the turbulent boundary layer generated by the flight of a high-speed aircraft. If the aircraft is flying at constant altitude and airspeed with a fixed configuration, it would be reasonable to assume that the resulting pressure data are stationary. On the other hand, if the aircraft is rapidly changing altitude, airspeed, and/or configuration, then nonstationarities in the resulting pressure data would be anticipated.

In practice, data are often collected under circumstances that do not permit an assumption of stationarity based on simple physical considerations. In such cases, the stationarity of the data must be evaluated by studies of available sample time history records. This evaluation might range from a visual inspection of the time histories by a talented analyst to detailed statistical tests of appropriate data parameters. In any case, there are certain important assumptions that must be made if the stationarity of data is to be ascertained from individual sample records. First, it must be assumed that any given sample record will properly reflect the nonstationary character of the random process in question. This is a reasonable assumption for those nonstationary random processes that involve deterministic trends, as discussed in Chapter 12. Second, it must be assumed that any given sample record is very long compared to the lowest frequency component in the data, excluding a nonstationary mean. In other words, the sample record must be long enough to permit nonstationary trends to be differentiated from the random fluctuations of the time history.

Beyond these basic assumptions, it is convenient (but not necessary) to assume further that any nonstationarity of interest will be revealed by time trends in the mean square value of the data. Of course, one can readily contrive a nonstationary random process with a stationary mean square value; for example, a process where each sample function is a constant amplitude oscillation with continuously increasing frequency and random initial phase. Nevertheless, such cases are unusual in practice because it is highly unlikely for nonstationary data to have a time-varying autocorrelation function at any time displacement τ without the value at $\tau=0$ varying. Because $R(0) = \psi^2$, the mean square value will usually reveal a time-varying autocorrelation. A similar argument applies to higher order properties.

With these assumptions in mind, the stationarity of random data can be tested by investigating a single time-history record $x(t)$ as follows:

1. Divide the sample record into N equal time intervals where the data in each interval may be considered independent.
2. Compute a mean square value (or mean value and variance separately) for each interval and align these sample values in time sequence as follows:

$$x_1^2, x_2^3, x_3^2, \ldots, x_N^2$$

3. Test the sequence of mean square values for the presence of underlying trends or variations other than those due to expected sampling variations.

The final test of the sample values for nonstationary trends may be accomplished in many ways. If the sampling distribution of the sample values is known, various statistical tests discussed in Chapter 4 could be applied. However, as noted in Section 8.2.2, the sampling distribution of mean square value estimates requires a knowledge of the frequency composition of the data. Such information is generally not available at the time one wishes to establish whether or not the data are stationary. Hence, a nonparametric approach that does not require a knowledge of the sampling distributions of the data parameters is more desirable. One such nonparametric test that is applicable to this problem is the reverse arrangements test outlined in Section 4.5.2. The *reverse arrangements test* may be directly applied as a test for stationarity as follows.

Let it be hypothesized that the sequence of sample mean square values $(x_1^2, x_2^2, x_3^2, \ldots, x_N^2)$ represents independent sample measurements of a stationary random variable with a mean square value of ψ_x^2. If this hypothesis is true, the variations in the sequence of sample values will be random and display no trends. Hence, the number of reverse arrangements will be as expected for a sequence of independent random observations of the random variable, as given by Equation (4.54). If the number of reverse arrangements is significantly different from this number, the hypothesis of stationarity would be rejected. Otherwise, the hypothesis would be accepted. Note that the above testing procedure does not require a knowledge of either the frequency bandwidth of the data or the averaging time used to compute the sample mean square values. Nor is it limited to a sequence of mean square values. It will work equally well on mean values, rms values, standard deviations, mean absolute values, or any other parameter estimate. Furthermore, it is not necessary for the data under investigation to be free of periodicities. Valid conclusions are obtained, even when periodicities are present, as long as the fundamental period is short compared to the averaging time used to compute sample values.

Example 10.3. **Test for Stationarity.** To illustrate the application of the reverse arrangement test as a test for stationarity, consider the sequence of 20 mean square value measurements plotted in Figure 10.9. The measurements were made on the output of an analog random noise generator as the gain level was slowly increased by about 20% during the measurement sequence. From Section 4.5.2, the number of reverse arrangements in the sequence are found to be as follows:

$$\begin{array}{llll} A_1 = 7 & A_6 = 4 & A_{11} = 7 & A_{16} = 0 \\ A_2 = 2 & A_7 = 0 & A_{12} = 6 & A_{17} = 2 \\ A_3 = 6 & A_8 = 8 & A_{13} = 3 & A_{18} = 0 \\ A_4 = 2 & A_9 = 0 & A_{14} = 0 & A_{19} = 1 \\ A_5 = 0 & A_{10} = 2 & A_{15} = 2 & \end{array}$$

The total number of reverse arrangements is then $A = 52$.

Now let it be hypothesized that the data are stationary. From Table A.6, this hypothesis would be accepted at the $\alpha = 0.05$ level of significance if the sequence of $N = 20$ measurements produced between $A_{20;0.975} = 64$ and $A_{20;0.025} = 125$ reverse arrangements. Since the sequence actually produced only $A = 52$ reverse arrangements, the hypothesis of stationarity is rejected at the 5% level of significance, meaning the data are correctly identified as being nonstationary. This concludes Example 10.3.

An assumption of stationarity can often be supported (or rejected) by a simple nonparametric test of sample mean square values (or related sample parameters) computed from the available data. However, if one is not prepared to accept time invariance of mean square values as sufficient evidence of time invariance of autocorrelation functions, then tests can still be performed by further segmenting of the data in the frequency domain. Specifically, the data can be segmented into several contiguous frequency ranges by bandpass filtering, and the sample mean square values in each frequency interval can then be individually tested for time invariance. Since spectral density functions and correlation functions are Fourier transform pairs, time invariance of one directly implies time invariance of the other.

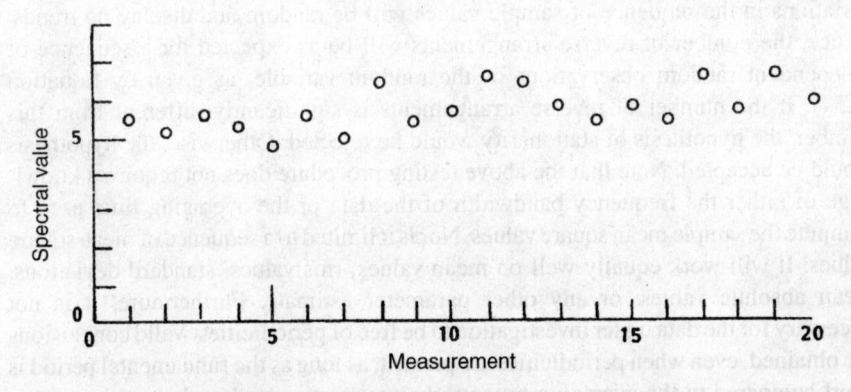

Figure 10.9 Sequence of mean square value measurements.

DATA QUALIFICATION

10.3.1.2 Test for Periodicities

Periodic and/or almost periodic components in otherwise random data will theoretically appear as delta functions in the autospectrum of the data. In practice, they will appear as sharp peaks in the autospectrum that might be confused with narrow bandwidth random contributions. Hence, it is desirable to identify the presence of periodic components so they will not be misinterpreted as narrow bandwidth random components with finite autospectral densities. If periodic components in the data are intense, their presence is usually obvious. However, less intense periodic components in random data may not be so obvious. The most effective procedures for detecting periodic components are those associated with the various analysis procedures that would be employed for random data analysis anyway. Hence, in practical terms, a test for periodicities usually evolves from analysis procedures that would be performed assuming the data are random. Specifically, the presence of periodic components in otherwise random data may often be detected by visual inspection of an amplitude probability density function, an autocorrelation function, and/or an autospectral density function measured from stationary data as illustrated in Figures 1.12–1.14. The autospectrum is the most commonly used analysis parameter for this application.

To be more specific, a highly resolved autospectral density estimate will reveal periodic components as sharp peaks, even when the periodicities are of relatively small intensity. A sharp peak in the autospectrum of sample data, however, may also represent narrow bandwidth random data. These two cases can usually be distinguished from one another by repeating the autospectral density analysis with a narrower resolution bandwidth. If the measured spectral peak represents a sine wave, the indicated bandwidth of the peak will always be equal to the resolution bandwidth of the analysis, no matter how narrow the bandwidth. Furthermore, the indicated spectral density will always increase in direct proportion to the reduction in the resolution bandwidth. This method of detection will clearly not work unless the resolution bandwidth of the analysis is smaller than the actual bandwidth of possible narrow bandwidth random data.

Example 10.4. **Autospectrum of Sine Wave in Noise.** To illustrate how an autospectrum can reveal the presence of a periodic component in otherwise random data, refer to Figure 10.10. In this example, the output of a Gaussian random number generator with a bandwidth of 400 Hz is mixed with a sinusoidal signal with a frequency of 200 Hz. The mean square value of the sine wave is one-twentieth that of the random signal. Figure 10.10(a), which shows the autospectrum computed with a relatively wide resolution bandwidth of $B_e = 50$ Hz, gives little or no indication of the presence of the sine wave. Figure 10.10(b), which was computed using one-fifth the previous resolution bandwidth, indicates a possible sine wave quite clearly. Figure 10.10(c), which was computed with a resolution bandwidth reduced by another factor of 5, gives a strong indication of the sine wave.

10.3.1.3 Test for Normality

Perhaps the most obvious way to test samples of stationary random data for normality is to measure the probability density function of the data and compare it with the theoretical normal distribution. If the same record is sufficiently long to permit a

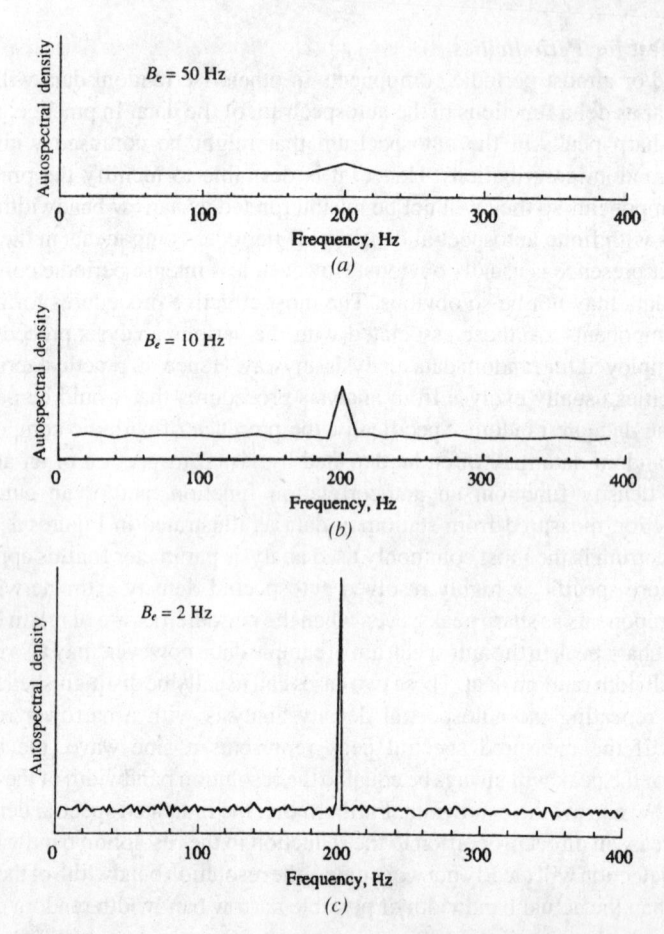

Figure 10.10 Measured autospectra of a sine wave in random noise.

measurement with small error compared to the deviations from normality, the lack of normality will be obvious. If the sampling distribution of the probability density estimate is known, various statistical tests for normality can be performed even when the random error is large. However, as for stationarity testing discussed earlier, a knowledge of the sampling distribution of a probability density computation requires frequency information for the data that may be difficult to obtain in practical cases. Hence a nonparametric test is desirable. One of the most convenient nonparametric tests for normality is the chi-square goodness-of-fit test outlined in Section 4.5.1. The details of applying the chi-square goodness-of-fit test with a numerical illustration are presented in Example 4.3.

10.3.2 Data Validation

Every reasonable effort should be made to design a data acquisition system that will provide valid data, as detailed in Refs 2–4. Unfortunately, random data are sometimes

DATA QUALIFICATION

acquired with faults introduced by the data acquisition system, and then they are analyzed and interpreted as if they were valid. Such errors can be dramatically suppressed if the acquired data are validated by a careful inspection for anomalies before the data analysis is performed. As for the data classification procedures discussed in Section 10.3.1, a detailed validation of data is not feasible when the data are acquired and analyzed in real time. However, when data are stored for later analysis, all data signals should be validated prior to data analysis.

Random data validation procedures can range from purely subjective techniques to sophisticated techniques using specialized computer programs. As an example of a subjective technique, experienced technicians and engineers can often detect subtle anomalies in random acoustic and/or vibration data in the audio frequency range by simply listening to the output of the data acquisition transducers with a headset; the human hearing system is a marvelous pattern recognition device for data in the audio frequency range. At the other extreme, knowledge-based digital data acquisition systems have been developed that detect anomalies in specific types of random data by automated procedures. In many cases, however, anomalies due to common data acquisition errors can be detected by a simple visual inspection of measured time history records, sometimes augmented by certain preliminary data analysis operations. From Ref 3, the most commonly occurring random data anomalies that can be detected in this manner are

a. Excessive instrumentation noise
b. Signal clipping
c. Intermittent noise spikes
d. Temporary signal dropouts
e. Power line pickup
f. Spurious trends

10.3.2.1 Excessive Instrumentation Noise

Excessive instrumentation noise occurs when the input sensitivity (gain) of one or more instruments in the data acquisition system is set too low, causing the measured data signals to have values that are not substantially greater than the noise floor of the data acquisition system; that is, the measurements are made with an inadequate signal-to-noise ratio, as discussed in Section 10.1.4. Because instrumentation noise (excluding power line pickup) is generally random in character with a wide bandwidth, it is often difficult to distinguish from the actual random data being acquired. Hence, the only sure way to correctly identify excessive instrumentation noise is to measure the noise floor of the data acquisition system. This might be done as part of the calibration procedure, as suggested in Section 10.1.3, but can also be done by preceding and/or following all data measurements with a quiescent noise measurement—that is, a measurement made by the data acquisition system with all sensitivities (instrument gains) set as they will be for the actual measurements—but before and/or after the physical phenomenon to be measured is applied.

Excessive instrumentation noise exaggerates the mean square value of the data and obscures the lower values of a computed autospectral density function. At the extreme, the instrumentation noise may dominate the measurement and cause the autospectrum of the data to appear to be near-white noise, as illustrated theoretically in Table 5.2.

10.3.2.2 Signal Clipping

Signal clipping occurs when the input sensitivity (gain) of an instrument in the data acquisition system (usually an amplifier or storage device) is set too high, causing the instrument to saturate (exceed its linear range) and produce an output time history record with a limited range of magnitudes. Clipping may limit either one or both sides of the data values, depending on the mean value of the data. An example of mild two-sided clipping of a random time history record with a zero mean value is shown in Figure 10.11(b), where the unclipped data record is shown in Figure 10.11(a). Even small amounts of clipping in measured random data can often be detected by an experienced analyst through a simple visual inspection of a time history record, although a stronger detection may be achieved by computing the probability density function of the measured data. Clipping will appear as small peaks on one or both tails of the probability density function at the clipping level, as illustrated for two-sided clipping in Figure 10.12(b), where the probability density function for the unclipped signal is shown in Figure 10.12(a).

Experience suggests that clipping at a level above ± 3 standard deviations of a Gaussian random signal has a negligible impact on the mean square value, autocorrelation function, and autospectral density function of the data. However, severe clipping at a level below ± 1.5 standard deviations significantly reduces the indicated mean square value and exaggerates the indicated autospectrum values of the data at the higher frequencies.

10.3.2.3 Intermittent Noise Spikes

Sometimes during the acquisition of random data, particularly dynamic load data where there is relative motion of the transducer cables, intermittent noise spikes ooeur. This problem is usually caused by a defective cable connector at the transducer or signal conditioner, which either open circuits or short circuits when the cable is moved. Intermittent noise spikes also sometimes appear in data transmitted by RF telemetry when the data signal level is too low at the receiver [3]. An example of intermittent noise spikes in a random data time history record is shown in Figure 10.11(c), where the data record without noise spikes is shown in Figure 10.11(a). As for clipping, an experienced analyst can often detect intermittent noise spikes by a visual inspection of a measured time history record, but the problem is even more apparent in a probability density plot. Specifically, assuming the random data being acquired are approximately Gaussian, intermittent noise spikes will cause the tails of the probability density function to become too thick. This is illustrated in Figure 10.12(c), where the probability density function for the noise-free data record is shown in Figure 10.12(a).

Because an intermittent noise spike approximates a delta function, and the Fourier transform of a delta function is white noise, it follows that intermittent noise spikes

DATA QUALIFICATION 343

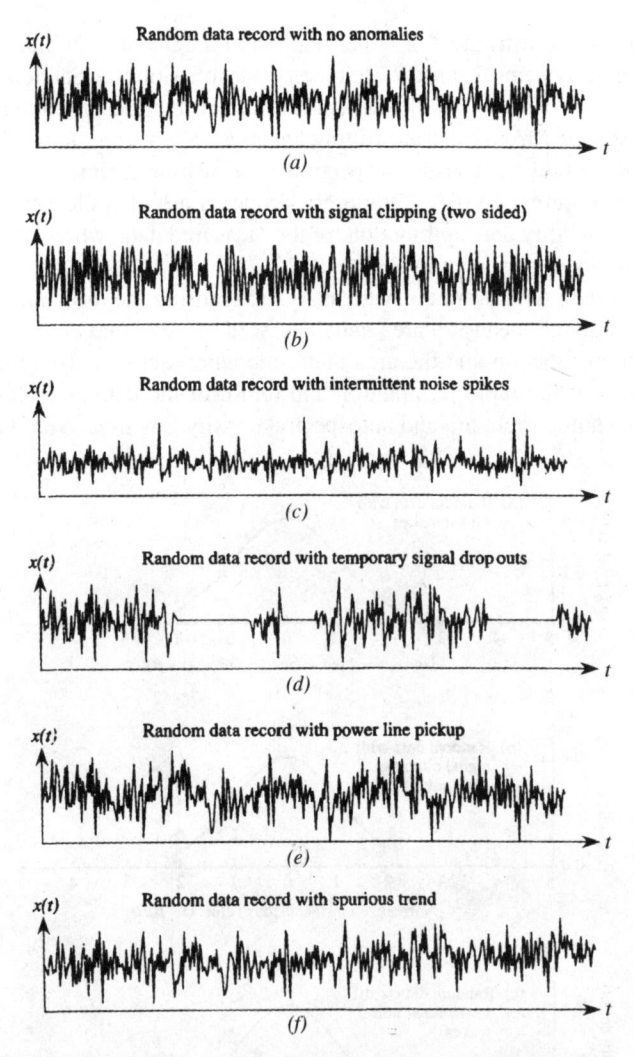

Figure 10.11 Examples of random data with anomalies.

will tend to flatten the autospectrum of the data. At the extreme, the intermittent noise spikes may dominate the measurement and, like excessive instrumentation noise, cause the autospectrum of the data to appear to be near-white noise.

10.3.2.4 Temporary Dropouts
Sometimes the output signal from a data acquisition system will diminish rapidly into the instrumentation noise floor for no apparent reason, and it may or may not return later in the measurement. Permanent dropouts usually indicate a major malfunction of the transducer or some other instrument in the data acquisition system, while temporary dropouts might occur because of a momentary saturation of a data

acquisition system instrument or a malfunction of a transmission link. In particular, data acquisition systems that use RF telemetry transmission (see Section 10.1.2) often reveal temporary dropouts on those occasions when the receiver antenna becomes physically shielded from the transmitting antenna. In any case, temporary dropouts are easily identified by a visual inspection of a measured time history record, as illustrated in Figure 10.11(*d*). Temporary dropouts are also clearly apparent in a computed probability density function for the measured data, where they appear as a spike at zero level, as shown in Figure 10.12(*d*).

If random data with dropouts were analyzed ignoring the dropouts, it is obvious that the computed mean square value, as well as the maximum value of the autocorrelation function and the area under the autospectrum, would be too small. Also, because of the rapid termination and return of the data at each dropout, the shapes of the autocorrelation and autospectral density functions would be distorted.

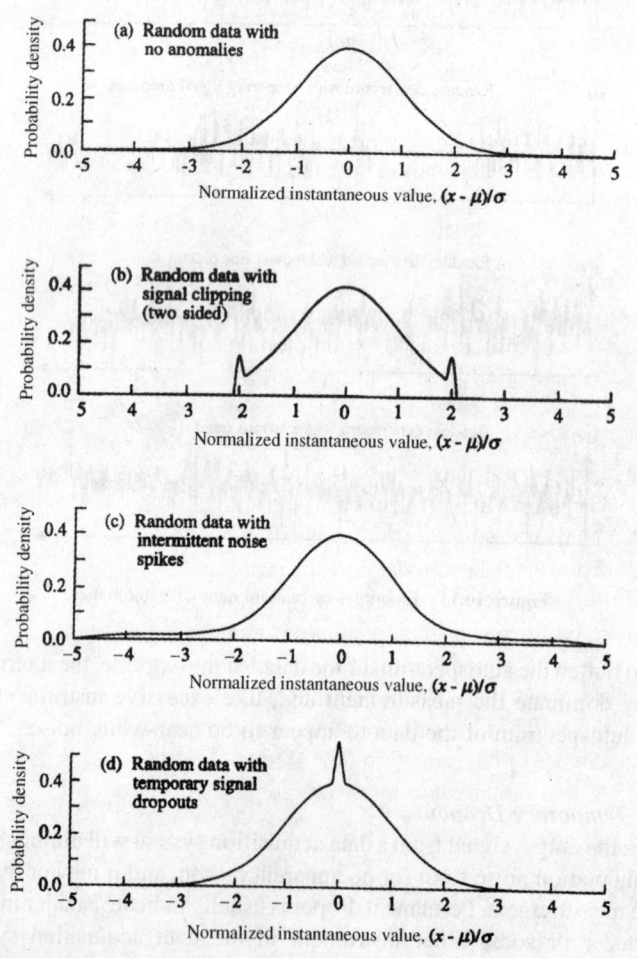

Figure 10.12 Probability density functions of random data with anomalies.

DATA QUALIFICATION

10.3.2.5 Power Line Pickup

All advanced countries have extensive ac electric power distribution systems that radiate substantial electromagnetic energy at the power-line frequency (60 Hz in the United States, but 50 Hz in many other regions of the world). This power line generated energy is commonly picked up by data acquisition systems that are improperly shielded or are grounded at two or more physical locations with a slight potential difference so as to cause a current to flow through the shield (commonly referred to as a *ground loop*). Such power line pickup appears in measured random data as a sine wave at the power line frequency. In extreme cases, power line pickup may saturate one or more instruments in the data acquisition system and produce signal contamination at the power line frequency and many of its harmonics. If sufficient in magnitude, an experienced analyst can often detect power line pickup in random data by a visual inspection of a measured time history record, as illustrated in Figure 10.11(*e*), where an uncontaminated record is shown in Figure 10.11(*a*). However, the most powerful way to detect power line pickup is through the computation of an autospectrum with a narrow bandwidth resolution, as previously demonstrated in Example 10.4.

Unless the power line pickup is sufficiently extreme to saturate one or more instruments in the data acquisition system, its only effect is to introduce a sine wave component into the data at the power line frequency and perhaps some harmonics thereof. Hence, it usually does not distort the desired information in the measured random data at all other frequencies.

10.3.2.6 Spurious Trends

A spurious trend (a time-varying mean value) may occur in a data acquisition system for any one of several reasons, the most common being temperature-induced drift in one or more instruments or an integration operation, which often produces a low-frequency trend due to the integration of low-frequency noise. Such spurious trends usually appear in a random time history record as illustrated in Figure 10.11(*f*), where the untrended record is shown in Figure 10.11(*a*). Assuming it is known that the mean value of the data is zero, or at least a constant, spurious trends can often be detected by an experienced analyst through a simple visual inspection of a time history record. However, a more powerful detection procedure is provided by a statistical trend test on a sequence of short time-averaged mean value computations, as discussed in Section 4.5.2 and illustrated for mean square value measurements in Example 10.4.

Spurious trends tend to exaggerate the values of a computed autospectrum at those frequencies below about $10/T_r$, where T_r is the total length of the acquired data record. In many cases, this will be below the frequency range of interest in the data. However, spurious trends also distort the autocorrelation and probability density functions of the data in a manner that might cause a misinterpretation of the results.

10.3.3 Data Editing

Conventional wisdom suggests that all random data measurements that reveal anomalies during the data validation process discussed in Section 10.3.2 should be discarded, or at least the results of any analysis of such data should be viewed as highly suspect. However, in those cases where repeating the experiment to acquire new data is costly or perhaps not even possible, an effort to correct the data for detected anomalies may be warranted. Specifically, there are editing operations that sometimes can be applied to the measured data in digital form that will allow the recovery of at least some acceptably reliable information from the data analysis. From Ref. 3, possible editing operations to recover useful information from measured random data with one or more of the six anomalies discussed in Section 10.3.2 are now outlined. It should be emphasized that most of these editing operations involve assumptions about the basic characteristics of the data. If any of the noted assumptions are invalid, the editing operation may still produce data that could lead to misleading data analysis results. Also, as for the data classification and validation operations discussed in Sections 10.3.1 and 10.3.2, these editing procedures may be integrated as a preliminary step in the final data analysis. Finally, if editing operations are performed on any data, this fact should be noted on all plotted or tabulated data analysis results, and a report detailing the exact editing operations performed should be attached to the analysis results.

10.3.3.1 Excessive Instrumentation Noise

If the noise floor of the data acquisition system is measured during calibration, as suggested in Section 10.1.3, or a quiescent noise measurement is made before or after the actual measurement of the data, as discussed in Section 10.3.2, then the autospectrum computed from the measured random data can be corrected for excessive instrumentation noise by the following procedure:

1. Compute the autospectrum of the measured quiescent noise, $\hat{G}_{nn}(f)$, as well as the autospectrum of the measured data, $\hat{G}_{yy}(f)$.
2. Assuming the actual random data are statistically independent of the data acquisition system noise, the autospectrum of the actual random data, $G_{xx}(f)$ can be estimated by computing $\hat{G}_{xx}(f) = \hat{G}_{yy}(f) - \hat{G}_{nn}(f)$.
3. The mean square value of the actual data can be estimated from the area under the computed $\hat{G}_{xx}(f)$, and if desired, the autocorrelation function of the actual data can be estimated from the inverse Fourier transform of $\hat{G}_{xx}(f)$, as detailed in Section 11.4.2.

As the magnitude of the instrumentation noise increases relative to the magnitude of the actual random data, the estimate for the autospectrum becomes a difference between two large numbers with the associated inaccuracies. As a rule of thumb, $\hat{G}_{yy}(f) > 2\hat{G}_{nn}(f)$ will provide acceptable results.

10.3.3.2 Signal Clipping

As noted in Section 10.3.2, although modest amounts of clipping of measured random data can often be tolerable, severe clipping (i.e., at a level within ±1.5 standard deviations of the mean value of the data) will in most cases seriously distort the mean square value, autocorrelation function, and autospectral density function computed from those data. There is one special case, however, where useful autocorrelation and autospectrum results can be extracted from even the most severely clipped data. Specifically, if it can be assumed that the undistorted data being measured have a Gaussian probability density function, then the hard-clipping procedure detailed in Section 12.5.3 for the analysis of a certain class of nonstationary random data applies to clipped random data as well. However, this nonlinear procedure does not recover the correct mean square value of the data. Instead, the analyzed results will always have a mean square value of unity; hence, the computed autocorrelation function at zero time delay, as well as the area under the computed autospectrum, will also be unity.

10.3.3.3 Intermittent Noise Spikes

Intermittent noise spikes in digitized random data can easily be removed by an interpolation procedure as follows:

1. Remove all digital time history values defining each noise spike. The number of digital values N_s defining each noise spike will be a function of the sampling rate R_s (in samples/second) and the upper cutoff frequency of the data acquisition system, which is usually the cutoff frequency f_c of the anti-aliasing filters. As a rule of thumb, $N_s \approx R_s/(2f_c)$.
2. Replace the removed values for each spike with new values determined by an appropriate interpolation between the last value before and the first value after the noise spike. In most cases, a linear interpolation will suffice, particularly if oversampling procedures are used (see Section 10.3.3), because the final digital low-pass filtering and decimation prior to analysis will further smooth the interpolation.

For those cases where the data have a substantial frequency content up to the cutoff frequency f_c, it may be difficult to distinguish between a noise spike and a natural peak in the random data. A common rule of thumb to make this distinction is to assume that if any peak in the time history record has (a) approximately the number of data values given in Step 1 above and (b) a magnitude in excess of three standard deviations from the mean value of the data, then that peak should be considered a spurious noise spike.

10.3.3.4 Temporary Signal Dropouts

At first glance, it would seem reasonable that measured random data with temporary dropouts could be edited by simply removing the dropout regions from the time history record. This approach is often acceptable for those cases where the dropouts are known to be due to intermittent shielding between the transmitting and receiving antennas in an RF telemetry transmission link. Even in this case, however, if a continuous data record is reconstructed by splicing together the data segments with the dropout portions removed, a smooth interpolation must be made between the data values at the end of each segment and the beginning of the next segment to avoid introducing spurious high-frequency spectral components. For dropouts caused by other data acquisition problems, all the data must be considered suspect unless the exact source of the dropouts can be established and determined to have no significant influence on the other portions of the data.

10.3.3.5 Power Line Pickup

Assuming power line pickup is not sufficiently severe to saturate any of the data acquisition system instruments, it may be removed from digital time history records by the following procedure:

1. Compute the discrete Fourier transform of the time history record using the procedures detailed in Section 11.2. If the ultimate goal of the later data analysis is the computation of correlation and/or spectral density functions, this operation should be incorporated into the data analysis, and the Fourier transforms should be computed on the individual blocks of data used for the correlation and/or spectral computations, as detailed in Chapter 11.
2. Remove the digital spectral values defining a peak at the power-line frequency and at all multiples of the power-line frequency where a peak in the Fourier transform is apparent.
3. Replace the removed spectral values at the power-line frequency and its harmonics with appropriately interpolated values. In most cases, a linear interpolation will suffice.
4. If this editing operation is incorporated into the computation of correlation and/or spectral density functions, proceed with the correlation or spectral computations as detailed in Chapter 11. If an edited time history record of the data is desired, inverse Fourier transform the edited Fourier transform using the procedures in Section 11.2.5.

10.3.3.6 Spurious Trends

If the validation procedures detailed in Section 10.3.2 identify a spurious trend in measured random data, that spurious trend should be removed from the data by one of two procedures as follows:

1. If it is desired to retain all information in the measured random data down to the minimum frequency of $f_1 = 1/T_r$, where T_r is total record length, then the best way to remove a spurious trend is by the regression analysis procedure detailed in Section 11.1.2.
2. If it is acceptable to lose the information in the measured random data at frequencies below about $f_2 \approx 10/T_r$, then a spurious trend can be removed by a high-pass digital filtering operation, as outlined in Section 11.1.3, This approach is most appropriate when the goal of the final data analysis is the computation of spectral density functions, because the creation of data blocks for ensemble-averaged spectral computations, as described in Section 11.5.1, generally introduces a low-frequency limit into the computed spectrum that is much higher than the frequency f_2 defined above.

10.4 DATA ANALYSIS PROCEDURES

The procedures for analyzing the properties of random data may be divided logically into two categories: the procedure for analyzing individual sample records and the procedure for analyzing multiple sample records given the properties of the individual records. Applicable data analysis procedures for these two categories are now outlined.

10.4.1 Procedure for Analyzing Individual Records

An overall procedure for analyzing the pertinent statistical properties of individual sample time history records is presented in Figure 10.13. Note that many of the suggested steps in the procedure might be omitted for some applications, while additional steps would be required for other applications. Further note that the data qualification steps discussed in Section 10.3 are incorporated into the procedure to help clarify how these two parts of the overall data processing problem interact. Each block in Figure 10.13 will now be discussed.

10.4.1.1 Mean and Mean Square Value Analysis

The first step indicated by Block A is a mean and mean square value (or variance) computation. This step is almost universally performed for one or both of two valid

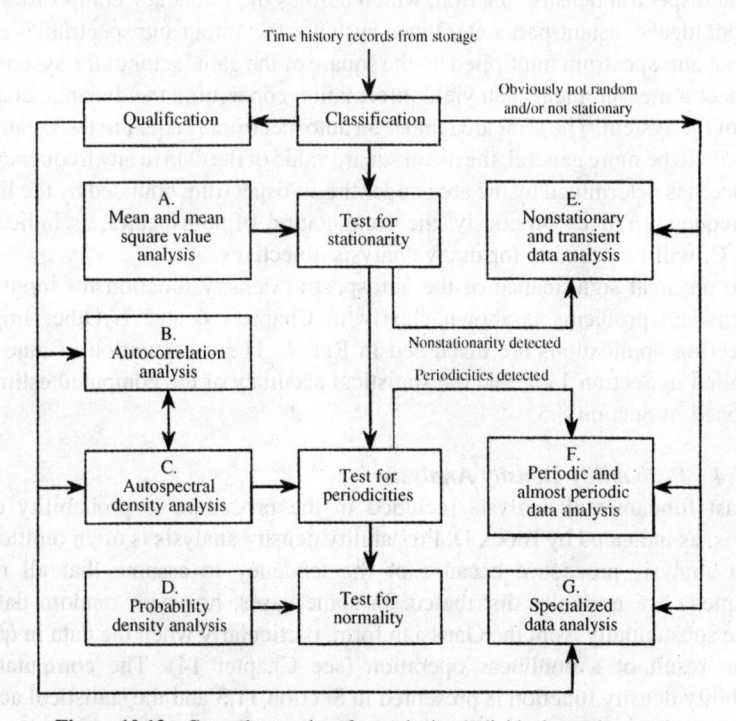

Figure 10.13 General procedure for analyzing individual sample records.

reasons. First, because the mean and mean square values are the basic measures of central tendency and dispersion, their calculation is generally required for even the most rudimentary applications. Second, the computation of short time-averaged mean and mean square value estimates provides a basis for evaluating the stationarity of the data, as indicated in Figure 10.13 and illustrated in Section 10.3.1. The computation of mean and mean square values is discussed in Section 11.1. The statistical accuracy of mean and mean square value estimates is developed in Section 8.2.

10.4.1.2 Autocorrelation Analysis

The autocorrelation function of stationary data is the inverse Fourier transform of the autospectral density function and thus produces no new information over the autospectrum. Because the autospectrum can be computed more efficiently and is generally easier to interpret for most applications, autocorrelation functions are often omitted. There may be special situations, however, where an autocorrelation estimate is desired. In such cases, the autocorrelation function is usually computed from a spectral density estimate, as detailed in Section 11.4.2. The statistical accuracy of autocorrelation estimates is discussed in Section 8.4. Engineering applications of correlation functions are discussed in Ref. 1.

10.4.1.3 Autospectral Density Analysis

Perhaps the most important single descriptive characteristic of stationary random data is the autospectral density function, which defines the frequency composition of the data. For ideal constant-parameter linear systems, the output autospectrum is equal to the input autospectrum multiplied by the square of the gain factor of the system. Thus autospectra measurements can yield information concerning the dynamic characteristics of the system. The total area under an autospectrum is equal to the mean square value ψ^2. To be more general, the mean square value of the data in any frequency range of concern is determined by the area under the autospectrum bounded by the limits of that frequency range. Obviously, the computation of autospectra, as indicated by Block C, will be valuable for many analysis objectives.

The physical significance of the autospectral density function for input/output random data problems is shown clearly in Chapters 6 and 7. Other important engineering applications are discussed in Ref. 1. The computation of autospectra is detailed in Section 11.5, and the statistical accuracy of the computed estimates is developed in Section 8.5.

10.4.1.4 Probability Density Analysis

The last fundamental analysis included in the procedure is probability density analysis, as indicated by Block D. Probability density analysis is often omitted from a data analysis procedure because of the tendency to assume that all random phenomena are normally distributed. In some cases, however, random data may deviate substantially from the Gaussian form, particularly when the data in question are the result of a nonlinear operation (see Chapter 14). The computation of probability density function is presented in Section 11.3 and the statistical accuracy of the computed estimates is discussed in Section 8.3.

10.4.1.5 Nonstationary and Transient Data Analysis

All of the analysis techniques discussed thus far apply only to sample records of stationary data. If the data are determined to be nonstationary during the qualification phase of the processing, then special analysis techniques will be required as indicated by Block E. The analysis of nonstationary and transient data is discussed in Chapter 12. Note that certain classes of nonstationary data can sometimes be analyzed using the same equipment or computer programs as employed for stationary data analysis. However, the results of such analyses must be interpreted with caution as illustrated in Chapter 12.

10.4.1.6 Periodic and Almost-Periodic Data Analysis

If sinusoidal components due to periodic or almost-periodic contributions are detected in the data during the classification phase discussed in Section 10.3.1, then analysis procedures appropriate for such data should be employed. The primary analysis procedure for periodic and almost-periodic data is the computation of Fourier series components (sometimes called a linear or line spectrum) using the techniques detailed in Section 11.2. More extensive analysis procedures for periodic and almost-periodic data are presented in Ref. 3.

10.4.1.7 Specialized Data Analysis

Various other analyses of individual time history records are often required, depending on the specific goals of the data processing. For example, studies of fatigue damage in mechanical systems may involve the calculation of peak probability density functions of strain data, as discussed in Section 5.5 and Ref. 5. An investigation of zero crossings or arbitrary level crossings might be warranted for certain communication noise problems, as detailed in Section 5.5.1. The computation of Hilbert transforms may be desired for special problems discussed in Chapter 13. Such specialized analyses, as indicated by Block G, must be established in the context of the engineering problem of concern.

10.4.2 Procedure for Analyzing Multiple Records

The preceding section presented methods for analyzing each individual sample record from an experiment. A procedure for analyzing further pertinent statistical properties of multiple sample records is presented in Figure 10.14. As for the analysis of individual sample records outlined in Figure 10.13, many of the suggested steps in Figure 10.14 might be omitted for some applications while additional steps would be required for others. Furthermore, the suggested steps assume the individual records are stationary. Each block in Figure 10.14 will now be discussed.

10.4.2.1 Analysis of Individual Records

This first step in the procedure is to analyze the pertinent statistical properties of the individual sample records, as outlined in Figure 10.13. Hence the applicable portions of Figure 10.13 constitute Block A in Figure 10.14.

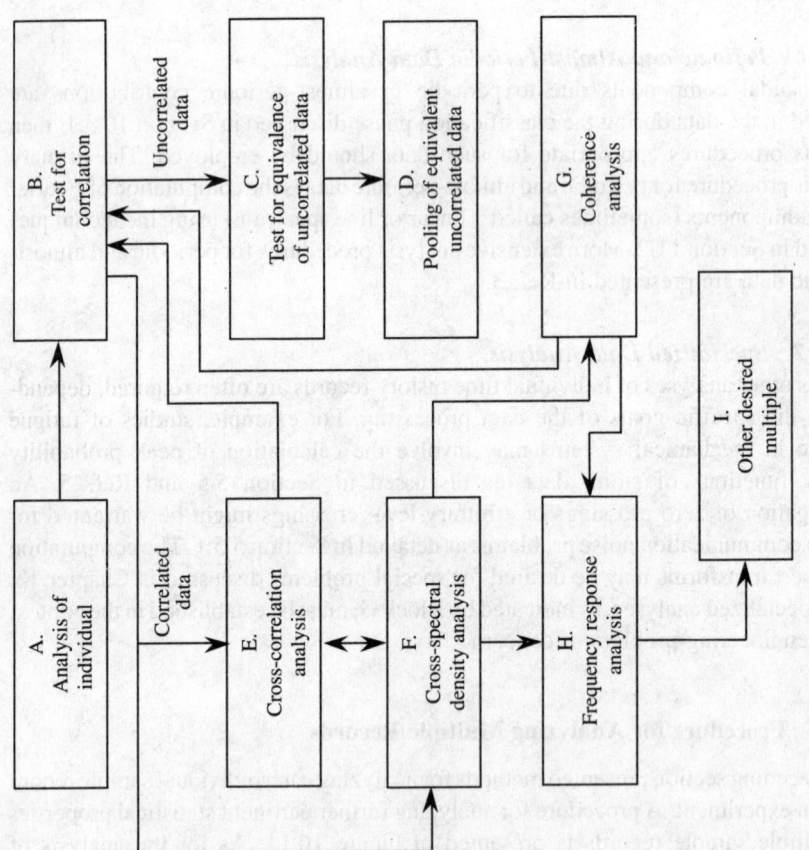

Figure 10.14 General procedure for analyzing multiple sample records.

DATA ANALYSIS PROCEDURES   **353**

10.4.2.2 Test for Correlation

The next step indicated by Block B is to determine whether or not the individual sample records are correlated. In many cases, this decision involves little more than a cursory evaluation of pertinent physical considerations. For example, if the collection of sample records represents measurements of a physical phenomenon over widely separated time intervals, then usually the individual records can be accepted as uncorrelated without further study. On the other hand, if the collection represents simultaneous measurements of the excitation and response of a physical system, then correlation would be anticipated. For those cases where a lack of correlation is not obvious from basic considerations, a test for correlation among the sample records should be performed using cross-correlation functions or coherence functions, as indicated in Figure 10.14.

10.4.2.3 Test for Equivalence of Uncorrelated Data

It sample records are found to be uncorrelated in Block B, then these records should be tested for equivalent statistical properties as indicated by Block C. This is an important but often overlooked step in the analysis of random data. Far too often the analyzed results for a large number of sample records are presented as individual plots when in fact the results differ only by amounts that fall within the acceptable limits of random error. The formal presentation of such redundant data is usually of no value and can actually be detrimental in several ways. First, large quantities of analyzed data will sometimes tend to overwhelm the user and unnecessarily complicate the interpretation of the results. Second, the unsophisticated user might interpret the statistical scatter in individual results as physically meaningful differences. Third, more accurate results could be presented for the equivalent data if they were pooled prior to plotting, as will be discussed next. Note that for most applications, an equivalence of autospectra is a sufficient criterion for equivalence of sampled data. A procedure for testing the equivalence of autospectra is presented in Section 8.5.5.

10.4.2.4 Pooling of Equivalent Uncorrelated Data

The analyzed results for individual sample records that are found to represent equivalent data should be pooled, as indicated by Block D. This is done by computing appropriately weighted averages of the results for the individual records. For example, assume two autospectral density function estimates were computed from two uncorrelated sample records that now are found to represent equivalent data. If $\hat{G}_1(f)$ and $\hat{G}_2(f)$ were the original autospectra estimates computed with n_{d1} and n_{d2} averages, respectively, a new pooled estimate of the autospectrum is given by

$$\hat{G}_p(f) = \frac{n_{d1}\hat{G}_1(f) + n_{d2}\hat{G}_2(f)}{n_{d1} + n_{d2}} \qquad (10.19)$$

where $\hat{G}_p(f)$ is essentially computed with $n_{dp} = n_{d1} + n_{d2}$ averages. Equation (10.19) may be generalized for q estimates from uncorrelated but equivalent samples as follows:

$$\hat{G}_p(f) = \frac{\sum_{i=1}^{q} n_{di}\hat{G}_i(f)}{\sum_{i=1}^{q} n_{di}} \qquad (10.20)$$

where $\hat{G}_p(f)$ is now computed with an equivalent number of averages given by

$$n_d = \sum_{i=1}^{q} n_{di} \qquad (10.21)$$

Noting from Section 8.5.4 that the random error in an autospectral density estimate is approximated by $\epsilon_r = 1/\sqrt{n_d}$, it follows from Equation (10.21) that the pooling operation produces an autospectrum estimate with a reduced random error. However, it also should be noted that the pooling operation generally will not suppress the systematic error (bias) in the autospectra estimates, as defined and discussed in Section 8.5.1. This fact often leads data analysts to reprocess sample records with equivalent statistical properties in a manner designed to reduce bias errors. For the case of autospectra estimates, the reprocessing might consist of a recomputation of autospectral density estimates from the original sample records using a greatly reduced resolution bandwidth to suppress the bias errors at the expense of increased random errors. The random errors in the individual estimates are then suppressed by the pooling operation.

10.4.2.5 *Cross-Correlation Analysis*
As for the case of autocorrelation and autospectral density functions, the cross-correlation and cross-spectral density functions are Fourier transform pairs. Hence, the measurement of a cross-correlation function will technically not yield any new information over the cross-spectrum. However, it sometimes presents the desired information in a more convenient format. An example is the measurement of time delays between two measurement points. Such measurements are the basis for a wide range of applications summarized in Ref. 1. Therefore, cross-correlation analysis is included in the procedures as a separate step indicated by Block E. Note that a cross-correlation estimate can be used as a test for correlation between two records.

Cross-correlation functions are usually estimated by computing the inverse Fourier transform of a cross-spectral density estimate, as detailed in Section 11.6.2. The statistical accuracy of cross-correlation estimates is discussed in Section 8.4.

10.4.2.6 *Cross-Spectral Density Analysis*
The most important joint computation for a collection of correlated sample records is the cross-spectral density analysis indicated by Block F. Cross-spectral density functions provide information concerning the linear relationships that might exist among the collection of sample records. When interpreted into a physical context, such information often leads directly to problem solutions as developed in Chapters 6 and 7, and illustrated extensively in Ref. 1.

The computation of cross-spectral density functions is detailed in Section 11.6.3. The statistical accuracy of cross-spectra estimates is developed in Section 9.1.

10.4.2.7 *Coherence Function Analysis*
Block G indicates the calculation of coherence functions based on autospectral and cross-spectral density estimates. Coherence functions of various types (ordinary, multiple, and partial) are valuable in several ways. First, they can be used to test for

correlation among the collection of sample records. Second, they constitute a vital parameter in assessing the accuracy of frequency response function estimates. Third, they can provide a direct solution for certain types of problems.

The computation of coherence functions is detailed in Sections 11.6.6 and 11.7. Illustrations of their applications to many engineering problems are presented in Ref. 1. The statistical accuracy of coherence function estimates is developed in Sections 9.2.3 and 9.3.

10.4.2.8 Frequency Response Function Analysis

The ultimate goal in the analysis of a collection of sample records is often to establish linear relationships among the data represented by the various records. The existence of such linear relationships can be detected from cross-correlation, cross-spectral density, or coherence function estimates. However, a meaningful description of the linear relationships is best provided by computing the frequency response functions of the relationships, as indicated by Block H.

The computation of frequency response functions is developed in Sections 11.6.4 and 11.7. The statistical accuracy of frequency response function estimates is discussed in Sections 9.2.4, 9.2.5, and 9.3.

10.4.2.9 Other Desired Multiple Analysis

Block I indicates other joint analyses of a collection of sample records needed to satisfy special data processing goals. Included might be advanced spectral calculations such as generalized spectra used in nonstationary data analysis discussed in Chapter 12, or Hilbert transform techniques discussed in Chapter 13.

PROBLEMS

10.1 If an end-to-end electrical calibration and an end-to-end mechanical calibration are performed on a data acquisition system, and there is a significant difference in the results of the two calibrations, which is more likely to be correct and why?

10.2 Assume the autospectral density function of a sample record of analog random data is to be computed by digital procedures. If it is known that the data exist only at frequencies below 1 kHz,

(a) what is the minimum sampling rate that can be used to digitize the original analog record?

(b) is this minimum sampling rate also required for the computation of an autocorrelation function?

(c) is this minimum sampling rate also required for the computation of a probability density function?

10.3 Suppose an analog random process represents band-limited white noise with a uniform autospectral density function of $G = 0.1$ V^2/Hz over the frequency range of $0 \leq f \leq 500$ Hz and zero for $f > 500$ Hz. If a sample record of the random process is digitized for analysis with a sampling rate of 200 sps, and no anti-aliasing filter is used,

(a) what will be the frequency range of autospectral density function computed from the digital data?

(b) what will be the value (on the average) of the autospectral density function computed from the digital data at 50 Hz?

10.4 Suppose the probability density function $p(x)$ computed from an acquired random data record reveals (a) a sharp peak at $x = 0$ and (b) a second sharp peak at $x = \mu_x + 1.5\sigma_x$ and is zero beyond $x = \mu_x + 1.5\sigma_x$. What type of data acquisition errors would be suspected?

10.5 Suppose an otherwise random data record includes a sine wave with an rms value of 1 V. Assume the autospectral density function of the data is measured using a resolution filter bandwidth of $B_e = 10$ Hz. If the spectral density of the random portion of the data in the vicinity of the sine wave frequency is $G = 0.1$ V^2/Hz, what will be the indicated spectral density (on the average) at the frequency of the sine wave?

10.6 The input gain to an analog-to-digital converter is set to make 1V full scale. If the ADC produces 8-bit words, what is the standard deviation of the digital noise floor (the quantization error) for the ADC?

10.7 Referring to the general data analysis procedure for individual sample records presented in Figure 10.3, explain why a test for stationarity is suggested prior to a test for periodicities and/or normality.

10.8 Referring to the general data analysis procedure for multiple sample records presented in Figure 10.14, explain why a coherence function estimate should always accompany a frequency response function estimate.

10.9 Assume a random vibration is measured using a piezoelectric accelerometer, as illustrated in Figure 10.2, where the natural frequency and damping ratio of the accelerometer sensing element are $f_n = 1$ kHz and $\zeta = 0.01$, respectively. If the autospectral density function of the vibration data is computed at frequencies up to 500 Hz, determine the bias error in the resulting autospectral density estimate at 500 Hz due to the nonuniform gain factor of the accelerometer.

10.10 In Problem 10.1, how will the nonuniform phase factor of the accelerometer influence the autospectral density estimate for the random vibration of 400 Hz?

REFERENCES

1. Bendat, J. S., and Piersol, A. G., *Engineering Applications of Correlation and Spectral Analysis*, 2nd ed., Wiley–Interscience, New York, 1993.

2. Doebelin, E. O., *Measurement Systems: Application and Design*, 5th ed., McGraw-Hill, New York, 2004.
3. Himelblau, H., and Piersol, A. G., *Handbook/or Dynamic Data Acquisition and Analysis*, 2nd ed., IEST RD-DTE012.2, Institute of Environmental Sciences and Technology, Arlington Heights, IL, 2006.
4. Wright, C. F., *Applied Measurement Engineering: How to Design Effective Mechanical Measurement Systems*, Prentice-Hall, Englewood Cliffs, NJ 1995.
5. Wirsching, P. H., Paez, T. L., and Ortiz, H., *Random Vibrations: Theory and Practice*, Wiley, New York, 1995.

CHAPTER 11

Data Analysis

This chapter details the basic operations required to estimate various properties of random data. The computations to be presented assume that the data are in the form of discrete values representing sample records from stationary (ergodic) random processes. Techniques for the analysis of nonstationary data are presented in Chapter 12, procedures for the computation of Hilbert transforms are developed in Chapter 13, and procedures for the analysis of data representing the response of nonlinear systems are summarized in Chapter 14.

11.1 DATA PREPARATION

As noted in Chapter 10, some random data occur naturally in digital form—for example, neutron emission data and some forms of economic data. In most cases, however, the data originate in analog form and must be converted to digital values with proper concern for (a) the aliasing and quantification problems detailed in Section 10.2 and (b) the data qualification procedures discussed in Section 10.3. Also, the data may be a function of an independent variable other than time—for example, a spatial variable as discussed in Section 5.2.4, Nevertheless, in this chapter, all computations are presented with time as the independent variable (i.e., the data are processed as time-series records) where it is assumed that the actual independent variable for the data record can be made proportional to time. The time parameter in the computed properties of the data can then be replaced by the actual independent variable for the data, as illustrated in Table 5.3.

With the above assumptions, let a discrete-valued random process be given by

$$\{u_n\} \quad n = 1, 2, 3, \ldots, N \tag{11.1}$$

Random Data: Analysis and Measurement Procedures, Fourth Edition. By Julius S. Bendat and Allan G. Piersol
Copyright © 2010 John Wiley & Sons, Inc.

where the data values are associated with the equally spaced times

$$t_n = t_0 + n\Delta t \quad n = 1, 2, 3, \ldots, N \tag{11.2}$$

It follows that a sample record of $\{u_n\}$ is given by

$$u_n = u(t_0 + n\Delta t) \quad n = 1, 2, 3, \ldots N \tag{11.3}$$

where the initial time t_0 is arbitrary and does not enter into later formulas so long as the data represent a stationary random process. It is clear in Equation (11.3) that the total record length represented by the sample data is $T_r = N\Delta t$. Also, from the developments in Section 10.2, the Nyquist frequency associated with the sample data is given by

$$f_A = \frac{1}{2\Delta t} \tag{11.4}$$

Various preliminary operations might be applied to the data as noted previously in Sections 10.2 and 10.3. Special operations of common interest include (a) data standardization, (b) trend removal, and (c) digital filtering.

11.1.1 Data Standardization

The mean value of the sample record u_n, $n = 1, 2, \ldots, N$, is given by

$$\bar{u} = \frac{1}{N} \sum_{n=1}^{N} u_n \tag{11.5}$$

For stationary ergodic data, the quantity $\bar{u}$ is an unbiased estimate of the mean value μ as demonstrated in Section 4.1. It is convenient for later calculations to transform the sample values u_n to a new set of values x_n that have a zero sample mean by computing

$$x_n = x(t_0 + n\Delta t) = u_n - \bar{u} \quad n = 1, 2, \ldots, N \tag{11.6}$$

All subsequent formulas will be stated in terms of the transformed data values x_n, where $\bar{x} = 0$.

The standard deviation of the transformed sample record x_n is given by

$$s = \left[\frac{1}{N-1} \sum_{n=1}^{N} x_n^2 \right]^{1/2} \tag{11.7}$$

The quantities s and s^2 are unbiased estimates of the standard deviation σ_x and the variance σ_x^2, respectively, as proved in Section 4.1. If later computer calculations are to be performed using fixed-point as opposed to floating-point arithmetic or if divisions are required, as in frequency response function computations, then it will be desirable to further standardize the data by transforming the values x_n to a new set of values z_n by computing

$$z_n = \frac{x_n}{s} \quad n = 1, 2, \ldots, N \tag{11.8}$$

11.1.2 Trend Removal

Situations sometimes occur where the sample data include spurious trends or low-frequency components with a wavelength longer than the record length $T_r = N\Delta t$, as discussed in Section 10.3.2 and illustrated in Figure 10.11(f). The most common technique for trend removal is to fit a low-order polynomial to the data using the least squares procedures detailed in Section 4.6.2. Specifically, let the original data values u_n be fit with a polynomial of degree K defined by

$$\tilde{u}_n = \sum_{k=0}^{K} b_k (n\Delta t)^k \quad n = 1, 2, \ldots, N \tag{11.9}$$

A "least squares" fit is obtained by minimizing the squared discrepancies between the data values and the polynomial given by

$$Q = \sum_{n=1}^{N} (u_n - \tilde{u}_n)^2 = \sum_{n=1}^{N} \left[u_n - \sum_{k=0}^{K} b_k (n\Delta t)^k \right]^2 \tag{11.10}$$

Taking the partial derivatives of Q with respect to b_k and setting them equal to zero yields $K + 1$ equations of the form

$$\sum_{k=0}^{K} b_k \sum_{n=1}^{N} (n\Delta t)^{k+m} = \sum_{n=1}^{N} u_n (n\Delta t)^m \quad m = 0, 1, 2, \ldots K \tag{11.11}$$

which can be solved for the desired regression coefficients $\{b_k\}$. For example, when $K = 0$, Equation (11.11) becomes

$$b_0 \sum_{n=1}^{N} (n\Delta t)^0 = \sum_{n=1}^{N} u_n (n\Delta t)^0 \tag{11.12}$$

giving the result

$$b_0 = \frac{1}{N} \sum_{n=1}^{N} u_n = \bar{u} \tag{11.13}$$

For $K = 1$, Equation (11.11) becomes

$$b_0 \sum_{n=1}^{N} (n\Delta t)^m + b_1 \sum_{n=1}^{N} (n\Delta t)^{1+m} = \sum_{n=1}^{N} u_n (n\Delta t)^m \quad m = 0, 1 \tag{11.14}$$

Noting the identities

$$\sum_{n=1}^{N} n = \frac{N(N+1)}{2} \quad \sum_{n=1}^{N} n^2 = \frac{N(N+1)(2N+1)}{6} \tag{11.15}$$

Equation (11.14) yields the results

$$b_0 = \frac{2(2N+1)\sum_{n=1}^{N} u_n - 6\sum_{n=1}^{N} nu_n}{N(N-1)} \quad (11.16a)$$

$$b_1 = \frac{12\sum_{n=1}^{N} nu_n - 6(N+1)\sum_{n=1}^{N} u_n}{\Delta t N(N-1)(N+1)} \quad (11.16b)$$

Equation (11.16) defines a linear regression line with an intercept of b_0 and a slope of b_1, which should then be subtracted from the original data values u_n. Note that Equation (11.16) is equivalent to Equation (4.66), where $u_n = y_i$, $n\Delta t = x_i$, $b_0 = A$, and $b_1 = B$. An example of linear trend removal is illustrated in Figure 11.1. More complex trends can be removed by higher order polynomial fits, but trend removal using an order of greater than $K = 3$ is generally not recommended because fits with $K > 3$ may remove actual low-frequency information in the data.

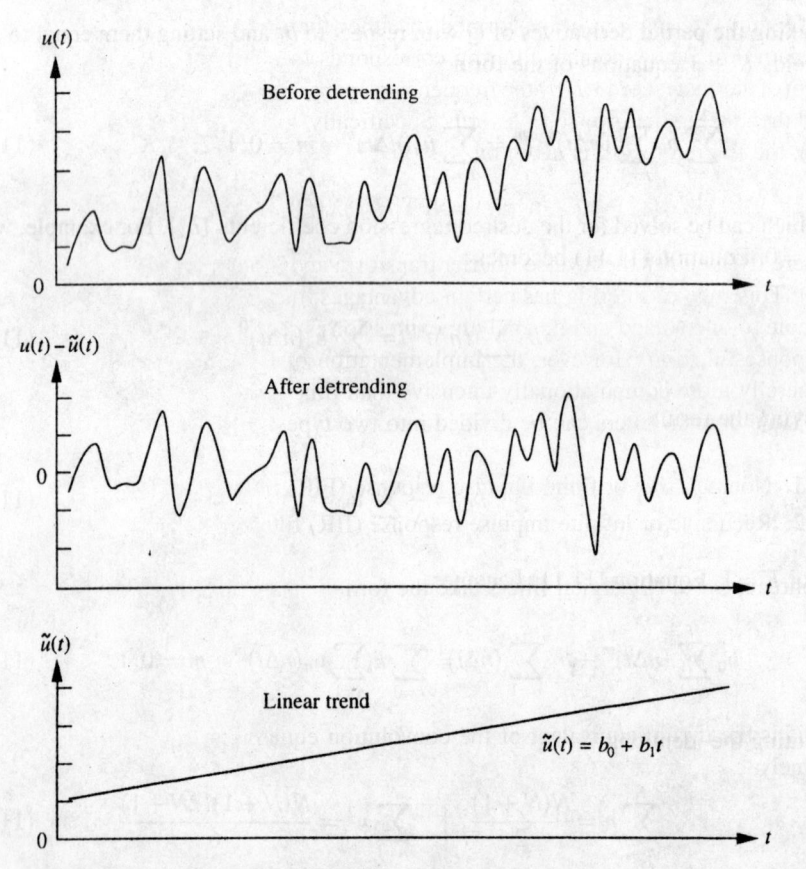

Figure 11.1 Illustration of linear trend removal.

11.1.3 Digital Filtering

The filtering of data prior to more detailed analyses may be desired for various reasons, including either the isolation or elimination of periodic components, as an integral step in "zoom" transform operations to be discussed in Section 11.5.4, or as an anti-aliasing step prior to data decimation. The last-mentioned application is of particular importance since decimation of sample data is often carried out to decrease the amount of data for later analysis. By definition, a dth-order decimation of sample data consists of keeping every dth data value and discarding all other data values. Hence, data that were originally sampled with a sampling interval of Δt are reduced to data with a new sampling interval of $d\Delta t$. It follows that the new Nyquist frequency becomes $f'_N = 1/(2d\Delta t)$ and all information above this frequency will be folded (aliased) back into the frequency interval from 0 to $1/(2d\Delta t)$. To avoid aliasing, the original sample data should be filtered prior to decimation to remove information in the frequency range above $1/(2d\Delta t)$ by using a low-pass digital filter. Note that this does not negate the requirement to remove all information in the original data above $f_N = 1/(2\Delta t)$ by low-pass analog filtering.

Digital filtering can be performed in either the time domain or the frequency domain. Frequency-domain filtering corresponds to multiplying the Fourier transform of the data record $x(t)$ by the frequency response function $H(f)$ of the desired filter and then taking the inverse transform. Specifically, given a transformed data record $x(t)$, the filtered record is given by

$$y(t) = \text{IFT}[H(f)X(f)] \tag{11.17}$$

where IFT denotes the inverse Fourier transform and $X(f)$ is the Fourier transform of $x(t)$. This type of filtering has certain advantages, the primary ones being that it is simple to understand and no analytic expression is required for the filter frequency response function. However, the implementation of frequency-domain filtering is generally more computationally intensive than time-domain filtering procedures.

Time-domain filters can be divided into two types:

1. Nonrecursive or finite impulse response (FIR) filters.
2. Recursive or infinite impulse response (IIR) filters.

Nonrecursive (FIR) digital filters take the form

$$y_i = \sum_{k=0}^{M} h_k x_{i-k} \tag{11.18}$$

This is the digital equivalent of the convolution equation given in Equation (6.1), namely,

$$y(t) = \int_0^\infty h(\tau) x(t-\tau) d\tau \tag{11.19}$$

where $h(\tau)$ is the unit impulse response function of the desired filter. In a similar manner, $\{h_k\}$ defines the unit impulse response of the digital filter. Classical smoothing, interpolation, extrapolation, differentiation, and integration techniques are all examples of FIR filters.

A recursive (IIR) digital filter is that type of filter where the output time series is generated not only using a finite sum of input terms but also using previous outputs as input terms (a procedure engineers call feedback). A simple type of IIR filter is given by

$$y_n = cx_n + \sum_{k=1}^{M} h_k y_{n-k} \qquad (11.20)$$

which uses M previous outputs and only one input. More general recursive filters involve M outputs and larger numbers of inputs. Equation (11.20) is illustrated in Figure 11.2. The triangles represent multiplication by the values shown within the triangles, the rectangles represent a delay of Δt from one point to another, and the circles represent summing operations.

The Fourier transform of Equation (11.20) yields the result

$$Y(f) = cX(f) + Y(f) \sum_{k=1}^{M} h_k e^{-j2\pi fk\Delta t} \qquad (11.21)$$

where the summation involves a polynomial in powers of the exponential exp $(-j2\pi f\Delta t)$. (Replacing this exponential by the letter z leads to a procedure for analyzing digital niters in terms of what is called z-transform theory.) From Equation (11.21), the frequency response function of the entire system is given by

$$H(f) = \frac{Y(f)}{X(f)} = \frac{c}{1 - \sum_{k=1}^{M} h_k e^{-j2\pi fk\Delta t}} \qquad (11.22)$$

Studies of the properties of $H(f)$ are thus reduced to determining the location and nature of the poles in the denominator of this last result.

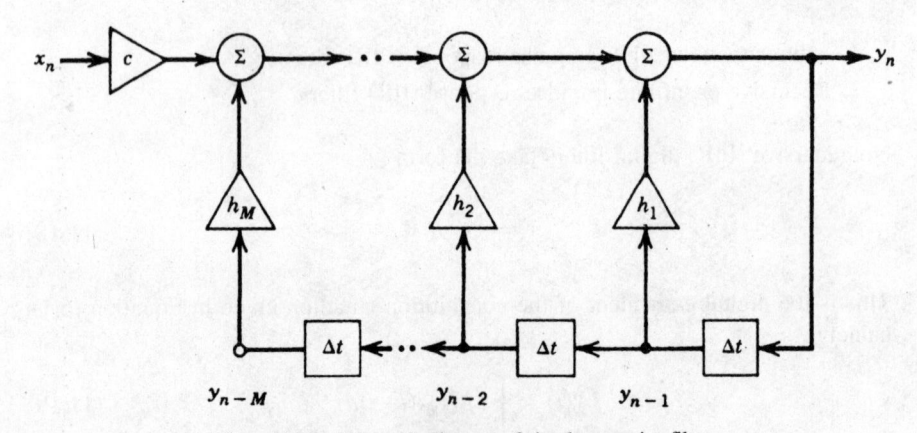

Figure 11.2 Schematic diagram of simple recursive filter.

DATA PREPARATION

As an example of this procedure, consider the IIR filter denned by

$$y_n = (1-a)x_n + ay_{n-1} \tag{11.23}$$

where $a = \exp(-\Delta t/RC)$. This can behave like a low-pass filter as defined previously in Example 6.1. To verify this property, note that from Equation (11.22) we obtain

$$H(f) = \frac{1-a}{1-ae^{-j2\pi f \Delta t}} \tag{11.24}$$

The square of the filter gain factor is then given by

$$|H(f)|^2 = \frac{(1-a)^2}{(1+a^2) - 2a \cos 2\pi f \Delta t} \tag{11.25}$$

Observe that if $RC \gg \Delta t$, then $a = \exp(-\Delta t/RC) \approx 1 - (\Delta t/RC)$ and $(1-a) \simeq \Delta t/RC$. Also, if $2\pi f \Delta t \ll 1$, then $e^{-j2\pi f \Delta t}$ may be approximated by $(1 - j2\pi f \Delta t)$. For this situation

$$H(f) \approx \frac{1}{1+j2\pi fRC}$$

and

$$|H(f)|^2 \approx \frac{1}{1+(2\pi fRC)^2} \tag{11.26}$$

which are the usual low-pass RC filter results.

Recursive digital niters that give good approximations to Butterworth filters have been synthesized with the aid of Equation (11.22) by finding a set of numerical weights $\{h_k\}$ and a coefficient c such that the resulting $|H(f)|^2$ has the form

$$|H(f)|^2 = \frac{1}{1 + (\sin \pi f \Delta t / \sin \pi f_0 \Delta t)^{2M}} \quad 0 \leq f \leq \frac{1}{2\Delta t} \tag{11.27}$$

Note that $|H(f)|^2 = 1$ for $f = 0$ and $|H(f)|^2 = 0.5$ for $f = f_0$. At $f = 1/(2\Delta t)$, the Nyquist frequency, the quantity $H(f)$ approaches zero for large M. Thus, over the frequency range from 0 to $1/(2\Delta t)$, the filter described by Equation (11.27) acts like a low-pass Butterworth filter of the form

$$|H(f)|^2 = \frac{1}{1+(f/f_0)^K} \tag{11.28}$$

where f_0 is the half-power point and K determines the rolloff rate. More complete mathematical details for the synthesis of digital filters appear in Refs 1–4.

Example 11.1. Illustration of Recursive Digital Filter. Assume digital data have been collected with a sampling rate of 1000 sps. It is now desired to low-pass filter the data using a simple RC-type filter with a half-power point cutoff frequency of $f_0 = 10$ Hz. Determine an appropriate recursive digital filter to accomplish this task.

From Equation (11.26), the half-power point cutoff frequency f_0 occurs where $|H(f_0)|^2 = \frac{1}{2}|H(f)|^2_{max} = \frac{1}{2}|H(10)|^2 = 0.5$. Because $RC \gg \Delta t = 10^{-3}$ for this case,

$$|H(10)|^2 \approx \frac{1}{1 + (20\pi RC)^2} = 0.5$$

It follows that $RC = 0.016$ and $a = \exp(-0.063) = 0.94$. This result is checked by substituting $a = 0.94$ into Equation (11.25), which yields $|H(10)|^2 = 0.5$. Hence, the desired low-pass filter is given from Equation (11.23) as

$$y_n = 0.06x_n + 0.94y_{n-1}$$

11.2 FOURIER SERIES AND FAST FOURIER TRANSFORMS

Fourier series and Fourier transforms of data differ in their theoretical properties but not, for most practical purposes, in their digital computational details. This is because only a finite-range Fourier transform can actually be computed with digitized data, and this finite range can always be considered as the period of an associated Fourier series. From the discussions in Section 5.2.2, one of the main reasons for the importance of fast Fourier transforms is that they can be used to provide estimates of desired spectral density and correlation functions. Before explaining the basis for the methods to compute fast Fourier transforms, it is instructive to review a standard Fourier series procedure.

11.2.1 Standard Fourier Series Procedure

If a stationary sample record $x(t)$ is periodic with a period of T_p and a fundamental frequency $f_1 = 1/T_p$, then $x(t)$ can be represented by the Fourier series

$$x(t) = \frac{a_0}{2} + \sum_{q=1}^{\infty}(a_q \cos 2\pi q f_1 t + b_q \sin 2\pi q f_1 t) \qquad (11.29)$$

where

$$a_q = \frac{2}{T_p}\int_0^{T_p} x(t)\cos 2\pi q f_1 t\, dt \quad q = 0, 1, 2, \ldots$$

$$b_q = \frac{2}{T_p}\int_0^{T_p} x(t)\sin 2\pi q f_1 t\, dt \quad q = 1, 2, 3, \ldots$$

Assume a sample record $x(t)$ is of finite length $T_r = T_p$, the fundamental period of the data. Further assume that the record is sampled at an even number of N equally spaced points a distance Δt apart, where Δt has been selected to produce a sufficiently high Nyquist frequency $f_A = 1/2\Delta t$. Consider the time of the initial data point to be Δt

and denote the transformed data values, as before, by

$$x_n = x(n\Delta t) \quad n = 1, 2, \ldots, N \tag{11.30}$$

Proceed now to calculate the finite version of a Fourier series that will pass through these N data values. For any point t in the interval $(0, T_p)$, the result is

$$x(t) = A_0 + \sum_{q=1}^{N/2} A_q \cos\left(\frac{2\pi qt}{T_p}\right) + \sum_{q=1}^{(N/2)-1} B_q \sin\left(\frac{2\pi qt}{T_p}\right) \tag{11.31}$$

At the particular points $t = n\Delta t$, $n = 1, 2, \ldots, N$, where $T_p = N\Delta t$,

$$x_n = x(n\Delta t) = A_0 + \sum_{q=1}^{N/2} A_q \cos\left(\frac{2\pi qn}{N}\right) + \sum_{q=1}^{(N/2)-1} B_q \sin\left(\frac{2\pi qn}{N}\right) \tag{11.32}$$

The coefficients A_q and B_q are given by

$$\begin{aligned}
A_0 &= \frac{1}{N} \sum_{n=1}^{N} x_n = \bar{x} = 0 \\
A_q &= \frac{2}{N} \sum_{n=1}^{N} x_n \cos \frac{2\pi qn}{N} \quad q = 1, 2, \ldots, \frac{N}{2} - 1 \\
A_{N/2} &= \frac{1}{N} \sum_{n=1}^{N} x_n \cos n\pi \\
B_q &= \frac{2}{N} \sum_{n=1}^{N} x_n \sin \frac{2\pi qn}{N} \quad q = 1, 2, \ldots, \frac{N}{2} - 1
\end{aligned} \tag{11.33}$$

The computation of A_q and B_q involves the following steps:

1. Evaluate $\theta = 2\pi qn/N$ for fixed q and n
2. Compute $\cos \theta$, $\sin \theta$
3. Compute $x_n \cos \theta$, $x_n \sin \theta$
4. Accumulate both sums for $n = 1, 2, \ldots, N$
5. Increment q and repeat operations

This procedure requires a total of approximately N^2 *real* multiply–add operations.

For large N, these standard digital computation methods for determining the coefficients A_q and B_q can be time-consuming since the required number of computations is a function of N^2. To greatly reduce these standard computational times, alternative methods have been proposed and developed, known as *fast Fourier transform* (FFT) procedures. These methods will now be discussed in some detail because of their importance in digital processing of random data.

11.2.2 Fast Fourier Transforms

An infinite-range Fourier transform of a real-valued or a complex-valued record $x(t)$ is defined by the complex-valued quantity

$$X(f) = \int_{-\infty}^{\infty} x(t)e^{-j2\pi ft} dt \qquad (11.34)$$

Theoretically, as noted previously, this transform $X(f)$ will not exist for an $x(t)$ that is a representative member of a stationary random process when the infinite limits are used. However, by restricting the limits to a finite time interval of $x(t)$, say in the range $(0, T)$, the finite-range Fourier transform will exist, as defined by

$$X(f, T) = \int_0^T x(t)e^{-j2\pi ft} dt \qquad (11.35)$$

Assume now that this $x(t)$ is sampled at N equally spaced points a distance Δt apart, where Δt has been selected to produce a sufficiently high Nyquist frequency. As before, the sampling times are $t_n = n\Delta t$. However, it is convenient here to start with $n = 0$. Hence, in place of Equation (11.30), let

$$x_n = x(n\Delta t) \quad n = 0, 1, 2, \ldots, N-1$$

Then, for arbitrary f, the discrete version of Equation (11.35) is

$$X(f, T) = \Delta t \sum_{n=0}^{N-1} x_n \exp[-j2\pi fn\Delta t] \qquad (11.36)$$

The usual selection of discrete frequency values for the computation of $X(f, T)$ is

$$f_k = \frac{k}{T} = \frac{k}{N\Delta t} \quad k = 0, 1, 2, \ldots, N-1 \qquad (11.37)$$

At these frequencies, the transformed values give the Fourier components defined by

$$X_k = \frac{X(f_k)}{\Delta t} = \sum_{n=0}^{N-1} x_n \exp\left[-j\frac{2\pi kn}{N}\right] \quad k = 0, 1, 2, \ldots N-1 \qquad (11.38)$$

where Δt has been included with $X(f_k)$ to have a scale factor of unity before the summation. Note that results are unique only out to $k = N/2$ since the Nyquist frequency occurs at this point. The function defined in Equation (11.38) is often referred to as the *discrete Fourier transform* (DFT).

To simplify the notation, let

$$W(u) = \exp\left[-j\frac{2\pi u}{N}\right] \qquad (11.39)$$

Observe that $W(N) = 1$, and for all u and v,

$$W(u+v) = W(u)W(v)$$

Also, let

$$X(k) = X_k \quad \text{and} \quad x(n) = x_n$$

Then Equation (11.38) becomes

$$X(k) = \sum_{n=0}^{N-1} x(n) W(kn) \quad k = 0, 1, 2, \ldots, N-1 \qquad (11.40)$$

Equations (11.38) and (11.40) should be studied so as to be easily recognized as the Fourier transform of $x(n)$ when $x(n)$ is expressed by a series of N terms. Such equations require a total of approximately N^2 *complex* multiply-add operations (where 1 complex multiply-add = 4 real multiply-adds) to compute all of the $X(k)$ terms involved.

11.2.2.1 Basis for FFT Procedures

The fast Fourier transform procedures are now based on decomposing N into its composite (nonunity) factors and carrying out Fourier transforms over the smaller number of terms in each of the composite factors. In particular, if N is the product of p factors such that

$$N = \prod_{i=1}^{p} r_i = r_1 r_2 \cdots r_p \qquad (11.41)$$

where the r's are all integers greater than unity, then as will be proved below, the $X(k)$ in Equation (11.40) can be found by computing in an iterative fashion the sum of p terms,

$$\begin{array}{l} (N/r_1) \text{ Fourier transforms requiring } 4r_1^2 \text{ real operations each} \\ (N/r_2) \text{ Fourier transforms requiring } 4r_2^2 \text{ real operations each} \\ \qquad\qquad\qquad\qquad \vdots \\ (N/r_p) \text{ Fourier transforms requiring } 4r_p^2 \text{ real operations each} \end{array} \qquad (11.42)$$

Hence, the total number of real operations becomes

$$4(Nr_1 + Nr_2 + Nr_3 + \cdots + Nr_p) = 4N \sum_{i=1}^{p} r_i \qquad (11.43)$$

The resulting speed ratio of these FFT procedures to the standard method is then

$$\text{Speed ratio} = \frac{N^2}{4N \sum_{i=1}^{p} r_i} = \frac{N}{4 \sum_{i=1}^{p} r_i} \qquad (11.44)$$

11.2.2.2 Relation of Equation (11.33) to Equation (11.38)

It is useful to show the relation between A_q and B_q in Equation (11.33) and X_k in Equation (11.38). To this end, let X_k be replaced by X_q where starting with $n=1$,

$$X_q = \sum_{n=1}^{N} x_n \exp(-j2\pi qn/N)$$

$$q = 1, 2, \ldots, (N/2)-1$$

$$X_{N-q} = \sum_{n=1}^{N} x_n \exp(j2\pi qn/N)$$

$$X_0 = \sum_{n=1}^{N} x_n$$

$$X_{N/2} = \sum_{n=1}^{N} x_n \cos(n\pi)$$

$$\text{Real}(X_q + X_{N-q}) = 2\sum_{n=1}^{N} x_n \cos(2\pi qn/N)$$

$$\text{Imag}(X_{N-q} - X_N) = 2\sum_{n=1}^{N} x_n \sin(2\pi qn/N)$$

$$A_0 = (1/N)X_0$$

$$A_{N/2} = (1/N)X_{N/2}$$

$$A_q = (1/N)\text{Real}(X_q + X_{N-q})$$

$$q = 1, 2, \ldots, (N/2)-1$$

$$B_q = (1/N)\text{Imag}(X_{N-q} - X_N)$$

Example 11.2. **FFT Speed Ratio for Powers of Two.** If $N = 2^p$, then $\Sigma_{i=1}^{p} r_i = 2p = 2\log_2 N$. In this case, the speed ratio by Equation (11.44) appears to be

$$\text{Speed ratio} = \frac{N^2}{8Np} = \frac{N}{8p}$$

However, a doubling of the speed can be achieved in practice by noting that the values for $W(kn)$, when N is a power of 2, all turn out to be $+1$ or -1, so that multiplications are replaced by additions and subtractions. This yields a higher speed ratio of the order

$$\text{Speed ratio} = \frac{N}{4p} \qquad (11.45)$$

For example, if $N = 2^{13} = 8192$, Equation (11.45) gives a speed ratio of $(8192/52) \approx 158$. This result is deemed to be a conservative estimate since a further speed improvement of at most two can be obtained by dividing a single record into two parts and computing as indicated later in Section 11.2.4.

FOURIER SERIES AND FAST FOURIER TRANSFORMS   371

11.2.2.3 Derivation of General Procedure

To derive the result stated in Equation (11.42), express the indices k and n in Equation (11.40) in the following way:

$$k = \sum_{v=0}^{p-1} k_v \prod_{i=0}^{v} r_i \qquad \text{where } k_v = 0, 1, 2, \ldots, r_{v+1}-1$$

$$r_0 = 1 \qquad (11.46)$$

$$n = \sum_{v=0}^{p-1} n_v \prod_{i=0}^{v} r_{m+1-i} \qquad \text{where } n_v = 0, 1, 2, \ldots, r_{p-v}-1$$

$$r_{p+1} = 1$$

Note the indices k and n are replaced by new indices k_v and n_v as defined above. Equation (11.46) has the following interpretation:

$$\begin{aligned} k &= k_0 + k_1 r_1 + k_2 r_1 r_2 + \cdots + k_{p-1}(r_1 r_2 \cdots r_{p-1}) \\ n &= n_0 + n_1 r_p + n_2 r_p r_{p-1} + \cdots + n_{p-1}(r_p r_{p-1} \cdots r_2) \end{aligned} \qquad (11.47)$$

where

$$\begin{aligned} k_0 &= 0, 1, 2, \ldots, r_1 - 1 & n_0 &= 0, 1, 2, \ldots, r_p - 1 \\ k_1 &= 0, 1, 2, \ldots, r_2 - 1 & n_1 &= 0, 1, 2, \ldots, r_{p-1} - 1 \\ &\vdots & &\vdots \\ k_{p-1} &= 0, 1, 2, \ldots, r_p - 1 & n_{p-1} &= 0, 1, 2, \ldots, r_1 - 1 \end{aligned}$$

By fixing the values of k_v and n_v in turn, it is a straightforward exercise to verify that k and n will each vary from 0 to $N-1$, where N is the product of all the r's as per Equation (11.41). Equation (11.40) can now be rewritten as

$$\begin{aligned} X(k) &= X(k_0, k_1, \ldots, k_{p-1}) \\ &= \sum_{n_0=0}^{r_p-1} \sum_{n_1=0}^{r_{p-1}-1} \cdots \sum_{n_{p-2}=0}^{r_2-1} \sum_{n_{p-1}=0}^{r_1-1} x(n_0, n_1, \ldots, n_{p-2}, n_{p-1}) W(kn) \end{aligned} \qquad (11.48)$$

where

$$W(kn) = W(k[n_0 + n_1 r_p + \cdots + n_{p-v}(r_p r_{p-1} \cdots r_{v+1}) + \cdots \\ + n_{p-1}(r_p r_{p-1} \cdots r_2)]) \qquad (11.49)$$

with k given by Equation (11.46).

An alternative way to write k is as follows:

$$\begin{aligned} k &= (k_0 + k_1 r_1 + \cdots + k_{v-1} r_1 r_2 \cdots r_{v-1}) \\ &+ (r_1 r_2 \cdots r_v)(k_v + k_{v+1} r_{v+1} + \cdots + k_{p-1} r_{v+1} r_{v+2} \cdots r_{p-1}) \end{aligned}$$

Hence, a representative term in Equation (11.49) is such that

$$
\begin{aligned}
kn_{p-v}(r_p r_{p-1} \cdots r_{v+1}) = {} & (k_0 + k_1 r_1 + \cdots + k_{v-1} r_1 r_2 \cdots r_{v-1}) \\
& \times n_{p-v}(r_p r_{p-1} \cdots r_{v+1}) \\
& + N n_{p-v}(k_v + k_{v+1} r_{v+1} + \cdots \\
& + k_{p-1} r_{v+1} r_{v+2} \cdots r_{p-1})
\end{aligned}
\quad (11.50)
$$

Then, because W for any integer power of N is equal to unity, it follows for $v = 1, 2, \ldots, p$ that

$$
\begin{aligned}
W(kn_{p-v} r_p r_{p-1} \cdots r_{v+1}) = {} & W[(k_0 + k_1 r_1 + \cdots + k_{v-1} r_1 r_2 \cdots r_{v-1}) \\
& \times n_{p-v} r_p r_{p-1} \cdots r_{v+1}]
\end{aligned}
\quad (11.51)
$$

Equation (11.51) will now be interpreted. For $v = 1$, observe that

$$
W(kn_{p-1} r_p r_{p-1} \cdots r_2) = W(k_0 n_{p-1} r_p r_{p-1} \cdots r_2) \\
= W\left(\frac{k_0 n_{p-1} N}{r_1}\right) = \exp\left[-j \frac{2\pi k_0 n_{p-1}}{r_1}\right] \quad (11.52)
$$

This is the exponential required in a Fourier transform of $x(n_{p-1})$ as expressed by a series of r_1 terms, instead of N terms as shown in Equations (11.36) and (11.40). Note also that the indices k_0 and n_{p-1} each vary over the values $0, 1, 2, \ldots, r_1 - 1$, thus requiring a total of r_1^2 multiply–add operations to compute each of the associated $X(k_0)$ that might be involved here. For $v = 2, 3, \ldots, p$, Equation (11.51) with the aid of $W(u+v) = W(u) W(v)$ becomes the product of two factors, namely,

$$
W[(k_0 + k_1 r_1 + \cdots + k_{v-2} r_1 r_2 \cdots r_{v-2}) n_{p-v} r_p r_{p-1} \cdots r_{v+1}]
\quad (11.53)
$$

multiplied by $W(k_{v-1} r_1 r_2 \cdots r_{v-1} n_{p-v} r_p r_{p-1} \cdots r_{v+1})$

where only the second factor contains k_{v-1}. This second factor is the quantity

$$
W\left(\frac{k_{v-1} n_{p-v} N}{r_v}\right) = \exp\left[-j \frac{2\pi k_{v-1} n_{p-v}}{r_v}\right] \quad (11.54)
$$

which is the exponent required in a Fourier transform of $x(n_{p-v})$ as expressed by a series of r_v terms. Furthermore, the indices k_{v-1} and n_{p-v} each vary over the values $0, 1, 2, \ldots, r_v - 1$. Hence, a total of r_v^2 multiply–add operations are needed to compute each of the associated $X(k_{v-1})$ that might be involved here.

11.2.2.4 The FFT Algorithm
From the development in Equations (11.50) through (11.52), Equation (11.49) becomes

$$
W(kn) = \prod_{v=1}^{p} T(k_0, k_1, \ldots, k_{v-2}) W\left(\frac{k_{v-1} n_{p-v} N}{r_v}\right) \quad (11.55)
$$

where

$$T(k_0, k_1, \ldots, k_{v-2}) = 1 \quad \text{for } v = 1$$
$$= W[(k_0 + k_1 r_1 + \cdots + k_{v-2} r_1 r_2 \cdots r_{v-2})$$
$$\times (n_{p-v} r_p r_{p-1} \cdots r_{v+1})] \quad (11.56)$$
$$\text{for } v = 2, 3, \ldots, p$$

Quantities such as the T terms in Equation (11.56) are often called *twiddle factors*. The result of Equation (11.55) should now be substituted into Equation (11.48). Regrouping of terms then yields

$$\begin{aligned} X(k_0, k_1, \ldots, k_{p-1}) &= \sum_{n_0=0}^{r_p-1} T(k_0, k_1, \ldots, k_{p-2}) W\left(\frac{k_{p-1} n_0 N}{r_p}\right) \\ &\times \sum_{n_1=0}^{r_{p-1}-1} T(k_0, k_1, \ldots, k_{p-3}) W\left(\frac{k_{p-2} n_1 N}{r_{p-1}}\right) \\ &\times \cdots \\ &\times \sum_{n_{p-2}=0}^{r_2-1} T(k_0) W\left(\frac{k_1 n_{p-2} N}{r_2}\right) \\ &\times \sum_{n_{p-1}=0}^{r_1-1} x(n_0, n_1, \ldots, n_{p-2}, n_{p-1}) W\left(\frac{k_0 n_{p-1} N}{r_1}\right) \end{aligned} \quad (11.57)$$

Thus, the desired Fourier transform can be computed in p successive iterative steps as shown by Equation (11.57). The principal remaining question of concern here is the understanding of these steps.

Consider the last innermost sum of terms in Equation (11.57). Let

$$A_1(k_0, n_0, n_1, \ldots, n_{p-2}) = \sum_{n_{p-1}=0}^{r_1-1} x(n_0, n_1, \ldots, n_{p-2}, n_{p-1}) W\left(\frac{k_0 n_{p-1} N}{r_1}\right) \quad (11.58)$$

Then, holding $n_0, n_1, \ldots, n_{p-2}$ fixed for each of their possible values, Equation (11.58) gives a total of (N/r_1) Fourier transforms of $x(n_{p-1})$ requiring r_1^2 operations each. At the next innermost sum of terms in Equation (11.57), let

$$\begin{aligned} &A_2(k_0, k_1, n_0, n_1, \ldots, n_{p-3}) \\ &= \sum_{n_{p-2}=0}^{r_2-1} A_1(k_0, n_0, n_1, \ldots, n_{p-2}) T(k_0) W\left(\frac{k_1 n_{p-2} N}{r_2}\right) \end{aligned} \quad (11.59)$$

Here, holding $k_0, n_0, n_1, \ldots, n_{p-3}$ fixed for each of their possible values, Equation (11.59) gives a total of (N/r_2) Fourier transforms of $x(n_{p-2})$ requiring r_2^2 operations each. Continuing in this way, at the vth step, where $v = 2, 3, \ldots$,

$p-1$, let

$$A_v(k_0, k_1, \ldots, k_{v-1}, n_0, n_1, \ldots, n_{p-v-1})$$
$$= \sum_{n_{p-v}=0}^{r_v-1} A_{v-1}(k_0, k_1, \ldots, k_{v-2}, n_0, n_1, \ldots, n_{p-v}) \qquad (11.60)$$
$$\times T(k_0, k_1, \ldots, k_{v-2}) W\left(\frac{k_{v-1} n_{p-v} N}{r_v}\right)$$

Here, holding $k_0, k_1, \ldots, k_{v-2}, n_0, n_1, \ldots, n_{p-v-1}$ fixed for each of their possible values gives a total of (N/r_v) Fourier transforms of $x(n_{p-v})$ requiring r_v^2 operations each. At the last step, Equation (11.57) yields

$$X(k_0, k_1, \ldots, k_{p-1}) = A_p(k_0, k_1, \ldots, k_{p-1})$$
$$= \sum_{n_0=0}^{r_p-1} A_{p-1}(k_0, k_1, \ldots, k_{p-2}, n_0) \qquad (11.61)$$
$$\times T(k_0, k_1, \ldots, k_{p-2}) W\left(\frac{k_{p-1} n_0 N}{r_p}\right)$$

Holding $k_0, k_1, \ldots, k_{p-2}$ fixed for each of their possible values produces a total of (N/r_p) Fourier transforms of $x(n_0)$ requiring r_p^2 operations each. The sequence of steps in Equations (11.58)–(11.61) proves the result stated in Equation (11.42), making allowance for complex to real operations.

The formula derived in Equation (11.60) is a general *fast Fourier transform algorithm* and is the basis for many Fourier transform computational procedures in use today. See Ref. 5 for further details.

11.2.3 Cooley–Tukey Procedure

The Cooley–Tukey procedure, first introduced in 1965 in Ref. 6, is a special case of the general algorithm of Equation (11.60) that is appropriate for binary digital computers. In particular, it applies to those situations where the number of data samples N is a power of 2, namely,

$$N = 2^p \qquad (11.62)$$

If necessary, zeros are added to the data sequence to satisfy this requirment. Here, the iterative procedures of Equation (11.57) become the sum of p terms, where every term involves $(N/2)$ Fourier transforms requiring four operations each. This gives a total of $2Np$ complex multiply–add operations.

It is desirable to write down the special equations that apply to this case because of their widespread importance. This will be done by substituting into previous results. Equation (11.47) becomes

$$k = k_0 + 2k_1 + 2^2 k_2 + \cdots + 2^{p-1} k_{p-1}$$
$$n = n_0 + 2n_1 + 2^2 n_2 + \cdots + 2^{p-1} n_{p-1} \qquad (11.63)$$

where each k and n, respectively, take on the values 0 and 1 only. Equation (11.54) becomes for all $v = 1, 2, \ldots, p$,

$$W\left(\frac{k_{v-1}n_{p-v}N}{r_v}\right) = \exp(-j\pi k_{v-1}n_{p-v}) \tag{11.64}$$

which takes on the values 1 and -1 only. Equation (11.56) becomes

$$T(k_0, k_1, \ldots, k_{v-2}) = 1 \quad \text{for } v = 1$$
$$= W[(k_0 + 2k_1 + \cdots + 2^{v-2}k_{v-2})2^{p-v}n_{p-v}] \tag{11.65}$$
$$\text{for } v = 2, 3, \ldots, p$$

The Fourier transform iteration of Equation (11.57) can be expressed in this special case by the formula

$$X(k_0, k_1, \ldots, k_{p-1})$$
$$= \sum_{n_0=0}^{1} \sum_{n_1=0}^{1} \cdots \sum_{n_{p-2}=0}^{1} \sum_{n_{p-1}=0}^{1} x(n_0, n_1, \ldots, n_{p-2}, n_{p-1}) W(kn) \tag{11.66}$$

where

$$W(kn) = \prod_{v=1}^{p} T(k_0, k_1, \ldots, k_{v-2}) \exp(-j\pi k_{v-1} n_{p-v})$$

The first step in this iteration is now from Equation (11.58)

$$A_1(k_0, n_0, n_1, \ldots, n_{p-2}) = \sum_{n_{p-1}=0}^{1} x(n_0, n_1, \ldots, n_{p-2}, n_{p-1}) \exp(-j\pi k_0 n_{p-1}) \tag{11.67}$$

The vth step, for $v = 2, 3, \ldots, p-1$, becomes from Equation (11.60)

$$A_v(k_0, k_1, \ldots, k_{v-1}, n_0, n_1, \ldots, n_{p-v-1})$$
$$= \sum_{n_{p-v}=0}^{1} A_{v-1}(k_0, k_1, \ldots, k_{v-2}, n_0, n_1, \ldots, n_{p-v}) \tag{11.68}$$
$$\times T(k_0, k_1, \ldots, k_{v-2}) \exp(-j\pi k_{v-1} n_{p-v})$$

This result is called the *Cooley–Tukey fast Fourier transform algorithm*. The last step in the iteration, Equation (11.61), is

$$X(k_0, k_1, \ldots, k_{p-1}) = A_p(k_0, k_1, \ldots, k_{p-1})$$
$$= \sum_{n_0=0}^{1} A_{p-1}(k_0, k_1, \ldots, k_{p-2}, n_0) \tag{11.69}$$
$$\times T(k_0, k_1, \ldots, k_{p-2}) \exp(-j\pi k_{p-1} n_0)$$

and completes the procedure for this special case. A detailed discussion of these matters appears in Refs 2–6.

11.2.4 Procedures for Real-Valued Records

Fourier transforms of two real-valued records may be computed simultaneously by inserting one record $x(n)$ as the real part and one record $y(n)$ as the imaginary part of a complex record $z(n)$. In equation form, let

$$z(n) = x(n) + jy(n) \quad n = 0, 1, \ldots, N-1 \tag{11.70}$$

The Fourier transform of $z(n)$ by Equation (11.38) is

$$Z(k) = \sum_{n=0}^{N-1} [x(n) + jy(n)] \exp\left[-j\frac{2\pi kn}{N}\right] \quad k = 0, 1, 2, \ldots, N-1 \tag{11.71}$$

This can be computed by the fast Fourier transform procedures described in Section 11.2.2. It is usually assumed in Equations (11.70) and (11.71) that N data points in $x(n)$ and $y(n)$ are transformed into N frequency points that are spaced $1/T$ apart. For these situations, the Nyquist frequency occurs when $k = N/2$ so that for N even, unique results occur only for $k = 0, 1, 2, \ldots, (N/2)$. To obtain $X(k)$ and $Y(k)$, observe that

$$\exp\left[j\frac{2\pi n(N-k)}{N}\right] = \exp\left[-j\frac{2\pi nk}{N}\right]$$

because $\exp[j2\pi n] = 1$ for any n. Hence, if $Z^*(k)$ is the complex conjugate of $Z(k)$, then

$$Z^*(N-k) = \sum_{n=0}^{N-1} [x(n) - jy(n)] \exp\left[-j\frac{2\pi nk}{N}\right]$$

It follows that

$$Z(k) + Z^*(N-k) = 2\sum_{n=0}^{N-1} x(n) \exp\left[-j\frac{2\pi nk}{N}\right] = 2X(k)$$

$$Z(k) - Z^*(N-k) = 2j\sum_{n=0}^{N-1} y(n) \exp\left[-j\frac{2\pi nk}{N}\right] = 2jY(k)$$

Thus, the two real-valued records $x(n)$ and $y(n)$ have Fourier transforms $X(k)$ and $Y(k)$ given by

$$\begin{aligned} X(k) &= \frac{Z(k) + Z^*(N-k)}{2} \\ Y(k) &= \frac{Z(k) - Z^*(N-k)}{2j} \end{aligned} \quad k = 0, 1, \ldots, N-1 \tag{11.72}$$

The same principle is used to calculate a double-length transform where a single, real-valued record $v(n)$, $n = 0, 1, \ldots, 2N-1$, is divided into two records, one consisting of the values $v(n)$ where n is even and the other where n is odd. Specifically, let

$$\begin{aligned} x(n) &= v(2n) \\ y(n) &= v(2n+1) \end{aligned} \quad n = 0, 1, 2, \ldots, N-1 \qquad (11.73)$$

Now compute the Fourier transforms of $z(n) = x(n) + jy(n)$, $n = 0, 1, \ldots, N-1$, using Equation (11.71), and then the individual transforms, $X(k)$ and $Y(k)$, using Equation (11.72). These transforms can now be combined to obtain the desired Fourier transform of $v(n)$ by

$$\begin{aligned} V(k) &= X(k) + Y(k)\exp\left[-j\frac{\pi}{N}\right] \\ V(N+k) &= X(k) - Y(k)\exp\left[-j\frac{\pi}{N}\right] \end{aligned} \quad k = 0, 1, \ldots, N-1 \qquad (11.74)$$

Note that the operation calculates the Fourier transform of $2N$ real data values using a single N-point complex transform. See Ref. 3 for details on the practical implementation of the FFT algorithm on a digital computer.

11.2.5 Further Related Formulas

Referring to Equation (11.34), the inverse Fourier transform of $X(f)$ is

$$x(t) = \int_{-\infty}^{\infty} X(f) e^{j2\pi ft} df \qquad (11.75)$$

This leads to the discrete inverse Fourier transform formula

$$x_n = \frac{1}{N} \sum_{k=0}^{N-1} X_k \exp\left[j\frac{2\pi kn}{N}\right] \quad n = 0, 1, 2, \ldots, N-1 \qquad (11.76)$$

where the Fourier components X_k of Equation (11.38) are computed by the FFT procedures. The constant $(1/N)$ in Equation (11.76) is a scale factor only and is not otherwise important. This inverse Fourier transform can be computed by the same FFT procedures previously described by merely interchanging k and n and replacing x_n by X_k and $W(kn)$ by $W(-kn)$.

As a final topic here, it should be noted that the FFT computation always operates on a function with a nonnegative independent variable and produces a transformed function also with a nonnegative independent variable. Specifically, an input function of time is always defined as $x(t)$ over $0 \leq t \leq T$, not $-T/2 \leq t \leq T/2$. Similarly, the transformed function $X(f)$ is defined over $0 \leq f \leq 2f_A$, not $-f_A \leq f \leq f_A$. In digital terms, $x_n = x(n\Delta t)$, $n = 0, 1, \ldots, N-1$, and $X(k) = X(k/N\Delta t)/\Delta t$, $k = 0, 1, \ldots, N-1$, where $k = N/2$ corresponds to the Nyquist frequency f_A defined in Equation (10.12). However, from Equation (11.72),

$$X(k) = X^*(N-k) \quad k = 0, 1, \ldots N-1 \qquad (11.77)$$

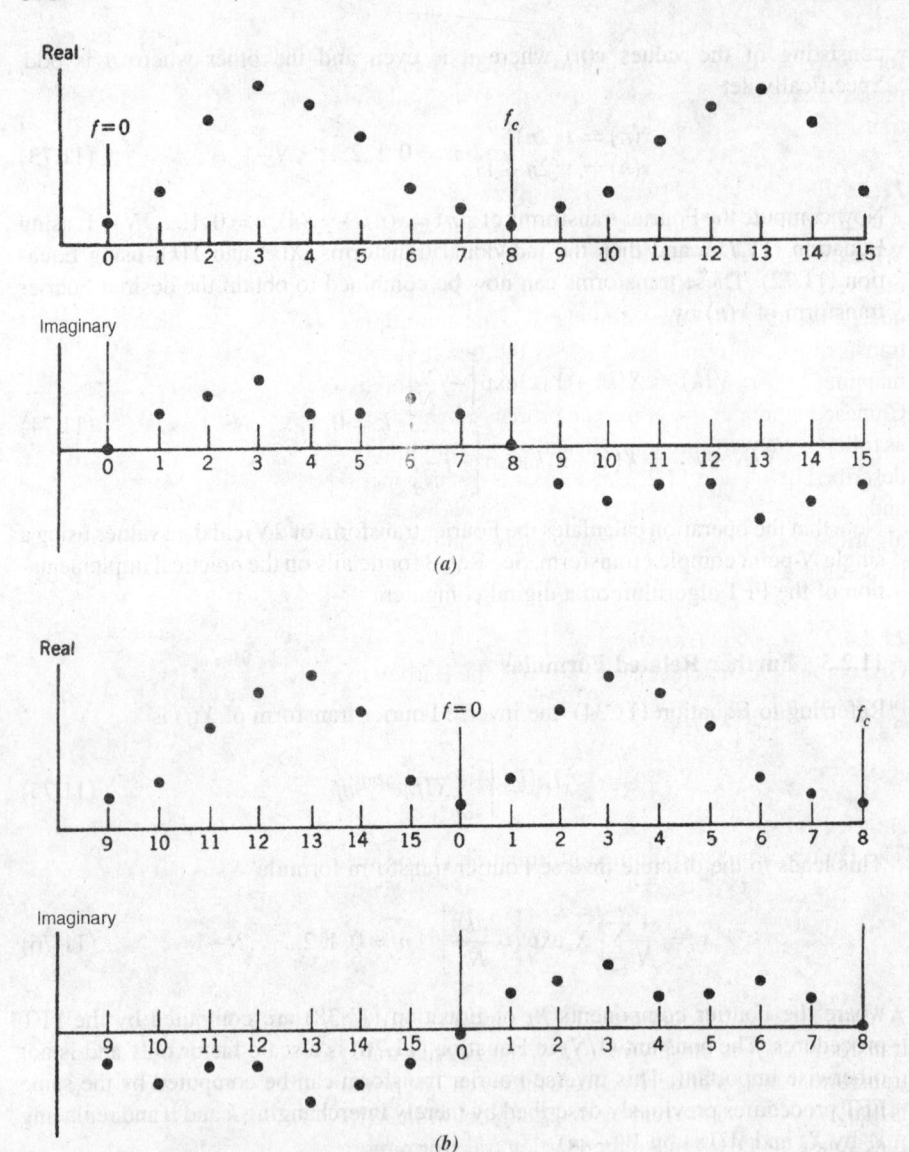

Figure 11.3 Illustration of frequency components for $N = 16$-point FFT. (a) Components as produced by FFT. (b) Transposed components defining two-sided spectrum.

where the values at frequencies above $N/2$ may be interpreted as the negative frequency values if desired to obtain a two-sided spectral function, as illustrated in Figure 11.3.

11.2.6 Other Algorithms

New procedures for computing Fourier transforms or equivalent transforms are continually being devised. Most are modifications of the standard FFT optimized for a specific use or mechanization, but a few involve different concepts. Two such procedures that deserve mention are the Winograd Fourier transform and the Hartley transform.

11.2.6.1 Winograd Fourier Transform

A totally different procedure for computing fast Fourier transforms was introduced by Winograd in Ref. 7. Essentially, the procedure maps a one-dimensional time sequence of N values into a multidimensional array where each array dimension corresponds to one of the prime numbers of the N. The multidimensional array is then Fourier transformed and remapped back to the one-dimensional frequency sequence. The mapping is performed according to number-theoretic concepts using the so-called Chinese remainder theorem. The primary advantages of the Winograd algorithm are as follows: (a) It requires significantly less computational time than the FFT algorithm described in Section 11.2.2, and (b) it is easily generalized to radices other than two and, especially, to mixed radices. The primary disadvantage of the Winograd algorithm is that it is significantly more complex than the FFT algorithm described in Section 11.2.2. See Ref. 7 for details.

11.2.6.2 Hartley Transform

Given a sample time history record $x(t)$, the Hartley transform, which was originally proposed in Ref. 8, is defined as

$$X_H(f) = \int_{-\infty}^{\infty} x(t)[\cos(2\pi ft) + \sin(2\pi ft)]\, dt \qquad (11.78)$$

The Fourier transform defined in Equation (11.34) can be written as

$$X(f) = \int_{-\infty}^{\infty} x(t)[\cos(2\pi ft) - j\sin(2\pi ft)]\, dt \qquad (11.79)$$

A comparison of Equations (11.78) and (11.79) clearly shows that the Hartley transform $X_H(f)$ is closely related to the Fourier transform $X(f)$; the result of either transformation can be derived from the other. The primary difference between the two is that $X_H(f)$ is always a real-valued function, while $X(f)$ is generally a complex-valued function. This might make the Hartley transform more attractive to some engineers who prefer to work only with real-valued functions. Also, assuming that the time history function $x(t)$ is real valued, it is argued in Ref. 9 that a fast Hartley transform can be computed with fewer computations than a fast Fourier transform. See Refs 8 and 9 for details.

11.3 PROBABILITY DENSITY FUNCTIONS

Consider N data values $\{x_n\}, n = 1, 2, \ldots, N$, sampled at equally spaced time intervals Δt from a data record $x(t) = x(n\Delta t)$ that is stationary with $\bar{x} = 0$. It follows from

Equations (3.4) and (8.69) that the probability density function of $x(t)$ can be estimated by

$$\hat{p}(x) = \frac{N_x}{NW} \qquad (11.80)$$

where W is a narrow interval centered at x and N_x is the number of data values that fall within the range $x \pm W/2$. Hence, an estimate $\hat{p}(x)$ is obtained digitally by dividing the full range of x into an appropriate number of equal-width class intervals, tabulating the number of data values in each class interval, and dividing by the product of the class interval width W and the sample size N. Note that the estimate $\hat{p}(x)$ is not unique, because it clearly is dependent on the number of class intervals and their width selected for the analysis.

A formal statement of this procedure will now be given. Let K denote the number of constant-width class intervals selected to cover the entire range of the data values from a to b. Then the width of each interval is given by

$$W = \frac{b-a}{K} \qquad (11.81)$$

and the end point of the ith interval is defined by

$$d_i = a + iW \quad i = 0, 1, 2, \ldots, K \qquad (11.82)$$

Note that $d_0 = a$ and $d_K = b$. Now define a sequence of $K+2$ numbers $\{N_i\}, i = 0, 1, 2, \ldots, K+1$, by the conditions

$$N_0 = [\text{number of } x \text{ such that } x \leq d_0]$$
$$N_1 = [\text{number of } x \text{ such that } d_0 < x \leq d_1]$$
$$\vdots$$
$$N_i = [\text{number of } x \text{ such that } d_{i-1} < x \leq d_i]$$
$$\vdots$$
$$N_K = [\text{number of } x \text{ such that } d_{K-1} < x \leq d_K]$$
$$N_{K+1} = [\text{number of } x \text{ such that } x > d_K]$$

This procedure will sort out the N data values of x so that the number sequence $\{N_i\}$ satisfies

$$N = \sum_{i=0}^{K+1} N_i \qquad (11.83)$$

One method of doing this scoring on a digital computer is to examine each value x_n, $n = 1, 2, \ldots, N$, in turn as follows:

1. If $x_n \leq a$, add the integer 1 to N_0.
2. If $a < x_n \leq b$, compute $I = (x_n - a)/W$. Then, select i as the largest integer less than or equal to I, and add the integer 1 to N.
3. If $x_n > b$, add the integer 1 to N_{K+1}.

Four output forms of the sequence $\{N_i\}$ can be used. The first output is the *histogram*, which is simply the sequence $\{N_i\}$ without changes. The second output is the sample percentage of data in each class interval defined for $i = 0, 1, 2, \ldots, K + 1$, by

$$\hat{P}_i = \text{Prob}[d_{i-1} < x \leq d_i] = \frac{N_i}{N} \quad (11.84)$$

The third output is the sequence of sample probability density estimates $\{\hat{p}_i\}$ defined at the midpoints of the K class intervals in $[a, b]$ by

$$\hat{p}_i = \frac{\hat{P}_i}{W} = \left(\frac{N_i}{N}\right)\left(\frac{K}{b-a}\right) \quad i = 1, 2, \ldots, K \quad (11.85)$$

The fourth output is the sequence of sample probability distribution estimates $\{\hat{P}(i)\}$ defined at the class interval end points where $i = 0, 1, 2, \ldots, K + 1$, by

$$\hat{P}(i) = \text{Prob}[-\infty < x \leq d_i] = \sum_{j=0}^{i} \hat{P}_j = W \sum_{j=0}^{i} \hat{p}_j \quad (11.86)$$

11.4 AUTOCORRELATION FUNCTIONS

There are two ways to compute autocorrelation estimates. The first is the direct method, involving the computation of average products among the sample data values. The second way is the indirect approach of first computing an autospectral density estimate using FFT procedures and then computing the inverse transform of the autospectrum. The direct method is the easier to program and represents the more logical approach from the viewpoint of basic definitions. The second approach takes advantage of the dramatic computational efficiency of FFT algorithms and hence requires fewer computations to execute.

11.4.1 Autocorrelation Estimates via Direct Computations

Consider N data values $\{x_n\}$, $n = 1, 2, \ldots, N$, sampled at equally spaced time intervals Δt from a data record $x(t) = x(n\Delta t)$ that is stationary with $\bar{x} = 0$. From the basic definition in Equation (8.95), the autocorrelation function of $x(t)$ will be estimated from the sample values at the time delay $r\Delta t$ by

$$\hat{R}_{xx}(r\Delta t) = \frac{1}{N-r} \sum_{n=1}^{N-r} x_n x_{n+r} \quad r = 0, 1, 2, \ldots, m \quad (11.87)$$

where r is called the *lag number* and m is the maximum lag number ($m < N$). Note that the number of possible products at each lag number r in Equation (11.87) is only $N - r$. Hence, the division by $N - r$ is needed to obtain an unbiased estimate of the autocorrelation function. The number of real multiply-add operations required to compute the autocorrelation estimate is approximately Nm.

11.4.2 Autocorrelation Estimates via FFT Computations

The indirect method of computing autocorrelation estimates is based on the Weiner–Khinchine relations defined in Equation (5.28). Specifically, the autocorrelation function is computed by taking the inverse Fourier transform of the autospectrum

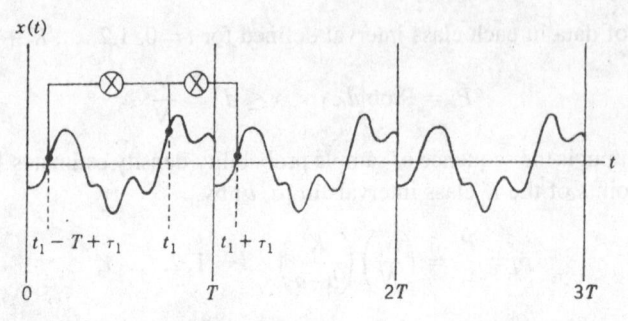

Figure 11.4 Illustration of circular effect in correlation analysis via FFT calculations.

estimate. However, due to the underlying periodic assumption of the finite Fourier transform, the autocorrelation function computed by this procedure is "circular" in character. This occurs because the FFT algorithm essentially treats a record of length $T = N\Delta t$ as one period of an ongoing periodic function. Hence, the resulting correlation function appears as if it were calculated from a periodic function, as illustrated in Figure 11.4. For a time t_1 and delay τ_1 such that $T - t_1 < \tau_1$, the product $x(t_1)x(t_1 + \tau_1) = x(t_1)x(t_1 - T + \tau_1)$. It follows that the resulting correlation function at any delay τ will be a composite of terms involving $R_{xx}(\tau)$ and $R_{xx}(T - \tau)$.

To evaluate this case, let the finite Fourier transform of a record $x(t)$, $0 \le t \le T$, and its complex conjugate be given by

$$X(f) = \int_0^T x(\alpha)e^{-j2\pi f \alpha}d\alpha \qquad X^*(f) = \int_0^T x(\beta)e^{j2\pi f \beta}d\beta$$

It follows that

$$|X(f)|^2 = \int_0^T \int_0^T x(\alpha)x(\beta)[e^{-j2\pi f(\beta-\alpha)}]d\beta d\alpha \qquad (11.88)$$

With the transformation of variables $\tau = \beta - \alpha$, $d\tau = d\beta$, and $\beta = \alpha + \tau$, Equation (11.88) becomes

$$|X(f)|^2 = \int_0^T \int_{-\alpha}^{T-\alpha} x(\alpha)x(\alpha+\tau)e^{-j2\pi f \tau}d\tau d\alpha \qquad (11.89)$$

From Equation (5.67), the two-sided autospectral density function of $x(t)$ is estimated by

$$\hat{S}_{xx}(f) = \frac{1}{T}E\left[|X(f)|^2\right] = \frac{1}{T}\int_0^T \int_{-\alpha}^{T-\alpha} \hat{R}_{xx}(\tau)e^{-j2\pi f \tau}d\tau d\alpha \qquad (11.90)$$

By reversing the order of integration as shown in the sketch below, Equation (11.90) can be written as

$$\hat{S}_{xx}(f) = \frac{1}{T}\int_{-T}^{0}\int_{-\tau}^{T}\hat{R}_{xx}(\tau)e^{-j2\pi f \tau}d\alpha d\tau + \frac{1}{T}\int_0^T \int_0^{T-\tau}\hat{R}_{xx}(\tau)e^{-j2\pi f \tau}d\alpha d\tau$$
$$= \frac{1}{T}\int_{-T}^{0}(T+\tau)\hat{R}_{xx}(\tau)e^{-j2\pi f \tau}d\tau + \frac{1}{T}\int_0^T(T-\tau)\hat{R}_{xx}(\tau)e^{-j2\pi f \tau}d\tau \qquad (11.91)$$

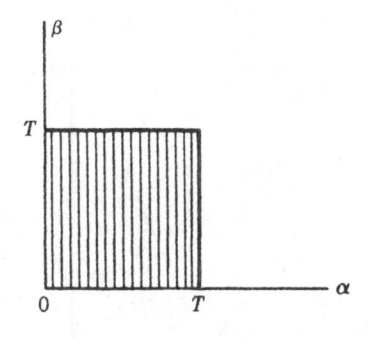

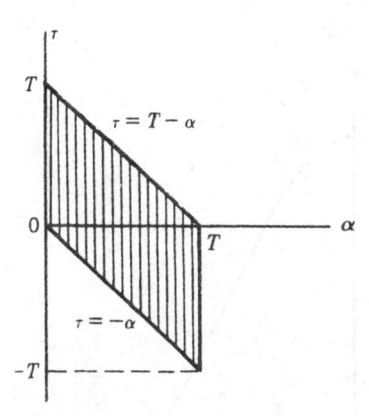

AUTOCORRELATION FUNCTIONS

In the first term of Equation (11.91), let $u = -\tau$ and $du = -d\tau$ to obtain

$$\int_{-T}^{0} (T+\tau)\hat{R}_{xx}(\tau)e^{-j2\pi f\tau}d\tau = \int_{0}^{T} (T-u)\hat{R}_{xx}(u)e^{j2\pi fu}du$$

where $\hat{R}_{xx}(-u)$ is replaced by $\hat{R}_{xx}(u)$. Next, change the variables again by letting $\tau = T - u$, $d\tau = -du$, to give

$$\int_{0}^{T} (T-u)\hat{R}_{xx}(u)e^{j2\pi fu}du = \int_{0}^{T} \tau\hat{R}_{xx}(T-\tau)e^{-j2\pi f\tau}d\tau$$

Here, use is made of the fact that $e^{j2\pi fT} = 1$ for any $f = f_k = k\Delta f = (k/T)$ where k is an integer. Thus Equation (11.91) is the same as

$$\hat{S}_{xx}(f) = \frac{1}{T}\int_{0}^{T} \tau\hat{R}_{xx}(T-\tau)e^{-j2\pi f\tau}d\tau + \frac{1}{T}\int_{0}^{T} (T-\tau)\hat{R}_{xx}(\tau)e^{-j2\pi f\tau}d\tau$$

$$= \int_{0}^{T} \hat{R}^{c}_{xx}(\tau)e^{-j2\pi f\tau}d\tau \qquad (11.92)$$

where

$$\hat{R}^{c}_{xx}(\tau) = \frac{(T-\tau)}{T}\hat{R}_{xx}(\tau) + \frac{\tau}{T}\hat{R}_{xx}(T-\tau) \qquad (11.93)$$

It follows that the inverse Fourier transform of $\hat{S}_{xx}(f)$ in Equation (11.92) will yield $\hat{R}^{c}_{xx}(\tau)$ as defined in Equation (11.93). For a digital sample $\{x_n\}, n = 0, 1, \ldots, N-1$, the *circular correlation function* in Equation (11.93) becomes

$$\hat{R}^{c}_{xx}(r\Delta t) = \frac{N-r}{N}\hat{R}_{xx}(r\Delta t) + \frac{r}{N}\hat{R}_{xx}[(N-r)\Delta t] \qquad (11.94)$$

The two parts of Equation (11.94) are illustrated in Figure 11.5.

In practice, for correlation functions that decay rapidly, the circular effect is not of great concern for maximum lag values of, say, $m < 0.1N$. In any case, the problem can be avoided by adding zeros to the original data. The effect of adding zeros to the data is to spread the two portions of the circular correlation function. In particular, if N zeros

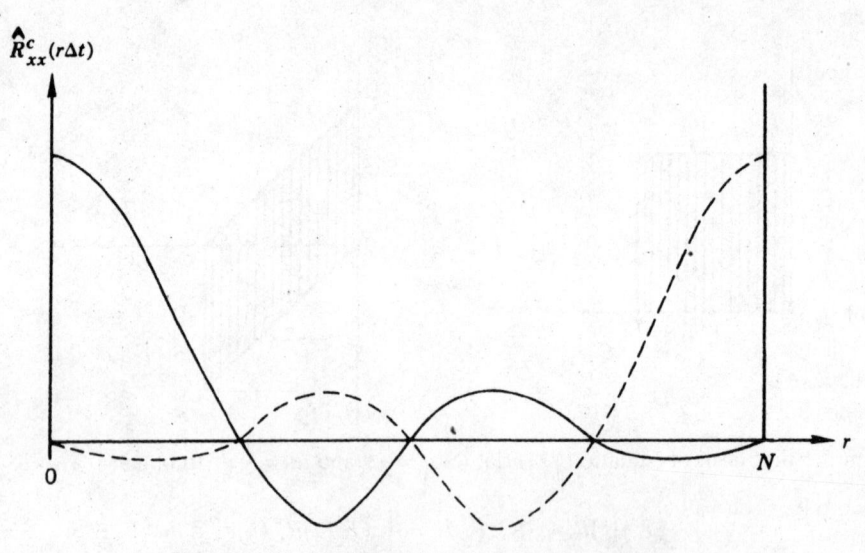

Figure 11.5 Illustration of circular correlation function.

are added to the original N data values, then the two portions will separate completely giving

$$\hat{R}^s_{xx}(r\Delta t) = \begin{cases} \dfrac{(N-r)}{N}\hat{R}_{xx}(r\Delta t) & r = 0, 1, \ldots, N-1 \\ \dfrac{(r-N)}{N}\hat{R}_{xx}[(2N-r)\Delta t] & r = N, N+1, \ldots, 2N-1 \end{cases} \quad (11.95)$$

The two parts of Equation (11.95) are shown in Figure 11.6. Note that the first half of the estimate where $0 \leq r \leq N-1$ represents the autocorrelation function values for positive lags ($0 \leq r \leq m$), while the second half of the estimate where $N \leq r \leq 2N-1$ constitutes the autocorrelation function values for negative lags ($-m \leq r \leq 0$). However, because autocorrelation functions are always even functions of r, the second half

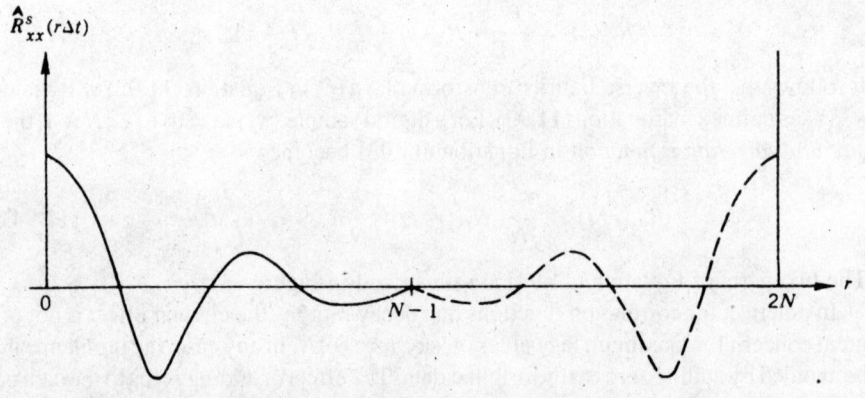

Figure 11.6 Circular correlation function when N zeros are added.

of the estimate can be discarded, so the final unbiased autocorrelation estimate is computed from

$$\hat{R}_{xx}(r\Delta t) = \frac{N}{N-r}\hat{R}^s_{xx}(r\Delta t) \quad r = 0, 1, \ldots, N-1 \qquad (11.96)$$

The correlation estimate given by Equation (11.96) is statistically equivalent to the directly computed correlation estimate defined in Equation (11.87). However, depending on the maximum lag value m, the indirect FFT approach might require substantially less calculation. Specifically, the indirect method requires first the computation of a spectral density estimate, which involves FFT calculations over n_d independent records, each with N data values augmented by N zeros for a total of $2N$ values for each FFT. This is followed by an inverse FFT over the $2N$ data points of the averaged spectral density estimate to give a total of $(n_d + 1)$ FFT calculations, each requiring $(4Np)$ real operations as detailed in Section 11.2.2. For an equivalent total record length of $n_d N$ data points, the direct method requires approximately $mn_d N$ real operations. Hence for a similar maximum lag value, $m = N$, the speed ratio is

$$\text{Speed ratio} = \frac{n_d N^2}{(n_d + 1)4Np} \approx \frac{N}{4p} \qquad (11.97)$$

For example, if $N = 1024 = 2^{10}$, the speed ratio is $1024/40 \simeq 26$. In practice, because only real number sequences are involved in autocorrelation and autospectra estimates, an additional speed increase of almost two can be achieved by using the FFT procedures detailed in Section 11.2.4.

In summary, the following steps are recommended to compute the autocorrelation function via FFT procedures. The available sample size for the record $x(n\Delta t)$ is assumed to be Nn_d, where $N = 2^p$.

1. Determine the maximum lag number m of interest and divide the available data record into n_d blocks, each consisting of $N \geq m$ data values.
2. Augment each block of N data values, $\{x_n\}$, $n = 1, 2, \ldots, N$, with N zeros to obtain a new sequence of $2N$ values.
3. Compute the $2N$-point FFT giving $X(f_k)$, $k = 0, 1, \ldots, 2N-1$, using Equation (11.36) with $2N$ replacing N.
4. Compute the two-sided autospectral density estimate $\hat{S}_{xx}(f_k)$ for $k = 0, 1, \ldots, 2N-1$ using Equation (11.101), to follow.
5. Compute the inverse FFT of $\hat{S}_{xx}(f_k)$ to obtain $\hat{R}^s_{xx}(r\Delta t)$ for $r = 0, 1, \ldots, 2N-1$, using Equation (11.76) with N replaced by $2N$, $X_k = \hat{S}_{xx}(f_k)$, and $x_n = \hat{R}^s_{xx}(r\Delta t)$.
6. Discard the last half of $\hat{R}^s_{xx}(r\Delta t)$ to obtain results for $r = 0, 1, \ldots, N-1$.
7. Multiply $\hat{R}^s_{xx}(r\Delta t)$, $r = 1, 2, \ldots, N-1$, by the scale factor $N/(N-r)$ to obtain the desired $\hat{R}_{xx}(r\Delta t)$.

It should be noted that the inverse transform in Step 5 requires that all values of the spectral estimate be used; that is, $\hat{S}_{xx}(f_k)$, $k = 0, 1, \ldots, 2N-1$, even though the Nyquist frequency occurs at $k = N$. This matter is discussed further in Section 11.5.1. It should also be noted from Section 8.4 that the variance of an autocorrelation estimate is inversely proportional to $2B_e T_r = N n_d$. Hence, an acceptably accurate autocorrelation estimate can often be obtained from a single FFT spectrum ($n_d = 1$) if N is sufficiently large. Finally, the calculation of the autospectra estimate in Step 4 should be accomplished without tapering operations of the type discussed in Section 11.5.2.

11.5 AUTOSPECTRAL DENSITY FUNCTIONS

Prior to 1967, the digital computation of autospectral density functions were usually accomplished by procedures based on the definition in Equation (5.34). Specifically, an autocorrelation function was first computed using Equation (11.87) and then Fourier transformed over an appropriate range of lag values to obtain a spectral estimate. This approach, which was first detailed in Ref. 10, is commonly referred to as the *Blackman–Tukey* procedure. Following the introduction of the fast Fourier transform algorithm in 1965 (see Ref. 6), a direct FFT computational procedure based upon the definition in Equation (5.67) was proposed in Ref. 11. This direct FFT approach, referred to as the *Welch* procedure or the direct FFT procedure, requires substantially fewer computer computations than the Blackman–Tukey approach and, hence, rapidly came into wide use. The basic computations for the direct FFT approach are straightforward, but there are various "grooming" operations that are often added to the computations to improve the quality of the resulting estimates. These matters will now be discussed.

11.5.1 Autospectra Estimates by Ensemble Averaging

Consider a transformed data record $x(t)$ of total length T_r that is stationary with $\bar{x} = 0$. Let the record be divided into n_d contiguous segments, each of length T, as shown in Figure 11.7. It follows that each segment of $x(t)$ is $x_i(t)$, $(i - 1)T \leq t \leq iT$, $i = 1, 2, \ldots, n_d$. Using Equation (8.157) and dividing by 2, an estimate $\hat{S}_{xx}(f)$ of the two-sided autospectral density function $\hat{S}_{xx}(f)$ for an arbitrary f is given by

$$\hat{S}_{xx}(f) = \frac{1}{n_d T} \sum_{i=1}^{n_d} |X_i(f, T)|^2 \qquad (11.98)$$

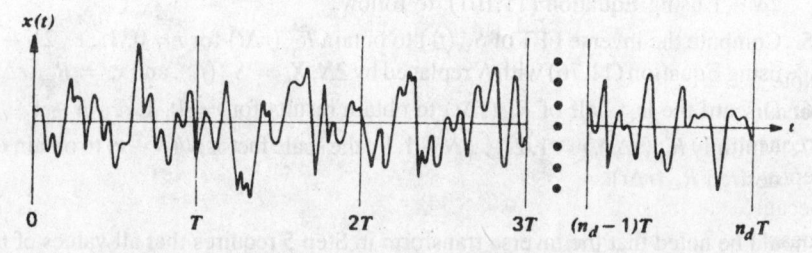

Figure 11.7 Subdivision of data into n_d records of individual length T.

where

$$X_i(f,T) = \int_0^T x_i(t)e^{-j2\pi ft}dt$$

The ensemble-averaging operation over the n_d records in Equation (11.98) approximates the expected value operation in Equation (5.67).

In digital terms, let each record segment $x_i(t)$ be represented by N data values $\{x_{in}\}$, $n = 0, 1, \ldots, N-1$, $i = 1, 2, \ldots, n_d$. The finite Fourier transform in Equation (11.98) will produce values at the discrete frequencies

$$f_k = \frac{k}{T} = \frac{k}{N\Delta t} \quad k = 0, 1, \ldots, N-1 \qquad (11.99)$$

The Fourier components for each segment are then given from Equation (11.38) by

$$X_i(f_k) = \Delta t X_{ik} = \Delta t \sum_{n=0}^{N-1} x_{in}\exp\left[\frac{-j2\pi kn}{N}\right] \qquad (11.100)$$

Two two-sided autospectral density function estimate of Equation (11.98) now becomes

$$\hat{S}_{xx}(f_k) = \frac{1}{n_d N \Delta t}\sum_{i=1}^{n_d}|X_i(f_k)|^2 \quad k = 0, 1, \ldots, N-1 \qquad (11.101)$$

As discussed in Section 11.2.4, when FFT procedures are used, the Nyquist frequency f_A occurs where $k = N/2$. Hence, the first $(N/2) + 1$ spectral values at $k = 0, 1, \ldots, N/2$ define the autospectral density estimate in the frequency range $0 \leq f_k \leq f_A$, while the last $(N/2) - 1$ spectral values at $k = (N/2) + 1, (N/2) + 2, \ldots, N-1$, can be interpreted as the autospectral density estimate in the frequency range $-f_A < f < 0$. Because autospectra functions are always real valued, it follows from Equation (11.77) that $\hat{S}_{xx}(f_k) = \hat{S}_{xx}(2f_A - f_k)$.

The one-sided autospectral density function is estimated directly from Equation (11.101) by

$$\hat{G}_{xx}(f_k) = \begin{cases} \dfrac{2}{n_d N \Delta t}\sum_{i=1}^{n_d}|X_i(f_k)|^2 & k = 1, 2, 3, \ldots, [(N/2)-1] \\ \dfrac{1}{n_d N \Delta t}\sum_{i=1}^{n_d}|X_i(f_k)|^2 & k = 0, (N/2) \end{cases} \qquad (11.102)$$

Note that the $k = 0$ and $k = N/2$ components theoretically do not double in value because there are no redundant components in the Fourier transforms at these frequencies, as illustrated in Figure 11.3. However, the $k = 0$ component, which represents the autospectral density estimate at zero frequency, is usually ignored because it is vulnerable to errors caused by the delta function representing a nonzero mean value; there will always be some round-off error in the standardization operations given by Equations (11.5) and (11.6). The $N/2$ component, which represents the spectral density estimate at the Nyquist frequency, is also usually ignored because it generally will be well above the cutoff frequency of the anti-aliasing filter used for the data conversion operations discussed in Section 10.3.3.

The number of data values N used for each FFT in Equations (11.101) and (11.102) is often called the *block size* for the calculation and is the key parameter in determining the frequency resolution bandwidth of the analysis given by

$$\Delta f = 1/T = 1/(N\Delta t) \quad (11.103)$$

On the other hand, the number of averages n_d determines the random error of the estimate as detailed in Section 8.5.4. Note that for a Cooley–Tukey FFT algorithm, it is convenient to select an analysis block size that is a power of 2—that is, $N = 2^p$, as discussed in Section 11.2.3.

11.5.2 Side-Lobe Leakage Suppression Procedures

The finite Fourier transform of $x(t)$ defined in Equation (11.98) can be viewed as the Fourier transform of an unlimited time history record $v(t)$ multiplied by a rectangular time window $u(t)$, where

$$u(t) = \begin{cases} 1 & 0 \leq t \leq T \\ 0 & \text{otherwise} \end{cases} \quad (11.104)$$

In other words, the sample time history record $x(t)$ can be considered to be the product

$$x(t) = u(t)v(t) \quad (11.105)$$

as illustrated in Figure 11.8. It follows that the Fourier transform of $x(t)$ is the *convolution* of the Fourier transforms of $u(t)$ and $v(t)$, namely,

$$X(f) = \int_{-\infty}^{\infty} U(\alpha)V(f-\alpha)d\alpha \quad (11.106)$$

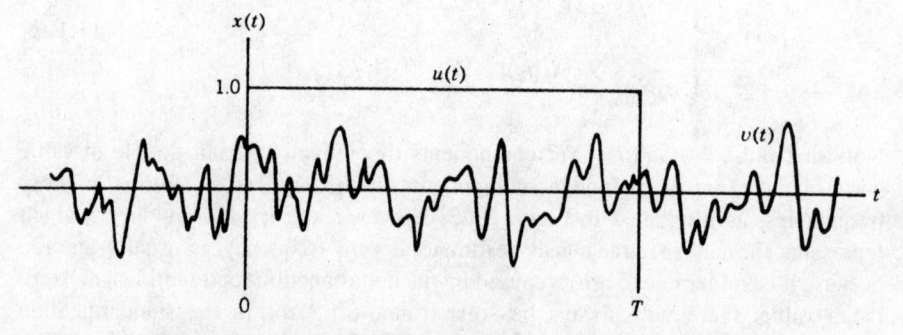

Figure 11.8 Illustration of inherent time window in special analysis.

AUTOSPECTRAL DENSITY FUNCTIONS

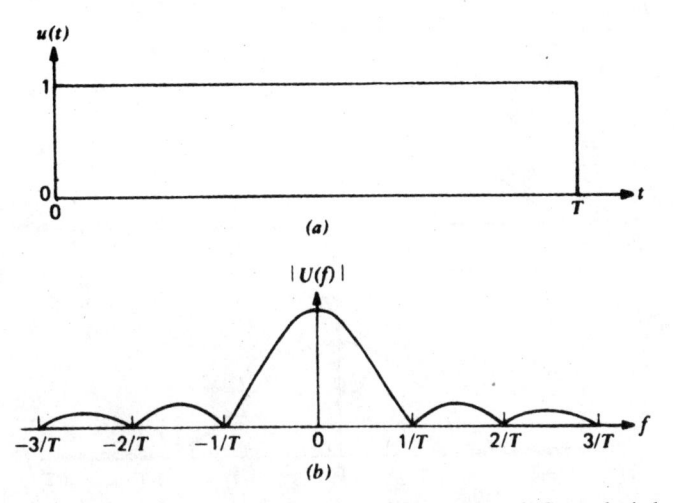

Figure 11.9 Rectangular analysis window. (a) Time window. (b) Spectral window.

For the case where $u(t)$ is the rectangular function defined by Equation (11.104), its Fourier transform is

$$U(f) = T\left(\frac{\sin \pi f T}{\pi f T}\right) e^{-j\pi f T} \qquad (11.107)$$

A plot of $|U(f)|$ is shown in Figure 11.9. Note that the first side lobe is about 13 dB down from the main lobe, and the side lobes fall off at a rate of 6 dB/octave thereafter. This function constitutes the basic "spectral window" of the analysis. The large side lobes of $|U(f)|$ allow the leakage of power at frequencies well separated from the main lobe of the spectral window and may introduce significant distortions of the estimated spectra, particularly when the data have a narrow bandwidth. The leakage problem will not arise in the analysis of periodic data with a period T_p as long as the record length T is an exact number of periods, that is, $T = kT_p, k = 1, 2, 3, \ldots$. In this case, the Fourier components at $f = kf_p = (k/T_p)$ cannot leak into the main lobe, because $U(f)$ in Equation (11.107) is always zero at these frequencies. However, if $T \neq kT_p$, then leakage will occur in the analysis of periodic data as well.

11.5.2.1 Time History Tapering

To suppress the leakage problem, it is common in practice to introduce a time window that tapers the time history data to eliminate the discontinuities at the beginning and end of the records to be analyzed. There are numerous such windows in current use, but one of the earliest and still commonly employed is a full cosine tapering window, called the *cosine squared* or *Hanning* window, which is given by

$$u_h(t) = \begin{cases} \frac{1}{2}\left(1 - \cos\frac{2\pi t}{T}\right) = 1 - \cos^2\left(\frac{\pi t}{T}\right) & 0 \leq t \leq T \\ 0 & \text{otherwise} \end{cases} \qquad (11.108)$$

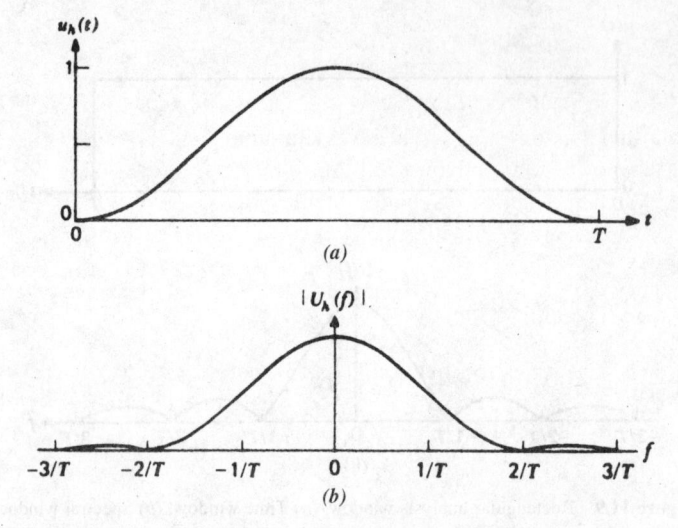

[Figure 11.10: Hanning analysis window. (a) Time window. (b) Spectral window.]

as shown in Figure 11.10(a). The Fourier transform of Equation (11.108) is

$$U_h(f) = \frac{1}{2}U(f) - \frac{1}{4}U(f-f_1) - \frac{1}{4}U(f+f_1) \qquad (11.109)$$

where $f_1 = 1/T$ and $U(f)$ is as defined in Equation (11.107). Note that

$$U(f-f_1) = -T\left[\frac{\sin \pi(f-f_1)T}{\pi(f-f_1)T}\right]e^{-j\pi fT}$$

$$U(f+f_1) = -T\left[\frac{\sin \pi(f+f_1)T}{\pi(f+f_1)T}\right]e^{-j\pi fT} \qquad (11.110)$$

A plot of $|U_h(f)|$ is shown in Figure 11.10(b). The first side lobe of the Hanning spectral window is some 32 dB below the mainlobe, and the side lobes fall off at 18 dB/octave thereafter.

Consider now any function $v(t)$ that is not periodic of periodic T and let

$$x(t) = u_h(t)v(t) \qquad (11.111)$$

The Fourier transform of Equation (11.111) is

$$X(f) = \int_0^T x(t)e^{-j2\pi ft}dt = \int_{-\infty}^{\infty} U_h(\alpha)V(f-\alpha)d\alpha \qquad (11.112)$$

At the discrete frequency values $f_k = (k/T)$ for $k = 0, 1, 2, \ldots, (N/2)$, one obtains

$$X(f_k) = \frac{1}{2}V(f_k) - \frac{1}{4}V(f_{k-1}) - \frac{1}{4}V(f_{k+1}) \qquad (11.113)$$

AUTOSPECTRAL DENSITY FUNCTIONS

where

$$V(f_k) = \int_0^T v(t) e^{-j2\pi kt/T} dt$$

To proceed further, assume that $v(t)$ behaves similar to bandwidth-limited white noise over the frequency resolution bandwidth $\Delta f = (1/T)$. It then follows that for any two discrete frequencies f and g calculated at the points $k\Delta f = (k/T)$, expected value operations on $V^*(f)$ and $V(g)$ will give

$$E[V^*(f)V(g)] = \begin{cases} 0 & \text{for } f \neq g \\ 1 & \text{for } f = g \end{cases} \quad (11.114)$$

Applying these properties to Equation (11.113) yields

$$E[|X(f_k)|^2] = \left(\frac{1}{2}\right)^2 + \left(\frac{1}{4}\right)^2 + \left(\frac{1}{4}\right)^2 = \frac{3}{8} \quad (11.115)$$

for any $f_k = (k/T)$, $k = 0, 1, 2, \ldots, (N/2)$. This represents a loss factor due to using the Hanning window of Equation (11.108) to compute spectral density estimates by Fourier transform techniques. Hence one should multiply Equation (11.100) by the scale factor $\sqrt{8/3}$ to obtain the correct magnitudes in later spectral density estimates using Equations (11.101) and (11.102). Specifically, the autospectral density estimate with Hanning is computed by Equations (11.101) and (11.102) using

$$X_i(f_k) = \Delta t \sqrt{\frac{8}{3}} \sum_{n=0}^{N-1} x_{in}\left(1 - \cos^2\frac{\pi n}{N}\right) \exp\left[-\frac{j2\pi kn}{N}\right] \quad (11.116)$$

where $f_k = k/(N\Delta t)$, $k = 0, 1, \ldots, (N/2)$. It should be mentioned that the loss factor determined in Equations (11.109)–(11.115) can also be computed directly from

$$\frac{\int_0^T u_h^2(t) dt}{\int_0^T u^2(t) dt} = \frac{3}{8} \quad (11.117)$$

where $u(t)$ and $u_h(t)$ are as defined in Equations (11.104) and (11.108), respectively. See Refs 12 and 13 for discussions of other tapering operations.

Example 11.3. Spectral Errors Due to Side-Lobe Leakage. To illustrate the effect of side-lobe leakage on spectral density estimates, consider the two autospectra estimates shown in Figure 11.11. Both spectra were computed from the same record of particle velocities measured in a water basin by a laser velocimeter during a long sequence of stationary wave activity scaled to 10 times real-time rates. The spectra were computed using $n_d = 400$ averages and a resolution of $\Delta f = 0.0488$ Hz ($T = 20.49$ s) from digital data sampled at a rate of 50 sps ($f_c = 25$ Hz). The only difference between the two spectral density estimates is that the solid line was computed with cosine squared tapering (Hanning) of the time history records and the dashed line was calculated with no tapering.

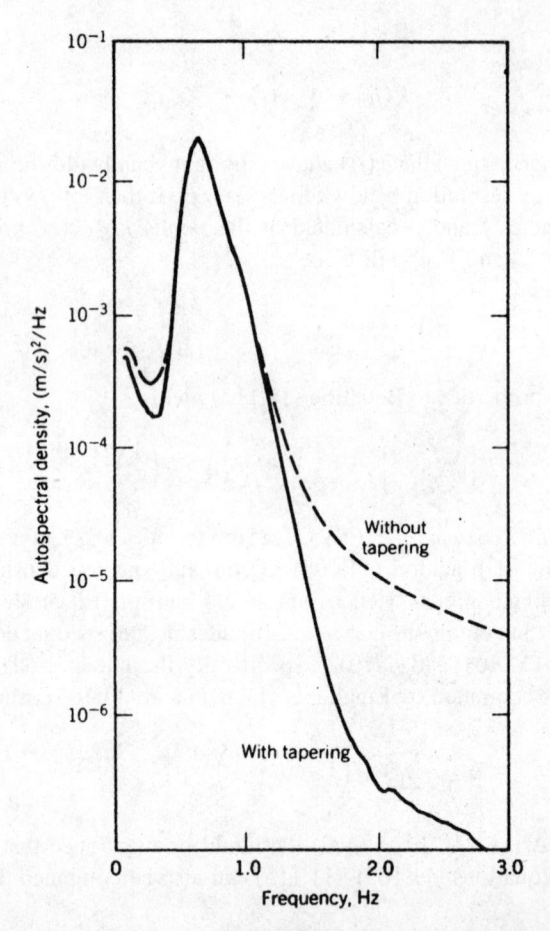

Figure 11.11 Autospectral density function of particle velocity in simulated ocean waves computed with and without tapering. These data resulted from studies funded by Shell Internationale Petroleum Maatschappij B.V., The Hague, Netherlands.

The results in Figure 11.11 clearly demonstrate the errors in autospectral density estimates that can be caused by spectral side-lobe leakage. Specifically, the spectral estimates at frequencies off a spectral peak are increased in value by leakage of power through the side lobes positioned at the frequency of a spectral peak. Note that the frequency resolution in this example ($\Delta f = 0.0488$ Hz) complies with the requirement for a negligible bias error given in Example 8.6. Thus, the leakage error can be a problem even when the usual resolution bias error is controlled. This concludes Example 11.3.

11.5.2.2 Overlapped Processing
From Figures 11.9 and 11.10, it is seen that the time history tapering used to suppress side-lobe leakage also increases the width of the main lobe of the spectral window;

that is, it reduces the basic resolving power of the analysis. For Hanning, the increase in the half-power bandwidth of the main lobe is about 60%. This is generally an acceptable penalty to pay for the suppression of leakage from frequencies outside the region of the main lobe. However, there may be cases where maintaining a minimum main-lobe bandwidth is critical to the analysis. This can be achieved by simply increasing the record length T for each FFT to provide the same bandwidth with tapering that would have occurred without tapering. Of course, this would also increase the total data record length T_r required to obtain a given random error, assuming the analysis is performed on n_d independent segments. If the data are limited such that the total record length cannot be increased, the result will be fewer independent segments (a smaller value of n_d) and, hence, an increased variability in the spectral estimates.

To counteract the increase in variability caused by time history tapering for sidelobe suppression, overlapped processing techniques are sometimes used. Specifically, instead of dividing a record $x(t)$ into n_d independent segments, $x_i(t)$, $(i-1)T \leq t \leq iT$, $i = 1, 2, \ldots, n_d$, the record is divided into overlapped segments $x(t)$ covering the time intervals

$$[q(i-1)]T \leq t \leq [q(i-1)+1]T \quad i = 1, 2, \ldots, (n_d/q) \quad q < 1 \quad (11.118)$$

A common selection in overlapped processing is $q = 0.5$, which produces 50% overlapping, as illustrated in Figure 11.12. This not only will retrieve about 90% of the stability lost due to the tapering operation but also will double the required number of FFT operations, See Ref. 11 for details.

11.5.2.3 Correlation Function Tapering

Another method for suppressing side-lobe leakage involves tapering the autocorrelation function of the data rather than the original time history. This approach, sometimes called *lag weighting*, causes very little increase in the variance of the resulting spectral estimates, and hence eliminates the need for overlapped processing. It also requires fewer computations. The general procedure is as follows.

1. Compute the two sided autospectral density function $\hat{S}_{xx}(f)$ from long, untapered time-history records using Equation (11.101).

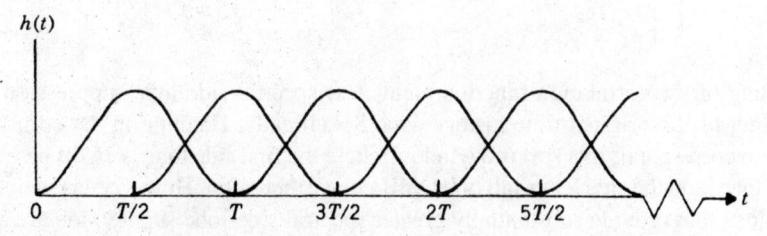

Figure 11.12 Sequence of tapered time windows for 50% overlapped processing.

2. Compute the autocorrelation function $\hat{R}_{xx}(\tau)$ by taking the inverse FFT of the autospectrum estimate as described in Section 11.4.2 (use of the circular correlation function is acceptable for this application).
3. Apply a taper $u(\tau)$ to the autocorrelation estimate such that $u(\tau) = 1$ at $\tau = 0$ and $u(\tau) = 0$ at $\tau = \tau_{max} \ll T$.
4. Based on Equation (5.34), recompute the smoothed, one-sided autospectral density function $\hat{G}_{xx}(f)$ by taking the FFT of $u(\tau)\hat{R}_{xx}(\tau)$ over the interval $0 \leq \tau \leq \tau_{max}$ and multiplying by 4.

Because the mean square value of the data is determined by the value of the autocorrelation function at $\tau = 0$, the tapering operation described above causes no change in the mean square value and hence no loss in the values of the calculated spectrum.

In computing spectra with lag weighting, one should calculate the original autospectrum from Equation (11.101) with a longer block length than needed to obtain the desired resolution in the final autospectrum. This will yield spectral estimates with smaller values of Δf and n_d than desired in the final estimates. However, because the final spectral estimates are given by the FFT of $u(\tau)\hat{R}_{xx}(\tau)$, the resolution of the final estimates will be

$$\Delta f = \frac{1}{\tau_{max}} = \frac{1}{m \Delta t} \qquad (11.119)$$

where $m < N$ is the maximum lag number. Furthermore, the normalized random error of the final estimates will be approximated by

$$\varepsilon_r = \sqrt{\frac{\tau_{max}}{n_d T}} = \sqrt{\frac{m}{n_d N}} \qquad (11.120)$$

Hence, the resulting spectral estimates will have essentially the same variance as if they were computed using time history tapering and overlapped processing procedures with the same resolution.

As for time history tapering, a full cosine tapering window (Hanning) is often used for correlation function tapering. In this case,

$$u_h(\tau) = \begin{cases} \frac{1}{2}\left(1 + \cos\frac{\pi\tau}{\tau_{max}}\right) = \frac{1}{2}\left(1 + \cos\frac{\pi r}{m}\right) & r = 0, 1, 2, \ldots m \\ 0 & r > m \end{cases} \qquad (11.121)$$

Hanning of the correlation function yields less spectral side-lobe suppression than Hanning of the original time history data. Specifically, Hanning in the correlation domain corresponds to a spectral window where the first side lobe is 16 dB below the main lobe, and the side lobes fall off at 9 dB/octave thereafter. However, lag weighting functions that provide substantially greater spectral side-lobe suppression are available, as detailed in Ref. 13.

11.5.3 Recommended Computational Steps for Ensemble-Averaged Estimates

Given a digitized sample record u_n, $n = 0, 1, \ldots, (n_d N - 1)$, the following steps are recommended to compute ensemble-averaged autospectral density estimates. An alternative procedure based upon frequency averaging is presented in Section 11.5.5.

1. Compute the mean value of the data record u_n, $n = 0, 1, \ldots, (n_d N - 1)$, using Equation (4.3) and subtract the mean value $\bar{u}$ from all data values to obtain a new data record x_n, $n = 0, 1, \ldots, (n_d N - 1)$, with a mean value of zero.
2. Divide the data record x_n, $n = 0, 1, \ldots, (n_d N - 1)$, into n_d contiguous blocks, each consisting of N values, to obtain a collection of n_d records given by x_{in}, $i = 1, 2, \ldots, n_d$, $n = 0, 1, \ldots, (N - 1)$.
3. To suppress side-lobe leakage, taper the data values of each block x_n, $n = 0, 1, \ldots, (N - 1)$, by the Hanning window described in Equation (11.108) or some other appropriate tapering function. The correlation function tapering procedure described in Section 11.5.2 may be used as an alternative.
4. Compute the N-point Fourier transform for each block of data using the FFT procedures detailed in Section 11.2.2 to obtain $X(f_k)$, $k = 0, 1, \ldots, (N - 1)$. If necessary to reduce the increase in resolution bandwidth caused by the tapering operation without increasing the random error in the estimates, compute the FFTs for overlapped records as described in Equation (11.118).
5. Adjust the scale factor of $X(f_k)$ for the loss due to the tapering operation (for Hanning tapering, multiple by $\sqrt{8/3}$).
6. Compute the autospectral density estimate from the n_d blocks of data using Equation (11.101) for a two-sided estimate, or Equation (11.102) for a one-sided estimate.

As a final point on the estimation of autospectra by the foregoing ensemble-averaging technique, for those cases where the original data are acquired as a continuous analog signal, *oversampling procedures* are often used to prepare data for digital computations. For example, one may wish to estimate the autospectral density function of a random data record that is believed to contain no information of interest at frequencies above 1 kHz. From the discussions in Section 10.3.3, to avoid aliasing errors, the usual data conversion procedure would be as follows:

1. Low-pass filter the original analog data record with a cutoff frequency of $f_c = 1$ kHz.
2. Convert the low-pass filtered analog data to a digital format using a sampling rate of 3000 to 4000 samples per second (3 to 4 ksps), depending on the rolloff rate of the low-pass filter, to achieve a Nyquist frequency of $f_N = 1.5$–2 kHz.

With the increasing availability of high-speed, inexpensive analog-to-digital converters (see Section 10.3.1), an alternative procedure can be used. Specifically, one could oversample the data at, say, 1 Msps, which produces a Nyquist frequency of

$f_N = 500$ kHz, and then low-pass digital filter and decimate the data as discussed in Section 11.1.3. The data conversion procedure would be as follows:

1. Low-pass filter the original analog data record with a cutoff frequency that is conservative for a sampling rate of 1 Msps, say $f_c = 100$ kHz.
2. Convert the low-pass filtered analog data to a digital format using a sampling rate of 1 Msps.
3. Low-pass filter the digital data using a digital filter (see Section 11.1.3) with a cutoff frequency of $f_c = 1$ kHz and a rapid rolloff above the cutoff frequency.
4. Decimate the low-pass filtered digital data by retaining, say, one of every 333 values to reduce the sampling rate to 3 ksps, corresponding to a Nyquist frequency of $f_N = 1.5$ kHz.

In the above procedure, the low-pass filtering operation on the original analog record is sometimes omitted under the assumption that there is no spectral content at frequencies above the Nyquist frequency for data sampled at such a high rate. Nevertheless, because of the possibility of high-frequency noise in the data collection system and the severe consequences of aliasing, it is recommended that analog low-pass filtering be performed on all data prior to analog-to-digital conversion, no matter how high the sampling rate.

The primary advantages of the oversampling procedure are as follows:

1. Although low-pass filtering of the original analog data is still recommended, a relatively simple, inexpensive filter can be used because the cutoff frequency can be set at a small fraction of the Nyquist frequency of the sampled data.
2. The digital filter used for the final suppression of potential aliasing errors can be carefully designed with any desired characteristics and implemented in software at a much lower cost than an equivalent analog filter.
3. If editing operations are performed to remove anomalies from the data, as described in Section 10.4.3, the digital filter used for the final suppression of potential aliasing errors will also interpolate out any discontinuities in the data that might have been introduced by the editing operations.
4. From Ref. 14, the oversampling procedure enhances the signal-to-noise ratio of the resulting digital computations.

11.5.4 Zoom Transform Procedures

A major problem in spectral analysis using FFT procedures is the computation of spectral values at relatively high frequencies with a very small resolution— that is, those cases where $f_A/\Delta f$ is very large. Of course, if there are no limits on the block size N that can be Fourier transformed, any desired resolution at higher frequencies can be obtained because

$$f_A/\Delta f = 1/(2\Delta t) \bigg/ 1/(N\Delta t) = N/2 \qquad (11.122)$$

However, there are practical limits on the block size N that can be Fourier transformed by a computer, and the required computations using a Cooley–Tukey FFT algorithm increase in proportion to Np when $N = 2^p$. Hence, it is desirable to use a computational technique that will permit the calculation of an autospectrum with a Nyquist frequency of f_A and a resolution Δf using fewer data points than suggested in Equation (11.122). Such techniques are commonly referred to as *zoom transform* procedures.

There are several ways to achieve a zoom transform, but the most common approach is first to convert the original data into a collection of band-limited records, and then to apply the principles of complex demodulation to move the lower frequency limit of each band-limited record down to zero frequency. To be specific, let the original data record $x(t)$ be bandpass filtered to produce a new record

$$y(t) = \begin{cases} x(t) & f_0 - (B/2) \leq f \leq f_0 + (B/2) \\ 0 & \text{otherwise} \end{cases} \quad (11.123)$$

Now multiply $y(t)$ by an exponential function to obtain the modulated signal

$$v(t) = y(t)e^{j2\pi f_1 t} \quad (11.124)$$

where f_1 is the modulating frequency. The Fourier transform of $v(t)$ yields

$$\begin{aligned} V(f) &= \int_0^T y(t)e^{j2\pi f_1 t}e^{-j2\pi ft}\,dt \\ &= \int_0^T y(t)e^{-j2\pi(f-f_1)t}\,dt = Y(f - f_1) \end{aligned} \quad (11.125)$$

so the autospectral density function of $v(t)$ becomes

$$G_{vv}(f) = \lim_{T \to \infty} \frac{2}{T} E\left[|V(f)|^2\right] = G_{yy}(f - f_1) \quad (11.126)$$

It follows from Equation (11.126) that if the modulating frequency f_1 is set at $f_1 = f_0 - B/2$ then the autospectrum of the original band-limited data will be transposed in frequency down to the frequency range, $0 \leq f \leq B$, from the original frequency range, $f_0 - (B/2) \leq f \leq f_0 + (B/2)$, as indicated in Figure 11.13. The data can now be sampled at a minimum rate of $2B$ sps without aliasing, as opposed to a minimum rate of $2(f_0 + B/2)$ for the original data. Hence, a much finer resolution can be obtained for a given block size N, namely,

$$\begin{aligned} \text{original data}: \quad & \Delta f \geq 2(f_0 + B/2)/N \\ \text{zoom data}: \quad & \Delta f \geq 2B/N \end{aligned} \quad (11.127)$$

Of course, the analysis must be repeated for individual zoom transforms of the data in all frequency ranges of interest.

In earlier times, the bandpass filtering and demodulation operations required to perform a zoom transform were sometimes accomplished using analog devices prior to the digitization of the data. This permitted a relatively low-rate analog-to-digital

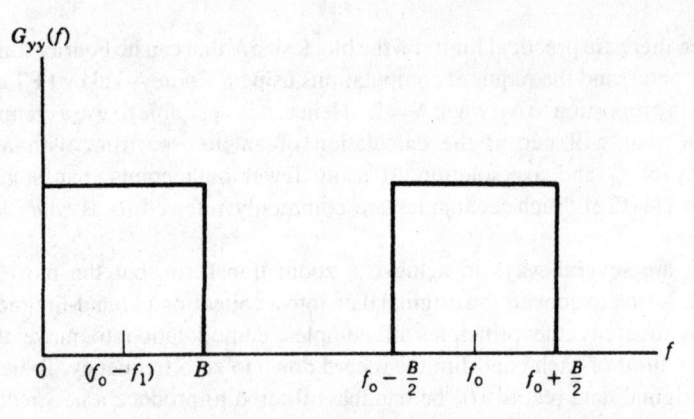

Figure 11.13 Illustration of frequency shift due to complex demodulation.

converter (ADC) to be used to analyze data at frequencies well above the ADC rate. With modern high-speed ADC equipment (see Section 10.3), it is now common to sample the data at a rate appropriate for the original data $x(t)$, and then accomplish the zoom transform operations digitially. Specifically, the original record $x(n\Delta t)$, $n = 1, 2,\ldots, N$, is first bandpass filtered by digital filtering procedures outlined in Section 11.1.3 to obtain $y(n\Delta t)$, $n = 1, 2,\ldots, N$, in the frequency range $k_1/(N\Delta t) \leq f_k \leq k_2/(N\Delta t)$. The values of $y(n\Delta t)$ are next modulated to obtain

$$v(n\Delta t) = y(n\Delta t)\exp[-j2\pi nk_1/N] \quad n = 1, 2, \ldots, N \qquad (11.128)$$

The sample values $v(n\Delta t)$ can now be decimated by a ratio of

$$d = k_2/(k_2 - k_1) \qquad (11.129)$$

to obtain $v(nd\Delta t)$, $n = 1, 2, \ldots, N$. Note that the required record length for each block is now $T = Nd\Delta t$ seconds. The Fourier transform of the decimated data then yields

$$Y\left(\frac{k}{Nd\Delta t}\right) = d\Delta t \sum_{n=0}^{N} v(nd\Delta t)\exp[-j2\pi kn/Nd] \quad k = 0, 1, \ldots, N/2 \qquad (11.130)$$

These operations are repeated over n_d independent records of $x(t)$, and the autospectrum is computed using Equation (11.102). The resulting spectrum will have a resolution of $\Delta f = 1/(Nd\Delta t)$ over the frequency range $k_1/(N\Delta t) \leq f_k \leq k_2/(N\Delta t)$, where $f_k = k/(Nd\Delta t)$ and $k = dk_1$ to dk_2.

Example 11.4. **Parameter Selections for Zoom Transform.** Assume the autospectrum of a stationary random data record $x(t)$ is to be computed with a normalized random error of $\varepsilon = 0.10$ and a resolution of $\Delta f = 1$ Hz over the frequency range 0–5120 Hz. Further assume the calculations are to be accomplished using a fixed block size of $N = 1024$ data points. Determine the total amount of data needed for the analysis.

To obtain a resolution of $\Delta f = 1$ Hz with $N = 1024$ data points, it follows from Equation (11.102) that the sampling interval must be

$$\Delta t = 1/(N\Delta f) = 0.000977$$

which provides a Nyquist frequency of

$$f_A = \frac{1}{2\Delta t} = 512 \text{ Hz}$$

Hence to analyze the data over the frequency range 0–5120 Hz, it will be necessary to zoom transform the data sequentially into 10 contiguous frequency bands of width $B = 512$ Hz. From Equation (8.158), to achieve an error of $\varepsilon = 0.10$, a total of $n_d = 100$ averages in each frequency band will be required. Hence, the total amount of data needed for the analysis in each frequency band is

$$T_r = n_d N \Delta t = 100 \text{ s}$$

If the original time history data are available in storage, then all 10 frequency bands can be analyzed with the 100 s of data. If the analysis is being performed on line, however, then a total of 1000 s of data would be needed to accomplish a sequential analysis in each of the 10 frequency bands.

11.5.5 Autospectra Estimates by Frequency Averaging

An alternative approach to the estimation of autospectral density functions is to average a single autospectral density estimate over frequency rather than averaging a collection of autospectral density estimates over an ensemble of records, as given in Equation (11.102). Specifically, consider a single sample record $u(t)$ of total length $T_r = n_d T = n_d N \Delta t$ that is converted to a digital data record

$$u_n = u(n\Delta t), \quad n = 0, 1, \ldots, (n_d N - 1) \tag{11.131}$$

where the total number of sample values $N_r = n_d N$ is a power of two. The procedure for computing a frequency-averaged autospectral density estimate is as follows:

1. Compute the mean value $\bar{u}$ of the digital data record u_n using Equation (11.5) and subtract this mean value from all data values to obtain a new digital data record x_n with zero mean value defined by

$$x_n = x(n\Delta t) = u_n - \bar{u} \quad n = 0, 1, \ldots, (n_d N - 1) \tag{11.132}$$

2. Compute the $n_d N$-point Fourier transform for the entire data record x_n using the FFT procedures detailed in Section 11.2.2 with $\Delta f = (1/T_r) = (1/n_d T)$ at the frequencies

$$f_k = k\Delta f \quad k = 0, 1, 2, \ldots, (n_d N - 1) \tag{11.133}$$

to obtain the Fourier transform values

$$X(f_k) = X(k\Delta f) \quad k = 0, 1, 2, \ldots, (n_d N - 1) \tag{11.134}$$

3. Compute the "raw" one-sided autospectral density estimates defined by

$$\tilde{G}_{xx}(f_k) = (2/T_r)|X(f_k)|^2 \quad k = 1, 2, \ldots, (N/2)n_d \quad (11.135)$$

Note that the $k=0$ component, which corresponds to the spectral component at $f=0$, is omitted. This component is commonly spurious for the reasons discussed in Section 11.5.1. Also, omitting the $k=0$ component provides an even number of $N/2$ contiguous frequency bands, each containing n_d "raw" spectral components.

4. Compute the final "smooth" one-sided autospectral density estimates by averaging the "raw" estimates over the n_d adjacent frequency components in each of the set of $(N/2)$ contiguous frequency bands with center frequencies denoted by

$$q_i = i\Delta f \quad i = 0, 1, 2, \ldots, [(N/2)-1] \quad (11.136)$$

where

$$\begin{aligned} q_i &= f_{[(2i+1)/2]n_d} \quad i = 1, 2, \ldots, [(N/2)-1] \\ q_0 &= f_{(1+n_d)/2} \quad \text{when } i = 0 \end{aligned} \quad (11.137)$$

Thus, $q_1 = f_{(3/2)n_d}$, $q_2 = f_{(5/2)n_d}$, and so on up to $q_{[(N/2)-1]} = f_{[(N-1)/2]n_d}$. The reason for changing the notation for these $(N/2)$ center frequencies is to avoid confusion with the original $(N/2)n_d$ computed frequencies. Figure 11.14 illustrates how the new $N/2$ center frequencies q_i, $i = 0, 1, 2, \ldots, [(N/2) - 1]$, are related to the original $(N/2)n_d$ computed frequencies f_k, $k = 1, 2, \ldots, (N/2)n_d$, by showing the correspondence between the indices i and k.

5. By this frequency-averaging procedure, the final "smooth" one-sided autospectral density function estimate computed from each frequency band of n_d adjacent frequency components is given at the $N/2$ center frequencies by

$$\hat{G}_{xx}(q_i) = \frac{1}{n_d} \sum_{k=in_d+1}^{(i+1)n_d} \tilde{G}_{xx}(f_k), i = 0, 1, 2, \ldots, [(N/2)-1] \quad (11.138)$$

From Equation (11.114), the components of the Fourier transform $X(f)$ at any two frequencies spaced $(1/T)$ apart are statistically independent. Hence, Equation (11.138) shows that, by averaging over n_d adjacent frequency components, the autospectral density estimates computed from a single record of total length $T_r = n_d T = n_d N \Delta t$ will produce results with the same random error as averaging over an ensemble of

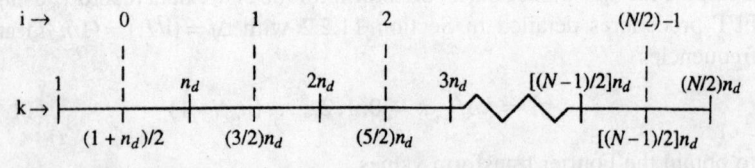

Figure 11.14 Relation of center frequencies to original computed frequencies for frequency-averaged autospectral density estimates.

AUTOSPECTRAL DENSITY FUNCTIONS

autospectral density estimates computed using Equation (11.102) from n_d different records, each of length $T = N\Delta t$. In addition, because the bandwidth resolution of the frequency-averaged estimates will be $B_e = n_d T_r = (1/T)$, the bias error in the frequency-averaged estimates will be essentially the same as the bias error in the ensemble-averaged estimates. However, the spectral window for frequency-averaged estimates will be quite different from the spectral window for ensemble-averaged estimates. Specifically, the square of the net spectral window for frequency-averaged estimates, $|U_i|^2$, will be the sum of the squares of n_d adjacent spectral windows, $|U_k|^2$, each as defined in Equation (11.107), namely,

$$|U_i|^2 = \sum_{k=in_d+1}^{(i+1)n_d} |U_k|^2 \quad i = 0, 1, 2, \ldots, [(N/2)-1] \qquad (11.139)$$

The window in Equation (11.139) approaches a rectangular shape as n_d becomes large. It still has side lobes, but they become very small compared to the main lobe because the width of the side lobes is now $(1/T_r) = (1/n_d T)$ rather than $(1/T)$ as shown in Figure 11.9. This fact is illustrated in Figure 11.15 for the case when $n_d = 16$. Even with this relatively modest amount of averaging, the power of the leakage through the first side lobe, as measured by the area under the side lobe, is over 20 dB below the power passed by the main lobe. For $n_d = 100$, the power passed by the first side lobe is over 30 dB below the power passed by the main lobe, approximately equivalent to the side-lobe leakage suppression provided by the Hanning window shown in Figure 11.10.

The frequency-averaging approach offers three important advantages over the more common ensemble-averaging procedure in Section 11.5.3 as follows:

1. Because the frequency-averaging approach provides autospectra estimates with low side-lobe leakage from untapered records, no tapering of the sample records and a resulting power loss correction of the autospectra estimates are required.
2. The frequency-averaging approach allows the computation of autospectra estimates with a resolution bandwidth that is proportional to frequency, which is more desirable than a constant-resolution bandwidth for certain applications.

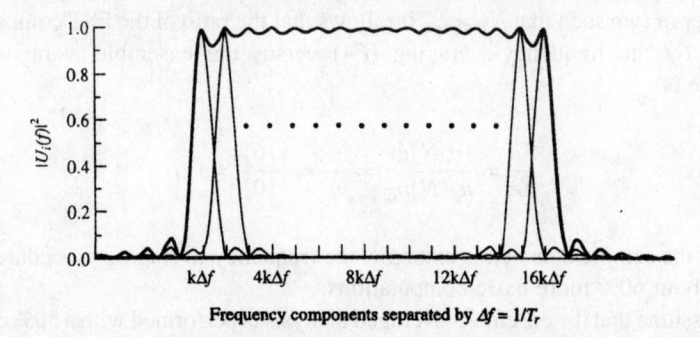

Figure 11.15 Spectral window for frequency averaging over 16 contiguous autospectral density values.

Specifically, it is shown in Example 8.7 that a proportional resolution bandwidth will provide autospectral density estimates with a near-minimum mean square error for data representing the resonant response of lightly damped mechanical and electrical systems.

3. The frequency-averaging approach allows the first resolution bandwidth to be placed at a lower frequency than provided by the autospectral density estimates computed using Equation (11.102). Specifically, excluding the estimate at $f=0$, the first frequency-averaged spectral window will start at $f=1/T_r = 1/(n_d T)$ and end at $f=n_d/T_r = 1/T$, giving a center frequency of $q_0 = [1 + (1/n_d)]/(2T)$ for the first resolution bandwidth. For example, if $n_d = 100$, the center frequency for the first resolution bandwidth is $q_0 = 0.505/T$. For estimates computed using Equation (11.102), the first resolution bandwidth, excluding the estimate at $f=0$, is always centered at $f_1 = 1/T$. This feature of frequency averaging constitutes a significant advantage in those cases where the spectral content of the data below the frequency $1/T$ may be of interest.

On the other hand, the frequency-averaging approach involves the computation of one FFT over a sequence of $n_d N$ data values, as opposed to n_d FFTs, each over N data values, as for the ensemble-averaging approach in Section 11.2.3 with no overlapping. Hence, the frequency-averaging approach requires substantially greater computer memory and, in some cases, more basic computations, as illustrated in Example 11.5. However, with the growing capacity and speed of digital computers, these issues no longer constitute a significant drawback to the frequency-averaging approach.

Example 11.5. Number of Computations for Frequency- versus Ensemble-Averaged Autospectra Estimates. Assume a sample record of stationary random data has been digitized into a total of $n_d N = 65,536$ data values, where it is desired to estimate the autospectral density function of the data with $n_d = 64$ averages. Using the ensemble-averaging approach of Equation (11.102) without overlapping, the basic computations would require $n_d = 64$ FFTs, each over $N = 1024 = 2^{10}$ data values. On the other hand, using the frequency-averaging approach of Equation (11.138), the basic computations would require a single FFT over $n_d N = 65,536 = 2^{16}$ data values. From Section 11.2.3, using the Cooley–Tukey algorithm, the number of multiply-add opertions required for an FFT over N_T data values is proportional to $N_T p$, where p is that power of two such that $N_T = 2^p$. It follows that the ratio of the FFT computations required by the frequency-averaging (FA) versus the ensemble-averaging (EA) procedure is

$$\frac{FA}{EA} = \frac{(n_d N)p_F}{n_d(N)p_E} = \frac{p_F}{p_E} = \frac{(16)}{(10)} = 1.6$$

Here, for the sample data in this example, the frequency-averaging procedure would require about 60% more basic computations.

Now assume that the ensemble-averaged analysis is performed with a 50% overlap. The number of required FFTs is $(2n_d - 1)$, and the ratio of the FFT computations required by the frequency–averaging versus the ensemble-averaging procedure is

$$\frac{FA}{EA} = \frac{(n_d N)p_F}{(2n_d - 1)(N)p_E} = \frac{p_F}{[2 - (1/n_d)]p_E} \approx \frac{16}{2(10)} \approx 0.8$$

Thus, the frequency-averaging procedure in this case would require about 20% fewer basic computations.

11.5.6 Other Spectral Analysis Procedures

This chapter summarizes only conventional spectral analysis techniques that involve Fourier transforms that inherently produce spectral estimates with a minimum resolution of $\Delta f = 1/T$. Problems often arise in practice where it is difficult or impossible to acquire a sufficiently long record to ensure the resolution needed for a proper analysis. This is particularly true in the analysis of seismic, oceanographic, atmospheric turbulence, and some biomedical data. Over the years, a number of spectral estimation techniques based on modeling procedures have been developed in an effort to resolve this problem. Such techniques are often referred to as *parametric spectral estimation procedures*.

Essentially, these techniques construct a model for the process generating the data from the data itself. The model assumes that white noise is played through a linear system with a frequency response function $H(f)$ to produce the data. The frequency response function is of the form

$$H(f) = \frac{\sum_{l=0}^{N} a_l z^l}{\sum_{k=0}^{M} b_k z^k} \qquad (11.140)$$

where $z = \exp(-j2\pi f \Delta t)$ is the z transform mentioned in Section 11.1.3. The model is then described by the difference equation

$$y_i = \sum_{l=0}^{N} a_l x_{i-l} + \sum_{k=1}^{M} b_k y_{i-k} \qquad (11.141)$$

If the b_k are identically zero, the model is termed a *moving average* (MA). If all the a_l except a_0 are identically zero, then the model is called *autoregressive* (AR). If neither the a_l nor the b_k is zero, the model is referred to as ARMA. Determination of the type of model selected (AR, MA, or ARMA) must be made by the data analyst prior to attempting a spectral estimation. This is usually done from some knowledge of the physical phenomenon being measured. If the wrong model is selected, the estimated spectra will be misleading and probably worse than those obtained by standard techniques.

After model selection, the model coefficients are derived by least squares techniques. The AR least squares technique is termed *maximum entropy spectral analysis* (MESA) because it was derived from the principle that the spectral estimate obtained must be the most random (have maximum entropy, in communication theory terms) of any autospectrum consistent with the measured data. An MA model gives rise to what is known as *maximum likelihood spectral analysis*, while no special name is given to the technique used in developing the ARMA model coefficients. The most difficult task in parametric spectral estimation is the order selection. This is a classic problem in least squares polynomial approximation. Tests have been devised to determine, in the statistical sense, an optimum model order. See Refs 15 and 16 for detailed discussions of these procedures.

11.6 JOINT RECORD FUNCTIONS

In the formulas to follow, it is assumed that two time history records $u(t)$ and $v(t)$ are from stationary (ergodic) random processes and exist only for $t_0 \leq t \leq t_0 + T$, where t_0 is arbitrary and does not enter into later formulas because of the stationary assumption. Assume the sampling interval is Δt, which corresponds to a Nyquist frequency of $f_c = 1/(2\Delta t)$. Let the respective sample values of $u(t)$ and $v(t)$ be denoted by

$$u_n = u(t_0 + n\Delta t) \quad n = 1, 2, \ldots, N$$
$$v_n = v(t_0 + n\Delta t) \quad T = N\Delta t \tag{11.142}$$

The first quantities to compute are the sample mean values given from Equation (11.5) by

$$\bar{u} = \frac{1}{N}\sum_{n=1}^{N} u_n \qquad \bar{v} = \frac{1}{N}\sum_{n=1}^{N} v_n \tag{11.143}$$

The transformed data values can then be calculated by

$$x_n = u_n - \bar{u} \quad y_n = v_n - \bar{v} \quad n = 1, 2, \ldots, N \tag{11.144}$$

where $\bar{x} = 0$ and $\bar{y} = 0$. Various preliminary operations might also be performed, as summarized in Chapter 10 and Section 11.1.

11.6.1 Joint Probability Density Functions

It follows from Equations (3.26) and (8.92) that the joint probability density function of two stationary records $x(t)$ and $y(t)$ can be estimated from digitized data by

$$\hat{p}(x, y) = \frac{N_{x,y}}{NW_x W_y} \tag{11.145}$$

where W_x and W_y are narrow intervals centered on x and y, respectively, and $N_{x,y}$ is the number of pairs of data values that simultaneously fall within these intervals. Hence, an estimate $\hat{p}(x, y)$ is obtained by dividing the full ranges of x and y into appropriate numbers of equal-width class intervals forming two-dimensional rectangular cells, tabulating the number of data values in each cell, and dividing by the product of the cell area $W_x W_y$ and the sample size N. Computer procedures for sorting the data values into appropriate cells are similar to those outlined for probability density estimates in Section 11.3.

11.6.2 Cross-Correlation Functions

As for autocorrelation functions, there are two basic approaches to the estimation of cross-correlation functions, namely, the direct approach and the roundabout FFT approach. Procedures for both cases will now be discussed.

11.6.2.1 Direct Procedures

Similar to the development presented in Section 11.4.1, unbiased estimates of the sample cross-correlation functions at lag numbers $r = 0, 1, 2, \ldots, m$ with $m < N$ are defined by

$$\hat{R}_{xy}(r\Delta t) = \frac{1}{N-r} \sum_{n=1}^{N-r} x_n y_{n+r} \quad (11.146a)$$

$$\hat{R}_{yx}(r\Delta t) = \frac{1}{N-r} \sum_{n=1}^{N-r} y_n x_{n+r} \quad (11.146b)$$

Note that the two cross-correlation functions $\hat{R}_{xy}(r\Delta t)$ and $\hat{R}_{yx}(r\Delta t)$ differ by the interchange of the x_n and y_n data values.

The sample cross-correlation function $\hat{R}_{xy}(r\Delta t)$ may be normalized to have values between plus and minus one through a division by $\sqrt{\hat{R}_{xx}(0)}\sqrt{\hat{R}_{yy}(0)}$. This defines a sample cross-correlation coefficient function

$$\hat{\rho}_{xy}(r\Delta t) = \frac{\hat{R}_{xy}(r\Delta t)}{\sqrt{\hat{R}_{xx}(0)}\sqrt{\hat{R}_{yy}(0)}} \quad r = 0, 1, 2, \ldots, m \quad (11.147)$$

which theoretically should satisfy $-1 \leq \hat{\rho}_{xy}(r\Delta t) \leq 1$, as proved in Section 5.1.3. A similar formula exists for $\hat{\rho}_{yx}(r\Delta t)$.

11.6.2.2 Via Fast Fourier Transforms

Similar to the development outlined in Section 11.4.2, the cross-correlation function can also be computed via FFT procedures. The initial sample size for both $x(t)$ and $y(t)$ is assumed to be $N = 2^p$. For these computations, the cross-correlation function is obtained from the cross-spectral density function and involves two separate sets of FFTs, one for $x(t)$ and the other for $y(t)$. These two sets of FFTs may be computed simultaneously by using the method in Section 11.2.4.

In summary, the following steps are recommended to compute the cross-correlation function via FFT procedures. The available sample size for the two records $x(n\Delta t)$ and $y(n\Delta t)$ is assumed to be $n_d N$, where $N = 2^p$.

1. Determine the maximum lag number m of interest and divide the available data records into n_d blocks, each consisting of $N \geq m$ data values.
2. Augment each block of N data values, $\{x_n\}$ and $\{y_n\}$, $n = 1, 2, \ldots, N$, with N zeros to obtain a new sequence of $2N$ data values.

3. Compute the 2N-point FFT giving $Z(k)$ for $k = 0, 1, \ldots, 2N - 1$, using the FFT procedure of Equation (11.71).
4. Compute the $X(k)$ and $Y(k)$ values for $k = 0, 1, \ldots, 2N - 1$, using Equation (11.72).
5. Compute the two-sided cross-spectral density function estimate $\hat{S}_{xy}(f_k)$ for $k = 0, 1, \ldots, 2N - 1$, using the procedure in Section 11.6.3.
6. Compute the inverse FFT of $\hat{S}_{xy}(f_k)$ to obtain $\hat{R}^s_{xy}(r\Delta t)$ for $r = 0, 1, \ldots, 2N - 1$, using Equation (11.76).
7. Multiply $\hat{R}^s_{xy}(r\Delta t)$, $r = 0, 1, \ldots, (N - 1)$, by the scale factor $N/(N - r)$ to obtain the unbiased cross-correlation estimate $\hat{R}_{xy}(r\Delta t)$ for positive lag values.
8. Multiply $\hat{R}^s_{xy}(r\Delta t)$, $r = N + 1, N + 2, \ldots, 2N - 1$, by the scale factor $N/(r - N)$ to obtain the unbiased cross-correlation estimate $\hat{R}_{xy}(r\Delta t)$ for negative lag values.

The justifications for these various steps are similar to those discussed for autocorrelation analysis in Section 11.4.2.

11.6.3 Cross-Spectral Density Functions

Similar to the ensemble-averaged computational procedure for autospectral density estimates in Section 5.5.3, the following steps are recommended to compute cross-spectral density estimates.

1. Compute the mean values of the two data records using Equation (4.5) and subtract the mean values from the data records to obtain new data records x_n, $n = 0, 1, 2, \ldots, (n_d N - 1)$ and y_n, $n = 0, 1, 2, \ldots, (n_d N - 1)$, both with mean values of zero.
2. Divide the available data records for x_n and y_n into n_d pairs of blocks, each consisting of N data values.
3. If needed to suppress side-lobe leakage, taper the data values in each pair of blocks, x_n and y_n, $n = 0, 1, \ldots, N - 1$, by the Hanning taper described in Section 11.5.2 or some other appropriate tapering function (the correlation function tapering described in Section 11.5.2 may be used as an alternative).
4. Store the tapered x_n values in the real part and the tapered y_n values in the imaginary part of $z_n = x_n + jy_n$, $n = 0, 1, \ldots, N - 1$.
5. Compute the N-point FFT for each block of data by Equation (11.71) giving $Z(k)$, $k = 0, 1, \ldots, N - 1$. If necessary to reduce the variance increase caused by tapering, compute the FFTs for overlapping records as described in Section 11.5.2.
6. Compute $X(k)$ and $Y(k)$, $k = 0, 1, \ldots, N - 1$, for each block of data using Equation (11.72).
7. Adjust the scale factor of $X(k)$ and $Y(k)$ for the loss due to tapering (for Hanning tapering, multiply by $\sqrt{8/3}$).

8. Compute the raw cross-spectral density estimate for each pair of blocks of data from $X^*(f_k) = \Delta t X^*(k)$ and $Y(f_k) = \Delta t Y(k)$ by

$$\tilde{S}_{xy}(f_k) = \frac{1}{N\Delta t}[X^*(f_k)Y(f_k)] \quad k=0,1,\ldots,N-1 \quad (11.148)$$

for a two-sided estimate, or

$$\tilde{G}_{xy}(f_k) = \frac{2}{N\Delta t}[X^*(f_k)Y(f_k)] \quad k=0,1,\ldots,N/2 \quad (11.149)$$

for a one-sided estimate.

9. Average the raw cross-spectral density estimates from the n_d blocks of data to obtain the final smooth estimate of $\hat{S}_{xy}(f_k), k=0,1,\ldots,N-1$, or $\hat{G}_{xy}(f_k), k=0, 1,\ldots, N/2$. The smooth estimate

$$\hat{G}_{xy}(f_k) = \hat{C}_{xy}(f_k) - j\hat{Q}_{xy}(f_k) = |\hat{G}_{xy}(f_k)|e^{-j\hat{\theta}_{xy}(f_k)} \quad (11.150)$$

As an alternative to the above procedure, cross-spectral density functions can be estimated using the frequency-averaging procedures discussed for autospectral density functions in Section 11.5.5.

11.6.4 Frequency Response Functions

For either single-input/single-output linear systems where extraneous noise is present only at the output or multiple-input/single-output linear systems where the inputs are uncorrelated, the recommended method for estimating the system frequency response function (including both gain and phase factors) is given by Equation (9.53), namely,

$$\hat{H}(f) = \frac{\hat{G}_{xy}(f)}{\hat{G}_{xx}(f)} = |\hat{H}(f)|e^{-j\hat{\phi}(f)} \quad (11.151)$$

It follows that

$$|\hat{H}(f)| = \frac{|\hat{G}_{xy}(f)|}{\hat{G}_{xx}(f)} \quad \text{and} \quad \hat{\phi}(f) = \hat{\theta}_{xy}(f) \quad (11.152)$$

Hence, in terms of the digital computation at the discrete frequencies $f_k = k/(N\Delta t)$, $k=0, 1,\ldots, N/2$, the gain factor the and phase factor can be estimated by

$$|\hat{H}(f_k)| = \frac{[\hat{C}_{xy}^2(f_k) + \hat{Q}_{xy}^2(f_k)]^{1/2}}{\hat{G}_{xx}(f_k)} \quad (11.153)$$

$$\hat{\phi}(f_k) = \tan^{-1}[\hat{Q}_{xy}(f_k)/\hat{C}_{xy}(f_k)] \quad (11.154)$$

where $\hat{G}_{xx}(f_k)$ is the autospectrum estimate computed from $x_n, n=0, 1,\ldots, N-1$, as detailed in Section 11.5, and $\hat{C}_{xy}(f_k)$ and $\hat{Q}_{xy}(f_k)$ are the real and imaginary parts, respectively, of the cross-spectrum estimate $\tilde{G}_{xy}(f_k)$ computed from x_n and $y_n, n=0, 1,\ldots, N-1$, as outlined in Section 11.6.3.

11.6.5 Unit Impulse Response (Weighting) Functions

The inverse Fourier transform of $\hat{H}(f)$ yields a circular biased estimate of the unit impulse response (weighting) function $\hat{h}(\tau)$ similar to the way the inverse Fourier transforms of $\hat{S}_{xx}(f)$ and $\hat{S}_{xy}(f)$ yield circular biased estimates of $\hat{R}_{xx}(\tau)$ and $\hat{R}_{xy}(\tau)$, respectively. If one desires to obtain $\hat{h}(\tau)$ from $\hat{H}(f)$, the two quantities $\hat{G}_{xx}(f)$ and $\hat{G}_{xy}(f)$ in Equations (11.102) and (11.149) should be replaced by two-sided quantities obtained by padding the original data with N zeros as described in Sections 11.4.2 and 11.6.2. The inverse Fourier transform of this new ratio will then yield $\hat{h}^s(r\Delta t)$ for values of $r = 0, 1, 2,\ldots, 2N-1$, where the last half should be discarded. Multiplication by the scale factor $N/(N-r)$ gives the desired $\hat{h}(r\Delta t)$ for $r = 0, 1, 2,\ldots, N-1$.

11.6.6 Ordinary Coherence Functions

From Equation (9.54), the ordinary coherence function $\gamma_{xy}^2(f)$ between two stationary records $x(t)$ and $y(t)$ is estimated by

$$\hat{\gamma}_{xy}^2(f) = \frac{|\hat{G}_{xy}(f)|^2}{\hat{G}_{xx}(f)\hat{G}_{yy}(f)} \qquad (11.155)$$

where $\hat{G}_{xx}(f)$ and $\hat{G}_{yy}(f)$ are the estimated autospectral density functions of $x(t)$ and $y(t)$ respectively, and $\hat{G}_{xy}(f)$ is the estimated cross-spectral density function between $x(t)$ and $y(t)$. Hence, in terms of digital calculations at the discrete frequencies $f_k = k/(N\Delta t)$, $k = 0, 1,\ldots, N/2$, the ordinary coherence function is estimated by

$$\hat{\gamma}_{xy}^2(f_k) = \frac{|\hat{G}_{xy}(f_k)|^2}{\hat{G}_{xx}(f_k)\hat{G}_{yy}(f_k)} \qquad (11.156)$$

where $\hat{G}_{xx}(f_k)$ and $\hat{G}_{yy}(f_k)$ are the autospectra estimates computed from x_n and y_n, $n = 0, 1,\ldots, N-1$, as detailed in Section 11.5, and $\hat{G}_{xy}(f_k)$ is the cross-spectrum estimate computed from x_n and y_n, $n = 0, 1,\ldots, N-1$, as outlined in Section 11.6.3.

11.7 MULTIPLE-INPUT/OUTPUT FUNCTIONS

Iterative algebraic procedures will now be listed to solve multiple-input/single-output problems using the formulas derived in Section 7.3. These results are based on the algorithm in Section 7.3.4 that computes conditioned spectral density functions from the original spectral density functions. Multiple-input/multiple-output problems should be treated as combinations of these multiple-input/single-output problems by merely repeating the same procedures on each different desired output record.

Multiple-input/single-output models for arbitrary inputs and for an ordered set of conditioned inputs are shown in Figures 7.11 and 7.12, respectively. Wherever possible, the original collected arbitrary input records should be ordered so as to agree with physical cause-and-effect conditions. Otherwise, as noted in Section 7.3, a general rule is to order the input records based on their ordinary coherence functions between each input record and the output record. It is sufficient to do this ordering at selected frequencies of interest, usually corresponding to peaks in the output autospectrum.

11.7.1 Fourier Transforms and Spectral Functions

For every stationary random input record $x_i(t)$, $i = 1, 2, \ldots, q$, and for the stationary random output record $y(t) = x_{q+1}(t)$, divide their total record lengths T_r into n_d disjoint parts, each of length T, so that $T_r = n_d T$. Finite Fourier transforms should be computed for every subrecord of length T from all of the $(q + 1)$ input and output records at the discrete frequencies $f_k = k\Delta f$, $k = 1, 2, \ldots, (N/2)$, where $\Delta f = 1/(N\Delta t)$ is the frequency resolution of the analysis. Hence, one will obtain a grand total of $(q + 1)n_d$ different finite Fourier transforms, each of which is computed at $(N/2)$ different frequencies. This provides the basic information to compute estimates of autospectral and cross-spectral density functions based on n_d averages of similar quantities calculated at each of the $(N/2)$ different frequencies. One-sided spectral density functions will be denoted by

$$G_{ij}(f_k) = G_{x_i x_j}(f_k) \quad i, j = 1, 2, \ldots, q, q+1$$
$$G_{iy}(f_k) = G_{x_i y}(f_k) \quad k = 1, 2, \ldots, (N/2) \quad (11.157)$$

The $G_{iy}(f_k)$ terms can be obtained by setting $j = q + 1 = y$. This gives the augmented $(q-1) \times (q+1)$ input/output measured spectral density matrix $\{G_{ij}\}$ that can be stored, as shown in Figure 11.16, at the successive frequencies f_k where $k = 1, 2, \ldots$, $(N/2)$. Note that this is a Hermitian matrix, where terms on the main diagonal are real valued and terms off the main diagonal are complex conjugate of each other. This Hermitian property is also true for all of the conditioned spectral density matrices in the next section.

11.7.2 Conditioned Spectral Density Functions

The general algorithm derived of Equation (7.94) in Section 7.3.4 to obtain conditioned spectral density functions by algebraic operations only is as follows. For any $j \geq i$ and any $r < j$, where $i, j = 1, 2, \ldots, q, q+1$ and $r = 1, 2, \ldots, q$, and at any fixed frequency f_k,

$$G_{ij \cdot r!}(f_k) = G_{ij \cdot (r-1)!}(f_k) - L_{rj}(f_k) G_{ir \cdot (r-1)!}(f_k)$$
$$L_{rj}(f_k) = \frac{G_{rj \cdot (r-1)!}(f_k)}{G_{rr \cdot (r-1)!}(f_k)} \quad (11.158)$$

This algorithm yields results for the output $y(t)$ by letting $y(t) = x_{q+1}(t)$. To simplify the notation, the dependence on frequency will now be omitted.

Starting from $r = 1$, results are computed for successive terms from previous terms. For $r = 1$, the algorithm in Equation (11.158) gives at any frequency f_k the $q \times q$

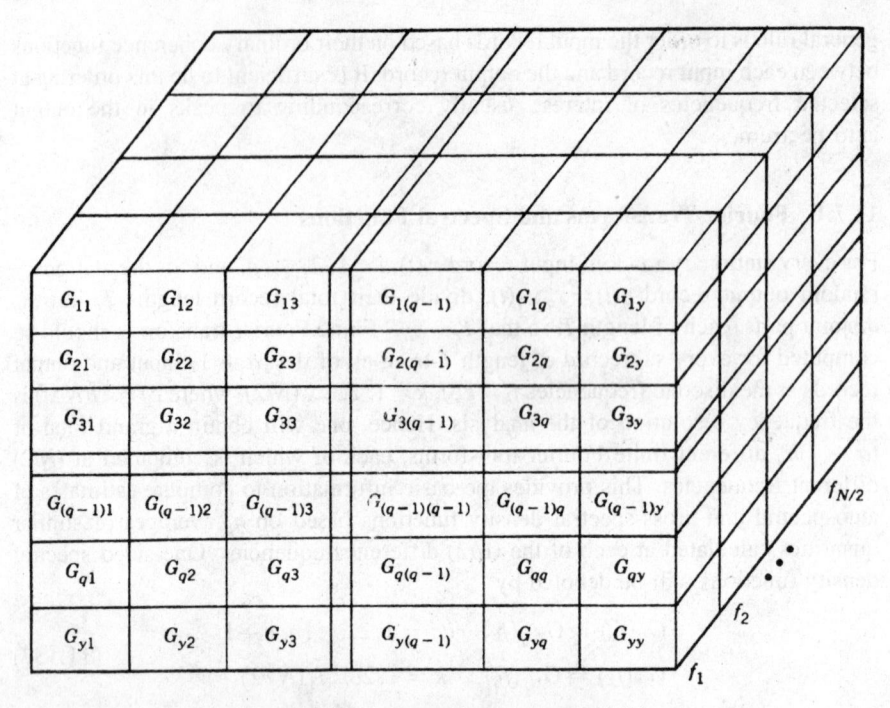

Figure 11.16 Augmented spectral matrix $\{G_{ij}\}$.

conditional spectral matrix as shown in Figure 11.17. For $r = 2$, the algorithm gives at any frequency f_k the $(q-1) \times (q-1)$ conditioned spectral matrix shown in Figure 11.18. This procedure continues until, after $(q-2)$ steps, one obtains from Equation (11.158) the 3×3 conditioned spectral matrix in Figure 11.19. The $(q-1)$th step from Equation (11.158) yields the 2×2 conditioned spectral matrix in Figure 11.20. The final qth step from Equation (11.158) yields at each frequency f_k the single term in Figure 11.21, namely,

$$G_{yy \cdot q!} = G_{yy \cdot (q-1)!} - L_{qy} G_{yq \cdot (q-1)!}$$

$$L_{qy} = \frac{G_{qy \cdot (q-1)!}}{G_{qq \cdot (q-1)!}} \quad (11.159)$$

$G_{22 \cdot 1}$	$G_{23 \cdot 1}$	$G_{2(q-1) \cdot 1}$	$G_{2q \cdot 1}$	$G_{2y \cdot 1}$
$G_{32 \cdot 1}$	$G_{33 \cdot 1}$	$G_{3(q-1) \cdot 1}$	$G_{3q \cdot 1}$	$G_{3y \cdot 1}$
$G_{(q-1)2 \cdot 1}$	$G_{(q-1)3 \cdot 1}$	$G_{(q-1)(q-1) \cdot 1}$	$G_{(q-1)q \cdot 1}$	$G_{(q-1)y \cdot 1}$
$G_{q2 \cdot 1}$	$G_{q3 \cdot 1}$	$G_{q(q-1) \cdot 1}$	$G_{qq \cdot 1}$	$G_{qy \cdot 1}$
$G_{y2 \cdot 1}$	$G_{y3 \cdot 1}$	$G_{y(q-1) \cdot 1}$	$G_{yq \cdot 1}$	$G_{yy \cdot 1}$

Figure 11.17 Conditioned spectral matrix $\{G_{ij \cdot 1}\}$.

MULTIPLE-INPUT/OUTPUT FUNCTIONS

$G_{33\cdot 2!}$	$G_{3(q-1)\cdot 2!}$	$G_{3q\cdot 2!}$	$G_{3y\cdot 2!}$
$G_{(q-1)3\cdot 2!}$	$G_{(q-1)(q-1)\cdot 2!}$	$G_{(q-1)q\cdot 2!}$	$G_{(q-1)y\cdot 2!}$
$G_{q3\cdot 2!}$	$G_{q(q-1)\cdot 2!}$	$G_{qq\cdot 2!}$	$G_{qy\cdot 2!}$
$G_{y3\cdot 2!}$	$G_{y(q-1)\cdot 2!}$	$G_{yq\cdot 2!}$	$G_{yy\cdot 2!}$

Figure 11.18 Conditioned spectral matrix $\{G_{ij\cdot 2!}\}$.

$G_{(q-1)(q-1)\cdot(q-2)!}$	$G_{(q-1)q\cdot(q-2)!}$	$G_{(q-1)y\cdot(q-2)!}$
$G_{q(q-1)\cdot(q-2)!}$	$G_{qq\cdot(q-2)!}$	$G_{qy\cdot(q-2)!}$
$G_{y(q-1)\cdot(q-2)!}$	$G_{yq\cdot(q-2)!}$	$G_{yy\cdot(q-2)!}$

Figure 11.19 Conditioned spectral matrix $\{G_{ij\cdot(q-2)!}\}$.

$G_{qq\cdot(q-1)!}$	$G_{qy\cdot(q-1)!}$
$G_{yq\cdot(q-1)!}$	$G_{yy\cdot(q-1)!}$

Figure 11.20 Conditioned spectral matrix $\{G_{ij\cdot(q-1)!}\}$.

$$G_{yy\cdot q!}$$

Figure 11.21 Conditioned term $G_{yy\cdot q!}$.

Note that $G_{yy\cdot q!}$ is the output noise spectrum G_{nn} in the q-input/single-output models of Figures 7.11 and 7.12. Thus, G_{nn} can be computed from the original measured data by following all of the steps outlined above, even though G_{nn} cannot be measured directly.

The information contained in Figures 11.16–11.21 represents the basis for identifying and interpreting various useful system properties and other relations from the measured multiple-input/output data. These matters are treated in Sections 7.3 and 7.4, as well as in Chapter 10 of Ref. 2 of Chapter 7.

11.7.3 Three-Input/Single-Output Models

Consider the special case of a three-input/single-output linear model as illustrated in Figures 7.18 and 7.19. The first three inputs in Figure 7.16 lead to the first three

(a)

G_{11}	G_{12}	G_{13}	G_{1y}
G_{21}	G_{22}	G_{23}	G_{2y}
G_{31}	G_{32}	G_{33}	G_{3y}
G_{y1}	G_{y2}	G_{y3}	G_{yy}

(b)

$G_{22 \cdot 1}$	$G_{23 \cdot 1}$	$G_{2y \cdot 1}$
$G_{32 \cdot 1}$	$G_{33 \cdot 1}$	$G_{3y \cdot 1}$
$G_{y2 \cdot 1}$	$G_{y3 \cdot 1}$	$G_{yy \cdot 1}$

(c)

$G_{33 \cdot 2!}$	$G_{3y \cdot 2!}$
$G_{3y \cdot 2!}$	$G_{yy \cdot 2!}$

(d)

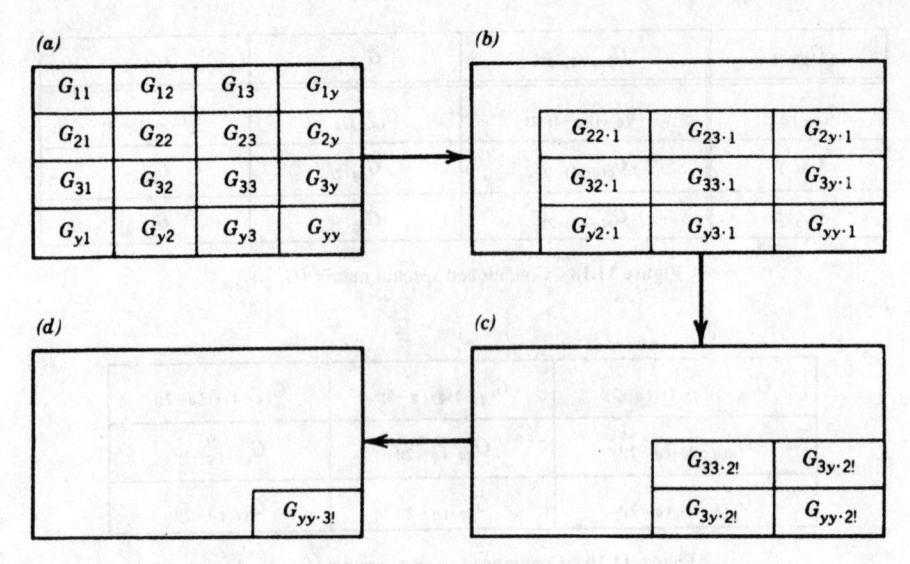

$G_{yy \cdot 3!}$

Figure 11.22 Conditioned results for three-input/one-output system.

modified SI/SO spectral models shown in Figure 7.17. Formulas will now be listed to compute various functions that apply to Figure 7.17.

Start with the augmented spectral matrix corresponding to Figure 11.16 when $q=3$ and apply the algorithm of Equation (11.158) three times to obtain the successive conditioned spectral results shown in Figure 11.22 at each frequency f_k of interest.

The $\{G_{ij \cdot 1}\}$ terms are computed by the formulas

$$
\begin{aligned}
G_{22 \cdot 1} &= G_{22} - L_{12} G_{21} \\
G_{23 \cdot 1} &= G_{23} - L_{13} G_{21} \\
G_{2y \cdot 1} &= G_{2y} - L_{1y} G_{21} \\
G_{33 \cdot 1} &= G_{33} - L_{13} G_{31} \\
G_{3y \cdot 1} &= G_{3y} - L_{1y} G_{31} \\
G_{yy \cdot 1} &= G_{yy} - L_{1y} G_{y1} \\
G_{32 \cdot 1} &= G_{23 \cdot 1}^{*} \quad G_{y2 \cdot 1} = G_{2y \cdot 1}^{*} \quad G_{y3 \cdot 1} = G_{3y \cdot 1}^{*}
\end{aligned}
\tag{11.160}
$$

where

$$L_{12} = (G_{12}/G_{11}) \tag{11.161}$$

$$L_{13} = (G_{13}/G_{11}) \tag{11.162}$$

$$L_{1y} = (G_{1y}/G_{11}) \tag{11.163}$$

MULTIPLE-INPUT/OUTPUT FUNCTIONS

The $\{G_{ij\cdot 2!}\}$ terms are computed by the formulas

$$G_{33\cdot 2!} = G_{33\cdot 1} - L_{23}G_{32\cdot 1}$$
$$G_{3y\cdot 2!} = G_{3y\cdot 1} - L_{2y}G_{32\cdot 1}$$
$$G_{yy\cdot 2!} = G_{yy\cdot 1} - L_{2y}G_{y2\cdot 1}$$
$$G_{y3\cdot 2!} = G^*_{3y\cdot 2!}$$
(11.164)

where

$$L_{23} = (G_{23\cdot 1}/G_{22\cdot 1}) \quad (11.165)$$
$$L_{2y} = (G_{2y\cdot 1}/G_{22\cdot 1}) \quad (11.166)$$

Finally, the output noise spectrum $G_{yy\cdot 3!}$ term is computed from the formula

$$G_{yy\cdot 3!} = G_{yy\cdot 2!} - L_{3y}G_{y3\cdot 2!} \quad (11.167)$$

where

$$L_{3y} = \frac{G_{3y\cdot 2!}}{G_{33\cdot 2!}} \quad (11.168)$$

The following ordinary and partial coherence functions can now be computed at each frequency f_k of interest.

$$\gamma^2_{1y} = \frac{|G_{1y}|^2}{G_{11}G_{yy}} \quad (11.169)$$

$$\gamma^2_{2y\cdot 1} = \frac{|G_{2y\cdot 1}|^2}{G_{22\cdot 1}G_{yy}} \quad (11.170)$$

$$\gamma^2_{3y\cdot 2!} = \frac{|G_{3y\cdot 2!}|^2}{G_{33\cdot 2!}G_{yy}} \quad (11.171)$$

The multiple coherence function is given by

$$\gamma^2_{y:3!} = 1 - \frac{G_{yy\cdot 3!}}{G_{yy}} \quad (11.172)$$

Various coherent output spectral density functions of interest are computed by the formulas

$$G_{y:1} = \gamma^2_{1y}G_{yy} = \frac{|G_{1y}|^2}{G_{11}} \quad (11.173)$$

$$G_{y:2\cdot 1} = \gamma^2_{2y\cdot 1}G_{yy} = \frac{|G_{2y\cdot 1}|^2}{G_{22\cdot 1}} \quad (11.174)$$

$$G_{y:3\cdot 2!} = \gamma^2_{3y\cdot 2!}G_{yy} = \frac{|G_{3y\cdot 2!}|^2}{G_{33\cdot 2!}} \quad (11.175)$$

The total output spectrum $G_{yy} = G_{yy}(f_k)$ is decomposed here into the sum of four terms as follows.

$$G_{yy} = G_{y:1} + G_{y:2 \cdot 1} + G_{y:3 \cdot 2!} + G_{yy \cdot 3!} \qquad (11.176)$$

The systems $\{A_{iy}\}$, $i = 1, 2, 3$, in Figure 7.18 can be computed using Equation (7.108) because $\{A_{iy}\}$ is the same as $\{H_{iy}\}$.

11.7.4 Functions in Modified Procedure

With the modified procedure in Section 7.4, the three inputs in Figure 7.19 are denoted by the simpler notation $U_1(f) = X_1(f)$, $U_2(f) = X_{2 \cdot 1}(f)$, $U_3(f) = X_{3 \cdot 2!}(f)$. This leads to easier interpretations of the analyzed results. Formulas to compute the various functions in Figure 7.19 with this modified notation are listed in Section 7.4.2. Formulas with the more complicated notation are given in Section 11.7.3.

1. Equations (7.122)–(7.124) for the three L-systems in Figure 7.19 give the same results as Equations (11.163)–(11.166) and (11.168).
2. Equation (7.133) for the first ordinary coherence function is exactly the same as Equation (11.169).
3. Equations (7.134) and (7.135) for the second and third ordinary coherence functions give the same results as Equations (11.170) and (11.171).
4. Equation (7.136) for the multiple coherence function gives the same result as Equation (11.172).
5. Equations (7.128)–(7.130) for the three coherent output spectral density functions give the same results as Equations (11.173)–(11.175).

PROBLEMS

11.1 Consider a sequence of $N = 16,384$ data points that are complex numbers. How many real operations would be required to Fourier transform the data values

(a) using conventional calculations.

(b) using Cooley-Tukey FFT procedures.

11.2 Determine the equation for a first-order IIR (recursive) filter that will behave like a high-pass RC filter.

11.3 A set of sample values $\{u_n\}$, $n = 1, 2, \ldots, N$, have a standard deviation of s_u. Determine the standard deviation of the transformed data values $\{x_n\} = \{u_n - \bar{u}\}$, $n = 1, 2, \ldots, N$.

11.4 Assume a set of sample values $\{u_n\}$, $n = 1, 2, \ldots, N$, are to be detrended using a polynomial of degree $K = 2$. Determine the coefficients (b_0, b_1, b_2) required for a least squares fit of the polynomial to the sample data.

11.5 In computing an autospectral density function estimate by FFT procedures, suppose a record of total length $T_r = 4$ s is digitized at a sampling rate of 4096 sps. If a resolution of $\Delta f = 16$ Hz is desired, determine

(a) the approximate number of real operations required to perform the calculations.

(b) the normalized random error of the resulting estimate.

11.6 Assume an autocorrelation function is estimated from a sample record $x(t)$ of stationary random data where the autocorrelation function can be approximated by

$$\hat{R}_{xx}(\tau) = e^{-2|\tau|} \cos 18.85\tau$$

If the sample record is $T = 1$ s long, what is the equation for the circular correlation function that would be obtained by computing the inverse Fourier transform of an autospectrum estimate without zero padding?

11.7 A sequence of $N_r = 8192$ sample values of a stationary random signal are available to compute an autocorrelation function estimate. It is desired to compute the autocorrelation estimate by the indirect FFT approach to a maximum lag value of $m = 256$. This could be accomplished by using a single block of $N = 8192$ data points versus $n_d = 32$ blocks of $N = 256$ data points. Which approach would require fewer calculations?

11.8 Assume a cross-correlation function is to be estimated from two sample records, each digitized into a sequence of $N_r = 4096$ data points. Further assume the estimate is desired for lag values out to $m = 256$. Determine the speed ratio between the direct computational approach and the indirect FFT approach.

11.9 The *noise bandwidth* of a spectral window is defined as the bandwidth of an ideal rectangular bandpass filter that would produce the same output mean square value as the spectral window when analyzing white noise. Determine the noise bandwidth of the spectral window produced by a rectangular (untapered) time window of length T.

11.10 The Fourier coefficients of a record $x(t) = A \sin 100\pi t$ are calculated from a simple record of length $T = 1.015$ s. Assuming a very high sampling rate, determine the magnitude of the Fourier coefficient with the largest value that would be calculated using

(a) a rectangular time window.

(b) a Hanning time window.

REFERENCES

1. Hamming, R. W., *Digital Filters*, 2nd ed., Prentice-Hall, Englewood Cliffs, NJ, 1983.
2. Stearns, S. D., and Rush, D. R., *Digital Signal Analysis*, 2nd ed., Prentice-Hall, Englewood Cliffs, NJ, 1990.

3. Oppenheim, A. V., Schafer, R. W., and Buck, J. R., *Discrete-Time Signal Processing*, 2nd ed., Prentice-Hall, Englewood Cliffs, NJ, 1998.
4. Mitra, S. K., and Kaiser, J. F., *Handbook for Digital Signal Processing*, Wiley, New York, 1993.
5. Brigham, E. O., *The Fast Fourier Transform and Its Applications*, Prentice-Hall, Englewood Cliffs, NJ, 1988.
6. Cooley, J. W., and Tukey, J. W., "An Algorithm for the Machine Calculation of Complex Fourier Series," *Mathematics of Computations*, Vol. 19, p. 297, 1965.
7. Winograd, S., "On Computing the Discrete Fourier Transform," *Mathematics of Computations*, Vol. 32, p. 175, 1978.
8. Hartley, R. V. L., "A More Symmetrical Fourier Analysis Applied to Transmission Problems," *Proceedings of the IRE*, Vol. 30, p. 144, 1942.
9. Bracewell, R. N., *The Hartley Transform*, Oxford University Press, New York, 1986.
10. Blackman, R. B., and Tukey, J. W., *The Measurement of Power Spectra*, Dover, New York, 1958.
11. Welch, P. D., "The Use of Fast Fourier Transform for the Estimation of Power Spectra: A Method Based on Time Averaging Over Short, Modified Periodograms," *IEEE Transactions on Audio and Electroacoustics*, Vol. AU-15, No. 2, June 1967.
12. Harris, F. J., "On the Use of Windows for Harmonic Analysis with Discrete Fourier Transform," *Proceedings of the IEEE*, Vol. 66, p. 51, January 1978.
13. Nuttall, A. H., and Carter, G. C, "Spectral Estimation Using Combined Time and Lag Weighting," *Proceedings of the IEEE*, Vol. 70, p. 1115, September 1982.
14. Hauser, M. W., "Principles of Oversampling A/D Conversion," *Journal of the Audio Engineering Society*, Vol. 39, p. 3, January/February 1991.
15. Marple, L. S., *Digital Spectral Analysis with Applications*, Prentice-Hall, Engle-wood Cliffs, NJ, 1987.
16. Kay, S. M., *Modern Spectral Estimation: Theory and Application*, Prentice-Hall, Englewood Cliffs, NJ, 1988.

CHAPTER 12

Nonstationary Data Analysis

The material presented in previous chapters has been restricted largely to the measurement and analysis of stationary random data, that is, data with statistical properties that are invariant with translations in time (or any other independent variable of the data). The theoretical ideas, error formulas, and processing techniques do not generally apply when the data are nonstationary. Special considerations are required in these cases. Such considerations are the subject of this chapter.

12.1 CLASSES OF NONSTATIONARY DATA

Much of the random data of interest in practice is nonstationary when viewed as a whole. Nevertheless, it is often possible to force the data to be at least piecewise stationary for measurement and analysis purposes. To repeat the example from Section 10.4.1, the pressure fluctuations in the turbulent boundary layer generated by a high-speed aircraft during a typical mission will generally be nonstationary because they depend on the airspeed and altitude, which vary during the mission. However, one can easily fly the aircraft under a specific set of fixed flight conditions so as to produce stationary boundary layer pressures for measurement purposes. The flight conditions can then be changed sequentially to other specific sets of fixed conditions, producing stationary data for measurement purposes until the entire mission environment has been represented in adequate detail by piecewise stationary segments. Such procedures for generating stationary data to represent a generally nonstationary phenomenon are commonly used and are strongly recommended to avoid the need for nonstationary data analysis procedures.

There are a number of situations where the approach to data collection and analysis described above is not feasible, and individual sample records of data must be analyzed as nonstationary data. From a purely computational viewpoint, the most desirable situation is that in which an experiment producing the nonstationary data of

---

Random Data: Analysis and Measurement Procedures, Fourth Edition. By Julius S. Bendat and Allan G. Piersol
Copyright © 2010 John Wiley & Sons, Inc.

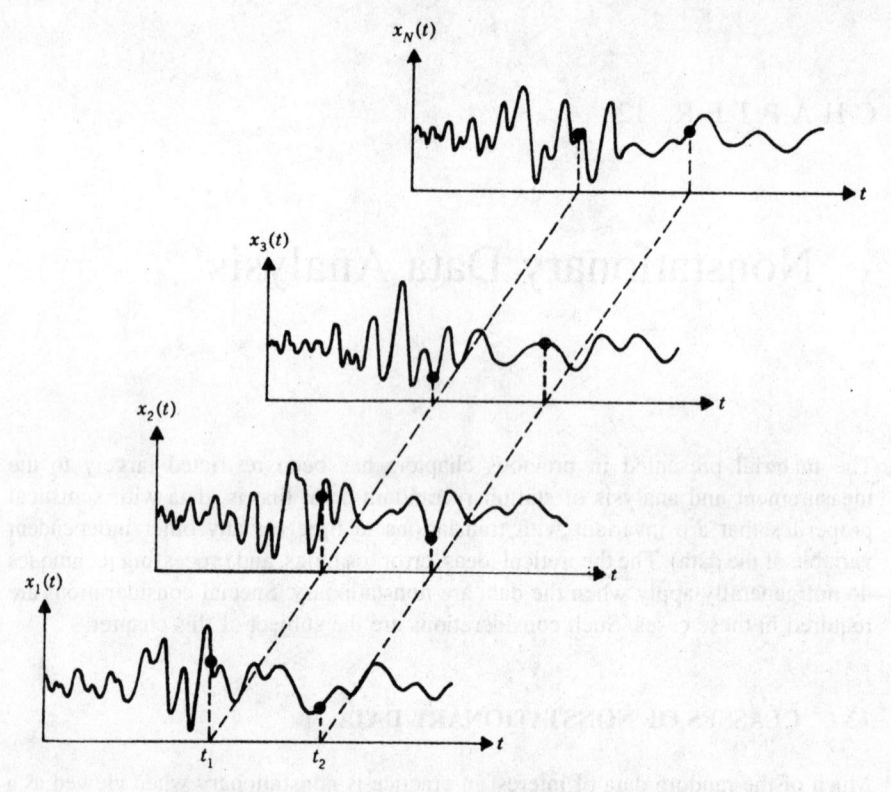

Figure 12.1 Sample records of nonstationary random process.

interest can be repeated under statistically similar conditions. This allows an ensemble of sample records to be measured on a common time base, as illustrated in Figure 12.1. A more common situation, however, is that in which the nonstationary phenomenon of interest is unique and cannot be reproduced under statistically similar conditions. Examples include nonstationary ocean waves, atmospheric turbulence, and economic time-series data. The basic factors producing such data are too complex to allow the performance of repeated experiments under similar conditions. The analysis of data in these cases must be accomplished by computations on single sample records.

An appropriate general methodology does not exist for analyzing the properties of all types of nonstationary random data from individual sample records. This is due partly to the fact that a nonstationary conclusion is a negative statement specifying only a lack of stationary properties, rather than a positive statement defining the precise nature of the nonstationarity. It follows that special techniques must be developed for nonstationary data that apply only to limited classes of these data. The usual approach is to hypothesize a specific model for each class of nonstationary data of interest that consists of deterministic factors operating on an otherwise stationary random process. Three examples are shown in Figure 12.2. These nonstationary time history records are constructed from

PROBABILITY STRUCTURE OF NONSTATIONARY DATA 419

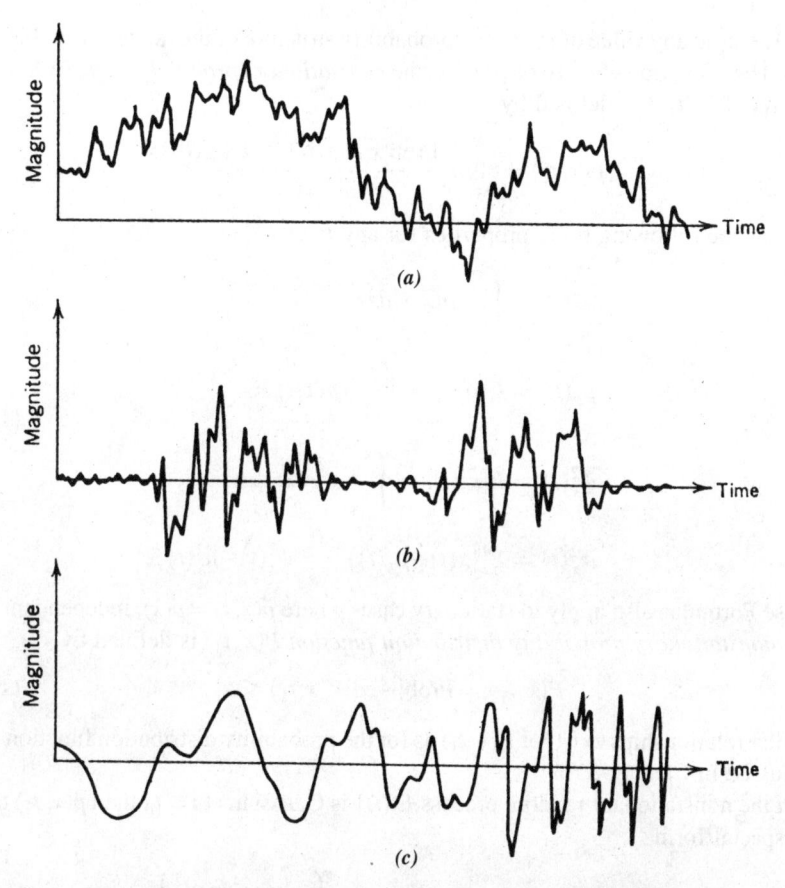

Figure 12.2 Examples of nonstationary data, (*a*) Time-varying mean value, (*b*) Time-varying mean square value, (*c*) Time-varying frequency structure.

$$
\begin{aligned}
&\text{(a)}\ x(t) = a(t) + u(t)\\
&\text{(b)}\ x(t) = a(t)u(t)\\
&\text{(c)}\ x(t) = u(t^n)
\end{aligned}
\quad (12.1)
$$

where $u(t)$ is a sample record of a stationary random process $\{u(t)\}$ and $a(t)$ is a deterministic function that is repeated exactly on each record. Such elementary nonstationary models can be combined or extended to generate more complex models as required to fit various physical situations.

12.2 PROBABILITY STRUCTURE OF NONSTATIONARY DATA

For a nonstationary random process $\{x(t)\}$ as illustrated in Figure 12.1, statistical properties over the ensemble at any time t are not invariant with respect to translations in t. Hence at any value of $t = t_1$, the probability structure of the random variable $x(t_1)$ would be a function of t_1. To be precise, the *nonstationary probability density function* $p(x, t_1)$ of $\{x(t_1)\}$ is defined by

$$p(x, t_1) = \lim_{\Delta x \to 0} \frac{\text{Prob}[x < x(t_1) \leq x + \Delta x]}{\Delta x} \quad (12.2)$$

and has the following basic properties for any t:

$$1 = \int_{-\infty}^{\infty} p(x, t) dx$$

$$\mu_x(t) = E[x(t)] = \int_{-\infty}^{\infty} x p(x, t) dx$$

$$\psi_x^2(t) = E[x^2(t)] = \int_{-\infty}^{\infty} x^2 p(x, t) dx \quad (12.3)$$

$$\sigma_x^2(t) = E[\{x(t) - \mu_x(t)\}^2] = \psi_x^2(t) - \mu_x^2(t)$$

These Formulas also apply to stationary cases where $p(x, t) = p(x)$, independent of t. The *nonstationary probability distribution function* $P(x, t_1)$ is defined by

$$P(x, t_1) = \text{Prob}[-\infty < x(t_1) \leq x] \quad (12.4)$$

Similar relationships exist for $P(x, t_1)$ as for the probability distribution function $P(x)$ discussed in Chapter 3.

If the nonstationary random process $\{x(t)\}$ is Gaussian at $t = t_1$, then $p(x, t_1)$ takes the special form

$$p(x, t_1) = [\sigma_x(t_1)\sqrt{2\pi}]^{-1} \exp\left\{\frac{-[x - \mu_x(t_1)]^2}{2\sigma_x^2(t_1)}\right\} \quad (12.5)$$

which is completely determined by the nonstationary mean and mean square values of $x(t)$ at $t = t_1$. This result indicates that the measurement of these two quantities may be quite significant in many nonstationary applications just as in previous stationary applications.

12.2.1 Higher Order Probability Functions

For a pair of times t_1 and t_2, the *second-order nonstationary probability density function* of $x(t_1)$ and $x(t_2)$ is defined by

$$p(x_1, t_1; x_2, t_2) = \lim_{\substack{\Delta x_1 \to 0 \\ \Delta x_2 \to 0}} \frac{\text{Prob}[x_1 < x(t_1) \leq x_1 + \Delta x_1 \text{ and } x_2 < x(t_2) \leq x_2 + \Delta x_2]}{(\Delta x_1)(\Delta x_2)}$$

$$(12.6)$$

and has the following basic properties for any t_1, t_2:

PROBABILITY STRUCTURE OF NONSTATIONARY DATA

$$1 = \iint_{-\infty}^{\infty} p(x_1, t_1; x_2, t_2) dx_1 dx_2$$

$$p(x_1, t_1) = \int_{-\infty}^{\infty} p(x_1, t_1; x_2, t_2) dx_2$$

$$p(x_2, t_2) = \int_{-\infty}^{\infty} p(x_1, t_1; x_2, t_2) dx_1 \qquad (12.7)$$

$$R_{xx}(t_1, t_2) = E[x(t_1)x(t_2)] = \iint_{-\infty}^{\infty} x_1 x_2 p(x_1, t_1; x_2, t_2) dx_1 dx_2$$

For stationary cases, $p(x_1, t_1; x_2, t_2) = p(x_1, 0; x_2, t_2-t_1)$. *Second-order nonstationary probability distribution functions* may be defined analogous to Equation (12.4) by the quantity

$$P(x_1, t_1; x_2, t_2) = \text{Prob}[-\infty < x(t_1) \le x_1 \text{ and } -\infty < x(t_2) \le x_2] \qquad (12.8)$$

Continuing in this way, higher order nonstationary probability distribution and density functions may be defined that describe the nonstationary random process $\{x(t)\}$ in more detail. This procedure supplies a rigorous characterization of the nonstationary random process $\{x(t)\}$.

Consider next two different nonstationary random processes $\{x(t)\}$ and $\{y(t)\}$. For $x(t_1)$ and $y(t_2)$, the *joint* (*second-order*) *nonstationary probability density function* is defined by

$$p(x_1, t_1; y, t_2) = \lim_{\substack{\Delta x \to 0 \\ \Delta y \to 0}} \frac{\text{Prob}[x < x(t_1) \le x + \Delta x \text{ and } y < y(t_2) \le y + \Delta y]}{(\Delta x)(\Delta y)} \qquad (12.9)$$

and has basic properties similar to Equation (12.7). In particular, the nonstationary cross-correlation function, which is discussed in Section 12.5, satisfies the relation

$$R_{xy}(t_1, t_2) = E[x(t_1)y(t_2)] = \iint_{-\infty}^{\infty} xy p(x, t_1; y, t_2) dx\, dy \qquad (12.10)$$

For stationary cases, $p(x, t_1; y, t_2) = p(x, 0; y, t_2-t_1)$.

The measurement of nonstationary probability density functions can be a formidable task. Even for the first-order density function defined in Equation (12.2), all possible combinations of x and t_1 must be considered. This will require the analysis of a large collection of sample records. If a Gaussian assumption can be made, Equation (12.5) reduces the problem of measuring $p(x, t_1)$ to measuring $\mu_x(t_1)$ and $\sigma_x^2(t_1)$, which is a much simpler undertaking. Nevertheless, ensemble averaging of a collection of sample records is still generally required, as discussed in Sections 12.3 and 12.4.

12.2.2 Time-Averaged Probability Functions

It often occurs in practice that only one or a very few sample records of data are available for a nonstationary random process of interest. There may be a strong temptation in such cases to analyze the data by time-averaging procedures as would be appropriate if the data were a sample record from a stationary (ergodic) random process. For some nonstationary data parameters, time-averaging analysis procedures can produce meaningful results in certain special cases, as will be discussed later. For the case of probability density functions, however, time-averaging procedures will generally produce severely distorted results. In particular, the probability density function computed by time-averaging data with a nonstationary mean square value will tend to exaggerate the probability density of low- and high-amplitude values at the expense of intermediate values, as demonstrated in the illustration to follow.

Example 12.1. **Illustration of Time-Averaged Probability Density Function.**
Assume a sample record of data consists of a normally distributed stationary time history with a zero mean and a variance σ_1^2 over the first half of the record, and a second normally distributed stationary time history with a zero mean and a variance $\sigma_2^2 > \sigma_1^2$ over the second half of the record. Then the time history $x(t)$ is given by

$$x(t) = \begin{cases} x_1(t) & 0 \le t \le T/2 \\ x_2(t) & T/2 \le t \le T \end{cases}$$

and the probability density function of $x(t)$ is given by

$$p(x,t) = \begin{cases} \dfrac{1}{\sigma_1\sqrt{2\pi}} e^{-x^2/2\sigma_1^2} & 0 \le t \le T/2 \\ \dfrac{1}{\sigma_2\sqrt{2\pi}} e^{-x^2/2\sigma_2^2} & T/2 \le t \le T \end{cases}$$

Now, if this lack of stationarity is ignored in the computation of a probability density function for $x(t)$, $0 \le t \le T$, the resulting density calculated at any level x will simply be the average of the densities for the two halves of the record at level x. That is,

$$\hat{p}(x) = \frac{1}{2\sqrt{2\pi}} \left[\frac{1}{\sigma_1} e^{-x^2/2\sigma_1^2} + \frac{1}{\sigma_2} e^{-x^2/2\sigma_2^2} \right]$$

For example, let $\sigma_1^2 = 1$ and $\sigma_2^2 = 16$. The nonstationary resultant probability density function that would be obtained for this case is computed and illustrated graphically in Figure 12.3. Observe that $\hat{\sigma} = 2.9$ in $\hat{p}(x)$ because $\hat{\sigma}^2 = \frac{1}{2}(\sigma_1^2 + \sigma_2^2) = 8.5$. The equivalent Gaussian probability density function for $\sigma = 2.9$ is also shown in Figure 12.3.

12.3 NONSTATIONARY MEAN VALUES

Consider the problem of estimating the time-varying mean value of nonstationary data. Given a collection of sample records $x_i(t), 0 \le t \le T, i = 1, 2, \ldots, N$, from a

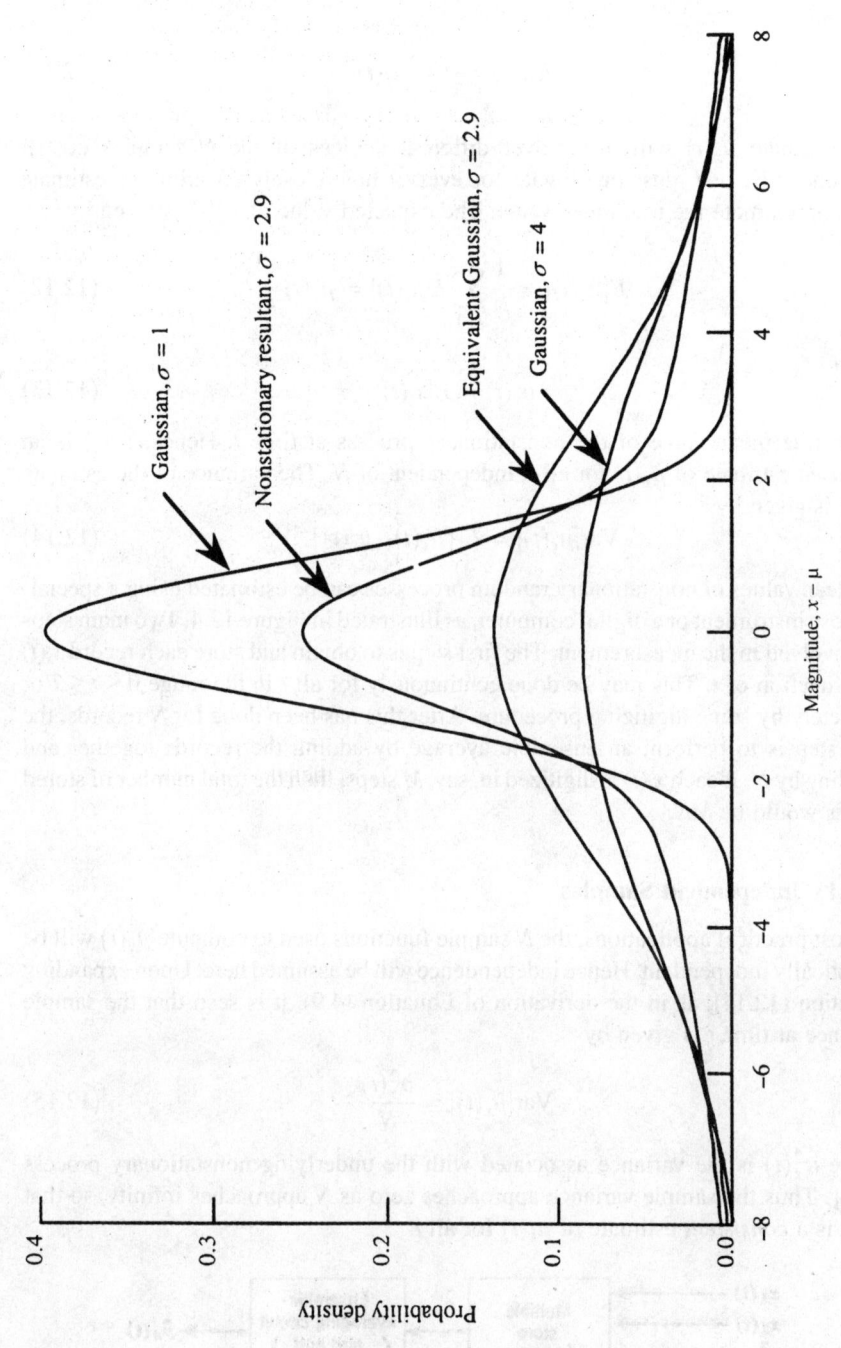

Figure 12.3 Illustration of probability density function of nonstationary data.

nonstationary process $\{x(t)\}$, the mean value at any time t is estimated by the ensemble average

$$\hat{\mu}_x(t) = \frac{1}{N}\sum_{i=1}^{N} x_i(t) \qquad (12.11)$$

The estimate $\hat{\mu}_x(t)$ will differ over different choices of the N samples $\{x_i(t)\}$. Consequently, one must investigate for every t how closely an arbitrary estimate will approximate the true mean value. The expected value of $\hat{\mu}_x(t)$ is given by

$$E[\hat{\mu}_x(t)] = \frac{1}{N}\sum_{i=1}^{N} E[x_i(t)] = \mu_x(t) \qquad (12.12)$$

where

$$\mu_x(t) = E[x_i(t)] \qquad (12.13)$$

is the true mean value of the nonstationary process at time t. Hence, $\hat{\mu}_x(t)$ is an *unbiased* estimate of $\mu_x(t)$ for all t, independent of N. The variance of the estimate $\hat{\mu}_x(t)$ is given by

$$\text{Var}[\hat{\mu}_x(t)] = E[\{\hat{\mu}_x(t) - \mu_x(t)\}^2] \qquad (12.14)$$

Mean values of nonstationary random processes can be estimated using a special-purpose instrument or a digital computer, as illustrated in Figure 12.4. Two main steps are involved in the measurement. The first step is to obtain and store each record $x_i(t)$ as a function of t. This may be done continuously for all t in the range $0 \le t \le T$ or discretely by some digitizing procedure. After this has been done for N records, the next step is to perform an ensemble average by adding the records together and dividing by N. If each $x_i(t)$ is digitized in, say, M steps, then the total number of stored values would be MN.

12.3.1 Independent Samples

In most practical applications, the N sample functions used to compute $\hat{\mu}_x(t)$ will be statistically independent. Hence independence will be assumed here. Upon expanding Equation (12.14), as in the derivation of Equation (4.9), it is seen that the sample variance at time t is given by

$$\text{Var}[\hat{\mu}_x(t)] = \frac{\sigma_x^2(t)}{N} \qquad (12.15)$$

where $\sigma_x^2(t)$ is the variance associated with the underlying nonstationary process $\{x(t)\}$. Thus the sample variance approaches zero as N approaches infinity, so that $\hat{\mu}_x(t)$ is a *consistent* estimate of $\mu_x(t)$ for all t.

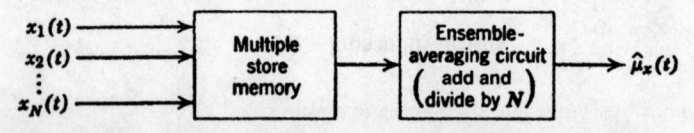

Figure 12.4 Procedure for nonstationary mean value measurement.

Confidence intervals for the nonstationary mean value $\mu_x(t)$ can be constructed based on the estimate $\hat{\mu}_x(t)$ using the procedures detailed in Section 4.4. Specifically, the $(1-\alpha)$ confidence interval at any time t is

$$\left[\hat{\mu}_x(t) - \frac{\hat{\sigma}_x(t) t_{n;\alpha/2}}{\sqrt{N}} \leq \mu_x(t) < \hat{\mu}_x(t) + \frac{\hat{\sigma}_x(t) t_{n;\alpha/2}}{\sqrt{N}}\right] \quad (12.16)$$

where $\hat{\sigma}_x(t)$ is an unbiased estimate of the standard deviation of $\{x(t)\}$ at time t given by Equation (4.12) as

$$\hat{\sigma}_x(t) = \left\{\frac{1}{N-1} \sum_{i=1}^{N} [x_i(t) - \hat{\mu}_x(t)]^2\right\}^{1/2} \quad (12.17)$$

and $t_{n;\alpha/2}$ is the $\alpha/2$ percentage point of Student's t variable with $n = N - 1$ degrees of freedom defined in Section 4.2.3. Note that Equation (12.16) applies even when $\{x(t)\}$ is not normally distributed, assuming the sample size is greater than, say, $N = 10$. This follows from the central limit theorem in Section 3.3.1, which applies to the nonstationary mean value computation in Equation (12.11).

12.3.2 Correlated Samples

Consider a general situation where sample functions $x_i(t)$, $0 \leq t \leq T$, $i = 1, 2, \ldots, N$, from a nonstationary random process are correlated such that, for every t,

$$E[x_i(t) x_j(t)] = R_{xx}(k, t) \quad \text{where } k = j - i \quad (12.18)$$

The quantity $R_{xx}(k, t)$ is called a *nonstationary spatial cross-correlation function* at time t between all pairs of records $x_i(t)$ and $x_j(t)$ satisfying $k = j - i$. It follows from the definition of Equation (12.18) that, by interchanging i and j,

$$R_{xx}(-k, t) = R_{xx}(k, t) \quad (12.19)$$

When the sample functions $x_i(t)$ and $x_j(t)$ are independent, for $i \neq j$ corresponding to $k \neq 0$,

$$R_{xx}(k, t) = E[x_i(t) x_j(t)] = E[x_i(t)] E[x_j(t)] = \mu_x^2(t) \quad \text{for } k \neq 0 \quad (12.20)$$

At $k = 0$, Equation (12.18) becomes

$$R_{xx}(0, t) = E[x_i^2(t)] = \sigma_x^2(t) + \mu_x^2(t) \quad (12.21)$$

These relations yield the independent sample case in the preceding section.

For correlated samples, Equation (12.15) now takes the general form

$$\text{Var}[\hat{\mu}_x(t)] = \frac{\sigma_x^2(t)}{N} + \frac{1}{N^2} \sum_{\substack{i,j=1 \\ i \neq j}}^{N} E\{[x_i(t)-\mu_x(t)][x_j(t)-\mu_x(t)]\}$$

$$= \frac{\sigma_x^2(t)}{N} + \frac{1}{N^2} \sum_{\substack{i,j=1 \\ i \neq j}}^{N} [R_{xx}(j-i,t)-\mu_x^2(t)] \qquad (12.22)$$

The next problem is to simplify the double sum appearing in Equation (12.22). The index $k = j - i$ takes on values $k = 1, 2, \ldots, N-1$. Altogether, there are $N^2 - N$ terms. Because $R_{xx}(-k,t) = R_{xx}(k,t)$, the $N^2 - N$ terms in this double sum can be arranged so that there are two terms where $k = N-1$ of the form $R_{xx}(N-1,t)$, four terms where $k = N-2$ of the form $R_{xx}(N-2,t), \ldots$, and $2(N-1)$ terms where $k = 1$ of the form $R_{xx}(1,t)$. Thus, one derives the simplified expression

$$\sum_{\substack{i,j=1 \\ i \neq j}}^{N} R_{xx}(j-i,t) = 2 \sum_{k=1}^{N-1} (N-k) R_{xx}(k,t) \qquad (12.23)$$

As a check, note that the sum

$$2 \sum_{k=1}^{N-1} (N-k) = N^2 - N \qquad (12.24)$$

Substitution of Equation (12.23) into Equation (12.22) now yields

$$\text{Var}[\hat{\mu}_x(t)] = \frac{\sigma_x^2(t)}{N} + \frac{2}{N^2} \sum_{k=1}^{N-1} (N-k) [R_{xx}(k,t)-\mu_x^2(t)] \qquad (12.25)$$

Equation (12.20) shows that Equation (12.25) reduces to Equation (12.15) when the records are independent, providing another check on the validity of Equation (12.25). The result of Equation (12.25) is an important extension of Equation (12.15) and should be used in place of Equation (12.15) for correlated samples.

A special situation of *complete dependence* between all samples is worthy of mention. For this case,

$$R_{xx}(k,t) = R_{xx}(0,t) = \sigma_x^2(t) + \mu_x^2(t) \quad \text{for all } k \qquad (12.26)$$

Equation (12.25) now becomes

$$\text{Var}[\hat{\mu}_x(t)] = \frac{\sigma_x^2(t)}{N} + \frac{1}{N^2} (N^2-N) \sigma_x^2(t) = \sigma_x^2(t) \qquad (12.27)$$

Thus, no reduction in variance occurs when the samples are completely dependent.

For physical situations where a partial correlation may exist between the different samples, the following example may be helpful in giving quantitative results.

NONSTATIONARY MEAN VALUES

Example 12.2. **Variance of Mean Value Estimate for Exponential Correlation Between Samples.** An exponential form for the nonstationary cross-correlation function $R_{xx}(k, t)$ will now be assumed so as to obtain some quantitative results to characterize different degrees of correlation. To be specific, assume that

$$R_{xx}(k,t) = \mu_x^2(t) + \sigma_x^2(t)e^{-kc}$$

where k and c are positive constants. Determine the corresponding sample variance for nonstationary mean value estimates.

From Equation (12.25), the sample variance is given by

$$\text{Var}[\hat{\mu}_x(t)] = \frac{\sigma_x^2(t)}{N} + \frac{2\sigma_x^2(t)}{N^2}\sum_{k=1}^{N-1}(N-k)e^{-kc}$$

To evaluate the sum above, let

$$f(c) = \sum_{k=1}^{N-1} e^{-kc} = \frac{1-e^{-(N-1)c}}{e^c-1}$$

Then

$$f'(c) = -\sum_{k=1}^{N-1} ke^{-kc} = \frac{Ne^{-N(N-2)c}-(N-1)e^{-(N-1)c}-e^c}{(e^c-1)^2}$$

Now

$$F(c) = \sum_{k=1}^{N-1}(N-k)e^{-kc} = Nf(c) + f'(c) = \frac{(N-1)e^c - N + e^{-(N-1)c}}{(e^c-1)^2}$$

Substitution into the variance expression gives

$$\text{Var}[\hat{\mu}_x(t)] = \frac{\sigma_x^2(t)}{N} + \frac{2\sigma_x^2(t)}{N^2}\left[\frac{(N-1)e^c - N + e^{-(N-1)c}}{(e^c-1)^2}\right]$$

The result given above can be used to generate a set of curves for different values of $\sigma_x^2(t)$, N, and c. Experimental results would enable one to estimate the constant c for the application of these curves.

12.3.3 Analysis Procedures for Single Records

As noted in Section 12.1, it often occurs in practice that only one sample record of data is available for a nonstationary process of interest. In such cases, nonstationary mean values are often estimated from a single sample record by one of several operations equivalent to low-pass filtering. This technique can be employed profitably for certain classes of nonstationary data. To be more specific, consider a nonstationary random process of the sum form

$$\{x(t)\} = a(t) + \{u(t)\} \tag{12.28}$$

where $a(t)$ is a deterministic function and $\{u(t)\}$ is a random process with a stationary mean value of zero, as illustrated in Figure 12.2(a). Note that the variance and autocorrelation function of $\{u(t)\}$ need not be stationary. The mean value of the nonstationary random process $\{x(t)\}$ at any time t is given by

$$E[x(t)] = E[a(t) + u(t)] = E[a(t)] + E[u(t)] = a(t) \qquad (12.29)$$

It follows that $a(t)$ can be interpreted as the instantaneous mean value of $\{x(t)\}$. If it is assumed that the variations of $a(t)$ are very slow compared to the lowest frequency in $\{u(t)\}$, then $a(t)$ can be separated from $\{u(t)\}$ by low-pass filtering operations on a single sample record $x(t)$. Such filtering operations may be physically accomplished in several ways, including the following:

a. Digital low-pass filtering with either recursive or nonrecursive filters as discussed in Section 11.1.3
b. Polynomial curve fitting (regression analysis) as introduced in Section 4.6.2 and discussed for trend removal applications in Section 11.1.2
c. Segmented mean value estimates (short time-averaging operations)

In any case, the resulting mean value estimates will involve a bias error that is a function of the low-pass filter cutoff frequency (the number of terms in the polynomial fit or the short averaging time) relative to the rate of variation of $a(t)$.

For example, consider the short time-averaged estimate of the mean value $\mu_x(t)$ given by

$$\hat{\mu}_x(t) = \int_{t-T/2}^{t+T/2} x(t)dt = \int_{t-t/2}^{t+T/2} [a(t) + u(t)]dt \qquad (12.30)$$

where T is a short averaging time. It is readily shown that

$$E[\hat{\mu}_x(t)] = E\left[\int_{t-T/2}^{t+T/2} [a(t) + u(t)]dt\right] = \int_{t-t/2}^{t+T/2} \{E[a(t)] + E[u(t)]\}dt$$
$$= \int_{t-t/2}^{t+T/2} a(t)dt \neq a(t) \qquad (12.31)$$

Hence this estimate $\hat{\mu}_x(t)$ will generally be *biased*. A development similar to that presented in Section 8.3.1 yields a first-order approximation for the bias error at any time t as

$$b[\hat{\mu}_x(t)] = \frac{T^2}{24} a''(t) \qquad (12.32)$$

where $a''(t)$ is the second derivative of $a(t)$ with respect to t. It is clear from Equation (12.32) that the bias error in the mean value estimate diminishes as the averaging time T becomes small. However, the random error in the estimate increases as T becomes small in a manner similar to that developed for stationary data in Section 8.2.1. Thus, the selection of an appropriate averaging time T involves a compromise

12.4 NONSTATIONARY MEAN SQUARE VALUES

A similar analysis to the one given in Section 12.3 will now be carried out to determine how the nonstationary mean square values change with time. This can be estimated by using a special-purpose instrument or a computer that performs the following operation to calculate a sample mean square value from a sample of size N. Specifically, for N sample functions $x_i(t)$, $0 \le t \le T$, $i = 1, 2, 3, \ldots, N$, from a nonstationary process $\{x(t)\}$, fix t and compute the ensemble average estimate

$$\hat{\psi}_x^2(t) = \frac{1}{N} \sum_{i=1}^{N} x_i^2(t) \qquad (12.33)$$

Independent of N, the quantity $\hat{\psi}_x^2(t)$ is an *unbiased* estimate of the true mean square value of the nonstationary process $\{x(t)\}$ at any time t because the expected value is given by

$$E\left[\hat{\psi}_x^2(t)\right] = \frac{1}{N} \sum_{i=1}^{N} E\left[x_i^2(t)\right] = \psi_x^2(t) \qquad (12.34)$$

The quantity

$$\psi_x^2(t) = E\left[x_i^2(t)\right] = \mu_x^2(t) + \sigma_x^2(t) \qquad (12.35)$$

is the true mean square value of the nonstationary process at time t. Figure 12.4 indicates how to measure $\hat{\psi}_x^2(t)$ by merely replacing $x_i(t)$ by $x_i^2(t)$.

12.4.1 Independent Samples

It will now be assumed that the N sample functions $x_i(t)$ are independent so that for all i and j,

$$E[x_i(t)x_j(t)] = E[x_i(t)]E[x_j(t)] = \mu_x^2(t) \qquad (12.36)$$

The sample variance associated with the estimates $\hat{\psi}_x^2(t)$ are calculated as follows. By definition,

$$\text{Var}\left[\hat{\psi}_x^2(t)\right] = E\left[\{\hat{\psi}_x^2(t) - \psi_x^2(t)\}^2\right] = E\left[\{\hat{\psi}_x^2(t)\}^2\right] - \psi_x^4(t) \qquad (12.37)$$

where $\hat{\psi}_x^2(t)$ is given by Equation (12.33) and

$$E\left[\{\hat{\psi}_x^2(t)\}^2\right] = \frac{1}{N^2}\sum_{i,j=1}^{N} E[x_i^2(t)x_j^2(t)]$$

$$= \frac{1}{N^2}\left[\sum_{i=1}^{N} E[x_i^4(t)] + \sum_{\substack{i,j=1 \\ i \neq j}}^{N} E[x_i^2(t)x_j^2(t)]\right] \quad (12.38)$$

Thus, the problem reduces to an evaluation of the expected values appearing in Equation (12.38).

In order to obtain reasonable closed-form answers, it will be assumed now that the random process $\{x_i(t)\}$ at any time t follows a Gaussian distribution with mean value $\mu_x(t)$ and variance $\sigma_x^2(t)$. One can then derive

$$E[x_i^4(t)] = 3\psi_x^4(t) - 2\mu_x^4(t) \quad (12.39)$$

$$E[x_i^2(t)x_j^2(t)] = \psi_x^4(t) \quad \text{for } i \neq j \quad (12.40)$$

The derivation of Equations (12.39) and (12.40) is based on a nonstationary form of the fourth-order Gaussian relation of Equation (3.78), namely,

$$\begin{aligned}E[x_i(t)x_j(t)x_m(t)x_n(t)] &= E[x_i(t)x_j(t)]E[x_m(t)x_n(t)] \\ &+ E[x_i(t)x_m(t)]E[x_j(t)x_n(t)] \\ &+ E[x_i(t)x_n(t)]E[x_j(t)x_m(t)] - 2\mu_x^4(t)\end{aligned} \quad (12.41)$$

Substitution into Equations (12.37) and (12.38) yields the result

$$\text{Var}\left[\hat{\psi}_x^2(t)\right] = \frac{2}{N}\left[\psi_x^4(t) - \mu_x^4(t)\right] \quad (12.42)$$

Thus the sample variance approaches zero as N approaches infinity, so that $\hat{\psi}_x^2(t)$ is a *consistent* estimate of $\hat{\psi}_x^2(t)$ for all t.

To arrive at confidence intervals for $\hat{\psi}_x^2(t)$, it is more convenient to work with the nonstationary variance estimate given from Equation (12.35) by

$$\hat{\sigma}_x^2(t) = \hat{\psi}_x^2(t) - \mu_x^2(t) \quad (12.43)$$

Assuming $x_i(t)$, $i = 1, 2, \ldots, N$, is normally distributed, $\hat{\sigma}_x^2(t)$ will have a sampling distribution for each value of t given from Section 4.3.2 as

$$\hat{\sigma}_x^2(t) = \hat{\sigma}_x^2(t)\chi_n^2 \quad n = N-1 \quad (12.44)$$

where χ_n^2 is the chi-square variable with $n = N-1$ degrees of freedom defined in Section 4.2.2. Hence, the $(1-\alpha)$ confidence interval at any time t is

$$\left[\frac{n\hat{\sigma}_x^2(t)}{\chi_{n;\alpha/2}^2} \leq \sigma_x^2(t) < \frac{n\hat{\sigma}_x^2(t)}{\chi_{n;1-\alpha/2}^2}\right] \quad n = N-1 \quad (12.45)$$

12.4.2 Correlated Samples

For situations involving correlated samples, it is assumed as in Section 12.3.2 that the sample records satisfy the relation

$$E[x_i(t)x_j(t)] = R_{xx}(k,t) \quad \text{where } k = j-i \tag{12.46}$$

Equation (12.40) where $i \neq j$ is now replaced by

$$E[x_i^2(t)x_j^2(t)] = \psi_x^4(t) + 2[R_{xx}^2(k,t) - \mu_x^4(t)] \tag{12.47}$$

where $k = j - i \neq 0$. When $i = j$, Equation (12.46) becomes

$$E[x_i^2(t)] = R_{xx}(0,t) = \psi_x^2(t) \tag{12.48}$$

Proper steps for including $R_{xx}(k,t)$ in the analysis are developed in Section 12.3.2. A similar procedure here yields the result

$$\text{Var}\left[\hat{\psi}_x^2(t)\right] = \frac{2}{N}\left[\psi_x^4(t) - \mu_x^4(t)\right] + \frac{4}{N^2}\sum_{k=1}^{N-1}(N-k)\left[R_{xx}^2(k,t) - \mu_x^4(t)\right] \tag{12.49}$$

which is a useful generalization of Equation (12.42).

Example 12.3. Variance of Mean Square Value Estimate for Exponential Correlation Between Samples. In order to obtain some quantitative expressions corresponding to Equation (12.42) that will characterize different degrees of correlation, assume that $R_{xx}(k,t)$ has an exponential form such that

$$R_{xx}(k,t) = \mu_x^2(t) + \sigma_x^2(t)e^{-kc}$$

where k and c are positive constants. Determine the corresponding sample variance for mean square value estimates.

The sample variance is given by Equation (12.49). To carry out this evaluation, let $f(c)$ and $F(c)$ be defined as in Example 12.2. It then follows that

$$R_{xx}^2(k,t) - \mu_x^4(t) = \sigma_x^2(t)\left[2\mu_x^2(t)e^{-kc} + \sigma_x^2(t)e^{-2kc}\right]$$

Hence, the second term in Equation (12.49) is

$$\frac{4\sigma_x^2(t)}{N^2}\sum_{k=1}^{N-1}(N-k)\left[2\mu_x^2(t)e^{-kc} + \sigma_x^2(t)e^{-2kc}\right]$$

$$= \frac{4\sigma_x^2(t)}{N^2}\left[2\mu_x^2(t)F(c) + \sigma_x^2(t)F(2c)\right]$$

The desired variance is now given by the above result and the first term in Equation (12.49).

12.4.3 Analysis Procedures for Single Records

There is one important class of nonstationary random data where the time-varying mean square value can be estimated from a single sample record. Specifically, assume a nonstationary random process $\{x(t)\}$ can be represented by

$$\{x(t)\} = a(t)\{u(t)\} \qquad (12.50)$$

where $a(t)$ is a deterministic function and $\{u(t)\}$ is a random process with a stationary mean value and variance of zero and unity, respectively, as illustrated in Figure 12.2(b). Note that the autocorrelation function of $\{u(t)\}$ need not be stationary for this application. The mean square value of the nonstationary random process $\{x(t)\}$ is given by

$$E[x^2(t)] = \psi_x^2(t) = E[a^2(t)u^2(t)] = a^2(t)E[u^2(t)] = a^2(t) \qquad (12.51)$$

It follows that $a^2(t)$ can be interpreted as the instantaneous mean square value of $\{x(t)\}$.

Similar to the time-varying mean value estimation procedures discussed in Section 12.3.3, if the variations of $a(t)$ in Equation (12.50) are slow compared to the lowest frequency of $\{u(t)\}$, then $a^2(t)$ can be separated from $\{[u^2(t)]\}$ by a low-pass filtering operation on the squared values of a single record $x(t)$. The most common approach here is to use a short time-averaging procedure where, from Equation (12.51), a moving mean square value estimate averaged over a short interval T is computed by

$$\hat{\psi}_x^2(t) = \int_{t-T/2}^{t+T/2} a^2(t)dt \qquad (12.52)$$

Of course, the resulting mean square value estimate versus time will generally be biased, specifically,

$$E\left[\hat{\psi}_x^2(t)\right] = E\left[\int_{t-T/2}^{t+T/2} a^2(t)dt\right] = \int_{t-T/2}^{t+T/2} E[a^2(t)]dt = \int_{t-T/2}^{t+T/2} a^2(t)dt \neq a^2(t) \qquad (12.53)$$

A development similar to that presented in Section 8.3.1 yields a first-order approximation for the normalized time interval bias error at any time t as

$$\varepsilon_b\left[\hat{\psi}_x^2\right] = \frac{T^2}{24}\left\{\frac{[a^2(t)]''}{a^2(t)}\right\} \qquad (12.54)$$

where $[a^2(t)]''$ is the second derivative of $a^2(t)$ with respect to t. It is clear from Equation (12.54) that the time interval bias error diminishes as the averaging time T becomes small. However, from Equation (8.51), assuming the record $x(t)$ is approximately stationary over each short time interval T, the normalized random error is

NONSTATIONARY MEAN SQUARE VALUES

approximated by

$$\varepsilon_r\left[\hat{\psi}_x^2(t)\right] = \frac{1}{\sqrt{B_s T}} \tag{12.55}$$

where B_s is defined in Equation (8.52). It follows from Equation (8.5) that the total mean square error for the estimated mean square value at any time t can be approximated by

$$\varepsilon^2\left[\hat{\psi}_x^2(t)\right] = \frac{1}{B_s T} + \frac{T^4}{576} C_T(t) \tag{12.56}$$

where

$$C_T(t) = \left\{\frac{[a^2(t)]''}{a^2(t)}\right\}^2 \tag{12.57}$$

It is clear from Equation (12.56) that the selection of an appropriate averaging time T is a compromise between a time interval bias error and a random error. A common approach is to select this compromise averaging time by a trial-and-error procedure as follows:

a. Compute a moving average for the mean square value of the nonstationary data using Equation (12.52) with an averaging time T that is too short to smooth out variations in the mean square value versus time.

b. Continuously recompute the moving average with an increasing averaging time until it is clear that the averaging time is smoothing out variations in the mean square value versus time.

Example 12.4. Illustration of Nonstationary Mean Square Value Estimates using a Moving Average. The trial-and-error approach to selecting an appropriate averaging time for mean square value estimates computed from a sample record of nonstationary data using a moving average is illustrated in Figure 12.5, which is taken directly from Ref. 1. Figure 12.5(a) shows the moving average computed with three different averaging times for the mean square value of the acoustical pressure measured inside the payload fairing of a Titan IV launch vehicle during liftoff. Figure 12.5(b) presents the average autospectrum of the acoustical pressures during the liftoff event. It is clear from these results that the variation of the mean square value with time is slow compared to the lowest frequency of the data, as required for the application of Equation (12.52). Referring to Figure 12.5(a), the first moving average computed with an averaging time of $T = 0.1$ s reveals substantial variations from one averaging interval to the next that are typical of random sampling errors. When the averaging time is increased to $T = 1.0$ s, the random errors are suppressed, but there is no evidence that the underlying nonstationary trend in the mean square value has been significantly altered. When the averaging time is further increased to $T = 4.0$ s, it is clear that the nonstationary trend in the mean square value is substantially distorted. It follows that an averaging time of about $T = 1$ s is appropriate

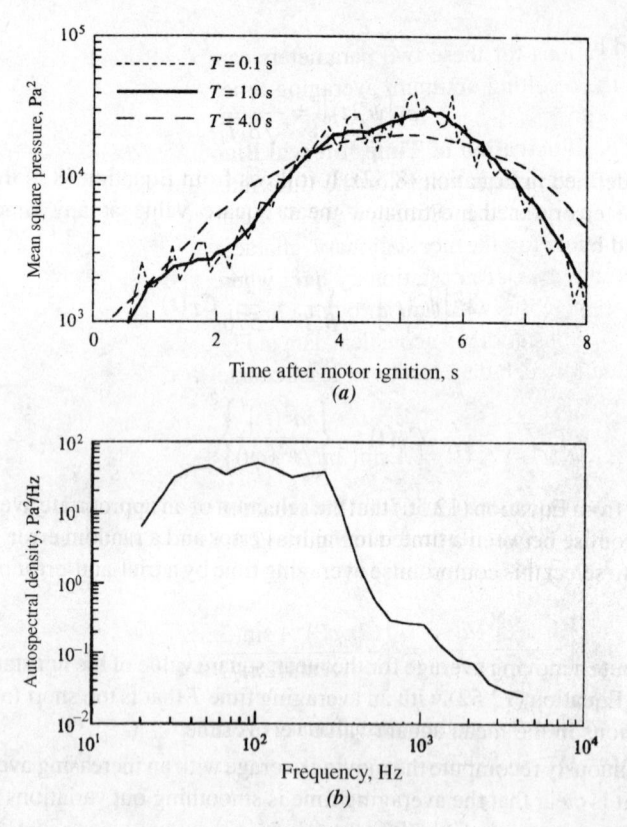

Figure 12.5 Running mean square value and average autospectrum estimates for nonstationary acoustic data. (*a*) Running mean square values. (*b*) Average autospectrum.

for the computation of a moving average of the nonstationary mean square value for these data. This concludes Example 12.4.

Beyond trial-and-error procedures, an optimum averaging time that minimizes the total mean square error given by Equation (12.56) can be estimated given sufficient information. Specifically, taking the derivative of Equation (12.56) with respect to T and equating to zero yields an optimum averaging time given by

$$T_0 = \left[\frac{144}{B_s C_T(t)}\right]^{1/5} \tag{12.58}$$

where B_s and $C_T(t)$ are defined in Equations (8.52) and (12.57), respectively. The value for B_s in Equation (12.58) can be approximated using the average autospectrum of the nonstationary data to solve Equation (8.52). The maximum value for $C_T(t)$ in Equation (12.58) can be approximated from a preliminary moving average computation of the mean square value of the data. Noting that the optimum averaging time T_0 in Equation (12.58) is a function of the one-fifth power of both B_s and $C_T(t)$, it follows

NONSTATIONARY MEAN SQUARE VALUES

that the approximations for these two parameters can be relatively coarse without major errors in the resulting optimum averaging time.

Example 12.5. Illustration of Time Interval Bias Error Determination. The determination of a maximum value for the time interval bias error term $C_T(t)$ in Equation (12.58), as defined in Equation (12.57), can often be accomplished by a simple approximation for the nonstationary character of the data. For example, consider a common class of nonstationary data where the mean square value of a sample record $x(t)$ increases with time through a maximum value and then decreases, as illustrated by the nonstationary acoustical data in Figure 12.5(a). The time-varying mean square value for such data can be at least coarsely approximated by half-sine function given by

$$\psi_x^2(t) = a^2(t) = A \sin(2\pi t/P) \quad 0 \le t \le P/2 \tag{12.59}$$

where P is the period of the sine wave. It follows that the maximum mean square value occurs at the time $t_m = P/4$, as illustrated in Figure 12.6. Substituting Equation (12.59) into Equation (12.57) yields

$$C_T(t) = \left[\frac{d^2\psi_x^2(t)/dt^2}{\psi_x^2(t)}\right] = \left[\frac{(2\pi/P)^2 A \sin(2\pi t/P)}{A \sin(2\pi t/P)}\right]^2 = \left[\frac{2\pi}{P}\right]^4$$

Now let the *effective duration* of the nonstationary event be defined as the half-power point duration $T_D = t_2 - t_1$, where

$$\psi_x^2(t_1) = \psi_x^2(t_2) = \frac{1}{2}\psi_x^2(t_m)$$

as illustrated in Figure 12.6. It follows from Equation (12.59) that $t_1 = P/12$ and $t_2 = 5P/12$. Hence $T_D = P/3$ and the value of Equation (12.57) at t_m is given by

$$C_T(t_m) = \left[\frac{2\pi}{3T_D}\right]^4 \tag{12.60}$$

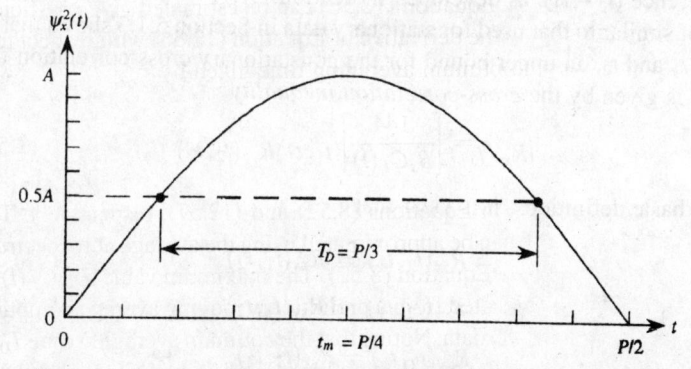

Figure 12.6 Half-sine approximation for time-varying mean square value.

where T_D can be estimated from a preliminary computation of $\hat{\psi}_x^2(t)$ or from past experience with similar nonstationary data. For example, given the moving average for the data in Figure 12.5(a) computed with $T \leq 1$ s, the half-power point duration for the nonstationary event is $T_D \approx 3$ s. Solving Equation (8.52) using the average autospectrum in Figure 12.5(b) yields a statistical bandwidth of $B_s \approx 320$ Hz. Substituting these values into Equation (12.58) gives an optimum averaging time of $T_0 \approx 1.1$ s, which is very close to the optimum averaging time determined by trial-and-error procedures in Example 12.4.

12.5 CORRELATION STRUCTURE OF NONSTATIONARY DATA

Consider any pair of real-valued nonstationary random processes $\{x(t)\}$ and $\{y(t)\}$. The *mean values* at arbitrary fixed times t are defined by the expected values

$$\mu_x(t) = E[x(t)]$$
$$\mu_y(t) = E[y(t)] \tag{12.61}$$

Original data can always be transformed to have zero mean values by replacing $x(t)$ by $x(t) - \mu_x(t)$ and $y(t)$ by $y(t) - \mu_y(t)$. This will be assumed henceforth.

12.5.1 Double-Time Correlation Functions

The *correlation functions* at any pair of fixed times t_1 and t_2 are defined by the expected values

$$R_{xx}(t_1, t_2) = E[x(t_1)x(t_2)]$$
$$R_{yy}(t_1, t_2) = E[y(t_1)y(t_2)] \tag{12.62}$$

$$R_{xy}(t_1, t_2) = E[x(t_1)y(t_2)] \tag{12.63}$$

The quantities $R_{xx}(t_1, t_2)$ and $R_{yy}(t_1, t_2)$ are called *nonstationary autocorrelation functions*, whereas $R_{xy}(t_1, t_2)$ is called a *nonstationary cross-correlation function*. For stationary random data, these results would not be functions of t_1 and t_2 but only of their difference $(t_2 - t_1)$, as developed in Section 5.1.1.

A proof similar to that used for stationary data in Section 5.1.3 shows that for any values of t_1 and t_2, an upper bound for the nonstationary cross-correlation function $R_{xy}(t_2, t_2)$ is given by the *cross-correlation inequality*

$$|R_{xy}(t_1, t_2)|^2 \leq R_{xx}(t_1, t_1) R_{yy}(t_2, t_2) \tag{12.64}$$

From the basic definitions, it is clear that

$$R_{xx}(t_2, t_1) = R_{xx}(t_1, t_2)$$
$$R_{yy}(t_2, t_1) = R_{yy}(t_1, t_2) \tag{12.65}$$

$$R_{xy}(t_2, t_1) = R_{yx}(t_1, t_2) \tag{12.66}$$

CORRELATION STRUCTURE OF NONSTATIONARY DATA

Consider the problem of measuring $R_{xx}(t_1, t_2)$ using a set of N sample functions $x_i(t)$, $i = 1, 2, \ldots, N$, from the nonstationary random process. In place of Equation (12.62), one would compute the ensemble average estimate

$$\hat{R}_{xx}(t_1, t_2) = \frac{1}{N} \sum_{i=1}^{N} x_i(t_1) x_i(t_2) \tag{12.67}$$

A recommended procedure to perform this computation is as follows. Let $t_1 = t$, and $t_2 = t - \tau$, where τ is a fixed time-delay value. This yields

$$\hat{R}_{xx}(t, t-\tau) = \frac{1}{N} \sum_{i=1}^{N} x_i(t) x_i(t-\tau) \tag{12.68}$$

which for stationary processes would be a function of τ only, but for nonstationary processes would be a function of both t and τ. For each fixed delay value τ and each record $x_i(t)$, calculate and store the product $x_i(t)x_i(t-\tau)$ for all t. Repeat for all N records, and then perform an ensemble average to yield the estimate of Equation (12.68). This whole operation must be repeated for every different τ of concern. Figure 12.7 illustrates this procedure for measuring nonstationary autocorrelation functions. A similar procedure may be followed for nonstationary cross-correlation function measurements.

12.5.2 Alternative Double-Time Correlation Functions

A different double-time correlation function can be defined by making the following transformations. Let

$$t_1 = t - \frac{\tau}{2} \qquad t_2 = t + \frac{\tau}{2} \tag{12.69}$$

Then

$$\tau = t_2 - t_1 \qquad t = \frac{t_1 + t_2}{2} \tag{12.70}$$

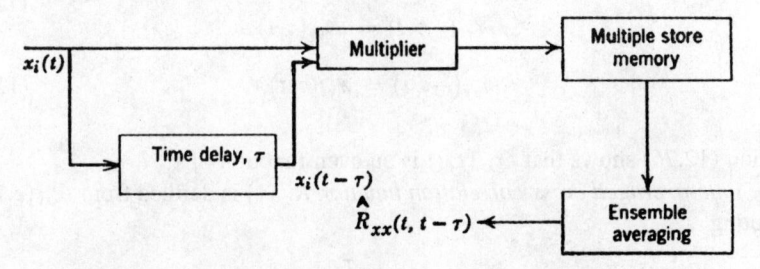

Figure 12.7 Procedure for nonstationary autocorrelation measurement.

Here τ is the time difference between t_1 and t_2, and t is the midtime between t_1 and t_2. Now

$$R_{xy}(t_1, t_2) = R_{xy}\left(t - \frac{\tau}{2}, t + \frac{\tau}{2}\right) \quad (12.71)$$

$$= E\left[x\left(t - \frac{\tau}{2}\right) y\left(t + \frac{\tau}{2}\right)\right] = \mathcal{R}_{xy}(\tau, t)$$

Also,

$$\mathcal{R}_{xx}(\tau, t) = E\left[x\left(t - \frac{\tau}{2}\right) x\left(t + \frac{\tau}{2}\right)\right] \quad (12.72)$$

$$\mathcal{R}_{yy}(\tau, t) = E\left[y\left(t - \frac{\tau}{2}\right) y\left(t + \frac{\tau}{2}\right)\right]$$

The above functions of τ and t are often referred to as *instantaneous correlation functions*. A script $\mathcal{R}$ is used in place of R to distinguish the (τ, t) plane from the (t_1, t_2) plane. Note that at the point $\tau = 0$, assuming $\mu_x(t) = \mu_y(t) = 0$,

$$\mathcal{R}_{xx}(0, t) = E[x^2(t)] = \sigma_x^2(t)$$
$$\mathcal{R}_{yy}(0, t) = E[y^2(t)] = \sigma_y^2(t) \quad (12.73)$$

$$\mathcal{R}_{xy}(0, t) = E[x(t)y(t)] = \sigma_{xy}(t) \quad (12.74)$$

where $\sigma_x^2(t)$ and $\sigma_y^2(t)$ are the variances of $x(t)$ and $y(t)$ at time t, and $\sigma_{xy}(t)$ is the covariance between $x(t)$ and $y(t)$ at time t. For any $\mathcal{R}(\tau, t)$, one has the relations

$$\mathcal{R}_{xx}(\tau, 0) = E\left[x\left(-\frac{\tau}{2}\right) x\left(\frac{\tau}{2}\right)\right] \quad (12.75)$$

Also,

$$\mathcal{R}_{xx}(-\tau, t) = \mathcal{R}_{xx}(\tau, t)$$
$$\mathcal{R}_{yy}(-\tau, t) = \mathcal{R}_{yy}(\tau, t) \quad (12.76)$$

$$\mathcal{R}_{xy}(-\tau, t) = \mathcal{R}_{yx}(\tau, t) \quad (12.77)$$

Equation (12.76) shows that $\mathcal{R}_{xx}(\tau, t)$ is an even function of τ.

The *time-averaged cross-correlation function* $\bar{R}_{xy}(\tau)$ is defined from $\mathcal{R}_{xy}(\tau, t)$ by computing

$$\bar{R}_{xy}(\tau) = \lim_{T \to \infty} \frac{1}{T} \int_0^T \mathcal{R}_{xy}(\tau, t) dt \quad (12.78)$$

CORRELATION STRUCTURE OF NONSTATIONARY DATA

The *time-averaged autocorrelation function* $\bar{R}_{xx}(\tau)$ is defined from $\mathscr{R}_{xx}(\tau, t)$ by

$$\bar{R}_{xx}(\tau) = \lim_{T \to \infty} \frac{1}{T} \int_0^T \mathscr{R}_{xx}(\tau, t) dt \qquad (12.79)$$

Because $\mathscr{R}_{xx}(-\tau, t) = \mathscr{R}_{xx}(\tau, t)$, it follows that

$$\bar{R}_{xx}(-\tau) = \bar{R}_{xx}(\tau) \qquad (12.80)$$

Thus $\bar{R}_{xx}(\tau)$ is a real-valued even function of τ, representing the usual autocorrelation function of stationary random data. From Equation (12.77), since $\mathscr{R}_{xy}(-\tau, t) = \mathscr{R}_{yx}(\tau, t)$, one obtains

$$\bar{R}_{xy}(-\tau) = \bar{R}_{yx}(\tau) \qquad (12.81)$$

so that $\bar{R}_{xy}(\tau)$ represents the usual cross-correlation function of stationary random data.

Example 12.6. Instantaneous Autocorrelation Function of Modulated Random Data. Consider a cosine-modulated random process defined by

$$\{x(t)\} = [\cos 2\pi f_0 t]\{u(t)\}$$

where f_0 is a constant and $\{u(t)\}$ is a zero mean value stationary random process. From Equations (12.62) and (12.72),

$$R_{xx}(t_1, t_2) = E[x(t_1)x(t_2)] = [\cos 2\pi f_0 t_1 \cos 2\pi f_0 t_2] R_{uu}(t_2 - t_1)$$

$$\mathscr{R}_{xx}(\tau, t) = E\left[x\left(t - \frac{\tau}{2}\right) x\left(t - \frac{\tau}{2}\right)\right] = \frac{1}{2}[\cos 2\pi f_0 \tau + \cos 4\pi f_0 t] R_{uu}(\tau)$$

For this example, the nonstationary component in $\mathscr{R}_{xx}(\tau, t)$ separates into a function of t and τ multiplied by a function of τ alone. Note that, for all t,

$$\mathscr{R}_{xx}(0, t) = E[x^2(t)] = \frac{1}{2}[1 + \cos 4\pi f_0 t] R_{uu}(0) \geq 0$$

In general, however, for $\tau \neq 0$, the instantaneous autocorrelation function $\mathscr{R}_{xx}(\tau, t)$ may be positive or negative.

12.5.3 Analysis Procedures for Single Records

Given a single sample record $x(t)$ of length T from an arbitrary nonstationary process $\{x(t)\}$, one might compute the instantaneous autocorrelation function defined in Equation (12.72) with no averaging, that is,

$$\hat{\mathscr{R}}_{xx}(\tau, t) = x\left(t - \frac{\tau}{2}\right) x\left(t + \frac{\tau}{2}\right) \quad 0 \leq t \leq T \qquad (12.82)$$

If the data are at least partially deterministic in character, Equation (12.82) is sometimes used to compute a frequency–time spectral function discussed in

Section 12.6.4. However, if the data are from a nonstationary random process, the statistical sampling (random) errors in the estimate given by Equation (12.82) will be comparable to those for unaveraged estimates of stationary correlation functions in Section 8.4. The random errors might be somewhat suppressed by using a short time-averaging operation similar to that employed to estimate nonstationary mean square values in Section 12.3.3, but the short time-averaging approach is best accomplished in the frequency domain, as detailed in Section 12.6.4.

There is a special class of nonstationary random data where at least a normalized version of the autocorrelation function can be accurately estimated from a single sample record. Specifically, assume that a nonstationary random process $\{x(t)\}$ can be represented by

$$\{x(t)\} = a(t)\{u(t)\} \qquad (12.83)$$

where $a(t)$ is a deterministic function and $\{u(t)\}$ is a stationary random process with a mean and a variance of zero and unity, respectively. Moreover, unlike the $\{u(t)\}$ in Equation (12.50), the $\{u(t)\}$ in Equation (12.83) must have a stationary autocorrelation function, as well as a stationary mean and variance. Equation (12.83) is commonly referred to as the *product model* for a nonstationary random process and is simply a generalization of the modulated random process evaluated in Example 12.6. Now let the product model in Equation (12.83) be further restricted by the following assumptions:

a. The deterministic function $a(t)$ is nonnegative; that is, $a(t) \geq 0$.
b. The stationary random function $u(t)$ is a sample record from a stationary Gaussian random process $\{u(t)\}$.

With the first assumption, from Equation (12.51), $a(t)$ can be interpreted as the instantaneous rms value of $\{x(t)\}$. Because the rms value is nonnegative, it is clear that a sample record $x(t)$ will produce zero crossings identical to $u(t)$, as illustrated in Figure 12.8. With the second assumption, from Ref. 2, the autocorrelation function of $\{u(t)\}$ can be computed from a single nonstationary sample record $x(t)$ by the following procedure:

1. Given a nonstationary sample record $x(t)$, compute a new stationary sample record $y(t)$ using the nonlinear operation

$$y(t) = \begin{cases} 1 & \text{if } x(t) \text{ nonnegative} \\ -1 & \text{if } x(t) \text{ negative} \end{cases} \qquad (12.84)$$

The operation in Equation (12.84) is often referred to as *hard clipping* and essentially retains only the zero crossing information from the original nonstationary record $x(t)$.

CORRELATION STRUCTURE OF NONSTATIONARY DATA

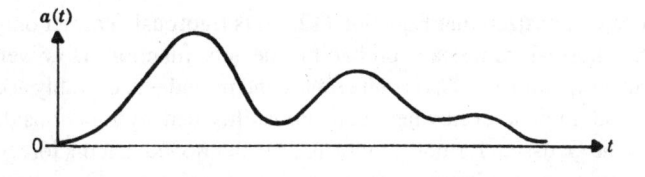

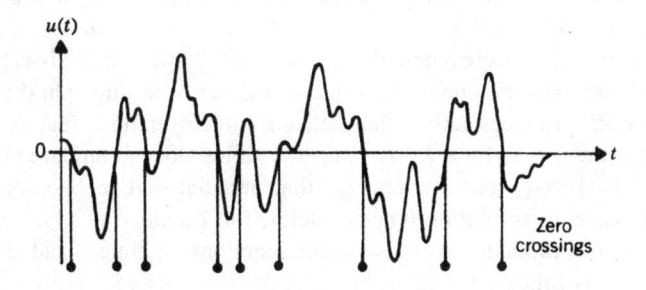

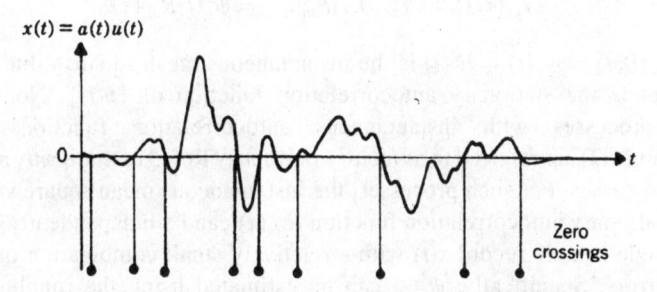

Figure 12.8 Zero crossings of product model nonstationary data.

2. Estimate the autocorrelation function of the hard clipped record $y(t)$ over the entire available record length T using

$$\hat{R}_{yy}(\tau) = \frac{1}{(T-\tau)} \int_0^{T-\tau} y(t)y(t+\tau)dt \qquad (12.85)$$

3. It is shown in Ref. 2 that the autocorrelation function of any Gaussian random process $\{u(t)\}$ can be computed from the hard clipped random process $\{y(t)\}$ using the formula known as the *arc-sine law*, which states that

$$R_{uu}(\tau) = \sin\left[\frac{\pi}{2} R_{yy}(\tau)\right] \qquad (12.86)$$

Hence, an estimate for the autocorrelation function of $\{u(t)\}$ is obtained by solving Equation (12.86) using the estimate $\hat{R}_{yy}(\tau)$ computed in Equation (12.85).

It should be emphasized that Equation (12.86) is rigorously correct only for random data with a normal (Gaussian) probability density function. However, experience suggests that Equation (12.86) is quite robust and provides acceptably accurate results for most random data, even when their probability density functions deviate somewhat from the Gaussian form. It should also be mentioned that the foregoing analysis procedure can be applied to recover meaningful correlation and spectral information from Gaussian random data that were distorted by clipping during data acquisition, as discussed in Section 10.4.3.

The analysis procedure detailed in Equations (12.84)–(12.86) is valid no matter how rapidly the nonstationary rms value $a(t)$ varies with time. On the other hand, the procedure produces only a normalized autocorrelation; that is, $R_{uu}(0) = 1$. However, if the nonstationary rms value $a(t)$ varies slowly compared to the lowest frequency in $\{u(t)\}$, then for reasons that are clarified in Section 12.6.4, the instantaneous autocorrelation function defined in Equation (12.72) can be approximated by the product of two separate functions of time t and time delay τ, respectively, as follows:

$$\mathcal{R}_{xx}(\tau, t) \approx \mathcal{R}_{xx}(0, t) R_{uu}(\tau) = \psi_x^2(t) R_{uu}(\tau) \qquad (12.87)$$

where $\mathcal{R}_{xx}(0, t) = \psi_x^2(t) = a^2(t)$ is the instantaneous mean square value of $\{x(t)\}$, and $R_{uu}(\tau)$ is the stationary autocorrelation function of $\{u(t)\}$. Nonstationary random processes with instantaneous autocorrelation functions that fit Equation (12.87) are referred to as *locally stationary* Ref. 3 or *uniformly modulated* random processes. For such processes, the instantaneous mean square value $\psi_x^2(t)$ and the stationary autocorrelation function $R_{uu}(\tau)$ can be independently estimated from a single sample record $x(t)$ with a relatively small combination of bias and random errors. Specifically, $\psi_x^2(t)$ can be estimated using the running average procedure detailed in Section 12.4.3, while $R_{uu}(\tau)$ can be estimated by averaging over the entire sample record length T in one of two ways. The first way is to estimate $R_{uu}(\tau)$ by the hard clipping procedure given in Equations (12.84)–(12.86). The second way is to approximate $R_{uu}(\tau)$ by computing the time-averaged autocorrelation function $\bar{R}_{xx}(\tau)$ over the nonstationary record $x(t)$ using Equation (12.79) and normalizing to make $\bar{R}_{xx}(0) = 1$. Substituting Equation (12.87) into Equation (12.79) shows that the normalized $\bar{R}_{xx}(\tau) \approx R_{uu}(\tau)$. Because the normalized $\bar{R}_{xx}(\tau)$ is easier to compute and does not require a Gaussian assumption, it is more commonly used than an estimate of $R_{uu}(\tau)$ via Equation (12.86) for the autocorrelation analysis of locally stationary random processes. On the other hand, the normalized $\bar{R}_{xx}(\tau)$ deviates from $R_{uu}(\tau)$ as the rate of change of $a(t)$ with time increases, as will be clarified in Section 12.6.4.

12.6 SPECTRAL STRUCTURE OF NONSTATIONARY DATA

Two distinct theoretical methods will be studied that define the spectral structure of nonstationary data, namely, double frequency (generalized) spectra and frequency–time (instantaneous) spectra. Two types of double frequency spectra are detailed in

SPECTRAL STRUCTURE OF NONSTATIONARY DATA

Sections 12.6.1 and 12.6.2. Frequency–time spectra are discussed in Section 12.6.3. Practical procedures for estimating frequency–time spectra from single sample records of nonstationary random processes are covered in Section 12.6.4.

12.6.1 Double-Frequency Spectral Functions

Assume that any $x(t)$ and any $y(t)$ from real-valued nonstationary random processes $\{x(t)\}$ and $\{y(t)\}$ have finite Fourier transforms given by

$$X(f,T) = \int_0^T x(t) e^{-j2\pi ft} dt$$
$$Y(f,T) = \int_0^T y(t) e^{-j2\pi ft} dt \tag{12.88}$$

where $x(t)$ and $y(t)$ are assumed to be zero outside of the range $(0, T)$. For simplicity in notation, the dependence on T will be omitted by letting

$$X(f) = X(f,T) \qquad Y(f) = Y(f,T) \tag{12.89}$$

Also, the limits in Equation (12.88) and in following formulas will be omitted. Spectral density functions at any pair of fixed frequencies f_1 and f_2 are defined by the expected values

$$S_{xx}(f_1,f_2) = E[X^*(f_1)X(f_2)]$$
$$S_{yy}(f_1,f_2) = E[Y^*(f_1)Y(f_2)] \tag{12.90}$$

$$S_{xy}(f_1,f_2) = E[X^*(f_1)Y(f_2)] \tag{12.91}$$

where X^* and Y^* are complex conjugates of X and Y. The quantities $S_{xx}(f_1,f_2)$ and $S_{yy}(f_1,f_2)$ are called *double-frequency (generalized) autospectral density functions*, whereas $S_{xy}(f_1,f_2)$ is called a *double-frequency (generalized) cross-spectral density function*. Note that these functions are complex valued where f_1 and f_2 can take on any positive or negative values in the range $(-\infty, \infty)$.

For any values of f_1 and f_2, a proof similar to the one detailed for stationary data in Section 5.2.5 shows that an upper bound for this double-frequency cross-spectral density function is given by the *cross-spectrum inequality*

$$|S_{xy}(f_1,f_2)|^2 \leq S_{xx}(f_1,f_2)S_{yy}(f_1,f_2) \tag{12.92}$$

From the basic definitions, it is clear that

$$S_{xx}(f_2,f_1) = S_{xx}^*(f_1,f_2)$$
$$S_{yy}(f_2,f_1) = S_{yy}^*(f_1,f_2) \tag{12.93}$$

$$S_{xy}(f_2,f_1) = S_{yx}^*(f_1,f_2) \tag{12.94}$$

Equations (12.90) and (12.93) show that $S_{xx}(f,f)$ is a real-valued positive even function of f.

From Equation (12.88), one may write

$$X^*(f_1)Y(f_2) = \left[\int x(t_1)e^{j2\pi f_1 t_1}dt_1\right]\left[\int y(t_2)e^{-j2\pi f_2 t_2}dt_2\right] \quad (12.95)$$

Taking expected values of both sides of Equation (12.95) shows that

$$S_{xy}(f_1,f_2) = \iint R_{xy}(t_1,t_2)e^{j2\pi(f_1 t_1 - f_2 t_2)}dt_1 dt_2 \quad (12.96)$$

Hence, $S_{xy}(f_1,f_2)$ does *not* equal the double Fourier transform of $R_{xy}(t_1,t_2)$, which is given by

$$\text{DFT}[R_{xy}(t_1,t_2)] = \iint R_{xy}(t_1,t_2)e^{-j2\pi(f_1 t_1 + f_2 t_2)}dt_1 dt_2 \quad (12.97)$$

Instead, it is the inverse Fourier transform *of* $R_{xy}(t_1,t_2)$ over t_1 followed by the direct Fourier transform over t_2. Equation (12.96) when $y(t) = x(t)$ shows how $S_{xx}(f_1,f_2)$ can be obtained from $R_{xx}(t_1,t_2)$.

The inverse single Fourier transform pairs to Equation (12.88) are

$$x(t) = \int X(f)e^{j2\pi ft}dt$$
$$y(t) = \int Y(f)e^{j2\pi ft}dt \quad (12.98)$$

where the limits of integration may be from $-\infty$ to ∞. Because $x(t)$ is real valued, one can also write

$$x(t) = \int X^*(f)e^{-j2\pi ft}dt \quad (12.99)$$

Now, from Equations (12.98) and (12.99), it follows that

$$x(t_1)y(t_2) = \left[\int X^*(f_1)e^{-j2\pi f_1 t_1}df_1\right]\left[\int Y(f_2)e^{j2\pi f_2 t_2}df_2\right] \quad (12.100)$$

Taking expected values of both sides of Equation (12.100) yields

$$R_{xy}(t_1,t_2) = \iint S_{xy}(f_1,f_2)e^{-j2\pi(f_1 t_1 - f_2 t_2)}df_1 df_2 \quad (12.101)$$

This is *not* the inverse double Fourier transform of $S_{xy}(f_1,f_2)$, which is given by

$$\text{DFT}[S_{xy}(f_1,f_2)] = \iint S_{xy}(f_1,f_2)e^{j2\pi(f_1 t_1 + f_2 t_2)}df_1 df_2 \quad (12.102)$$

Instead, it is the direct Fourier transform of $S_{xy}(f_1,f_2)$ over f_1 followed by the inverse Fourier transform over f_2. Equation (12.101) when $y(t) = x(t)$ shows how $R_{xx}(t_1,t_2)$ can be obtained from $S_{xx}(f_1,f_2)$.

12.6.2 Alternative Double-Frequency Spectral Functions

A different double-frequency spectral function can be defined by making the following transformations of variables. Let

$$f_1 = f - \frac{g}{2} \qquad f_2 = f + \frac{g}{2} \qquad (12.103)$$

Then

$$g = f_2 - f_1 \qquad f = \frac{f_1 + f_2}{2} \qquad (12.104)$$

Now the double-frequency cross-spectrum can be written as

$$S_{xy}(f_1, f_2) = S_{xy}\left(f - \frac{g}{2}, f + \frac{g}{2}\right) = E\left[X^*\left(f - \frac{g}{2}\right)Y\left(f - \frac{g}{2}\right)\right] = \mathscr{S}_{xy}(f, g) \quad (12.105)$$

where script $\mathscr{S}$ is used in place of S to distinguish the (f, g) plane from the (f_1, f_2) plane. For the double-frequency autospectra,

$$\mathscr{S}_{xx}(f, g) = E\left[X^*\left(f - \frac{g}{2}\right)X\left(f + \frac{g}{2}\right)\right]$$

$$\mathscr{S}_{yy}(f, g) = E\left[Y^*\left(f - \frac{g}{2}\right)Y\left(f + \frac{g}{2}\right)\right] \qquad (12.106)$$

Note that at the point $g = 0$, the functions

$$\mathscr{S}_{xx}(f, 0) = E\left[|X(f)^2|\right]$$

$$\mathscr{S}_{yy}(f, 0) = E\left[|Y(f)^2|\right] \qquad (12.107)$$

$$\mathscr{S}_{xy}(f, 0) = E[X^*(f)Y(f)] \qquad (12.108)$$

represent the *energy autospectral density functions* of $x(t)$ and $y(t)$ at frequency f, and the *energy cross-spectral density function* between $x(t)$ and $y(t)$ at frequency f. Observe that

$$\mathscr{S}_{xx}(-f, g) = E\left[X^*\left(-f - \frac{g}{2}\right)X\left(-f + \frac{g}{2}\right)\right]$$

$$= E\left[X^*\left(f - \frac{g}{2}\right)X\left(f + \frac{g}{2}\right)\right] = \mathscr{S}_{xx}(f, g) \qquad (12.109)$$

Hence $\mathscr{S}_{xx}(f, g)$ is an even function of f. Also,

$$\mathscr{S}^*_{xx}(f, g) = E\left[X^*\left(f + \frac{g}{2}\right)X\left(f - \frac{g}{2}\right)\right] = \mathscr{S}_{xx}(f, -g) \qquad (12.110)$$

shows that $\mathscr{S}_{xx}(f, -g)$ is the complex conjugate of $\mathscr{S}_{xx}(f, g)$. Similarly, it follows for arbitrary $x(t)$ and $y(t)$ that

$$\begin{aligned}\mathscr{S}_{xy}(-f, g) &= \mathscr{S}_{yx}(f, g) \\ \mathscr{S}_{xy}^*(f, g) &= \mathscr{S}_{yx}(f, -g)\end{aligned} \quad (12.111)$$

Equation (12.111) gives Equations (12.109) and (12.110) when $x(t) = y(t)$.

Referring back to Equation (12.88) and letting $t_1 = t - (\tau/2)$ and $dt_1 = -(d\tau/2)$, it follows that

$$X^*\left(f - \frac{g}{2}\right) = \int x(t_1) e^{j2\pi(f - g/2)t_1} dt_1 = \int x\left(t - \frac{\tau}{2}\right) e^{j2\pi(f - g/2)(t - \tau/2)} \left(\frac{d\tau}{2}\right)$$

Similarly, from Equation (12.98), by letting $u = f + (g/2)$ and $du = (dg/2)$

$$y\left(t + \frac{\tau}{2}\right) = \int Y(u) e^{j2\pi(t + \tau/2)u} du = \int Y\left(f + \frac{g}{2}\right) e^{j2\pi(f + g/2)(t + \tau/2)} \left(\frac{dg}{2}\right).$$

Now, because

$$\left(f + \frac{g}{2}\right)\left(t + \frac{\tau}{2}\right) = \left(f - \frac{g}{2}\right)\left(t + \frac{\tau}{2}\right) + f\tau + gt$$

it follows that

$$y\left(t + \frac{\tau}{2}\right) e^{-j2\pi f\tau} = \int Y\left(f + \frac{g}{2}\right) e^{j2\pi(f - g/2)(t - \tau/2)} e^{j2\pi gt} \left(\frac{dg}{2}\right)$$

Multiplication of both sides by $x(t - \tau/2)$ and integration over τ yields

$$\int x\left(t - \frac{\tau}{2}\right) y\left(t + \frac{\tau}{2}\right) e^{-j2\pi f\tau} d\tau$$

$$= \int \left[\int x\left(t - \frac{\tau}{2}\right) e^{j2\pi(f - g)/2)(t - \tau/2)} \left(\frac{d\tau}{2}\right)\right] Y\left(f + \frac{g}{2}\right) e^{j2\pi gt} dg$$

$$= \int X^*\left(f - \frac{g}{2}\right) Y\left(f + \frac{g}{2}\right) e^{j2\pi gt} dg$$

Taking expected values of both sides proves that

$$\int \mathscr{R}_{xy}(\tau, t) e^{-j2\pi f\tau} d\tau = \int \mathscr{S}_{xy}(f, g) e^{j2\pi gt} dg \quad (12.112)$$

Special cases occur when $y(t) = x(t)$ to show how $\mathscr{R}_{xx}(\tau, t)$ relates to $\mathscr{S}_{xx}(f, g)$.

The left-hand side of Equation (12.112) is the Fourier transform of $\mathscr{R}_{xy}(\tau, t)$ with respect to τ, holding f and t fixed. The right-hand side of Equation (12.112) is the inverse Fourier transform of $\mathscr{S}_{xy}(f, g)$ with respect to g, holding f and t fixed. Either of these operations defines the *frequency-time* function.

$$\mathscr{W}_{xy}(f, t) = \int \mathscr{R}_{xy}(\tau, t) e^{-j2\pi f\tau} d\tau \quad (12.113)$$

SPECTRAL STRUCTURE OF NONSTATIONARY DATA

which will be studied in the next section. This quantity $\mathscr{W}_{xy}(f,t)$ should never be confused with $\mathscr{S}_{xy}(f,g)$. It also follows from Equation (12.112) that

$$\mathscr{S}_{xy}(f,g) = \iint \mathscr{R}_{xy}(\tau,t) e^{-j2\pi(f\tau+gt)} d\tau\, dt \qquad (12.114)$$

In words, $\mathscr{S}_{xy}(f,g)$ is the double Fourier transform of $\mathscr{R}_{xy}(\tau,t)$ with respect to τ and t.

For the special case of stationary random data, the previous nonstationary relations simplify because the two-parameter correlation results of Equations (12.63) and (12.71) become one-parameter results, namely,

$$R_{xy}(t_1, t_2) = R_{xx}(t_2 - t_1) \qquad (12.115)$$

$$\mathscr{R}_{xy}(\tau,t) = R_{xy}(\tau) \qquad (12.116)$$

with corresponding special results when $x(t) = y(t)$. From Equation (12.101), in general,

$$R_{xy}(t,t) = \iint S_{xy}(f_1, f_2) e^{-j2\pi t(f_1 - f_2)} df_1\, df_2 \qquad (12.117)$$

where the dependence on t appears in the exponent. For stationary data, one obtains

$$R_{xy}(t,t) = R_{xy}(0) = \iint S_{xy}(f_1, f_2) df_1\, df_2 = \int S_{xy}(f_1) df_1 \qquad (12.118)$$

where

$$S_{xy}(f_1) = \int S_{xy}(f_1, f_2) df_2 \qquad (12.119)$$

Hence, for stationary data

$$S_{xy}(f_1, f_2) = S_{xy}(f_1) \delta_1(f_2 - f_1) \qquad (12.120)$$

where $\delta_1(f)$ is a finite delta function defined by

$$\delta_1(f) = \begin{cases} T & (-1/2T) < f < (1/2T) \\ 0 & \text{otherwise} \end{cases} \qquad (12.121)$$

It follows that $S_{xy}(f_1, f_2)$ exists only on the line $f_2 = f_1$ in the (f_1, f_2) plane, assuming frequencies f_1 and f_2 are spaced $(1/T)$ apart. Thus,

$$E[X^*(f_1)Y(f_2)] = 0 \qquad \text{for } f_2 \neq f_1$$

$$E[X^*(f_1)Y(f_1)] = TS_{xy}(f_1) \qquad \text{for } f_2 = f_1 \qquad (12.122)$$

which shows that

$$S_{xy}(f_1) = \frac{1}{T}E[X^*(f_1)Y(f_1)] \tag{12.123}$$

This development proves that, for consistency, one must define the cross-spectral density functions for stationary random data by Equation (12.123), as done previously in Equation (5.67). Also, letting $x(t) = y(t)$, Equation (12.122) proves that there is no correlation between the Fourier components of stationary random data at the two different frequencies.

Now considering the double-frequency result of Equation (12.105), it is clear that

$$\mathscr{S}_{xy}(f,g) = S_{xy}(f)\delta_1(g) \tag{12.124}$$

with $\delta_1(g)$ satisfying Equation (12.121). This means that $\mathscr{S}_{xy}(f,g)$ exists only on the line $g = 0$ in the (f, g) plane, assuming frequencies of g are spaced $(1/T)$ apart. Thus, for stationary random data,

$$\mathscr{S}_{xy}(f,g) = E\left[X^*\left(f-\frac{g}{2}\right)Y\left(f+\frac{g}{2}\right)\right] = 0 \quad \text{for } g \neq 0$$

$$\mathscr{S}_{xy}(f,0) = E[X^*(f)Y(f)] = TS_{xy}(f) \quad \text{for } g = 0 \tag{12.125}$$

Again

$$S_{xy}(f) = \frac{1}{T}E[X^*(f)Y(f)] \tag{12.126}$$

in agreement with Equation (12.123). The definition of autospectral density functions for stationary random data is merely a special case, namely,

$$S_{xx}(f) = \frac{1}{T}E[X^*(f)X(f)] = \frac{1}{T}E\left[|X(f)|^2\right] \tag{12.127}$$

Example 12.7. Double-Frequency Autospectrum of Modulated Random Data. Consider a cosine-modulated random process defined by

$$\{x(t)\} = [\cos 2\pi f_0 t]\{u(t)\}$$

where f_0 is a constant and $\{u(t)\}$ is a zero mean value stationary random process. From Example 12.6,

$$\mathscr{R}_{xx}(\tau, t) = \frac{1}{2}[\cos 2\pi f_0 \tau + \cos 4\pi f_0 t]R_{uu}(\tau)$$

SPECTRAL STRUCTURE OF NONSTATIONARY DATA

Then from Equation (12.114)

$$
\begin{aligned}
\mathscr{S}_{xx}(f,g) &= \iint \mathscr{R}_{xx}(\tau,t) e^{-j2\pi(f\tau+gt)} d\tau\, dt \\
&= \frac{1}{2}\delta(g) \int (\cos 2\pi f_0 \tau) R_{uu}(\tau) d\tau \\
&\quad + \frac{1}{2} \int (\cos 4\pi f_0 t) e^{-j2\pi g t} dt \int R_{uu}(\tau) e^{-j2\pi f\tau} d\tau \\
&= \frac{1}{4}\delta(g)[S_{uu}(f-f_0) + S_{uu}(f+f_0)] \\
&\quad + \frac{1}{4}[\delta(g-2f_0) + \delta(g+2f_0)] S_{uu}(f)
\end{aligned}
$$

This shows that the function $\mathscr{S}_{xx}(f,g)$ exists only along the three lines $g=0$ and $g=\pm 2f_0$ in the (f, g) plane. The autospectrum $S_{uu}(f)$ is shifted by $\pm 2f_0$ along the line $g=0$ and is unchanged along the lines $g=\pm 2f_0$. See Figure 12.9 for a plot of $\mathscr{S}_{xx}(f,g)$ for positive f when $S_{uu}(f)$ is narrow bandwidth noise.

12.6.3 Frequency Time Spectral Functions

Consider any pair of nonstationary random processes $\{x(t)\}$ and $\{y(t)\}$ with zero mean values. As defined in Sections 12.5.2 and 12.6.2, assume that one can compute the nonstationary correlation functions $\mathscr{R}_{xx}(\tau,t)$, $\mathscr{R}_{yy}(\tau,t)$, and $\mathscr{R}_{xy}(\tau,t)$, where

$$\mathscr{R}_{xy}(\tau,t) = E\left[x\left(t-\frac{\tau}{2}\right)y\left(t+\frac{\tau}{2}\right)\right] \qquad (12.128)$$

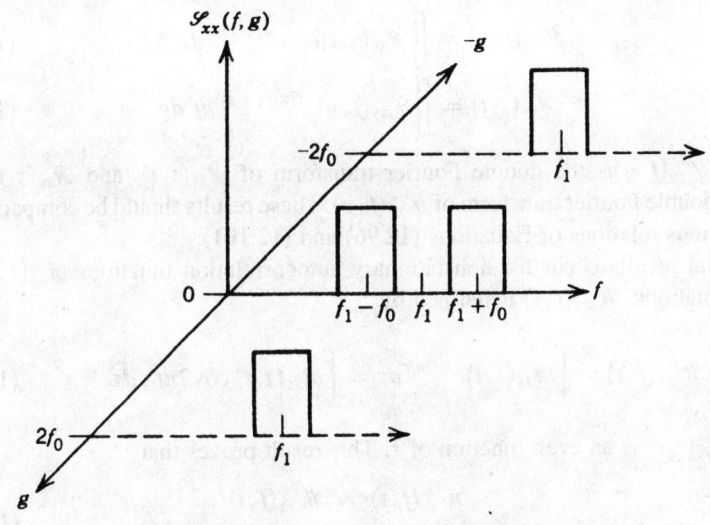

Figure 12.9 Illustration of double-frequency autospectrum for cosine-modulated narrow bandwidth noise.

and the nonstationary spectral density functions $\mathscr{S}_{xx}(f,g)$, $\mathscr{S}_{yy}(f,g)$, and $\mathscr{S}_{xy}(f,g)$, where

$$\mathscr{S}_{xy}(f,g) = E\left[X^*\left(f-\frac{g}{2}\right)Y\left(f+\frac{g}{2}\right)\right] \qquad (12.129)$$

The fourier transform of the nonstationary cross-correlation function $\mathscr{R}_{xy}(\tau,t)$ with respect to τ while holding t constant is given by

$$\mathscr{W}_{xy}(f,t) = \int \mathscr{R}_{xy}(\tau,t)e^{-j2\pi f\tau}d\tau \qquad (12.130)$$

This defines a *frequency–time spectral density function*, which is often called the *instantaneous spectrum*. The previous derivation of Equation (12.112) proves that

$$\mathscr{W}_{xy}(f,t) = \int \mathscr{S}_{xy}(f,g)e^{j2\pi gt}dg \qquad (12.131)$$

Thus, $\mathscr{W}_{xy}(f,t)$ is also the inverse Fourier transform of $\mathscr{S}_{xy}(f,g)$ with respect to g while holding f constant.

Corresponding to Equations (12.130) and (12.131), the inverse relations can be written

$$\mathscr{R}_{xy}(\tau,t) = \int \mathscr{W}_{xy}(f,t)e^{j2\pi f\tau}df \qquad (12.132)$$

$$\mathscr{S}_{xy}(f,g) = \int \mathscr{W}_{xy}(f,t)e^{-j2\pi gt}dt \qquad (12.133)$$

Substitution of Equation (12.130) into Equation (12.133) and Equation (12.131) into Equation (12.132) yields

$$\mathscr{S}_{xy}(f,g) = \iint \mathscr{R}_{xy}(\tau,t)e^{-j2\pi(f\tau+gt)}d\tau\,dt \qquad (12.134)$$

$$\mathscr{R}_{xy}(\tau,t) = \iint \mathscr{S}_{xy}(f,g)e^{j2\pi(f\tau+gt)}df\,dg \qquad (12.135)$$

Hence, $\mathscr{S}_{xy}(f,g)$ is the double Fourier transform of $\mathscr{R}_{xy}(\tau,t)$, and $\mathscr{R}_{xy}(\tau,t)$ is the inverse double Fourier transform of $\mathscr{S}_{xy}(f,g)$. These results should be compared with the previous relations of Equations (12.96) and (12.101).

Special results occur for nonstationary autocorrelation functions $\mathscr{R}_{xx}(\tau,t)$. For these situations, $\mathscr{W}_{xx}(f,t)$ is defined by

$$\mathscr{W}_{xx}(f,t) = \int \mathscr{R}_{xx}(\tau,t)e^{-j2\pi f\tau}d\tau = \int \mathscr{R}_{xx}(\tau,t)\cos 2\pi f\tau\,d\tau \qquad (12.136)$$

since $\mathscr{R}_{xx}(\tau,t)$ is an even function of τ. This result proves that

$$\begin{aligned}\mathscr{W}_{xx}^*(f,t) &= \mathscr{W}_{xx}(f,t) \\ \mathscr{W}_{xx}(-f,t) &= \mathscr{W}_{xx}(f,t)\end{aligned} \qquad (12.137)$$

In words, $\mathcal{W}_{xx}(f,t)$ is a real-valued even function of f. The inverse relation of Equation (12.136) gives

$$\mathcal{R}_{xx}(\tau,t) = \int \mathcal{W}_{xx}(f,t)e^{j2\pi f\tau}df = \int \mathcal{W}_{xx}(f,t)\cos 2\pi f\tau\, df \qquad (12.138)$$

because $\mathcal{W}_{xx}(f,t)$ is an even function of f.

From Equation (12.131), for nonstationary autospectral density functions $\mathcal{S}_{xx}(f,g)$, the associated relation with the aid of Equations (12.109) and (12.110) becomes

$$\begin{aligned}
\mathcal{W}_{xx}(f,t) &= \int_{-\infty}^{\infty} \mathcal{S}_{xx}(f,g)e^{j2\pi gt}dg \\
&= \int_{0}^{\infty}[\mathcal{S}_{xx}(f,g)+\mathcal{S}_{xx}^{*}(f,g)]\cos 2\pi gt\, dg \\
&\quad +j\int_{0}^{\infty}[\mathcal{S}_{xx}(f,g)-\mathcal{S}_{xx}^{*}(f,g)]\sin 2\pi gt\, dg
\end{aligned} \qquad (12.139)$$

The inverse relation of Equation (12.139) gives

$$\begin{aligned}
\mathcal{S}_{xx}(f,g) &= \int \mathcal{W}_{xx}(f,t)e^{-j2\pi gt}dt \\
&= \int \mathcal{W}_{xx}(f,t)\cos 2\pi gt\, dt - j\int \mathcal{W}_{xx}(f,t)\sin 2\pi gt\, dt
\end{aligned} \qquad (12.140)$$

where t may vary over $(-\infty, \infty)$. From Equation (12.137), it follows that

$$\begin{aligned}
\mathcal{S}_{xx}(-f,g) &= \mathcal{S}_{xx}(f,g) \\
\mathcal{S}_{xx}^{*}(f,g) &= \mathcal{S}_{xx}(f,-g)
\end{aligned} \qquad (12.141)$$

in agreement with Equations (12.109) and (12.110).

It is worth noting that one can change nonstationary formulas from two-dimensional correlation time spaces to two-dimensional spectral frequency spaces by using the frequency–time spectra and appropriate changes of variables. The order can go in both directions, as shown in Table 12.1.

Table 12.1 Nonstationary Correlation and Spectral Functions

Function	Space
$R_{xy}(t_1,t_2)$	(time, time)
$\updownarrow$	$\updownarrow$
$\mathcal{R}_{xy}(\tau,t)$	(time, time)
$\updownarrow$	$\updownarrow$
$\mathcal{W}_{xy}(f,t)$	(frequency, time)
$\updownarrow$	$\updownarrow$
$\mathcal{S}_{xy}(f,g)$	(frequency, frequency)
$\updownarrow$	$\updownarrow$
$S_{xy}(f_1,f_2)$	(frequency, frequency)

Now consider special properties of the frequency–time (instantaneous) spectrum $\mathscr{W}_{xx}(f,t)$. At the special point $\tau = 0$, it follows from Equations (12.73) and (12.138) that

$$\mathscr{R}_{xx}(0,t) = \int \mathscr{W}_{xx}(f,t)df = E[x^2(t)] \qquad (12.142)$$

Thus, *integration of $\mathscr{W}_{xx}(f,t)$ over all f gives the nonstationary mean square value (instantaneous power) of $\{x(t)\}$ at time t.* Also, at $g = 0$, from Equations (12.107) and (12.140),

$$\mathscr{S}_{xx}(f,0) = \int \mathscr{W}_{xx}(f,t)dt = E[|X(f)|^2] \qquad (12.143)$$

Thus, *integration of $\mathscr{W}_{xx}(f,t)$ over all t gives the energy autospectral density function of $\{x(t)\}$ at frequency f.*

Let t vary over $(-\infty, \infty)$ and f vary over $(-\infty, \infty)$. Then the energy contained in $\{x(t)\}$ in the time interval from t_a to t_b is given by

$$\int_{t_a}^{t_b} E[x^2(t)]dt = \int_{t_a}^{t_b} \left[\int_{-\infty}^{\infty} \mathscr{W}_{xx}(f,t)df\right]dt \qquad (12.144)$$

On the other hand, the energy contained in $\{x(t)\}$ in the frequency interval from f_a to f_b is given by

$$\int_{f_a}^{f_b} E[|X(f)|^2]dt = \int_{f_a}^{f_b} \left[\int_{-\infty}^{\infty} \mathscr{W}_{xx}(f,t)dt\right]df \qquad (12.145)$$

The total energy in $\{x(t)\}$ over the whole (f, t) plane is given by

$$\int_{-\infty}^{\infty} \int \mathscr{W}_{xx}(f,t)df\, dt = \int_{-\infty}^{\infty} \int \mathscr{W}_{xx}(f,t)dt\, df \qquad (12.146)$$

These relations show the physical importance of the instantaneous autospectrum $\mathscr{W}_{xx}(f,t)$ to describe the properties of $\{x(t)\}$.

Now consider the instantaneous cross-spectrum $\mathscr{W}_{xy}(f,t)$. From Equations (12.74) and (12.132),

$$\mathscr{R}_{xy}(0,t) = \int \mathscr{W}_{xy}(f,t)df = \sigma_{xy}(t) \qquad (12.147)$$

In words, *integration of $\mathscr{W}_{xy}(f,t)$ over all f gives the covariance between $\{x(t)\}$ and $\{y(t)\}$ at time t.* Also, from Equations (12.108) and (12.133),

$$\mathscr{S}_{xy}(f,0) = \int \mathscr{W}_{xy}(f,t)dt = E[X^*(f)Y(f)] \qquad (12.148)$$

In words, *integration of $\mathscr{W}_{xy}(f,t)$ over all t gives the energy cross-spectral density function between $\{x(t)\}$ and $\{y(t)\}$ at frequency f.*

SPECTRAL STRUCTURE OF NONSTATIONARY DATA

Returning to Equation (12.131), taking the complex conjugate of both sides yields, with the aid of Equation (12.111),

$$\begin{aligned}
\mathcal{W}_{xy}^*(f,t) &= \int \mathcal{S}_{xy}^*(f,g)e^{-j2\pi gt}dg \\
&= \int \mathcal{S}_{yx}(f,-g)e^{-j2\pi gt}dg \qquad (12.149) \\
&= \int \mathcal{S}_{yx}(f,g)e^{j2\pi gt}dg = \mathcal{W}_{yx}(f,t)
\end{aligned}$$

Also, from Equations (12.111) and (12.131), one obtains

$$\mathcal{W}_{xy}(-f,t) = \int \mathcal{S}_{xy}(-f,g)e^{j2\pi gt}dg = \int \mathcal{S}_{yx}(f,g)e^{j2\pi gt}dg = \mathcal{W}_{yx}(f,t) \quad (12.150)$$

When $x(t) = y(t)$, these equations become

$$\begin{aligned}
\mathcal{W}_{xx}^*(f,t) &= \mathcal{W}_{xx}(f,t) \\
\mathcal{W}_{xx}(-f,t) &= \mathcal{W}_{xx}(f,t)
\end{aligned} \qquad (12.151)$$

to give another proof of Equation (12.137) that $\mathcal{W}_{xx}(f,t)$ is a real-valued even function of f. Note that there is no restriction that $\mathcal{W}_{xx}(f,t)$ must be nonnegative. In fact, $\mathcal{W}_{xx}(f,t)$ can take on negative values, as shown in later examples. Also, Equations (12.150) and (12.151) allow one-sided instantaneous spectral density functions to be defined as follows:

$$W_{xy}(f) = \begin{cases} 2\mathcal{W}_{xy}(f) & f > 0 \\ \mathcal{W}_{xy}(f) & f = 0 \\ 0 & f < 0 \end{cases} \qquad (12.152)$$

$$W_{xx}(f) = \begin{cases} 2\mathcal{W}_{xx}(f) & f > 0 \\ \mathcal{W}_{xx}(f) & f = 0 \\ 0 & f < 0 \end{cases} \qquad (12.153)$$

The *time-averaged cross-spectral density function* $\bar{S}_{xy}(f)$ is defined from $\mathcal{W}_{xy}(f,t)$ by computing

$$\bar{S}_{xy}(f) = \lim_{T \to \infty} \frac{1}{T}\int_0^T \mathcal{W}_{xy}(f,t)dt \qquad (12.154)$$

The *time-averaged autospectral density function* $\bar{S}_{xx}(f)$ is defined from $\mathcal{W}_{xx}(f,t)$ by

$$\bar{S}_{xx}(f) = \lim_{T \to \infty} \frac{1}{T}\int_0^T \mathcal{W}_{xx}(f,t)dt \qquad (12.155)$$

Because $\mathcal{W}_{xy}(f,t)$ is the Fourier transform ($\mathcal{F}$) of $\mathcal{R}_{xy}(\tau,t)$ assuming that various limiting operations may be interchanged,

$$\begin{aligned}
\bar{S}_{xy}(f) &= \mathcal{F}[\bar{R}_{xy}(\tau)] \\
\bar{S}_{xx}(f) &= \mathcal{F}[\bar{R}_{xx}(\tau)]
\end{aligned} \qquad (12.156)$$

where the time-averaged correlation functions are defined in Equations (12.78) and (12.79).

Equation (12.143) indicates that the quantity $\bar{S}_{xx}(f)$ will be nonnegative for all values of f because, for large T,

$$\bar{S}_{xx}(f) = \frac{1}{T} E\left[|X(f)|^2\right] \geq 0 \qquad (12.157)$$

This is the usual definition for the autospectral density function of stationary random data. Similarly, from Equations (12.148) and (12.154), one obtains, for large T,

$$\bar{S}_{xy}(f) = \frac{1}{T} E[X^*(f) Y(f)] \qquad (12.158)$$

This is the usual definition for cross-spectral density functions of stationary random data. One-sided time-averaged spectral density functions are given as before by

$$\bar{G}_{xy}(f) = \begin{cases} 2\bar{S}_{xy}(f) & f > 0 \\ \bar{S}_{xy}(f) & f = 0 \\ 0 & f < 0 \end{cases} \qquad (12.159)$$

$$\bar{G}_{xx}(f) = \begin{cases} 2\bar{S}_{xx}(f) & f > 0 \\ \bar{S}_{xx}(f) & f = 0 \\ 0 & f < 0 \end{cases} \qquad (12.160)$$

For the special case of stationary random data, the nonstationary correlation function becomes

$$\mathcal{R}_{xy}(\tau, t) = R_{xy}(\tau) \qquad (12.161)$$

Hence,

$$\mathcal{W}_{xy}(f, t) = \int \mathcal{R}_{xy}(\tau, t) e^{-j2\pi f \tau} d\tau = S_{xy}(f) \qquad (12.162)$$

This shows that the frequency–time cross-spectrum $\mathcal{W}_{xy}(f, t)$ is now independent of t and is the usual stationary cross-spectral density function $S_{xy}(f)$. Similarly, for stationary random data, the nonstationary spectral density function is given by

$$\mathcal{S}_{xy}(f, g) = S_{xy}(f) \delta(g) \qquad (12.163)$$

It follows again that

$$\mathcal{W}_{xy}(f, t) = \int \mathcal{S}_{xy}(f, g) e^{j2\pi g t} dg = S_{xy}(f) \qquad (12.164)$$

Thus, $\mathcal{W}_{xy}(f, t)$ includes $S_{xy}(f)$ as a special case when data are stationary.

***Example 12.8.* Instantaneous Autospectrum of Modulated Random Data.**
Consider a cosine-modulated random process defined by

$$\{x(t)\} = [\cos 2\pi f_0 t]\{u(t)\}$$

where f_0 is a constant and $\{u(t)\}$ is a zero mean value stationary random process. From Example 12.6,

$$\mathscr{R}_{xx}(\tau,t) = \frac{1}{2}[\cos 2\pi f_0\tau + \cos 4\pi f_0 t]R_{uu}(\tau)$$

Then from Equation (12.136)

$$\mathscr{W}_{xx}(f,t) = \int \mathscr{R}_{xx}(\tau,t)e^{-j2\pi f\tau}d\tau$$
$$= \frac{1}{4}[S_{uu}(f-f_0) + S_{uu}(f+f_0)] + \frac{1}{2}(\cos 4\pi f_0 t)S_{uu}(f)$$

Observe the following;

a. The stationary component $S_{uu}(f)$ is shifted by $\pm f_0$.
b. The nonstationary component is periodic with a frequency $2f_0$.
c. $\mathscr{W}_{xx}(f,t)$ can take on negative values.

The *instantaneous power* in these data is given by Equation (12.73) as

$$\mathscr{R}_{xx}(0,t) = E[\,^2(t)] = R_{uu}(0)\cos^2 2\pi f_0 t$$

This agrees with integrating $\mathscr{W}_{xx}(f,t)$ over all f. The *energy autospectral density function* in these data is given by Equation (12.143) as

$$\mathscr{S}_{xx}(f,0) = E[|X(f)|^2]$$

where

$$X(f) = \frac{1}{2}[U(f-f_0) + U(f+f_0)]$$

Hence, for finite T, where $E\left[|U(f)|^2\right] = TS_{uu}(f)$, one obtains

$$\mathscr{S}_{xx}(f,0) = \frac{T}{4}[S_{uu}(f-f_0) + S_{uu}(f+f_0)]$$

This agrees with integrating $\mathscr{W}_{xx}(f,t)$ over t for the record length T. A plot of the one-sided instantaneous autospectrum $W_{xx}(f,t)$ when the one-sided $G_{uu}(f)$ is narrow bandwidth noise centered at $f = f_1$ is shown in Figure 12.10. The time-averaged results for this example are

$$\bar{R}_{xx}(\tau) = \frac{1}{T}\int_0^T \mathscr{R}_{xx}(\tau,t)dt = \frac{1}{2}(\cos 2\pi f_0\tau)R_{uu}(\tau)$$

$$\bar{G}_{xx}(f) = \frac{1}{2}\int_0^T W_{xx}(f,t)dt = \frac{1}{4}[G_{uu}(f_1-f_0) + G_{uu}(f_1+f_0)]$$

Note that the time-averaged spectrum includes only the two stationary spectral components centered at $f = f_1 \pm f_0$; the time-varying component centered at $f = f_1$ is removed by the averaging operation. These two stationary components are commonly referred to as the *sidebands* produced by the modulation process.

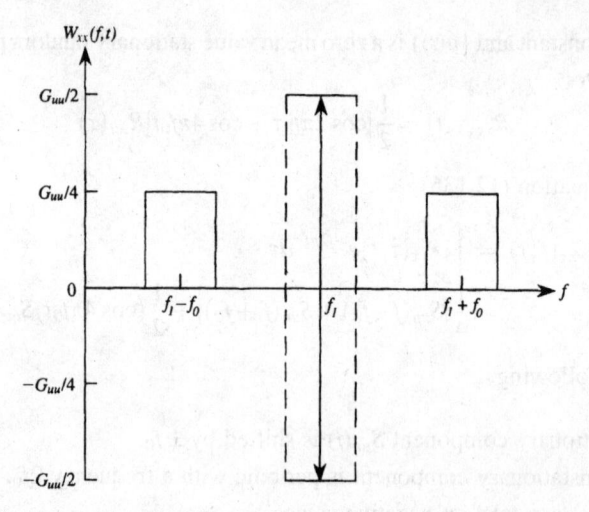

Figure 12.10 Illustration of instantaneous autospectrum for cosine-modulated narrow bandwidth noise.

12.6.4 Analysis Procedures for Single Records

Given a sample record $x(t)$ of length T from an arbitrary nonstationary random process $\{x(t)\}$, the procedures for estimating spectral functions are similar to those discussed for correlation functions in Section 12.5.3. Specifically, assume that the nonstationary random data can be represented by the product model in Equation (12.83). To repeat,

$$\{x(t)\} = a(t)\{u(t)\} \qquad (12.165)$$

where $a(t)$ is a deterministic function and $\{u(t)\}$ is a stationary random process with a mean and a variance of zero and unity, respectively. Further assume $a(t) \geq 0$ and $\{u(t)\}$ is a Gaussian random process. With these assumptions, an estimate for the autocorrelation function of $\{u(t)\}$, denoted by $\hat{R}_{uu}(\tau)$ can be computed from a single sample record $x(t)$ by the hard clipping procedure detailed in Equations (12.84)–(12.86), and the autospectrum of $\{u(t)\}$ can then be estimated by taking the Fourier transform of $\hat{R}_{uu}(\tau)$; that is,

$$\hat{G}_{uu}(f) = 4\int_0^{\tau_{\max}} \hat{R}_{uu}(\tau)\cos(2\pi f\tau)d\tau \qquad (12.166)$$

where the frequency resolution of the resulting spectral estimate is given by $\Delta f = 1/\tau_{\max}$. Of course, the autospectrum given by Equation (12.166) is normalized; that is, the area under the spectrum is unity independent of the instantaneous mean square value of the data. However, for some applications, the relative spectral content of nonstationary random data may be the only data property of interest. An example is atmospheric turbulence data, where measured sample records are commonly nonstationary, but important characteristics of the turbulence phenomenon can be obtained from only the relative spectral content of the data. Because such data are known to be approximately Gaussian and fit the product model, the analysis procedure leading to Equation (12.166) provides valuable information, as detailed with an illustration in Ref. 4.

Again referring to Equation (12.165), if it is further assumed that $a(t)$ varies slowly relative to the lowest frequency of $\{u(t)\}$, then the instantaneous autocorrelation function of $\{x(t)\}$ reduces to the locally stationary form given in Equation (12.87). Taking the Fourier transform of Equation (12.87) over τ yields the one-sided instantaneous autospectrum

$$W_{xx}(f,t) = \psi_x^2(t) G_{uu}(f) \qquad (12.167)$$

where $G_{uu}(f)$ is estimated by Equation (12.166). It follows from Equation (12.167) that the instantaneous autospectrum for locally stationary data is always nonnegative and separates into a time-dependent function, which is the instantaneous mean square value of $\{x(t)\}$, and a frequency-dependent function, which is the autospectrum of $\{u(t)\}$. The instantaneous mean square value $\psi_x^2(t)$ can be estimated by the running average procedure detailed in Section 12.3.3, while the stationary autospectrum $G_{uu}(f)$ can be estimated by averaging over the entire sample record length T in one of two ways. The first way is to estimate $G_{uu}(f)$ using Equation (12.166), where $R_{uu}(\tau)$ is computed by the hard clipped procedure in Equations (12.84)–(12.86). The second way is to approximate $G_{uu}(f)$ by computing a time-averaged autospectral density function $\bar{G}_{uu}(f)$ over the nonstationary record $x(t)$ find normalizing to make $\int \bar{G}_{xx}(f) df = 1$. The fact that the normalized $\bar{G}_{xx}(f) \approx G_{uu}(f)$ when the variations of $a(t)$ with time are slow compared to the lowest frequency of $\{u(t)\}$ is demonstrated by the instantaneous autospectrum for the modulation process in Figure 12.10. Specifically, as the modulating frequency f_0 becomes small compared to the center frequency f_1, the two stationary spectral components at $f_1 \pm f_0$ collapse into a single stationary autospectrum approximated by $\frac{1}{2} G_{uu}(f)$. This net stationary autospectrum then sums with the time-varying spectral component centered at f_1 to produce an instantaneous autospectrum with a time-averaged value of $\bar{G}_{xx}(f) \approx \frac{1}{2} G_{uu}(f)$. Replacing $G_{uu}(f)$ in Equation (12.167) with the normalized $\bar{G}_{xx}(f)$ eliminates the need for assuming that $\{u(t)\}$ has a normal (Gaussian) probability density function and is easier to compute, but it is clear from Figure 12.10 that the bandwidth of $\bar{G}_{xx}(f)$ will increase relative to $G_{uu}(f)$ as the rate of change of $a(t)$ with time increases.

Finally, consider the more general case where the autospectrum of $\{u(t)\}$ in Equation (12.163) is not stationary; that is, the mean and variance of $\{u(t)\}$ are still stationary with values of zero and unity, respectively, but the autospectrum of $\{u(t)\}$ varies with time. In many cases, an instantaneous autospectrum for $\{x(t)\}$ can still be estimated with acceptable bias and random errors using short time-averaging operations. Specifically, based on the definition of the autospectrum in Section 5.2.3, let the time-varying autospectrum of a nonstationary random process $\{x(t)\}$ be estimated by the filtering–squaring–averaging operation illustrated in Figure 12.11, where a running average of the output of each bandpass filter with a bandwidth B_i is computed using a short averaging time T_i. Such an analysis procedure is easily implemented using digital filters (see Section 11.1.3). From Equation (5.68), the running average

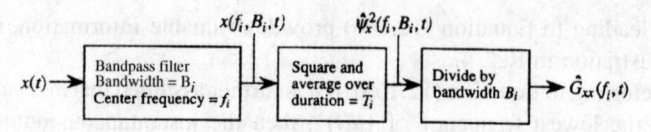

Figure 12.11 Procedure for estimating instantaneous autospectrum by filtering, squaring, and averaging.

autospectrum estimate at the center frequency of the ith bandpass filter is given by

$$\hat{G}_{xx}(f_i, t) = \frac{1}{B_i T_i} \int_{t-T_i/2}^{t+T_i/2} x^2(f_i, B_i, u)\, du \quad i = 1, 2, \ldots, M \tag{12.168}$$

where M is the total number of bandpass filters required to cover the frequency range of the analysis. The estimation procedure is then similar to that presented for nonstationary mean square values in Section 12.4.3, except the running average is now computed for the output of each of a collection of M bandpass filters. As for time-varying mean square value estimates, there will be (a) a time resolution bias error that can be approximated by Equation (12.54) and (b) a random error given by Equation (12.55) where $B_s = B_i$. However, there is now a third error, namely, a frequency resolution bias error that can be approximated by Equation (8.139). It follows that the total normalized mean square error of the running average autospectrum estimate in Equation (12.168) at each frequency $f = f_i$ is given by

$$\varepsilon^2[\hat{G}_{xx}(f, t)] = \frac{1}{B_i T_i} + \frac{T_i^4}{576} C_{T_i}(f, t) + \frac{B_i^4}{576} C_{B_i}(f, t) \tag{12.169}$$

where

$$C_{T_i}(f, t) = \left\{ \frac{d^2[G_{xx}(f, t)]/dt^2}{G_{xx}(f, t)} \right\}^2 \quad C_{B_i}(f, t) = \left\{ \frac{d^2[G_{xx}(f, t)]/df^2}{G_{xx}(f, t)} \right\}^2 \tag{12.170}$$

From Section 12.3.4 in Ref. 1, an optimum estimate of a time-varying autospectrum can be accomplished by solving for those values of T_i and B_i that minimize the total mean square error of the estimate. This is done by taking the partial derivative of Equation (12.169), first with respect to T_i and then with respect to B_i, setting these two partial derivatives equal to zero, and solving the resulting simultaneous equations. The partial derivatives of Equation (12.169) equated to zero are

$$\frac{\partial\{\varepsilon^2[\hat{G}_{xx}(f, t)]\}}{\partial T_i} = \frac{-1}{B_i T_i^2} + \frac{T_i^3}{144} C_{T_i}(f, t) = 0$$

$$\frac{\partial\{\varepsilon^2[\hat{G}_{xx}(f, t)]\}}{\partial B_i} = \frac{-1}{B_i^2 T_i} + \frac{B_i^3}{144} C_{B_i}(f, t) = 0$$

The solution of the above two simultaneous equations for the optimum values T_0 and B_0 in the ith frequency band yields

$$T_{0i} = 2.29 \frac{C_{B_i}^{1/24}(f, t)}{C_{T_i}^{5/24}(f, t)} \quad \text{and} \quad B_{0i} = 2.29 \frac{C_{T_i}^{1/24}(f, t)}{C_{B_i}^{5/24}(f, t)} \tag{12.171}$$

Note that the $C_T(f, t)$ and $C_B(f, t)$ terms appear in Equation (12.171) raised to the 1/24 or 5/24 power, meaning that the estimation of values for these terms can be coarse without introducing major errors in the resulting optimum parameters. Also, note that the $C_T(f, t)$ and $C_B(f, t)$ terms are both functions of frequency and time. However, the maximum value of $C_T(f, t)$ for the time-varying mean square value of the data can often be used in all frequency bands with acceptable results. One possible procedure for estimating this value is detailed in Example 12.4. An appropriate value for $C_B(f, t)$ as a function of frequency might be estimated from a preliminary analysis of the data, past experience, or theoretical considerations.

Example 12.9. Selection of Optimum Analysis Parameters for Nonstationary Data. Assume that a sample record $x(t)$ from a nonstationary random process $\{x(t)\}$ is to be analyzed by the running average procedure in Equation (12.168). Further assume that the time-varying mean square value of the data is similar to that shown in Figure 12.5(a), where $T_D \approx 3$ s. It follows from Equation (12.60) that

$$C_T(t_m) \approx 0.24 \text{s}^{-4}$$

which will be used as an approximation for $C_B(f, t)$ in all frequency bands. Finally, assume the nonstationary data represent the vibration response of a resonant structure where each resonance can be described by the frequency response function illustrated in Figure 2.3. From Section 12.3.4 in Ref. 1, the maximum value of $C_B(f, t)$ at each resonance frequency is given by $C_B(f, t) \approx 4(\zeta_i f_i)^{-4} \text{Hz}^{-4}$. Let the estimated damping ratio for the response at all resonant frequencies be $\zeta \approx 0.05$ so that

$$C_B(f, t) \approx 640,000 f_i^{-4} \text{Hz}^{-4}$$

Because it is not known in advance of the analysis which frequency bands will include a resonance frequency, the above value for $C_B(f, t)$ will be used for the analysis in all frequency bands. Substituting these values into Equation (12.171) gives

$$T_0(f) \approx 5.39 f^{-1/6} \text{s} \quad \text{and} \quad B_0(f) \approx 0.134 f^{5/6} \text{Hz}$$

The above optimum analysis parameters are plotted in Figure 12.12 for the frequency range from 10 to 1000 Hz. Note from this figure that the optimum averaging time $T_0(f)$

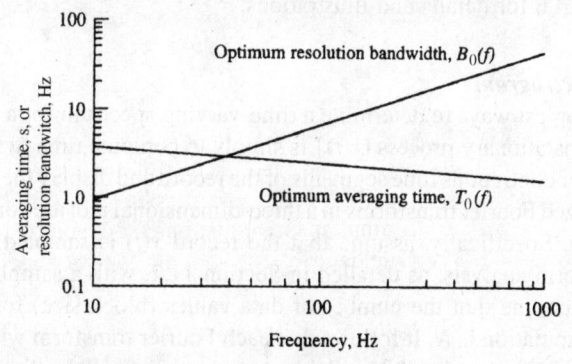

Figure 12.12 Optimum averaging time and resolution bandwidth for nonstationary structural vibration data.

is closely approximated by a constant T_0, while the optimum frequency resolution bandwidth $B_0(f)$ is almost proportional to frequency. This explains why spectra for structural vibration and acoustical data, both stationary and nonstationary, are often estimated using a fixed averaging time and a proportional bandwidth. This concludes Example 12.9.

There are other procedures for estimating the spectral properties of nonstationary data from a single sample record that are most effective when the data are deterministic, but are sometimes applied to the analysis of nonstationary data that are at least partially random in character. Three widely used procedures are the Wigner distribution, spectrograms, and wavelet analysis.

12.6.4.1 Wigner Distribution

Given a sample record $x(t)$ from a nonstationary process $\{x(t)\}$, the *Wigner distribution* (sometimes called the *Wigner–Ville distribution*) is usually defined as the Fourier transform of the unaveraged instantaneous autocorrelation function in Equation (12.82) over τ, that is,

$$WD_{xx}(f,t) = \int \left[x\left(t - \frac{\tau}{2}\right) x\left(t + \frac{\tau}{2}\right) \right] e^{-j2\pi f \tau} d\tau \qquad (12.172)$$

Comparing Equations (12.172) and (12.136), it is clear that the Wigner distribution is essentially an instantaneous autospectrum computed with no averaging. Hence, the Wigner distribution at certain times can take on negative values. For example, an *average* Wigner distribution for the cosine-modulated narrow bandwidth noise studied in Example 12.8 would be the same as pictured in Figure 12.10. However, given a sample record $x(t)$ of length T, the computation in Equation (12.172) can be performed only over a finite range of time delay values $\tau \leq T$, which produces an estimate of $WD_{xx}(f, t)$ with a frequency resolution of $B_e = 1/\tau_{max}$. The maximum frequency resolution is obtained with $\tau_{max} = T$, meaning $B_e T = 1$. For this case, the estimate of $WD_{xx}(f, t)$ would have a normalized random error of about 100% $(\varepsilon_r[\hat{W}D_{xx}(f,t)] \approx 1)$. It follows that the Wigner distribution is most applicable to data that are primarily deterministic in character so that the statistical sampling (random) errors in the resulting estimates will be small—for example, speech signals. See Refs. 5 and 6 for details and illustrations.

12.6.4.2 Spectrogram

One of the simplest ways to determine a time-varying spectrum for a sample record $x(t)$ from a nonstationary process $\{x(t)\}$ is simply to compute time-averaged Fourier transforms over contiguous time segments of the record and display the magnitudes of the time averaged Fourier transforms in a three-dimensional plot are commonly called a *spectrogram*. Specifically, assume that the record $x(t)$ is sampled for a discrete Fourier transform analysis, as detailed in Section 11.2, with a sampling interval of Δt s. Further assume that the number of data values (block size) for each Fourier transform computation is N. It follows that each Fourier transform will cover a time segment of $T_B = N \Delta t$ s so that the available record length T will be divided into (T/T_B)

SPECTRAL STRUCTURE OF NONSTATIONARY DATA

(a) Waterfall display

(b) Two-dimensional display

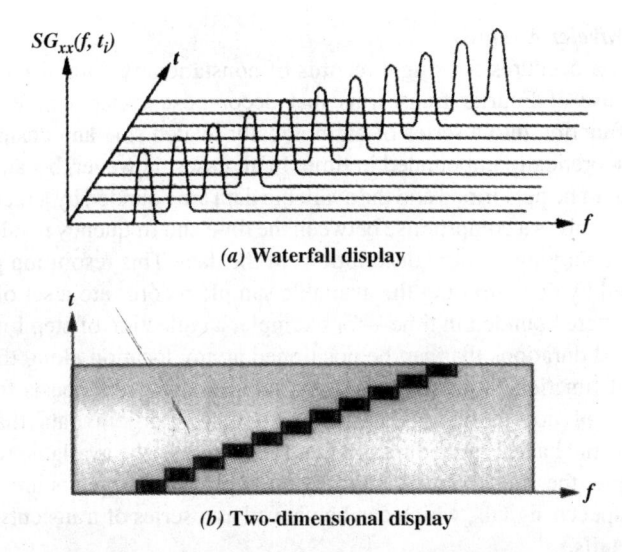

Figure 12.13 Spectrograms for sine wave with linearly increasing instantaneous frequency.

segments. The collection of time-averaged Fourier transform magnitudes for these segments is then given by

$$SG_{xx}(f, t_i) = \frac{1}{T_B} \left| \int_{(i-1)T_B}^{iT_B} x(t)e^{-j2\pi ft}dt \right| \quad i = 1, 2, 3, \ldots, (T/T_B) \quad (12.173)$$

The spectrogram for a sine wave with a linearly increasing instantaneous frequency is illustrated in Figure 12.13(a), where the lowest instantaneous frequency is $f > (1/T_B)$. When presented in this manner, spectrograms are often called *waterfall displays*. A less quantitative way to present a spectrogram is as data points in a two-dimensional display of time versus frequency where the magnitude of the spectral components is proportional to the darkness of the data points, as illustrated in Figure 12.13(b). In either format, the computation of a spectrogram involves a compromise between the time resolution given by T_B and the frequency resolution given by $1/T_B$, which must be decided based upon the specific characteristics of the data being analyzed. Note that, unlike the Wigner distribution, spectrograms can never have negative values. On the other hand, like the Wigner distribution, the computation involves a BT product of unity and, hence, the results will include large random errors if the data being analyzed are random in character. Specifically, if $x(t)$ is a sample record from a random process $\{x(t)\}$, then Equation (12.173) produces only an estimate $S\hat{G}_{xx}(f, t)$. From Sections 8.5.4 and 4.2.2, assuming the estimates at each time t are computed from an approximately stationary segment, the ratio $[S\hat{G}_{xx}(f, t)/SG_{xx}(f, t)]$ has a probability distribution equivalent to the square root of chi-square with two degrees of freedom, which is the Rayleigh distribution detailed in Section 3.4.2. Thus, from Equations (3.99) and (3.100), the normalized random error for the estimate is $\varepsilon_r[S\hat{G}_{xx}(f, t)] = \sqrt{2}/1.25 = 1.13$ (113%). See Ref. 5 for detailed discussions of spectrograms.

12.6.4.3 Wavelet Analysis

The analysis procedures for single records of nonstationary data discussed thus far involve the use of Fourier transforms that decompose either a time history or a correlation function into a series of harmonically related sine and cosine functions, which are theoretically unbounded in time. In all cases, however, because ensemble averages cannot be performed and the available data are bounded by a record length T, the analysis involves a compromise between the time and frequency resolutions of the resulting time-varying spectral descriptions of the data. This resolution problem can be suppressed by decomposing the available sample record into a set of orthogonal functions that are bounded in time—for example, a collection of step functions with integer-related durations that can be positioned at any location along the time axis. Such a set of functions are called *wavelets*, and they provide a basis for analyzing certain types of nonstationary data—in particular, transient data that are near-deterministic and have a finite duration that is covered by the available record length T, for example, the shock wave caused by an explosion. Wavelets are also used to decompose speech signals, which can be viewed as a series of transients. See Refs 6 and 7 for details.

12.7 INPUT/OUTPUT RELATIONS FOR NONSTATIONARY DATA

Consider sample functions from a nonstationary random process $\{x(t)\}$ acting as the input to a time-varying linear system with a weighting function $h(\tau, t)$ and a frequency response function $H(f, t)$, where

$$H(f,t) = \int h(\tau,t)e^{-j2\pi f\tau}d\tau \qquad (12.174)$$

For an arbitrary input $x(t)$ belonging to $\{x(t)\}$, the output $y(t)$ belonging to $\{y(t)\}$ is

$$y(t) = \int h(\tau,t)x(t-\tau)d\tau \qquad (12.175)$$

It is clear that, in general, $\{y(t)\}$ will be a nonstationary random process because its statistical properties will be a function of t when either $\{x(t)\}$ is nonstationary or $h(\tau, t)$ is a function of t. For constant-parameter linear systems, $h(\tau, t) = h(\tau)$ and $H(f, t) = H(f)$, independent of t. Input/output relations in both the double-time correlation domain and the double-frequency spectral domain will now be derived for four cases:

1. Nonstationary input and time-varying linear system
2. Nonstationary input and constant-parameter linear system
3. Stationary input and time-varying linear system
4. Stationary input and constant-parameter linear system

The last case reduces to the familiar single time correlation domain and the single frequency spectral domain, as covered in Chapter 6.

INPUT/OUTPUT RELATIONS FOR NONSTATIONARY DATA   463

12.7.1 Nonstationary Input and Time-Varying Linear System

For a pair of times t_1, t_2, the product of $y(t_1)$ with $y(t_2)$ is given by

$$y(t_1)y(t_2) = \iint h(\alpha,t_1)h(\beta,t_2)x(t_1-\alpha)x(t_2-\beta)d\alpha\,d\beta$$

Taking expected values produces the nonstationary input/output autocorrelation relation

$$R_{yy}(t_1,t_2) = \iint h(\alpha,t_1)h(\beta,t_2)R_{xx}(t_1-\alpha,t_2-\beta)d\alpha\,d\beta \qquad (12.176)$$

Similarly, the product of $x(t_1)$ with $y(t_2)$ is given by

$$x(t_1)y(t_2) = \int h(\beta,t_2)x(t_1)x(t_2-\beta)d\beta$$

Again taking expected values yields

$$R_{xy}(t_1,t_2) = \int h(\beta,t_2)R_{xx}(t_1,t_2-\beta)d\beta \qquad (12.177)$$

Equations (12.176) and (12.177) are general results where all operations take place in a real-valued time domain.

To transform to a complex-valued frequency domain, let

$$J(f,g) = \int H(f,t)e^{-j2\pi gt}dt \qquad (12.178)$$

Then from Equation (12.174)

$$J(f,g) = \iint h(\tau,t)e^{-j2\pi(f\tau+gt)}d\tau\,dt \qquad (12.179)$$

In words, $J(f, g)$ is the double Fourier transform of $h(\tau, t)$. Also,

$$h(\tau,t) = \iint J(f,g)e^{j2\pi(f\tau+gt)}df\,dg \qquad (12.180)$$

Equation (12.175) is thus the same as

$$y(t) = \iiint J(f,g)e^{j2\pi(f\tau+gt)}x(t-\tau)d\tau\,df\,dg \qquad (12.181)$$

Now let $g = f_1 - f$, $dg = df_1$, $\alpha = t - \tau$, and $d\alpha = -d\tau$. It follows that

$$y(t) = \iiint J(f,f_1-f)e^{j2\pi f_1 t}e^{-j2\pi f\alpha}x(\alpha)d\alpha\,df\,df_1$$

$$= \iint J(f,f_1-f)X(f)e^{j2\pi f_1 t}df\,df_1 \qquad (12.182)$$

$$= \int Y(f_1)e^{j2\pi f_1 t}df_1$$

where

$$X(f) = \int x(\alpha)e^{-j2\pi f\alpha}d\alpha \tag{12.183}$$

$$Y(f_1) = \int J(f, f_1 - f)X(f)df \tag{12.184}$$

Equation (12.184) is the key to obtaining the desired nonstationary input/output spectral density relations. Specifically, for a pair of frequencies f_1 and f_2, the product $Y^*(f_1)Y(f_2)$ is given by

$$Y^*(f_1)Y(f_2) = \iint J^*(\lambda, f_1 - \lambda)J(\eta, f_2 - \eta)X^*(\lambda)X(\eta)\,d\lambda\,d\eta$$

Taking expected values of both sides yields the result

$$S_{yy}(f_1, f_2) = \iint J^*(\lambda, f_1 - \lambda)J(\eta, f_2 - \eta)S_{xx}(\lambda, \eta)\,d\lambda\,d\eta \tag{12.185}$$

Similarly, the product of $X^*(f_1)$ with $Y(f_2)$ yields

$$X^*(f_1)Y(f_2) = \int J(\eta, f_2 - \eta)X^*(f_1)X(\eta)\,d\eta$$

Taking expected values, one obtains

$$S_{xy}(f_1, f_2) = \int J(\eta, f_2 - \eta)S_{xx}(f_1, \eta)\,d\eta \tag{12.186}$$

Equations (12.185) and (12.186) are general results where all operations take place in a complex-valued frequency domain. These general results are henceforth referred to as the Case 1 results.

12.7.2 Results for Special Cases

Further results will now be stated for special cases that follow from the general formulas for in Section 12.7.1.

CASE 1. *Nonstationary Input and Constant-Parameter Linear System*

For the case where the linear system has constant parameters, it follows that

$$\begin{aligned} h(\tau, t) &= h(\tau) & J(f, g) &= H(f)\delta(g) \\ H(f, t) &= H(f) & Y(f_1) &= H(f_1)X(f_1) \end{aligned} \tag{12.187}$$

Then Equations (12.176) and (12.177) become

$$R_{yy}(t_1, t_2) = \iint h(\alpha)h(\beta)R_{xx}(t_1 - \alpha, t_2 - \beta)\,d\alpha\,d\beta \tag{12.188}$$

$$R_{xy}(t_1, t_2) = \int h(\beta)R_{xx}(t_1, t_2 - \beta)\,d\beta \tag{12.189}$$

and Equations (12.185) and (12.186) become

$$S_{yy}(f_1,f_2) = H^*(f_1)H(f_2)S_{xx}(f_1,f_2) \qquad (12.190)$$

$$S_{xy}(f_1,f_2) = H(f_2)S_{xx}(f_1,f_2) \qquad (12.191)$$

Note that this last equation involves $H(f_2)$ and *not* $H(f_1)$.

CASE 2. *Stationary Input and Time-Varying Linear System*

For the case where the input is stationary, it follows that

$$\begin{aligned} R_{xx}(t_1,t_2) &= R_{xx}(t_2-t_1) \\ S_{xx}(f_1,f_2) &= S_{xx}(f_1)\delta(f_2-f_1) \end{aligned} \qquad (12.192)$$

Hence, Equations (12.176) and (12.177) become

$$R_{yy}(t_1,t_2) = \iint h(\alpha,t_1)h(\beta,t_2)R_{xx}(t_2-t_1+\alpha-\beta)\, d\alpha\, d\beta \qquad (12.193)$$

$$R_{xy}(t_1,t_2) = \int h(\beta,t_2)R_{xx}(t_2-t_1-\beta)\, d\beta \qquad (12.194)$$

and Equations (12.185) and (12.186) become

$$S_{yy}(f_1,f_2) = \int J^*(f,f_1-f)J(f,f_2-f)S_{xx}(f)\, df \qquad (12.195)$$

$$S_{xy}(f_1,f_2) = J(f_1,f_2-f_1)S_{xx}(f_1) \qquad (12.196)$$

Note that this last result involves $S_{xx}(f_1)$ and not $S_{xx}(f_2)$.

CASE 3. *Stationary Input and Constant-Parameter Linear System*

For the case where the input is stationary and the linear system has constant parameters, all the special relations in Equations (12.187) and (12.192) apply, giving the following well-known results as the simplest form of Equations (12.176), (12.177), (12.185), and (12.186).

$$R_{yy}(\tau) = \iint h(\alpha)h(\beta)R_{xx}(\tau+\alpha-\beta)\, d\alpha\, d\beta \qquad (12.197)$$

$$R_{xy}(\tau) = \int h(\beta)R_{xx}(\tau-\beta)\, d\beta \qquad (12.198)$$

$$S_{yy}(f) = |H(f)|^2 S_{xx}(f) \qquad (12.199)$$

$$S_{xy}(f) = H(f)S_{xx}(f) \qquad (12.200)$$

The results from all four cases are summarized in Table 12.2.

12.7.3 Frequency–Time Spectral Input/Output Relations

Consider Case from the previous section, where nonstationary data pass through a constant-parameter linear system. Frequency–time spectral input/output relations are now derived, starting from the double-frequency spectral relations of Equations (12.190) and (12.191).

Table 12.2 Nonstationary Input/Output Correlation and Spectral Relations

Case	Correlation Relations	Spectral Relations
Nonstationary input, time-varying system	$R_{yy}(t_1,t_2) = \iint h(\alpha,t_1)h(\beta,t_2)R_{xx}(t_1-\alpha,t_2-\beta)\,d\alpha\,d\beta$ $R_{xy}(t_1,t_2) = \int h(\beta,t_2)R_{xx}(t_1,t_2-\beta)\,d\beta$	$S_{yy}(f_1,f_2) = \iint J^*(\lambda,f_1-\lambda)J(\eta,f_2-\eta)S_{xx}(\lambda,\eta)\,d\lambda\,d\eta$ $S_{xy}(f_1,f_2) = \int J(\eta,f_2-\eta)S_{xx}(f_1,\eta)\,d\eta$
Nonstationary input, constant-parameter system	$R_{yy}(t_1,t_2) = \iint h(\alpha)h(\beta)R_{xx}(t_1-\alpha,t_2-\beta)\,d\alpha\,d\beta$ $R_{xy}(t_1,t_2) = \int h(\beta)R_{xx}(t_1,t_2-\beta)\,d\beta$	$S_{yy}(f_1,f_2) = H^*(f_1)H(f_2)S_{xx}(f_1,f_2)$ $S_{xy}(f_1,f_2) = H(f_2)S_{xx}(f_1,f_2)$
Stationary input, time-varying system	$R_{yy}(t_1,t_2) = \iint h(\alpha,t_1)h(\beta,t_2)R_{xx}(t_2-t_1+\alpha-\beta)\,d\alpha\,d\beta$ $R_{xy}(t_1,t_2) = \int h(\beta,t_2)R_{xx}(t_2-t_1-\beta)\,d\beta$	$S_{yy}(f_1,f_2) = \int J^*(f,f_1-f)J(f,f_2-f)S_{xx}(f)\,df$ $S_{xy}(f_1,f_2) = J(f_1,f_2-f_1)S_{xx}(f_1)$
Stationary input, constant-parameter system	$R_{yy}(\tau) = \iint h(\alpha)h(\beta)R_{xx}(\tau+\alpha-\beta)\,d\alpha\,d\beta$ $R_{xy}(\tau) = \int h(\beta)R_{xx}(\tau-\beta)\,d\beta$	$S_{yy}(f) = \|H(f)\|^2 S_{xx}(f)$ $S_{xy}(f) = H(f)S_{xx}(f)$

INPUT/OUTPUT RELATIONS FOR NONSTATIONARY DATA

Let the following transformations be made:
$$f_1 = f - \frac{g}{2} \qquad f_2 = f + \frac{g}{2} \tag{12.201}$$

It then follows that
$$S_{xx}(f_1,f_2) = \mathscr{S}_{xx}(f,g)$$
$$S_{yy}(f_1,f_2) = \mathscr{S}_{yy}(f,g) \tag{12.202}$$
$$S_{xy}(f_1,f_2) = \mathscr{S}_{xy}(f,g) \tag{12.203}$$

This gives in place of Equations (12.190) and (12.191) the spectral input/output results

$$\mathscr{S}_{yy}(f,g) = H^*\left(f - \frac{g}{2}\right)H\left(f + \frac{g}{2}\right)\mathscr{S}_{xx}(f,g) \tag{12.204}$$

$$\mathscr{S}_{xy}(f,g) = H\left(f + \frac{g}{2}\right)\mathscr{S}_{xx}(f,g) \tag{12.205}$$

The frequency–time (instantaneous) spectra are now calculated from Equations (12.131) and (12.139) by

$$W_{xx}(f,t) = \int \mathscr{S}_{xx}(f,g)e^{j2\pi gt}\,dg$$
$$W_{yy}(f,t) = \int \mathscr{S}_{yy}(f,g)e^{j2\pi gt}\,dg \tag{12.206}$$

$$W_{xy}(f,t) = \int \mathscr{S}_{xy}(f,g)e^{j2\pi gt}\,dg \tag{12.207}$$

Let the following functions be defined:
$$\mathscr{S}_{HH}(f,g) = H^*\left(f - \frac{g}{2}\right)H\left(f + \frac{g}{2}\right) \tag{12.208}$$
$$W_{HH}(f,t) = \int \mathscr{S}_{HH}(f,g)e^{j2\pi gt}\,dg \tag{12.209}$$

Then Equation (12.204) becomes
$$\mathscr{S}_{yy}(f,g) = \mathscr{S}_{HH}(f,g)\mathscr{S}_{xx}(f,g) \tag{12.210}$$

and the frequency–time spectral input/output relation is now
$$W_{yy}(f,t) = \int W_{HH}(f,\alpha)W_{xx}(f,t-\alpha)\,d\alpha \tag{12.211}$$

showing that $W_{yy}(f,t)$ is the convolution of $W_{HH}(f,t)$ with $W_{xx}(f,t)$. This result in Equation (12.211) can be negative for some values of f and t.

12.7.4 Energy Spectral Input/Output Relations

A special class of nonstationary data are those that physically exist only within a finite, measurable time interval, that is, where the input process $\{x(t)\}$ and the output process $\{y(t)\}$ have nonzero values only for $0 \le t \le T$. Such data are commonly referred to as *transients* and allow a greatly simplified analysis because for a pair of sample records $x(t)$ and $y(t)$ with zero mean values,

$$X(f) = \int_0^T x(t)e^{-j2\pi ft} dt = \int_{-\infty}^{\infty} x(t)e^{-j2\pi ft} dt$$
$$Y(f) = \int_0^T y(t)e^{-j2\pi ft} dt = \int_{-\infty}^{\infty} y(t)e^{-j2\pi ft} dt \tag{12.212}$$

From Equation (12.148), the expected value of the product of $X^*(f)$ and $Y(f)$ yields the *energy cross-spectral density function* defined by

$$\mathscr{S}_{xy}(f) = E[X^*(f)Y(f)] = \int_0^T \mathscr{W}_{xy}(f,t)\, dt \tag{12.213}$$

Similarly, the energy autospectral density functions are defined by

$$\mathscr{S}_{xx}(f) = E[X^*(f)X(f)] = \int_0^T \mathscr{W}_{xx}(f,t)\, dt$$
$$\mathscr{S}_{yy}(f) = E[Y^*(f)Y(f)] = \int_0^T \mathscr{W}_{yy}(f,t)\, dt \tag{12.214}$$

It then follows from the input/output relations in Equations (12.204) and (12.205) for $g = 0$ that

$$\mathscr{S}_{yy}(f) = H(f)^2 \mathscr{S}_{xx}(f) \tag{12.215}$$
$$\mathscr{S}_{xy}(f) = H(f) \mathscr{S}_{xx}(f) \tag{12.216}$$

In terms of one-sided energy spectral density functions that exist only for $f \geq 0$,

$$\mathscr{G}_{yy}(f) = H(f)^2 \mathscr{G}_{xx}(f) \tag{12.217}$$
$$\mathscr{G}_{yy}(f) = H(f) \mathscr{G}_{xx}(f) \tag{12.218}$$

Note that the input/output relations given above for transients are identical to those developed for stationary random data in Equations (6, 7, 8, 9), except "energy" spectra replace "power" spectra. For transient data, the averaging operation needed to compute the energy spectral estimates $\mathscr{G}_{xy}(f)$ and $\mathscr{G}_{xx}(f)$ theoretically requires that the experiment producing the data be repeated many times. In practice, however, the frequency averaging procedures detailed in Section 11.5.5 for stationary random data can be applied to transient data as well. Also, transient input/output data often involve sufficiently high signal-to-noise ratios to allow the computation of a meaningful frequency response function magnitude from a single experiment using Equation (12.217) with unaveraged energy spectra, as illustrated in Example 12.10.

Example 12.10. Illustration of Energy Spectrum Estimate. Consider an automobile traveling at a speed of 30 mph that collides head-on with a second automobile traveling at the same speed in the opposite direction. The automobile is carrying a simulated passenger restrained by a conventional seat belt and shoulder harness in the front passenger seat (right side). Figure 12.14 shows the acceleration time histories measured (a) on the vehicle frame just right of the passenger seat and (b) in the chest of the simulated passenger. The energy autospectra for these time histories are

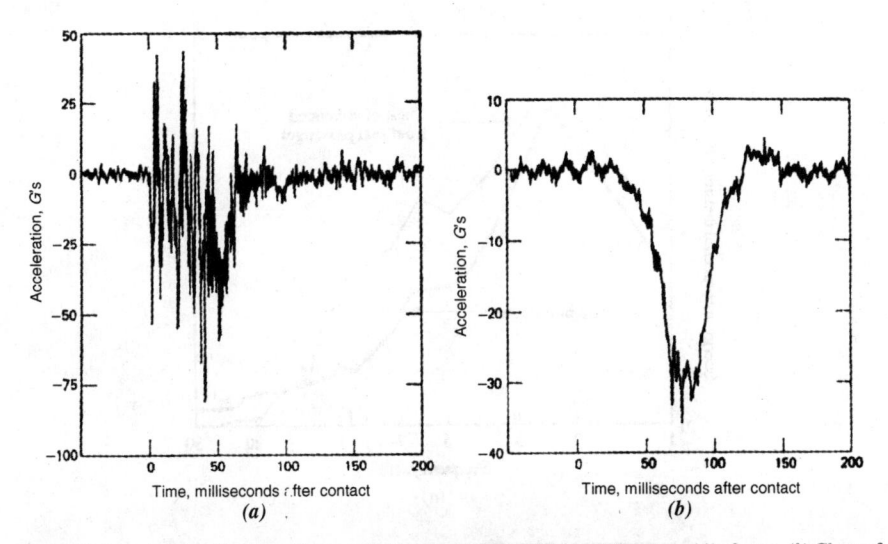

Figure 12.14 Acceleration time histories during automobile collision, (a) Automobile frame, (b) Chest of simulated front seat passenger. (c) These data resulted from studies funded by the FHWA National Highway Safety Bureau, Washington, D.C., under Contract FH-11-7218.

presented in Figure 12.15(a). These spectra were calculated from single records with a frequency resolution of $\Delta f = 1.16$ Hz.

From Equation (12.217), an acceleration gain factor between the vehicle frame and the simulated passenger's chest is given by $|H(f)| = [\mathcal{G}_{yy}(f)/\mathcal{G}_{xx}(f)]^{1/2}$, where $\mathcal{G}_{yy}(f)$ is the energy autospectrum of the passenger acceleration and $\mathcal{G}_{xx}(f)$ is the energy autospectrum of the vehicle acceleration. The results of this calculation are presented in Figure 12.15(b). A comparison of these results with the transmissibility function illustrated in Figure 2.5 shows that the restrained simulated passenger responds to the vehicle impact much like a heavily damped spring supported mass with a natural frequency of about 10 Hz.

PROBLEMS

12.1 Consider a nonstationary random process defined by

$$\{x(t)\} = A \sin \frac{\pi t}{T_r} + \{u(t)\} \quad 0 \leq t \leq T_r$$

where A is a constant and $\{u(t)\}$ is a stationary random process with zero mean and unity variance. Assume the mean value of $\{x(t)\}$ is estimated by short time-averaging procedures with an averaging time of $T = 0.1 T_r$. Determine the bias error in the mean value estimate at $t = 0.5 T_r$.

(a) exactly.
(b) using the approximation in Equation (12.32).

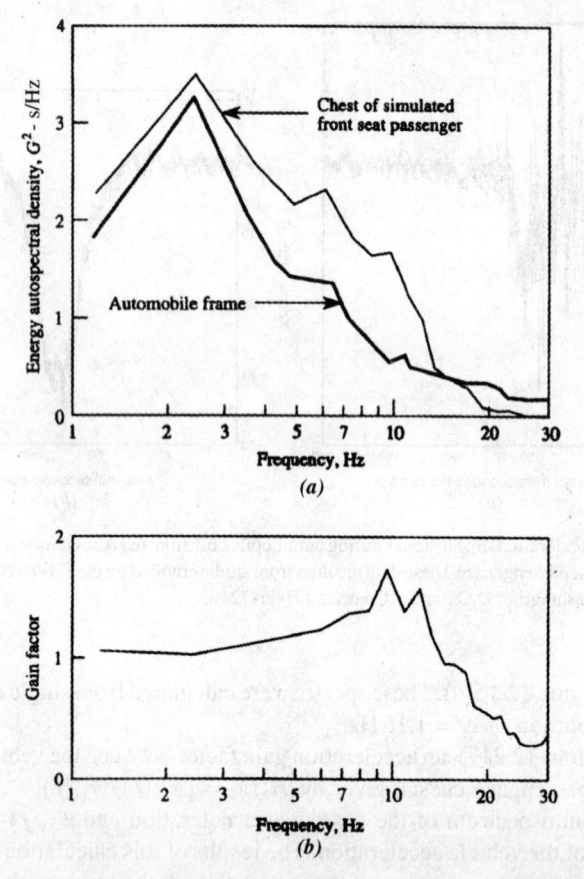

Figure 12.15 Energy autospectra and gain factor for simulated passenger response to automotive collision. (a) Energy spectra. (b) Gain factor. These data resulted from studies funded by the FHWA National Highway Safety Bureau, Washington, D.C., under Contract FH-11-7218.

12.2 Assume a nonstationary random process is defined by

$$\{x(t)\} = a(t) + b(t)\{u(t)\}$$

where $a(t)$ and $b(t)$ are deterministic functions and $\{u(t)\}$ is a stationary random process with zero mean and unity variance. Determine for $\{x(t)\}$ at any time t

(a) the mean value.

(b) the variance

(c) the mean square value.

12.3 For the nonstationary random process in Problem 12.2, write the equation for probability density function of $\{x(t)\}$ at any time t assuming $\{u(t)\}$ is Gaussian.

12.4 Assume a nonstationary random process has a double-frequency autospectrum given by

$$\mathscr{S}_{xx}(f,g) = Ae^{-a(|f|+|g|)}$$

where A and a are positive constants. Determine
(a) the frequency-time autospectrum $\mathscr{W}_{xx}(f,t)$ for the process.
(b) the energy autospectral density function for the process.

12.5 For the nonstationary random process in Problem 12.7, determine the double-time autocorrelation function $\mathscr{R}_{xx}(\tau,t)$.

12.6 Assume a nonstationary random process has the form

$$\{x(t)\} = Ae^{-at}\{u(t)\}$$

where A and a are positive constants and $\{u(t)\}$ is a stationary random process with zero mean and unity variance. Determine the double-time autocorrelation function of $\{x(t)\}$ in terms of
(a) $R_{xx}(t_1, t_2)$ defined in Equation (12.62).
(b) $\mathscr{R}_{xx}(\tau,t)$ defined in Equation (12.72).

12.7 For the nonstationary random process in Problem 12.6 if $\mathscr{R}_{xx}(\tau,t)$ is an even function of t, determine the double-frequency autospectrum in terms of
(a) $S_{xx}(f_1, f_2)$ defined in Equation (12.77).
(b) $\mathscr{S}_{xx}(f,g)$ defined in Equation (12.93).

Hint: Equations (12.96) and (12.114) will be helpful.

12.8 For the nonstationary random process in Problem 12.6, determine the frequency–time autospectrum $\mathscr{W}_{xx}(f,t)$ defined in Equation (12.136).

12.9 Consider a time-varying linear system with a frequency response function defined by

$$H(f,t) = \frac{1}{1+j2\pi ft}$$

Assume that a stationary random input to the system is white noise with an autospectrum of $G_{xx}(f) = G$. Determine the autospectrum of the output of the system in terms of a double-frequency spectrum.

12.10 Assume that a single degree-of-freedom system with a natural frequency of $f_n = 100$ Hz and a damping ratio of $\zeta = 0.05$ is excited by a nonstationary white noise input $x(t)$ with a time-varying mean square value given by

$$\psi_x^2(t) = 1 - \cos(\pi t/15) \quad 0 \le t \le 30 \text{ s}$$

If the instantaneous autospectral density function of the output of the system is to be estimated by short time-averaging procedures, determine the optimum averaging time and frequency resolution bandwidth that will minimize the total mean square error of the spectral estimate at 100 Hz.

REFERENCES

1. Bendat, J. S., and Piersol, A. G., *Engineering Applications of Correlation and Spectral Analysis*, 2nd ed., Wiley–Interscience, New York, 1993.
2. Bendat, J. S., *Nonlinear System Techniques and Applications*, Wiley–Interscience, New York, 1998.
3. Silverman, R. A., "Locally Stationary Random Processes," *Transactions of the IRE, Information Theory*, Vol. IT-3, p. 182, September 1957.
4. Mark, W. D., and Fischer, R. W.,"Investigation of the Effects of Non-homogeneous (or Nonstationary) Behavior on the Spectra of Atmospheric Turbulence," NASA CR-2745, NASA Langley Research Center, Virginia, 1967.
5. Cohen, L., *Time–Frequency Analysis*, Prentice-Hall PTR, Upper Saddle River, New Jersey, 1995.
6. Newland, D., E., *Random Vibrations, Spectral & Wavelet Analysis*, 3rd ed., Addison-Wesley Longman, Harlow, Essex, England, 1993.
7. Teolis, A., *Computational Signal Processing with Wavelets*, Birkhauser, Boston, 1998.

CHAPTER 13

The Hilbert Transform

The Hilbert transform of a real-valued time-domain signal $x(t)$ is another real-valued time-domain signal, denoted by $\tilde{x}(t)$, such that $z(t) = x(t) + j\tilde{x}(t)$ is an analytic signal. The Fourier transform of $x(t)$ is a complex-valued frequency domain signal $X(f)$, which is clearly quite different from the Hilbert transform $\tilde{x}(t)$ or the quantity $z(t)$. From $z(t)$, one can define a magnitude function $A(t)$ and a phase function $\theta(t)$, where $A(t)$ describes the envelope of the original function $x(t)$ versus time, and $\theta(t)$ describes the instantaneous phase of $x(t)$ versus time. Section 13.1 gives three equivalent mathematical definitions for the Hilbert transform, followed by examples and basic properties. The intrinsic nature of the Hilbert transform to causal functions and physically realizable systems is also shown. Section 13.2 derives special formulas for the Hilbert transform of correlation functions and their envelopes. Applications are outlined for both nondispersive and dispersive propagation problems. Section 13.3 discusses the computation of two envelope signals followed by correlation of the envelope signals. Further material on the Hilbert transform and its applications appears in Refs 1–5.

13.1 HILBERT TRANSFORMS FOR GENERAL RECORDS

The Hilbert transform for general records can be defined in three ways as follows, where all integrals shown will exist in practice:

1. *Definition as Convolution Integral.* The *Hilbert transform* of a real-valued function $x(t)$ extending over the range $-\infty < t < \infty$ is a real-valued function $\tilde{x}(t)$ defined by

---

Random Data: Analysis and Measurement Procedures, Fourth Edition. By Julius S. Bendat and Allan G. Piersol
Copyright © 2010 John Wiley & Sons, Inc.

$$\tilde{x}(t) = \mathcal{H}[x(t)] = \int_{-\infty}^{\infty} \frac{x(u)}{\pi(t-u)} du \quad (13.1)$$

Thus $\tilde{x}(t)$ is the convolution integral of $x(t)$ and $(1/\pi t)$, written as

$$\tilde{x}(t) = x(t) * (1/\pi t) \quad (13.2)$$

Like Fourier transforms, Hilbert transforms are linear operators where

$$\mathcal{H}[a_1 x_1(t) + a_2 x_2(t)] = a_1 \mathcal{H}[x_1(t)] + a_2 \mathcal{H}[x_2(t)] \quad (13.3)$$

for any constants a_1, a_2 and any functions $x_1(t)$, $x_2(t)$.

2. *Definition as $(\pi/2)$ Phase Shift System.* Let $\tilde{X}(f)$ be the Fourier transform of $\tilde{x}(t)$, namely,

$$\tilde{X}(f) = \mathcal{F}[\tilde{x}(t)] = \int_{-\infty}^{\infty} \tilde{x}(t) e^{-j2\pi ft} dt \quad (13.4)$$

Then, from Equation (13.2), it follows that $\tilde{X}(f)$ is the Fourier transform $X(f)$ of $x(t)$, multiplied by the Fourier transform of $(1/\pi t)$. The Fourier transform of $(1/\pi t)$ is given by

$$\mathcal{F}[1/\pi t] = -j \operatorname{sgn} f = \begin{cases} -j & \text{for } f > 0 \\ j & \text{for } f < 0 \end{cases} \quad (13.5)$$

At $f=0$, the function $\operatorname{sgn} f = 0$. Hence, Equation (13.2) is equivalent to the passage of $x(t)$ through a system defined by $(-j \operatorname{sgn} f)$ to yield

$$\tilde{X}(f) = (-j \operatorname{sgn} f) X(f) \quad (13.6)$$

This complex-valued quantity $\tilde{X}(f)$ is *not* the Hilbert transform of the complex-valued quantity $X(f)$. Its relation to $\tilde{x}(t)$ is

$$\tilde{x}(t) = \int_{-\infty}^{\infty} \tilde{X}(f) e^{j2\pi ft} df \quad (13.7)$$

In words, $\tilde{x}(t)$ is the inverse Fourier transform of $\tilde{X}(f)$.

The Fourier transform of $(-j \operatorname{sgn} f)$ can be represented by

$$B(f) = -j \operatorname{sgn} f = \begin{cases} e^{-j(\pi/2)} & f > 0 \\ e^{j(\pi/2)} & f < 0 \end{cases} \quad (13.8)$$

with $B(0) = 0$. Also,

$$B(f) = |B(f)| e^{-j\phi_b(f)} \quad (13.9)$$

Hence, $B(f)$ is a $(\pi/2)$ phase shift system where

$$|B(f)| = 1 \quad \text{for all } f \neq 0 \quad (13.10)$$

$$\phi_b(f) = \begin{cases} \pi/2 & \text{for } f > 0 \\ -\pi/2 & \text{for } f < 0 \end{cases} \quad (13.11)$$

HILBERT TRANSFORMS FOR GENERAL RECORDS

If one lets

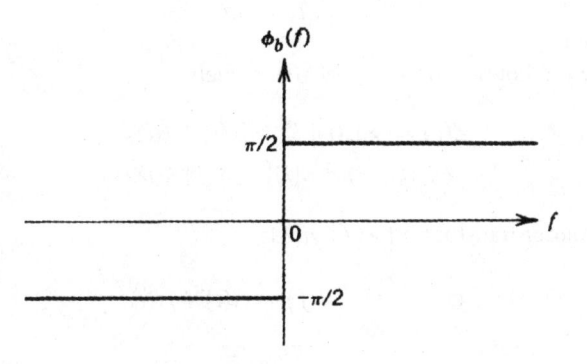

$$X(f) = |X(f)|e^{-j\phi_x(f)} \qquad (13.12)$$

[Graph showing $\phi_b(f)$ as a step function: $\pi/2$ for $f > 0$ and $-\pi/2$ for $f < 0$]

It follows that

$$\tilde{X}(f) = \tilde{X}(f)e^{-j\tilde{\phi}_x(f)} = |X(f)|e^{-j[\phi_x(f)+\phi_b(f)]} \qquad (13.13)$$

Thus, the Hilbert transform consists of passing $x(t)$ through a system which leaves the magnitude of $X(f)$ unchanged, but changes the phase from $\phi_x(f)$ to $\phi_x(f) + \phi_b(f)$ using the $\phi_b(f)$ of Equation (13.11), that is,

$$\begin{aligned} \phi_x(f) &\to \phi_x(f) + (\pi/2) \quad \text{for } f > 0 \\ \phi_x(f) &\to \phi_x(f) - (\pi/2) \quad \text{for } f < 0 \end{aligned} \qquad (13.14)$$

In words, shift $(\pi/2)$ for positive frequencies and shift $(-\pi/2)$ for negative frequencies as sketched above.

3. *Definition as Imaginary Part of Analytic Signal.* A third useful way to understand and to compute the Hilbert transform $\tilde{x}(t)$ of $x(t)$ is via the *analytic signal* $z(t)$ associated with $x(t)$, defined by

$$z(t) = x(t) + j\tilde{x}(t) \qquad (13.15)$$

One can also write

$$z(t) = A(t)e^{j\theta(t)} \qquad (13.16)$$

where $A(t)$ is called the *envelope signal* of $x(t)$ and $\theta(t)$ is called the *instantaneous phase signal* of $x(t)$. In terms of $x(t)$ and $\tilde{x}(t)$, it is clear that

$$A(t) = [x^2(t) + \tilde{x}^2(t)]^{1/2} \qquad (13.17)$$

$$\theta(t) = \tan^{-1}\left[\frac{\tilde{x}(t)}{x(t)}\right] = 2\pi f_0 t \qquad (13.18)$$

The "instantaneous frequency" f_0 is given by

$$f_0 = \left(\frac{1}{2\pi}\right)\frac{d\theta(t)}{dt} \qquad (13.19)$$

Let $Z(f)$ be the Fourier transform of $z(t)$, namely,

$$\begin{aligned}Z(f) &= \mathscr{F}[z(t)] = \mathscr{F}[x(t) + j\tilde{x}(t)] \\ &= \mathscr{F}[x(t)] + j\mathscr{F}[\tilde{x}(t)] = X(f) + j\tilde{X}(f)\end{aligned} \qquad (13.20)$$

The inverse Fourier transform of $Z(f)$ yields

$$z(t) = \mathscr{F}^{-1}[Z(f)] = x(t) + j\tilde{x}(t) \qquad (13.21)$$

where

$$\tilde{x}(t) = \mathscr{H}[x(t)] = \text{Im}[z(t)] \qquad (13.22)$$

13.1.1 Computation of Hilbert Transforms

To compute $Z(f)$, note from Equation (13.6) that

$$\tilde{X}(f) = (-j\,\text{sgn}\,f)X(f)$$

Hence, Equation (13.20) becomes

$$Z(f) = [1 + \text{sgn}\,f]X(f) = B_1(f)X(f) \qquad (13.23)$$

where, as shown in the sketch, $B_1(0) = 1$ and

$$B_1(f) = \begin{cases} 2 & \text{for } f > 0 \\ 0 & \text{for } f < 0 \end{cases} \qquad (13.24)$$

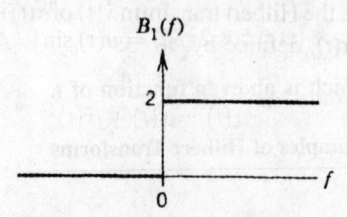

This is a very simple transformation to obtain $Z(f)$ from $X(f)$. One should compute $X(f)$ for all f and then define $Z(f)$ by $Z(0) = X(0)$ and

$$Z(f) = \begin{cases} 2X(f) & \text{for } f > 0 \\ 0 & \text{for } f < 0 \end{cases} \qquad (13.25)$$

The inverse Fourier transform of $Z(f)$ then gives $z(t)$ with $\tilde{x}(t) = \text{Im}[z(t)]$. This is the recommended way to compute the Hilbert transform. From Equation (13.25),

$$x(t) = \text{Re}\left[2\int_0^\infty X(f)e^{j2\pi ft}df\right]$$
$$\tilde{x}(t) = \text{Im}\left[2\int_0^\infty X(f)e^{j2\pi ft}df\right]$$
(13.26)

Example 13.1. Digital Formulas for $x(t)$ and $\tilde{x}(t)$. For digital computations, from Equations (11.76) and (11.77), one obtains for $n = 0, 1, 2, \ldots, (N-1)$,

$$x(n\Delta t) = 2\Delta f \, \text{Re}\left[\sum_{k=1}^{N/2} X(k\Delta f)\exp\left(j\frac{2\pi kn}{N}\right)\right] + X_0 \Delta f$$

$$\tilde{x}(n\Delta t) = 2\Delta f \, \text{Im}\left[\sum_{k=1}^{N/2} X(k\Delta f)\exp\left(j\frac{2\pi kn}{N}\right)\right]$$

Here, the factor $\Delta f = (1/N\Delta t)$ with

$$X(k\Delta f) = \Delta t \sum_{n=0}^{N-1} x(n\Delta t)\exp\left(-j\frac{2\pi kn}{N}\right)$$

Note that values of $X(k\Delta f)$ are needed only from $k = 0$ up to $k = (N/2)$, where the Nyquist frequency occurs, to obtain the digitized values of $x(n\Delta t)$ and its Hilbert transform $\tilde{x}(n\Delta t)$. The envelope signal of $x(t)$ is given by

$$A(n\Delta t) = [x^2(n\Delta t) + \tilde{x}^2(n\Delta t)]^{1/2}$$

13.1.2 Examples of Hilbert Transforms

Table 13.1 gives several $x(t)$ with their associated $\tilde{x}(t)$ and envelopes $A(t)$. Proofs of these results follow directly from previous definitions. These examples are plotted in Figure 13.1. The last result in Table 13.1 is a special case of a general theorem that

$$\mathcal{H}[u(t)\cos 2\pi f_0 t] = u(t)\sin 2\pi f_0 t \quad (13.27)$$

for any function $u(t)$ which is an even function of t.

Table 13.1 Examples of Hilbert Transforms

$x(t)$	$\tilde{x}(t)$	$A(t)$
$\cos 2\pi f_0 t$	$\sin 2\pi f_0 t$	1
$\sin 2\pi f_0$	$-\cos 2\pi f_0 t$	1
$\dfrac{\sin t}{t}$	$\dfrac{1-\cos t}{t}$	$\left\|\dfrac{\sin(t/2)}{(t/2)}\right\|$
$\dfrac{1}{1+t^2}$	$\dfrac{t}{1+t^2}$	$\left[\dfrac{1}{1+t^2}\right]^{1/2}$
$e^{-c\|t\|}\cos 2\pi f_0 t$	$e^{-c\|t\|}\sin 2\pi f_0 t$	$e^{-c\|t\|}$

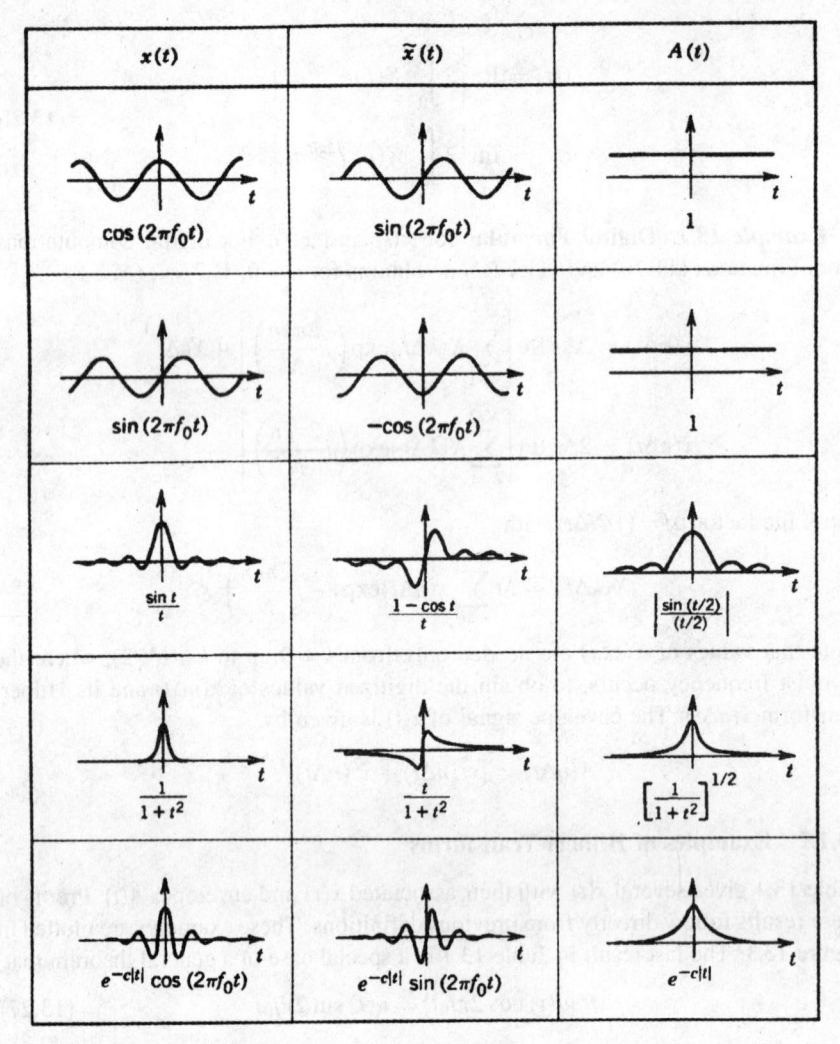

$x(t)$	$\tilde{x}(t)$	$A(t)$
$\cos(2\pi f_0 t)$	$\sin(2\pi f_0 t)$	1
$\sin(2\pi f_0 t)$	$-\cos(2\pi f_0 t)$	1
$\dfrac{\sin t}{t}$	$\dfrac{1-\cos t}{t}$	$\left|\dfrac{\sin(t/2)}{(t/2)}\right|$
$\dfrac{1}{1+t^2}$	$\dfrac{t}{1+t^2}$	$\left[\dfrac{1}{1+t^2}\right]^{1/2}$
$e^{-c|t|}\cos(2\pi f_0 t)$	$e^{-c|t|}\sin(2\pi f_0 t)$	$e^{-c|t|}$

Figure 13.1 Examples of Hilbert transforms.

13.1.3 Properties of Hilbert Transforms

A number of properties will now be stated for Hilbert transforms, which follow readily from the basic definitions or are proved in the references. Let $\tilde{x}(t) = \mathscr{H}[x(t)]$ and $\tilde{y}(t) = \mathscr{H}[y(t)]$ be Hilbert transforms of $x(t)$ and $y(t)$, with corresponding Fourier transforms $X(f)$ and $Y(f)$.

a. *Linear Property*

$$\mathscr{H}[ax(t) + by(t)] = a\tilde{x}(t) + b\tilde{y}(t) \qquad (13.28)$$

for any functions $x(t)$, $y(t)$ and any constants a, b.

b. Shift Property

$$\mathcal{H}[x(t-a)] = \tilde{x}(t-a) \tag{13.29}$$

c. Hilbert Transform of Hilbert Transform

$$\mathcal{H}[\tilde{x}(t)] = -x(t) \tag{13.30}$$

In words, the application of two successive Hilbert transforms gives the negative of the original function.

d. Inverse Hilbert Transform of $\tilde{x}(t)$

$$x(t) = \mathcal{H}^{-1}[\tilde{x}(t)] = -\int_{-\infty}^{\infty} \frac{\tilde{x}(u)}{\pi(t-u)} du \tag{13.31}$$

Thus $x(t)$ is the convolution of $\tilde{x}(t)$ with $(-1/\pi t)$. Alternatively, $x(t)$ can be defined by

$$x(t) = \mathcal{F}^{-1}[(j\,\text{sgn}\,f)\tilde{X}(f)] \tag{13.32}$$

where

$$\tilde{X}(f) = \mathcal{F}[\tilde{x}(t)] \tag{13.33}$$

e. Even and Odd Function Properties

If $x(t)$ is an even (odd) function of t, then $\tilde{x}(t)$ is an odd (even) function of t:

$$\begin{aligned} x(t) \text{ even} &\leftrightarrow \tilde{x}(t) \text{ odd} \\ x(t) \text{ odd} &\leftrightarrow \tilde{x}(t) \text{ even} \end{aligned} \tag{13.34}$$

f. Similarity Property

$$\mathcal{H}[x(at)] = \tilde{x}(at) \tag{13.35}$$

g. Energy Property

$$\int_{-\infty}^{\infty} x^2(t)\,dt = \int_{-\infty}^{\infty} \tilde{x}^2(t)\,dt \tag{13.36}$$

This follows from Parseval's theorem because

$$\begin{aligned} \int_{-\infty}^{\infty} x^2(t)\,dt &= \int_{-\infty}^{\infty} |X(f)|^2\,df \\ \int_{-\infty}^{\infty} \tilde{x}^2(t)\,dt &= \int_{-\infty}^{\infty} |\tilde{X}(f)|^2\,df \end{aligned} \tag{13.37}$$

and the fact that

$$|\tilde{X}(f)|^2 = |X(f)|^2 \tag{13.38}$$

h. *Orthogonal Property*

$$\int_{-\infty}^{\infty} x(t)\tilde{x}(t)\, dt = 0 \qquad (13.39)$$

This follows from Parseval's theorem because

$$\int_{-\infty}^{\infty} x(t)\tilde{x}(t)\, dt = \int_{-\infty}^{\infty} X^*(f)\tilde{X}(f)\, df \qquad (13.40)$$

and the fact that

$$X^*(f)\tilde{X}(f) = (-j\,\mathrm{sgn}\,f)|X(f)|^2 \qquad (13.41)$$

is an odd function of f so that the right-hand side of Equation (13.40) is zero.

i. *Modulation Property*

$$\mathcal{H}[x(t)\cos 2\pi f_0 t] = x(t)\sin 2\pi f_0 t \qquad (13.42)$$

if $x(t)$ is a signal whose Fourier transform $X(f)$ is bandwidth limited; that is,

$$X(f) = \begin{cases} X(f) & |f| \le F \\ 0 & \text{otherwise} \end{cases} \qquad (13.43)$$

provided that f_0 is such that $f_0 > F$. Also,

$$\mathcal{H}[x(t)\sin 2\pi f_0 t] = -x(t)\cos 2\pi f_0 t \qquad (13.44)$$

j. *Convolution Property*

$$\mathcal{H}[x(t) * y(t)] = \tilde{x}(t) * y(t) = x(t) * \tilde{y}(t) \qquad (13.45)$$

This follows from the fact that

$$\mathcal{F}[x(t) * y(t)] = X(f)Y(f) \qquad (13.46)$$

and

$$\begin{aligned}[(-j\,\mathrm{sgn}\,f)X(f)]Y(f) &= \tilde{X}(f)Y(f) \\ &= X(f)[(-j\,\mathrm{sgn}\,f)Y(f)] = X(f)\tilde{Y}(f)\end{aligned} \qquad (13.47)$$

k. *Lack of Commutation Property*

$$\mathcal{F}\{\mathcal{H}[x(t)]\} \ne \mathcal{H}\{\mathcal{F}[x(t)]\} \qquad (13.48)$$

In words, Fourier transforms and Hilbert transforms do *not* commute.

13.1.4 Relation to Physically Realizable Systems

A *physically realizable constant-parameter linear system* is defined by a weighting function $h(\tau)$ satisfying Equation (2.3), that is,

$$h(\tau) = 0 \quad \text{for } r < 0 \qquad (13.49)$$

The corresponding frequency response function $H(f)$ of Equation (2.13) is given by

$$H(f) = \mathscr{F}[h(\tau)] = \int_0^\infty h(\tau)e^{-j2\pi f\tau} d\tau \qquad (13.50)$$
$$= H_R(f) - jH_I(f)$$

Here, $H_R(f)$ equals the real part of $H(f)$ and $H_I(f)$ equals the imaginary part of $H(f)$ as defined by

$$H_R(f) = \int_0^\infty h(\tau)\cos 2\pi f\tau\, d\tau$$
$$H_I(f) = \int_0^\infty h(\tau)\sin 2\pi f\tau\, d\tau \qquad (13.51)$$

It will now be proved that for a system to be physically realizable, it is necessary and sufficient that $H_I(f)$ be the Hilbert transform of $H_R(f)$.

This result is a special case of a more general theorem that applies to all causal functions. By definition, a real-valued function $y(t)$ is a *causal function* if

$$y(t) = 0 \quad \text{for } t < 0 \qquad (13.52)$$

Any function $y(t)$ can always be broken down into the sum of an even function $y_e(t)$ plus an odd function $y_o(t)$ by writing

$$y(t) = y_e(t) + y_o(t) \qquad (13.53)$$

where

$$y_e(t) = \tfrac{1}{2}[y(t) + y(-t)]$$
$$y_o(t) = \tfrac{1}{2}[y(t) - y(-t)] \qquad (13.54)$$

This gives $y_e(-t) = y_e(t)$ and $y_o(-t) = -y_o(t)$. The resolution of any causal function into its even and odd components is illustrated in Figure 13.2.

Assume now that $y(t)$ is a causal function. Then, from Equations (13.52) and (13.54), for $t > 0$,

$$y_e(t) = \tfrac{1}{2}y(t)$$
$$y_o(t) = \tfrac{1}{2}y(t) = y_e(t) \qquad (13.55)$$

For $t < 0$, however,

$$y_e(t) = \tfrac{1}{2}y(-t)$$
$$y_o(t) = -\tfrac{1}{2}y(-t) = -y_e(t) \qquad (13.56)$$

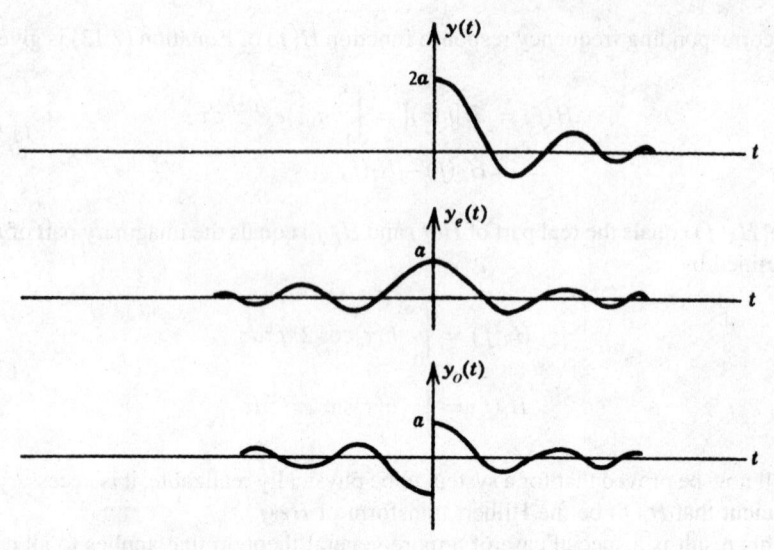

Figure 13.2 Even and odd components of a causal function.

Hence, for a causal function,
$$y_o(t) = (\operatorname{sgn} t) y_e(t) \tag{13.57}$$
where
$$\operatorname{sgn} t = \begin{cases} 1 & t > 0 \\ -1 & t < 0 \end{cases} \tag{13.58}$$

For any causal function $y(t)$, its Fourier transform $Y(f)$ must satisfy
$$Y(f) = \mathscr{F}[y(t)] = \mathscr{F}[y_e(t) + y_o(t)] = Y_R(f) - jY_I(f) \tag{13.59}$$
where
$$\begin{aligned} \mathscr{F}[y_e(t)] &= Y_R(f) \\ \mathscr{F}[y_o(t)] &= -jY_I(f) \end{aligned} \tag{13.60}$$

From Equation (13.57),
$$\mathscr{F}[y_o(t)] = \mathscr{F}[(\operatorname{sgn} t) y_e(t)] = \mathscr{F}[\operatorname{sgn} t] * \mathscr{F}[y_e(t)]$$
where
$$\mathscr{F}[\operatorname{sgn} t] = \frac{-j}{\pi f}$$

Hence,
$$\mathscr{F}[y_o(t)] = \int_{-\infty}^{\infty} \frac{-jY_R(u)}{\pi(f-u)} du$$

This proves that

$$Y_I(f) = \int_{-\infty}^{\infty} \frac{Y_R(u)}{\pi(f-u)} du = \mathcal{H}[Y_R(f)] \quad (13.61)$$

In words, $Y_I(f)$ is the Hilbert transform of $Y_R(f)$ when $y(t)$ is a causal function. This completes the proof.

A direct way to determine whether or not a computed $H(f)$ can represent a physically realized (causal) system is now available. It will be physically realizable if $H_I(f)$ is the Hilbert transform of $H_R(f)$ since Equation (13.61) is equivalent to Equation (13.57). Thus, Equation (13.61) is both a necessary and a sufficient condition for a system to be physically realizable. In equation form,

$$H(f) = H_R(f) - jH_I(f) \quad \text{with } H_I(f) = \tilde{H}_R(f) \quad (13.62)$$

It follows that

$$\tilde{H}_I(f) = \tilde{\tilde{H}}_R(f) = -H_R(f) \quad (13.63)$$

and

$$\tilde{H}(f) = \tilde{H}_R(f) - j\tilde{H}_I(f) = H_I(f) + jH_R(f) = jH(f) \quad (13.64)$$

Deviations from these results can be used to study nonlinear systems.

Example 13.2. Exponential Causal Function. Consider the causal function

$$y(t) = \pi e^{-2\pi t} \quad t > 0 \text{ (otherwise zero)}$$

Here,

$$y_e(t) = \frac{\pi}{2} e^{-2\pi|t|} \quad \text{all } t$$

and

$$y_o(t) = \begin{cases} \dfrac{\pi}{2} e^{-2\pi t} & t > 0 \\ -\dfrac{\pi}{2} e^{2\pi t} & t < 0 \end{cases}$$

Taking Fourier transforms yields

$$Y_e(f) = Y_R(f) = \frac{1}{2(1+f^2)}$$

and

$$Y_o(f) = Y_I(f) = \frac{f}{2(1+f^2)}$$

Thus, $Y_R(f)$ is an even function of f and $Y_I(f)$ is an odd function of f with

$$Y_I(f) = \mathcal{H}[Y_R(f)]$$

The total Fourier transform of $y(t)$ is then

$$Y(f) = Y_R(f) - jY_I(f) = \frac{1}{2(1+jf)}$$

Example 13.3. Exponential-Cosine Causal Function. Consider the causal function

$$y(t) = e^{-at}\cos 2\pi b t \quad a > 0, t > 0 \text{ (otherwise zero)}$$

For this case, the Fourier transform of $y(t)$ is given by

$$Y(f) = \frac{a + j2\pi f}{(a+j2\pi f)^2 + (2\pi b)^2} = Y_R(f) - jY_I(f)$$

where the separate formulas for $Y_R(f)$ and $Y_I(f)$ are quite complicated. Because $y(t)$ is a causal function, however, one will have

$$Y_I(f) = \mathcal{H}[Y_R(f)]$$

with $Y_R(f)$ an even function of f, and $Y_I(f)$ an odd function of f.

13.2 HILBERT TRANSFORMS FOR CORRELATION FUNCTIONS

One of the more important applications for Hilbert transforms involves the calculation of correlation function envelopes to estimate time delays in energy propagation problems. The principles behind such applications are now developed for both nondispersive and dispersive propagations.

13.2.1 Correlation and Envelope Definitions

Let $x(t)$ and $y(t)$ represent zero mean value stationary random data with autocorrelation functions $R_{xx}(\tau)$ and $R_{yy}(\tau)$ and a cross-correlation function $R_{xy}(\tau)$. Let the associated two-sided autospectral density functions be $S_{xx}(f)$ and $S_{yy}(f)$ and the associated two-sided cross-spectral density function be $S_{xy}(f)$. As defined in Section 5.2.1, such associated functions are Fourier transform pairs. For each stationary random record $x(t)$ or $y(t)$, let $\tilde{x}(t) = \mathcal{H}[x(t)]$ and $\tilde{y}(t) = \mathcal{H}[y(t)]$ be their Hilbert transforms. Because Hilbert transforms are linear operations, it follows that $\tilde{x}(t)$ and $\tilde{y}(t)$ will also be stationary random data. Various correlation and spectral density functions for $\tilde{x}(t)$ and $\tilde{y}(t)$ can be defined the same as for $x(t)$ and $y(t)$ to yield $R_{\tilde{x}\tilde{x}}(\tau)$, $R_{\tilde{y}\tilde{y}}(\tau)$, $R_{\tilde{x}\tilde{y}}(\tau)$ and $S_{\tilde{x}\tilde{x}}(f)$, $S_{\tilde{y}\tilde{y}}(f)$, $S_{\tilde{x}\tilde{y}}(f)$, where the associated functions are Fourier transform pairs. To be specific, the definitions are

$$R_{\tilde{x}\tilde{x}}(\tau) = E[\tilde{x}(t)\tilde{x}(t+\tau)]$$
$$R_{\tilde{y}\tilde{y}}(\tau) = E[\tilde{y}(t)\tilde{y}(t+\tau)] \quad (13.65)$$
$$R_{\tilde{x}\tilde{y}}(\tau) = E[\tilde{x}(t)\tilde{y}(t+\tau)]$$

Then their Fourier transforms give

$$S_{\tilde{x}\tilde{x}}(\tau) = \mathcal{F}[R_{\tilde{x}\tilde{x}}(\tau)]$$
$$S_{\tilde{y}\tilde{y}}(f) = \mathcal{F}[R_{\tilde{y}\tilde{y}}(\tau)] \quad (13.66)$$
$$S_{\tilde{x}\tilde{y}}(f) = \mathcal{F}[R_{\tilde{x}\tilde{y}}(\tau)]$$

Except for a scale factor (which is unimportant for theoretical derivations, since it will appear on both sides of equations and therefore cancel out), one can also use the definitions

$$S_{\tilde{x}\tilde{x}}(f) = E[\tilde{X}^*(f)\tilde{X}(f)] = E[|\tilde{X}(f)|^2]$$
$$S_{\tilde{y}\tilde{y}}(f) = E[\tilde{Y}^*(f)\tilde{Y}(f)] = E[|\tilde{Y}(f)|^2] \quad (13.67)$$
$$S_{\tilde{x}\tilde{y}}(f) = E[\tilde{X}^*(f)\tilde{Y}(f)]$$

Mixing functions and their Hilbert transforms leads to $R_{x\tilde{y}}(\tau)$, $R_{\tilde{x}y}(\tau)$ and the associated $S_{x\tilde{y}}(f)$, $S_{\tilde{x}y}(f)$ defined by

$$R_{x\tilde{y}}(\tau) = E[x(t)\tilde{y}(t+\tau)]$$
$$R_{\tilde{x}y}(\tau) = E[\tilde{x}(t)y(t+\tau)] \quad (13.68)$$

$$S_{x\tilde{y}}(f) = \mathcal{F}[R_{x\tilde{y}}(\tau)]$$
$$S_{\tilde{x}y}(f) = \mathcal{F}[R_{\tilde{x}y}(\tau)] \quad (13.69)$$

Special cases are $R_{x\tilde{x}}(\tau)$, $R_{\tilde{x}x}(\tau)$, $S_{x\tilde{x}}(f)$, and $S_{\tilde{x}x}(f)$. Except for a scale factor, as noted previously, one can also define $S_{x\tilde{y}}(f)$ and $S_{\tilde{x}y}(f)$ directly by

$$S_{x\tilde{y}}(f) = E[X^*(f)\tilde{Y}(f)]$$
$$S_{\tilde{x}y}(f) = E[\tilde{X}^*(f)Y(f)] \quad (13.70)$$

Envelope functions for $R_{xx}(\tau)$, $R_{yy}(\tau)$, and $R_{xy}(\tau)$ are defined in terms of Hilbert transforms $\tilde{R}_{xx}(\tau)$, $\tilde{R}_{yy}(\tau)$, and $\tilde{R}_{xy}(\tau)$ as follows. The envelope function for $R_{xx}(\tau)$ is

$$A_{xx}(\tau) = [R_{xx}^2(\tau) + \tilde{R}_{xx}^2(\tau)]^{1/2} \quad (13.71)$$

The envelope function for $R_{yy}(\tau)$ is

$$A_{yy}(\tau) = [R_{yy}^2(\tau) + \tilde{R}_{yy}^2(\tau)]^{1/2} \quad (13.72)$$

The envelope function for $R_{xy}(\tau)$ is

$$A_{xy}(\tau) = [R_{xy}^2(\tau) + \tilde{R}_{xy}^2(\tau)]^{1/2} \quad (13.73)$$

Various relationships and properties for all of the above quantities will now be stated.

Table 13.2 Hilbert Transform Relationships

$$R_{\tilde{x}\tilde{x}}(\tau) = R_{xx}(\tau) \quad S_{\tilde{x}\tilde{x}}(f) = S_{xx}(f)$$

$$R_{\tilde{x}\tilde{x}}(-\tau) = R_{\tilde{x}\tilde{x}}(\tau), \text{an even function of } \tau$$

$$\sigma_{\tilde{x}}^2 = R_{\tilde{x}\tilde{x}}(0) = R_{xx}(0) = \sigma_x^2$$

$$\tilde{R}_{xx}(\tau) = R_{x\tilde{x}}(\tau) = -R_{\tilde{x}x}(\tau) \quad \tilde{S}_{xx}(f) = S_{x\tilde{x}}(f) = -S_{\tilde{x}x}(f)$$

$$\tilde{R}_{xx}(-\tau) = -\tilde{R}_{xx}(\tau), \text{an odd function of } \tau$$

$$\tilde{R}_{xx}(0) = R_{x\tilde{x}}(0) = R_{\tilde{x}x}(0) = 0$$

$$R_{\tilde{x}\tilde{y}}(\tau) = R_{xy}(\tau) \quad S_{\tilde{x}\tilde{y}}(f) = S_{xy}(f)$$

$$\sigma_{\tilde{x}\tilde{y}} = R_{\tilde{x}\tilde{y}}(0) = R_{xy}(0) = \sigma_{xy}$$

$$\tilde{R}_{xy}(\tau) = R_{x\tilde{y}}(\tau) = -R_{\tilde{x}y}(\tau) \quad \tilde{S}_{xy}(f) = S_{x\tilde{y}}(f) = -S_{\tilde{x}y}(f)$$

$$\tilde{R}_{xy}(-\tau) = R_{\tilde{y}x}(\tau) \quad \tilde{S}_{xy}^*(f) = S_{\tilde{y}x}(f)$$

13.2.2 Hilbert Transform Relations

Table 13.2 gives a number of useful relationships for autocorrelation (auto-spectral density) and cross-correlation (cross-spectral density) functions. Proofs of these results represent straightforward exercises.

Some results in Table 13.2 are worthy of attention. Specifically,

$$\tilde{R}_{xx}(\tau) = \mathscr{H}[R_{xx}(\tau)] = R_{x\tilde{x}}(\tau) \tag{13.74}$$

In words, the Hilbert transform of $R_{xx}(\tau)$ is the cross-correlation function between $x(t)$ and its Hilbert transform $\tilde{x}(t)$. Also, note that $\tilde{R}_{xx}(\tau)$ is an odd function of τ because $R_{xx}(\tau)$ is an even function of τ. This gives

$$\tilde{R}_{xx}(0) = R_{x\tilde{x}}(0) = 0 \tag{13.75}$$

Thus, a zero crossing of $\tilde{R}_{xx}(\tau)$ occurs at $\tau = 0$, corresponding to a maximum value of $R_{xx}(\tau)$ at $\tau = 0$. This crossing of zero by $\tilde{R}_{xx}(\tau)$ will be with positive slope, that is,

$$\tilde{R}_{xx}(0-) < 0 \quad \text{and} \quad \tilde{R}_{xx}(0+) > 0 \tag{13.76}$$

as can be verified for any of the examples in Table 13.1. This property is just the reverse of the zero crossings by derivative functions $R'_{xx}(\tau)$ stated in Equation (5.146).

13.2.3 Analytic Signals for Correlation Functions

The analytic signal $z_x(t)$ corresponding to a stationary random record $x(t)$ is defined as in Equation (13.15) by

$$z_x(t) = x(t) + j\tilde{x}(t)$$

where $\tilde{x}(t) = \mathcal{H}[x(t)]$. The *complex-valued* autocorrelation function $R_{z_x z_x}(\tau)$ is defined by

$$R_{z_x z_x}(\tau) = E[z_x^*(t)z_x(t+\tau)] = E[\{x(t)-j\tilde{x}(t)\}\{x(t+\tau)+j\tilde{x}(t+\tau)\}]$$
$$= R_{xx}(\tau) + R_{\tilde{x}\tilde{x}}(\tau) + j[R_{x\tilde{x}}(\tau) - R_{\tilde{x}x}(\tau)]$$

But, from Table 13.2,

$$R_{\tilde{x}\tilde{x}}(\tau) = R_{xx}(\tau) \quad \text{and} \quad R_{\tilde{x}x}(\tau) = -R_{x\tilde{x}}(\tau)$$

Hence,

$$R_{z_x z_x}(\tau) = 2[R_{xx}(\tau) + jR_{x\tilde{x}}(\tau)] = 2[R_{xx}(\tau) + j\tilde{R}_{xx}(\tau)]$$

This proves that

$$\frac{R_{z_x z_x}(\tau)}{2} = R_{xx}(\tau) + j\tilde{R}_{xx}(\tau) \tag{13.77}$$

is the analytic signal for $R_{xx}(\tau)$.

The Fourier transform of $R_{z_x z_x}(\tau)$ is $S_{z_x z_x}(f)$, where

$$S_{z_x z_x}(f) = \mathscr{F}[R_{z_x z_x}(\tau)] = 2[S_{xx}(f) + j\tilde{S}_{xx}(f)]$$
$$= 2[1 + \operatorname{sg}\mathit{1}f]S_{xx}(f)$$

Hence, the autospectrum relation is

$$S_{z_x z_x}(f) = \begin{cases} 4S_{xx}(f) & \text{for } f > 0 \\ 0 & \text{for } f < 0 \end{cases} \tag{13.78}$$

From Equation (13.77), one obtains

$$\mathscr{F}^{-1}[S_{z_x z_x}(f)/2] = R_{xx}(\tau) + j\tilde{R}_{xx}(\tau) \tag{13.79}$$

Theoretical formulas are now

$$R_{xx}(\tau) = 2\int_0^\infty S_{xx}(f)\cos 2\pi\tau\pi\, df$$
$$\tilde{R}_{xx}(\tau) = 2\int_0^\infty S_{xx}(f)\sin 2\pi f\tau\, df \tag{13.80}$$

The analytic signal for $R_{xy}(\tau)$ corresponding to stationary random records $x(t)$ and $y(t)$ is defined from

$$z_x(t) = x(t) + j\tilde{x}(t) \qquad z_y(t) = y(t) + j\tilde{y}(t)$$

The *complex-valued* cross-correlation function $R_{z_x z_y}(\tau)$ is defined by

$$R_{z_x z_y}(\tau) = E[z_x^*(t)z_y(t+\tau)] = E[\{x(t)-j\tilde{x}(t)\}\{y(t+\tau)+j\tilde{y}(t+\tau)\}]$$
$$= R_{xy}(\tau) + R_{\tilde{x}\tilde{y}}(\tau) + j[R_{x\tilde{y}}(\tau) - R_{\tilde{x}y}(\tau)]$$

But, from Table 13.2,
$$R_{\tilde{x}\tilde{y}}(\tau) = R_{xy}(\tau) \quad \text{and} \quad R_{\tilde{x}y}(\tau) = -R_{x\tilde{y}}(\tau)$$
Hence,
$$R_{z_x z_y}(\tau) = 2[R_{xy}(\tau) + jR_{x\tilde{y}}(\tau)] = 2[R_{xy}(\tau) + j\tilde{R}_{xy}(\tau)]$$
This proves that
$$\frac{R_{z_x z_y}(\tau)}{2} = R_{xy}(\tau) + \tilde{R}_{xy}(\tau) \tag{13.81}$$
is the analytic signal for $R_{xy}(\tau)$.

The Fourier transform of $R_{z_x z_y}(\tau)$ is $S_{z_x z_y}(f)$, where
$$\begin{aligned}S_{z_x z_y}(f) &= \mathscr{F}[R_{z_x z_y}(\tau)] = 2[S_{xy}(f) + j\tilde{S}_{xy}(f)] \\ &= 2[1 + \operatorname{sgn} f]S_{xy}(f)\end{aligned}$$

Hence, the cross-spectrum relation is
$$S_{z_x z_y}(f) = \begin{cases} 4S_{xy}(f) & \text{for } f > 0 \\ 0 & \text{for } f < 0 \end{cases} \tag{13.82}$$

From Equation (13.81), one obtains
$$\mathscr{F}^{-1}\left[\frac{S_{z_x z_y}(f)}{2}\right] = R_{xy}(\tau) + j\tilde{R}_{xy}(\tau) \tag{13.83}$$

This yields the theoretical formulas
$$\begin{aligned}R_{xy}(\tau) &= \operatorname{Re}\left[2\int_0^\infty S_{xy}(f)e^{j2\pi f\tau}df\right] \\ \tilde{R}_{xy}(\tau) &= \operatorname{Im}\left[2\int_0^\infty S_{xy}(f)e^{j2\pi f\tau}df\right]\end{aligned} \tag{13.84}$$

Example 13.4. **Digital Formulas for $R_{xy}(\tau)$ and $\tilde{R}_{xy}(\tau)$.** For digital computations, as discussed in Sections 11.4.2 and 11.6.2, augment each of the N data values in $\{x(n\Delta t)\}$ and $\{y(n\Delta t)\}$ with N zeros so as to obtain new data sequences with $2N$ terms. With $\Delta f = (1/2N\Delta t)$, for $k = 0, 1, 2, \ldots, N$, compute
$$X(k\Delta f) = \Delta t \sum_{n=0}^{N-1} x(n\Delta t)\exp\left(-j\frac{\pi kn}{N}\right)$$
$$Y(k\Delta f) = \Delta t \sum_{n=0}^{N-1} y(n\Delta t)\exp\left(-j\frac{\pi kn}{N}\right)$$
$$G_{xy}(k\Delta f) = \frac{2}{N\Delta t}[X^*(k\Delta f)Y(k\Delta f)]$$

HILBERT TRANSFORMS FOR CORRELATION FUNCTIONS

For $r = 0, 1, 2, \ldots, (N-1)$, one then obtains

$$R_{xy}(r\Delta t) = \left(\frac{N\Delta f}{N-r}\right) \text{Re}\left[\sum_{k=0}^{N} G_{xy}(k\Delta f)\exp\left(j\frac{\pi k r}{N}\right)\right]$$

$$\tilde{R}_{xy}(r\Delta t) = \left(\frac{N\Delta f}{N-r}\right) \text{Im}\left[\sum_{k=0}^{N} G_{xy}(k\Delta f)\exp\left(j\frac{\pi k r}{N}\right)\right]$$

The squared envelope signal of $R_{xy}(\tau)$ is given by

$$A_{xy}^2(r\Delta t) = R_{xy}^2(r\Delta t) + \tilde{R}_{xy}^2(r\Delta t)$$

Autocorrelation functions are special cases where

$$R_{xx}(r\Delta t) = \left(\frac{N\Delta f}{N-r}\right)\left[\sum_{k=0}^{N} G_{xx}(k\Delta f)\cos(\pi k r/N)\right]$$

$$\tilde{R}_{xx}(r\Delta t) = \left(\frac{N\Delta f}{N-r}\right)\left[\sum_{k=0}^{N} G_{xx}(k\Delta f)\sin(\pi k r/N)\right]$$

$$A_{xx}^2(r\Delta t) = R_{xx}^2(r\Delta t) + \tilde{R}_{xx}^2(r\Delta t)$$

13.2.4 Nondispersive Propagation Problems

Consider the basic nondispersive propagation case previously defined in Equation (5.19), For simplicity, assume that $n(t)$ is essentially zero, so that

$$y(t) = \alpha x(t - \tau_0) \tag{13.85}$$

with

$$\begin{aligned} R_{yy}(\tau) &= \alpha^2 R_{xx}(\tau) \\ R_{xy}(\tau) &= \alpha R_{xx}(\tau - \tau_0) \\ \rho_{xy}(\tau) &= \frac{R_{xy}(\tau)}{\sqrt{R_{xx}(0)R_{yy}(0)}} = \rho_{xx}(\tau - \tau_0) \end{aligned} \tag{13.86}$$

Consider the case where $x(t)$ is bandwidth-limited white noise as defined by Equation (5.48), namely,

$$R_{xx}(\tau) = aB\left(\frac{\sin \pi B \tau}{\pi B \tau}\right)\cos 2\pi f_0 \tau \tag{13.87}$$

Now

$$\begin{aligned} R_{xx}(0) &= aB \\ R_{yy}(0) &= \alpha^2(aB) \end{aligned} \tag{13.88}$$

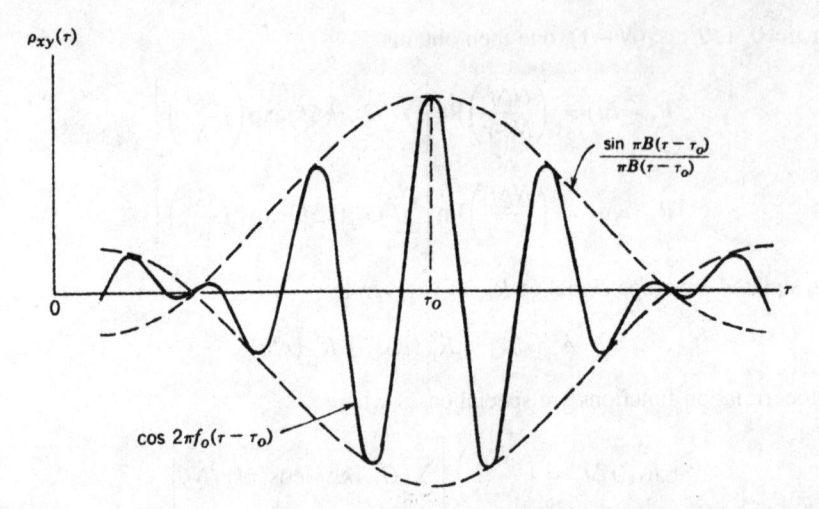

Figure 13.3 Typical cross-correlation coefficient function for nondispersive propagation through a single path.

$$\rho_{xy}(\tau) = \left[\frac{\sin \pi B(\tau-\tau_0)}{\pi B(\tau-\tau_0)}\right] \cos 2\pi f_0(\tau-\tau_0) \qquad (13.89)$$

Here, f_0 is the center of an ideal rectangular filter of bandwidth B, where the autospectral density function $G_{xx}(f)$ is a constant within this band and zero outside. The time delay τ_0 is a constant. Equation (13.89) is plotted in Figure 13.3.

A number of properties of Equation (13.89) for nondispersive propagation are worthy of note.

1. The cosine function $\cos 2\pi f_0 \tau$ at the center frequency f_0 is modulated by the envelope function $[(\sin \pi B\tau)/\pi B\tau]$ that is defined by the bandwidth B.
2. The peak value of the envelope function occurs at the time delay $\tau_0 = (d/c)$, a fixed value independent of frequency.
3. Peak values of the cosine function occur at time delays $\tau_n = \tau_0 \pm (n/f_0)$, where n is any integer. In particular, a peak value of the cosine function coincides with the peak value of the envelope function.
4. The main lobe of the envelope function extends from $[\tau_0 - (1/B)]$ to $[\tau_0 + (1/B)]$, a width of $(2/B)$ s. The number of oscillations of the cosine function contained in the main lobe of the envelope function is $(2f_0/B)$.

Three important types of nondispersive propagation problems where one desires to measure the envelope of cross-correlation functions are illustrated in the following examples. As in all engineering problems, it is necessary to derive statistical error analysis criteria to help design experiments and to evaluate the estimates of the computed results. In particular, formulas are required to determine the statistical errors in (a) magnitude estimates of the envelope peak values and (b) location

HILBERT TRANSFORMS FOR CORRELATION FUNCTIONS

estimates of the time delays where the envelope peak values occur. These matters are covered in Ref. 1 based upon material in Section 8.4.

Example 13.5. Low-Pass White Noise. Consider the case of low-pass white noise $x(t)$ with bandwidth B from $0 \leq f \leq B$. From Equation (5.50), the autocorrelation function $R_{xx}(\tau)$ of $x(t)$ is

$$R_{xx}(\tau) = R_{xx}(0)\left(\frac{\sin 2\pi B\tau}{2\pi B\tau}\right)$$

This is plotted in Figure 13.4. The maximum value of $R_{xx}(\tau)$ occurs at $\tau = 0$ where $R_{xx}(\tau) = R_{xx}(0)$. The first positive value of τ where $R_{xx}(\tau) = 0$ is at $\tau = (1/2B)$. The first negative value of τ where $R_{xx}(\tau) = 0$ is at $\tau = (-1/2B)$. Thus, the width of the main lobe around $R_{xx}(0)$ is $(1/B)$.

From Table 13.1, the Hilbert transform $\tilde{R}_{xx}(\tau)$ is given by

$$\tilde{R}_{xx}(\tau) = R_{xx}(0)\left(\frac{1-\cos 2\pi B\tau}{2\pi B\tau}\right)$$

This is plotted in Figure 13.5. Note that the Hilbert transform $\tilde{R}_{xx}(\tau) = 0$ at $\tau = 0$ where the maximum value of $R_{xx}(\tau)$ occurs. It is easier to locate this zero-crossing point where $\tilde{R}_{xx}(\tau) = 0$ than to locate the value of τ where $R_{xx}(\tau)$ has its maximum value.

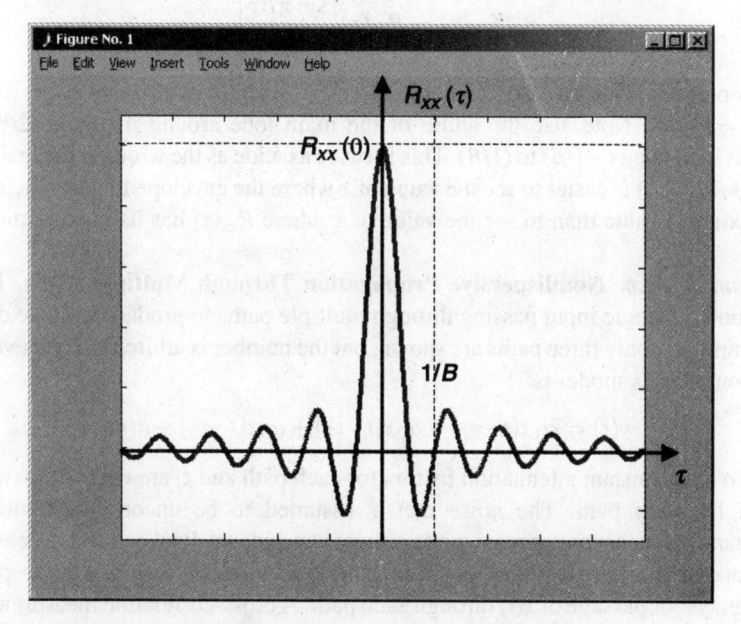

Figure 13.4 Autocorrelation function of low-pass white noise.

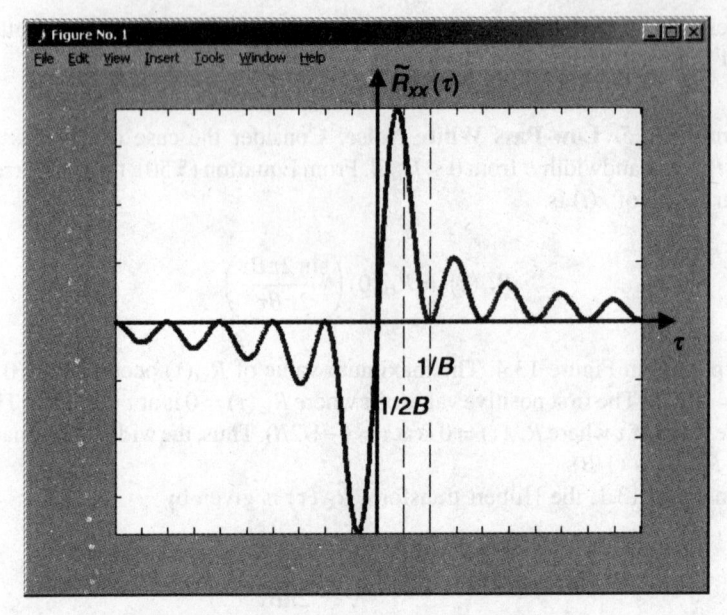

Figure 13.5 Hilbert transform of autocorrelation function.

The envelope function for $R_{xx}(\tau)$ from Equation (13.71) is given by

$$A_{xx}(\tau) = R_{xx}(\tau) \left| \frac{\sin \pi B \tau}{\pi B \tau} \right|$$

This is plotted in Figure 13.6. Note that $A_{xx}(\tau)$ has its maximum value at $\tau = 0$ where $A_{xx}(0) = R_{xx}(0)$. Note also the width of the main lobe around $A_{xx}(0)$ is $(2/B)$ and extends here from $(-1/B)$ to $(1/B)$. This is twice as wide as the width of the main lobe around $R_{xx}(0)$. It is easier to see the value of τ where the envelope function $A_{xx}(\tau)$ has its maximum value than to see the value of τ where $R_{xx}(\tau)$ has its maximum value.

Example 13.6. **Nondispersive Propagation Through Multiple Paths.** Figure 13.7 shows a single input passing through multiple paths to produce a single output. For simplicity, only three paths are shown, but the number is arbitrary. The governing equation for this model is

$$y(t) = \alpha_1 x(t-\tau_1) + \alpha_2 x(t-\tau_2) + \alpha_3 x(t-\tau_3) + n(t)$$

where α_i are constant attenuation factors for each path and τ_i are the respective time delays for each path. The noise $n(t)$ is assumed to be uncorrelated with $x(t)$. Simultaneous measurements are made only of $x(t)$ and $y(t)$. It is required to determine the proportion of the output power in $y(t)$ that goes via each path and the respective time delays for passage of $x(t)$ through each path. A cross-correlation measurement is made between $x(t)$ and $y(t)$, followed by Hilbert transform computations for its

HILBERT TRANSFORMS FOR CORRELATION FUNCTIONS

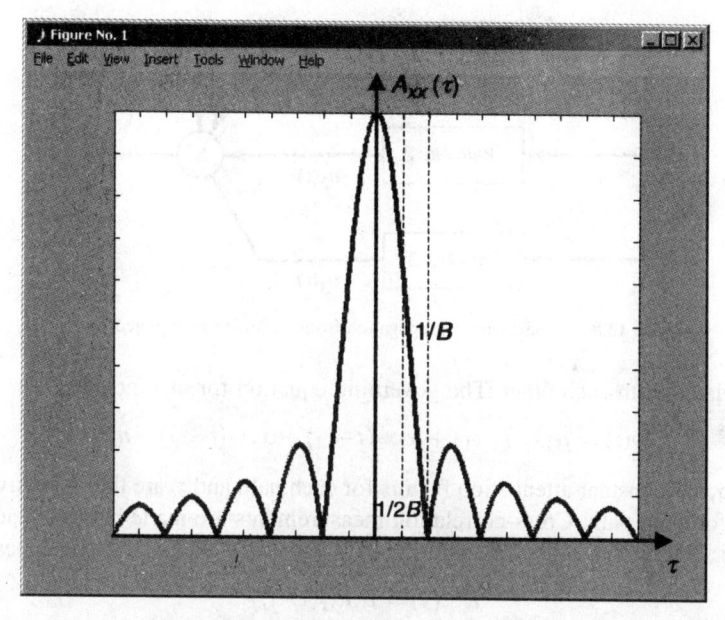

Figure 13.6 Envelope of autocorrelation function.

envelope. Here,

$$R_{xy}(\tau) = \alpha_1 R_{xx}(\tau-\tau_1) + \alpha_2 R_{xx}(\tau-\tau_2) + \alpha_3 R_{xx}(\tau-\tau_3)$$

Example 13.7. Nondispersive Propagation from Multiple Uncorrelated Sources. Figure 13.8 shows separate inputs with different paths to produce a single output. Simultaneous measurements are made of all inputs and the output. For simplicity, only three sources and associated paths are shown, but the number of uncorrelated sources can be arbitrary. It is required to determine the proportion of the output power in $y(t)$ that comes from each source and the respective time delays for passage of each source through its particular path. The output noise $n(t)$ is assumed to be uncorrelated with the inputs $x_i(t)$, and the three sources are also assumed to be

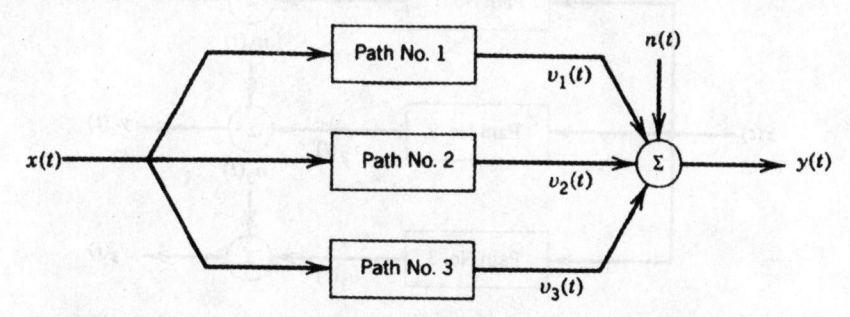

Figure 13.7 Nondispersive propagation through multiple paths.

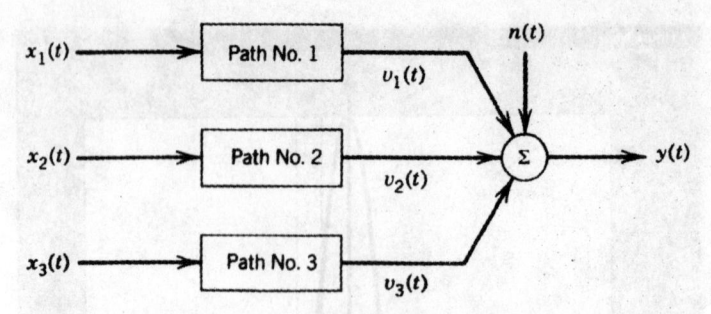

Figure 13.8 Nondispersive propagation from multiple uncorrelated sources.

uncorrelated with each other. The governing equation for this model is

$$y(t) = \alpha_1 x_1(t-\tau_1) + \alpha_2 x_2(t-\tau_2) + \alpha_3 x_3(t-\tau_3) + n(t)$$

where α_i are constant attenuation factors for each path and τ_i are the respective time delays for each path. Cross-correlation measurements are made between each $x_i(t)$ and $y(t)$, followed by Hilbert transform computations to obtain their envelopes. Here

$$R_{x_i y}(\tau) = \alpha_i R_{xx}(\tau - \tau_i)$$

Example 13.8. Nondispersive Propagation from an Unmeasured Single Source to Measured Multiple Outputs. Figure 13.9 shows separate outputs due to an unmeasured single output. Simultaneous measurements are made of all output signals. For simplicity, only three outputs are shown, but the number of different outputs can be arbitrary. It is required to determine the relative time delay between all pairs of output signals without knowing the actual time delays from the input $x(t)$ to any of the outputs, assuming $x(t)$ is not or cannot be measured. The extraneous noise terms $n_i(t)$ are all assumed to be uncorrelated with each other and with $x(t)$. The

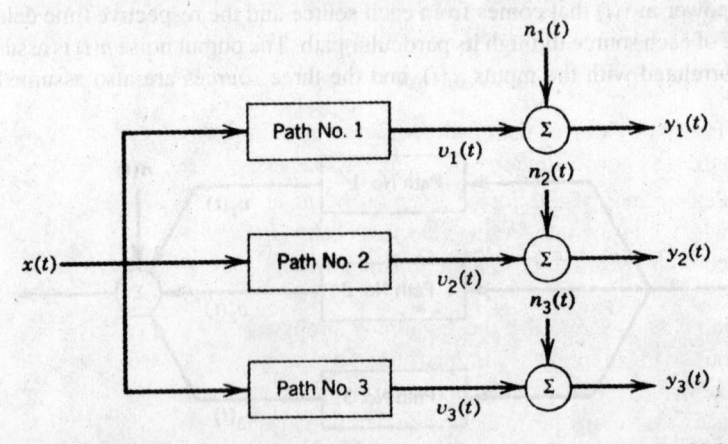

Figure 13.9 Nondispersive propagation from an unmeasured single source to measured multiple outputs.

governing equations for this model are that each output for $i = 1, 2, 3$ is of the form
$$y_i(t) = v_i(t) + n_i(t) = \alpha_i x(t-\tau_i) + n_i(t)$$

Cross-correlation measurements are made between pairs of output records, followed by Hilbert transform computations of their envelopes. Here
$$R_{y_i y_j}(\tau) = \alpha_i \alpha_j R_{xx}(\tau + \tau_i - \tau_j)$$

13.2.5 Dispersive Propagation Problems

The material in Section 13.2.4 applies to nondispersive propagation problems where the velocity of propagation is a constant independent of frequency. Consider other situations where the propagation paths are frequency dispersive as discussed in Refs 6 and 7. In particular for flexural waves in structures, the "apparent" propagation speed of the waves at a given frequency is called the *group velocity* c_g. This c_g is related but not equal to the *phase velocity* c_p. It is known that the group velocity of flexural waves in thin beams satisfies

$$c_g = 2c_p \sim \sqrt{f} \tag{13.90}$$

In words, c_g is twice c_p and both are proportional to the square root of frequency.

For dispersive propagation problems governed by Equation (13.90), as a first order of approximation, Ref. 7 proves that the cross-correlation coefficient function for narrow bandwidth data corresponding to Equation (13.89) now takes the form

$$\rho_{xy}(\tau) \approx \left[\frac{\sin \pi B_0(\tau-\tau_2)}{\pi B_0(\tau-\tau_2)} \right] \cos 2\pi f_0(\tau-\tau_1) \tag{13.91}$$

where

$$\tau_1 = (d/c_p) \sim f_0^{-1/2} \tag{13.92}$$
$$\tau_2 = (d/c_g) \sim f_0^{-1/2} \tag{13.93}$$

with $\tau_1 = 2\tau_2$ because $c_g = 2c_p$. Equation (13.91) is plotted in Figure 13.10.

Observe that Equation (13.91) is similar in nature to Equation (13.89), but has two important differences.

1. The peak value of the envelope function occurs at the time delay $\tau_2 = (d/c_g)$, which is now a function of frequency because $c_g \sim \sqrt{f_0}$.
2. Peak values of the cosine function occur at the time delays $\tau_n = \tau_1 \pm (n/f_0)$, where n is any integer. In general, a peak value of the cosine function does *not* coincide with the peak value of the envelope function.

Equation (13.91) shows that the "apparent" propagation speed given by the envelope function at a given frequency is determined by the group velocity c_g rather than by the phase velocity c_p. For such dispersive propagation problems, the peak value of $\rho_{xy}(\tau)$ from its fine structure due to the cosine function in Equation (13.91) may *not* coincide with the envelope peak value that occurs at the time delay τ_2. To find τ_2, one must

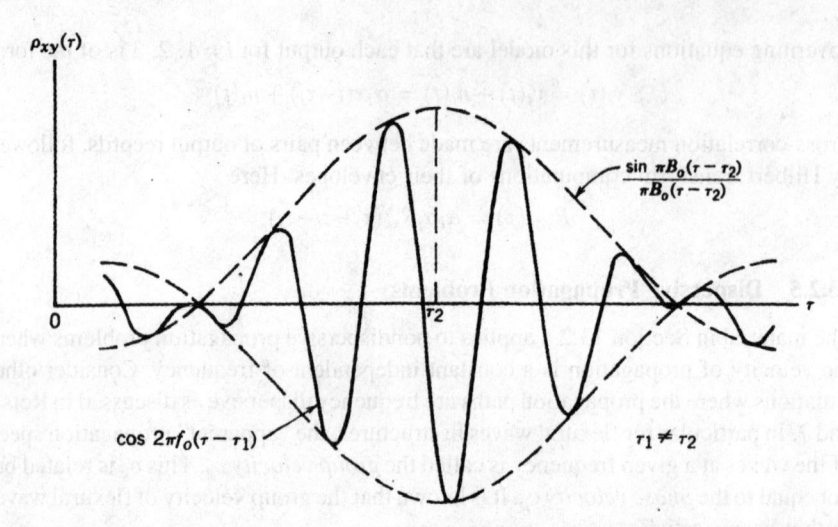

Figure 13.10 Typical narrow bandwidth cross-correlation coefficient function for dispersive propagation through a single path.

compute the envelope function of $\rho_{xy}(\tau)$, as can be done using Hilbert transform techniques.

The derivation of Equation (13.91) is based on the following ideas. Start with the general relation

$$R_{xy}(\tau) = \int_{-\infty}^{\infty} S_{xy}(f) e^{j2\pi f \tau} df \qquad (13.94)$$

For dispersive cases leading to Equation (13.91), the corresponding $S_{xy}(f)$ is

$$S_{xy}(f) = \alpha S_{xx}(f) e^{-j2\pi f \tau_p} \qquad (13.95)$$

where the delay $\tau_p = (d/c_p)$ is a function of frequency since the phase velocity $c_p \sim \sqrt{f}$. Here, $\tau_p = \tau_p(f)$ can be expressed at frequency f as

$$\tau_p = \frac{d}{c_p} = \frac{a}{\sqrt{2\pi f}} \qquad (13.96)$$

with a as a suitable proportionality constant. Substitution of Equation (13.95) into Equation (13.94) gives

$$\begin{aligned} R_{xy}(\tau) &= \alpha \int_{-\infty}^{\infty} S_{xx}(f) e^{j2\pi f(\tau - \tau_p)} df \\ &= \alpha \int_{0}^{\infty} G_{xx}(f) \cos 2\pi f(\tau - \tau_p) df \end{aligned} \qquad (13.97)$$

where the one-sided autospectrum $G_{xx}(f) = 2S_{xx}(f)$ for $f \geq 0$ and is otherwise zero. For bandwidth-limited white noise,

$$G_{xx}(f) = \begin{cases} K & 0 \leq f_0 - (B_0/2) \leq f \leq f_0 + (B_0/2) \\ 0 & \text{otherwise} \end{cases} \qquad (13.98)$$

Thus,
$$R_{xy}(\tau) = \alpha K \int_{f_0-(B_0/2)}^{f_0+(B_0/2)} \cos 2\pi f(\tau-\tau_p)\,df \qquad (13.99)$$

Also,
$$R_{xx}(0) = K \int_{f_0-(B_0/2)}^{f_0+(B_0/2)} df = KB_0 \qquad (13.100)$$
$$R_{yy}(0) = \alpha^2 R_{xx}(0) = \alpha^2 KB_0$$

Hence, the cross-correlation coefficient function becomes
$$\rho_{xy}(\tau) = \frac{1}{B_0} \int_{f_0-(B_0/2)}^{f_0+(B_0/2)} \cos 2\pi f(\tau-\tau_p)\,df \qquad (13.101)$$

Consider situations where the frequency bandwidth B_0 is less than one octave, so that for any $\varepsilon < 1$, f can be replaced by
$$f = f_0(1+\varepsilon) \quad df = f_0\,d\varepsilon \qquad (13.102)$$

This change of variable gives
$$\rho_{xy}(\tau) = \frac{f_0}{B_0} \int_{B_0/2f_0}^{B_0/2f_0} \cos 2\pi f_0(1+\varepsilon)(\tau-\tau_p)\,d\varepsilon \qquad (13.103)$$

and the τ_p of Equation (13.96) becomes
$$\tau_p = \frac{a}{\sqrt{2\pi f}} = \frac{a}{\sqrt{2\pi f_0(1+\varepsilon)}} \qquad (13.104)$$

For small ε, neglecting terms of order ε^2,
$$2\pi f_0(1+\varepsilon)(\tau-\tau_p) = 2\pi f_0(1+\varepsilon)\tau - a\sqrt{2\pi f_0(1+\varepsilon)}$$
$$\approx 2\pi f_0(1+\varepsilon)\tau - a\sqrt{2\pi f_0}\left(1+\frac{\varepsilon}{2}\right) \qquad (13.105)$$
$$\approx 2\pi f_0\left(\tau - \frac{a}{\sqrt{2\pi f_0}}\right) + 2\pi f_0\left(\tau - \frac{a}{2\sqrt{2\pi f_0}}\right)\varepsilon$$

Then, neglecting sine terms compared to cosine terms,
$$\cos 2\pi f_0(1+\varepsilon)(\tau-\tau_1) \approx \cos[2\pi f_0(\tau-\tau_1) + 2\pi f_0(\tau-\tau_2)\varepsilon]$$
$$\approx [\cos 2\pi f_0(\tau-\tau_1)][\cos 2\pi f_0(\tau-\tau_2)\varepsilon] \qquad (13.106)$$

where
$$\tau_1 = \frac{a}{\sqrt{2\pi f_0}} = \frac{d}{c_p} \qquad (13.107)$$

$$\tau_2 = \frac{a}{2\sqrt{2\pi f_0}} = \frac{d}{c_g} \tag{13.108}$$

Here, c_p and c_g represent the phase velocity at frequency f_0 and the group velocity at frequency f_0 with $c_g = 2c_p$. Finally, one should substitute Equation (13.106) into Equation (13.103) and integrate to obtain

$$\begin{aligned}\rho_{xy}(\tau) &\approx \left(\frac{f_0}{B_0}\right) \cos 2\pi f_0(\tau - \tau_1) \int_{-B_0/2f_0}^{B_0/2f_0} \cos 2\pi f_0(\tau - \tau_2)\varepsilon \, d\varepsilon \\ &\approx \left[\frac{\sin \pi B_0(\tau - \tau_2)}{\pi B_0(\tau - \tau_2)}\right] \cos 2\pi f_0(\tau - \tau_1)\end{aligned} \tag{13.109}$$

which is the stated result of Equation (13.91).

13.3 ENVELOPE DETECTION FOLLOWED BY CORRELATION

Consider Figure 13.11 where

$$\begin{aligned}u(t) &= x^2(t) + \tilde{x}^2(t) = \text{squared envelope of } x(t) \\ v(t) &= y^2(t) + \tilde{y}^2(t) = \text{squared envelope of } y(t)\end{aligned} \tag{13.110}$$

The cross-correlation function $R_{uv}(\tau)$ of these squared envelope signals is given by

$$\begin{aligned}R_{uv}(\tau) &= E[u(t)v(t+\tau)] = E[\{x^2(t) + \tilde{x}^2(t)\}\{y^2(t+\tau) + \tilde{y}^2(t+\tau)\}] \\ &= E[x^2(t)y^2(t+\tau)] + E[x^2(t)\tilde{y}^2(t+\tau)] \\ &\quad + E[\tilde{x}^2(t)\tilde{y}^2(t+\tau)] + E[\tilde{x}^2(t)\tilde{y}^2(t+\tau)]\end{aligned} \tag{13.111}$$

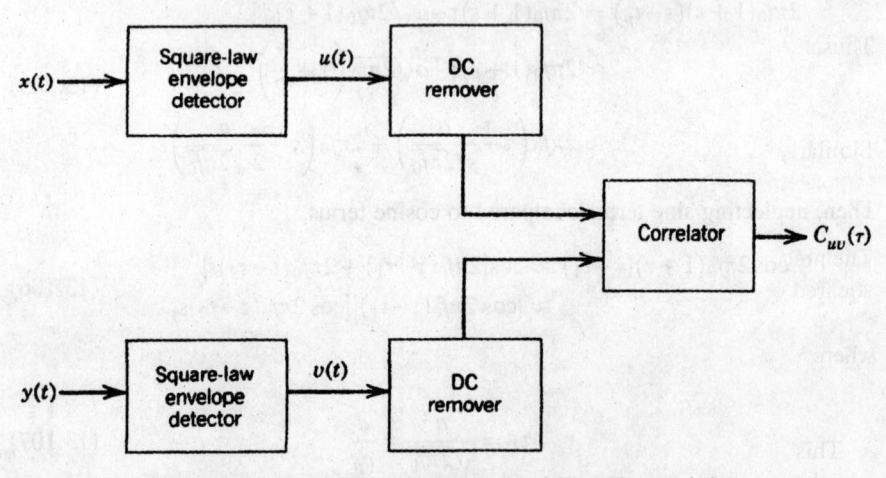

Figure 13.11 Square-law envelope detection followed by correlation.

ENVELOPE DETECTION FOLLOWED BY CORRELATION

Assume that $x(t)$, $\tilde{x}(t)$, $y(t)$, and $\tilde{y}(t)$ are jointly normally distributed with zero mean values. Then

$$E[x^2(t)y^2(t+\tau)] = \sigma_x^2\sigma_y^2 + 2R_{xy}^2(\tau)$$

$$E[x^2(t)\tilde{y}^2(t+\tau)] = \sigma_x^2\sigma_{\tilde{y}}^2 + 2R_{x\tilde{y}}^2(\tau)$$

$$E[\tilde{x}^2(t)y^2(t+\tau)] = \sigma_{\tilde{x}}^2\sigma_y^2 + 2R_{\tilde{x}y}^2(\tau)$$

$$E[\tilde{x}^2(t)\tilde{y}^2(t+\tau)] = \sigma_{\tilde{x}}^2\sigma_{\tilde{y}}^2 + 2R_{\tilde{x}\tilde{y}}^2(\tau) \quad (13.112)$$

Substituting Equation (13.112) into (13.111) and using results from Table 13.2 yields

$$R_{uv}(\tau) = 4\sigma_x^2\sigma_y^2 + 4[R_{xy}^2(\tau) + \tilde{R}_{xy}^2(\tau)] \quad (13.113)$$

Also,

$$\bar{u} = E[u(t)] = 2\sigma_x^2$$
$$\bar{v} = E[v(t)] = 2\sigma_y^2 \quad (13.114)$$

Hence,

$$R_{uv}(\tau) - (\bar{u})(\bar{v}) = 4[R_{xy}^2(\tau) + \tilde{R}_{xy}^2(\tau)] = 4A_{xy}^2(\tau) \quad (13.115)$$

where, as shown in Equation (13.73), the quantity $A_{xy}^2(\tau)$ is the squared envelope of $R_{xy}(\tau)$. Now

$$R_{uu}(0) = E[u^2(t)] = E[\{x^2(t) + \tilde{x}^2(t)\}^2]$$
$$= E[x^4(t)] + 2E[x^2(t)\tilde{x}^2(t)] + E[\tilde{x}^4(t)] \quad (13.116)$$
$$= 3\sigma_x^4 + 2\sigma_x^2\sigma_{\tilde{x}}^2 + 3\sigma_{\tilde{x}}^4 = 8\sigma_x^4$$

Thus,

$$R_{uu}(0) - (\bar{u})^2 = 4\sigma_x^4 \quad (13.117)$$

Similarly,

$$R_{vv}(0) - (\bar{v})^2 = 4\sigma_y^4 \quad (13.118)$$

The preceding relations prove that the correlation coefficient function $\rho_{uv}(\tau)$ for the squared envelope signals $u(t)$ and $v(t)$ is given by

$$\rho_{uv}(\tau) = \frac{R_{uv}(\tau) - (\bar{u})(\bar{v})}{\sqrt{[R_{uu}(0) - (\bar{u})^2][R_{vv}(0) - (\bar{v})^2]}} = \frac{A_{xy}^2(\tau)}{\sigma_x^2\sigma_y^2} \quad (13.119)$$

This particular result in Equation (13.119) should be compared with the usual correlation coefficient function $\rho_{xy}(\tau)$ for the original signals $x(t)$ and $y(t)$ as given by

Equation (5.16), namely,

$$\rho_{xy}(\tau) = \frac{R_{xy}(\tau) - (\bar{x})(\bar{y})}{\sqrt{[R_{xx}(0) - (\bar{x})^2][R_{yy}(0) - (\bar{y})^2]}} = \frac{R_{xy}(\tau)}{\sigma_x \sigma_y} \quad (13.120)$$

Upon taking Hilbert transforms

$$\tilde{\rho}_{xy}(\tau) = \mathscr{H}[\rho_{xy}(\tau)] = \frac{\tilde{R}_{xy}(\tau)}{\sigma_x \sigma_y} = \frac{R_{x\tilde{y}}(\tau)}{\sigma_x \sigma_y} = \rho_{x\tilde{y}}(\tau) \quad (13.121)$$

It follows now using Equation (13.73) that

$$\rho_{uv}(\tau) = \rho_{xy}^2(\tau) + \tilde{\rho}_{xy}^2(\tau) \quad (13.122)$$

Thus, the function $\rho_{uv}(\tau)$, with mean values removed prior to correlation, measures the squared envelope value of $\rho_{xy}(\tau)$. The quantity $\rho_{uv}(\tau)$ is the correlation coefficient function for

$$C_{uv}(\tau) = R_{uv}(\tau) - (\bar{u})(\bar{v}) = E[\{u(t) - \bar{u}\}\{v(t+\tau) - \bar{v}\}] \quad (13.123)$$

where $u(t)$, $v(t)$, $\bar{u}$, and $\bar{v}$ satisfy Equations (13.110) and (13.114). The computation of $C_{uv}(\tau)$ is sketched in Figure 13.11.

Three special points should be noted from Equation (13.122) regarding the nature of the envelope correlation coefficient $\rho_{uv}(\tau)$ compared to its underlying $R_{xy}(\tau)$ and its envelope $A_{xy}(\tau)$.

1. The quantity $\rho_{uv}(\tau)$, like $A_{xy}(\tau)$, will be independent of the fine structure in $R_{xy}(\tau)$.
2. The quantity $\rho_{uv}(\tau)$ will sharpen the correlation function of $R_{xy}(\tau)$ and of $\rho_{xv}(\tau)$ in the vicinity of τ where the peak value occurs.
3. The quantity $\rho_{uv}(\tau)$ will also sharpen the correlation function of $A_{xy}(\tau)$ in the vicinity of τ where the peak value occurs.

Thus, the result $\rho_{uv}(\tau)$ is *superior* to both $\rho_{xy}(\tau)$ and $A_{xy}(\tau)$ in locating where peak values occur.

Example 13.9. Exponential-Cosine Cross-Correlation Function. Consider a cross-correlation coefficient function of the form

$$\rho_{xy}(\tau) = \frac{R_{xy}(\tau)}{\sigma_x \sigma_y} = e^{-b|\tau|} \cos 2\pi f_0 \tau$$

The Hilbert transform is then

$$\tilde{\rho}_{xy}(\tau) = \frac{\tilde{R}_{xy}(\tau)}{\sigma_x \sigma_y} = e^{-b|\tau|} \sin 2\pi f_0 \tau$$

It follows that

$$A_{xy}(\tau) = \sigma_x \sigma_y e^{-b|\tau|}$$

and
$$\rho_{uv}(\tau) = \frac{A_{xy}^2(\tau)}{\sigma_x^2 \sigma_y^2} = e^{-2b|\tau|}$$

Observe that $\rho_{uv}(\tau)$ and $A_{xy}(\tau)$ are both independent of the modulating frequency f_0. Also, near $\tau = 0$, where the peak value of $\rho_{xy}(\tau)$ occurs, both $\rho_{xy}(\tau)$ and $A_{xy}(\tau)$ behave like $e^{-b|\tau|}$ but the associated $\rho_{uv}(\tau)$ behaves like $e^{-2b|\tau|}$. Clearly, $\rho_{uv}(\tau)$ will have a sharper peak at $\tau = 0$ than $A_{xy}(\tau)$. This concludes the example.

Consider next the cross-spectral density functions and the autospectral density functions for the squared envelope signals $u(t)$ and $v(t)$ given in Equation (13.110). From Equation (13.115), the envelope cross-spectral density function

$$S_{uv}(f) = \mathscr{F}[R_{uv}(\tau) - \bar{u}\bar{v}] = 4\mathscr{F}[A_{xy}^2(\tau)] \tag{13.124}$$

The squared envelope of $R_{xy}(\tau)$, namely,

$$A_{xy}^2(\tau) = R_{xy}^2(\tau) + \tilde{R}_{xy}^2(\tau) \tag{13.125}$$

can be computed by the procedure outlined in Example 13.4. Now

$$\mathscr{F}[R_{xy}^2(\tau)] = \int_{-\infty}^{\infty} S_{xy}(\alpha) S_{xy}(f-\alpha) \, d\alpha \tag{13.126}$$

$$\mathscr{F}[\tilde{R}_{xy}^2(\tau)] = \int_{-\infty}^{\infty} \tilde{S}_{xy}(\alpha) \tilde{S}_{xy}(f-\alpha) \, d\alpha$$
$$= \int_{-\infty}^{\infty} B(\alpha) B(f-\alpha) S_{xy}(\alpha) S_{xy}(f-\alpha) \, d\alpha \tag{13.127}$$

where $B(f) = (-j \operatorname{sgn} f)$ as in Equation (13.8). Hence,

$$S_{uv}(f) = 4 \int_{-\infty}^{\infty} [1 + B(\alpha)B(f-\alpha)] S_{xy}(\alpha) S_{xy}(f-\alpha) \, d\alpha \tag{13.128}$$

For any $f > 0$, the quantity

$$B(\alpha)B(f-\alpha) = \begin{cases} 1 & \alpha < 0 \\ -1 & 0 < \alpha < f \\ 1 & \alpha > f \end{cases} \tag{13.129}$$

It follows by straightforward steps that for any $f > 0$,

$$S_{uu}(f) = 16 \int_0^{\infty} S_{xx}(\alpha) S_{xx}(f+\alpha) \, d\alpha$$
$$S_{uv}(f) = 16 \int_0^{\infty} S_{yx}^*(\alpha) S_{xy}(f+\alpha) \, d\alpha \tag{13.130}$$

Thus, knowledge of the basic spectral density functions for the signals $x(t)$ and $y(t)$ enables one to compute the associated spectral density functions for the squared envelope signals $u(t)$ and $v(t)$.

PROBLEMS

13.1 Consider a function $x(t)$ with a Fourier transform given by

$$X(f) = \frac{1}{1+j2\pi f}$$

Determine the Fourier transform of the Hilbert transform $\tilde{x}(t)$.

13.2 Determine the Hilbert transform of the function

$$x(t) = \frac{t-a}{1+(t-a)^2}$$

13.3 Determine the Hilbert transform of the function

$$x(t) = ae^{-b|t|} \quad \text{where } b > 0$$

13.4 Which of the following statements are correct?
(a) The Hilbert transform is a linear operator.
(b) The Hilbert transform of a time-dependent function is also a time-dependent function.
(c) Given $x(t)$ and its Hilbert transform $\tilde{x}(t)$ with Fourier transforms $X(f)$ and $\tilde{X}(f)$, respectively, $\tilde{X}(f)$ equals the Hilbert transform of $X(f)$.
(d) Given $x(t)$ and its Hilbert transform $\tilde{x}(t)$, the magnitude of the Fourier transforms of $x(t)$ and $\tilde{x}(t)$ is equal.
(e) If the Fourier transform of $x(t)$ is real valued, the Fourier transform of $\tilde{x}(t)$ will also be real valued.

13.5 The real part of the frequency response function for a physically realizable constant-parameter linear system is given by

$$H_R(f) = \frac{1-f^2}{(1-f^2)^2 + (af)^2}$$

Determine the imaginary part of the frequency response function.

13.6 Given a complex-valued function $z(t) = x(t) + jy(t)$, under what circumstances will the Hilbert transform of $z(t)$, denoted by $\tilde{z}(t)$, be equal to $jz(t)$?

13.7 Consider an analytic function $z(t) = x(t) + j\tilde{x}(t)$ where the two-sided autospectrum of $x(t)$ is given by

$$S_{xx}(f) = \frac{2a}{a^2 + 4\pi^2 f^2}$$

Determine the autospectra of (a) $\tilde{x}(t)$ and (b) $z(t)$.

13.8 Given a modulated signal $y(t) = x(t) \cos 2\pi f_0 t$ where the spectrum of $x(t)$ includes no frequency components above $F < f_0$, determine the following:
   (a) The Hilbert transform of $y(t)$, denoted by $\tilde{y}(t)$.
   (b) The correlation function of $y(t)$, denoted by $R_{yy}(\tau)$, in terms of $R_{xx}(\tau)$.
   (c) The Hilbert transform of the correlation function $R_{yy}(\tau)$, denoted by $\tilde{R}_{yy}(\tau)$.
   (d) The envelope of the correlation function $R_{yy}(\tau)$.

13.9 Assume that the cross-correlation function between the excitation and response of a physical system has the form

$$R_{xy}(\tau) = aB\left(\frac{\sin \pi B|\tau-\tau_2|}{\pi B|\tau-\tau_2|}\right) \cos 2\pi f_0|\tau-\tau_1|$$

where $B < f_0$. If $\tau_1 = \tau_2$, what is the propagation time through the system at frequency $f = f_0 + B$?

13.10 In Problem 13.9, if $\tau_1 \neq \tau_2$, what is the propagating time through the system at frequency $f = f_0 + B$ assuming the group velocity of propagating waves is $c_g \sim \sqrt{f}$?

REFERENCES

1. Bendat, J. S., *The Hilbert Transform and Applications to Correlation Measurements*, Bruel and Kjaer Publication, Denmark, 1985.
2. Bracewell, R., *The Fourier Transform and Its Applications*, McGraw-Hill, New York, 1965.
3. Oppenheim, A. V., and Schafer, R. W., *Discrete-Time Signal Processing*, Prentice-Hall, Englewood Cliffs, NJ, 1989.
4. Dugundji, J., "Envelopes and Pre-Envelopes of Real Waveforms," *IRE Transactions on Information Theory*, Vol. IT-4, p. 53, March 1958.
5. Huang, N. E., et al. "The Empirical Mode Decomposition and the Hilbert Spectrum for Nonlinear and Non-Stationary Time Series Analysis," *Proceedings, Royal Society A*, Vol. 454, p. 903, 1998.
6. Cremer, L., Heckl, M., Unger, E. E., *Structure-Borne Sound*, Springer-Verlag, New York, 1973.
7. White, P. H., "Cross-Correlation in Structural Systems: Dispersive and Nondispersive Waves," *Journal of Acoustical Society of America*, Vol. 45, p. 1118, May 1969.

CHAPTER 14

Nonlinear System Analysis

This chapter reviews some recommended techniques to identify the frequency domain properties of nonlinear systems from measured input/output random data. Procedures are discussed for the following five types of nonlinear systems and models.

1. Zero-memory and finite-memory nonlinear systems
2. Square-law and cubic nonlinear models
3. Volterra nonlinear models
4. Single-Input/Single-Output (SI/SO) models with parallel linear and nonlinear systems
5. SI/SO models with nonlinear feedback

Where appropriate, square-law and cubic nonlinear models are basic systems to apply. Formulas for Volterrra models involve multidimensional functions for Gaussian random data that are difficult to compute and interpret. Formulas for the SI/SO nonlinear models are valid for arbitrary random data and apply to broad classes of nonlinear operations. Direct multiple-input/single-output (MI/SO) linear techniques from Chapters 7 and 9 can be used to solve the SI/SO nonlinear models with parallel linear and nonlinear systems. Reverse MI/SO linear techniques, where input data and output data are interchanged, can be used to solve the SI/SO models with nonlinear feedback. Many examples and applications of these SI/SO models and techniques to solve nonlinear system problems are in Ref. 1 and Chapter 13 of Ref. 2.

14.1 ZERO-MEMORY AND FINITE-MEMORY NONLINEAR SYSTEMS

Two main properties distinguish nonlinear systems from linear systems. First, nonlinear systems do not satisfy the additive and homogeneous requirements of linear

---

Random Data: Analysis and Measurement Procedures, Fourth Edition. By Julius S. Bendat and Allan G. Piersol
Copyright © 2010 John Wiley & Sons, Inc.

```
                    ┌─────────────┐
                    │ Zero-memory │
        x(t) ──────▶│  nonlinear  │──────▶ y(t) = g[x(t)]
                    │ system, g(x)│
                    └─────────────┘
```

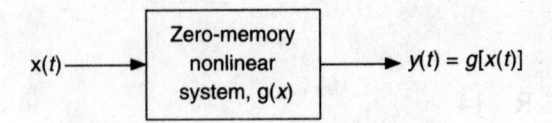

Figure 14.1 Zero-memory nonlinear system.

systems. Second, the passage of Gaussian input data through any nonlinear system produces non-Gaussian output data. A general spectral analysis technique exists as detailed in Chapters 6 and 7 to identify the frequency response properties in SI/SO and MI/SO linear systems. No general spectral analysis technique exists that applies to all nonlinear systems. Instead, special techniques are required for particular types of nonlinear systems that can occur in different fields. This chapter reviews analysis and identification techniques for nonlinear system models found to be important and practical.

A zero-memory nonlinear system, shown in Figure 14.1, is a system where the output $y(t)$ at any time t is a single-valued nonlinear function $g(x)$ of the input $x(t)$ at the *same* instant of time, namely,

$$y(t) = g[x(t)] \tag{14.1}$$

Note that $g(x)$ is a function of x. It is not a function of t. For any constants a_1, a_2 and any inputs x_1, x_2 the nonlinear function $g(x)$ is neither additive or homogeneous, namely,

$$g(a_1 x_1 + a_1 x_2) \neq a_1 g(x_1) + a_2 g(x_2) \tag{14.2}$$

The nonlinear system $g(x)$ is a constant-parameter nonlinear system if the output $y(t)$ becomes $y(t + \tau)$ when the input $x(t)$ becomes $x(t + \tau)$. For stationary random input data passing through a constant-parameter nonlinear system $g(x)$, the output data will also be stationary random data. Examples of zero-memory nonlinear systems are illustrated in Chapter 2 of Ref. 1.

Chapter 2 of Ref. 1 also derives four useful theorems to predict input/output relations when stationary random data pass through specified zero-memory nonlinear systems. *Theorem 1* applies to arbitrary input data and predicts the output probability density function from knowledge of the input probability density function. *Theorem 2* shows how to identify a possible zero-memory nonlinear system $g(x)$ that is single valued and one-to-one from simultaneous measurements of input/output probability density functions. Theorems 3 and 4 apply only to Gaussian input data. *Theorem 3* predicts the output autocorrelation function from knowledge of the input autocorrelation function. *Theorem 4* predicts the input/output cross-correlation function from knowledge of the input autocorrelation function.

When memory operations are desired along with the zero-memory nonlinear operations, they can often be modeled by inserting a linear system either "*after*" or "*before*" the zero-memory nonlinear system. The finite-memory nonlinear system in Figure 14.2 shows a linear system $A(f)$ that is "*after*" the zero-memory nonlinear system. The finite-memory nonlinear system in Figure 14.3 shows a linear system $B(f)$ that is "*before*" the zero-memory nonlinear system.

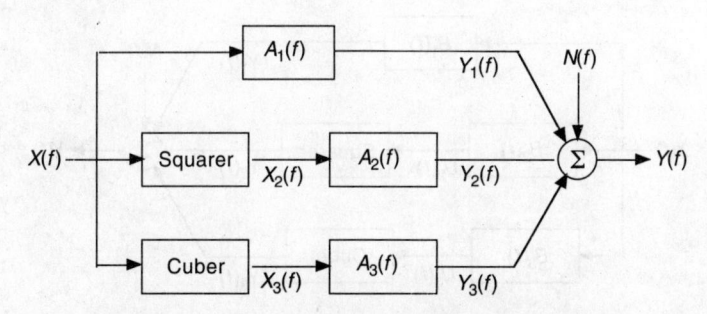

SQUARE-LAW AND CUBIC NONLINEAR MODELS

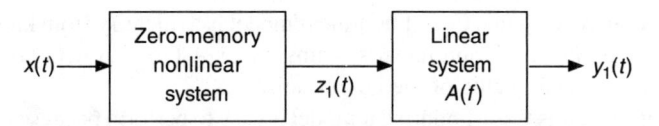

Figure 14.2 Finite-memory nonlinear system with a linear system after zero-memory linear system.

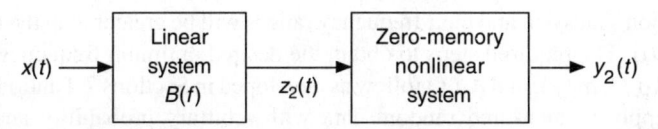

Figure 14.3 Finite-memory nonlinear system with a linear system before the zero-memory nonlinear system.

14.2 SQUARE-LAW AND CUBIC NONLINEAR MODELS

Two nonlinear models of physical interest are Case 1 and Case 2 square-law and cubic nonlinear models because they represent finite–memory nonlinear extensions of optimum third-order polynomial approximations to zero-memory nonlinear operations.

The Case 1 square-law and cubic nonlinear model is pictured in Figure 14.4, where the squarer and cuber that produce the outputs $x^2(t)$ and $x^3(t)$ from the input $x(t)$ are followed by linear systems $A_2(f)$ and $A_3(f)$. The terms in Figure 14.4 are

$X(f) = X_1(f) =$ Fourier transform of measured input $x(t)$
$Y(f) =$ Fourier transform of measured total output $y(t)$
$N(f) =$ Fourier transform of unmeasured noise output $n(t)$
$X_2(f) =$ Fourier transform of squarer output $x^2(t)$
$X_3(f) =$ Fourier transform of cuber output $x^3(t)$
$Y_1(f) = A_1(f)X_1(f)$
$Y_2(f) = A_2(f)X_2(f)$
$Y_3(f) = A_3(f)X_3(f)$
$Y(f) = Y_1(f) + Y_2(f) + Y_3(f) + N(f)$

Figure 14.4 Case 1 square-law and cubic nonlinear model.

The objective in solving this Case 1 nonlinear model is to identify from knowledge of $x(t)$ and $y(t)$ the three optimum linear systems $A_1(f), A_2(f)$, and $A_3(f)$ that give the minimum mean square value of the output noise.

The solution of this Case 1 nonlinear model is easy to perform because Figure 14.4 can be replaced by a three-input/single-output linear model like Figure 7.18, where the three known inputs are $x(t)$, $x^2(t)$, and $x^3(t)$. Note that $x^2(t)$ and $x^3(t)$ will always be non-Gaussian and their frequency ranges will be greater than the frequency range for $x(t)$. The required steps to obtain the desired optimum frequency response functions $A_1(f), A_2(f)$, and $A_3(f)$ follow as developed in Sections 7.4 and 11.7. These formulas apply to measured random data with arbitrary probability and spectral properties. For the special case of Gaussian input data, simple closed-form spectral results are derived in Section 13.3.3 of Ref. 2 that solve this Case 1 nonlinear model.

The Case 2 square-law and cubic nonlinear model is pictured in Figure 14.5 where the squarer and cuber are preceded by linear systems $B_2(f)$ and $B_3(f)$. The terms in Figure 14.5 are

$X(f) =$ Fourier transform of measured input $x(t)$

$Y(f) =$ Fourier transform of measured total output $y(t)$

$N(f) =$ Fourier transform of unmeasured noise output $n(t)$

$U_2(f) = B_2(f)X(f) =$ Fourier transform of output $u_2(t)$

$U_3(f) = B_3(f)X(f) =$ Fourier transform of output $u_3(t)$

$Y_1(f) = B_1(f)X(f) =$ Fourier transform of output $y_1(t)$

$Y_2(f) =$ Fourier transform of output $y_2(t) = u_2^2(t)$

$Y_3(f) =$ Fourier transform of output $y_3(t) = u_3^2(t)$

$Y(f) = Y_1(f) + Y_2(f) + Y_3(f) + N(f)$

The objective in solving this Case 2 nonlinear model is to identify from knowledge of $x(t)$ and $y(t)$ the three optimum linear systems $B_1(f), B_2(f)$, and $B_3(f)$ that give the minimum mean square value of the output noise.

This Case 2 nonlinear model cannot be replaced by an equivalent three-input/single-output linear model as done for the Case 1 nonlinear model because the records $u_2(t)$ and $u_3(t)$ cannot be determined for arbitrary input data $x(t)$ without the knowl-

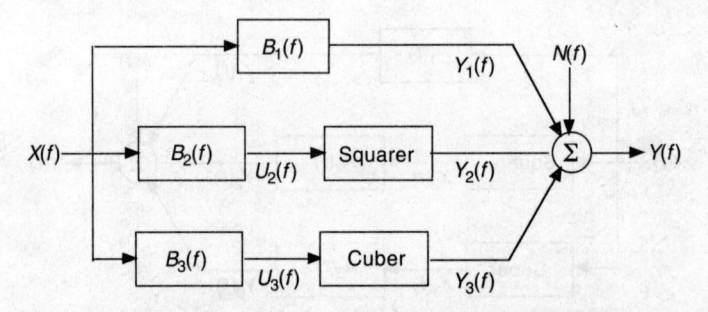

Figure 14.5 Case 2 square-law and cubic nonlinear model.

edge of $B_2(f)$ and $B_3(f)$. No practical procedures are known to solve Case 2 models for arbitrary input data. For the special case of Gaussian input data, complicated spectral formulas are derived in Section 9.4.4 of Ref. 1 that solve this Case 2 nonlinear model.

14.3 VOLTERRA NONLINEAR MODELS

Volterra nonlinear models consist of a sum of Volterra functionals where the total output $y(t)$ to an arbitrary input $x(t)$ is the sum of a linear system output, a bilinear system output, a trilinear system output, and so on to as many terms as desired. A third-order Volterra nonlinear model is pictured in Figure 14.6. Computations beyond the trilinear system are extremely complicated and rarely carried out in practice. Linear systems are described by first-order frequency response functions, $H_1(f)$, bilinear systems are described by second-order frequency functions, $H_2(f,g)$, third-order trilinear systems are described by third-order frequency functions, $H_3(f,g,h)$, and so on. Past work on Volterra models is in Refs 1, 3, and 4.

In Figure 14.6, the terms are

$x(t)$ = measured input
$y(t)$ = measured total output
$n(t)$ = unmeasured noise output
$y_1(t)$ = linear system output
$y_2(t)$ = bilinear system output
$y_3(t)$ = trilinear system output
$H_1(f)$ = linear system frequency response function
$H_2(f,g)$ = bilinear system frequency response function
$H_3(f,g,h)$ = trilinear system frequency response function

The objective in solving this Volterra nonlinear model is to identify from knowledge of $x(t)$ and $y(t)$ the optimum linear, bilinear, and trilinear frequency response functions that give the minimum mean square value of the output noise.

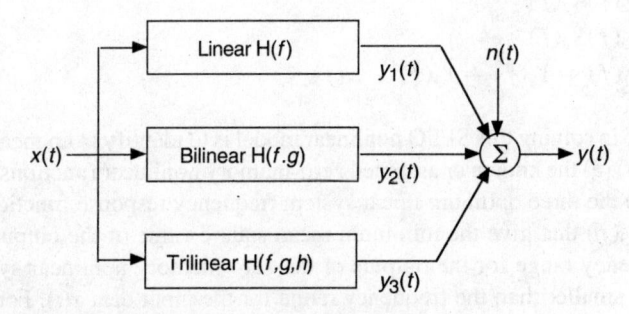

Figure 14.6 Third-order Volterra nonlinear model.

General solutions to solve the third-order Volterra nonlinear model of Figure 14.6 for arbitrary input data are not known. For zero mean value Gaussian input data, the desired optimum frequency response functions can be obtained by computing appropriate first-order spectral density functions, second-order bispectral density functions, and third-order trispectral density functions. The second-order and third-order functions are complicated to compute and difficult to interpret. Clear and complete derivations of the data processing formulas required to identify the desired optimum linear, bilinear, and trilinear systems from Gaussian input data are carried out in Chapters 8 and 9 of Ref. 1. These Volterra models and techniques should not be used except as a last resort because they can often be replaced by the simpler practical SI/SO nonlinear models and techniques recommended here in Sections 14.4 and 14.5.

14.4 SI/SO MODELS WITH PARALLEL LINEAR AND NONLINEAR SYSTEMS

A general SI/SO nonlinear model of wide interest is shown in Figure 14.7 where a linear system $A_1(f)$ is in parallel with two nonlinear systems. The nonlinear systems consist of two known or assumed zero-memory nonlinear systems $g_2(x)$ and $g_3(x)$ that are followed by linear systems $A_2(f)$ and $A_3(f)$. The case of only one parallel nonlinear system occurs when $g_3(x) = 0$. More parallel nonlinear systems can be included as needed for cases of three or more parallel nonlinear systems. This class of SI/SO models with parallel linear and nonlinear systems represents appropriate nonlinear models to use for many engineering and scientific applications that are discussed in the references.

In Figure 14.7, the terms are

$x(t) = x_1(f) = $ measured input
$y(t) = $ measured total output
$n(t) = $ unmeasured noise output
$x_2(t) = g_2[x(t)] = $ input to linear system $A_2(f)$
$x_3(t) = g_3[x(t)] = $ input to linear system $A_3(f)$
$Y_1(f) = A_1(f)X_1(f)$
$Y_2(f) = A_2(f)X_2(f)$
$Y_3(f) = A_3(f)X_3(f)$
$Y(f) = Y_1(f) + Y_2(f) + Y_3(f) + N(f)$

The objective in solving this SI/SO nonlinear model is to identify from measurements of $x(t)$ and $y(t)$ (a) the known or assumed zero-memory nonlinear functions, $g_2(x)$ and $g_3(x)$, and (b) the three optimum linear system frequency response functions, $A_1(f)$, $A_2(f)$, and $A_3(f)$ that give the minimum mean square value of the output noise.

The frequency range for the outputs of the zero-memory nonlinear systems can be greater or smaller than the frequency range for the input data $x(t)$. For example, in a nonlinear wave force model (discussed in Ref. 1), where $x_2(t)$ is proportional to

SI/SO MODELS WITH PARALLEL LINEAR AND NONLINEAR SYSTEMS

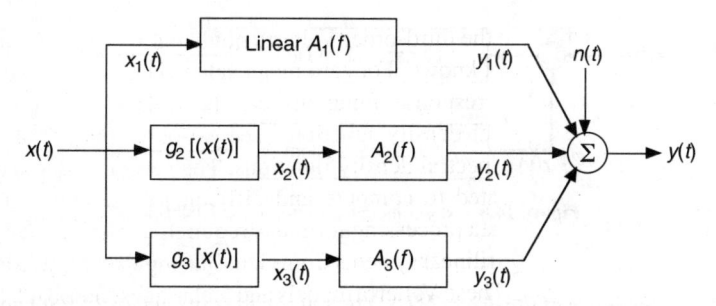

Figure 14.7 SI/SO model with parallel linear and nonlinear systems.

$x(t)|x(t)|$ (a squarer with sign), the output frequency range will be greater. In a nonlinear drift force model (discussed in Section 14.8), where $x_2(t)$ is proportional to the squared envelope of $x(t)$, the output frequency range will be smaller.

For some problems, the properties of the two zero-memory nonlinear functions will be known from previous theoretical or experimental work, such as by computation of input/output probability density functions. For other problems, trial properties of these two zero-memory nonlinear functions should be assumed based on engineering judgment and justified later by coherence analysis. In either situation, one will be able to compute the two non-Gaussian records, $x_2(t)$ and $x_3(t)$, that are the inputs to the systems $A_2(f)$ and $A_3(f)$. One can then obtain their Fourier transforms, $X_2(f)$ and $X_3(f)$, as well as their spectral density functions for the later analysis of Figure 14.7.

The key to solving this SI/SO nonlinear model is to recognize that Figure 14.7, like Figure 14.4, can be replaced by the three-input/single-output MI/SO linear model of Figure 7.18 where the three input records and the total output record are known. The three desired optimum linear system frequency response functions, $A_1(f), A_2(f)$, and $A_3(f)$ in Figure 14.7, are the same functions that are desired in Figure 7.18. They can be identified by the following procedure:

1. The first step is to compute from the correlated input records $\{X_i(f)\}, i = 1, 2, 3$, a new set of mutually uncorrelated input records $\{U_i(f)\}, i = 1, 2, 3$, using ordered conditioned spectral density functions.
2. The second step is to replace Figure 7.18 by Figure 7.19 where the mutually uncorrelated input records $\{U_i(f)\}$ now pass through new linear systems $\{L_i(f)\}, i = 1, 2, 3$.
3. Simple SI/SO spectral analysis formulas should next be used to identify the optimum linear systems $\{L_i(f)\}$ in Figure 7.19 from each uncorrelated input $\{U_i(f)\}$ to the total output record $Y(f)$.
4. The percentage of the output spectrum of $Y(f)$ due to each of the uncorrelated inputs and the multiple coherence function can be computed to determine the validity of this nonlinear model.
5. The optimum linear systems $\{A_i(f)\}$ in Figure 7.18 from the original correlated input records $\{X_i(f)\}$ to the total output record $Y(f)$ can be computed by Equations (7.125), (7.126), and (7.127).

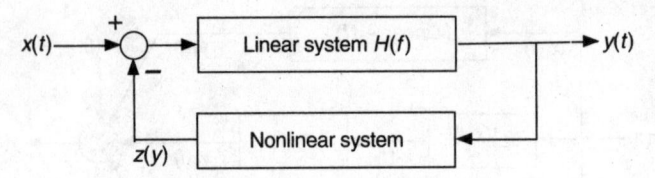

Figure 14.8 SI/SO model with nonlinear feedback.

6. This is the basis of the direct MI/SO technique to solve general SI/SO nonlinear models with parallel linear and nonlinear systems.

14.5 SI/SO MODELS WITH NONLINEAR FEEDBACK

A general SI/SO model with nonlinear feedback is shown in Figure 14.8 where a linear system is in parallel with a known or unknown nonlinear feedback system. In the past, from knowledge of measured input/output random data, it was usually very difficult, if not impossible, to identify the linear and nonlinear system frequency response properties in this model except for very special cases. In Figure 14.8, the terms are

$x(t)$ = measured input
$y(t)$ = measured output
$H(f)$ = linear system frequency response function
$z(y)$ = nonlinear feedback function of $y(t)$ = nonlinear system output

The objective in solving this SI/SO model with nonlinear feedback is to identify from measurements of $x(t)$ and $y(t)$ the linear system frequency response function $H(f)$ and the frequency properties of the known or unknown nonlinear feedback system that will produce the output $y(t)$ from the input $x(t)$.

The key to solving this nonlinear feedback model is to define a mathematical reverse SI/SO nonlinear model *without feedback* as pictured in Figure 14.9 where the measured physical input and the measured physical output are reversed. The physical input $x(t)$ now becomes a mathematical output, and the physical output $y(t)$ now becomes a mathematical input. The linear system $H(f)$ is replaced by its reciprocal system $A_1(f) = [H(f)]^{-1}$. The nonlinear function $z(y)$ remains the same as before. The mathematical total output $x(t)$ is now the sum of $z(y)$ and the output of the linear system $A_1(f)$.

In Figure 14.9, the terms are

$x(t)$ = mathematical total output = measured input
$y(t)$ = mathematical input = measured output
$A_1(f) = [H(f)]^{-1}$ = linear system frequency response function
$z(y)$ = nonlinear feedback function of $y(t)$ = nonlinear system output

SI/SO MODELS WITH NONLINEAR FEEDBACK

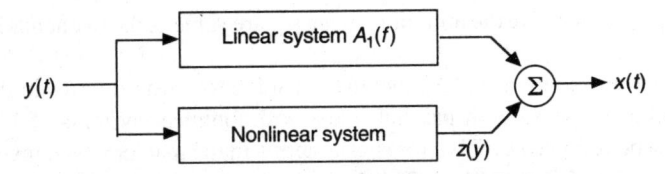

Figure 14.9 Reverse SI/SO nonlinear model without feedback.

Further work to identify the frequency properties in Figure 14.9 can now be carried out for problems where the nonlinear system output $z(y)$ can be modeled by a collection of known or assumed zero-memory nonlinear systems that are followed by linear systems. For example, with two parallel nonlinear paths as shown in Figure 14.10, one would have the two nonlinear systems $g_2(y)$ and $g_3(y)$ whose computed outputs are $y_2(t)$ and $y_3(t)$. These two mathematical output records are the mathematical input records to the linear systems $A_2(f)$ and $A_3(f)$ to be determined. The mathematical input record $y(t)$ goes through the linear system $A_1(f)$ to be determined.

In Figure 14.10, the terms are

$x(t)$ = mathematical total output = measured input
$y(t) = y_1(t)$ = mathematical input = measured output
$n(t)$ = mathematical output noise
$y_2(t) = g_2[y(t)]$ = input to linear system $A_2(f)$
$y_3(t) = g_3[y(t)]$ = input to linear system $A_3(f)$
$X_1(f) = A_1(f)Y_1(f)$
$X_2(f) = A_2(f)Y_2(f)$
$X_3(f) = A_3(f)Y_3(f)$
$X(f) = X_1(f) + X_2(f) + X_3(f) + N(f)$

The objective in solving this mathematical reverse SI/SO nonlinear model with parallel linear and nonlinear systems of Figure 14.10 is to identify from measurements of $x(t)$ and $y(t)$ (a) the known or assumed zero-memory nonlinear functions, $g_2(y)$ and $g_3(y)$, and (b) the three optimum linear system frequency response functions, $A(f)$,

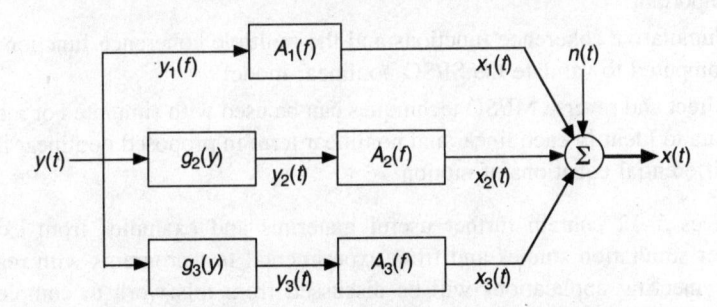

Figure 14.10 Reverse SI/SO model with parallel linear and nonlinear systems.

$A_2(f)$, and $A(f)$, that give the minimum mean square value of the mathematical output noise.

The same procedure as used previously to solve for desired terms in the general SI/SO nonlinear model with parallel linear and nonlinear systems of Figure 14.7 should now be followed to solve for similar terms in the mathematical reverse SI/SO nonlinear model of Figure 14.10. *This is the basis of the reverse MI/SO technique to solve SI/SO models with nonlinear feedback.*

14.6 RECOMMENDED NONLINEAR MODELS AND TECHNIQUES

Whenever appropriate for engineering and scientific applications, one should try to establish desired SI/SO nonlinear models to be either

  a. SI/SO models with parallel linear and nonlinear systems, or
  b. SI/SO models with nonlinear feedback.

These two types of SI/SO nonlinear models are recommended for the following reasons:

1. Frequency-domain results can be obtained using established data processing procedures and computer programs by changing the SI/SO nonlinear models into equivalent MI/SO linear models.
2. The recommended direct and reverse MI/SO techniques to solve these two types of SI/SO nonlinear models are valid for input/output random data with arbitrary probability and spectral properties.
3. There are no restrictions on the forms of the zero-memory nonlinear operations in these SI/SO nonlinear models.
4. Nonlinear system amplitude properties can be determined from the zero-memory nonlinear operations, as well as the frequency properties of coefficients for physical parameters of linear and nonlinear system.
5. The percentage of the output spectrum due to each linear and nonlinear system operation can be evaluated using appropriate coherence functions to show the particular frequencies where each linear and nonlinear system operation is important.
6. Cumulative coherence functions and the multiple coherence function can be computed to validate the SI/SO nonlinear model.
7. Direct and reverse MI/SO techniques can be used with simulated or measured data to identify each linear and nonlinear term in proposed nonlinear integro-differential equations of motion.

References 5–12 contain further useful materials and examples from extensive computer simulation studies and from experimental test programs with real data. Two engineering applications will be discussed from this work to complete this chapter:

a. Duffing SDOF nonlinear system.
b. Nonlinear drift force problem.

14.7 DUFFING SDOF NONLINEAR SYSTEM

A Duffing SDOF nonlinear system is a nonlinear feedback system described by the constant-parameter differential equation

$$m\ddot{u}(t) + c\dot{u}(t) + ku(t) + k_3 u^3(t) = F(t) \tag{14.3}$$

where

$F(t)$ = applied input force
$u(t)$ = displacement output response
m = system mass
c = linear viscous damping coefficient
k = linear elastic stiffness coefficient
k_3 = nonlinear feedback cubic stiffness coefficient

The basic SDOF linear case without feedback occurs when $k_3 = 0$.

This Duffing SDGF nonlinear system and the basic SDOF linear case were studied by computer simulations in Ref. 9. In these studies, the applied input force $F(t)$ was broadband random data with unit variance that followed a Gaussian distribution, This was achieved using a random number generator provided in the 386-MATLAB computer code. The digital data processing parameters for the later analysis are listed in Table 14.1. Note that the spectral and frequency response function estimates are based on 16 averages with a bandwidth resolution of 0.977 Hz. A Hanning window was used to reduce the effects of leakage. Also, a 256-point overlap was employed to recover information lost by the windowing operation.

The linear frequency response function $H(f)$ in Equation (14.3) for the physical input and output records is

Table 14.1 Digital Data Processing Parameters

f_s = sampling frequency = 50 Hz
$\Delta t = 1/f_s$ = discretization time = 0.02 s
$f_c = 1/f_s$ = Nyquist cutoff frequency = 25 Hz
N = number of sample values per subrecord = 512
$T = N \Delta t$ = time of each subrecord = 1.24 s
n_d = number of distinct subrecords = 16
$N_{total} = n_d N$ = total number of sample values = 8192
$T_{total} = n_d T$ = total time for all subrecords = 163.84 s
$\Delta f = 1/T$ = bandwidth resolution = 0.0977 Hz

$$H(f) = [k-(2\pi f)^2 m + j(2\pi f)c]^{-1} \tag{14.4}$$

with undamped natural frequency and damping ratio given by

$$f_n = \frac{1}{2\pi}\sqrt{k/m}$$

$$\zeta = \frac{c}{2\sqrt{km}} = \frac{c}{4\pi f_n m} \tag{14.5}$$

For a reverse dynamic linear system as described in Section 14.5 where

$u(t) =$ mathematical displacement input
$F(t) =$ mathematical force output

the linear system frequency response function $A_1(f)$ is the reciprocal of the $H(f)$ of Equation (14.4), namely,

$$A_1(f) = k-(2\pi f)^2 m + j(2\pi f)c \tag{14.6}$$

With the terms in Equation (14.5), this $A_1(f)$ can also be expressed as

$$A_1(f) = k[1-(f/f_n)^2 + j2\zeta(f/f_n)] \tag{14.7}$$

The connection between a measured $A_1(f)$ and the physical parameters m, c, and k of the SDOF linear system can be found by noting that the minimum value of $|A_1(f)|$ occurs at $f=f_n$ where $|A_1(f_n)| = 2\zeta k$. These parameters are

$$\begin{aligned} k &= A_1(0) \\ m &= k/(2\pi f_n)^2 = A_1(0)/(2\pi f_n)^2 \\ c &= 2\zeta\sqrt{km} = |A_1(f_n)|/(2\pi f_n)^2 \\ \zeta &= |A_1(f_n)|2k \end{aligned} \tag{14.8}$$

Table 14.2 shows the simulated system parameters that were used in Ref. 9 to study the basic SDOF linear system and the Duffing SDOF nonlinear system.

14.7.1 Analysis for SDOF Linear System

The applied excitation source is illustrated in Figure 14.11. This shows a time history segment from 0 to 10 s and the force autospectrum using a bandwidth resolution of 0.098 Hz. This force autospectrum has the appearance of bandwidth-limited white noise from 0 to 10 Hz. In Figure 14.12, the associated force histogram using 8192 sample values has a Gaussian shape.

Table 14.2 Simulated System Parameters

System Type	k	c	f_n	ζ	k_3
Linear	355.3	3.77	3.0 Hz	0.10	0
Duffing	355.3	3.77	3.0 Hz	0.10	2×10^7

DUFFING SDOF NONLINEAR SYSTEM

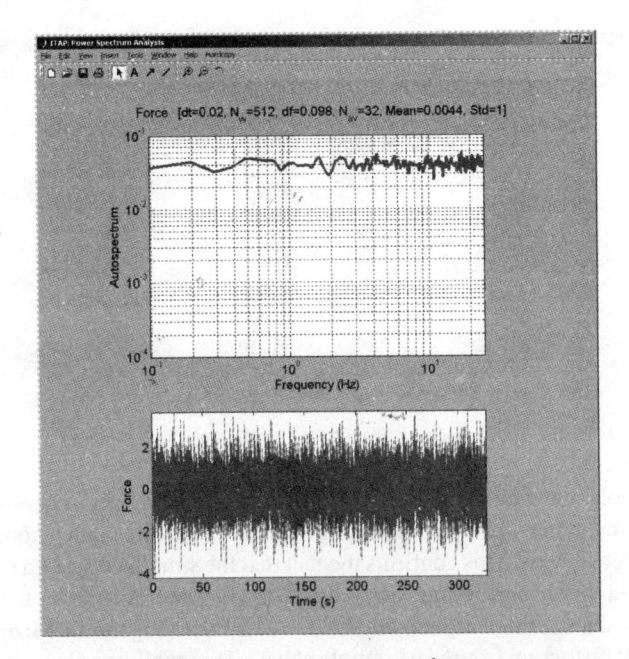

Figure 14.11 Force history segment and autospectrum.

Figure 14.13(a) and (b) shows the analyzed results for the magnitude and phase of the frequency response function $A_1(f)$ of Equation (14.7) for the simulated reverse dynamic SDOF linear system where $f_n = 3.0$ Hz and $k_3 = 0$. Note that the magnitude of $A_1(f)$ has a dip at this resonance frequency instead of the usual peak value. The

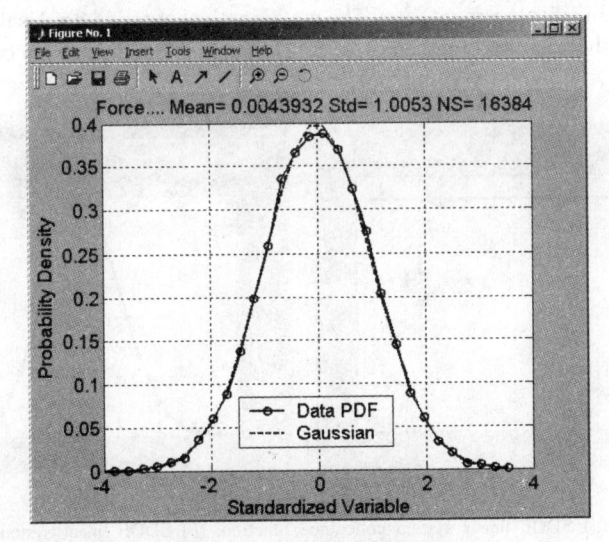

Figure 14.12 Force historgram.

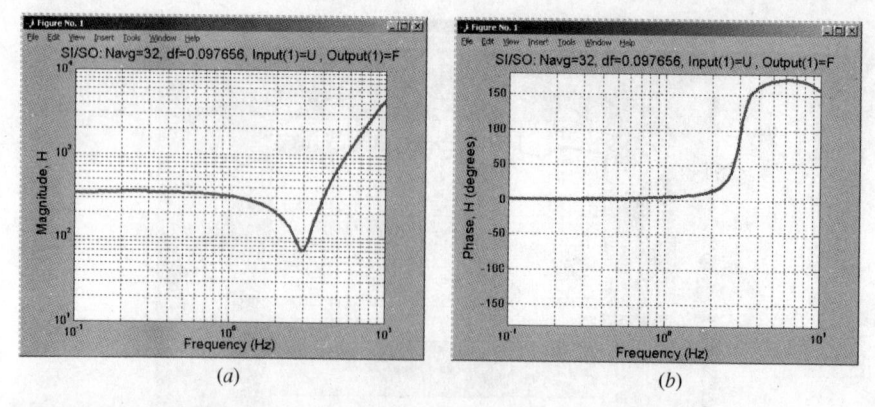

Figure 14.13 (a) SDOF linear system magnitude. (b) SDOF linear system phase.

cumulative coherence function in Figure 14.14(a) is the ordinary coherence function between the mathematical input record and the mathematical output record and is near unity at all frequencies. This confirms the fact that the simulated system is linear with no significant noise corruption. The slight dip in coherence near the resonance frequency is due to the well-known effect of leakage. Figure 14.14(b) shows the displacement histogram from 8192 sample values. This exhibits a Gaussian shape like the force histogram that further confirms the system is linear.

14.7.2 Analysis for Duffing SDOF Nonlinear System

Figures 14.15–14.17 show the analyzed results for the computer-simulated Duffing SDOF nonlinear system where $f_n = 3.0$ Hz and $k_3 = 2 \times 10^7$. For this MI/SO reverse dynamic analysis, two mathematical inputs are required: the displacement $u(t)$ and the correlated cubic displacement $u^3(t)$. The mathematical output record is the force $F(t)$. Estimates of the magnitude and phase of the Duffing system linear frequency response

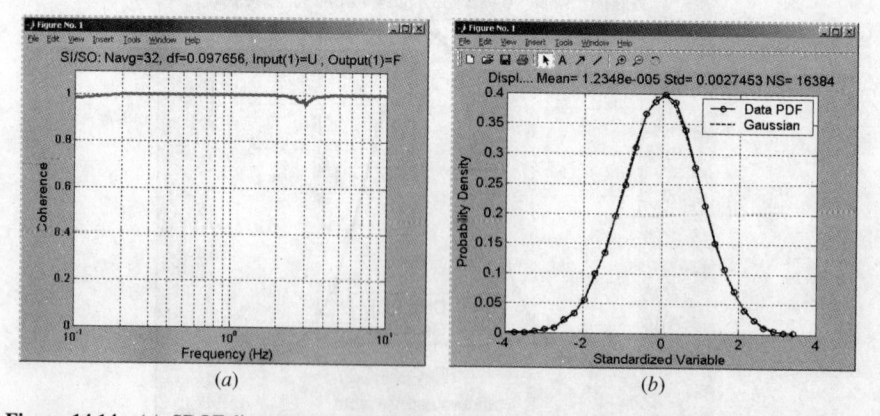

Figure 14.14 (a) SDOF linear system coherence function. (b) SDOF linear system displacement histogram.

DUFFING SDOF NONLINEAR SYSTEM

(a)

(b)

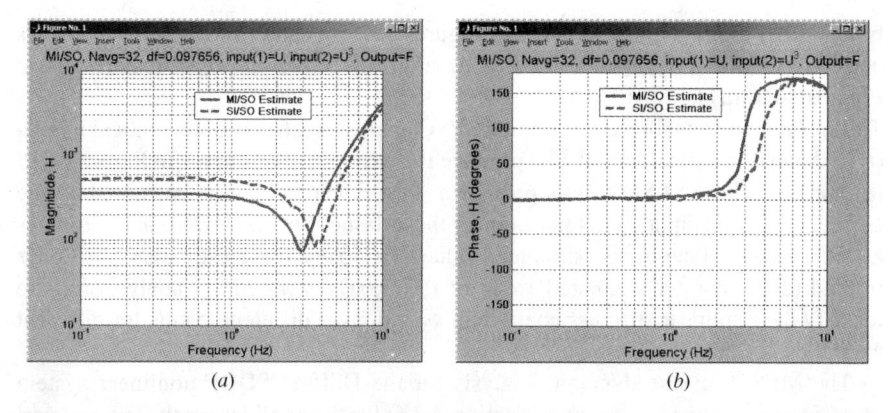

Figure 14.15 (a) Duffing system linear magnitude and SI/SO magnitude. (b) Duffing system linear phase and SI/SO phase.

(a)

(b)

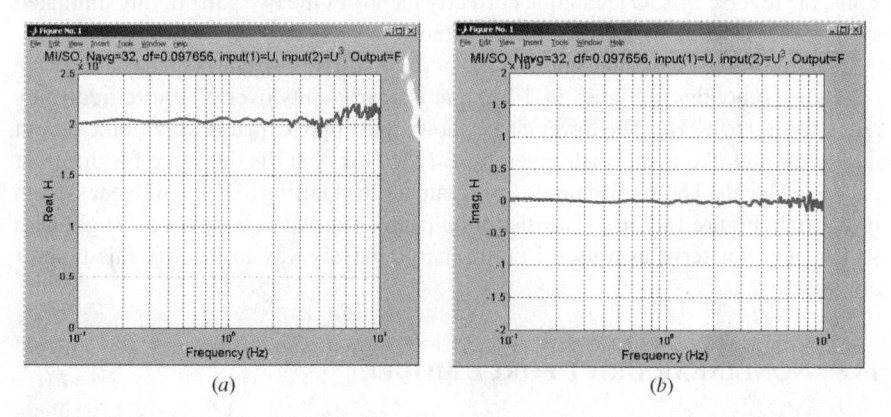

Figure 14.16 Duffing system nonlinear frequency response function. (a) Real part. (b) Imaginary part.

(a)

(b)

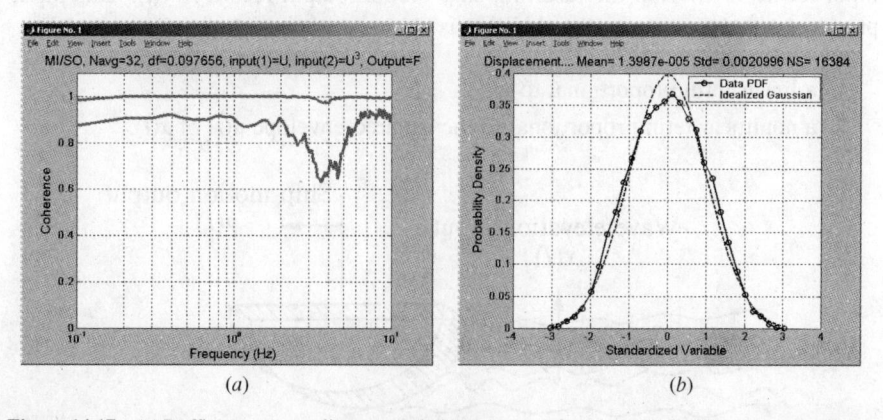

Figure 14.17 (a) Duffing system nonlinear cumulative coherence functions. (b) Duffing system nonlinear displacement histogram.

function $A_1(f)$ are the solid curves in Figures 14.15(a) and (b). These solid curves correctly identify $A_1(f)$ since they agree with the SDOF linear system results in Figures 14.13(a) and (b).

The analyzed results for a conventional SI/SO analysis with one mathematical input $u(t)$ to the mathematical output $F(t)$ produce the wrong dashed curves in Figure 14.15(a) and (b). These SI/SO results provide a "best linear fit" that is corrupted by the correlated second input $u^3(t)$. Inspection of these dashed curves shows that it estimates $k = 500$ instead of the correct simulated value $k = 355$ and that it estimates $f_n = 3.6$ Hz instead of the correct simulated value of $f_n = 3.0$ Hz. This SI/SO analysis fails to identify the nonlinear stiffness coefficient k_3 and gives different results for different excitation levels.

The MI/SO reverse dynamic analysis for the Duffing SDOF nonlinear system identifies the frequency response function $A_2(f)$ for the nonlinear path. The real part of $A_2(f)$, shown in Figure 14.16(a), gives the value of $k_3 = 2 \times 10^7$ as used in the simulation. The imaginary part of $A_2(f)$, shown in Figure 14.6(b), is essentially zero. Thus, the reverse MI/SO technique correctly identifies the two parts of this simulated system as a Duffing SDOF nonlinear system.

The validity of this conclusion is further confirmed by inspection of the cumulative coherence functions in Figure 14.17(a) that is nearly unity over the entire frequency range from 0 to 10 Hz. The lower curve shows that approximately 90% of the output passes through the linear path given by $L_1(f)$. This result is the same for different excitation levels. The displacement histogram for the Duffing SDOF nonlinear system is shown in Figure 14.17(b). The distortion from a Gaussian shape is very slight here so it would not serve as a useful preliminary analysis way to identify this type of nonlinearity.

14.8 NONLINEAR DRIFT FORCE MODEL

The general problem to be analyzed is shown in Figure 14.18 where the wave elevation input record is $x(t)$ and the resulting ship motion output record is $y(t)$. This input produces a force acting on the ship that is assumed to consist of two components:

1. a linear term proportional to $x(t)$.
2. a nonlinear term proportional to the squared envelope $u(t)$ of $x(t)$.

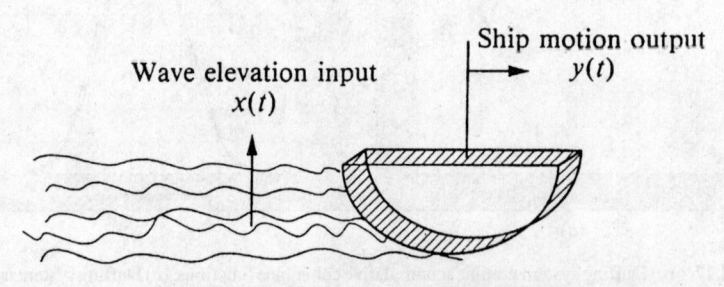

Figure 14.18 Illustration of drift force problem.

NONLINEAR DRIFT FORCE MODEL

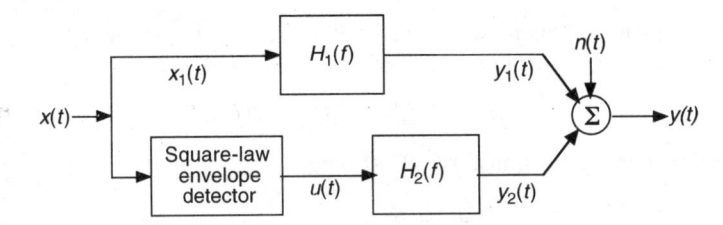

Figure 14.19 Nonlinear drift force model with parallel linear and square-law envelope detector systems.

The nonlinear term $u(t)$, called the *slowly varying drift force*, has output frequencies that are lower than the input frequencies.

The ship motion output $y(t)$ thus takes the form

$$y(t) = k_1 x(t) + k_2 u(t) \tag{14.9}$$

where the coefficients k_1 and k_2 are usually assumed to be constants, independent of frequency. This nonlinear operation is poorly represented by a third-order polynomial approximation like the nonlinear model of Figure 14.4, where the output frequencies are higher than the input frequencies.

A generalization of Equation (14.9) is drawn in Figure 14.19 where the coefficients k_1 and k_2 are replaced by linear frequency response functions $H_1(f)$ and $H_2(f)$. For Gaussian input data, the records $x(t)$ and $u(t)$ will be uncorrelated. This makes Figure 14.9 equivalent to a simple two-input/single-output linear problem with uncorrelated inputs $x(t)$ and $u(t)$ passing through $H_1(f)$ and $H_2(f)$ to give the outputs $y_1(t)$ and $y_2(t)$.

14.8.1 Basic Formulas for Proposed Model

The following basic formulas apply to the proposed nonlinear drift force model of Figure 14.19. From Section 13.3, the square-taw envelope detector output $u(t)$ is given by

$$u(t) = x^2(t) + \tilde{x}^2(t) \tag{14.10}$$

where

$$\tilde{x}(t) = \text{Hilbert transform of } x(t) \tag{14.11}$$

This Hilbert transform can be computed as per Section 13.1.1. The symbol $\sim$ used here should not be confused with "raw" estimates. When $x(t)$ has a zero mean value, $\tilde{x}(t)$ will also have a zero mean value. However, the mean value of $u(t)$, denoted by $E[u(t)]$, is not zero. Instead,

$$E[u(t)] = E[x^2(t)] + E[\tilde{x}^2(t)] = 2\sigma_x^2 \tag{14.12}$$

where σ_x^2 is the variance of $x(t)$.

In the frequency-domain, with mean values removed prior to taking Fourier transforms, the Fourier transform $Y(f)$ of the total output $y(t)$ is

$$Y(f) = Y_1(f) + Y_2(f) + N(f) \tag{14.13}$$

where $N(f)$ is the Fourier transform of $n(t)$ and

$$Y_1(f) = H_1(f)X(f) \tag{14.14}$$

$$Y_2(f) = H_2(f)U(f) \tag{14.15}$$

Here, $X(f)$ is the Fourier transform of $x(t)$ and $U(f)$ is the Fourier transform of the square-law envelope detector output $u(t)$.

From Equation (14.10),

$$U(f) = \int_{-\infty}^{+\infty} \left[X(\alpha)X(f-\alpha) + \tilde{X}(\alpha)\tilde{X}(f-\alpha) \right] d\alpha \tag{14.16}$$

where the quantity $\tilde{X}(f)$ is defined by

$$\tilde{X}(f) = B(f)X(f) \tag{14.17}$$

using the same $B(f)$ as in Equation (13.8), namely,

$$B(f) = -j\,\mathrm{sgn}\,f = \begin{cases} -j & f > 0 \\ 0 & f = 0 \\ +j & f < 0 \end{cases} \tag{14.18}$$

Hence,

$$U(f) = \int_{-\infty}^{+\infty} \left[1 + B(\alpha)B(f-\alpha) \right] X(\alpha)X(f-\alpha)\,d\alpha \tag{14.19}$$

For any $f > 0$, the product quantity

$$B(\alpha)B(f-\alpha) = \begin{cases} 1 & \alpha < 0 \\ -1 & 0 < \alpha < f \\ 1 & \alpha > f \end{cases} \tag{14.20}$$

Substitutions then prove after several steps that

$$U(f) = 4 \int_0^\infty X^*(\alpha)X(f+\alpha)\,d\alpha \tag{14.21}$$

This shows how to compute $U(f)$ from $X(f)$ for any $f > 0$.

Two problems will now be treated for this nonlinear drift force model of Figure 14.19.

1. *Spectral Decomposition Problem.* Given $H_1(f)$ and $H_2(f)$ plus measurement only of $x(t)$, determine the spectral properties of the two outputs $y_1(t)$ and $y_2(t)$. If $y(t)$ is also measured, determine the spectral properties of the noise $n(t)$.
2. *System Identification Problem.* From simultaneous measurements of both $x(t)$ and $y(t)$, identify the optimum frequency response properties $H_1(f)$ and $H_2(f)$ to minimize the autospectrum of $n(t)$.

14.8.2 Spectral Decomposition Problem

In Figure 14.19, for Gaussian input data, the linear output term $y_1(t)$ and the nonlinear output term $y_2(t)$ will be uncorrelated. This is because $y_1(t)$ is uncorrelated with both $x^2(t)$ and $\tilde{x}^2(t)$, the two parts of $u(t)$. Hence, the total output spectral density function $G_{yy}(f)$ is given by the simple sum

$$G_{yy}(f) = G_{y_1 y_1}(f) + G_{y_2 y_2}(f) + G_{nn}(f) \tag{14.22}$$

where

$$G_{y_1 y_1}(f) = |H_1(f)|^2 G_{xx}(f) \tag{14.23}$$

$$G_{y_2 y_2}(f) = |H_2(f)|^2 G_{uu}(f) \tag{14.24}$$

The spectral quantity $G_{xx}(f)$ can be computed directly from $X(f)$ for an ensemble of stationary random records of length T by the expected value operation

$$G_{xx}(f) = \frac{2}{T} E|X^*(f)X(f)| \tag{14.25}$$

Similarly, the spectral quantity $G_{uu}(f)$ can be computed directly from $U(f)$ for an ensemble of stationary random records of length T by the expected value operation

$$G_{uu}(f) = \frac{2}{T} E[U^*(f)U(f)] \tag{14.26}$$

where $U(f)$ is obtained from $X(f)$ by Equation (14.21).

Another formula to compute $G_{uu}(f)$ from knowledge of $G_{xx}(f)$ is derived in Equation (13.130). For any $f > 0$, this formula is

$$G_{uu}(f) = 8 \int_0^\infty G_{xx}(\alpha) G_{xx}(f-\alpha) d\alpha \tag{14.27}$$

With knowledge of $G_{xx}(f)$ and $G_{uu}(f)$, Equations (14.23) and (14.24) can now be used to compute the spectral properties of $y_1(t)$ and $y_2(t)$ from $H_1(f)$ and $H_2(f)$. To further obtain the spectral properties of $n(t)$, the total output record $y(t)$ must be measured to give $G_{yy}(f)$. One can then compute $G_{nn}(f)$ from Equation (14.22). These formulas solve the spectral decomposition problem.

14.8.3 System Identification Problem

Assume that the properties of the linear systems $H_1(f)$ and $H_2(f)$ are *not* known in the nonlinear drift force model of Figure 14.19. Optimum properties are to be determined from simultaneous measurements of the input $x(t)$ and the total output $y(t)$, based upon minimizing the autospectrum $G_{nn}(f)$ of $n(t)$ over all possible choices of linear systems to predict $y(t)$ from $x(t)$. It is assumed that the input data follow a Gaussian distribution with zero mean value.

From Equations (14.13) and (14.14), the cross-spectral density function $G_{xy}(f)$ between $x(t)$ and $y(t)$ is given by

$$G_{xy}(f) = G_{xy_1}(f) = H_1(f)G_{xx}(f) \tag{14.28}$$

because

$$G_{xu}(f) = 0 \tag{14.29}$$

and

$$G_{xn}(f) = 0 \tag{14.30}$$

Equation (14.29) occurs because $x(t)$ and $u(t)$ are uncorrelated for Gaussian $x(t)$. Equation (14.30) occurs because $H_1(f)$ is the same as the optimum linear system $H_o(f)$ and the optimum linear system makes $n(t)$ uncorrelated with $x(t)$. The optimum linear system is given by

$$H_o(f) = \frac{G_{xy}(f)}{G_{xx}(f)} = H_1(f) \tag{14.31}$$

Thus, $H_1(f)$ can be Identified using $x(t)$ and $y(t)$.

From Equations (14.13) and (14.15), the cross-spectral density function $G_{uy}(f)$ between $u(t)$ and $y(t)$ is given by

$$G_{uy}(f) = H_2(f)G_{uu}(f) \tag{14.32}$$

The autospectral density function $G_{uu}(f)$ can be computed by Equation (14.26). Similarly, the cross-spectral density function $G_{uy}(f)$ can be computed for an ensemble of stationary random records of length T by the expected value operation

$$G_{uy}(f) = \frac{2}{T}E|U^*(f)Y(f)| \tag{14.33}$$

Thus, $H_2(f)$ can also be identified from Equation (14.32) using $x(f)$ and $y(t)$ since $u(t)$ is a function of $x(t)$. These formulas solve the system identification problem.

PROBLEMS

14.1 A nonlinear square-law system with sign is defined by the relation $y(t) = g[x(t)] = x(t)|x(f)|$. Prove that $y(t)$ is a constant-parameter nonlinear system.

14.2 Determine the output probability density function $p_2(y)$ as a function of y when zero mean value Gaussian input data $x = x(t)$ passes through a square-law system $y(t) = g[x(t)] = x^2(t)$.

14.3 In Figures 14.2 and 14.3, assume that the two linear systems $A(f) = B(f)$. Assume also that the same zero-memory nonlinear system transformation $g[]$ is involved where $z_1(t) = g[x(t)]$ and $Y_2(t) = g[z_2(t)]$. Prove that the same input data $x(t)$ to Figures 14.2 and 14.3 produce two different output data $y_1(t)$ and $y_2(t)$.

14.4 Assume that zero mean value Gaussian input data $x(t)$ passes through a nonlinear cubic system $y(t) = g[x(t)] = x^3(t)$. Determine the optimum linear system $H_o(f) = [G_{xy}(f)/G_{xx}(f)]$.

14.5 Assume that zero mean value Gaussian input data $x(t)$ passes through a fourth-order system $y(t) = g[x(t)] = x^4(t)$. Prove that the optimum linear system $H_o(f)$ is now zero. How can one determine the part of the output due to $x^4(t)$?

14.6 Consider the general SI/SO nonlinear model of Figure 14.7. Show that computation of the optimum linear system $H_o(f)$ is not the same as the computation of the linear system $A_1(f)$ in Figure 14.7. Also, show that computation of $H_o(f)$ does not determine the nonlinear terms in Figure 14.7.

14.7 Assume in Figure 14.7 that the linear record $x_1(t)$ and the two nonlinear records $x_2(t)$ and $x_3(t)$ are mutually uncorrelated. Determine the percentage of the output spectrum of $y(t)$ that is due to these three linear and nonlinear records.

14.8 Show that Figure 14.9 gives the same result as Figure 14.8 when the input data and the output data are reversed.

14.9 A Duffing nonlinear system is defined by the equation

$$m\ddot{y}(t) + c\dot{y}(t) + ky(t) + k_3 y^3(t) = x(t)$$

where $x(t)$ = measured input, $y(t)$ = measured output, and the coefficients are physical parameters to be determined. Show how the mathematical reverse SI/SO nonlinear model of Figure 14.10 can be used to solve for the physical parameters.

14.10 Show that conventional SI/SO linear analysis of the Duffing nonlinear system in Problem 14.9 gives the wrong physical parameters.

REFERENCES

1. Bendat, J. S., *Nonlinear System Techniques and Applications*, Wiley–Interscience, New York, 1998.

2. Bendat, J. S., and Piersol, A. G., *Engineering Application of Correlation and Spectral Analysis*, 2nd ed., Wiley–Interscience, New York, 1993.
3. Schetzen, M., *The Volterra, Wiener Theories of Nonlinear Systems*, Wiley–Interscience, New York, 1980.
4. Rugh, W. J., *Nonlinear System Theory: The Volterra/Wiener Approach*, Johns Hopkins University Press, Baltimore, MD, 1981.
5. Bendat, J. S., and Piersol, A. G., "Spectral Analysis of Nonlinear Systems Involving Square-Law Operations," *Journal of Sound and Vibration*, Vol. 81, p. 199, 1982.
6. Bendat, J. S., and Piersol, A. G., "Decomposition of Wave Forces into Linear and Nonlinear Components," *Journal of Sound and Vibration*, Vol. 106, p. 391, 1986.
7. Rice, H. J., and Fitzpatrick, J. S., "A Generalized Technique for Spectral Analysis of Nonlinear Systems," *Mechanical Systems and Signal Processing*, Vol. 2, p. 95, 1988.
8. Bendat, J. S., and Palo, P. A.,"Practical Techniques for Nonlinear System Analysis and Identification," *Sound and Vibration*, Bay Village, OH, June 1990.
9. Bendat, J. S., Palo, P. A., and Coppolino, R. N., "A General Identification Technique for Nonlinear Differential Equations of Motion," *Probabilistic Engineering Mechanics*, Vol. 7, p. 43, 1992.
10. Bendat, J. S., "Spectral Techniques for Nonlinear System Analysis and Identification," *Shock and Vibration*, Vol. 1, p. 21, 1993.
11. Bendat, J. S., Palo, P. A., and Coppolino, R. N., "Identification of Physical Parameters with Memory in Nonlinear Systems, *International Journal of Nonlinear Mechanics*, Vol. 30, p. 841, 1995.
12. Chertoff, M. E., et al. "Characterizing Cochlear Mechano-Electric Transduction Using a Nonlinear Systems Identification Procedure," *Journal of the Acoustical Society of America*, Vol. 100, p. 3741, 1996.

Bibliography

1. Anon., *"Military Standard, Calibration System Requirements,"* MIL-STD-45562A, Department of Defense, Washington, D.C., 1988.
2. Bendat, J. S., *Principles and Applications of Random Noise Theory*, Wiley, New York, 1958. Reprinted by Krieger, Melbourne, Florida, 1977.
3. Bendat, J. S., "The Hilbert Transform and Applications to Correlation Measurements," *Bruel & Kjaer*, Denmark, 1985.
4. Bendat, J. S., "Spectral Techniques for Nonlinear System Analysis and Identification," *Shock and Vibration*, Vol. 1, p. 21, 1993.
5. Bendat, J. S., *Nonlinear System Techniques and Applications*, Wiley-Interscience, New York, 1998.
6. Bendat, J. S., and Palo, P. A., *"Practical Techniques for Nonlinear System Analysis and Identification,"* Sound and Vibration, Bay Village, OH, June 1990.
7. Bendat, J. S., Palo, P. A., and Coppolino, R. N., "A General Identification Technique for Nonlinear Differential Equations of motion," *Probabilistic Engineering Mechanics*, Vol. 7, p. 43, 1992.
8. Bendat, J, S., Palo, P. A., and Coppolino, R. N., "Identification of Physical Parameters with Memory in Nonlinear Systems," *International Journal of Nonlinear Mechanics*, Vol. 30, p. 841, 1995.
9. Bendat, J. S., and Piersol, A. G., "Spectral Analysis of Nonlinear Systems Involving Square-Law Operations," *Journal of Sound and Vibration*, Vol. 81, p. 199, 1982.
10. Bendat, J. S., and Piersol, A. G., "Decomposition of Wave Forces into Linear and Nonlinear Components," *Journal of Sound and Vibration*, Vol. 106, p. 391, 1986.
11. Bendat, J. S., and Piersol, A. G., *Engineering Applications of Correlation and Spectral Analysis*, 2nd ed., Wiley-Interscience, New York, 1993.
12. Blackman, R. B., and Tukey, J. W., *The Measurement of Power Spectra*, Dover, New York, 1958.

Random Data: Analysis and Measurement Procedures, Fourth Edition. By Julius S. Bendat and Allan G. Piersol
Copyright © 2010 John Wiley & Sons, Inc.

13. Bracewell, R., *The Fourier Transform and its Applications*, McGraw-Hill, New York, 1965.
14. Bracewell, R. N., *The Hartley Transform*, Oxford University Press, New York, 1986.
15. Brigham, E. O., *The Fast Fourier Transform and its Applications*, Prentice-Hall, Englewood Cliffs, New Jersey, 1988.
16. Camras, M., *Magnetic Recording Handbook*, Van Nostrand Reinhold, NY, 1988.
17. Carter, G. G, Knapp, C. H., and Nuttall, A. H., "Estimation of the Magnitude- Squared Coherence via Overlapped Fast Fourier Transform Processing," *IEEE Transactions on Audio and Electroacoustics*, Vol. AU-21, p. 337, August 1973.
18. Chertoff, M. E., et al., "Characterizing Cochlear Mechano-Electric Transduction Using a Nonlinear Systems Identification Procedure," *Journal of the Acoustical Society of America*, Vol. 100, p. 3741, 1996.
19. Cohen, L., *Time-Frequency Analysis*, Prentice-Hall, Upper Saddle River, New Jersey, 1995.
20. Cooley, J. W., and Tukey, J. W., "An Algorithm for the Machine Calculation of Complex Fourier Series," *Mathematics of Computations*, Vol. 19, p 297, April 1965.
21. Crandall, S. H., and Mark, W. D., *Random Vibration in Mechanical Systems*, Academic Press, New York, 1963.
22. Cremer, L., Heckl, M., and Ungar, E. E., *Structure-Borne Sound*, Springer-Verlag, New York, 1973.
23. Davenport, W. B., Jr., and Root, W. L., *Random Signals and Noise*, McGraw-Hill, New York, 1958.
24. Dodds, C. J., and Robson, J. D., "Partial Coherence in Multivariate Random Processes," *Journal of Sound and Vibration*, Vol. 42, p. 243, 1975.
25. Doebelin, E. O., *Measurement Systems: Application and Design*, 4th edition, McGraw-Hill, New York, 1990.
26. Doebelin, E. O., *Measurement Systems: Application and Design*, 5th ed., McGraw-Hill, NY, 2004.
27. Doob, J. L., *Stochastic Processes*, Wiley, New York, 1953.
28. Dugundj, J., "Envelopes and Pre-Envelopes of Real Waveforms," *IRE Transactions on Information Theory*, Vol. IT-4, p. 53, March 1958.
29. Forlifer, W. R., "Effects of Filter Bandwidth in Spectrum Analysis of Random Vibration," *Shock and Vibration Bulletin*, No. 33, Part 2, p. 273, 1964.
30. Goodman, N. R., *"Measurement of Matrix Frequency Response Functions and Multiple Coherence Functions,"* AFFDL TR 65-56, Air Force Flight Dynamics Laboratory, Wright-Patterson AFB, Ohio, February 1965.
31. Guttman, I., Wilks, S. S., and Hunter, J. S., *Introductory Engineering Statistics*, 3rd ed., Wiley, New York, 1982.
32. Hamming, R. W., *Digital Filters*, 2nd ed., Prentice-Hall, Englewood Cliffs, New Jersey, 1983.
33. Harris, F. J., "On the Use of Windows for Harmonic Analysis with Discrete Fourier Transform," *Proceedings of the IEEE*, Vol. 66, p. 51, January 1978.
34. Hartley, R. V. L., "A More Symmetrical Fourier Analysis Applied to Transmission Problems," *Proceedings of the IRE*, Vol. 30, p. 144, March 1942.

35. Hauser, M. W., "Principles of Oversampling A/D Conversion," *Journal of Audio Engineering Society*, Vol. 39, p. 3, January/February 1991.
36. Himelblau, H., Piersol, A. G., Wise, J. H., and Grundvig, M. R., *Handbook for Dynamic Data Acquisition and Analysis*, IEST-RP-DTE012.1, Institute of Environmental Sciences and Technology, Mount Prospect, Illinois, 1994.
37. Himelblau, H., and Piersol, A. G., *Handbook for Dynamic Data Acquisition and Analysis*, 2nd ed., IEST RD-DTE012.2, Institute of Environmental Sciences and Technology, Arlington Heights, IL, 2006.
38. Hines, W. H., and Montgomery, D. C, *Probability and Statistics in Engineering and Management Sciences*, 3rd ed., Wiley, New York, 1990.
39. Hnatek, E. R., *A Users Handbook of D/A and A/D Converters*, Wiley, NY, 1976.
40. Huang, N. E., et al., "The Empirical Mode Decomposition and its Hilbert Spectrum for Nonlinear and Non-Stationary Time Series Analysis," *Proceedings, Royal Society A*, Vol. 454, p. 903, 1998.
41. Jenkins, G. M., and Watts, D. G., *Spectral Analysis and its Applications*, Holden-Day, San Francisco, 1968.
42. Kay, S. M., *Modern Spectral Estimation: Theory and Application*, Prentice-Hall, Englewood Cliffs, New Jersey, 1988.
43. Kendall, M. G., and Stuart, A., The Advanced Theory of Statistics, Vol. 2, *"Inference and Relationships,"* Hafner, New York, 1961.
44. Laning, J. H., Jr., and Battin, R. H., *Random Processes in Automatic Control*, McGraw-Hill, New York, 1956.
45. Liebeck, H., *Algebra for Scientists and Engineers*, Wiley, New York, 1969.
46. Loeve, M. M., *Probability Theory*, 4th ed., Springer-Verlag, New York, 1977.
47. Mark, W. D., and Fischer, R. W., "Investigation of the Effects of Nonhomogeneous (or Nonstationary) Behavior on the Spectra of Atmospheric Turbulence," NASA CR-2745, NASA Langley Research Center, Virginia, 1967.
48. Marple, L. S., *Digital Spectral Analysis with Applications*, Prentice-Hall, Englewood Cliffs, New Jersey, 1987.
49. Miller, K. S., *Engineering Mathematics*, Reinhart, New York, 1957.
50. Mitra, S. K., and Kaiser, J. F., *Handbook for Digital Signal Processing*, Wiley, New York, 1993.
51. Newland, D. E., *Random Vibrations, Spectral & Wavelet Analysis*, 3rd ed., Addisor Wesley Longman, Harlow, Essex, England, 1993.
52. Nuttall, A. H., and Carter, G. C, "Spectral Estimation Using Combined Time and Lag Weighting," *Proceedings of the IEEE*, Vol. 70, p. 1115, September 1982.
53. Ochi, M. K., *Applied Probability and Stochastic Processes*, Wiley-Interscience, New York, 1990.
54. Oppenheim, A. V., and Schafer, R. W., *Discrete-Time Signal Processing*, Prentice-Hall Englewood Cliffs, New Jersey, 1989.
55. Oppenheim, A. V., Schafer, R. W., and Buck, J. R., *Discrete-Time Signal Processing*, 2nd ed., Prentice-Hall, Englewood Cliffs, NJ, 1998.
56. Papoulis, A., *Probability, Random Variables, and Stochastic Processes*, 3rd ed., McGraw-Hill, 1991.
57. Patel, J. K., and Read, C. B., *Handbook of the Normal Distribution*, Dekker, New York 1982.

58. Piersol, A. G., "Time Delay Estimation using Phase Data," *IEEE Transactions on Acoustics, Speech, and Signal Processing*, Vol. ASSP-29, p. 471, June 1981.
59. Piersol, A. G., "Optimum Resolution Bandwidth for Spectral Analysis of Stationary Random Vibration Data," *Shock and Vibration*, Vol. 1, p. 33, 1993/1994.
60. Rice, S. O., "Statistical Properties of a Sine Wave plus Random Noise," *Bell System Technical Journal*, Vol. 27, p. 109, January 1948.
61. Rice, S. O., "Mathematical Analysis of Random Noise," in *Selected Papers on Noise and Stochastic Processes*, (N. Wax, ed.) Dover, New York, 1954.
62. Rice, H. J., and Fitzpatrick, J. S., "A Generalized Technique for Spectral Analysis of Nonlinear Systems," *Mechanical Systems and Signal Processing*, Vol. 2, p. 95, 1988.
63. Ross, S. M., *Introduction to Probability and Statistics for Engineers and Scientists*, Wiley, New York, 1987.
64. Rugh, W. J., *Nonlinear System Theory: The Volterra/Wiener Approach*, Johns Hopkins University Press, Baltimore, MD, 1981.
65. Schaeffer, H. G., "Finite Element Methods," Chapter 28, Part II in *Shock and Vibration Handbook*, 4th ed. (C. M. Harris, ed.), McGraw-Hill, New York, 1996.
66. Schetzen, M., *The Volterra and Wiener Theories of Nonlinear Systems*, Wiley–Interscience, New York, 1980.
67. Schmidt, H., "Resolution Bias Errors in Spectral Density, Frequency Response and Coherence Function Measurements," *Journal of Sound and Vibration*, Vol. 101, No. 3, p. 347, 1985.
68. Silverman, R. A., "Locally Stationary Random Processes," *Transactions of the IRE Information Theory*, Vol. IT-3, p. 182, September 1957.
69. Smallwood, D. O., "Using Singular Value Decomposition to Compute the Conditioned Cross-Spectral Density Matrix and Coherence Functions," *Proceedings of the 66th Shock and Vibration Symposium*, Vol. 1, p. 109, November 1995.
70. Stearns, S. D., and Rush, D. R., *Digital Signal Analysis*, 2nd ed., Prentice-Hall, Englewood Cliffs, New Jersey, 1990.
71. Stokey, W. F., "Vibrations of Systems Having Distributed Mass and Elasticity, Chapter 7 in *Shock and Vibration Handbook*, 4th ed. (C. M. Harris,ed.) McGraw-Hill, New York, 1996.
72. Taylor, J. L., *Computer-Based Data Acquisition Systems*, 2nd ed., Instrument Society of America, Research Triangle Park, NC, 1990.
73. Telemetry Group, Range Commander's Council, "Telemetry Applications Handbook," IRIG Document 119-88, White Sands, New Mexico, 1988.
74. Telemetry Group, Range Commander's Council, *"Telemetry Standards,"* IRIG Standard 106-93, White Sands, New Mexico, 1993.
75. Teolis, A., *Computational Signal Processing with Wavelets*, Birkhauser, Boston, 1998.
76. Welch, P. D., "The Use of Fast Fourier Transform for the Estimation of Power Spectra: A Method Based on Time Averaging Over Short, Modified Periodograms," *IEEE Transactions on Audio and Electroacoustics*, Vol. AU-15, No. 2, June 1967.
77. White, P. H., "Cross-Correlation in Structural Systems: Dispersive and Nondispersive Waves," *Journal of Acoustical Society of America*, Vol. 45, p. 1118, May 1969.
78. Winograd, S., "On Computing the Discrete Fourier Transform," *Mathematics of Computations*, Vol. 32, p. 175, January 1978.

79. Wirsching, P. H., Paez, T. L., and Ortiz, H., *Random Vibrations: Theory and Practice*, Wiley-Interscience, New York, 1995.
80. Wright, C. F., *Applied Measurement Engineering: How to Design Effective Mechanical Measurement Systems*, Prentice-Hall, Englewood Cliffs, NJ, 1995.
81. Yang, C. Y., *Random Vibration of Structures*, Wiley-Interscience, New York, 1986.
82. Zayed, A. I., *Advances in Shannon's Sampling Theory*, CRC Press, Boca Raton, Florida, 1993.

APPENDIX A

Statistical Tables

Table A.1   Ordinates of the Standardized Normal Density Function

$$p(x) = \frac{1}{\sqrt{2\pi}} e^{-z^2/2}$$

z	0.00	0.01	0.02	0.03	0.04	0.05	0.06	0.07	0.08	0.09
0.0	0.3989	0.3989	0.3989	0.3988	0.3986	0.3986	0.3982	0.3980	0.3977	0.3973
0.1	0.3970	0.3966	0.3961	0.3956	0.3951	0.3945	0.3939	0.3932	0.3925	0.3918
0.2	0.3910	0.3902	0.3894	0.3884	0.3876	0.3867	0.3857	0.3847	0.3836	0.3825
0.3	0.3814	0.3802	0.3790	0.3778	0.3765	0.3752	0.3739	0.3725	0.3712	0.3697
0.4	0.3683	0.3668	0.3653	0.3637	0.3621	0.3605	0.3589	0.3572	0.3555	0.3538
0.5	0.3521	0.3503	0.3485	0.3467	0.3448	0.3429	0.3410	0.3391	0.3372	0.3352
0.6	0.3332	0.3312	0.3292	0.3271	0.3251	0.3230	0.3209	0.3187	0.3166	0.3144
0.7	0.3123	0.3101	0.3079	0.3056	0.3034	0.3011	0.2989	0.2966	0.2943	0.2920
0.8	0.2897	0.2874	0.2850	0.2827	0.2803	0.2780	0.2756	0.2732	0.2709	0.2685
0.9	0.2661	0.2637	0.2613	0.2589	0.2565	0.2541	0.2516	0.2492	0.2468	0.2444
1.0	0.2420	0.2396	0.2371	0.2347	0.2323	0.2299	0.2275	0.2251	0.2227	0.2203
1.1	0.2179	0.2155	0.2131	0.2107	0.2083	0.2059	0.2036	0.2012	0.1989	0.1965
1.2	0.1942	0.1919	0.1895	0.1872	0.1849	0.1826	0.1804	0.1781	0.1758	0.1736
1.3	0.1714	0.1691	0.1669	0.1647	0.1626	0.1605	0.1582	0.1561	0.1539	0.1518
1.4	0.1497	0.1476	0.1456	0.1435	0.1415	0.1394	0.1374	0.1354	0.1334	0.1315
1.5	0.1295	0.1276	0.1257	0.1238	0.1219	0.1200	0.1282	0.1163	0.1145	0.1127
1.6	0.1109	0.1092	0.1074	0.1057	0.1040	0.1023	0.1006	0.0989	0.0973	0.0957
1.7	0.0940	0.0925	0.0909	0.0893	0.0878	0.0863	0.0848	0.0833	0.0818	0.0804
1.8	0.0790	0.0775	0.0761	0.0748	0.0734	0.0721	0.0707	0.0694	0.0681	0.0669
1.9	0.0656	0.0644	0.0632	0.0620	0.0608	0.0596	0.0584	0.0573	0.0562	0.0051

(*Continued*)

Random Data: Analysis and Measurement Procedures, Fourth Edition. By Julius S. Bendat and Allan G. Piersol
Copyright © 2010 John Wiley & Sons, Inc.

Table A.1 (*Continued*)

$$p(x) = \frac{1}{\sqrt{2\pi}} e^{-z^2/2}$$

z	0.00	0.01	0.02	0.03	0.04	0.05	0.06	0.07	0.08	0.09
2.0	0.0540	0.0529	0.0519	0.0508	0.0498	0.0488	0.0478	0.0468	0.0459	0.0449
2.1	0.0440	0.0431	0.0422	0.0413	0.0404	0.0396	0.0387	0.0379	0.0371	0.0363
2.2	0.0355	0.0347	0.0339	0.0332	0.0325	0.0317	0.0310	0.0303	0.0297	0.0290
2.3	0.0283	0.0277	0.0270	0.0264	0.0258	0.0252	0.0246	0.0241	0.0235	0.0229
2.4	0.0224	0.0219	0.0213	0.0208	0.0203	0.0198	0.0194	0.0189	0.0184	0.0180
2.5	0.0175	0.0171	0.0167	0.0163	0.0158	0.0154	0.0151	0.0147	0.0143	0.0139
2.6	0.0136	0.0132	0.0129	0.0126	0.0122	0.0119	0.0116	0.0113	0.0110	0.0107
2.7	0.0104	0.0101	0.0099	0.0096	0.0093	0.0091	0.0088	0.0086	0.0084	0.0081
2.8	0.0079	0.0077	0.0075	0.0073	0.0071	0.0069	0.0067	0.0065	0.0063	0.0061
2.9	0.0060	0.0058	0.0056	0.0055	0.0053	0.0051	0.0050	0.0048	0.0047	0.0046
3.0	0.0044	0.0043	0.0042	0.0040	0.0039	0.0038	0.0037	0.0036	0.0035	0.0034
3.1	0.0033	0.0032	0.0031	0.0030	0.0029	0.0028	0.0027	0.0026	0.0025	0.0025
3.2	0.0024	0.0023	0.0022	0.0022	0.0021	0.0020	0.0020	0.0019	0.0018	0.0018
3.3	0.0017	0.0017	0.0016	0.0016	0.0015	0.0015	0.0014	0.0014	0.0013	0.0013
3.4	0.0012	0.0012	0.0012	0.0011	0.0011	0.0010	0.0010	0.0010	0.0009	0.0009
3.5	0.0009	0.0008	0.0008	0.0008	0.0008	0.0007	0.0007	0.0007	0.0007	0.0006
3.6	0.0006	0.0006	0.0006	0.0005	0.0005	0.0005	0.0005	0.0005	0.0005	0.0004
3.7	0.0004	0.0004	0.0004	0.0004	0.0004	0.0004	0.0003	0.0003	0.0003	0.0003
3.8	0.0003	0.0003	0.0003	0.0003	0.0003	0.0002	0.0002	0.0002	0.0002	0.0002
3.9	0.0002	0.0002	0.0002	0.0002	0.0002	0.0002	0.0002	0.0002	0.0001	0.0001

Table A.2 Areas under Standardized Normal Density Function

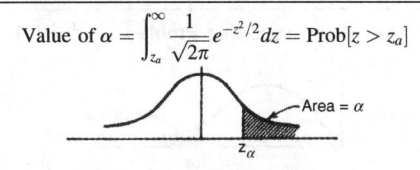

$$\text{Value of } \alpha = \int_{z_a}^{\infty} \frac{1}{\sqrt{2\pi}} e^{-z^2/2} dz = \text{Prob}[z > z_a]$$

z_α	0.00	0.01	0.02	0.03	0.04	0.05	0.06	0.07	0.08	0.09
0.0	0.5000	0.4960	0.4920	0.4880	0.4840	0.4801	0.4761	0.4721	0.4681	0.4641
0.1	0.4602	0.4562	0.4522	0.4483	0.4443	0.4404	0.4364	0.4325	0.4286	0.4247
0.2	0.4207	0.4168	0.4129	0.4090	0.4052	0.4013	0.3974	0.3936	0.3897	0.3859
0.3	0.3821	0.3783	0.3745	0.3707	0.3669	0.3632	0.3594	0.3557	0.3520	0.3483
0.4	0.3446	0.3409	0.3372	0.3336	0.3300	0.3264	0.3228	0.3192	0.3156	0.3121
0.5	0.3085	0.3050	0.3015	0.2981	0.2946	0.2912	0.2877	0.2843	0.2810	0.2776
0.6	0.2743	0.2709	0.2676	0.2643	0.2611	0.2578	0.2546	0.2514	0.2483	0.2451
0.7	0.2420	0.2389	0.2358	0.2327	0.2296	0.2266	0.2236	0.2206	0.2177	0.2148
0.8	0.2119	0.2090	0.2061	0.2033	0.2005	0.1977	0.1949	0.1922	0.1894	0.1867
0.9	0.1841	0.1814	0.1788	0.1762	0.1736	0.1711	0.1685	0.1660	0.1635	0.1611
1.0	0.1587	0.1562	0.1539	0.1515	0.1492	0.1469	0.1446	0.1423	0.1401	0.1379
1.1	0.1357	0.1335	0.1314	0.1292	0.1271	0.1251	0.1230	0.1210	0.1190	0.1170
1.2	0.1151	0.1131	0.1112	0.1093	0.1075	0.1056	0.1038	0.1020	0.1003	0.0985
1.3	0.0968	0.0951	0.0934	0.0918	0.0901	0.0885	0.0869	0.0853	0.0838	0.0823
1.4	0.0808	0.0793	0.0778	0.0764	0.0749	0.0735	0.0721	0.0708	0.0694	0.0681
1.5	0.0668	0.0655	0.0643	0.0630	0.0618	0.0606	0.0594	0.0582	0.0571	0.0539
1.6	0.0548	0.0537	0.0526	0.0516	0.0505	0.0495	0.0485	0.0475	0.0465	0.0455
1.7	0.0446	0.0436	0.0427	0.0418	0.0409	0.0401	0.0392	0.0384	0.0375	0.0367
1.8	0.0359	0.0351	0.0344	0.0336	0.0329	0.0322	0.0314	0.0307	0.0301	0.0294
1.9	0.0287	0.0281	0.0274	0.0268	0.0262	0.0256	0.0250	0.0244	0.0239	0.0233
2.0	0.0228	0.0222	0.0217	0.0212	0.0207	0.0202	0.0197	0.0192	0.0188	0.0183
2.1	0.0179	0.0174	0.0170	0.0166	0.0162	0.0158	0.0154	0.0150	0.0146	0.0143
2.2	0.0139	0.0136	0.0132	0.0129	0.0125	0.0122	0.0119	0.0116	0.0113	0.0110
2.3	0.0107	0.0104	0.0102	0.00990	0.00964	0.00939	0.00914	0.00889	0.00866	0.00842
2.4	0.00820	0.00798	0.00776	0.00755	0.00734	0.00714	0.00695	0.00676	0.00657	0.00639
2.5	0.00621	0.09604	0.00587	0.00570	0.00554	0.00539	0.00523	0.00508	0.00494	0.00480
2.6	0.00466	0.00453	0.00440	0.00427	0.00415	0.00402	0.00391	0.00379	0.00368	0.00357
2.7	0.00347	0.00336	0.00326	0.00317	0.00307	0.00298	0.00289	0.00280	0.00272	0.00264
2.8	0.00256	0.00248	0.00240	0.00233	0.00226	0.00219	0.00212	0.00205	0.00199	0.00193
2.9	0.00187	0.00181	0.00175	0.00169	0.00164	0.00159	0.00154	0.00149	0.00144	0.00139

Table A.3 Percentage Points of Chi-Square Distribution

Value of $\chi^2_{n;\alpha}$ such that $\text{Prob}[\chi^2_n > \chi^2_{n;\alpha}] = \alpha$

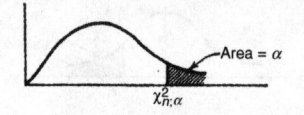

n	0.995	0.990	0.975	0.950	0.900	0.10	0.05	0.025	0.010	0.005
1	0.000039	0.00016	0.00098	0.0039	0.0158	2.71	3.84	5.02	6.63	7.88
2	0.0100	0.0201	0.0506	0.103	0.211	4.61	5.99	7.38	9.21	10.60
3	0.0717	0.115	0.216	0.352	0.584	6.25	7.81	9.35	11.34	12.84
4	0.207	0.297	0.484	0.711	1.06	7.78	9.49	11.14	13.28	14.86
5	0.412	0.554	0.831	1.15	1.61	9.24	11.07	12.83	15.09	16.75
6	0.676	0.872	1.24	1.64	2.20	10.64	12.59	14.45	16.81	18.55
7	0.989	1.24	1.69	2.17	2.83	12.02	14.07	16.01	18.48	20.28
8	1.34	1.65	2.18	2.73	3.49	13.36	15.51	17.53	20.09	21.96
9	1.73	2.09	2.70	3.33	4.17	14.68	16.92	19.02	21.67	23.59
10	2.16	2.56	3.25	3.94	4.87	15.99	18.31	20.48	23.21	25.19
11	2.60	3.05	3.82	4.57	5.58	17.28	19.68	21.92	24.73	26.76
12	3.07	3.57	4.40	5.23	6.30	18.55	21.03	23.34	26.22	28.30
13	3.57	4.11	5.01	5.89	7.04	19.81	22.36	24.74	27.69	29.82
14	4.07	4.66	5.63	6.57	7.79	21.06	23.68	26.12	29.14	31.32
15	4.60	5.23	6.26	7.26	8.55	22.31	25.00	27.49	30.58	32.80
16	5.14	5.81	6.91	7.96	9.31	23.54	26.30	28.85	32.00	34.27
17	5.70	6.41	7.56	8.67	10.08	24.77	27.59	30.19	33.41	35.72
18	6.26	7.01	8.23	9.39	10.86	25.99	28.87	31.53	34.81	37.16
19	6.84	7.63	8.91	10.12	11.65	27.20	30.14	32.85	36.19	38.58
20	7.43	8.26	9.59	10.85	12.44	28.41	31.41	34.17	37.57	40.00
21	8.03	8.90	10.28	11.59	13.24	29.62	32.67	35.48	38.93	41.40
22	8.64	9.54	10.98	12.34	14.04	30.81	33.92	36.78	40.29	42.80
23	9.26	10.20	11.69	13.09	14.85	32.01	35.17	38.08	41.64	44.18
24	9.89	10.86	12.40	13.85	15.66	33.20	36.42	39.36	42.98	45.56
25	10.52	11.52	13.12	14.61	16.47	34.38	37.65	40.65	44.31	46.93
26	11.16	12.20	13.84	13.38	17.29	35.56	38.88	41.92	45.64	48.29
27	11.81	12.88	14.57	16.15	18.11	36.74	40.11	43.19	46.96	49.64
28	12.46	13.56	15.31	16.93	18.94	37.92	41.34	44.46	48.28	50.99
29	13.12	14.26	16.05	17.71	19.77	39.09	42.56	45.72	49.59	52.34
30	13.79	14.95	16.79	18.49	20.60	40.26	43.77	46.98	50.89	53.67
40	20.71	22.16	24.43	26.51	29.05	51.81	55.76	59.34	63.69	66.77
60	35.53	37.48	40.48	43.19	46.46	74.40	79.08	83.30	88.38	91.95
120	83.85	86.92	91.58	95.70	100.62	140.23	146.57	152.21	158.95	163.65

For $n > 120$, $\chi^2_{n;\alpha} \approx n\left[1 - \frac{2}{9n} + z_\alpha \sqrt{\frac{2}{9n}}\right]^2$ where z_α is the desired percentage point for a standardized normal distribution.

Table A.4 Percentage Points of t Distribution

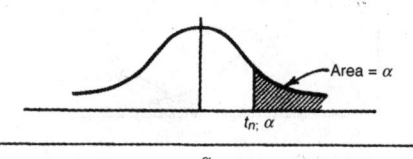

Value of $t_{n;\alpha}$ such that $\text{Prob}[t_n > t_{n;\alpha}] = \alpha$

n	0.10	0.050	0.025	0.010	0.005
1	3.078	6.314	12.706	31.821	63.657
2	1.886	2.920	4.303	6.965	9.925
3	1.638	2.353	3.182	4.541	5.841
4	1.533	2.132	2.776	3.747	4.604
5	1.476	2.015	2.571	3.365	4.032
6	1.440	1.943	2.447	3.143	3.707
7	1.415	1.895	2.365	2.998	3.499
8	1.397	1.860	2.306	2.896	3.355
9	1.383	1.833	2.262	2.821	3.250
10	1.372	1.812	2.228	2.764	3.169
11	1.363	1.796	2.201	2.718	3.106
12	1.356	1.782	2.179	2.681	3.055
13	1.350	1.771	2.160	2.650	3.012
14	1.345	1.761	2.145	2.624	2.977
15	1.341	1.753	2.131	2.602	2.947
16	1.337	1.746	2.120	2.583	2.921
17	1.333	1.740	2.110	2.567	2.898
18	1.330	1.734	2.101	2.552	2.878
19	1.328	1.729	2.093	2.539	2.861
20	1.325	1.725	2.086	2.528	2.845
21	1.323	1.721	2.080	2.518	2.831
22	1.321	1.717	2.074	2.508	2.819
23	1.319	1.714	2.069	2.500	2.807
24	1.318	1.711	2.064	2.492	2.797
25	1.316	1.708	2.060	2.485	2.787
26	1.315	1.706	2.056	2.479	2.779
27	1.314	1.703	2.052	2.473	2.771
28	3.313	1.701	2.048	2.467	2.763
29	1.311	1.699	2.045	2.462	2.756
30	1.310	1.697	2.042	2.457	2.750
40	1.303	1.684	2.021	2.423	2.704
60	1.296	1.671	2.000	2.390	2.660
120	1.289	1.658	1.980	2.358	2.617

$\alpha = 0.995, 0.990, 0.975, 0.950$, and 0.900 follow from $t_{n;1-\alpha} = -t_{n;\alpha}$

Table A.5(a) Percentage Points of F Distribution

Values of $F_{n_1,n_2;0.05}$ such that $\text{Prob}[F_{n_1,n_2} > F_{n_1 n_2;0.05}] = 0.05$

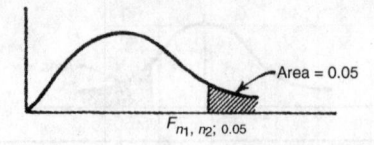

n_2 \ n_1	1	2	3	4	5	6	7	8	9	10	11	12	13	14	16
1	161	200	216	225	230	234	237	239	241	242	243	244	245	245	246
2	18.5	19.0	19.2	19.2	19.3	19.3	19.4	19.4	19.4	19.4	19.4	19.4	19.4	19.4	19.4
3	10.1	9.55	9.28	9.12	9.01	8.94	8.89	8.85	8.81	8.79	8.76	8.74	8.73	8.71	8.69
4	7.71	6.94	6.59	6.39	6.26	6.16	6.09	6.04	6.00	5.96	5.94	5.91	5.89	5.87	5.84
5	6.61	5.79	5.41	5.19	5.05	4.95	4.88	4.82	4.77	4.73	4.70	4.68	4.66	4.64	4.60
6	5.99	5.14	4.76	4.53	4.39	4.28	4.21	4.15	4.10	4.06	4.03	4.00	3.98	3.96	3.92
7	5.59	4.74	4.35	4.12	3.97	3.87	3.79	3.73	3.68	3.64	3.60	3.57	3.55	3.53	3.49
8	5.32	4.46	4.07	3.84	3.69	3.58	3.50	3.44	3.39	3.35	3.31	3.28	3.26	3.24	3.20
9	5.12	4.26	3.86	3.63	3.48	3.37	3.29	3.23	3.18	3.14	3.10	3.07	3.05	3.03	2.99
10	4.96	4.10	3.71	3.48	3.33	3.22	3.14	3.07	3.02	2.98	2.94	2.91	2.89	2.86	2.83
11	4.84	3.98	3.59	3.36	3.20	3.09	3.01	2.95	2.90	2.85	2.82	2.79	2.76	2.74	2.70
12	4.75	3.89	3.49	3.25	3.11	3.00	2.91	2.85	2.80	2.75	2.72	2.69	2.66	2.64	2.60
13	4.67	3.81	3.41	3.18	3.03	2.92	2.83	2.77	2.71	2.67	2.63	2.60	2.58	2.55	2.51
14	4.60	3.74	3.35	3.11	2.96	2.85	2.76	2.70	2.65	2.60	2.57	2.53	2.51	2.48	2.44
16	4.49	3.63	3.24	3.01	2.85	2.74	2.66	2.59	2.54	2.49	2.46	2.42	2.40	2.37	2.33
18	4.41	3.55	3.16	2.93	2.77	2.66	2.58	2.51	2.46	2.41	2.37	2.34	2.31	2.29	2.25
20	4.35	3.49	3.10	2.87	2.71	2.60	2.51	2.45	2.39	2.35	2.31	2.28	2.25	2.22	2.18
22	4.30	3.44	3.05	2.82	2.66	2.55	2.46	2.40	2.34	2.30	2.26	2.23	2.20	2.17	2.13
24	4.26	3.40	3.01	2.78	2.62	2.51	2.42	2.36	2.30	2.25	2.21	2.18	2.15	2.13	2.09
26	4.23	3.37	2.98	2.74	2.59	2.47	2.39	2.32	2.27	2.22	2.18	2.15	2.12	2.09	2.05
28	4.20	3.34	2.95	2.71	2.56	2.45	2.36	2.29	2.24	2.19	2.15	2.12	2.09	2.06	2.02
30	4.17	3.32	2.92	2.69	2.53	2.42	2.33	2.27	2.21	2.16	2.13	2.09	2.06	2.04	1.99
40	4.08	3.23	2.84	2.61	2.45	2.34	2.25	2.18	2.12	2.08	2.04	2.00	1.97	1.95	1.90
50	4.03	3.18	2.79	2.56	2.40	2.29	2.20	2.13	2.07	2.03	1.99	1.95	1.92	1.89	1.85
60	4.00	3.15	2.76	2.53	2.37	2.25	2.17	2.10	2.04	1.99	1.95	1.92	1.89	1.86	1.82
80	3.96	3.11	2.72	2.49	2.33	2.21	2.13	2.06	2.00	1.95	1.91	1.88	1.84	1.82	1.77
100	3.94	3.09	2.70	2.46	2.31	2.19	2.10	2.03	1.97	1.93	1.89	1.85	1.82	1.79	1.75
200	3.89	3.04	2.65	2.42	2.26	2.14	2.06	1.98	1.93	1.88	1.84	1.80	1.77	1.74	1.69
500	3.86	3.01	2.62	2.39	2.23	2.12	2.03	1.96	1.90	1.85	1.81	1.77	1.74	1.71	1.66
∞	3.84	3.00	2.60	2.37	2.21	2.10	2.01	1.94	1.88	1.83	1.79	1.75	1.72	1.69	1.64

Table A.5(a) (Continued)

18	20	22	24	26	28	30	40	50	60	80	100	200	500	∞	n_1 / n_2
247	248	249	249	249	250	250	251	252	252	252	253	254	254	254	1
19.4	19.5	19.5	19.5	19.5	19.5	19.5	19.5	19.5	19.5	19.5	19.5	19.5	19.5	19.5	2
8.67	8.66	8.65	8.64	8.63	8.62	8.62	8.59	8.59	8.57	8.56	8.55	8.54	8.53	8.53	3
5.82	5.80	5.79	5.77	5.76	5.75	5.75	5.72	5.70	5.69	5.67	5.66	5.65	5.64	5.63	4
4.58	3.56	4.54	4.53	4.52	4.50	4.50	4.46	4.44	4.43	4.41	4.41	4.39	4.37	4.37	5
3.90	3.87	3.86	3.84	3.83	3.82	3.81	3.77	3.75	3.74	3.72	3.71	3.69	3.68	3.67	6
3.47	3.44	3.43	3.41	3.40	3.39	3.38	3.34	3.32	3.30	3.29	3.27	3.25	3.24	3.23	7
3.17	3.15	3.13	3.12	3.10	3.09	3.08	3.04	3.02	3.01	2.99	2.97	2.95	2.94	2.93	8
2.96	2.94	2.92	2.90	2.89	2.87	2.86	2.83	2.80	2.79	2.77	2.76	2.73	2.72	2.71	9
2.80	2.77	2.75	2.74	2.72	2.71	2.70	2.66	2.64	2.62	2.60	2.59	2.56	2.55	2.54	10
2.67	2.65	2.63	2.61	2.59	2.58	2.57	2.53	2.51	2.49	2.47	2.46	2.43	2.42	2.40	11
2.57	2.54	2.52	2.51	2.49	2.48	2.47	2.43	2.40	2.38	2.36	2.35	2.32	2.31	2.30	12
2.48	2.46	2.44	2.42	2.41	2.39	2.38	2.34	2.31	2.30	2.27	2.26	2.23	2.22	2.21	13
2.41	2.38	2.37	2.35	2.33	2.32	2.31	2.27	2.24	2.22	2.20	2.19	2.16	2.14	2.13	14
2.30	2.28	2.25	2.24	2.22	2.21	2.19	2.15	2.12	2.11	2.08	2.07	2.04	2.02	2.01	16
2.22	2.19	2.17	2.15	2.13	2.12	2.11	2.06	2.04	2.02	1.99	1.98	1.95	1.93	1.92	18
2.15	2.12	2.10	2.08	2.07	2.05	2.04	1.99	1.97	1.95	1.92	1.91	1.88	1.86	1.84	20
2.10	2.07	2.05	2.03	2.01	2.00	1.98	1.94	1.91	1.89	1.86	1.85	1.82	1.80	1.78	22
2.05	2.03	2.00	1.98	1.97	1.95	1.94	1.89	1.86	1.84	1.82	1.80	1.77	1.75	1.73	24
2.02	1.99	1.97	1.95	1.93	1.91	1.90	1.84	1.82	1.80	1.78	1.76	1.73	1.71	1.69	26
1.99	1.96	1.93	1.91	1.90	1.88	1.87	1.82	1.79	1.77	1.74	1.73	1.69	1.67	1.65	28
1.96	1.93	1.91	1.89	1.87	1.85	1.84	1.79	1.76	1.74	1.71	1.70	1.66	1.64	1.62	30
1.87	1.84	1.81	1.79	1.77	1.76	1.74	1.69	1.66	1.64	1.61	1.59	1.55	1.53	1.51	40
1.81	1.78	1.76	1.74	1.72	1.70	1.69	1.63	1.60	1.58	1.54	1.52	1.48	1.46	1.44	50
1.78	1.75	1.72	1.70	1.68	1.66	1.65	1.59	1.56	1.53	1.50	1.48	1.44	1.41	1.39	60
1.73	1.70	1.68	1.65	1.63	1.62	1.60	1.54	1.51	1.48	1.45	1.43	1.38	1.35	1.32	80
1.71	1.68	1.65	1.63	1.61	1.59	1.57	1.52	1.48	1.45	1.41	1.39	1.34	1.31	1.28	100
1.66	1.62	1.60	1.57	1.55	1.53	1.52	1.46	1.41	1.39	1.35	1.32	1.26	1.22	1.19	200
1.62	1.59	1.56	1.54	1.52	1.50	1.48	1.42	1.38	1.34	1.30	1.28	1.21	1.16	1.11	500
1.60	1.57	1.54	1.52	1.50	1.48	1.46	1.39	1.35	1.32	1.27	1.24	1.17	1.11	1.00	∞

Table A.5 (b) Percentage Points of F Distribution

Values of $F_{n_1,n_2;0.025}$ such that $\text{Prob}[F_{n_1,n_2} > F_{n_1 n_2;0.025}] = 0.025$

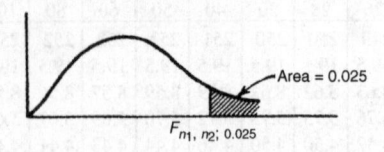

n_2 \ n_1	1	2	3	4	5	6	7	8	9	10	11	12	13	14	16
1	648	800	864	900	922	937	948	957	963	969	973	977	980	983	987
2	38.5	39.0	39.2	39.2	39.3	39.3	39.4	39.4	39.4	39.4	39.4	39.4	39.4	39.4	39.4
3	17.4	16.0	15.4	15.1	14.9	14.7	14.6	14.5	14.5	14.4	14.4	14.3	14.3	14.3	14.2
4	12.2	10.6	9.98	9.60	9.36	9.20	9.07	8.98	8.90	8.84	8.79	8.75	8.72	8.69	8.64
5	10.0	8.43	7.76	7.39	7.15	6.98	6.85	6.76	6.68	6.62	6.37	6.52	6.49	6.46	6.41
6	8.81	7.26	6.60	6.23	5.99	5.82	5.70	5.60	5.52	5.46	5.41	5.37	5.33	5.30	5.25
7	8.07	6.54	5.89	5.52	5.29	5.12	4.99	4.90	4.82	4.76	4.71	4.67	4.63	4.60	4.54
8	7.57	6.06	5.42	5.05	4.82	4.65	4.53	4.43	4.36	4.30	4.24	4.20	4.16	4.13	4.08
9	7.21	5.71	5.08	4.72	4.48	4.32	4.20	4.10	4.03	3.96	3.91	3.87	3.83	3.60	3.74
10	6.94	5.46	4.83	4.47	4.24	4.07	3.95	3.85	3.78	3.72	3.66	3.62	3.58	3.55	3.50
11	6.72	5.26	4.63	4.28	4.04	3.88	3.76	3.66	3.59	3.53	3.47	3.43	3.39	3.36	3.30
12	6.55	5.10	4.47	4.12	3.89	3.73	3.61	3.51	3.44	3.37	3.32	3.28	3.24	3.21	3.15
13	6.41	4.97	4.35	4.00	3.77	3.60	3.48	3.39	3.31	3.25	3.20	3.15	3.12	3.08	3.03
14	6.30	4.86	4.24	3.89	3.66	3.50	3.38	3.29	3.21	3.15	3.09	3.05	3.01	2.98	2.92
16	6.12	4.69	4.08	3.73	3.50	3.34	3.22	3.12	3.05	2.99	2.93	2.89	2.85	2.82	2.76
18	5.98	4.56	3.95	3.61	3.38	3.22	3.10	3.01	2.93	2.87	2.81	2.77	2.73	2.70	2.64
20	5.87	4.46	3.86	3.51	3.29	3.13	3.01	2.91	2.84	2.77	2.72	2.68	2.64	2.60	2.55
22	5.79	4.38	3.78	3.44	3.22	3.05	2.93	2.84	2.76	2.70	2.65	2.60	2.56	2.53	2.47
24	5.72	4.32	3.72	3.38	3.15	2.99	2.87	2.78	2.70	2.64	2.59	2.54	2.50	2.47	2.41
26	5.66	4.27	3.67	3.33	3.10	2.94	2.82	2.73	2.65	2.59	2.54	2.49	2.45	2.42	2.36
28	5.61	4.22	3.63	3.29	3.06	2.90	2.78	2.69	2.61	2.55	2.49	2.45	2.41	2.37	2.32
30	5.57	4.18	3.59	3.25	3.03	2.87	2.75	2.65	2.57	2.51	2.46	2.41	2.37	2.34	2.28
40	5.42	4.05	3.46	3.13	2.90	2.74	2.62	2.53	2.45	2.39	2.33	2.29	2.25	2.21	2.15
50	5.34	3.98	3.39	3.06	2.83	2.67	2.55	2.46	2.38	2.32	2.26	2.22	2.18	2.14	2.08
60	5.29	3.93	3.34	3.01	2.79	2.63	2.51	2.41	2.33	2.27	2.22	2.17	2.13	2.09	2.03
80	5.22	3.86	3.28	2.95	2.73	2.57	2.45	2.36	2.38	2.21	2.16	2.11	2.07	2.03	1.97
100	5.18	3.83	3.25	2.92	2.70	2.54	2.42	2.32	2.24	2.18	2.12	2.08	2.04	2.00	1.94
200	5.10	3.76	3.18	2.85	2.63	2.47	2.35	2.26	2.18	2.11	2.06	2.01	1.97	1.93	1.87
500	5.05	3.72	3.14	2.81	2.59	2.43	2.31	2.22	2.14	2.07	2.02	1.97	1.93	1.89	1.83
∞	5.02	3.69	3.12	2.79	2.57	2.41	2.29	2.19	2.11	2.05	1.99	1.94	1.90	1.87	1.80

Table A.5(b)   (*Continued*)

18	20	22	24	26	28	30	40	50	60	80	100	200	500	∞	n_1 / n_2
990	993	995	997	999	1000	1001	1006	1008	1010	1012	1013	1016	1017	1018	1
39.4	39.4	39.5	39.5	39.5	39.5	39.5	39.5	39.5	39.5	39.5	39.5	39.5	39.5	39.5	2
14.2	14.2	14.1	14.1	14.1	14.1	14.1	14.0	14.0	14.0	14.0	14.0	13.9	13.9	13.9	3
8.60	8.56	8.53	8.51	8.49	8.48	8.46	8.41	8.38	8.36	8.33	8.32	8.29	8.27	8.26	4
6.37	6.33	6.30	6.28	6.26	6.24	6.23	6.18	6.14	6.12	6.10	6.08	6.05	6.03	6.01	5
5.21	5.17	5.14	5.12	5.10	5.08	5.07	5.01	4.98	4.96	4.93	4.92	4.88	4.86	4.85	6
4.50	4.47	4.44	4.42	4.39	4.38	4.36	4.31	4.28	4.25	4.23	4.21	4.18	4.16	4.14	7
4.03	4.00	3.97	3.95	3.93	3.91	3.89	3.84	3.81	3.78	3.76	3.74	3.70	3.68	3.67	8
3.70	3.67	3.64	3.61	3.59	3.58	3.56	3.51	3.47	3.45	3.42	3.40	3.37	3.35	3.33	9
3.45	3.42	3.39	3.37	3.34	3.33	3.31	3.26	3.22	3.20	3.17	3.15	3.12	3.09	3.08	10
3.26	3.23	3.20	3.17	3.15	3.13	3.12	3.06	3.03	3.00	2.97	2.96	2.92	2.90	2.88	11
3.11	3.07	3.04	3.02	3.00	2.98	2.96	2.91	2.87	2.85	2.82	2.80	2.76	2.74	2.72	12
2.98	2.95	2.92	2.89	2.87	2.85	2.84	2.78	2.74	2.72	2.69	2.67	2.63	2.61	2.60	13
2.88	2.84	2.81	2.79	2.77	2.75	2.73	2.67	2.64	2.61	2.58	2.56	2.53	2.50	2.49	14
2.72	2.68	2.65	2.63	2.60	2.58	2.57	2.51	2.47	2.45	2.42	2.40	2.36	2.33	2.32	16
2.60	2.56	2.53	2.50	2.48	2.46	2.44	2.38	2.35	2.32	2.29	2.27	2.23	2.20	2.19	18
2.50	2.46	2.43	2.41	2.39	2.37	2.35	2.29	2.25	2.22	2.19	2.17	2.13	2.10	2.09	20
2.43	2.39	2.36	2.33	2.31	2.29	2.27	2.21	2.17	2.14	2.11	2.09	2.05	2.02	2.00	22
2.36	2.33	2.30	2.27	2.25	2.23	2.21	2.15	2.11	2.08	2.05	2.02	1.98	1.95	1.94	24
2.31	2.28	2.24	2.22	2.19	2.17	2.16	2.09	2.05	2.03	1.99	1.97	1.92	1.90	1.88	26
2.27	2.23	2.20	2.17	2.15	2.13	2.11	2.05	2.01	1.98	1.94	1.92	1.88	1.85	1.83	28
2.23	2.20	2.16	2.14	2.11	2.09	2.07	2.01	1.97	1.94	1.90	1.88	1.84	1.81	1.79	30
2.11	2.07	2.03	2.01	1.98	1.96	1.94	1.88	1.83	1.80	1.76	1.74	1.69	1.66	1.64	40
2.03	1.99	1.96	1.93	1.91	1.88	1.87	1.80	1.75	1.72	1.68	1.66	1.60	1.57	1.55	50
1.98	1.94	1.91	1.88	1.86	1.83	1.82	1.74	1.70	1.67	1.62	1.60	1.54	1.51	1.48	60
1.93	1.88	1.85	1.82	1.79	1.77	1.75	1.68	1.63	1.60	1.55	1.53	1.47	1.43	1.40	80
1.89	1.85	1.81	1.78	1.76	1.74	1.71	1.64	1.59	1.56	1.51	1.48	1.42	1.38	1.35	100
1.82	1.78	1.74	1.71	1.68	1.66	1.64	1.56	1.51	1.47	1.42	1.39	1.32	1.27	1.23	200
1.78	1.74	1.70	1.67	1.64	1.62	1.60	1.51	1.46	1.42	1.37	1.34	1.25	1.19	1.14	500
1.75	1.71	1.67	1.64	1.61	1.59	1.57	1.48	1.43	1.39	1.33	1.30	1.21	1.13	1.00	∞

Table A.5(c)   Percentage Points of F Distribution

Values of $F_{n_1,n_2;0.01}$ such that $\text{Prob}[F_{n_1,n_2} > F_{n_1 n_2;0.01}] = 0.01$

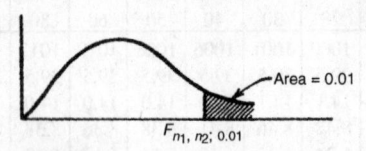

Area = 0.01

$F_{n_1, n_2; 0.01}$

n_2 \ n_1	1	2	3	4	5	6	7	8	9	10	11	12	13	14	16
*1	405	500	540	563	576	586	593	598	602	606	608	611	613	614	617
2	98.5	99.0	99.2	99.2	99.3	99.3	99.4	99.4	99.4	99.4	99.4	99.4	99.4	99.4	99.4
3	34.1	30.8	29.5	28.7	28.2	27.9	27.7	27.5	27.3	27.2	27.1	27.1	27.0	26.9	26.8
4	21.2	18.0	16.7	16.0	15.5	15.2	15.0	14.8	14.7	14.5	14.4	14.4	14.3	14.2	14.2
5	16.3	13.3	12.1	11.4	11.0	10.7	10.5	10.3	10.2	10.1	9.96	9.89	9.82	9.77	9.68
6	13.7	10.9	9.78	9.15	8.75	8.47	8.26	8.10	7.98	7.87	7.79	7.72	7.66	7.60	7.52
7	12.2	9.55	8.45	7.85	7.46	7.19	6.99	6.84	6.72	6.62	6.54	6.47	6.41	6.36	6.27
8	11.3	8.65	7.59	7.01	6.63	6.37	6.18	6.03	5.91	5.81	5.73	5.67	5.61	5.56	5.48
9	10.6	8.02	6.99	6.42	6.06	5.80	5.61	5.47	5.35	5.26	5.18	5.11	5.05	5.00	4.92
10	10.0	7.56	6.55	5.99	5.64	5.39	5.20	5.06	4.94	4.85	4.77	4.71	4.65	4.60	4.52
11	9.65	7.21	6.22	5.67	5.32	5.07	4.89	4.74	4.63	4.54	4.46	4.40	4.34	4.29	4.21
12	9.33	6.93	5.95	5.41	5.06	4.82	4.64	4.50	4.39	4.30	4.22	4.16	4.10	4.05	3.97
13	9.07	6.70	5.74	5.21	4.86	4.62	4.44	4.30	4.19	4.10	4.02	3.96	3.91	3.86	3.78
14	8.86	6.51	5.56	5.04	4.70	4.46	4.28	4.14	4.03	3.94	3.86	3.80	3.75	3.70	3.62
16	8.53	6.23	5.29	4.77	4.44	4.20	4.03	3.89	3.78	3.69	3.62	3.55	3.50	3.45	3.37
18	8.29	6.01	5.09	4.58	4.25	4.01	3.84	3.71	3.60	3.51	3.43	3.37	3.32	3.27	3.19
20	8.10	5.85	4.94	4.43	4.10	3.87	3.70	3.56	3.46	3.37	3.29	3.23	3.18	3.13	3.05
22	7.95	5.72	4.82	4.31	3.99	3.76	3.59	3.45	3.35	3.26	3.18	3.12	3.07	3.02	2.94
24	7.82	5.61	4.72	4.22	3.90	3.67	3.50	3.36	3.26	3.17	3.09	3.03	2.98	2.93	2.85
26	7.72	5.53	4.64	4.14	3.82	3.59	3.42	3.29	3.18	3.09	3.02	2.96	2.90	2.86	2.78
28	7.64	5.45	4.57	4.07	3.75	3.53	3.36	3.23	3.12	3.03	2.96	2.90	2.84	2.79	2.72
30	7.56	5.39	4.51	4.02	3.70	3.47	3.30	3.17	3.07	2.98	2.91	2.84	2.79	2.74	7.66
40	7.31	5.18	4.11	3.83	3.51	3.29	3.12	2.99	2.89	2.80	2.73	2.66	2.61	2.56	2.48
50	7.17	5.06	4.20	3.72	3.41	3.19	3.02	2.89	2.79	2.70	2.63	2.56	2.51	2.46	2.38
60	7.08	4.98	4.13	3.65	3.34	3.12	2.95	2.82	2.72	2.63	2.56	2.50	2.44	2.39	2.31
80	6.96	4.88	4.04	3.56	3.26	3.04	2.87	2.74	2.64	2.55	2.48	2.42	2.36	2.31	2.23
100	6.90	4.82	3.98	3.51	3.21	2.99	2.82	2.69	2.59	2.50	2.43	2.37	2.31	2.26	2.19
200	6.76	4.71	3.88	3.41	3.11	2.89	2.73	2.60	2.50	2.41	2.34	2.27	2.22	2.17	2.09
500	6.69	4.65	3.82	3.36	3.05	2.84	2.68	2.55	2.44	2.36	2.28	2.22	2.17	2.12	2.04
∞	6.63	4.61	3.78	3.32	3.02	2.80	2.64	2.51	2.41	2.32	2.25	2.18	2.13	2.08	2.00

Table A.5(c) (Continued)

18	20	22	24	26	28	30	40	50	60	80	100	200	500	∞	n_1 / n_2
619	621	622	623	624	625	626	629	630	631	633	633	635	636	637	1
99.4	99.4	99.5	99.5	99.5	99.5	99.5	99.5	99.5	99.5	99.5	99.5	99.5	99.5	99.5	2
26.8	26.7	26.6	26.6	26.6	26.5	26.5	26.4	26.4	26.3	26.3	26.2	26.2	26.1	26.1	3
14.1	14.0	14.0	13.9	13.9	13.9	13.8	13.7	13.7	13.7	13.6	13.6	13.5	13.5	13.5	4
9.61	9.55	9.51	9.47	9.43	9.40	9.38	9.29	9.24	9.20	9.16	9.13	9.08	9.04	9.02	5
7.45	7.40	7.35	7.31	7.28	7.25	7.23	7.14	7.09	7.06	7.01	6.99	6.93	6.90	6.88	6
6.21	6.16	6.11	6.07	6.04	6.02	5.99	5.91	5.86	5.82	5.78	5.75	5.70	5.67	5.65	7
5.41	5.36	5.32	5.28	5.25	5.22	5.20	5.12	5.07	5.03	4.99	4.96	4.91	4.88	4.85	8
4.86	4.81	4.77	4.73	4.70	4.67	4.65	4.57	4.52	4.48	4.44	4.42	4.36	4.33	4.31	9
4.46	4.41	4.36	4.33	4.30	4.27	4.25	4.17	4.12	4.08	4.04	4.01	3.96	3.93	3.91	10
4.15	4.10	4.06	4.02	3.99	3.96	3.94	3.86	3.81	3.78	3.73	3.71	3.66	3.62	3.60	11
3.91	3.86	3.82	3.78	3.75	3.72	3.70	3.62	3.57	3.54	3.49	3.47	3.41	3.38	3.36	12
3.72	3.66	3.62	3.59	3.56	3.53	3.51	3.43	3.38	3.34	3.30	3.27	3.22	3.19	3.16	13
3.56	3.51	3.46	3.43	3.40	3.37	3.35	3.27	3.22	3.18	3.14	3.11	3.06	3.03	3.00	14
3.31	3.26	3.22	3.18	3.15	3.12	3.10	3.02	2.97	2.93	2.89	2.86	2.81	2.78	2.75	16
3.13	3.08	3.03	3.00	2.97	2.94	2.92	2.84	2.78	2.75	2.70	2.68	2.62	2.59	2.57	18
2.99	2.94	2.90	2.86	2.83	2.80	2.78	2.69	2.64	2.61	2.56	2.54	2.48	2.44	2.42	20
2.88	2.83	2.78	2.75	2.72	2.69	2.67	2.58	2.53	2.50	2.45	2.42	2.36	2.33	2.31	22
2.79	2.74	2.70	2.66	2.63	2.60	2.58	2.49	2.44	2.40	2.36	2.33	2.27	2.24	2.21	24
2.72	2.66	2.62	2.58	2.55	2.53	2.50	2.42	2.36	2.33	2.28	2.25	2.19	2.16	2.13	26
2.65	2.60	2.56	2.32	2.49	2.46	2.44	2.35	2.30	2.26	2.22	2.19	2.13	2.09	2.06	28
2.60	2.55	2.51	2.47	2.44	2.41	2.39	2.30	2.25	2.21	2.16	2.13	2.07	2.03	2.01	30
2.42	2.37	2.33	2.29	2.26	2.23	2.20	2.11	2.06	2.02	1.97	1.94	1.87	1.83	1.80	40
2.32	2.27	2.22	2.18	2.15	2.12	2.10	2.01	1.95	1.91	1.86	1.82	1.76	1.71	1.68	50
2.25	2.20	2.15	2.12	2.08	2.05	2.03	1.94	1.88	1.84	1.78	1.75	1.68	1.63	1.60	60
2.17	2.12	2.07	2.03	2.00	1.97	1.94	1.85	1.79	1.75	1.69	1.66	1.58	1.53	1.49	80
2.12	2.07	2.02	1.98	1.94	1.92	1.89	1.80	1.73	1.69	1.63	1.60	1.52	1.47	1.43	100
2.02	1.97	1.93	1.89	1.85	1.82	1.79	1.69	1.63	1.58	1.52	1.48	1.39	1.33	1.28	200
1.97	1.92	1.87	1.83	1.79	1.76	1.74	1.63	1.56	1.52	1.45	1.41	1.31	1.23	1.16	500
1.93	1.88	1.83	1.79	1.76	1.72	1.70	1.59	1.52	1.47	1.40	1.36	1.25	1.15	1.00	∞

* Multiply the number of the first row ($n_2 = 1$) by 10.

Table A.6 Percentage Points of Reverse Arrangement Distribution

Values of $A_{N;\alpha}$ such that $\text{Prob}[A_N > A_{N;\alpha}] = \alpha$, where $N =$ total number of measurements

N	α					
	0.99	0.975	0.95	0.05	0.025	0.01
10	9	11	13	31	33	35
12	16	18	21	44	47	49
14	24	27	30	60	63	66
16	34	38	41	78	81	85
18	45	50	54	98	102	107
20	59	64	69	120	125	130
30	152	162	171	263	272	282
40	290	305	319	460	474	489
50	473	495	514	710	729	751
60	702	731	756	1013	1038	1067
70	977	1014	1045	1369	1400	1437
80	1299	1344	1382	1777	1815	1860
90	1668	1721	1766	2238	2283	2336
100	2083	2145	2198	2751	2804	2866

APPENDIX B

Definitions for Random Data Analysis

Autocorrelation Function

The autocorrelation function $R_{xx}(\tau)$ of a quantity $x(t)$ is the average of the product of the quantity at time t with the quantity at time $(t + \tau)$ for an appropriate averaging time T:

$$R_{xx}(\tau) = \frac{1}{T}\int_0^T x(t)x(t+\tau)dt$$

The delay τ can be either positive or negative. For an ergodic process, T should approach infinity, but, in practice, T must be finite. The total mean square value $\overline{x^2}$ can be estimated by

$$\overline{x^2} = R_{xx}(0) = \frac{1}{T}\int_0^T x^2(t)dt$$

Autospectral Density Function

By finite Fourier transform techniques, the autospectral (also called power spectral) density function $G_{xx}(f)$ is defined for $0 < f < \infty$ by

$$G_{xx}(f) = \frac{2}{T}E\left[|X(f,T)|^2\right]$$

where $E[\,]$ is an ensemble average, for fixed f, over n_d available sample records of $|X(f,T)|^2$. The quantity $X(f, T)$ is a finite Fourier transform of $x(t)$ of length T. The quantity $G_{xx}(f) = 0$ for $f < 0$.

Random Data: Analysis and Measurement Procedures, Fourth Edition. By Julius S. Bendat and Allan G. Piersol
Copyright © 2010 John Wiley & Sons, Inc.

For theoretical studies, a two-sided autospectral density function $S_{xx}(f)$ can be defined for $-\infty < f < \infty$ by setting

$$S_{xx}(f) = \tfrac{1}{2} G_{xx}(f) \text{ when } f > 0$$

$$S_{xx}(-f) = S_{xx}(f)$$

For stationary random data, the autospectral density function $G_{xx}(f)$ is twice the Fourier transform of the autocorrelation function $R_{xx}(\tau)$. The total mean square value $\overline{x^2}$ can be obtained by integrating $G_{xx}(f)$ or $S_{xx}(f)$ as follows:

$$\overline{x^2} = \int_0^\infty G_{xx}(f) df = \int_{-\infty}^\infty S_{xx}(f) df$$

Coherence Function

The coherence function $\gamma_{xy}^2(f)$ of two quantities $x(t)$ and $y(t)$ is the ratio of the square of the absolute value of the cross-spectral density function to the product of the autospectral density functions of the two quantities:

$$\gamma_{xy}^2(f) = \frac{|G_{xy}(f)|^2}{G_{xx}(f) G_{yy}(f)}$$

For all f, the quantity $\gamma_{xy}^2(f)$ satisfies $0 \leq \gamma_{xy}^2(f) \leq 1$. This ordinary coherence function measures the extent to which $y(t)$ may be predicted from $x(t)$ by an optimum linear least squares relationship.

Coherent Output Spectrum

The coherent output spectrum $G_{vv}(f)$ for a single-input/single-output problem is the product of the coherence function between the input signal $x(t)$ and the output signal $y(t)$, multiplied by the output autospectral density function:

$$G_{vv}(f) = \gamma_{xy}^2(f) G_{yy}(f)$$

The associated noise output spectrum $G_{nn}(f)$ is given by

$$G_{nn}(f) = [1 - \gamma_{xy}^2(f)] G_{yy}(f)$$

Cross-Correlation Coefficient Function

The cross-correlation coefficient function $\rho_{xy}(\tau)$ of two quantities $x(t)$ and $y(t)$ is the ratio of the cross-correlation function $R_{xy}(\tau)$ to the square root of the product of the autocorrelation functions of the two quantities at $\tau = 0$:

$$\rho_{xy}(\tau) = \frac{R_{xy}(\tau)}{\sqrt{R_{xx}(0) R_{yy}(0)}}$$

For all τ, the quantity $\rho_{xy}(\tau)$ satisfies $-1 \leq \rho_{xy}(\tau) \leq 1$. This cross-correlation coefficient function and the ordinary coherence function are *not* Fourier transforms of each other.

Cross-Correlation Function

The cross-correlation function $R_{xy}(\tau)$ of two quantities $x(t)$ and $y(t)$ is the average of the product of $x(t)$ at time t with $y(t)$ at time $(t + \tau)$ for an appropriate averaging time T:

$$R_{xy}(\tau) = \frac{1}{T}\int_0^T x(t)y(t+\tau)dt$$

For a pair of ergodic processes, T should approach infinity, but, in practice, T must be finite. The autocorrelation function $R_{xx}(\tau)$ is a special case of $R_{xy}(\tau)$ when $x(t) = y(t)$.

Cross-Spectral Density Function

By finite Fourier transform techniques, the cross-spectral density function is defined for $0 < f < \infty$ by

$$G_{xy}(f) = \frac{2}{T}E[X^*(f,T)Y(f,T)]$$

where $E[\,]$ is an ensemble average, for fixed f, over n_d available associated pairs of $X^*(f, T)$ and $Y(f, T)$ computed from sample records of $x(t)$ and $y(t)$, each of length T. The quantity $X^*(f, T)$ is the complex conjugate of the finite Fourier transform $X(f, T)$ of $x(t)$, while $Y(f, T)$ is the finite Fourier transform of $y(t)$. The quantity $G_{xy}(f) = 0$ for $f < 0$.

For theoretical studies, a two-sided cross-spectral density function $S_{xy}(f)$ can be defined for $-\infty < f < \infty$ by setting

$$S_{xy}(f) = \tfrac{1}{2}G_{xy}(f) \quad \text{when } f > 0$$

$$S_{xy}(-f) = S_{xy}^*(f)$$

For stationary random data, the cross-spectral density function $G_{xy}(f)$ is twice the Fourier transform of the cross-correlation function $R_{xy}(\tau)$.

Deterministic Data

Deterministic data are data that can be described by an explicit mathematical relationship.

Energy Autospectral Density Function

By finite Fourier transform techniques, the energy autospectral density function is defined for $0 < f < \infty$ by

$$\mathcal{G}_{xx}(f) = 2E[|X(f,T)|^2]$$

where $E[\,]$ is an ensemble average, for fixed f, over n_d available sample (transient) records of $x(t)$, each of finite length T. This quantity $\mathcal{G}_{xx}(f) = 0$ for $f < 0$. The energy autospectral density function for transient random data is related to the "power" autospectral density function for the same transient data by

$$\mathcal{G}_{xx}(f) = TG_{xx}(f)$$

where T is the length of the transient records. Observe that $G_{xx}(f)$ for transient data must approach zero as T approaches infinity. For theoretical studies, a two-sided energy autospectral density function can be defined for $-\infty < f < \infty$ by setting

$$\mathscr{S}_{xx}(f) = \frac{1}{2}\mathscr{G}_{xx}(f) \quad \text{when } f > 0$$

$$\mathscr{S}_{xx}(-f) = \mathscr{S}_{xx}(f)$$

Energy Cross-Spectral Density Function

By finite Fourier transform techniques, the energy cross-spectral density function is defined for $0 < f < \infty$ by

$$\mathscr{G}_{xy}(f) = 2E[X^*(f,T)Y(f,T)]$$

where $E[\,]$ is an ensemble average, for fixed f, over n_d available associated pairs of sample (transient) records of $x(t)$ and $y(t)$ each of finite length T. This quantity $\mathscr{G}_{xy}(f) = 0$ for $f < 0$. The energy cross-spectral density function for transient random data is related to the usual cross-spectral density function for the same transient data by

$$\mathscr{G}_{xy}(f) = TG_{xy}(f)$$

where T is the length of the transient records. For theoretical studies, a two-sided energy cross-spectral density function can be defined for $-\infty < f < \infty$ by setting

$$\mathscr{S}_{xy}(f) = \frac{1}{2}\mathscr{G}_{xy}(f) \quad \text{when } f > 0$$

$$\mathscr{S}_{xy}(-f) = \mathscr{S}_{xy}^*(f)$$

Ergodic Process

An ergodic process is a stationary random process involving a collection of time history records where time-averaged results are the same for every record. It follows that these time-averaged results from any single record will then be equal to corresponding ensemble-averaged results over the collection of records. To help explain this definition, consider a stationary random process $\{x_k(t)\}$ where $k = 1, 2, 3, \ldots$ represents the different records. For any particular record $x_k(t)$, a time-averaged result such as the mean square value is given theoretically by

$$\overline{x_k^2} = \lim_{T \to \infty} \frac{1}{T} \int_0^T x_k^2(t) dt$$

This result must be independent of k and the same for all records if the process is ergodic. The corresponding ensemble-averaged result over the collection of records is given theoretically by

$$E[x^2] = \lim_{k \to \infty} \frac{1}{K} \sum_{k=1}^{K} x_k^2(t)$$

APPENDIX B: DEFINITIONS FOR RANDOM DATA ANALYSIS   549

and is independent of t for stationary processes. For an ergodic process, the two types of averages given above will be equal.

Ergodic Random Data
See ergodic process.

Fourier Series
A Fourier series expresses a periodic quantity $x(t)$ in terms of its individual frequency components. If $x(t)$ is periodic of period T where $x(t) = x(t + T)$, then

$$x(t) = \frac{a_0}{2} + \sum_{n=1}^{\infty} a_n \cos 2\pi nft + \sum_{n=1}^{\infty} b_n \sin 2\pi nft$$

The frequency $f = (1/T)$ is the fundamental frequency. The coefficients

$$a_n = \frac{2}{T} \int_0^T x(u) \cos 2\pi nfu \, du$$
$$b_n = \frac{2}{T} \int_0^T x(u) \sin 2\pi nfu \, du \qquad n = 0, 1, 2, \ldots$$

where u is a dummy variable of integration.

Fourier Transform
The Fourier transform, also called the Fourier spectrum, $X(f)$ of a quantity $x(t)$, is a complex-valued function of frequency f defined by

$$X(f) = \int_{-\infty}^{\infty} x(t) e^{-j2\pi ft} dt \qquad -\infty < f < \infty$$

assuming $x(t)$ is such that $X(f)$ exists. The time function $x(t)$ is obtained from $X(f)$ by

$$x(t) = \int_{-\infty}^{\infty} X(f) e^{j2\pi ft} df \qquad -\infty < t < \infty$$

$X(f)$ and $x(t)$ are known as the direct and inverse Fourier transforms, respectively. In terms of real and imaginary parts,

$$X(f) = \text{Re}[X(f)] - j\text{Im}[X(f)]$$

where

$$\text{Re}[X(f)] = \int_{-\infty}^{\infty} x(t) \cos 2\pi ft \, dt$$

$$\text{Im}[X(f)] = \int_{-\infty}^{\infty} x(t) \sin 2\pi ft \, dt$$

In actual practice, $x(t)$ will be of finite length T, so that $X(f)$ is estimated by computing the finite Fourier transform

$$X(f, T) = \int_0^T x(t) e^{-j2\pi ft} dt$$

Such finite integrals always exist.

Frequency Response Function
The frequency response function $H(f)$ for a constant-parameter linear system is the Fourier transform of the unit impulse response function $h(\tau)$ that describes this system. In equation form,

$$H(f) = \int_{-\infty}^{\infty} h(\tau) e^{-j2\pi f \tau} d\tau$$

The quantity $H(f)$ is often called the transfer function by engineers, although the term transfer function should be reserved for the Laplace transform of the unit impulse response function. In complex polar notation,

$$H(f) = |H(f)| e^{-j\phi(f)}$$

where

$$|H(f)| = \text{gain factor of system}$$
$$\phi(f) = \text{phase factor of system}$$

For linear systems, $H(f)$ can be estimated using deterministic data, transient data, or stationary random data because its properties are independent of the nature of data passing through the system.

Gain Factor
See frequency response function.

Gaussian Process
A Gaussian process is a stationary random process $x(t)$ whose instantaneous values at any time t have the following probability density function:

$$p(x) = \frac{1}{\sigma_x \sqrt{2\pi}} \exp\left[-(x - \mu_x)^2 / 2\sigma_x^2\right] \quad -\infty < x < \infty$$

where μ_x is the true mean value of $x(t)$ and σ_x^2 is the true variance of $x(t)$. This probability density function defines the Gaussian distribution.

Gaussian Random Data
See Gaussian process.

Histogram
A histogram is a plot of the number of observed values of a quantity $x(t)$ that falls within various specified magnitude ranges, called class intervals.

Hilbert Transform
The Hilbert transform of a real-valued function $x(t)$ extending over the range $-\infty < t < \infty$ is a real-valued function $\tilde{x}(t)$ defined by

$$\tilde{x}(t) = \mathcal{H}[x(t)] = \int_{-\infty}^{\infty} \frac{x(u)}{\pi(t-u)} du$$

Thus, the Hilbert transform $\tilde{x}(t)$ is the original function $x(t)$ convolved with $(1/\pi t)$.

Line Spectrum
A line spectrum is a spectrum whose components occur at a number of discrete frequencies, as in a Fourier series representation.

Linear System
A linear system is one that is additive and homogeneous. Given two inputs x_1 and x_2 that individually produce outputs y_1 and y_2, the system is additive if the input $x_1 + x_2$ produces the output $y_1 + y_2$, and homogeneous if the input cx_1 produces the output cy_1 where c is an arbitrary constant.

Mean Value
The mean value $\bar{x}$ of a quantity $x(t)$ is the time average of the quantity for an appropriate averaging time T:

$$\bar{x} = \frac{1}{T} \int_0^T x(t)\, dt$$

For an ergodic process, the true mean value μ_x can be obtained by letting T approach infinity.

Mean Square Value
The mean square value $\overline{x^2}$ of a quantity $x(t)$ is the time average of the square of the quantity for an appropriate averaging time T:

$$\overline{x^2} = \frac{1}{T} \int_0^T x^2(t)\, dt$$

For an ergodic process, the true mean square value $\psi_x^2(f)$ can be obtained by letting T approach infinity. See also notes under autocorrelation and autospectral density functions.

Multiple Coherence Function

The multiple coherence function $\gamma_{y:x}^2(f)$ between a quantity $y(t)$ and a set of other quantities $x_i(t)$, $i = 1, 2, \ldots, q$, measures the extent to which $y(t)$ may be predicted from these various $x_i(t)$ by optimum linear least squares relationships. For all f, the multiple coherence function satisfies $0 \leq \gamma_{y:x}^2(f) \leq 1$. The multiple coherence function includes the ordinary coherence function as a special case.

Narrow Bandwidth Random Data

Narrow bandwidth random data are those data whose spectral values are significant only within a narrow frequency range relative to the center of the frequency range. If such data have instantaneous values that follow a Gaussian distribution, then their peak values approximate a Rayleigh distribution.

Noise Correlation Duration

The noise correlation duration T_n for a zero mean value stationary random process $\{x(t)\}$ with an autocorrelation function $R_{xx}(\tau)$ is defined by

$$T_n = \frac{2 \int_0^\infty |R_{xx}(\tau)| \, d\tau}{R_{xx}(0)}$$

It is a measure of the time interval over which the values of a sample record from this random process are correlated.

Noise Spectral Bandwidth

The noise spectral bandwidth B_n for a zero mean value stationary random process with autospectral density function $G_{xx}(f)$ is defined by

$$B_n = \frac{\int_0^\infty G_{xx}(f) \, df}{G_{xx}(f)|_{\max}}$$

It is the bandwidth for this stationary random process that has the same mean square value as for bandwidth-limited white noise with a bandwidth of $B = B_n$.

Nonlinear System

A nonlinear system is one that is either not additive or not homogeneous, as defined under linear system.

Nonstationary Process

A nonstationary random process is any process that is not a stationary process (refer to definition of stationary process). Statistical averages computed over an ensemble of time history records are not invariant with respect to translations in time but are a function of the times being analyzed. In general, time-averaged results from any single record do not represent this record or any other record, because information about essential time-varying properties are lost by the averaging operation.

Nonstationary Random Data
See nonstationary process.

Partial Coherence Function
The partial coherence function between a quantity $y(t)$ and any subset of a larger set of known quantities $x_i(t)$, $i = 1, 2, \ldots, q$, measures the extent to which $y(t)$ may be predicted from this subset by optimum linear least squares relationships. Such partial coherence functions will be bounded between zero and unity.

Peak Probability Density Function
The peak probability density function of a stationary random record describes the statistical properties of positive peaks for this record.

Peak Value
A peak value of a quantity $x(t)$ is the value of $x(t)$ at a maximum or minimum value. Peak counts per unit time can indicate the number of maxima only, the number of minima only, or both.

Phase Factor
See frequency response function.

Power Spectral Density Function
See autospectral density function.

Probability Density Function
The probability density function $p(x)$ of a quantity $x(t)$ is the probability that $x(t)$ at any value of t will assume the value x per unit magnitude window for an appropriate magnitude window W:

$$p(x) = \frac{P(x, W)}{W}$$

where $P(x, W)$ is the probability that $x(t)$ falls in the magnitude window W centered at x. In words, $p(x)$ is an estimate of the rate of change of probability with magnitude. For stationary random data, W should approach zero, but, in practice, W must be greater than zero. For all values of x, $p(x) \geq 0$, with the area under the probability density curve equal to unity.

Probability Distribution Function
The probability distribution function $P(x)$ defines the probability that $x(t) \leq x$ at any value of t. In terms of the probability density function $p(x)$,

$$P(x) = \int_{-\infty}^{x} p(u) \, du$$

where u is a dummy variable of integration. Observe that $P(-\infty) = 0$ and $P(\infty) = 1$.

Random Data
See random process

Random Process
A random process is a collection of time history records that can be described by appropriate statistical parameters, such as averaged properties of these records at a number of fixed times.

Rayleigh Probability Density Function
The Rayleigh probability density function $q_1(R)$ is defined for $R \geq 0$ by

$$q_1(R) = \frac{R}{\sigma_r^2} \exp\left(-\frac{R^2}{2\sigma_r^2}\right)$$

This function describes the statistical properties of the envelope $R(t)$ of a narrow bandwidth Gaussian random record $r(t)$ with zero mean value and variance σ_r^2. It also represents the peak probability density function for this record.

Root Mean Square Value
The root mean square (rms) value is the positive square root of the mean square value. The rms value is equal to the standard deviation if the mean value is zero.

Spectral Density
See autospectral and cross-spectral density functions.

Spectrum
A spectrum is a description of a quantity in terms of any function of frequency. The spectrum may be either a line spectrum or a continuous spectrum.

Standard Deviation
The standard deviation is the positive square root of the variance. The standard deviation is equal to the rms value if the mean value is zero.

Stationary Process
A stationary random process is a collection of time history records having statistical properties that are invariant with respect to translations in time. Stationary processes may be either ergodic or nonergodic.

Stationary Random Data
See stationary process.

Statistical Bandwidth
The statistical bandwidth B_s for a zero mean value Gaussian random process with an autospectral density function $G_{xx}(f)$ is defined by

$$B_s = \frac{\left[\int_0^\infty G_{xx}(f)df\right]^2}{\int_0^\infty G_{xx}^2(f)df}$$

It is the bandwidth for this Gaussian random process whose mean square value estimates have the same random error as for bandwidth-limited white noise with a bandwidth of $B = B_s$.

Time History Record
A time history record is the waveform of any quantity expressed as a function of time, where the data may be either deterministic or random. The reciprocal of the period for a record that is periodic in time is the frequency of the record. Any other independent variable may replace time in time history records, provided a corresponding change is made in the interpretation of frequency.

Transfer Function
The transfer function for a constant-parameter linear system is the Laplace transform of the unit impulse response function that describes this system. Along the imaginary axis, this quantity becomes the frequency response function of the system. See frequency response function.

Transient Data
Transient data are data of limited duration, which may be either deterministic or random.

Unit Impulse Response (Weighting) Function
The unit impulse response function, also called the weighting function, $h(\tau)$ of a constant-parameter linear system describes the response of this system to a unit impulse (delta) function. It is the inverse Fourier transform of the frequency response function of the system.

Variance
The variance s_x^2 of a quantity $x(t)$ is the time average of the square of the deviation from the mean value $\bar{x}$ for an appropriate averaging time T:

$$s_x^2 = \frac{1}{T}\int_0^T [x(t)-\bar{x}]^2 dt$$

For an ergodic process, the true variance σ_x^2 can be obtained by letting T approach infinity. The quantity $s_x^2 = \overline{x^2}$ if $\bar{x} = 0$.

Wavenumber Autospectral Density Function
The wavenumber autospectral density function $G_{xx}(\kappa)$ is the autospectra density function of a random process where each sample record $x(\delta)$ is a function of distance δ in meters rather than time t in seconds. The spectra density is a function of wave number κ in cycles/m rather than frequency f in cycles/s (Hz).

Wavenumber Cross-Spectral Density Function
The wavenumber cross-spectral density function $G_{xy}(\kappa)$ is the cross-spectra density function between two random processes where the sample records $x(\delta)$ and $y(\delta)$ are a function of distance S in meters rather than time t in seconds.

Wide Bandwidth Random Data
Wide bandwidth random data are data whose spectral values are significant over a wide frequency range relative to the center of the frequency range.

List of Figures

1.1	Simple spring mass system	2
1.2	Classifications of deterministic data	3
1.3	Time history and spectrum of sinusoidal data	4
1.4	Spectrum of complex periodic data	5
1.5	Spectrum of almost-periodic data	6
1.6	Illustrations of transient data	7
1.7	Spectra of transient data	8
1.8	Sample records of thermal noise generator outputs	9
1.9	Classifications of random data	9
1.10	Ensemble of time history records defining a random process	10
1.11	Four special time histories. (*a*) Sine wave. (*b*) Sine wave plus random noise. (*c*) Narrow bandwidth random noise. (*d*) Wide bandwidth random noise	15
1.12	Probability density function plots. (*a*) Sine wave. (*b*) Sine wave plus random noise. (*c*) Narrow bandwidth random noise. (*d*) Wide bandwidth random noise	16
1.13	Autocorrelation function plots. (*a*) Sine wave. (*b*) Sine wave plus random noise. (*c*) Narrow bandwidth random noise. (*d*) Wide bandwidth random noise	17
1.14	Autospectral density function plots. (*a*) Sine wave. (*b*) Sine wave plus random noise. (*c*) Narrow bandwidth random noise. (*d*) Wide bandwidth random noise	18
1.15	Single-input/single-output system with output noise	19
1.16	Single-input/multiple-output system with output noise	20
1.17	Multiple-input/single-output system with output noise	21
1.18	Random and bias errors in gun shoots at a target. (*a*) Gun A: large bias error and small random error. (*b*) Gun B: small bias error and large random error	22

Random Data: Analysis and Measurement Procedures, Fourth Edition. By Julius S. Bendat and Allan G. Piersol
Copyright © 2010 John Wiley & Sons, Inc.

2.1	Simple mechanical system	30
2.2	Mechanical system with force input	31
2.3	Frequency response function of mechanical system with force input, (*a*) Gain factor. (*b*) Phase factor.	33
2.4	Mechanical system with foundation motion input	35
2.5	Frequency response function of mechanical system with foundation motion input. (*a*) Gain factor. (*b*) Phase factor	37
2.6	Electrical system with voltage input	39
3.1	Discrete probability density and distribution functions. (*a*) Probability density function. (*b*) Probability distribution function	48
3.2	Uniform probability density and distribution functions. (*a*) Probability density function. (*b*) Probability distribution function	49
3.3	Sine wave probability density and distribution functions. (*a*) Probability density function. (*b*) Probability distribution function	52
3.4	Probability density function for sum of two independent uniformly distributed variables	58
3.5	Standardized Gaussian (normal) probability density and distribution functions. (*a*) Probability density function. (*b*) Probability distribution function	61
3.6	Time history and autospectrum for narrow bandwidth data	68
3.7	Standardized Rayleigh probability density and distribution functions. (*a*) Probability density function (*b*) Probability distribution function	70
3.8	Standardized probability density functions of a sine wave in Gaussian noise	75
4.1	Acceptance and rejection regions for hypothesis tests	91
4.2	Type II error regions for hypothesis tests	92
4.3	Illustration of varying degrees of correlation, (*a*) Perfect linear correlation, (*b*) Moderate linear correlation, (*c*) Nonlinear correlation, (*d*) No correlation	100
5.1	Model for time-delay problem	117
5.2	Typical cross-correlation function for time-delay problem	117
5.3	One-sided and two-sided autospectral density functions	120
5.4	Relation of phase angle to cross-spectral terms	122
5.5	Autospectrum estimate by filtering–squaring–averaging	129
5.6	Typical phase angle plot for time-delay problem	136
5.7	Illustration of nonergodic stationary sine wave process	144
5.8	Illustration of ergodic sine wave process	145
5.9	Illustration of derivatives of autocorrelation functions. (*a*) Original function. (*b*) First derivative. (*c*) Second derivative	152
5.10	Illustration of crossings of level with positive and negative slopes	156
5.11	Illustration of positive peaks above level α	160
5.12	Probability (positive peak $> \alpha$) for narrow bandwidth Gaussian data	161

LIST OF FIGURES

5.13	Probability density functions for peak values of Gaussian random data	164
6.1	Ideal single-input/single-output linear system	174
6.2	Input/output spectral relationships for linear systems, (*a*) Autospectra. (*b*) Cross-spectra	175
6.3	Airplane flying through atmospheric turbulence	181
6.4	Coherence function between gust velocity and response acceleration of airplane. These data resulted from studies funded by the NASA Langley Research Center, Hampton, Virginia, under Contract NAS 1-8538	181
6.5	Autospectra of gust velocity and response acceleration of airplane. These data resulted from studies funded by the NASA Langley Research Center, Hampton, Virginia, under Contract NAS 1-8538	182
6.6	Single-input/single-output system with extraneous noise	184
6.7	Single-input/single-output system with output noise	189
6.8	Single-input/two-output system with output noise	191
6.9	Single-input/multiple-output system with output noise	193
7.1	Multiple-input/signal-output model	202
7.2	Two-input/one-output model	207
7.3	Illustration of fully coherent inputs	209
7.4	Decomposition of $x_2(t)$ from $x_1(t)$	214
7.5	Illustration of erroneous high coherence	215
7.6	Model equivalent to Figure 7.2	216
7.7	Model equivalent to Figure 7.6	216
7.8	Model equivalent to Figure 7.7	216
7.9	Decomposition of $y(t)$ from $x_1(t)$	228
7.10	Decomposition of $y(t)$ from $x_{2 \cdot 1}(t)$	220
7.11	Multiple-input model for arbitrary inputs	221
7.12	Multiple-input model for ordered conditioned inputs	222
7.13	General conditioned-input/output model	226
7.14	Algorithm to compute conditioned spectral density functions (Results extend to any number of inputs.)	228
7.15	Special algorithm to compute conditioned autospectral density functions (Results extend to any number of inputs.)	229
7.16	Modified single-input/single-output models	233
7.17	Modified single-input/single-output spectral models	234
7.18	Three-input/single-output linear model where the inputs can be correlated	234
7.19	Revised three-input/single-output linear model equivalent to Figure 7.18 where the inputs are mutually uncorrelated	235
8.1	Normalized random error of mean square value and rms value estimates	258
8.2	Autospectral density function of example random process	259
8.3	Normalized random error of autocorrelation function estimates	270

8.4	Illustration of bias error introduced by frequency smoothing of spectral density estimates	275
8.5	Normalized bias error for autospectral density estimates of single degree-of-freedom system response to white noise	277
9.1	Single-input/single-output linear model	298
9.2	Normalized random error of coherent output spectral estimates when $n_d = 100$	304
9.3	Normalized random error of coherent output spectral estimates versus number of averages	304
9.4	Normalized random error of coherence function estimates when $n_d = 100$	307
9.5	Normalized random error of coherence function estimates versus number of averages	307
9.6	Normalized random error of gain factor estimates when $n_d = 100$	310
9.7	Normalized random error of gain factor estimates versus number of averages	311
10.1	Key steps in data acquisition and processing	318
10.2	Schematic diagram and frequency response characteristics of piezoelectric accelerometer (a) Schematic diagram, (b) Gain factor, (c) Phase factor	320
10.3	Schematic diagram of sigma-delta converter	327
10.4	Sampling of analog signal	328
10.5	Frequency aliasing due to an inadequate digital sampling rate	331
10.6	Folding about the Nyquist frequency	331
10.7	Illustration of aliasing error in the computation of an autospectral density function	332
10.8	Illustration of quantization error	333
10.9	Sequence of mean square value measurements	338
10.10	Measured autospectra of a sine wave in random noise	340
10.11	Examples of random data with anomalies	343
10.12	Probability density functions of random data with anomalies	344
10.13	General procedure for analyzing individual sample records	349
10.14	General procedure for analyzing multiple sample records	352
11.1	Illustration of linear trend removal	362
11.2	Schematic diagram of simple recursive filter	364
11.3	Illustration of frequency components for $N = 16$-point FFT, (a) Components as produced by FFT. (b) Transposed components defining two-sided spectrum	378
11.4	Illustration of circular effect in correlation analysis via FFT calculations	382
11.5	Illustration of circular correlation function	384
11.6	Circular correlation function when N zeros are added	384
11.7	Subdivision of data into n_d records of individual length T	386
11.8	Illustration of inherent time window in special analysis	388

LIST OF FIGURES

11.9	Rectangular analysis window. (*a*) Time window. (*b*) Spectral window	389
11.10	Hanning analysis window. (*a*) Time window. (*b*) Spectral window	390
11.11	Autospectral density function of particle velocity in simulated ocean waves computed with and without tapering. These data resulted from studies funded by Shell Internationale Petroleum Maatschappij B.V., The Hague, Netherlands	392
11.12	Sequence of tapered time windows for 50% overlapped processing	393
11.13	Illustration of frequency shift due to complex demodulation	398
11.14	Relation of center frequencies to original computed frequencies for frequency-averaged autospectral density estimates	400
11.15	Spectral window for frequency averaging over 16 contiguous autospectral density values	401
11.16	Augmented spectral matrix $\{G_{ij}\}$	410
11.17	Conditioned spectral matrix $\{G_{ij\cdot 1}\}$	410
11.18	Conditioned spectral matrix $\{G_{ij\cdot 2!}\}$	411
11.19	Conditioned spectral matrix $\{G_{ij\cdot(q-2)!}\}$	411
11.20	Conditioned spectral matrix $\{G_{ij\cdot(q-1)!}\}$	411
11.21	Conditioned term $G_{yy\cdot q!}$	411
11.22	Conditioned results for three-input/one-output system	412
12.1	Sample records of nonstationary random process	418
12.2	Examples of nonstationary data, (*a*) Time-varying mean value, (*b*) Time-varying mean square value, (*c*) Time-varying frequency structure	419
12.3	Illustration of probability density function of nonstationary data	423
12.4	Procedure for nonstationary mean value measurement	424
12.5	Running mean square value and average autospectrum estimates for nonstationary acoustic data, (*a*) Running mean square values, (*b*) Average autospectrum	434
12.6	Half-sine approximation for time-varying mean square value	435
12.7	Procedure for nonstationary autocorrelation measurement	437
12.8	Zero crossings of product model nonstationary data	441
12.9	Illustration of double-frequency autospectrum for cosine-modulated narrow bandwidth noise	449
12.10	Illustration of instantaneous autospectrum for cosine-modulated narrow bandwidth noise	456
12.11	Procedure for estimating instantaneous autospectrum by filtering, squaring, and averaging	458
12.12	Optimum averaging time and resolution bandwidth for nonstationary structural vibration data	459
12.13	Spectrograms for sine wave with linearly increasing instantaneous frequency	461

12.14	Acceleration time histones during automobile collision, (*a*) Automobile frame, (*b*) Chest of simulated front seat passenger. (*c*) These data resulted from studies funded by the FHWA National Highway Safety Bureau, Washington, D.C., under Contract FH-11-7218	469
12.15	Energy autospectra and gain factor for simulated passenger response to automotive collision, (*a*) Energy spectra, (*b*) Gain factor. These data resulted from studies funded by the FHWA National Highway Safety Bureau, Washington, D.C., under Contract FH-11-7218	470
13.1	Examples of Hilbert transforms	478
13.2	Even and odd components of a causal function	482
13.3	Typical cross-correlation coefficient function for nondispersive propagation through a single path	490
13.4	Autocorrelation function of low-pass white noise	491
13.5	Hilbert transform of autocorrelation function	492
13.6	Envelope of autocorrelation function	493
13.7	Nondispersive propagation through multiple paths	493
13.8	Nondispersive propagation from multiple uncorrelated sources	494
13.9	Nondispersive propagation from an unmeasured single source to measured multiple outputs	494
13.10	Typical narrow bandwidth cross-correlation coefficient function for dispersive propagation through a single path	496
13.11	Square-law envelope detection followed by correlation	498
14.1	Zero-memory nonlinear system	506
14.2	Finite-memory nonlinear system with a linear system after zero-memory linear system	507
14.3	Finite-memory nonlinear system with a linear system before the zero-memory nonlinear system	507
14.4	Case 1 square-law and cubic nonlinear model	507
14.5	Case 2 square-law and cubic nonlinear model	508
14.6	Third-order Volterra nonlinear model	509
14.7	SI/SO model with parallel linear and nonlinear systems	511
14.8	SI/SO model with nonlinear feedback	512
14.9	Reverse SI/SO nonlinear model without feedback	513
14.10	Reverse SI/SO model with parallel linear and nonlinear systems	513
14.11	Force history segment and autospectrum	517
14.12	Force historgram	517
14.13	(*a*) SDOF linear system magnitude. (*b*) SDOF linear system phase	518
14.14	(*a*) SDOF linear system coherence function. (*b*) SDOF linear system displacement histogram	518
14.15	(*a*) Duffing system linear magnitude and SI/SO magnitude. (*b*) Duffing system linear phase and SI/SO phase	519
14.16	Duffing system nonlinear frequency response function. (*a*) Real part. (*b*) Imaginary part	519

14.17 (a) Duffing system nonlinear cumulative coherence functions.
(b) Duffing system nonlinear displacement histogram 519
14.18 Illustration of drift force problem 520
14.19 Nonlinear drift force model with parallel linear and
square-law envelope detector systems 521

List of Tables

2.1	Summary of gain factors for simple mechanical system	38
2.2	Analogous terms for mechanical and electrical systems	40
2.3	Analogous characteristics for several physical systems	41
3.1	Special probability density functions	47
4.1	Sample observations arranged in increasing order	96
4.2	Calculations for goodness-of-fit test	97
4.3	Height and weight data for male students	101
5.1	Special autocorrelation functions	124
5.2	Special autospectral density functions	125
5.3	Related quantities for wavenumber and frequency	133
8.1	Record lengths and averages for basic estimates	285
9.1	Normalized random errors for spectral estimates	293
9.2	Covariance formulas for various estimates	297
9.3	Conditions for $\varepsilon[\hat{G}_{vv}] = 0.10$	305
9.4	Conditions for $\varepsilon[\hat{\gamma}_{xy}^2] = 0.10$	308
9.5	Conditions for $\varepsilon[|\hat{H}_{xy}|] = 0.10$	311
9.6	Summary of single-input/output random error formulas	312
12.1	Nonstationary correlation and spectral functions	451
12.2	Nonstationary input/output correlation and spectral relations	466
13.1	Examples of Hilbert transforms	477
13.2	Hilbert transform relationships	486
14.1	Digital data processing parameters	515
14.2	Simulated system parameters	516
A.1	Ordinates of the standardized normal density function	533
A.2	Areas under standardized normal density function	535
A.3	Percentage points of chi-square distribution	536
A.4	Percentage points of t distribution	537
A.5	Percentage points of F distribution	538
A.6	Percentage points of reverse arrangement distribution	544

List of Examples

2.1	Illustration of nonlinear system	26
2.2	Illustration of unstable system	27
2.3	Illustration of resonant system	34
3.1	Discrete distribution	46
3.2	Uniform (rectangular) distribution	48
3.3	Sine wave distribution with fixed amplitude	51
3.4	Illustration of probability intervals	54
3.5	Sum of two independent uniformly distributed variables	57
3.6	Sine wave distribution with random amplitudes	73
3.7	Sine wave in Gaussian noise	74
4.1	Illustration of confidence intervals	90
4.2	Illustration of hypothesis test design	93
4.3	Illustration of test for normality	96
4.4	Illustration of reverse arrangement test	98
4.5	Illustration of linear correlation analysis	101
4.6	Illustration of linear regression analysis	104
5.1	Autocorrelation function of sine wave process	113
5.2	Autocorrelation function of rectangular wave process	113
5.3	Autocorrelation function of sum of two processes	114
5.4	Uncorrelated-dependent random variables	114
5.5	Autospectral density function of sine wave process	124
5.6	Autospectral density function of rectangular wave process	126
5.7	Autospectral density function of sum of two processes	126
5.8	Low-pass white noise	139
5.9	Gaussian spectrum noise	139
5.10	Exponential autocorrelation function noise	140
5.11	Nonergodic stationary random process	144
5.12	Zero crossings of low-pass Gaussian white noise	158
5.13	Zero crossings of bandwidth-limited Gaussian white noise	158
5.14	Peak probability for narrow bandwidth Gaussian data	160

5.15	Expected number of positive peaks for narrow bandwidth Gaussian data	162
6.1	Response properties of low-pass filter to white noise	177
6.2	Response properties of low-pass filter to sine wave	178
6.3	Force-input/displacement-output system	178
6.4	Displacement-input/displacement-output system	179
6.5	Physical illustration of coherence measurement	181
6.6	Illustration of noisy measurements	197
7.1	Multiple coherence function for two uncorrelated inputs	213
7.2	Illustration of erroneous high coherence	214
8.1	Approximate 95% confidence intervals for mean square and rms value estimates	252
8.2	Random error in mean value estimate	255
8.3	Bandwidths for random noise with a nonuniform autospectrum	259
8.4	Bias in probability density estimate of Gaussian random data	263
8.5	Time-delay estimate from cross-correlation calculation	272
8.6	Illustration of bias error in autospectrum estimate	275
8.7	Illustration of optimum resolution bandwidth selection	279
9.1	Illustration of random errors in cross-spectral density estimate	298
9.2	Illustration of bias and random errors in coherent output spectrum estimate	303
9.3	Illustration of confidence interval for coherence function estimate	306
9.4	Illustration of random errors in frequency response function estimate	311
10.1	Illustration of piezoelectric accelerometer	319
10.2	Illustration of digitization	334
10.3	Test for stationarity	338
10.4	Autospectrum of sine wave in noise	339
11.1	Illustration of recursive digital filter	365
11.2	FFT speed ratio for powers of two	370
11.3	Spectral errors due to side-lobe leakage	391
11.4	Parameter selections for zoom transform	398
11.5	Number of computations for frequency- versus ensemble-averaged autospectra estimates	402
12.1	Illustration of time-averaged probability density function	422
12.2	Variance of mean value estimate for exponential correlation between samples	427
12.3	Variance of mean square value estimate for exponential correlation between samples	431
12.4	Illustration of nonstationary mean square value estimates using a moving average	433
12.5	Illustration of time interval bias error determination	435
12.6	Instantaneous autocorrelation function of modulated random data	439
12.7	Double-frequency autospectrum of modulated random data	448

12.8	Instantaneous autospectrum of modulated random data	454
12.9	Selection of optimum analysis parameters for nonstationary data	459
12.10	Illustration of energy spectrum estimate	486
13.1	Digital formulas for $x(t)$ and $\hat{x}(t)$	477
13.2	Exponential causal function	483
13.3	Exponential-cosine causal function	484
13.4	Digital formulas for $R_{xy}(\tau)$ and $R_{xy}(\tau)$	488
13.5	Low-Pass White Noise	491
13.6	Nondispersive propagation through multiple paths	492
13.7	Nondispersive propagation from multiple uncorrelated sources	493
13.8	Nondispersive propagation from an unmeasured single source to measured multiple outputs	494
13.9	Exponential-cosine cross-correlation function	500

Answers to Problems in Random Data

CHAPTER 1

1.1 Period $= 2\pi$
1.2 (a) and (c) are periodic; (b) and (d) are nonperiodic
1.3 The autocorrelation function $R_{xx}(\tau) \to \mu_x^2$ as $\tau \to \infty$
1.4 Variance $= 0.09$
1.5 $\varepsilon = \frac{E[(\hat{\phi}-\phi)^2]^{1/2}}{\phi} = \frac{0.50}{5} = 0.10$
1.6 (d) is always true
1.7 (c), (d), and (e) are always true
1.8 (a) or (b)
1.9 (b) and (c)
1.10 Only (b) now applies

CHAPTER 2

2.1 $f(x) = x|x|$
$f(x_1 + x_2) = (x_1 + x_2)|x_1 + x_2| \neq x_1|x_1| + x_2|x_2|$;
$f(cx) = cx|cx| \neq cx|x|$
2.2 $f(c_1 x_1 + c_2 x_2) = c_1 f(x_1) + c_2 f(x_2)$
2.3 (a) and (b)
2.4 $H(f) = \int\limits_0^\infty h(\tau) e^{-j2\pi f \tau} d\tau = \int\limits_0^\infty A e^{-(a+j2\pi f)\tau} d\tau = \frac{A}{a+j2\pi f}$.

Random Data: Analysis and Measurement Procedures, Fourth Edition. By Julius S. Bendat and Allan G. Piersol
Copyright © 2010 John Wiley & Sons, Inc.

2.5 (a) $f_n = \frac{1}{2\pi}\sqrt{\frac{k}{m}} = \frac{1}{2\pi}\sqrt{\frac{2000}{5}} = 3.18$ Hz

(b) $\varsigma = \frac{c}{2\sqrt{km}} = \frac{10}{2\sqrt{(2000)(5)}} = 0.05$

(c) $f_r = f_n\sqrt{1-2\varsigma^2} = 0.9975 f_n = 3.17$ Hz

(d) $|H(f_r)| = \frac{1/k}{2\varsigma\sqrt{1-\varsigma^2}} = \frac{0.0005}{0.0999} \approx 0.005$

2.6 For $\tau < 0$, $h(\tau) = 0$; for $\tau \geq 0$,

$$h(\tau) = \int_{-\infty}^{\infty} H(f)e^{j2\pi f\tau} df = \int_{-\infty}^{\infty} [k - (2\pi f)^2 m + j2\pi fc]^{-1} e^{j2\pi f\tau} df$$

$$= \frac{2\pi f_n}{k\sqrt{1-\varsigma^2}} e^{-2\pi f_n\varsigma\tau} \sin\left(2\pi f_n\sqrt{1-\varsigma^2}\right)\tau$$

2.7 From Equation (2.24),

$$H(f) = \frac{1/k}{A(f)} \text{ where } A(f) = [1 - (f/f_n)^2]^2 + [2\varsigma f/f_n]^2$$

The maximum response occurs where

$$\frac{dH(f)}{df} = \frac{A(f)(0) - (1/k)(dA(f)/df)}{A^2(f)} = 0$$

This requires

$$\frac{dA(f)}{df} = 2\left[1 - (f/f_n)^2\right](-2f/f_n)(1/f_n) + 2[2\varsigma f/f_n]2\varsigma/f_n = 0.$$

Hence, $1 - (f/f_n)^2 = 2\varsigma^2$ and $f = f_n\sqrt{1 - 2\varsigma^2} = f_r$

2.8 From Equation (2.24), assuming light damping, the half-power points of $|H(f)|$ occur approximately at those frequencies where

$$1 - (f/f_n)^2 \simeq \pm 2\varsigma f/f_n \approx \pm 2\varsigma$$

For the lower half-power point frequency, $f_1 = f_r - B_r/2$, it follows that

$$(f_1/f_r) = 1 - B_r/(2f_r)$$

Ignoring higher order terms,

$$(f/f_r)^2 \approx 1 - 2B_r/(2f_r) \quad \text{and} \quad 1 - (f_1/f_r)^2 \approx (B_r/f_r)$$

Since $f_r \approx f_n$,

$$1 - (f_1/f_r)^2 \approx 2\varsigma \approx (B_r/f_r)$$

A similar result is obtained for the upper half-power point frequency. Hence, for light damping, $B_r \approx 2\varsigma f_r$

2.9 From Problem 2.6,

$$h(\tau) = \frac{2\pi f_n}{k\sqrt{1-\varsigma^2}} e^{-2\pi f_n \varsigma \tau} \sin\left(2\pi f_n \sqrt{1-\varsigma^2}\right)\tau$$

Hence, $\left(2\pi f_n \sqrt{1-\varsigma^2}\right)\tau = \pi$ when $\tau = \frac{1}{2}\left[f_n\sqrt{1-\varsigma^2}\right]^{-1} = T$

2.10

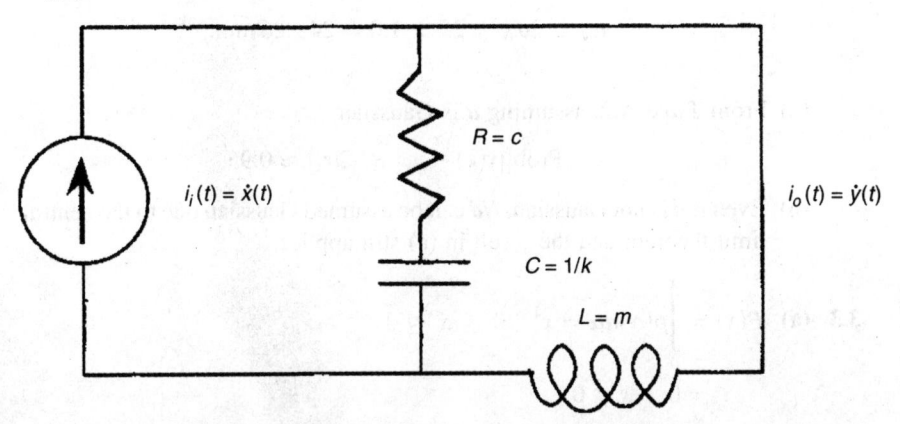

[Circuit diagram: current source $i_i(t) = \dot{x}(t)$ on left, parallel branches with $R = c$, $C = 1/k$, $L = m$ in series, output $i_o(t) = \dot{y}(t)$ on right.]

Letting the current $i(t) = \dot{q}(t)$ where $q(t)$ is charge, the loop equation is

$$L\ddot{q}_o + R[\dot{q}_o(t) - \dot{q}_i(t)] + \frac{1}{C}[q_o(t) - q_i(t)] = 0$$

Hence,

$$L\ddot{q}_o(t) + R\dot{q}_o(t) + \frac{1}{C}q_o(t) = \frac{1}{C}q_i(t) + R\dot{q}_i(t)$$

in agreement with Equation (2.29) for the mechanical system using analogies.

CHAPTER 3

3.1
A shaft will not fit in a bearing if $\Delta = b - s < 0$, where

$$\mu_\Delta = \mu_b - \mu_s = 0.01 \text{ cm}, \qquad \sigma_\Delta = \sqrt{\sigma_b^2 + \sigma_s^2} = 0.005 \text{ cm}$$

Assuming the diameters are normally distributed,

$$z = \frac{\Delta - 0.01}{0.005}$$

Then for $\Delta = 0$, $z = -2$ and the probability of $\Delta < 0$ is given from Table A.2 as $\text{Prob}[\Delta < 0] = \text{Prob}[z < -2] = 0.0228$

3.2 Since the mean values and variances sum, it follows that

$$\mu_N = N\mu_d = 25 \text{ cm}$$
$$\sigma_N^2 = N\sigma_d^2 = 25(0.1)^2 = 0.25 \text{ mm}^2$$
$$\sigma_N = 5(0.1) = 0.5 \text{ mm}$$

The desired interval is then

$$\mu_N \pm 2\sigma_N = 25 \pm 1.0 = 24-26 \text{ mm}$$

(a) From Table A.2, assuming d is Gaussian,

$$\text{Prob}[|x(k) - \mu_x| \leq 2\sigma_x] \approx 0.95$$

(b) Even if d is not Gaussian, Nd can be assumed Gaussian due to the central limit theorem and the result in (a) still applies.

3.3 (a) $P(x) = \int_0^x p(\alpha)d\alpha = x^4 \quad 0 \leq x \leq 1$

$$= 0; \quad x < 0$$
$$= 1; \quad x > 1$$

(b) $\mu_x = \int_0^1 xp(x)dx = 4\int_0^1 x^4 dx = \frac{4}{5}$

$\psi_x^2 = \int_0^1 x^2 p(x)dx = 4\int_0^1 x^5 dx = \frac{2}{3}$

$\sigma_x^2 = \psi_x^2 - \mu_x^2 = \frac{2}{75}$

3.4 (a) $p(x) = \frac{dP(x)}{dx} = \begin{cases} 0 & x \leq 0 \\ nx^{n-1} & 0 < x \leq 1 \\ 0 & x > 0 \end{cases}$

(b) $\mu_x = \int_0^1 xp(x)dx = \frac{n}{n+1}$

$\psi_x^2 = \int_0^1 x^2 p(x)dx = \frac{n}{n+2}$

$\sigma_x^2 = \psi_x^2 - \mu_x^2 = \frac{n}{(n+1)^2(n+2)}$

3.5 The probability density function for the random numbers is
$$p(x) = 0.1\delta(x-x_n) \quad \text{for} \quad x_n = 0, 1, 2, \ldots, 9$$
It follows that
$$\mu_x = \int_0^9 xp(x)dx = 4.5$$
$$\psi_x^2 = \int_0^9 x^2 p(x)dx = 28.5$$
$$\sigma_x^2 = \psi_x^2 - \mu_x^2 = 8.25$$
Since the sum of the numbers is
$$T = \sum_{n=1}^{N} x_n$$
then
$$\mu(T) = N\mu(x) = 4.5N$$
$$\sigma^2(T) = N\sigma^2(x) = 8.25N$$

3.6 From Equation (3.12),
$$p(y) = \frac{p(x)}{|dy/dx|} \quad \text{where} \quad y = 2x+1$$
It follows that
$$\left|\frac{dy}{dx}\right| = 2 \quad \text{and} \quad x = \frac{1}{2}(y-1)$$
so that
$$p(y) = \frac{1}{2}p\left(\frac{1}{2}(y-1)\right)$$
corresponding to $1 < y < 3$. Hence,
$$p(y) = \frac{1}{2} \quad \text{for} \quad 1 < y < 3$$
$$= 0 \quad \text{for} \quad y \leq 1 \text{ or } y \geq 3$$

3.7 For $y = x^2$, $x = \pm\sqrt{y}$, and $\frac{dy}{dx} = 2x$. Then from Equation (3.13),
$$p(y) = \frac{2p(x)}{|dy/dx|} = \frac{p(\sqrt{y})}{\sqrt{y}}$$
where
$$p(x) = \frac{1}{\sqrt{2\pi}}\exp(-x^2/2) \quad \text{for all } x$$

and

$$p(\sqrt{y}) = \frac{1}{\sqrt{2\pi}} \exp(-y/2) \quad \text{for } y \geq 0$$

Hence,

$$p(y) = \frac{1}{\sqrt{2\pi y}} \exp(-y/2) \quad \text{for } y \geq 0$$
$$= 0 \qquad \text{otherwise}$$

3.8 From Equation (3.99), $\mu_R = 2.50 = 1.25\sigma_r$; hence $\sigma_r = 2$. From Equation (3.96), Prob$[R > 5] = 1 - Q_1(R) = \exp[-R^2/(2\sigma_r^2)] = \exp\{-5^2/[2(2)^2]\} = \exp[-25/8]$
$= 0.0439$

3.9 The moment-generating function of Equation (3.17) becomes

$$m(s) = \sum_{x=0}^{\infty} e^{sx} e^{-\mu} (\mu^x/x!) = e^{-\mu} \sum_{x=0}^{\infty} (\mu e^s)^x/x!$$
$$= e^{-\mu} e^{\mu e^s} = e^{\mu(e^s - 1)}$$

It follows that

$$m'(s) = \mu e^{\mu(e^s - 1) + s}$$
$$m''(s) = \mu\{(\mu e^s + 1) e^{\mu(e^s - 1) + s}\}$$

Setting $s = 0$ yields

$$\mu = m'(0) = \mu$$
$$\psi^2 = m''(0) = \mu^2 + \mu$$
$$\sigma^2 = \psi^2 - \mu^2 = \mu$$

Hence, the mean and variance of the Poisson distribution are both equal to the parameter μ.

3.10 From the stated probability density functions,

$$\mu_x = 1, \sigma_x^2 = 2 \quad \text{and} \quad \mu_y = -1, \sigma_y^2 = 2$$

It follows that for $u = x - y$,

$$\mu_u = \mu_x - \mu_y = 2 \quad \text{and} \quad \sigma_u^2 = \sigma_x^2 + \sigma_y^2 = 4$$

while for $v = x + y$,

$$\mu_v = \mu_x + \mu_y = 0 \quad \text{and} \quad \sigma_v^2 = \sigma_x^2 + \sigma_y^2 = 4$$

Hence, the probability density functions for u and v are

(a) $p(u) = \frac{1}{2\sqrt{2\pi}} \exp\left[-(u-2)^2/8\right]$

(b) $p(v) = \frac{1}{2\sqrt{2\pi}} \exp[-v^2/8]$

CHAPTER 4

4.1 (a) $\mu_y = E[cx] = cE[x] = c\mu_x$
(b) $\psi_y^2 = E[(cx)^2] = c^2 E[x^2] = c^2 \psi_x^2$
(c) $\sigma_y^2 = \psi_y^2 - \mu_y^2 = c^2(\psi_x^2 - \mu_x^2) = c^2 \sigma_x^2$

4.2 The mean value and variance are $\mu_x = 1$ and $\sigma_x^2 = 4$.

4.3 (a) For $v = xy$, $\mu_v = \mu_x \mu_y$
(b) For $u = x - y$, $\sigma_u^2 = \sigma_x^2 + \sigma_y^2$

4.4 When the variance estimate is computed as in Equation (4.12), then

$$\frac{ns^2}{\sigma_x^2} = \chi_n^2 \quad \text{where } n = N - 1$$

It follows that

$$\text{Var}[\chi_n^2] = 2n = \frac{n^2}{\sigma_n^4} \text{Var}[s^2]$$

Hence,

$$\text{Var}[s^2] = \frac{2\sigma_x^4}{n} = \frac{2\sigma_x^4}{N-1}$$

and

$$\varepsilon_r = \frac{\{\text{Var}[s^2]\}^{1/2}}{E[s^2]} = \frac{\sqrt{2}}{\sqrt{N-1}} \approx 0.10$$

4.5 (a) Chi-square distribution with $n = 4$ dof
(b) Normal distribution with a mean value and variance of $\mu = 0$ and $\sigma^2 = 4$
(c) Student t distribution with $n = 3$ dof
(d) F distribution with $n_1 = 3$ and $n_2 = 1$ dof

4.6 (a) Normal distribution
(b) F distribution
(c) Chi-square distribution
(d) Student t distribution

4.7 From Equation (4.58), for $r = 0.77$,

$$w = \frac{1}{2} \ln\left[\frac{1 + r_{xy}}{1 - r_{xy}}\right] = \frac{1}{2} \ln\left[\frac{1.77}{0.23}\right] \approx 1.02$$

At the 1% level of significance, from Table A.2, $z_{\alpha/2} = z_{0.005} = 2.57$. Hence, the acceptance region for the hypothesis that $r_{xy} = 0$ is given by

Equation (4.61) with $N = 7$ as

$$\left[\frac{-2.57}{\sqrt{7-3}}\right] \leq \frac{1}{2}\ln\left[\frac{1+r_{xy}}{1-r_{xy}}\right] < \frac{-2.57}{\sqrt{7-3}}$$

Since 1.02 falls inside this interval, the hypothesis is accepted, meaning there is insufficient evidence to assert that correlation exists between the two variables.

4.8 Given $\hat{y} = 1 + x$, it follows that $a = 1$ and $b = 1$.

(a) From Equation (4.70),
$$r_{xy} = [bb']^{1/2} = 0.5, \text{ so } b' = 1/4$$

(b) From Equation (4.68),
$$\hat{x} = \bar{x} + b'(y - \bar{y}) = 1 + \frac{1}{4}(y-2) = \frac{1}{2} + \frac{1}{4}y$$

4.9 (a) $s^2 = \frac{1}{N}\sum_{i=1}^{N} x_i^2$

$$E[s^2] = E\left[\frac{1}{N}\sum_{i=1}^{N} x_i^2\right] = \frac{1}{N}\sum_{i=1}^{N} E[x_i^2] = \frac{1}{N}\sum_{i=1}^{N} \sigma_x^2 = \frac{1}{N}(N\sigma_x^2) = \sigma_x^2$$

(b) $s^2 = \frac{\sigma^2 \chi_n^2}{n}$ where $n = N$ dof

(c) $\text{Var}[s^2] = \frac{\text{Var}[\chi_n^2]\sigma^4}{n^2} = \frac{2N\sigma^4}{N^2} = \frac{2\sigma^4}{N}$

4.10 (a) The reverse arrangements for the sequence of $N = 20$ measurements are

$$\begin{array}{lllll}
A_1 = 4 & A_5 = 1 & A_9 = 2 & A_{13} = 2 & A_{17} = 0 \\
A_2 = 9 & A_6 = 6 & A_{10} = 6 & A_{14} = 2 & A_{18} = 1 \\
A_3 = 1 & A_7 = 11 & A_{11} = 0 & A_{15} = 2 & A_{19} = 0 \\
A_4 = 1 & A_8 = 0 & A_{12} = 11 & A_{16} = 3 & A = 62
\end{array}$$

From Table A.6, for $N = 20$ and $\alpha = 0.05$, $A_{20;0.975} = 64$ and $A_{20;0.025} = 125$. Since $A = 62$ falls outside this acceptance region, the hypothesis of stationarity is rejected at the 5% level of significance; that is, there is reason to doubt that the sequence of $N = 20$ measurements was acquired from a stationary random process.

(b) From Equation (4.66), the slope of the linear regression line for the sequence of $N = 20$ measurements is

$$b = \frac{\sum_{i=1}^{20} x_i y_i - N\bar{x}\bar{y}}{\sum_{i=1}^{20} x_i^2 - N\bar{x}^2} = \frac{2238.9 - 20(10.5)(10.53)}{2870 - 20(10.5)^2} = \frac{27.6}{665} = 0.042$$

From Equation (4.57), the correlation coefficient for the sequence of measurements is

$$r = \frac{\sum_{i=1}^{20} x_i y_i - N\bar{x}\bar{y}}{\left[\left(\sum_{i=1}^{20} x_i^2 - N\bar{x}^2\right)\left(\sum_{i=1}^{20} y_i^2 - N\bar{y}^2\right)\right]^{1/2}}$$

$$= \frac{25.7}{[(665)(2223.1 - 20(10.53)^2)]^{1/2}} = 0.46$$

From Equation (4.74), the standard error about the regression line is

$$\sigma_{y/x} = \left[\left(\frac{N-1}{N-2}\right)s_y^2(1-r_{xy}^2)\right]^{1/2} = \left[\frac{19}{18}(0.28)(1-0.21)\right]^{1/2} = 0.48$$

From Equation (4.72) the acceptance region for the hypothesis that $B=0$ is

$$|b| \le \frac{\pm s_{y/x} t_{N-2}}{\left(\sum_{i=1}^{N} x_i^2 - N\bar{x}^2\right)^{1/2}} = \frac{\pm 0.48(2.101)}{(665)^{1/2}} = \pm 0.039$$

Since $b = 0.042$ falls outside this acceptance region, the hypothesis that $B = 0$ is again rejected at the 5% level of significance.

The measurements in this problem were actual acquired from a random process with a mean value that increased linearly by about 10% from the first to the last measurement. Thus, both the nonparametric reverse arrangements test and the parametric test using the slope of the regression line correctly detected this modest linear trend at the 5% level of significance.

CHAPTER 5

5.1 (a), (c), (d), and (e) are always true
5.2 None
5.3 (a) For autospectra, (a), (b), (d), and (e) are always true
  (b) For cross-spectra, none are always true

5.4 (a) and (g) are always true

5.5 (a) $\mu_x = \sqrt{R_{xx}(\infty)} = 4$
  $\psi_x^2 = R_{xx}(0) = 41$
  $\sigma_x^2 = \psi_x^2 - \mu_x^2 = 25$
  (b) $G_{xx}(f) = 200\left[\frac{1}{16 + 4\pi^2(f+2)^2} + \frac{1}{16 + 4\pi^2(f-2)^2}\right] + 16\delta(f)$

5.6 (a) $\mu_x = 4$

$$\psi_x^2 = \int_{-\infty}^{\infty} S_{xx}(f)df = 216$$

$$\sigma_x^2 = \psi_x^2 - \mu_x^2 = 200$$

(b) $R_{xx}(\tau) = 16 + 40\int_0^{10}\left(1-\frac{f}{10}\right)\cos(2\pi f\tau)df = 16 + \dfrac{[1-\cos(20\pi\tau)]}{\pi^2\tau^2}$

5.7 From Equations (5.195), (5.188), and (5.189),

$$N_0 = \frac{1}{\pi}\left[\frac{\int_0^{25}(2\pi f)^2 G_{xx}(f)df}{\int_0^{25} G_{xx}(f)df}\right]^{1/2} = 16.24$$

This follows from the fact that

$$\int_0^{25}\frac{1}{25+f^2}df = \frac{1}{5}\tan^{-1}(5) = 0.275$$

and

$$\int_0^{25}\frac{(2\pi f)^2}{25+f^2}df = (2\pi)^2[25 - 5\tan^{-1}(5)] = (2\pi)^2(18.133)$$

5.8 From Equations (5.211), (5.215), and (5.216),

$$M = \frac{1}{2\pi}\left(\frac{\sigma_a}{\sigma_v}\right) = \frac{1}{2\pi}\left[\frac{(2\pi)^2 68.96}{(2\pi)4.26}\right] = 16.19$$

This follows from the fact that

$$\sigma_v^2 = \int_0^{25}\frac{(2\pi f)^2}{25+f^2}df = (2\pi)^2[25 - 5\tan^{-1}(5)] = (2\pi)^2 18.133$$

and

$$\sigma_a^2 = \int_0^{25}\frac{(2\pi f)^4}{25+f^2}df = (2\pi)^4\left[-625 + \frac{(25)^3}{3} + 125\tan^{-1}(5)\right] = (2\pi)^4 4755$$

Note that M is the number of positive peaks per second. The total number of positive and negative peaks (maxima and minima) per second is $2M = 32.38$.

ANSWERS TO PROBLEMS IN RANDOM DATA   581

5.9 (a) $S_{xy}(f) = (3/f^2) + j(4/f^3)$. Using the convention $S(f) = S_{Re}(f) - j\, S_{Im}(f)$,

$$\text{Real } S_{xy}(f) = (3/f^2) \text{ and Imag } S_{xy}(f) = -(4/f^3)$$

(b) $|S_{xy}(f)| = [(3/f^2)^2 + (4/f^3)^2]^{1/2}$, and

$$\theta_{xy}(f) = \tan^{-1}\left[\frac{-(4/f^3)}{(3/f^2)}\right] = \tan^{-1}\left(\frac{-4}{3f}\right)$$

5.10 From Equation (5.155),

$$R_{\ddot{x}\ddot{x}}(\tau) = -R''_{xx}(\tau)$$
$$= [(2\pi f_0)^2 - a^2]e^{-a|\tau|}\cos(2\pi f_0\tau) - 4\pi a f_0 e^{-a|\tau|}\sin(2\pi f_0|\tau|)$$

CHAPTER 6

6.1 (a) The magnitude of $G_{xy}(f)$ is given by

$$|G_{xy}(f)|^2 = (4/f^3)^2 + (4/f^2)^2 = 16\left(\frac{f^2+1}{f^6}\right)$$

It follows that

$$|H_{xy}(f)| = \frac{|G_{xy}(f)|}{G_{xx}(f)} = \frac{2}{f}(f^2+1)^{1/2}$$

(b) $\phi_{xy}(f) = \tan^{-1}(f)$

(c) $\tau_0 = \dfrac{\phi_{xy}(f)}{2\pi f} = \dfrac{\tan^{-1}(f)}{2\pi f}$

from Equation (5.97).

6.2 Each output spectrum is given by

$$G_{v_i v_i}(f) = |H(f)|^2 G_{x_i x_i}(f); \quad i = 1, 2, 3$$

Hence,

$$G_{v_1 v_1}(f) = 100;\ G_{v_2 v_2}(f) = 200;\ G_{v_3 v_3}(f) = 300$$

It follows that

$$G_{yy}(f) = G_{v_1 v_1}(f) + G_{v_2 v_2}(f) + G_{v_3 v_3}(f) + G_{nn}(f) = 700$$

and

$$\gamma^2_{x_1 y}(f) = \frac{100}{700} \approx 0.143;\ \gamma^2_{x_2 y}(f) = \frac{200}{700} \approx 0.286;\ \gamma^2_{x_3 y}(f) = \frac{300}{700} \approx 0.429$$

6.3 From Example 6.3, for a white noise input,

$$\psi^2_y = \frac{G\pi f_n}{4\zeta} = 25\pi \quad \text{and} \quad \psi_y = 5\sqrt{\pi} = 8.86$$

6.4 From Example 6.3, for a sine wave input,

$$\max \psi_y^2 = \frac{X^2}{8\varsigma^2} = 5000 \quad \text{and} \quad \max \psi_y = 70.71$$

6.5 $G_{yy}(f) = G_{vv}(f) + G_{nn}(f) = G_{vv}(f) + 0.1$

$$G_{vv}(f) = \frac{G_{xx}(f)}{[1 - (f/f_n)^2]^2 + [2\varsigma(f/f_n)]^2}$$

$G_{vv}(0) = 0.1$ $\quad\quad G_{yy}(0) = 0.25$
$G_{vv}(10) = 250$ $\quad\quad G_{yy}(10) = 250.1$
$G_{vv}(100) = 0.00001$ $\quad\quad G_{yy}(100) = 0.10001$

Hence, using $\gamma_{xy}^2(f) = [G_{vv}(f)/G_{yy}(f)]$,

(a) $\gamma_{xy}^2(0) = (0.1/0.2) = 0.5000$

(b) $\gamma_{xy}^2(10) = (250/250.1) = 0.9996$

(c) $\gamma_{xy}^2(100) = (0.00001/0.10001) = 0.0001$

6.6 Letting the input measurement be $x(t) = u(t) + m(t)$, it follows that $G_{xy}(f) = G_{uy}(f)$ and $G_{xx}(f) = G_{uu}(f) + G_{mm}(f) = 0.1 + 0.1$. Hence,

(a) $H_1(f) = \frac{G_{xy}(f)}{G_{xx}(f)} = \frac{G_{xy}(f)}{2G_{uu}(f)} = \frac{H(f)}{2}$

where $H(f)$ is as defined in Problem 6.1. Thus, the magnitude of the computed frequency response function $H_1(f)$ is only one-half the correct value.

(b) $H_2(f) = \frac{G_{yy}(f)}{G_{yx}(f)} = \frac{G_{yy}(f)}{G_{yu}(f)} = H(f)$

where $H(f)$ is as defined in Problem 6.1. Thus, the computed frequency response function $H_2(f)$ is correct.

6.7 The squared magnitude of the frequency response functions is given by

$$|H_1(f)|^2 = \frac{1}{1 + 16f^2} \quad \text{and} \quad |H_2(f)|^2 = \frac{1}{1 + 64f^2}$$

At $f = 1\,\text{Hz}$,

$G_{v_1 v_1} = (10/17) \approx 0.588, \quad G_{y_1 y_1} \approx 0.688$
$G_{v_2 v_2} = (10/65) \approx 0.154, \quad G_{y_2 y_2} \approx 0.254$

It follows that

$|G_{xy_1}|^2 = |H_1 G_{xx}|^2 = G_{v_1 v_1} G_{xx} = (100/17) \approx 5.88$

$|G_{xy_2}|^2 = |H_2 G_{xx}|^2 = G_{v_2 v_2} G_{xx} = (100/65) \approx 1.54$

$|G_{y_1 y_2}|^2 = |H_1^* H_2 G_{xx}|^2 = G_{v_1 v_1} G_{v_2 v_2} \approx 0.0906$

(a) $\gamma_{xy_1}^2 \approx \frac{0.588}{0.688} \approx 0.855 \quad \text{and} \quad \gamma_{xy_2}^2 \approx \frac{0.154}{0.254} \approx 0.606$

(b) $\gamma^2_{y_1y_2} \approx \dfrac{0.0906}{(0.688)(0.254)} \approx 0.518$

6.8 The squared magnitudes of the frequency response functions are

$$|H_1(f)|^2 = \frac{1}{1+16f^2} \quad \text{and} \quad |H_1(f)|^2 = \frac{1}{1+64f^2}$$

At $f = 1$ Hz

$G_{v_1v_1} = G_{y_1y_1} = (10/17) = 0.588; \qquad G_{v_2v_2} = G_{y_2y_2} = (10/65) = 0.154$

Since $G_{xx} = G_{uu} + G_{mm} = 10 + 10 = 20$, it follows that

$$|G_{xy_1}(f)|^2 = |H_1 G_{uu}(f)|^2 = G_{v_1v_1}(f)G_{uu}(f) = 5.88$$
$$|G_{xy_2}|^2 = |H_2 G_{uu}|^2 = G_{v_2v_2} G_{uu} = (100/65) = 1.54$$
$$|G_{y_1y_2}|^2 = |H_1^* H_2 G_{uu}|^2 = G_{v_1v_1} G_{v_2v_2} = 0.0906$$

(a)
$$\gamma^2_{xy_1} = \frac{|G_{xy_1}|^2}{G_{xx}G_{y_1y_1}} = \frac{5.88}{20(0.588)} = 0.500$$

$$\gamma^2_{xy_2} = \frac{|G_{xy_2}|^2}{G_{xx}G_{y_2y_2}} = \frac{1.54}{20(0.154)} = 0.500$$

(b) $\gamma^2_{y_1y_2} = \dfrac{|G_{y_1y_2}|^2}{G_{y_1y_1} G_{y_2y_2}} = \dfrac{0.0906}{(0.588)(0.154)} = 1.00$

6.9 As long as the input and output motions have the same units, the result in Example 6.4 applies. Hence,

$$\psi^2_{\dot{y}} = \frac{G\pi f_n(1+4\varsigma^2)}{4\varsigma} = \frac{(0.01)\pi(100)[1+4(0.7)^2]}{4(0.7)} = 3.32; \psi_{\dot{y}} = 1.82$$

6.10 From Table 2.1, the magnitude of the frequency response function for this case is

$$H_{\ddot{x}(y-x)}(f) = \frac{1}{(2\pi f_n)^2 \sqrt{\left[1-(f/f_n)^2\right]^2 + [2\varsigma f/f_n]^2}}$$

which is the frequency response function for the force input–displacement output system divided by $(2\pi f_n)^2$. Hence, from Example 6.3,

$$\psi^2_{(y-x)} = \frac{G\pi f_n}{(2\pi f_n)^4(4\varsigma)} = \frac{(0.01)\pi(100)}{(200\pi)^4(4)(0.7)} = 7.20 \times 10^{-12}; \psi_{(y-x)} = 2.68 \times 10^{-6}$$

CHAPTER 7

7.1 (a) No change in Equation (7.13).

(b) Equation (7.14) becomes

$$G_{yy}(f) + \mu_y^2 \delta(f) = \sum_{i=1}^{q} |H_1(f)|^2 G_{xx}(f) + G_{nn}(f) + \left[\sum_{i=1}^{q} H_i(0)\mu_{x_i}\right]^2 \delta(f)$$

where

$$\mu_y = \sum_{i=1}^{q} H_i(0)\mu_{x_i}$$

7.2 From Equations (7.52)–(7.54),

(a) $G_{22 \cdot 1} = \frac{4}{3} = 1.333$

(b) $G_{2y \cdot 1} = \frac{4}{3} = 1.333$

(c) $G_{yy \cdot 1} = \frac{17}{30} = 0.567$

(d) $H_{2y} = \frac{G_{2y \cdot 1}}{G_{22 \cdot 1}} = 1.000$

7.3 $L_{1y} = \frac{G_{1y}}{G_{11}} = (4/3) + j(1/3); |L_{1y}|^2 = \frac{17}{9}$

$L_{2y} = H_{2y} = 1.000; |L_{2y}|^2 = 1.000$

Then,

$$G_{y:1} = |L_{1y}|^2 G_{11} = \frac{17}{3}; G_{y:2 \cdot 1} = |L_{2y}|^2 G_{22 \cdot 1} = \frac{4}{3};$$

$$G_{y:2!} = \frac{17}{3} + \frac{4}{3} = 7; G_{yy} = 10.0$$

Hence,

$$\gamma_{y:2}^2 = \frac{G_{y:2!}}{G_{yy}} = 0.70$$

7.4 From Equation (7.26), if $G_{12} = 0.4A$, then $G_{yy} = 1.15A$. If $H_{12} = 0$, then $G_{yy} = 0.95A$.

7.5 Using Equations (7.20) and (7.21), $G_{12} = 0.4A$, $G_{1y} = 1.2A$, and $G_{2y} = 0.7A$. It follows that

$$\gamma_{12}^2 = 0.080, \gamma_{1y}^2 = \frac{1.44}{2.30} = 0.626, \gamma_{2y}^2 = \frac{0.49}{1.15} = 0.426$$

7.6 Using Equation (7.35), $\gamma_{y:2!}^2 = (0.95A)/(1.15A) = 0.826$

7.7 $L_{1y} = \frac{G_{1y}}{G_{11}} = \frac{1.2A}{2A} = 0.60$

$L_{2y} = \frac{G_{2y \cdot 1}}{G_{22 \cdot 1}} = \frac{0.46A}{0.92A} = 0.50$

7.8 $G_{32} = 1 - j2$ means power flow is from 3 to 2
$G_{12} = 2 + j1$ means power flow is from 2 to 1
$G_{13} = 3 + j3$ means power flow is from 3 to 1
Hence, the order should be x_3 to x_2 to x_1.

7.9 If $R_{11}(\tau) = 3\delta(f)$, then $S_{11}(f) = 3$ and $G_{11}(f) = 6$.

(a) $\gamma_{12}^2(f) = \frac{8}{9} = 0.889$

(b) $G_{yy}(f) = \frac{228}{25 + f^2}$ and $R_{yy}(\tau) = 22.8\pi e^{-10\pi|\tau|}$

(c) $R_{1y}(\tau) = 36\pi e^{-10\pi\tau}$ for $\tau \geq 0$
$= 0$ for $\tau < 0$
$G_{1y}(f) = \frac{36}{5 + jf}$

(d) $\gamma_{1y}^2(f) = \frac{18}{19} = 0.947$

7.10 Equations (7.125)–(7.127) follow directly from Equation (7.108) since $A_{iy}(f) = H_{iy}(f)$, $i = 1, 2, 3$. The physical reason why $L_{iy}(f)$ is not the same as $A_{1y}(f)$ is because $L_{1y}(f)$ represents the three possible ways that $U_1(f) = X_1(f)$ can reach $Y(f)$, but $A_{1y}(f)$ represents only one of the possible ways that $U_1(f) = X_1(f)$ can reach $Y(f)$.

CHAPTER 8

8.1 $\sigma[\hat{\mu}_x] = 0.10 = \frac{1}{\sqrt{2BT}}$ gives $BT = 50$.

(a) For $\mu_x = 0$, $\psi_x^2 = \sigma_x^2$, and $\varepsilon[\hat{\psi}_x^2] = \frac{1}{\sqrt{BT}} = \frac{1}{\sqrt{50}} = 0.1414$.

(b) $\varepsilon[\hat{\psi}_x] = \frac{1}{2\sqrt{BT}} = 0.0707$.

(c) For any μ_x, $\varepsilon_r[\hat{\sigma}_x] = \frac{1}{2\sqrt{BT}} = 0.0707$.

8.2 (a) $\varepsilon[\hat{\mu}_x] = \frac{1}{\sqrt{2BT}}\left(\frac{\sigma_x}{\mu_x}\right) = 0.0707$

(b) For $\mu_x \neq 0$,
$$\varepsilon[\hat{\psi}_x^2] = \frac{1}{\sqrt{2BT}}\left(\frac{\sigma_x}{\mu_x}\right)^2 + \frac{\sqrt{2}}{\sqrt{BT}}\left(\frac{\mu_x\sigma_x}{\psi_x}\right) = 0.040 + 0.0063 = 0.046$$

8.3 (c) and (e) involve a bias error.

8.4 From Sections 8.4.1 and 8.4.2,

(a) $\varepsilon[\hat{R}_{xx}(0)] = \varepsilon[\hat{R}_{yy}(0)] = \frac{1}{\sqrt{BT}}$

(b) $\varepsilon[\hat{R}_{xy}(0)] = \dfrac{1}{\sqrt{2BT}}\left[1 + \dfrac{(S+N_1)(S+N_2)}{S^2}\right]^{1/2}$

(c) $\varepsilon[\hat{R}_{xy}(0)] = \dfrac{1}{\sqrt{2BT}}\left[\left(\dfrac{N_1}{S}\right)\left(\dfrac{N_2}{S}\right)\right]^{1/2}$

(d) $\varepsilon[\hat{R}_{xy}(0)] = \dfrac{1}{\sqrt{2BT}}\left[\dfrac{N_2}{S}\right]^{1/2}$

8.5 From Equation (8.129),

$$\sigma_1(\tau) \approx \dfrac{0.93}{\pi B}\{\varepsilon[\hat{R}_{xy}(0)]\}^{1/2}$$

The maximum value of $\hat{R}_{xy}(\tau)$ occurs at $\tau = 0$ since $R_{xy}(\tau) = R_{ss}(\tau)$. Hence,

$$\text{Prob}[-2\sigma_1(\tau) \leq \hat{\tau} \leq 2\sigma_1(\tau)] = 0.95$$

8.6 The probability distribution function is given by

$$\hat{P}(x) = \hat{\text{Prob}}[x(t) \leq x] = \dfrac{T_x}{T} = \dfrac{N_x}{N}$$

$$E[\hat{P}(x)] = \lim_{N \to \infty}\left(\dfrac{N_x}{N}\right) = P(x)$$

Hence, $\hat{P}(x)$ is an unbiased estimate.

$$\sigma^2[\hat{P}(x)] = \dfrac{P(x)[1 - P(x)]}{N}$$

$$\varepsilon[\hat{P}(x)] = \dfrac{\sigma[\hat{P}(x)]}{P(x)} = \dfrac{\sqrt{1 - P(x)}}{\sqrt{NP(x)}}$$

At $x = \mu_x$, $P(x) = P(\mu) = (1/2)$ and

$$\varepsilon[\hat{P}(\mu)] = \dfrac{1}{\sqrt{N}} = 0.10$$

8.7 (a) At $x = \mu_x + 2.5\,\sigma_x$, a window of width $W = 0.25\,\sigma_x$ will cover

$$\mu_x - 2.375\sigma_x \leq x \leq \mu_x + 2.625\sigma_x$$

From Table A.2, the probability of being in this window is 0.0045, so the estimated probability density function is

$$\hat{p}(x) = \dfrac{0.0045}{0.25} = 0.0180$$

From Table A.1, the exact probability density function at $x = \mu_x + 2.5\,\sigma_x$ is $p(x) = 0.0175$, so the exact bias error is

$$b[\hat{p}(x)] = 0.0175 - 0.0180 = -0.0005$$

(b) From Equation (8.82) and Example 8.4, at $x = 2.5$,

$$p''(x) = \frac{-(1+x^2)}{\sqrt{2\pi}} e^{-x^2/2} = -0.127$$

For $W = 0.25\sigma_x$, the estimated bias error is

$$b[\hat{p}(x)] = \frac{W^2}{24} p''(x) = -0.0003$$

8.8 The spectral density corresponds to a system with a resonance frequency of $f_r \approx 100$ Hz and damping ratio of $\zeta = 0.05$. The half-power point bandwidth of the spectral peak is then $B_r \approx 2\zeta f_r = 10$ Hz.

(a) From Equation (8.141),

$$\varepsilon_b[\hat{G}(f)] = -\frac{1}{3}\left(\frac{B_e}{B_r}\right)^2 = -0.05$$

Hence, $B_e \leq \sqrt{0.15}(10) = 3.87$ Hz. From equation (8.147),

$$\varepsilon_r = \frac{1}{\sqrt{B_e T_r}} = 0.10$$

Hence, $T_r \geq 1/[(0.10)^2(3.87)] = 25.8$ s.

(b) From Equation (8.150),

$$B_o = 2\frac{(\zeta f_r)^{4/5}}{(T_r)^{1/5}} = 2\frac{[(0.05)(100)]^{4/5}}{(60)^{1/5}} = 3.20 \text{ Hz}$$

8.9 Let λ_m = maximum value of $\lambda(f)$. Then,

$$\lambda^2(f) = \frac{G_{xx}(f)}{G''_{xx}(f)}$$

From Equations (8.139) and (8.148),

$$\varepsilon_b[\hat{G}_{xx}(f)] \geq \frac{B_e^2}{24\lambda_m^2} \leq 0.05$$

$$\varepsilon_r[\hat{G}_{xx}(f)] \geq \frac{1}{\sqrt{n_d}} = \frac{1}{\sqrt{B_e T}} \leq 0.05$$

It follows that

$$B_e T \geq 400 \qquad T \geq (400/B_e)$$
$$B_e^2 \leq 1.2\lambda_m^2 \qquad B_e \geq 1.095\lambda_m$$

8.10 For $n_d = 12$, the degrees-of-freedom are $n = 2n_d = 24$ and from Table A.3, the values of the χ^2 variable are

$$\chi^2_{24;0.025} = 39.36; \quad \chi^2_{24;0.975} = 12.40$$

The 95% confidence interval from Equation (8.159) is then

$$[0.18 \leq G(f) \leq 0.58]$$

while the normalized random error is given by

$$\varepsilon_r = \frac{1}{\sqrt{n_d}} = \frac{1}{\sqrt{12}} = 0.29$$

CHAPTER 9

9.1 Set $\varepsilon = \dfrac{(1-\gamma^2)^{1/2}}{|\gamma|\sqrt{2n_d}} = 0.05$ with $\gamma^2 = 0.75$. Then $n_d = \dfrac{400}{6} = 67$.

9.2 Set $\dfrac{(1-\gamma^2)^{1/2}}{|\gamma|\sqrt{2n_d}} = \dfrac{1}{\sqrt{n_d}}$. Then $\gamma^2 = \frac{1}{3} = 0.333$.

9.3 From Table 9.1,

(a) $\varepsilon[\hat{G}_{xx}] = \varepsilon[\hat{G}_{yy}] = 0.10$
(b) $\varepsilon[\hat{G}_{xy}] = 0.1414$

9.4 From Table 9.1,

$$\varepsilon[\hat{C}_{xy}] = \varepsilon[\hat{Q}_{xy}] = 0.1414$$

9.5 $|G_{xy}|^2 = C^2 + Q^2 = 0.50; \; \gamma^2 = 0.50; \; G_{vv} = 0.5$

From Table 9.6,

$$\varepsilon[\hat{\gamma}^2_{xy}] = 0.100; \; \varepsilon[\hat{G}_{vv}] = 0.173$$

Hence,

$$\text{Prob}[0.30 \leq \hat{\gamma}^2_{xy} \leq 0.70] \approx 0.95$$
$$\text{Prob}[0.154 \leq \hat{G}_{vv} \leq 0.846] \approx 0.95$$

9.6 $\theta_{xy} = \tan^{-1}(1) = (\pi/4) = 0.7865$ rad. From Equation (9.52), $\sigma[\hat{\theta}_{xy}] = 0.0707$ rad. Hence, $\text{Prob}[0.645 \leq \hat{\theta}_{xy} \leq 0.928] \approx 0.95$.

9.7 From Equation (9.65),

$$\hat{G}_{xy} = G_{xy}\left(1 - \frac{\tau_1}{T}\right) = 0.80 \, G_{xy}$$

Hence, $\hat{H}_{xy} = 0.80 \, H_{xy}$ gives a biased estimate of H_{xy} due to a time delay. The true $G_{xy} = 10 G_{uu} \exp(-j2\pi f \tau_1)$ and the true $H_{xy} = \dfrac{G_{xy}}{G_{uu}} = 10 \exp(-j2\pi f \tau_1)$. The measured $\hat{H}_{xy} = \dfrac{G_{xy}}{G_{xx}} = \dfrac{G_{xy}}{2G_{uu}} = 5 \exp(-j2\pi f \tau_1)$, where $G_{xx} = G_{uu} + G_{mm} = 2G_{uu}$. Hence, $\hat{H}_{xy} = 0.50H_{xy}$ gives a biased estimate of H_{xy} due to input noise. The total biased estimate $\hat{H}_{xy}(f) = 0.4H_{xy}$.

9.8 (a) $G_{vv} = 0.50$ is the true value because $\gamma_{xy}^2 = 0.50$.
(b) $\hat{\gamma}_{xy}^2 = 0.64\gamma_{xy}^2 = 0.32$; $\hat{G}_{vv} = 0.64G_{vv} = 0.32$
$b[\hat{G}_{vv}] = -0.18$ due to the time-delay bias error.
(c) Using $\hat{\gamma}_{xy}^2 = 0.32$ in Equation (9.73), $\varepsilon[\hat{G}_{vv}] = 0.115$.

9.9 $G_{2y \cdot 1} = 4 - j3$; $G_{22 \cdot 1} = \frac{55}{4} = 13.75$; $G_{yy \cdot 1} = 20$; $\gamma_{2y \cdot 1}^2 = \frac{1}{11} = 0.0909$. This gives $\varepsilon[|\hat{H}_{2y}|] = \frac{1}{\sqrt{20}} = 0.224$; $\sigma[\hat{\phi}_{2y}] = 0.224$ rad $= 12.8°$.

9.10 $\hat{\gamma}_{y:x}^2 = \frac{6}{11} = 0.545$; $\varepsilon[\hat{\gamma}_{y:x}^2] = \frac{5}{33\sqrt{3}} = 0.087$

CHAPTER 10

10.1 The mechanical calibration is more likely to be correct because it includes the sensitivity of the transducer while the electrical calibration does not.

10.2 (a) The minimum sampling rate for $f_A = 1000$ Hz is $2f_A = 2000$ sps.
(b) Yes.
(c) No since the probability density function does not involve frequency information.

10.3 (a) For 200 sps, $f_A = 100$ Hz so the frequency range for the sampled data is $0 \leq f \leq 100$ Hz.
(b) The data in the four 100 Hz bands between 100 and 500 Hz will fold down into the frequency range below 100 Hz. Hence, for a white noise input of $G = 0.1$ V^2/Hz, the computed value of the autospectral density function at any frequency below 100 Hz, including 50 Hz, will be $5G = 5(0.1) = 0.5$ V^2/Hz.

10.4 (a) From Figure 10.13(d), a sharp peak at $x = 0$ suggests that one or more signal dropouts were present in the measured data.
(b) From Figure 10.13(b), a sharp peak at $x = \mu_x + 1.5s_x$ followed by zero values above this level suggests that one-sided clipping of the measured data occurred at this level.

10.5 The mean square value of the random data passed by the resolution filter in the vicinity of the sine wave is

$$\psi_{ran}^2 = B_e G = 10(0.1) = 1\text{V}^2$$

Hence, the total mean square value passed by the resolution filter in the vicinity of the sine wave is $\psi_{ran}^2 + \psi_{per}^2 = 1 + 1 = 2\text{V}^2$ and the computed autospectral density will be

$$G_{com} = \psi^2/B_e = 2/10 = 0.2 V^2/Hz$$

10.6 An 8-bit converter provides $2^8 = 256$ discrete levels over the full minimum to maximum range of 2 V. Hence, $\Delta x = 2/256 = 0.00781$ V and the standard deviation for the background noise is given by Equation (10.17) as

$$\sigma_x = 0.289 \Delta x = 0.00226 \text{ V}$$

10.7 Tests for periodic components and a normal distribution are generally valid only for stationary data, but the nonparametric test for stationary illustrated in Example 10.3 is valid for data that have periodic components and/or are not normally distributed.

10.8 The coherence function is a key parameter required to establish the accuracy of a frequency response function measurement, both gain and phase.

10.9 From Equation (10.1), for $f_n = 1000$ Hz and $\zeta = 0.01$, the magnitude of the frequency response function for a piezoelectric accelerometer is given by

$$|H(f)| = \frac{c}{(2\pi f_n)^2 \sqrt{[(1-f/f_n)^2]^2 + [2\zeta f/f_n]^2}}$$

At $f = 500$ Hz,

$$|H(f)| = \frac{c}{(2\pi f_n)^2 \sqrt{[(1-0.5)^2]^2 + [2(0.01)(0.5)]^2}} = \frac{1.333c}{(2\pi f_n)^2}$$

while the correct value at 0 Hz is

$$|H(f)| = \frac{c}{(2\pi f_n)^2}$$

Hence, the bias error in an autospectral density estimate, which is proportional to $|H(f)|^2$, is $(1.33)^2 = 1.78$ times the correct value, or about 78% to high.

10.10 Since the autospectral density function does not involve phase information, the nonuniform phase factor will have no influence on the measured autospectral density value at 500 Hz.

CHAPTER 11

11.1 (a) $N^2 = 2^{28} \approx 2.7 \times 10^8$
(b) $4Np = 4(2^{14})(14) \approx 9.2 \times 10^5$

11.2 Low-pass filter : $H_1(f) = \dfrac{1-a}{1-a\exp(-j2\pi f \Delta t)}$

High-pass filter : $H_2(f) = 1 - H_1(f) = \dfrac{a[1-\exp(-j2\pi f \Delta t)]}{1-a\exp(-j2\pi f \Delta t)} = \dfrac{Y(f)}{X(f)}$

ANSWERS TO PROBLEMS IN RANDOM DATA   591

$$Y(f) - a\exp(-j2\pi f \Delta t)Y(f) = aX(f) - a\exp(-j2\pi f \Delta t)X(f)$$
$$y(n) - a\,y_{n-1} = a\,x_n - a\,x_{n-1}$$

Hence, $y(n) = a\,x_n - a\,x_{n-1} + a\,y_{n-1}$

11.3 Since standard deviations are not dependent on the mean value of the data, $s_x = s_u$.

11.4 $\tilde{\mu}_n = b_0 + b_1(n\Delta t) + b_2(n\Delta t)^2$. Solve for b_0, b_1, and b_2 from

$$b_0 N + b_1 \Delta t \sum_{n=1}^{N} n + b_2 (\Delta t)^2 \sum_{n=1}^{N} n^2 = \sum_{n=1}^{N} u_n$$

$$b_0 \sum_{n=1}^{N} n + b_1 \Delta t \sum_{n=1}^{N} n^2 + b_2 (\Delta t)^2 \sum_{n=1}^{N} n^3 = \sum_{n=1}^{N} n u_n$$

$$b_0 \sum_{n=1}^{N} n^2 + b_1 \Delta t \sum_{n=1}^{N} n^3 + b_2 (\Delta t)^2 \sum_{n=1}^{N} n^4 = \sum_{n=1}^{N} n^2 u_n$$

Use
$$A = \sum_{n=1}^{N} n = \frac{N(N+1)}{2}$$

$$B = \sum_{n=1}^{N} n^2 = \frac{N(N+1)(2N+1)}{6}$$

$$C = \sum_{n=1}^{N} n^3 = \frac{N^2(N+1)^2}{4}$$

$$D = \sum_{n=1}^{N} n^4 = \frac{N(N+1)(2N+1)(3N^2+3N-1)}{30}$$

11.5 (a) For $B_e = 16\,\text{Hz}$, $T = 0.0625$ s and $n_d = 64$. Hence, $N = 256$ and $p = 8$, Assuming $4Np$ real operations for each FFT, the total n_d operations equal $64(4Np) = 5.24 \times 10^5$.

(b) $\varepsilon_r = 1/\sqrt{n_d} = 0.125$

11.6 From Equation (11.93),

$$\hat{R}_{xx}^c(\tau) = (1-\tau)\hat{R}_{xx}(\tau) + \tau\hat{R}_{xx}(1-\tau)$$
$$= (1-\tau)e^{-2|\tau|}\cos(18.85\tau) + \tau e^{-2|1-\tau|}\cos[18.85(1-\tau)]$$

11.7 Assuming $4Np$ real operations for an FFT, and if zero padding is used,
(a) Single block of $N = 8192$ points plus 8192 zeros requires approximately 1.84×10^6 operations.
(b) Thirty two blocks of $N = 256$ points plus 256 zeros requires approximately 1.18×10^6 operations.

11.8 To perform an analysis out to m = 256 lag values, the FFT analysis could be accomplished by averaging over 32 records from the original $N_i = 4096$ data values. From Equation (11.97) where $m = N$, $p = 12$ and the speed ratio = 16/3.

11.9 The rectangular window is defined by

$$h(t) = 1 \quad 0 \leq t \leq T$$
$$= 0 \quad \text{otherwise}$$

It follows that

$$H(f) = T\left[\frac{\sin(\pi fT)}{\pi fT}\right]e^{-2\pi ft} \quad \text{and} \quad \int_0^\infty |H(f)|^2 df = \frac{T}{2}$$

Hence, the noise bandwidth is

$$B_n = \frac{\int_0^\infty |H(f)|^2 df}{|H(f)|^2_{\max}} = \frac{(T/2)}{T^2} = \frac{1}{2T}$$

11.10 The signal is a sine wave with a frequency of $f_0 = 50$ Hz, Since $T = 1.015$ s, the frequency resolution of the computed Fourier spectrum is $\Delta f = (1/1.015)$ Hz. The largest spectral component will be the one closest to 50 Hz, which is the $k = 51$ component at $f_{51} = 50.2463$ Hz. From Equation (11.107), the magnitude of this component without tapering at $f = f_{51} - f_{50}$ 0.2463 Hz is

$$X_{51} = \frac{A\sin(0.2463\pi T)}{0.2463\pi T} = 0.899A$$

With the Hanning window, the magnitude of the largest spectral component is given by Equations (11.109) and (11.110) as

$$X_{51} = 2\left[\frac{A\sin(-0.7389\pi T)}{-0.7389(4\pi)T} + \frac{A\sin(0.2463\pi T)}{0.2463(2\pi)T} + \frac{A\sin(1.2315\pi T)}{1.2315(4\pi)T}\right] = 0.960A$$

The multiplication by two is required to correct for the power loss cause by the Hanning window operating on a sine wave.

CHAPTER 12

12.1 At $t = 0.5T_r$, the actual mean value is

$$\mu_x = A\sin(\pi/2) = A$$

(a) The estimated value is given by

$$\hat{\mu}_x(t) = \frac{1}{0.1T_r} \int_{0.45T_r}^{0.55T_r} A \sin\left(\frac{\pi t}{T_r}\right) dt = 0.996 A$$

so the actual bias error is

$$b[\hat{\mu}_x(t)] = 0.996A - A = -0.004A$$

(b) The bias error approximated by Equation (12.32) is

$$b[\hat{\mu}_x(t)] = \frac{(0.1T_r)^2}{24} \frac{d^2 a(t)}{dt^2} = -\left(\frac{\pi^2}{2400}\right) A = -0.004A$$

12.2 (a) $\mu_x(t) = a(t)$

(b) $\sigma_x^2 = b^2(t)$

(c) $\psi_x^2(t) = a^2(t) + b^2(t)$

12.3 $p(x,t) = \dfrac{1}{b(t)\sqrt{2\pi}} \exp\left\{-[x-a(t)]^2/2b^2(t)\right\}$

12.4 (a) By Equation (12.139),

$$\mathcal{W}_{xx}(f,t) = Ae^{-a|f|}\left(\frac{2a}{a^2 + (2\pi t)^2}\right)$$

(b) By Equation (12.143),

$$\mathcal{P}_{xx}(f,0) = Ae^{-a|f|}$$

12.5 By Equation (12.138),

$$\mathcal{B}_{xx}(\tau,t) = \frac{4Aa^2}{[a^2 + (2\pi t)^2][a^2 + (2\pi \tau)^2]}$$

12.6 (a) $R_{xx}(t_1, t_2) = A^2 e^{-a(t_1 + t_2)} R_{uu}(t_2 - t_1)$

(b) $\mathcal{R}_{xx}(\tau, t) = A^2 e^{-2at} R_{uu}(\tau)$

12.7 Solving Part (b) first, from Equation (12.114),

(b) $\mathcal{P}_{xx}(f,g) = \dfrac{A^2 a}{a^2 + \pi^2 g^2} S_{uu}(f)$

Then from Equation (12.104),

(a) $S_{xx}(f_1, f_2) = \dfrac{A^2 a}{a^2 + \pi^2(f_2 - f_1)^2} S_{uu}\left(\dfrac{f_1 + f_2}{2}\right)$

12.8 $\mathcal{W}_{xx}(f,t) = A^2 e^{-2a|t|} S_{uu}(f)$

12.9 From Equation (12.178),

$$J(f,g) = \frac{1}{f}e^{-g/f} \quad g \geq 0$$
$$= 0 \quad \text{otherwise}$$

From Equation (12.195),

$$S_{yy}(f_1,f_2) = \int_{-\infty}^{L} J^*(f,f_1-f)J(f,f_2-f)S_{xx}(f)df$$

$$= \frac{1}{f^2}\int_{-\infty}^{L} \exp[(2f-f_1-f_2)/f]S_{xx}(f)df$$

where the upper limit L is f_1 or f_2 satisfying $f \leq f_1$, and $f \leq f_2$.

12.10 The maximum spectral value will occur at $t = 15$ s and $f \approx 100$ Hz. Also, since the time-varying autospectral density of the output at all frequencies is proportional to the time-varying mean square value $\psi_x^2(t)$ of the input, $G_{yy}(f,t) \approx c(f)\psi_x^2(t)$, where $c(f)$ is a frequency-dependent coefficient of proportionality. From Equation (12.170),

$$C_T(f,t) = \left\{\frac{d^2[c(f)\psi_x^2(t)]/dt^2}{[c(f)\psi_x^2(t)]}\right\}^2 = \left\{\frac{d^2[1-\cos(\pi t/15)]/dt^2}{[1-\cos(\pi t/15)]}\right\}^2$$

$$= \left(\frac{(\pi/15)^2\cos(\pi t/15)}{[1-\cos(\pi t/15)]}\right)^2$$

It follows that

$$C_T(f,t) = (\pi/15)^4/4 = 0.000481 \text{ s}^{-4} \text{ at } t = 15 \text{ s}$$

From Example 12.9, for a single degree-of-freedom system with $f_n = 100$ and $\zeta = 0.05$,

$$C_B(f,t) = 4(\zeta f_n)^{-4} 4[0.05(100)]^{-4} = 0.00640 \text{ Hz}^{-4}$$

Then, from Equation (12.171), the averaging time and frequency resolution bandwidth that will minimize the mean square error of the estimate for the maximum spectral value are

$$T_0 = 2.29(0.0064)^{1/24}/(0.000481)^{5/24} = 9.11 \text{ s}$$

and

$$B_0 = 2.29(0.000481)^{1/24}/(0.0064)^{5/12} = 4.77 \text{ Hz}$$

CHAPTER 13

13.1 $$X(f) = \frac{1}{1+j2\pi f}$$

$$\tilde{X}(f) = (-j\operatorname{sgn}f)X(f) = \begin{cases} \dfrac{-j}{1+j2\pi f} & \text{for } f > 0 \\ \dfrac{j}{1-j2\pi f} & \text{for } f < 0 \end{cases}$$

13.2 $\tilde{x}(t) = \dfrac{-1}{1+(t-a)^2}$

This follows from
$$\tilde{x}(t-a) = x(t-a)$$
and
$$\mathcal{H}\left[\frac{1}{1+t^2}\right] = \frac{t}{1+t^2} \text{ gives } \mathcal{H}\left[\frac{t}{1+t^2}\right] = \frac{-1}{1+t^2}$$

13.3 From Eq. (13.27) by setting $f_0 = 0$, $\tilde{x}(t) = 0$

13.4 (a), (b), and (d) are correct

13.5 $H_{\text{Re}}(f) = \dfrac{(1-f^2)}{(1-f^2)^2 + (af)^2}$

$H_{\text{Im}}(f) = \tilde{H}_{\text{Re}}(f) = (-j\operatorname{sgn}f)H_{\text{Re}}(f)$

13.6 Given $z(t) = x(t) + jy(t)$, then $\tilde{z}(t) = \tilde{x}(t) + j\tilde{y}(t) = jz(t) = jx(t) - y(t)$ when $\tilde{x}(t) = -y(t)$ and $\tilde{y}(t) = x(t)$.

13.7 Given $z(t) = x(t) + j\tilde{x}(t)$ where $S_{xx}(f) = 2a/(a^2 + 4\pi^2 f^2)$,

(a) $S_{\tilde{x}\tilde{x}}(f) = S_{xx}(f) = \dfrac{2a}{a^2 + 4\pi^2 f^2}$

(b) $S_{zz}(f) = \dfrac{8a}{a^2 + 4\pi^2 f^2}$ for $f > 0$

$\quad\quad\quad = 0$ for $f < 0$

Part (b) comes from Equation (13.78).

13.8 $y(t) = x(t)\cos(2\pi f_0 t)$

(a) $\tilde{y}(t) = x(t)\sin(2\pi f_0 t)$

(b) $R_{yy}(\tau) = \dfrac{R_{xx}(\tau)}{2}\cos(2\pi f_0 \tau)$

(c) $\tilde{R}_{yy}(\tau) = \dfrac{R_{xx}(\tau)}{2} \sin(2\pi f_0 \tau)$

(d) $A_{yy}(\tau) = [R_{yy}^2(\tau) + \tilde{R}_{yy}^2(\tau)]^{1/2} = \dfrac{|R_{xx}(\tau)|}{2}$

13.9 Nondispersive propagation has constant propagation velocity v independent of frequency. The propagation time is $\tau_1 = d/v$.

13.10 Dispersive propagation is now involved. At the frequency $f = f_0 + B$, the propagation velocity is

$$\tau_2 = \dfrac{d}{c_g} \sim \dfrac{1}{\sqrt{f_0 + B}}$$

CHAPTER 14

14.1 Let the output be $y_1(t)$ when the input is $x_1(t) = x(t+\tau)$. Then $y_1(t) = x_1(t)|x_1(t)| = x(t+\tau)|x(t+\tau)| = y(t+\tau)$. This proves that $y(t)$ is a constant-parameter nonlinear system.

14.2 The passage of x(t) to the square-law system output y(t) represents a simple change of variable from x to y where $y = x^2$. One obtains here $x = \pm\sqrt{y}$ and $|dy/dx| = 2|x| = 2\sqrt{y}$. The zero mean value Gaussian probability density function for x is

$$p(x) = \dfrac{1}{\sigma_x\sqrt{2\pi}} \exp(-x^2/2\sigma_x^2).$$

From Equation (3.13), since x is a double-valued function of y, the output probability density function $p_2(y)$ for $y > 0$ is given by

$$p_2(y) = [2p(x)/|dy/dx|] = [p\sqrt{y}/\sqrt{y}]$$

where

$$p(\sqrt{y}) = \dfrac{1}{\sigma_x\sqrt{2\pi}} \exp(-y/2\sigma_x^2)$$

Hence for $y > 0$

$$p_2(y) = \dfrac{1}{\sigma_x\sqrt{2\pi}} \exp(-y/2\sigma_x^2)$$

This function is plotted as Figure 2.19 in Reference 14.2.

14.3 In Figure 14.2 where $z_1(t) = g[x(t)]$, Fourier transforms of both sides give $Z_1(f) = g[X(f)]$. The Fourier transform of the output $y_1(t)$ is $Y_1(f) = A(f)Z_1(f) = A(f)g[X(f)]$. Note here that the linear system $A(f)$ is *not* inside the nonlinear operation. In Figure 14.3, the output $y_2(t) = g[z_2(t)]$ with the Fourier transform relation $Y_2(f) = g[Z_2(f)]$, where $Z_2(f) = B(f)X(f)$. Here, $Y_2(f) = g[B(f)X(f)]$ with the linear system $B(f)$ inside the nonlinear operation. For $A(f) = B(f) \neq 1$, it follows that $Y_1(f) \neq Y_2(f)$ and $y_1(t) \neq y_2(t)$.

14.4 The cross-correlation function $R_{xy}(\tau)$ between the zero mean value Gaussian input $x(t)$ and the nonlinear cubic output $y(t) = x^3(t)$ is

$$R_{xy}(\tau) = E[x(t)y(t+\tau)] = E[x(t)x(t+\tau)x(t+\tau)x(t+\tau)].$$

By Equation (3.73), this fourth-order moment is given by

$$R_{xy}(\tau) = E[x_1 x_2]E[x_3 x_4] + E[x_1 x_3]E[x_2 x_4] + E[x_1 x_4]E[x_2 x_3]$$

where $x_1 = x(t)$ and $x_2 = x_3 = x_4 = x(t+\tau)$. The second-order moments

$$E[x_1 x_2] = E[x_1 x_3] = E[x_1 x_4] = R_{xx}(\tau)$$
$$E[x_3 x_4] = E[x_2 x_4] = E[x_2 x_3] = \sigma_x^2$$

Hence, $R_{xy}(\tau) = 3\sigma_x^2 R_{xx}(\tau)$. It follows that

$$G_{xy}(f) = 3\sigma_x^2 G_{xx}(f) \quad \text{and} \quad H_0(f) = 3\sigma_x^2$$

14.5 The cross-correlation function $R_{xy}(\tau)$ between the zero mean value Gaussian input $x(t)$ and the nonlinear output $y(t) = x^4(t)$ is zero by Equation (3.56) since this $R_{xy}(\tau)$ is a fifth-order moment, and all odd-order moments of Gaussian data are zero. It follows that $G_{xy}(f) = 0$ and $H_0(f) = 0$.
To determine that the nonlinear output $y(t)$ includes $x^4(t)$, one should consider a two-input/single-output model where the first input $x_1(t) = x(t)$ and the second input $x_2(t) = x^4(t)$.

14.6 The solution of Figure 14.7 requires changing the model of Figure 7.18 into the model of Figure 7.19.
The computation of $H_0(f)$ is the same as the computation of $L_{1y}(f)$ in Equation (7.122), namely, $H_0(f) = L_{1y}(f) = [G_{1y}/G_{11}(f)]$. The computation of $A_1(f)$ is the same as the computation of $A_{1y}(f)$ in Equation (7.117), namely,

$$A_1(f) = H_0(f) - [G_{12}(f)/G_{11}(f)]A_2(f) - [G_{13}(f)/G_{11}(f)]A_3(f)$$

Thus, in general, $A_1(f)$ and $H_0(f)$ give different results, and $H_0(f)$ does not determine the nonlinear terms.

14.7 For the three mutually uncorrelated records $x_1(t)$, $x_2(t)$, and $x_3(t)$ in Figure 14.7, the percentage of the output spectrum of $y(t)$ due to *each* record $x_i(t)$ for $i = 1, 2, 3$, is given by the coherence functions

$$\gamma_{iy}^2(f) = \frac{|G_{iy}(f)|^2}{G_{ii}(f)G_{yy}}$$

14.8 In Figure 14.8, let the Fourier transforms of $x(t)$, $y(t)$, and $z(t)$ be denoted by $X(f)$, $Y(f)$, and $Z(f)$, respectively. Then

$$Y(f) = H(f)[X(f) - Z(f)] = H(f)X(f) - H(f)Z(f)$$

Hence

$$H(f)X(f) = Y(f) + H(f)Z(f)$$

and

$$X(f) = [H(f)]^{-1}Y(f) + Z(f).$$

In Figure 14.9, one obtains

$$X(f) = A_1(f)Y(f) + Z(f)$$

where

$$A_1(f) = [H(f)]^{-1}.$$

14.9 The reverse SI/SO nonlinear model of Figure 14.10 considers the measured input $x(t)$ to be a mathematical output and the measured output $y(t)$ to be a mathematical input. Fourier transforms of both sides of the Duffing nonlinear equation give the two-input/single-output relation

$$A_1(f)Y_1(f) + A_3(f)Y_3(f) = X(f)$$

where

$$\begin{aligned} Y_1(f) &= Y(f) = \text{Fourier transform of } y(t) \\ Y_3(f) &= \text{Fourier transform of } y_3(t) = y^3(t) \\ X(f) &= \text{Fourier transform of } x(t) \\ A_1(f) &= k + j(2\pi f)c - (2\pi f)^2 m \\ A_3(f) &= k_3 \end{aligned}$$

The identification of $A_1(f)$ and $A_3(f)$ from knowledge of $Y_1(f)$, $Y_3(f)$, and $X(f)$ is straightforward to carry out and leads directly to determining the desired physical parameters by Equation (14.8).

14.10 From the Fourier transform relation for the Duffing nonlinear system in Problem 14.9, the associated spectral density relation is given by

$$A_1(f)G_{xy}(f) + A_3(f)G_{xv}(f) = G_{xx}(f)$$

where

$G_{xy}(f)$ = cross-spectral density function between $x(t)$ and $y(t)$
$G_{xv}(f)$ = cross-spectral density function between $x(t)$ and $v(t)$
$G_{xx}(f)$ = autospectral density function of $x(t)$

Conventional SI/SO modal analysis for the Duffing nonlinear system computes the optimum linear system frequency response function

$$H_0(f) = [G_{xy}(f)/G_{xx}(f)] = [A_1(f)]^{-1} - A_3(f)[G_{xv}(f)/G_{xx}(f)]$$

The gain and phase factors of this $H_0(f)$ give the wrong physical parameters for the Duffing nonlinear system. The correct results are contained in the computation of $A_1(f)$ and $A_3(f)$.

Index

Accelerometer, 319
Acceptance region, 91
Airplane test data, 181
Algorithm, for conditioned spectra, 225
   for conditioned Fourier transform, 224
   for fast Fourier transform, 372
Aliasing error, 330, 332
Aliasing frequency, *see* Nyquist frequency
Amplitude window, 261, 265
Analog-to-digital converter, 326
Analytic signal, 475, 486
Anti-aliasing filter, 332
Applications:
   Of correlation functions, 18
   of probability functions, 16
   Of spectral functions, 19
Arc-sine law, 441
Autocorrelation function, 111, 113, 124
   computation of, 381,385
   from autospectral density function, 119
   from hard clipping, 441
Automobile test data, 468
Autoregressive model, 403
Autospectral density function, 118, 123, 125
   computation of, 386, 395, 399
   equivalence test for, 282
   estimate of, 273, 275, 277, 280, 293

   from autocorrelation function, 118
   from filtering-squaring-averaging, 129
   from Fourier transform, 126
Autospectrum, *see* Autospectral density function
Average value, *see* Mean value

Bandwidth-limited white noise, 123, 254, 257, 260, 269, 271, 489
Bias error, 250, 251
   for autospectral density function, 274
   for coherence function, 305
   for correlation function, 267
   for frequency response function, 300
   for mean square value, 256
   for mean value, 253
   for probability density function, 263
   for variance, 260
Bilinear system, 509
Blackman-Tukey procedure, 386
Block size, 388

Case 1 nonlinear model, 507
Case 2 nonlinear model, 508
Causal function, 481
Central limit theorem, 60, 65, 86
Change of variables, 72,
Characteristic function, 53, 59, 63
Chebyshev inequality, 53

Random Data: Analysis and Measurement Procedures, Fourth Edition. By Julius S. Bendat and Allan G. Piersol
Copyright © 2010 John Wiley & Sons, Inc.

Chi-square distribution, 83, 87
  equivalence test from, 282
  goodness-of-fit test from, 94
  table for, 536
Circular correlation function, 382, 384
Coefficient of variation, 251
Coherence function, 135, 180, 299, 305
  computation of, 408
  linear transformation of, 183
Coherent output spectrum. 185, 303
  random error for, 304
Complex correlation function, 487
Complex demodulation, 397
Computer simulation study, 515–520
Conditioned record, 213, 216, 220
Conditioned spectra, 213, 217, 224, 409
Conditioned Fourier transform, 223
Confidence interval, 88, 90, 252, 425, 430
Consistent estimate, 80
Constant-parameter system, 25, 28, 173, 201
Convolution integral, 27
  for Hilbert transform, 473
Cooley-Tukey procedure, 374
Correlation coefficient, 56, 99, 116
Correlation function tapering, 393
Cosine-modulated random data, 439, 448, 454
Co-spectrum, 121
Covariance, 56, 110
Cross-correlation coefficient, 490
Cross-correlation function, 111
  computation of, 405
  from cross-spectral density function, 119
Cross-correlation inequality, 115
Cross-spectral density function, 119, 289
  computation of, 406
  from cross-correlation function, 118
Cross-spectrum, *see* Cross-spectral density function
Cross-spectrum inequality, 134
Cross-spectrum magnitude, 121
Cross-spectrum phase angle, 121
Cutoff frequency, *see* Nyquist frequency

Damping ratio, 32
Data acquisition, 318
Data analysis procedure:
  for individual sample records, 349
  for multiple sample records, 352
Data anomalies, 342
Data editing, 345
Data standardization, 360
Decimation of data, 398
Degrees-of-freedom, 83,
Delta function, 48, 122, 447
Derivative random data, 151
Detection of sine wave, 339
Deterministic data, 1, 3
Digital filters, 363
Direct MI/SO technique, 512
Discrete distribution, 46
Discrete Fourier transform, 368
Dispersive propagation, 495
Displacement-input system, 35, 179
Double-frequency spectra, 443, 445
Double-time correlation function, 436, 437
Duffing SDOF nonlinear system, 515
  computer simulation of, 515–520
Dynamic range, 324

Efficient estimate, 80
Electrical system, 39
Energy spectra, 177, 445
Ensemble of records, 10
Envelope function, *see* Envelope signal
Envelope signal, 475
  for correlation functions, 485
  from Hilbert transform, 477
  for narrow bandwidth data, 68
Equivalence test for spectra, 282
Ergodic random data, 11, 142, 145
Erroneous high coherence, 214
Error analysis criteria, 21
Expected value, *see* Mean value
Exponential autocorrelation function, 140
Exponential causal function, 483
Exponential-cosine cross-correlation function, 500

Fast Fourier transform, 368, 371, 372
  computation of, 369
F distribution, 84, 87
  table for, 538
FFT, *see* Fast Fourier transform
Finite delta function, 447

INDEX **601**

Finite Fourier transform, *see* Fast Fourier transform
Finite-memory nonlinear system, 507
Force-input system, 30, 178
Foundation-input system, 35, 179
Fourier series, 4, 366
Fourier transform, 7, 368
Fourth-order moment, 66
Frequency response function, 28, 30, 33, 37
  computation of 407
Frequency-time spectra, 450, 452

Gain factor, 29, 38, 300, 308
Gaussian data, 147
Gaussian distribution, 59, 62, 82
  tables for, 533, 535
Gaussian random process, 147
Gaussian spectrum noise, 139
Goodness-of-fit test, 94, 97
Group velocity, 495
Gun test, 22

Half-power point bandwidth, 34
Hanning window, 389, 394
Hard clipping of data, 440
Hartley transform, 379
Hilbert transform, 473
  computation of, 476
    envelope signal from, 477
  properties of, 478
Histogram, 380
Homogeneous data, 132
Hypothesis test, 91, 93

Ideal system, 25, 197
Impedance function, 40
Impulse response function, 26, 408
Independent variables, 55, 65
Input/output relations:
  for correlation functions, 174
  for linear systems, 173
  for nonstationary data, 462, 466
  for spectral functions, 174
  for stationary data, 173, 201
  for transient data, 177, 467
Instantaneous correlation function, 438
Instantaneous phase signal, 475
Instantaneous spectra, 450, 458

Inverse Fourier transform, 377
Inverse Hilbert transform, 479

Jacobian, 72
Joint Gaussian distribution, 62
Joint probability functions, 55

Lag number, 381
Lag weighting, 393
Laplace transform, 28
Least squares estimate, 188
Least squares fit, 102, 361
Level crossing, 155
Level of significance, 92
Linear correlation analysis, 99
Linear regression analysis, 102
Linear system, 27
Linear transformation, 149, 183
Linear trend, 361
Line spectra, 4
Locally stationary data, 442
Location of peak value, 137
Loss factor, 35
Low-pass filter, 177
Low-pass white noise, 123, 139, 491

Magnification function, 32
Magnitude window, 261
Markov process, 145
Matrix input/output formulas, 237
Maximum entropy analysis, 403
Maximum likelihood analysis, 403,
Mean square convergence, 150
Mean square error, 149
Mean square value, 50, 256
  computation of, 429
Mean value, 49, 80, 85, 110, 252
  computation of, 360, 424
Mechanical system, 30, 33, 37
Modified analysis procedure, 232
  for three-input system, 235, 313
Moment, 53
Moment generating function, 52, 57, 63
Moving average model, 403
Multidimensional central limit theorem, 65
Multiple coherence function, 212, 231, 237
Multiple coherent output spectra, 212

Multiple-input/multiple-output MI/MO system, 201, 312
　matrix formulas for, 238
Multiple-input/single-output MI/SO system, 21, 201, 202
　for arbitrary inputs, 205, 221, 229
　for conditioned inputs, 222, 225
　for uncorrelated inputs, 206
　modified procedure for, 232

Narrow bandwidth data, 67, 71, 159
Natural frequency, 35
N-dimensional Gaussian distribution, 69
Noise bandwidth, 259
Noise correlation duration, 138
Noise output spectrum, 185, 237
Noise spectral bandwidth, 138
Nondispersive propagation, 489, 493
Nonergodic stationary data, 74, 144, 184
Nonlinear drift force model, 520, 523, 524
Nonlinear feedback model, 512
　for Duffing nonlinear system, 515
Nonlinear system, 26, 505
　recommended model for, 514
Nonparametric trend test, 96
Nonrecursive digital filter, 363
Nonstationary cross-correlation inequality, 436
Nonstationary cross-spectrum inequality, 433
Nonstationary data, 12, 417, 419
　analysis for single records, 456
　correlation structure of, 436, 451
　input/output relations for, 462, 466
　mean square value of, 429, 432
　mean value of, 422, 427
　probability structure of, 419
　spectral structure of, 442, 451
Nonstationary random process, *see* Nonstationary data
Nonstationary spatial cross-correlation function, 425
Normal distribution, *see* Gaussian distribution
Normality test, 96
Normalized error, 251
Number of averages, 281, 285
Nyquist frequency, 331

One-sided spectra, 120, 387, 407
One-sided test, 92
Optimum frequency response function, 187, 211
　for MI/SO conditioned inputs, 225
　for MI/SO original inputs, 229
Optimum resolution bandwidth, 279
Ordinary coherence function, *see* Coherence function
Output noise spectrum, *see* Noise output spectrum
Overlapped processing, 392
Oversampling procedure, 395

Parametric spectral procedure, 403
Parseval theorem, 131
Partial coherence function, 219, 231
Peak correlation value, 115, 117
　location of, 137, 271
Peak gain factor, 34
Peak probability functions, 159, 162, 164
Peak signal-to-noise ratio, 325
Percentage point, 83, 84, 85
Periodic data, 3, 4, 6
　Fourier series for, 4, 366
Phase angle, 121
　estimate of, 297
　for time-delay problem, 136
　relation to cross-spectra, 122
Phase factor, 29, 300
　estimate of, 310
Phase shift system, 474
Phase velocity, 495
Physically realizable system, 27
　Hilbert transform for, 483
Poisson distribution, 123
Pooling of data, 353
Probability density function, 46, 420
　estimate of, 261
　computation of, 379, 404
　for sine wave, 52
Probability distribution function, 46, 420
　computation of, 381
　for sine wave, 52
Probability statement, 54, 86, 88, 251
Product model, 440, 456
Propagation problems, 489, 495
Propagation time delay error, 301

Quad-spectrum, 121
Quality factor, 35
Quantization error, 333

Random data, 2, 8, 13, 109, 417
Random error, 250, 251
  for autocorrelation function, 270
  for autospectral density function, 278, 281
  for coherence function, 306
  for coherent output spectrum, 303
  for gain factor, 309
  for mean square value, 257
  for mean value, 254
  for MI/SO problems, 313
  for probability density function, 265
  for SI/SO problems, 312
  for spectral estimates, 293
  for variance, 261
Random process, see Random data
Random variable, see Sample record
Raw estimate of spectra, 280, 290
Rayleigh distribution, 67, 70, 163
Record length requirements, 284
Rectangular distribution, 48
Rectangular wave process, 113, 126
Rectangular window, 388
Recursive digital filter, 364
Regression analysis, 102
Rejection region, 91
Removal, of extraneous noise, 194
  of linear trend, 361
Residual record, see Conditioned record
Residual spectra, see Conditioned spectra
Resolution bandwidth, 279
Resonance frequency, 34
Reverse arrangement test, 97, 337
  table for, 544
Reverse MI/SO technique, 514
Reverse SI/SO nonlinear model, 513
  for Duffing system, 518
Root mean square (rms) error, 250, 251, see also Bias error, Random error

Sample function, see Sample record
Sample record, 8, 12, 45, 54, 79, 109
Sample size, 80
Sample value, see Sample record
Sampling distribution, 85

Sampling theorem, 328
Short time-averaging procedure, 428, 432
Schwartz inequality, 142
Side-lobe leakage, 388, 391
Signal-to-noise ratio, 324, 325
Sine wave, 3
Sine wave distribution, 51, 73
Sine wave process, 113, 124, 144, 145
Single degree-of-freedom (SDOF) system, 30, 515
Single-input/multiple-output SI/MO system, 20, 192
Single-input/single-output SI/SO system, 19, 173, 298
SI/SO nonlinear model, 510, 511, 512
Single-input/two-output system, 191
Smooth estimate of spectra, 281, 290
Spectral bandwidth, 34, 138, 258
Spectra, see Autospectral density function, Cross-spectral density function
Spectral matrix, 410
Spectrogram, 460
Squared envelope signal, 498
Squared estimate, 251
Square-law envelope detector, 498, 521
Square-law and cubic nonlinear model, 507, 508
Standard deviation, 50, 360
  for phase estimate, 298, 310
Stationary random data, 9, 109, 111, 113
Stationary random process, see Stationary random data
Statistical bandwidth, 258
Statistical error, see Bias error, Random error
Statistical independence, 55, 65
Stochastic process, see Random data
Strongly stationary data, 11, 111

Tapering of data, 389, 393
t distribution, 84. 87
  table for, 537
Test, for normality, 96, 339
  for periodicities, 339
  for stationary data, 336
  for trend, 96
Three-input/single-output system, 234, 236, 412

Time-averaged correlation, 438
Time-averaged spectra, 453
Time-delay problem, 116, 136
Time history records, 15, 16, 17, 18
Time history tapering, 389
Time-invariant operator, 149
Time series, *see* Random data
Time-varying linear system, 462
Time window, 388
Transmissibility function, 36
Transducer, 318
Transfer function, 28. *See also* Frequency response function
Transient data, 7, 468
Trend removal, 361
Trilinear system, 509
Twiddle factor, 373
Two-input/single-output system, 207, 209, 211
Two-sided spectra 118, 386, 407
Two-sided test, 92
Type I, II error, 92

Unbiased estimate, 80, 82
Uncertainty principle, 141
Uncertainty relation, 138

Uncorrelated variable, 56, 114
Undamped natural frequency, 32
Uniform distribution, 48
Uniformly modulated data, 442
Unit impulse response function, 26, 408
Unstable system, 27

Variance, 50, 79, 110, 250, 260,
Volterra nonlinear model, 509

Waterfall display, 461
Wavelet analysis, 462
Wavelength, 132
Wave-number spectra, 133
Weakly stationary data, 11, 111
Weighting function, 26, 408
Welch procedure, 386
White noise, 123
Wide bandwidth data, 162
Wiener-Khinchine relation, 119, 381
Wigner distribution, 460
Winograd Fourier transform, 379

Zero crossing, 156, 157, 158
Zero-memory nonlinear system, 506
Zoom transform procedure, 396

WILEY SERIES IN PROBABILITY AND STATISTICS
ESTABLISHED BY WALTER A. SHEWHART AND SAMUEL S. WILKS

Editors: *David J. Balding, Noel A. C. Cressie, Garrett M. Fitzmaurice, Iain M. Johnstone, Geert Molenberghs, David W. Scott, Adrian F. M. Smith, Ruey S. Tsay, Sanford Weisberg*
Editors Emeriti: *Vic Barnett, J. Stuart Hunter, Jozef L. Teugels*

The *Wiley Series in Probability and Statistics* is well established and authoritative. It covers many topics of current research interest in both pure and applied statistics and probability theory. Written by leading statisticians and institutions, the titles span both state-of-the-art developments in the field and classical methods.

Reflecting the wide range of current research in statistics, the series encompasses applied, methodological and theoretical statistics, ranging from applications and new techniques made possible by advances in computerized practice to rigorous treatment of theoretical approaches.

This series provides essential and invaluable reading for all statisticians, whether in academia, industry, government, or research.

† ABRAHAM and LEDOLTER · Statistical Methods for Forecasting
  AGRESTI · Analysis of Ordinal Categorical Data
  AGRESTI · An Introduction to Categorical Data Analysis, *Second Edition*
  AGRESTI · Categorical Data Analysis, *Second Edition*
  ALTMAN, GILL, and McDONALD · Numerical Issues in Statistical Computing for the Social Scientist
  AMARATUNGA and CABRERA · Exploration and Analysis of DNA Microarray and Protein Array Data
  ANDĚL · Mathematics of Chance
  ANDERSON · An Introduction to Multivariate Statistical Analysis, *Third Edition*
* ANDERSON · The Statistical Analysis of Time Series
  ANDERSON, AUQUIER, HAUCK, OAKES, VANDAELE, and WEISBERG · Statistical Methods for Comparative Studies
  ANDERSON and LOYNES · The Teaching of Practical Statistics
  ARMITAGE and DAVID (editors) · Advances in Biometry
  ARNOLD, BALAKRISHNAN, and NAGARAJA · Records
* ARTHANARI and DODGE · Mathematical Programming in Statistics
* BAILEY · The Elements of Stochastic Processes with Applications to the Natural Sciences
  BALAKRISHNAN and KOUTRAS · Runs and Scans with Applications
  BALAKRISHNAN and NG · Precedence-Type Tests and Applications
  BARNETT · Comparative Statistical Inference, *Third Edition*
  BARNETT · Environmental Statistics
  BARNETT and LEWIS · Outliers in Statistical Data, *Third Edition*
  BARTOSZYNSKI and NIEWIADOMSKA-BUGAJ · Probability and Statistical Inference
  BASILEVSKY · Statistical Factor Analysis and Related Methods: Theory and Applications
  BASU and RIGDON · Statistical Methods for the Reliability of Repairable Systems
  BATES and WATTS · Nonlinear Regression Analysis and Its Applications
  BECHHOFER, SANTNER, and GOLDSMAN · Design and Analysis of Experiments for Statistical Selection, Screening, and Multiple Comparisons

*Now available in a lower priced paperback edition in the Wiley Classics Library.
†Now available in a lower priced paperback edition in the Wiley–Interscience Paperback Series.

BELSLEY · Conditioning Diagnostics: Collinearity and Weak Data in Regression
† BELSLEY, KUH, and WELSCH · Regression Diagnostics: Identifying Influential Data and Sources of Collinearity
BENDAT and PIERSOL · Random Data: Analysis and Measurement Procedures, *Fourth Edition*
BERRY, CHALONER, and GEWEKE · Bayesian Analysis in Statistics and Econometrics: Essays in Honor of Arnold Zellner
BERNARDO and SMITH · Bayesian Theory
BHAT and MILLER · Elements of Applied Stochastic Processes, *Third Edition*
BHATTACHARYA and WAYMIRE · Stochastic Processes with Applications
BILLINGSLEY · Convergence of Probability Measures, *Second Edition*
BILLINGSLEY · Probability and Measure, *Third Edition*
BIRKES and DODGE · Alternative Methods of Regression
BISWAS, DATTA, FINE, and SEGAL · Statistical Advances in the Biomedical Sciences: Clinical Trials, Epidemiology, Survival Analysis, and Bioinformatics
BLISCHKE AND MURTHY (editors) · Case Studies in Reliability and Maintenance
BLISCHKE AND MURTHY · Reliability: Modeling, Prediction, and Optimization
BLOOMFIELD · Fourier Analysis of Time Series: An Introduction, *Second Edition*
BOLLEN · Structural Equations with Latent Variables
BOLLEN and CURRAN · Latent Curve Models: A Structural Equation Perspective
BOROVKOV · Ergodicity and Stability of Stochastic Processes
BOULEAU · Numerical Methods for Stochastic Processes
BOX · Bayesian Inference in Statistical Analysis
BOX · R. A. Fisher, the Life of a Scientist
BOX and DRAPER · Response Surfaces, Mixtures, and Ridge Analyses, *Second Edition*
* BOX and DRAPER · Evolutionary Operation: A Statistical Method for Process Improvement
BOX and FRIENDS · Improving Almost Anything, *Revised Edition*
BOX, HUNTER, and HUNTER · Statistics for Experimenters: Design, Innovation, and Discovery, *Second Editon*
BOX, JENKINS, and REINSEL · Time Series Analysis: Forcasting and Control, *Fourth Edition*
BOX, LUCEÑO, and PANIAGUA-QUIÑONES · Statistical Control by Monitoring and Adjustment, *Second Edition*
BRANDIMARTE · Numerical Methods in Finance: A MATLAB-Based Introduction
† BROWN and HOLLANDER · Statistics: A Biomedical Introduction
BRUNNER, DOMHOF, and LANGER · Nonparametric Analysis of Longitudinal Data in Factorial Experiments
BUCKLEW · Large Deviation Techniques in Decision, Simulation, and Estimation
CAIROLI and DALANG · Sequential Stochastic Optimization
CASTILLO, HADI, BALAKRISHNAN, and SARABIA · Extreme Value and Related Models with Applications in Engineering and Science
CHAN · Time Series: Applications to Finance
CHARALAMBIDES · Combinatorial Methods in Discrete Distributions
CHATTERJEE and HADI · Regression Analysis by Example, *Fourth Edition*
CHATTERJEE and HADI · Sensitivity Analysis in Linear Regression
CHERNICK · Bootstrap Methods: A Guide for Practitioners and Researchers, *Second Edition*
CHERNICK and FRIIS · Introductory Biostatistics for the Health Sciences
CHILÈS and DELFINER · Geostatistics: Modeling Spatial Uncertainty
CHOW and LIU · Design and Analysis of Clinical Trials: Concepts and Methodologies, *Second Edition*
CLARKE · Linear Models: The Theory and Application of Analysis of Variance

---

*Now available in a lower priced paperback edition in the Wiley Classics Library.
†Now available in a lower priced paperback edition in the Wiley–Interscience Paperback Series.

CLARKE and DISNEY · Probability and Random Processes: A First Course with Applications, *Second Edition*
* COCHRAN and COX · Experimental Designs, *Second Edition*
COLLINS and LANZA · Latent Class and Latent Transition Analysis: With Applications in the Social, Behavioral, and Health Sciences
CONGDON · Applied Bayesian Modelling
CONGDON · Bayesian Models for Categorical Data
CONGDON · Bayesian Statistical Modelling
CONOVER · Practical Nonparametric Statistics, *Third Edition*
COOK · Regression Graphics
COOK and WEISBERG · Applied Regression Including Computing and Graphics
COOK and WEISBERG · An Introduction to Regression Graphics
CORNELL · Experiments with Mixtures, Designs, Models, and the Analysis of Mixture Data, *Third Edition*
COVER and THOMAS · Elements of Information Theory
COX · A Handbook of Introductory Statistical Methods
* COX · Planning of Experiments
CRESSIE · Statistics for Spatial Data, *Revised Edition*
CSÖRGŐ and HORVÁTH · Limit Theorems in Change Point Analysis
DANIEL · Applications of Statistics to Industrial Experimentation
DANIEL · Biostatistics: A Foundation for Analysis in the Health Sciences, *Eighth Edition*
* DANIEL · Fitting Equations to Data: Computer Analysis of Multifactor Data, *Second Edition*
DASU and JOHNSON · Exploratory Data Mining and Data Cleaning
DAVID and NAGARAJA · Order Statistics, *Third Edition*
* DEGROOT, FIENBERG, and KADANE · Statistics and the Law
DEL CASTILLO · Statistical Process Adjustment for Quality Control
DeMARIS · Regression with Social Data: Modeling Continuous and Limited Response Variables
DEMIDENKO · Mixed Models: Theory and Applications
DENISON, HOLMES, MALLICK and SMITH · Bayesian Methods for Nonlinear Classification and Regression
DETTE and STUDDEN · The Theory of Canonical Moments with Applications in Statistics, Probability, and Analysis
DEY and MUKERJEE · Fractional Factorial Plans
DILLON and GOLDSTEIN · Multivariate Analysis: Methods and Applications
DODGE · Alternative Methods of Regression
* DODGE and ROMIG · Sampling Inspection Tables, *Second Edition*
* DOOB · Stochastic Processes
DOWDY, WEARDEN, and CHILKO · Statistics for Research, *Third Edition*
DRAPER and SMITH · Applied Regression Analysis, *Third Edition*
DRYDEN and MARDIA · Statistical Shape Analysis
DUDEWICZ and MISHRA · Modern Mathematical Statistics
DUNN and CLARK · Basic Statistics: A Primer for the Biomedical Sciences, *Third Edition*
DUPUIS and ELLIS · A Weak Convergence Approach to the Theory of Large Deviations
EDLER and KITSOS · Recent Advances in Quantitative Methods in Cancer and Human Health Risk Assessment
* ELANDT-JOHNSON and JOHNSON · Survival Models and Data Analysis
ENDERS · Applied Econometric Time Series
† ETHIER and KURTZ · Markov Processes: Characterization and Convergence
EVANS, HASTINGS, and PEACOCK · Statistical Distributions, *Third Edition*

---

*Now available in a lower priced paperback edition in the Wiley Classics Library.
†Now available in a lower priced paperback edition in the Wiley–Interscience Paperback Series.

FELLER · An Introduction to Probability Theory and Its Applications, Volume I, *Third Edition,* Revised; Volume II, *Second Edition*
FISHER and VAN BELLE · Biostatistics: A Methodology for the Health Sciences
FITZMAURICE, LAIRD, and WARE · Applied Longitudinal Analysis
* FLEISS · The Design and Analysis of Clinical Experiments
FLEISS · Statistical Methods for Rates and Proportions, *Third Edition*
† FLEMING and HARRINGTON · Counting Processes and Survival Analysis
FUJIKOSHI, ULYANOV, and SHIMIZU · Multivariate Statistics: High-Dimensional and Large-Sample Approximations
FULLER · Introduction to Statistical Time Series, *Second Edition*
† FULLER · Measurement Error Models
GALLANT · Nonlinear Statistical Models
GEISSER · Modes of Parametric Statistical Inference
GELMAN and MENG · Applied Bayesian Modeling and Causal Inference from Incomplete-Data Perspectives
GEWEKE · Contemporary Bayesian Econometrics and Statistics
GHOSH, MUKHOPADHYAY, and SEN · Sequential Estimation
GIESBRECHT and GUMPERTZ · Planning, Construction, and Statistical Analysis of Comparative Experiments
GIFI · Nonlinear Multivariate Analysis
GIVENS and HOETING · Computational Statistics
GLASSERMAN and YAO · Monotone Structure in Discrete-Event Systems
GNANADESIKAN · Methods for Statistical Data Analysis of Multivariate Observations, *Second Edition*
GOLDSTEIN and LEWIS · Assessment: Problems, Development, and Statistical Issues
GREENWOOD and NIKULIN · A Guide to Chi-Squared Testing
GROSS, SHORTLE, THOMPSON, and HARRIS · Fundamentals of Queueing Theory, *Fourth Edition*
GROSS, SHORTLE, THOMPSON, and HARRIS · Solutions Manual to Accompany Fundamentals of Queueing Theory, *Fourth Edition*
* HAHN and SHAPIRO · Statistical Models in Engineering
HAHN and MEEKER · Statistical Intervals: A Guide for Practitioners
HALD · A History of Probability and Statistics and their Applications Before 1750
HALD · A History of Mathematical Statistics from 1750 to 1930
† HAMPEL · Robust Statistics: The Approach Based on Influence Functions
HANNAN and DEISTLER · The Statistical Theory of Linear Systems
HARTUNG, KNAPP, and SINHA · Statistical Meta-Analysis with Applications
HEIBERGER · Computation for the Analysis of Designed Experiments
HEDAYAT and SINHA · Design and Inference in Finite Population Sampling
HEDEKER and GIBBONS · Longitudinal Data Analysis
HELLER · MACSYMA for Statisticians
HINKELMANN and KEMPTHORNE · Design and Analysis of Experiments, Volume 1: Introduction to Experimental Design, *Second Edition*
HINKELMANN and KEMPTHORNE · Design and Analysis of Experiments, Volume 2: Advanced Experimental Design
HOAGLIN, MOSTELLER, and TUKEY · Fundamentals of Exploratory Analysis of Variance
* HOAGLIN, MOSTELLER, and TUKEY · Exploring Data Tables, Trends and Shapes
* HOAGLIN, MOSTELLER, and TUKEY · Understanding Robust and Exploratory Data Analysis
HOCHBERG and TAMHANE · Multiple Comparison Procedures
HOCKING · Methods and Applications of Linear Models: Regression and the Analysis of Variance, *Second Edition*

*Now available in a lower priced paperback edition in the Wiley Classics Library.
†Now available in a lower priced paperback edition in the Wiley–Interscience Paperback Series.

HOEL · Introduction to Mathematical Statistics, *Fifth Edition*
HOGG and KLUGMAN · Loss Distributions
HOLLANDER and WOLFE · Nonparametric Statistical Methods, *Second Edition*
HOSMER and LEMESHOW · Applied Logistic Regression, *Second Edition*
HOSMER, LEMESHOW, and MAY · Applied Survival Analysis: Regression Modeling of Time-to-Event Data, *Second Edition*
† HUBER and RONCHETTI · Robust Statistics, *Second Edition*
HUBERTY · Applied Discriminant Analysis
HUBERTY and OLEJNIK · Applied MANOVA and Discriminant Analysis, *Second Edition*
HUNT and KENNEDY · Financial Derivatives in Theory and Practice, *Revised Edition*
HURD and MIAMEE · Periodically Correlated Random Sequences: Spectral Theory and Practice
HUSKOVA, BERAN, and DUPAC · Collected Works of Jaroslav Hajek— with Commentary
HUZURBAZAR · Flowgraph Models for Multistate Time-to-Event Data
IMAN and CONOVER · A Modern Approach to Statistics
† JACKSON · A User's Guide to Principle Components
JOHN · Statistical Methods in Engineering and Quality Assurance
JOHNSON · Multivariate Statistical Simulation
JOHNSON and BALAKRISHNAN · Advances in the Theory and Practice of Statistics: A Volume in Honor of Samuel Kotz
JOHNSON and BHATTACHARYYA · Statistics: Principles and Methods, *Fifth Edition*
JOHNSON and KOTZ · Distributions in Statistics
JOHNSON and KOTZ (editors) · Leading Personalities in Statistical Sciences: From the Seventeenth Century to the Present
JOHNSON, KOTZ, and BALAKRISHNAN · Continuous Univariate Distributions, Volume 1, *Second Edition*
JOHNSON, KOTZ, and BALAKRISHNAN · Continuous Univariate Distributions, Volume 2, *Second Edition*
JOHNSON, KOTZ, and BALAKRISHNAN · Discrete Multivariate Distributions
JOHNSON, KEMP, and KOTZ · Univariate Discrete Distributions, *Third Edition*
JUDGE, GRIFFITHS, HILL, LÜTKEPOHL, and LEE · The Theory and Practice of Econometrics, *Second Edition*
JUREČKOVÁ and SEN · Robust Statistical Procedures: Aymptotics and Interrelations
JUREK and MASON · Operator-Limit Distributions in Probability Theory
KADANE · Bayesian Methods and Ethics in a Clinical Trial Design
KADANE AND SCHUM · A Probabilistic Analysis of the Sacco and Vanzetti Evidence
KALBFLEISCH and PRENTICE · The Statistical Analysis of Failure Time Data, *Second Edition*
KARIYA and KURATA · Generalized Least Squares
KASS and VOS · Geometrical Foundations of Asymptotic Inference
† KAUFMAN and ROUSSEEUW · Finding Groups in Data: An Introduction to Cluster Analysis
KEDEM and FOKIANOS · Regression Models for Time Series Analysis
KENDALL, BARDEN, CARNE, and LE · Shape and Shape Theory
KHURI · Advanced Calculus with Applications in Statistics, *Second Edition*
KHURI, MATHEW, and SINHA · Statistical Tests for Mixed Linear Models
KLEIBER and KOTZ · Statistical Size Distributions in Economics and Actuarial Sciences
KLEMELÄ · Smoothing of Multivariate Data: Density Estimation and Visualization
KLUGMAN, PANJER, and WILLMOT · Loss Models: From Data to Decisions, *Third Edition*
KLUGMAN, PANJER, and WILLMOT · Solutions Manual to Accompany Loss Models: From Data to Decisions, *Third Edition*

*Now available in a lower priced paperback edition in the Wiley Classics Library.
†Now available in a lower priced paperback edition in the Wiley–Interscience Paperback Series.

KOTZ, BALAKRISHNAN, and JOHNSON · Continuous Multivariate Distributions, Volume 1, *Second Edition*
KOVALENKO, KUZNETZOV, and PEGG · Mathematical Theory of Reliability of Time-Dependent Systems with Practical Applications
KOWALSKI and TU · Modern Applied U-Statistics
KRISHNAMOORTHY and MATHEW · Statistical Tolerance Regions: Theory, Applications, and Computation
KROONENBERG · Applied Multiway Data Analysis
KVAM and VIDAKOVIC · Nonparametric Statistics with Applications to Science and Engineering
LACHIN · Biostatistical Methods: The Assessment of Relative Risks
LAD · Operational Subjective Statistical Methods: A Mathematical, Philosophical, and Historical Introduction
LAMPERTI · Probability: A Survey of the Mathematical Theory, *Second Edition*
LANGE, RYAN, BILLARD, BRILLINGER, CONQUEST, and GREENHOUSE · Case Studies in Biometry
LARSON · Introduction to Probability Theory and Statistical Inference, *Third Edition*
LAWLESS · Statistical Models and Methods for Lifetime Data, *Second Edition*
LAWSON · Statistical Methods in Spatial Epidemiology
LE · Applied Categorical Data Analysis
LE · Applied Survival Analysis
LEE and WANG · Statistical Methods for Survival Data Analysis, *Third Edition*
LePAGE and BILLARD · Exploring the Limits of Bootstrap
LEYLAND and GOLDSTEIN (editors) · Multilevel Modelling of Health Statistics
LIAO · Statistical Group Comparison
LINDVALL · Lectures on the Coupling Method
LIN · Introductory Stochastic Analysis for Finance and Insurance
LINHART and ZUCCHINI · Model Selection
LITTLE and RUBIN · Statistical Analysis with Missing Data, *Second Edition*
LLOYD · The Statistical Analysis of Categorical Data
LOWEN and TEICH · Fractal-Based Point Processes
MAGNUS and NEUDECKER · Matrix Differential Calculus with Applications in Statistics and Econometrics, *Revised Edition*
MALLER and ZHOU · Survival Analysis with Long Term Survivors
MALLOWS · Design, Data, and Analysis by Some Friends of Cuthbert Daniel
MANN, SCHAFER, and SINGPURWALLA · Methods for Statistical Analysis of Reliability and Life Data
MANTON, WOODBURY, and TOLLEY · Statistical Applications Using Fuzzy Sets
MARCHETTE · Random Graphs for Statistical Pattern Recognition
MARDIA and JUPP · Directional Statistics
MASON, GUNST, and HESS · Statistical Design and Analysis of Experiments with Applications to Engineering and Science, *Second Edition*
McCULLOCH, SEARLE, and NEUHAUS · Generalized, Linear, and Mixed Models, *Second Edition*
McFADDEN · Management of Data in Clinical Trials, *Second Edition*
* McLACHLAN · Discriminant Analysis and Statistical Pattern Recognition
McLACHLAN, DO, and AMBROISE · Analyzing Microarray Gene Expression Data
McLACHLAN and KRISHNAN · The EM Algorithm and Extensions, *Second Edition*
McLACHLAN and PEEL · Finite Mixture Models
McNEIL · Epidemiological Research Methods
MEEKER and ESCOBAR · Statistical Methods for Reliability Data
MEERSCHAERT and SCHEFFLER · Limit Distributions for Sums of Independent Random Vectors: Heavy Tails in Theory and Practice
MICKEY, DUNN, and CLARK · Applied Statistics: Analysis of Variance and

---

*Now available in a lower priced paperback edition in the Wiley Classics Library.
†Now available in a lower priced paperback edition in the Wiley–Interscience Paperback Series.

Regression, *Third Edition*
* MILLER · Survival Analysis, *Second Edition*
MONTGOMERY, JENNINGS, and KULAHCI · Introduction to Time Series Analysis and Forecasting
MONTGOMERY, PECK, and VINING · Introduction to Linear Regression Analysis, *Fourth Edition*
MORGENTHALER and TUKEY · Configural Polysampling: A Route to Practical Robustness
MUIRHEAD · Aspects of Multivariate Statistical Theory
MULLER and STOYAN · Comparison Methods for Stochastic Models and Risks
MURRAY · X-STAT 2.0 Statistical Experimentation, Design Data Analysis, and Nonlinear Optimization
MURTHY, XIE, and JIANG · Weibull Models
MYERS, MONTGOMERY, and ANDERSON-COOK · Response Surface Methodology: Process and Product Optimization Using Designed Experiments, *Third Edition*
MYERS, MONTGOMERY, and VINING · Generalized Linear Models. With Applications in Engineering and the Sciences
† NELSON · Accelerated Testing, Statistical Models, Test Plans, and Data Analyses
† NELSON · Applied Life Data Analysis
NEWMAN · Biostatistical Methods in Epidemiology
OCHI · Applied Probability and Stochastic Processes in Engineering and Physical Sciences
OKABE, BOOTS, SUGIHARA, and CHIU · Spatial Tesselations: Concepts and Applications of Voronoi Diagrams, *Second Edition*
OLIVER and SMITH · Influence Diagrams, Belief Nets and Decision Analysis
PALTA · Quantitative Methods in Population Health: Extensions of Ordinary Regressions
PANJER · Operational Risk: Modeling and Analytics
PANKRATZ · Forecasting with Dynamic Regression Models
PANKRATZ · Forecasting with Univariate Box-Jenkins Models: Concepts and Cases
* PARZEN · Modern Probability Theory and Its Applications
PEÑA, TIAO, and TSAY · A Course in Time Series Analysis
PIANTADOSI · Clinical Trials: A Methodologic Perspective
PORT · Theoretical Probability for Applications
POURAHMADI · Foundations of Time Series Analysis and Prediction Theory
POWELL · Approximate Dynamic Programming: Solving the Curses of Dimensionality
PRESS · Bayesian Statistics: Principles, Models, and Applications
PRESS · Subjective and Objective Bayesian Statistics, *Second Edition*
PRESS and TANUR · The Subjectivity of Scientists and the Bayesian Approach
PUKELSHEIM · Optimal Experimental Design
PURI, VILAPLANA, and WERTZ · New Perspectives in Theoretical and Applied Statistics
† PUTERMAN · Markov Decision Processes: Discrete Stochastic Dynamic Programming
QIU · Image Processing and Jump Regression Analysis
* RAO · Linear Statistical Inference and Its Applications, *Second Edition*
RAUSAND and HØYLAND · System Reliability Theory: Models, Statistical Methods, and Applications, *Second Edition*
RENCHER · Linear Models in Statistics
RENCHER · Methods of Multivariate Analysis, *Second Edition*
RENCHER · Multivariate Statistical Inference with Applications
* RIPLEY · Spatial Statistics
* RIPLEY · Stochastic Simulation
ROBINSON · Practical Strategies for Experimenting
ROHATGI and SALEH · An Introduction to Probability and Statistics, *Second Edition*

---

*Now available in a lower priced paperback edition in the Wiley Classics Library.
†Now available in a lower priced paperback edition in the Wiley–Interscience Paperback Series.

ROLSKI, SCHMIDLI, SCHMIDT, and TEUGELS · Stochastic Processes for Insurance and Finance
ROSENBERGER and LACHIN · Randomization in Clinical Trials: Theory and Practice
ROSS · Introduction to Probability and Statistics for Engineers and Scientists
ROSSI, ALLENBY, and McCULLOCH · Bayesian Statistics and Marketing
† ROUSSEEUW and LEROY · Robust Regression and Outlier Detection
* RUBIN · Multiple Imputation for Nonresponse in Surveys
RUBINSTEIN and KROESE · Simulation and the Monte Carlo Method, *Second Edition*
RUBINSTEIN and MELAMED · Modern Simulation and Modeling
RYAN · Modern Engineering Statistics
RYAN · Modern Experimental Design
RYAN · Modern Regression Methods, *Second Edition*
RYAN · Statistical Methods for Quality Improvement, *Second Edition*
SALEH · Theory of Preliminary Test and Stein-Type Estimation with Applications
* SCHEFFE · The Analysis of Variance
SCHIMEK · Smoothing and Regression: Approaches, Computation, and Application
SCHOTT · Matrix Analysis for Statistics, *Second Edition*
SCHOUTENS · Levy Processes in Finance: Pricing Financial Derivatives
SCHUSS · Theory and Applications of Stochastic Differential Equations
SCOTT · Multivariate Density Estimation: Theory, Practice, and Visualization
† SEARLE · Linear Models for Unbalanced Data
† SEARLE · Matrix Algebra Useful for Statistics
† SEARLE, CASELLA, and McCULLOCH · Variance Components
SEARLE and WILLETT · Matrix Algebra for Applied Economics
SEBER · A Matrix Handbook For Statisticians
† SEBER · Multivariate Observations
SEBER and LEE · Linear Regression Analysis, *Second Edition*
† SEBER and WILD · Nonlinear Regression
SENNOTT · Stochastic Dynamic Programming and the Control of Queueing Systems
* SERFLING · Approximation Theorems of Mathematical Statistics
SHAFER and VOVK · Probability and Finance: It's Only a Game!
SILVAPULLE and SEN · Constrained Statistical Inference: Inequality, Order, and Shape Restrictions
SMALL and McLEISH · Hilbert Space Methods in Probability and Statistical Inference
SRIVASTAVA · Methods of Multivariate Statistics
STAPLETON · Linear Statistical Models, *Second Edition*
STAPLETON · Models for Probability and Statistical Inference: Theory and Applications
STAUDTE and SHEATHER · Robust Estimation and Testing
STOYAN, KENDALL, and MECKE · Stochastic Geometry and Its Applications, *Second Edition*
STOYAN and STOYAN · Fractals, Random Shapes and Point Fields: Methods of Geometrical Statistics
STREET and BURGESS · The Construction of Optimal Stated Choice Experiments: Theory and Methods
STYAN · The Collected Papers of T. W. Anderson: 1943–1985
SUTTON, ABRAMS, JONES, SHELDON, and SONG · Methods for Meta-Analysis in Medical Research
TAKEZAWA · Introduction to Nonparametric Regression
TAMHANE · Statistical Analysis of Designed Experiments: Theory and Applications
TANAKA · Time Series Analysis: Nonstationary and Noninvertible Distribution Theory
THOMPSON · Empirical Model Building
THOMPSON · Sampling, *Second Edition*
THOMPSON · Simulation: A Modeler's Approach
THOMPSON and SEBER · Adaptive Sampling

*Now available in a lower priced paperback edition in the Wiley Classics Library.
†Now available in a lower priced paperback edition in the Wiley–Interscience Paperback Series.

THOMPSON, WILLIAMS, and FINDLAY · Models for Investors in Real World Markets
TIAO, BISGAARD, HILL, PEÑA, and STIGLER (editors) · Box on Quality and Discovery: with Design, Control, and Robustness
TIERNEY · LISP-STAT: An Object-Oriented Environment for Statistical Computing and Dynamic Graphics
TSAY · Analysis of Financial Time Series, *Second Edition*
UPTON and FINGLETON · Spatial Data Analysis by Example, Volume II: Categorical and Directional Data
† VAN BELLE · Statistical Rules of Thumb, *Second Edition*
VAN BELLE, FISHER, HEAGERTY, and LUMLEY · Biostatistics: A Methodology for the Health Sciences, *Second Edition*
VESTRUP · The Theory of Measures and Integration
VIDAKOVIC · Statistical Modeling by Wavelets
VINOD and REAGLE · Preparing for the Worst: Incorporating Downside Risk in Stock Market Investments
WALLER and GOTWAY · Applied Spatial Statistics for Public Health Data
WEERAHANDI · Generalized Inference in Repeated Measures: Exact Methods in MANOVA and Mixed Models
WEISBERG · Applied Linear Regression, *Third Edition*
WELSH · Aspects of Statistical Inference
WESTFALL and YOUNG · Resampling-Based Multiple Testing: Examples and Methods for *p*-Value Adjustment
WHITTAKER · Graphical Models in Applied Multivariate Statistics
WINKER · Optimization Heuristics in Economics: Applications of Threshold Accepting
WONNACOTT and WONNACOTT · Econometrics, *Second Edition*
WOODING · Planning Pharmaceutical Clinical Trials: Basic Statistical Principles
WOODWORTH · Biostatistics: A Bayesian Introduction
WOOLSON and CLARKE · Statistical Methods for the Analysis of Biomedical Data, *Second Edition*
WU and HAMADA · Experiments: Planning, Analysis, and Parameter Design Optimization, *Second Edition*
WU and ZHANG · Nonparametric Regression Methods for Longitudinal Data Analysis
YANG · The Construction Theory of Denumerable Markov Processes
YOUNG, VALERO-MORA, and FRIENDLY · Visual Statistics: Seeing Data with Dynamic Interactive Graphics
ZACKS · Stage-Wise Adaptive Designs
ZELTERMAN · Discrete Distributions—Applications in the Health Sciences
* ZELLNER · An Introduction to Bayesian Inference in Econometrics
ZHOU, OBUCHOWSKI, and McCLISH · Statistical Methods in Diagnostic Medicine

*Now available in a lower priced paperback edition in the Wiley Classics Library.
†Now available in a lower priced paperback edition in the Wiley–Interscience Paperback Series.